Management**Accounting**

Analysis and Interpretation

The**Authors**

Cheryl S. McWatters

Cheryl McWatters is an Associate Professor in the Faculty of Management of McGill University, where she teaches management accounting and accounting thought. Dr. McWatters received her M.B.A. and Ph.D. in Management from Queen's University. She is also a CMA.

Dr. McWatters's main research interests are accounting history, and the organizational implications of manufacturing technologies. Her research has appeared in a variety of journals including *Accounting History, Accounting, Business and Financial History, The Accounting Historians Journal*, and the *Journal of Cost Management*. She has also contributed to collected volumes, including *Twentieth-Century Accounting Thinkers* and *Studies in Accounting History*. She is Book Review Editor of *The Accounting Historians Journal* and an editorial board member of *Accounting History*.

Cheryl McWatters is a member of the Canadian Academic Accounting Association, the American Accounting Association, the Society of Management Accountants of Ontario, the Academy of Accounting Historians, and the Administrative Sciences Association of Canada. Prior to academia, she worked in the public and private sectors, experiencing first-hand the organizational role of management accounting.

Dale C. Morse

Dale Morse is the Charles E. Johnson Professor of Accounting and Chairman of the Accounting Department at the University of Oregon. He received his M.B.A. in accounting from the University of Oregon and his Ph.D. in accounting from Stanford University. He was a faculty member at Cornell University in Ithaca, NY, from 1978–1991 and has held Visiting Professorships at the University of Auckland; the Dalian Institute of Technology, China; the University of Helsinki; the Universitas Merdeka Malang, Indonesia; and Koc University, Turkey. He also held a Fulbright Scholar position at the University of Nairobi, Kenya.

Dr. Morse's research has appeared in the *Journal of Accounting Research, Journal of Accounting and Economics, The Accounting Review*, and *Accounting Horizons*. His monograph, "Efficient Capital Markets and Accounting: A Critical Analysis," (with Tom Dyckman) is part of the Prentice-Hall "Contemporary Topics in Accounting" series. Dale Morse is a member of the American Accounting Association, American Finance Association, Institute of Management Accountants, and the Western Finance Association.

Jerold L. Zimmerman

Jerry Zimmerman is the Ronald L. Bittner Professor at the William E. Simon Graduate School of Business Administration, University of Rochester. He holds an undergraduate degree from the University of Colorado, Boulder, and a doctorate from the University of California, Berkeley. While at Rochester, Dr. Zimmerman has taught a variety of courses spanning accounting, finance, and economics. A deeper appreciation of the challenges of managing a complex organization was acquired by spending four years as Deputy Dean of the Simon School.

Dr. Zimmerman publishes widely in accounting on topics as diverse as cost allocations, municipal accounting, budgeting, taxes, auditing, financial accounting theory, mergers and acquisitions, trade unions, capital markets, and executive turnover. His paper, "The Costs and Benefits of Cost Allocations," won the American Accounting Association's competitive Manuscript Contest. He is recognized for developing Positive Accounting Theory. This work, co-authored with Ross Watts, also at the University of Rochester, received the 1978 and 1979 American Institute of Certified Public Accountants' Notable Contribution to the Accounting Literature Awards for "Towards a Positive Theory of the Determination of Accounting Standards" and "The Demand for and Supply of Accounting Theories: The Market for Excuses." Both papers appeared in the *Accounting Review*. They are also co-authors of the highly cited textbook, *Positive Accounting Theory* (Prentice Hall, 1986). Jerry Zimmerman was a founding editor of the *Journal of Accounting and Economics*, published by North-Holland, a scientific journal that is one of the most highly referenced accounting publications.

Second Edition

Management **Accounting**
Analysis and Interpretation

Cheryl S. McWatters
McGill University

Dale C. Morse
University of Oregon

Jerold L. Zimmerman
University of Rochester

 **Custom Publishing**

Boston   Burr Ridge, IL   Dubuque, IA   Madison, WI   New York
San Francisco   St. Louis   Bangkok   Bogotá   Caracas   Kuala Lumpur
Lisbon   London   Madrid   Mexico City   Milan   Montreal   New Delhi
Santiago   Seoul   Singapore   Sydney   Taipei   Toronto

Management Accounting Analysis and Interpretation

This book is a McGraw-Hill Custom Publishing textbook and contains all material from *Management Accounting: Analysis and Interpretation*, Second Edition by Cheryl S. McWatters, Dale C. Morse and Jerold L. Zimmerman. Copyright © 2001, 1997 by The McGraw-Hill Companies, Inc. Reprinted with permission of the publisher. Many custom published texts are modified versions or adaptations of our best-selling textbooks. Some adaptations are printed in black and white to keep prices at a minimum, while others are in color.

2 3 4 5 6 7 8 9 0   QSR QSR   0 9 8 7 6

ISBN 0-07-301627-6

Editor: Shirley Grall
Production Editor: Sue Culbertson
Printer/Binder: Quebecor World

To **Leslie**, **Jared**, **Tyler**, **Daneille**, **Amy**, and **John**

Preface

In a dynamic environment, organizations must evolve to keep pace with major forces, including technological change, globalization, and customer demand. Organizations and their managers depend on management accounting to provide information that enables them to deal successfully with a changing environment. Managers in all organizations, profit and not for profit, interact with their management accounting system. Sometimes the manager uses the accounting system to acquire information for making planning decisions. At other times, the accounting system measures the performance and influences the behavior of the manager. The management accounting system is both a source of information for making planning decisions and part of the organization's control mechanisms. Management accounting helps organizations to create value through improved decision making and control of organizational members.

This book provides students and managers with an understanding and appreciation of the strengths and limitations of an organization's accounting system, thereby allowing them to be more intelligent users of the system. This book is based on an analytical framework for organizational change that illustrates the way organizations must adapt to create customer and organizational value. This framework is a way of thinking about the organization's accounting system and a basis for analyzing proposed changes to the system. The text demonstrates that management accounting is an integral part of the firm's organizational strategy, not an isolated set of computational topics. The success of an organization is closely linked to having the appropriate management accounting system.

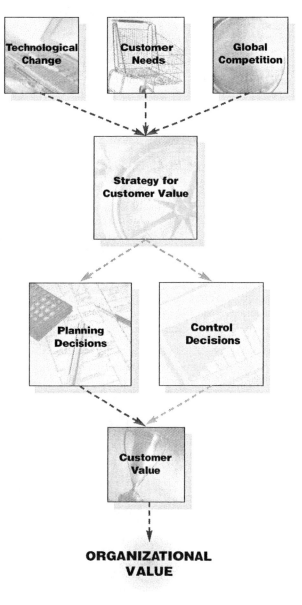

DISTINGUISHING FEATURES

Framework for Organizational Change

This book differs from other management accounting texts in several ways. The most important difference is the incorporation of the study of management accounting within an analytical framework for organizational change. Organizations must adapt to environmental forces by developing a strategy to create customer value. To implement this strategy, the management accounting system provides the organizational mechanisms to make planning and control decisions.

The conceptual framework depicted to the right is unique to this book. This framework is introduced in Chapter One, referenced at the opening of each chapter, and highlighted throughout the text with icons so that the student understands the "big picture" of management accounting. Most management accounting textbooks cover concepts in isolation, which provides only *half* of the picture. We believe that students learn best when they can relate important concepts to the overall objective of management accounting: helping to achieve customer and organizational value through sound business decision-making. We achieve this objective with the aid of this outstanding pedagogical tool.

Trade-Offs

This text emphasizes the fact that a single accounting system cannot always fulfill the information demands to make planning decisions and to control managers to successfully achieve organizational strategy. For example, an accounting system used as a control mechanism is likely to be less effective for making planning decisions. Most texts stress the importance of deriving different estimates of costs for different purposes. Existing books do a good job of illustrating how accounting costs developed for one purpose, such as inventory valuation, cannot be used without adjustment for other purposes, such as a make-or-buy decision. However, these books often leave the impression that one accounting system can be used for multiple purposes as long as the users make the appropriate adjustments in the data. Existing texts do not emphasize the trade-off between designing the accounting system for planning decisions and designing it for control. For example, the implementation of management innovations, such as activity-based management, TQM, and JIT, presumably improves the accounting system's ability to support planning decisions (pricing and product design), but existing texts do not address how the implementation of these innovations affects control decisions.

Logical Sequence

Another meaningful distinction between this text and others in the field is that the chapters in this text build on each other. The first chapter presents in detail the analytical framework for organizational change incorporated throughout the text. It also identifies the trade-off that exists among different uses of an accounting system. The next four chapters focus on strategy and planning decisions. Chapters Six and Seven utilize the framework to examine strategy and organizational problems of control. The next four chapters highlight planning and control issues by developing the basic theme of the trade-off that exists when using an accounting system for making planning decisions and control purposes. Chapter Twelve explores management accounting's role in a dynamic environment, especially in relation to new management innovations. This chapter both summarizes the remainder of the book and looks to the future in the context of recent trends in management accounting. It should be covered last. Chapters Thirteen (Investment Decisions) and Fourteen (Standard Costs and Variance Analysis) can be added to the sequence of the first 12 chapters (preferably after Chapter Eight) but are not necessary to understand the concepts introduced in the first 12 chapters.

Pedagogical Devices

This book adopts an analytical framework for organizational change that links management accounting to organizational strategy and uses the foundation concepts of opportunity cost and organizational theory. However, students are not expected to have any background in these areas. The book also can be read with a minimal understanding of financial accounting and is designed as an introductory text in management accounting appropriate for entry-level undergraduate students.

We encourage critical thinking by providing an organizational change framework for analyzing management accounting problems. Thought-provoking, real-world examples and recent events are integrated throughout the text to illustrate the diverse role of management accounting in organizations. Business Analyses are features that provide more detailed examples of management accounting in action. Many of these items have Internet links to encourage students to explore these situations and organizations beyond the textbook. The Business Analyses pose questions linked to the analytical framework; there are no "correct" answers to these questions, but students should enjoy analyzing and investigating these real-world situations.

Text material is written as simply and concisely as possible and with a minimum of technical jargon to avoid confusion. The text material is supplemented by examples from organizations familiar to students. Each chapter has an organizational example that continues throughout to illustrate the chapter concepts. Other simple examples, both numerical and conceptual, are provided. The numerical examples focus primarily on a specific concept.

Numerical Example 9.3

A motor pool allocates costs to other departments of the same organization based on the number of miles driven in company cars. The motor pool expects to incur annual fixed costs of $200,000 and variable costs of $0.20 per mile driven. Company cars are expected to be driven a total of 800,000 miles. What application rate does the motor pool use? How does that application rate lead to underuse of the motor pool and costly behavior by other departments?

Solution

The application rate is the total expected costs in the motor pool divided by the total expected miles driven:

$$\frac{\$200,000 + (\$0.20/\text{mile})(800,000 \text{ miles})}{800,000 \text{ miles}} = \$0.45/\text{mile}$$

This application rate, however, is higher than the incremental cost of operating an automobile, which is $0.20 per mile. The application rate acts as a transfer price. Therefore, managers in other departments will choose to use other means of transportation if the cost per mile of alternative transportation is less than the application rate of $0.45 per mile for the motor pool. The entire organization would benefit, however, if the motor pool were used whenever the cost of the alternative means of transportation exceeded $0.20 per mile.

A free student CD-ROM includes alternate versions of these numerical examples with hints and immediate feedback. Students can work through these additional examples at their own pace and improve their quantitative skills. When a numerical example is marked with a CD-ROM icon, students can go to the CD-ROM to work through several variations of similar problems.

Each chapter begins with a list of learning objectives, which are reinforced with conceptual review questions throughout the chapter. The summary of each chapter is a short description of these learning objectives.

LEARNING OBJECTIVES

1. Use budgeting for planning purposes.
2. Use budgeting for control purposes.
3. Identify the conflicts that exist between planning and control in the budgeting process.

Concept Review

1. What are the planning benefits of budgeting?
2. What are the control benefits of budgeting?
3. How do planning and control issues lead to conflict in the budgeting process?

SUMMARY

1 **Use budgeting for planning purposes.** Budgeting facilitates the flow of information from the bottom up for general planning and from the top down for coordination.

2 **Use budgeting for control purposes.** The budget is used to allocate responsibilities to different members of the organization and to establish performance measures, which are used to reward managers.

3 **Identify the conflicts that exist between planning and control in the budgeting process.** The flow of information in the budgeting process might be inhibited or biased because the information used for planning is often the same information used for performance evaluation.

long-term planning. Short-term budgets are used for both planning and control.

5 **Explain the responsibility implications of a line-item budget.** Line-item budgets constrain responsibilities by limiting managers' ability to shift resources from one use to another.

6 **Identify the costs and benefits of budget lapsing.** Budget lapsing constrains the manager to expend resources in the budget period. This policy provides increased control; however, managers are not able to use their specialized information to make more efficient decisions and frequently are motivated to consume excess resources during the budgeted period.

END-OF-CHAPTER MATERIAL

The end-of-chapter problem material is an integral part of this text. The first section of problems is a set of numerical exercises (NE) similar to the numerical examples in the body of the chapter; they are clearly identified in terms of the learning objectives and concepts addressed. Students should be able to refer to the numerical examples in the text to complete the problems. The second section provides longer numerical problems (NP) that frequently combine numerical computations, analysis, and interpretation with the concepts learned in the chapter. The next section is devoted to analysis and interpretation problems (AIP) that reinforce the text's framework for organizational change. The AIPs require students to develop critical thinking skills and to write short essays presenting their analyses. Good problems excite students about the material and generate lively class discussions. Many problems do not have a single correct answer; instead, they contain multiple dimensions demanding a broad management perspective. The last section of extended AIPs emphasizes the need for students to combine analysis and interpretation with numerical computations within the broader context of organizational change. End-of-chapter material ranges in level of difficulty, allowing instructors to tailor the course to their particular requirements.

CHANGES IN THE SECOND EDITION

Beginning with the title, this text has a number of important changes from the first edition. The new title, *Management Accounting: Analysis and Interpretation*, emphasizes the authors' goal to meet the call by managers and accounting professionals for the development and encouragement of students' critical thinking skills.

Throughout the text, the framework for organizational change is a unifying theme that offers students an analytical approach linking management accounting to the broader organizational context. In each chapter, icons identify the various components of the analytical framework.

Strategy for Customer Value

The role of management accounting in actual organizations is illustrated and reinforced through the integration within the text of real-world examples. The Business Analyses expand and replace the What's Happening sidebars of the first edition and provide students with increased opportunity to explore management accounting in action.

Each chapter has been rewritten with the pedagogical approach revised in terms of the analytical framework. Feedback from users has led to the inclusion of additional straightforward numerical examples and exercises tied to the learning objectives and concepts.

Difficult concepts and material of a more technical nature have been rewritten and often moved to an appendix at the end of the chapter. This approach allows instructors to determine the depth of topic coverage for nonaccounting as well as accounting majors.

The end-of-chapter material has been reorganized and expanded. The addition of Numerical Exercises provides a series of quick problems for student review and in-class use. The Numerical Problems have been extended with more emphasis on analysis and interpretation in both decision-making and control contexts. The Analysis and Interpretation Problems (previously Discussion Problems and Cases) have been supplemented. These problems challenge students to critically examine issues from multiple perspectives, not overlook the need for computational skills.

Chapter Fifteen, Managerial Accounting in International Organizations, of the first edition has been replaced with the integration of international examples and issues throughout the text. This approach should encourage students to understand the global context in which management accounting and organizations operate.

SUPPLEMENTS FOR THE INSTRUCTOR

Solutions Manual (0-07-290856-4)

Prepared by the authors, this manual contains detailed solutions for all end-of-chapter material in *Management Accounting*. The Solutions Manual has been accuracy checked by independent parties. Electronic files of the solutions manual are available at the text's Online Learning Center (www.mhhe.com/mm2) and on the Presentation Manager CD-ROM.

Instructor's Resource Guide (0-07-290858-0)

Prepared by the authors, this manual includes detailed teaching ideas for *Management Accounting*. The authors discuss ways to divide the text into class size sections for three- or four-credit quarters or semester courses, classify problem material according to difficulty, and suggest alternative teaching strategies for end-of-chapter material (including ways to use it to promote cooperative learning). Conversion notes to make the transition from leading competitors to *Management Accounting* are also provided and highlight some material available to adopters of *Management Accounting*. The Instructor's Resource Manual also provides additional "real-life" scenarios that include references to simple organizations that students understand and current events of better-known, larger organizations.

Ready Shows (0-07-561765-X)

Prepared by Jon A. Booker, Charles W. Caldwell, Susan C. Galbreath, and Richard S. Rand, all of Tennessee Technological University, Ready Shows is a comprehensive package of multimedia lecture enhancement aids that use PowerPoint® software to illustrate chapter concepts.

Test Bank (0-07-290824-6)

This comprehensive test bank contains more than 1,200 items. For each chapter of *Management Accounting*, adopters have the choice of objective questions, numerical problems, and discussion problems.

Presentation Manager (0-07-242241-6)

This all-in-one resource contains the Instructor's Manual, Test Bank, and Power-Point presentations organized by chapter. A computerized version of the test bank is available in Windows format and was developed using Diploma software—a new and easy-to-use software, this option provides more flexibility in designing your assessment tools. Thanks to the Presentation Manager, you can create a multimedia presentation that incorporates video, PowerPoint, solutions, and lecture outlines into one presentation.

Video Guide (0-07-561720-X)
Richard D. Irwin Managerial/Cost Video Library

These short, action-oriented videos provide the impetus for lively classroom discussion. This six-volume library includes videos of international and service companies as well as many manufacturing examples, as outlined here:

Richard D. Irwin Managerial /Cost Video Library I (0-256-13511-8)

"Behind the Bill"
"The Vancouver Door Company"
"How Many Bucks in a Bag"

Richard D. Irwin Managerial/Cost Video Library II (0-256-13512-6)

"Moving the Merchandise"
"Ogre Mills, after the Curtain Fell"

Richard D. Irwin Managerial /Cost Video Library III (0-256-14970-4)

"Lean Production"
"Quality"
"The Manufacturing Process"

Richard D. Irwin Managerial/Cost Video Library IV (0-256-14971-2)

"Computer-Integrated Manufacturing"
"Inventory Management"
"Service"

Richard D. Irwin Managerial/Cost Video Library V (0-256-14972-0)

"Manufacturing"
"Supplier Development Outreach"
"Program"
"Accounting Careers"

Richard D. Irwin Managerial/Cost Video Library VI (0-256-15924-6)

"Atlas Foundry and Machine Company"
"Management Accounting and Concepts"
"International Accounting"

SUPPLEMENTS FOR THE STUDENT
Free Interactive and Text-Integrated Student CD

A free, interactive student CD is provided to students that purchase a new textbook. This CD is designed to enhance the learning experience by providing additional practice in the **quantitative** and **qualitative** aspects of managerial accounting. As a result, the CD is divided into two sections: one providing additional practice on the numerical aspect of managerial accounting and the other providing additional practice in effective decision making. Students who use this innovative and valuable resource in conjunction with the textbook will achieve a balanced perspective of managerial accounting. As a result, they will better understand the **"big picture"** of managerial accounting—a major recommendation of the Accounting Education Change Commission (AECC).

The purpose of the first section of the CD is to provide additional practice and reinforcement for students that have difficulty with the quantitative aspect of managerial accounting. Each chapter in the textbook contains many *Numerical Examples* to help students gain a better understanding of how to quantify decision alternatives. Several of these *Numerical Examples* are marked with a CD icon to indicate to students that additional practice is available on the student CD. They will be provided with several variations to the corresponding *Numerical Example* in the textbook to aid in their comprehension. This interactive feature provides feedback to the student so they are able to improve this important skill set.

The purpose of the second section of the student CD is to place the student in the role of decision maker. Each chapter in the textbook contains a vignette woven throughout the chapter to highlight the key concepts in the context of a business setting. We have altered these vignettes for the student CD, and we have made them interactive. The unique conceptual framework presented in Chapter One, and referenced throughout the text, serves as the interface as students progress through a series of decision alternatives. Each scenario begins with either a technological change, a change in customer needs, or global competition that impacts the student's business. They must then decide, by selecting from strategic alternatives, how they will respond to this challenge in order to continue to provide customer value. Depending on their strategic decision, they will be prompted to select from planning and/or control decision alternatives. Based on the quality of their decisions, they will achieve either customer and organizational value, or they will be prompted to try again. This innovative and fun learning tool will improve the student's analytical skills.

Text Support Website
www.mhhe.com/business/accounting/mmz

Our marketing research indicates that when students visit text support websites an overwhelming majority gravitate to the online quizzing feature. As a result, we have greatly enhanced the quizzing component to our website. Most supporting websites provide 10–15 questions per chapter with minimal or no feedback. We provide students with 40–60 questions per chapter with feedback so they can obtain as much practice as necessary to better comprehend the important concepts presented in each chapter. They are particularly effective in preparation for exams to determine where additional studying is needed. Our research also indicates that many instructors like to quiz students prior to the start of class to motivate students to come to class prepared. For this reason we have provided an option for students to email their instructor their completed quiz. In addition to the enhanced quizzing component, we offer an array of additional online study tools.

PowerWeb

This content rich, online resource contains managerial and cost accounting specific articles, exercises, current events, additional self grading quizzes, interactive exercises, an interactive glossary, and daily news relevant to managerial accounting. The content was created by managerial and cost accounting professors and is frequently updated. Of course, the daily new is updated each day.

Acknowledgments

We received tremendous feedback from users and nonusers of the first edition. We began with a detailed survey to obtain more input regarding our framework, pedagogy, and end-of-chapter material, as well as other issues facing the managerial accounting course. More than 50 instructors responded, and their suggestions were instrumental in defining the look and feel of this text. We gratefully acknowledge all who participated in our survey:

Helen Adams, University of Washington
Felix E. Amenkhienan, Radford University
T. S. Amer, Northern Arizona University
Walter Austin, Mercer University
Ibrahim Badawi, St. John's University
James Bierstaker, University of Massachusetts–Boston
Marinus J. Bouwman, University of Arkansas
Rodger L. Brannan, University of Minnesota–Duluth
Robert Campbell, Miami University (Ohio)
Judith Cassidy, University of Mississippi
Chak-Tong Chau, University of Texas–San Antonio
John Core, University of Pennsylvania
Michael Dole, Marquette University
Paul J. Donadio, Marist College
Robert Elmore, Tennessee Technological University
Jerry W. Ferry, University of North Alabama
Michael L. Finch, Austin Peay State University
David R. Fordham, James Madison University
Lyal V. Gustafson, University of Wisconsin–Whitewater
Cynthia D. Heagy, University of Houston–Clear Lake
Jay Holmen, University of Wisconsin–Eau Claire
Bambi Hora, University of Central Oklahoma
Herbert G. Hunt, University of Vermont
Melvyn D. Hutt, Christopher Newport University
Paul Jensen, University of Central Arkansas
Sushila Kedia, Grambling State University
Saleha Khumawala, University of Houston
Mehmet Kocakulah, University of Southern Indiana
A. Ronald Kucic, University of Denver
Minwoo Lee, Western Kentucky University
Y. Robert Lin, California State University–Hayward
Cathy Lumbattis, Southern Illinois University
Mary D. Maury, St. John's University
Anita R. McKie, University of South Carolina–Aiken
Louella Moore, Arkansas State University
Liz Mulig, University of Texas–Tyler
Hossein Nouri, College of New Jersey

Joe O'Donnell, Canisius College
Robert R. Picard, Idaho State University
Andrew Potts, University of Southern Maine
Robert Putman, University of Tennessee at Martin
Vaughan Radcliffe, Case Western Reserve University
Sue Ravenscroft, Iowa State University
Manash Ray, Lehigh University
Roy W. Regel, University of Montana
Anne Rich, Quinnipiac College
Steve Rowley, University of Minnesota–Duluth
Stephen Ryan, New York University
Jeff Schatzberg, University of Arizona
James H. Sellers, University of Texas–Tyler
William Smith, Xavier University
David E. Stout, Villanova University
Scott Stovall, Harding University
Cathy Sullivan, James Madison University
Greg Thibadoux, University of Tennessee at Chattanooga
Lee Warren, Belmont University
Steven D. White, Western Kentucky University
Neil Wilner, University of North Texas
Katherine Wilson, Embry-Riddle University

We received extensive reviews of the first edition and the new manuscript from a wide range of instructors. Their chapter-by-chapter comments helped us fine-tune our presentation and significantly shaped the final draft. We wish to thank our reviewer panel for members' invaluable advice and suggestions:

Wagdy Abdallah, Seton Hall University
Lane Anderson, Texas Tech University
Roger Doost, Clemson University
Saurav Dutta, SUNY–Albany
Geoffrey Gurka, Southern Connecticut State University
Susan Gustin, West Virginia University
Jerry Haugland, Southeast Missouri State University
Afshad J. Irani, University of New Hampshire
Badr E. Ismail, Syracuse University
Melvin Jolly, Geneva College
Robert Koehler, Pennsylvania State University
Wendy Krislen-Adams, Linn Benton Community College
Thomas J. Krissek, Northeastern Illinois University
Robert G. Morgan, East Tennessee State University
Michael Mosebach, Old Dominion University
Gerald Myers, Pacific Lutheran University
Elizabeth Goad Oliver, Washington and Lee University
Sheila Shain, St. Mary's University
Dhinu Srinivasan, University of Pittsburgh
Bonnie Stivers, Kennesaw State University
Dan Stone, University of Illinois at Urbana-Champaign
Dan Swenson, University of Idaho

Lynda Thoman, Purdue University

Bernadette Vehec, Valencia Community College

Bente Villadsen, University of Iowa

Gary J. Vostok, Fitchburg State University

James J. Wallace, University of California–Irvine

In 1999, McGraw-Hill/Irwin collaborated with the Gary Siegel Organization, Inc. (GSO), on an extensive study of the management accounting course. The goals were to identify the way the management accounting course is changing and what textbook features and support materials would help address these changes. GSO conducted in-depth interviews with management accounting instructors at 150 schools.

Highlights from the interview results are available at our book's Online Learning Center (www.mhhe.com/mmz). The feedback we received was vital in determining the topics we emphasized, the types of problem material we developed, and the supplement package we created. We extend a special thanks to the many instructors who participated in these interviews and to the Gary Siegel Organization, Inc., for its superb work in conducting this research and analyzing the results.

Finally, we thank our colleagues at McGraw-Hill/Irwin for their help in developing and producing *Management Accounting: Analysis and Interpretation*.

Management accounting is an exciting and thought-provoking topic. We believe that this book should encourage students to pursue its study further. We appreciate any comments that help us to achieve this goal.

Cheryl S. McWatters

Dale C. Morse

Jerold L. Zimmerman

Brief**Contents**

Contents

ChapterThree
Measuring and Analyzing Product Costs   68

ChapterFour
Managing Activities   104

ChapterFive
Short-Term Decisions and Constraints 136

ChapterSix
Managing Organizations   168

ChapterSeven
Decentralized Organizations 194

ChapterEight
Budgeting 238

ChapterNine
Cost Allocations   *282*

ChapterTen
Absorption Costing Systems   *330*

ChapterEleven
Variable Costing and Capacity Costs   380

ChapterTwelve
Management Accounting in a Dynamic Environment   420

ChapterThirteen
Investment Decisions   *456*

ChapterFourteen
Standard Costs and Variance Analysis   *500*

Management**Accounting**

Analysis and Interpretation

Chapter**One**

Management Accounting in an Organizational Context

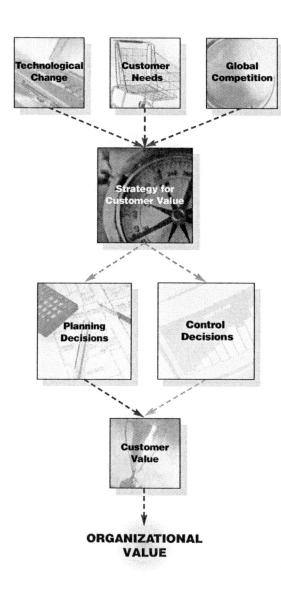

LEARNING OBJECTIVES

1 Explain how technological change, globalization, and customer needs can affect an organization and its management accounting system.

2 Identify strategies for achieving customer value.

3 Describe features of organizations that promote decisions to achieve their goals.

4 Explain the critical role played by management accounting in making planning and control decisions to help managers create organizational value.

5 Identify the trade-offs that exist in using information for making planning and control decisions and for external reporting.

6 Identify the roles of different types of management accountants.

7 Recognize the role of judgment and ethics in making management accounting choices.

COMPACT DISC STORES

Three years ago when Diane Johnson approached Janice Nishimura about investing in a compact disc store, Janice was not very excited. But Diane persisted. She explained to her friend that music stores don't have to pay for compact discs (CDs) until they are sold because any unsold CDs are returned to their producers. Therefore, no initial investment is required for inventory, and no risk of unsold inventory exists.

Diane's initial business strategy was to have low markups on CDs and attempt to sell large volumes. Diane also wanted to support local recording artists by reserving some shelf-space for their CDs.

Diane eventually convinced Janice to invest $50,000 along with her own $50,000 to form a partnership. Diane would receive an annual salary of $30,000 for managing the store, and she and Janice would share the remaining profits equally. Janice would not be involved in management. They were also able to borrow $200,000 from a bank and leased space in the center of town for the initial Compact Disc Store. After sales exceeded expectations, they opened two more Compact Disc Stores in suburban shopping malls and hired managers to operate them.

With the growth of the business, problems have begun to arise. Sales haven't been as high as expected at one of the new stores, and the other store appears to suffer from considerable shoplifting. Competition in the retail CD business has increased with a national chain's opening of a megastore near one of the mall stores. In addition, the Internet has become a factor with customers buying from Internet retailers such as Amazon.com or downloading music from MP3.com.

These new competitors have hurt sales. Diane and Janice must make some decisions to revise their strategy and operations and adapt to the increased competition. They realize that the stores must be much more sensitive to their customers and operate more efficiently, but they aren't sure exactly what to do.

MANAGEMENT ACCOUNTING IN A CHANGING ENVIRONMENT

ORGANIZATIONAL VALUE

Management accounting helps create organizational value through better decision making and management of the members of the organization. For example, management accounting information on costs helps managers to make decisions on products and services. Also, management accounting information is used in evaluating a manager's performance. Management accounting enables accountants to bring an integrating perspective to the organization's strategic and financial decisions.

Management accounting includes the design and use of information within organizations. Traditionally, management accounting has focused on financial information, such as the cost of a product or the revenues generated by a unit of the organization. But selecting and analyzing nonfinancial information, such as the time required to make a product or the percentage of defective products, has become an important part of management accounting. Nonfinancial information supplements financial information by providing a broader understanding of the organization, which can lead to better decisions.

Management accounting is not composed of a fixed set of rules. Organizations have different goals and are composed of different members; therefore, no universal rules of management accounting exist. Management accounting must adapt to each organization.

LO 1 Explain how technological change, globalization, and customer needs can affect an organization and its management accounting system.

Management accounting is not a static process. Instead, it adapts to organizational change. Three major forces cause organizations to evolve: technological change, globalization, and customer needs. Organizations that fail to adapt to these forces will not be able to survive in the long run. Organizations must meet the needs of other stakeholder groups beyond those of their customers. For example, the goals of shareholders and employees also must be satisfied to maintain the organization's viability.

Organizations depend on management accounting to provide information in a dynamic environment. If the evolution of the management accounting system lags behind the evolution of the organization, the system will act as an anchor preventing the organization from successfully dealing with a changing environment. Organizations must adapt to changing environments, and management accounting must adapt to changing organizations. Therefore, the study of management accounting is a study of a process, not a study of a set of procedures. The process of management accounting is linked to the characteristics of the organization, which are constantly changing. To understand management accounting, you must understand organizations and the forces that affect them.

The following sections describe the three major forces, technological change, globalization, and customer needs, that affect organizations. Organizations have chosen to adapt to these forces in different ways. Some of these adaptations, such as total quality management (TQM) and just-in-time (JIT) processes, have become well publicized. The following sections describe these adaptations and others; by identifying and understanding these changes in organizations, we can appreciate the role and process of management accounting.

Technological Change: Computers, Information Acquisition, and the Internet

Technology has dramatically changed the way we live. Computers, telecommunications, transportation systems, and medical and scientific discoveries affect the way we work, eat, and recreate. Organizations have been similarly influenced by technological change and will be continually influenced by breakthroughs in the future. For example, consider how e-mail and e-commerce have changed our lives.

Computers

The computing power of a digital watch today exceeds the computing power of the largest calculating machine just 50 years ago. Just 30 years ago, the slide rule was still an engineer's best friend. The proliferation of personal computers has occurred only in the last 15 years. The impact of computers on organizations has been enormous. They have affected the design and manufacture of products, the way organizations communicate with their suppliers and customers, and the way organizations are managed internally.

Computers also allow organizations to make better-quality products more efficiently through automation and precise operations. **Computer-integrated manufacturing (CIM)** is the term used to describe an organization that links all of its systems by computer. These links

CAD allows the design engineer to visualize the final product and the impact of changes in a three-dimensional format. Using this technology helps the organization to see the final product through the eyes of the customer. When linked with the management accounting system, CAD helps the organization determine the cost impact of product ideas and design changes prior to the production stage.

begin with **computer-assisted design (CAD)**, which allows engineers and designers to create new product ideas using three-dimensional plans. Car manufacturers such as DaimlerChrysler and airplane manufacturers such as Boeing rely heavily on CAD.

The computer design is then linked to the manufacturing process. **Computer-aided manufacturing (CAM)**, for example, allows organizations to make products through programmed machines. These machines perform the welding in the manufacture of cars and insert components in a circuit board in the electronics industry. In addition to saving on some labor costs, these machines have the advantage of being more precise and faster than humans are.

The CIM organization also has the advantage of real-time information. The Coors production facility in Virginia is a CIM facility. Its reporting system is tied to the manufacturing system and provides minute-by-minute displays. These systems feed process and operational data into a database that can be accessed by many users. All the employees at the Coors plant are trained to use the computer system.[1] Using real-time information, they can continually monitor quality and react quickly to design changes and market demand.

Technological Change

Information Acquisition and Dissemination

Probably the largest and most recent impact of technology on organizations relates to the proliferation of information products and services. The telecommunications and computer industries have revolutionized the way organizations operate; organizations can communicate with their members, suppliers, and customers almost instantly through devices such as cellular phones, fax machines, and the Internet. Restaurants use electronic pagers to inform customers their table is ready and servers that food orders are ready. Information on the changing demand for products and demographics is easily accessible. In addition, computers can

---

[1] K. Walker and T. Zinsli, "Coors Shenandoah: Brewing a Better Start-Up Operation," *Journal of Cost Management* 7, no. 2 (Summer 1993), pp. 5–12.

manipulate and simulate different scenarios to allow organizations to make better predictions about the future. To be successful, organizations must recognize the advantages of greater access to information.

A survey of financial executives indicated that many accounting systems are not adapting rapidly enough to new technology. Of the financial executives surveyed, 80% indicated that their company's accounting system produced useful data too slowly and inefficiently. Smithkline-Beecham, a large pharmaceutical firm, installed software to reduce the time to make certain budgeting comparisons from two to three weeks to two to three days.[2] Other companies are experimenting with real-time management with information available almost immediately.

Internet

The potential importance of the Internet for organizations can be seen in the stock market, with shares of Internet companies selling at high prices even though the companies currently are not generating any profit. Many industries operate almost solely through the Internet. Internet companies, such as Amazon.com and e-Trade.com, are challenging established firms for dominance in book and music retail sales, stock transactions, and banking. Technological advances, such as improved modems and mobile access, are motivating firms to expand operations to the Internet.[3]

Soon every organization will use the Internet as part of normal operations. The Internet provides information to potential customers as well as service to customers following purchase and is important in providing coordination with suppliers. A majority of all new car buyers now get basic information about prices and options via the Internet.[4] It allows organizations to "outsource" (subcontract) different organizational processes including manufacturing and billing. "Virtual" organizations may retain only some design functions.

Globalization: Low Costs, Operating Efficiently, and JIT

Global Competition

Globalization is the integration of national economies into a single international economy. Although trade and monetary barriers continue to exist among many countries, globalization has been a major force affecting business organizations in the last 40 years. In 1960, almost all cars and televisions purchased in the United States were made there. Today, however, most of the televisions and many of the cars purchased in the United States come from abroad. A simple examination of the tags on the clothes you are wearing indicates the extent of globalization. Shoes are made in Singapore, T-shirts in Guatemala, jeans in South Korea, and baseball caps in Costa Rica. Many products contain parts produced in a number of different countries. Financial markets and ownership also extend across national borders. Economic problems in one country frequently have a ripple effect around the world, as did those in Southeast Asia in 1999. Multinational organizations with operations in multiple countries are commonplace. In addition, the Internet has created an international marketplace. With the reduction of tariffs as a result of treaties such as the North American Free Trade Agreement (NAFTA), business organizations must consider the whole world as a source of competition, a source for parts, and an opportunity for new customers.

---

[2] *The Wall Street Journal*, February 2, 1995, B 2:5.

[3] "Survey: E-Commerce," *The Economist*, February 26, 2000.

[4] D. Tapscott, "Car Dealers Miss Web Retail Boat," *National Post*, February 19, 2000.

Low Costs

To be successful in a global economy, business organizations must be able to provide their products and services at a lower cost than their competition does. With the advent of the Internet, consumers can easily compare prices for products and services offered by different firms. No longer will businesses be able to sell products at high prices without offering a corresponding value or service.

With global competition limiting the prices that can be charged to customers, organizations must find ways to control the cost of creating products and services. One approach to reducing costs is to shift labor production costs to developing countries with lower labor rates. This procedure may cause temporary hardships and job losses, but an organization (and each individual) must continually look for its comparative advantage in a global economy to survive. Although the global economy threatens organizations and individuals that are unable to adapt, consumers in the current global economy enjoy the greatest diversity of products at the lowest prices and highest qualities in the history of the world.

Operating Efficiently

Seeking out places with lower labor costs is one way to reduce product costs. However, shifting production to take advantage of lower labor rates does not result necessarily in the lowest cost. Firms must also examine the efficiency of their low-cost workers compared to that of workers who command higher wage rates. If higher-paid employees can work more efficiently, organizations prefer to use them. These workers are more productive, suggesting that even if they are paid more, their employment results in lower costs overall. One of the basic theories of economics states that workers should be paid based on their productivity.

To improve efficiency and lower the cost of providing products and services, organizations must continually reevaluate and reengineer their processes. *Reengineering* refers to modifying processes within the organization to operate more efficiently, often by adopting new technologies.

Just-in-Time (JIT) Processes

Just-in-time (JIT) processes provide products and services on demand. JIT allows some organizations to operate more efficiently and at a lower cost. Manufacturing organizations using JIT make a product when an order is received rather than make it in advance and hold it until it is sold or discarded. Service organizations using JIT must adjust operations so that customers are served upon demand. With JIT, customers should no longer have long waits for delivery of the product or service. To make JIT work, the organization must design systems from order entry to delivery that operate efficiently and without delay. JIT is designed to eliminate or reduce activities that do not provide value to customers. One result of JIT is the elimination of inventory. By making the product only when it is ordered, there is no wasted product due to obsolescence or lack of demand. Moreover, the costs of warehousing and holding inventories are reduced. Gateway and Dell have combined the use of JIT and the Internet to compete successfully with IBM. In late 1999, IBM decided to pull its personal computer line from retail stores and to reinvent itself as an Internet retailer.

JIT works by supplying the product or service quickly only when demanded. If customers must wait, they will go elsewhere for the product or service. Organizations are able to shift to JIT, in part, because of technological changes. For example, the advent of bar-coding and the instant reporting of sales to grocery-store suppliers allowed Wal-Mart to hold less inventory and offer

At the production stage, mass production is shifting increasingly to mass customization. As always, firms strive to create customer value by operating efficiently and maintaining an adequate level of quality. In turn, organizational value is enhanced by eliminating non–value-added activities.

Customer Needs

customers lower prices. CAM allows manufacturers to change production quickly to accommodate unexpected changes in demand. Toyota's automated plants, for example, are designed to reduce the time of changing over from making one type of car to another. Computers also allow service organizations to satisfy customer demands more quickly. Automatic teller machines (ATMs) allow bank customers to obtain cash when needed rather than wait for normal operating hours. Internet banking even enables consumers to process many transactions from home.

Customers: TQM and Value Chain Analysis

Organizations must continually monitor technological change and global competition, but unless they identify and meet customer needs, all is for naught. Creating customer value by fulfilling their desires is critical to an organization's success. If customers want vanilla ice cream and you supply chocolate, your sales will suffer and some other organization will step in to supply vanilla. Organizations must continually seek to add value to customers by adapting to changing customer needs. For example, eBay.com has created an entire market for auctioning low-cost collectibles. Total quality management and value chain analysis help an organization have a customer focus.

Total Quality Management

The move to a customer orientation has been formalized through **total quality management (TQM)**. TQM is a philosophy of continually lowering costs and improving the provision of services and products to customers. TQM involves everyone within the organization. Quality is defined by the customer and designed into the product. Shifting to TQM means that the organization seeks to continually improve its operations and customer service.

Value Chain Analysis

Value chain analysis is associated with both JIT and TQM. The basic concept is to look at what the organization does through the eyes of the customer. Organizations do many things, but from a customer perspective, only some activities provide value. Those activities are called the *value chain*. A typical value chain might look like this:

Research and development → Design and engineering → Production → Distribution → Customer service

Any activities that are not on the value chain are considered **non–value-added activities;** they do not provide value for customers. Examples of such include moving and storing products and many administrative tasks. Elimination of non–value-added activities allows the organization to save resources and sell its products and services at a lower price without reducing the value to customers.

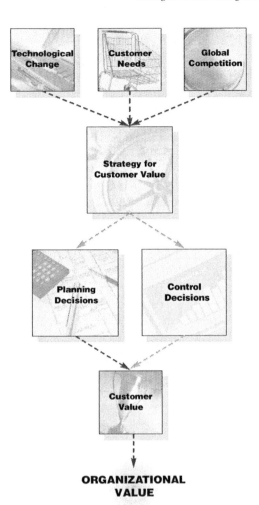

Figure 1.1

Framework for
Organizational Change

Adaptation to a Changing Environment

The preceding text has emphasized that organizations and their management accounting systems must adapt to a rapidly changing environment. Previous sections have outlined the impact of technological change, globalization, and customer needs and have introduced procedures for dealing with these external forces. Computer-integrated manufacturing, just-in-time processes, total quality management, and value chain analysis are methods that take advantage of technological changes and allow an organization to compete and to meet customer needs. Subsequent chapters review these procedures and introduce others. We will see that the success of an organization is closely tied to having the appropriate procedures and management accounting system.

This chapter develops a framework, outlined in Figure 1.1, to describe how organizations must adapt to technological change, globalization, and customer needs. The framework highlights that an organization's planning and control decisions must be consistent with its strategy. This model does not include all factors that affect a organization. For example, other approaches to organizational analysis and behavior emphasize decision making, human resources, leadership, and power. Each model provides insights into the complex nature of an organization. The framework in this book focuses on the need for organizations to make decisions and control behavior (and the trade-off between the two) so that organizational value is created. The remaining sections of this chapter describe the way that the organization adapts and the role of management accounting in the organization.

Concept**Review**

1. Why is management accounting an evolving process?
2. How can new technologies affect an organization?
3. What is the impact of globalization on an organization?
4. Why is meeting customer demand critical for an organization?

**COMPACT
DISC STORES**
(Continued)

Diane knows she must be aware of technological innovations that may make in-store sales of CDs obsolete. Most important is the need to adapt to the Internet revolution. She has identified some innovations that will help in operating her business. Bar-coding the CDs allows Diane and the suppliers of the CDs to track inventory. Also, antitheft magnetic tapes help reduce shoplifting.

Globalization is now affecting Diane's business. Through the Internet, retailers in Japan and Australia suddenly have become her competitors, but, if Diane gets on the Internet, the whole world can become her market.

Diane is also concerned about her shop customers. Although her stores sell CDs for low prices, she has ignored other aspects of customer satisfaction. Do customers find the CDs they want? Do they receive friendly service? Should the stores have more listening rooms? Diane realizes that her sales goal and her goal to help local artists depend on having satisfied customers. She is considering implementing a customer survey to discover what customers want and restructuring the organization to recognize the importance of customers. She plans to attend an upcoming seminar on TQM to make the organization more sensitive to customers.

STRATEGY FOR INCREASING CUSTOMER VALUE

**Strategy for
Customer Value**

Customers receive value from purchasing an organization's products and services. If the value the customers receive is less than the price they must pay for the product and/or service, they will not make the purchase. Therefore, an organization must offer its products and services at a price less than customer value. At the same time, the organization must be able to provide the product or service at a cost less than the price in order to sustain itself. For example, if customers value CDs at $17 each, CD stores must sell them for less than $17, say $16, and be able to buy them for $15. (The difference between the sales price and the purchase cost represents the *margin* on each CD.) To make matters more complex, the organization must accomplish this task in a world of technological change and globalization.

Organizations develop strategies by looking at the opportunities and threats posed by technological change, globalization, and customer needs. New technology offers opportunities to be more efficient and competitive but also threatens to make the existing technology of the organization outdated. Globalization provides the threat of new competitors entering an organization's market, but it also provides more opportunities to expand markets for an organization's products or services. Changing customer needs provide opportunities to develop new products and services but threaten the success of existing products and services.

At the same time, each organization must recognize its own strengths and weaknesses, given its existing and proposed characteristics. Personnel skills, access to capital, location, brand awareness and loyalty, and organizational structure help to determine an organization's strengths and weaknesses.

Given the existing and potential strengths and weaknesses of the organization and the opportunities and threats of the environment, the organization must decide how to create customer value. Organizations generally follow one of the following three strategies: innovative product/service design, high-quality products and services, or low-cost production. These strategies reflect the key variables that provide customer value.

LO 2   Identify strategies for achieving customer value.

Innovative Product/Service Design

With changes in technology and customer demand, some organizations are first at designing a new product or service that adds customer value. For example, Amazon.com was one of the first Internet booksellers. Being the "first mover" requires an organization to have excellent marketing and design skills. The marketing function is critical in identifying customer trends and niches that have not been previously identified. At the same time, an organization needs a good design team to take advantage of new technologies and meet changing customer demand.

By beating other global competitors to the market with a new product or service, an organization, such as eBay.com, temporarily can reap the rewards of adding customer value before profits are diluted as a result of price suppression. Obtaining patents can lengthen the time of profitable opportunities for a new product, but other organizations will soon find ways to make similar products.

The strategy of competing through innovative product/service design involves increased risk but offers the largest profit opportunities. Certain brand-name drug companies typically compete through innovative product design. They spend considerable amounts on research and development for new remedies for diseases. When it is successful, a new drug can be very profitable, but a drug company that cannot continually develop new drugs will have to invest in a different strategy to survive.

High-Quality Products and Services

Some organizations follow the strategy of providing high-quality products and services to achieve customer value. *High quality* in this case means delivering a product or service that conforms to the specifications of the design and meets or surpasses customers' expectations. High quality does not mean making a product with greater functionality than other products. A 5-bedroom house is a different product than a single-width trailer, yet both can be of high quality if they meet the specifications of what the customer ordered. Moreover, one customer can perceive two 5-bedroom houses differently in terms of quality as a result of other features such as size, layout, and location.

Successfully achieving a high-quality strategy requires the organization to pay considerable attention to the details of manufacturing and providing service. The organization must be aware of customer expectations and develop procedures that ensure that each product and service satisfies and even surpasses those expectations.

Grocery chains sell brand-name products as well as store brands, or generics, that provide customers with a lower-priced alternative often equal in quality. Grocery chains use management accounting data, such as product and marketing costs and profit margins, to evaluate the relative profitability of these products.

For example, online stock-trading companies must offer customers highly reliable, secure network connections.

Low-Cost Production

Another strategy to compete in a global economy is to be the low-cost producer of a product or service. Low-cost producers, such as Wal-Mart, can sell their products and services at a lower price than the competition does. By offering the products and services at a lower price, these organizations create customer value.

To be a low-cost producer, an organization must operate very efficiently. Low-cost producers cannot afford to have many non–value-added activities. At the same time, low-cost producers cannot completely sacrifice quality; customers still expect a certain level of quality.

Generic drug manufacturers are examples of low-cost producers. They spend very little on advertising and expect to be successful by charging a lower price for drugs than do brand-name drug companies. Grocery stores, such as Safeway in the United States and Loblaws in Canada, have their own store brands. These products compete with name brands but can sell at lower costs because of savings on advertising.

Strategies and Management Accounting

Whether an organization chooses to create customer value through innovation, quality, or low cost, management accounting plays an important role in the process. Strategies require planning and implementation, both of which are supported by management accounting. Management accounting methods should differ however, depending on the strategy chosen. Certain management accounting methods promote innovation while others promote quality or low-cost production. Matching management accounting methods with a strategy is critical to the organization's success. The role of strategy in achieving customer value is incorporated into the framework for organizational change in Figure 1.1.

Concept**Review**

1. What is customer value?

2. How can an organization create customer value?

COMPACT DISC STORES (Continued)

Diane needs a strategy to adapt to the opportunities and threats from technological changes, globalization, and customer demand. An examination of her own weaknesses has indicated that she has neither sufficient funds for major capital investments nor the technical expertise to develop new methods of recording or distributing music. Diane's strengths come from knowledge of local customers and recording artists. She decides not to expand her retail stores but to focus on excellent customer service in her existing stores. Better customer service will help to increase sales, especially at the weaker suburban store. In addition, she believes that CD sales can be expanded through an Internet site dedicated to local artists. This Internet strategy would reduce the need for a major input of capital.

ORGANIZATIONS AND DECISIONS

An *organization* is a group of individuals who have joined together to perform particular tasks to achieve particular goals. Organizations include schools, businesses, clubs, religious groups, hospitals, and governmental bodies. Organizations are formed because groups of individuals can perform particular tasks more easily than individuals operating alone can.

An organization performs tasks to achieve goals. Its goals reflect the interests of its **stakeholders.** The organization's stakeholders include any parties affected by the organization: owners, creditors, employees, customers, and society. Typical goals might include providing cash or nonmonetary benefits to the owners, maximizing profits, satisfying customers, improving the welfare of members of the organization, and providing services to society. To survive, however, an organization must receive sufficient resources through sales, donations, or other means to support its expenditures.

To achieve these goals, an organization must continually adapt to a changing environment. Decisions that will lead to customer value must be made. The following sections describe how organizations make decisions to achieve customer value and meet the organization's goals.

Organizational Structure

Although an organization forms to achieve goals not easily accomplishable by individuals, not all individuals within the organization will agree on how it should operate. An organization has a formal or informal structure that describes how decisions are made. An organization's structure is composed of three related processes: (1) assigning responsibilities, (2) measuring performance, and (3) rewarding individuals within the organization.

LO 3   Describe features of organizations that promote decisions to achieve their goals.

Assigning Responsibilities

The first component of the organizational structure determines the responsibilities of the organization's different members. These responsibilities define the duties that a member is expected to perform. Job descriptions specify the responsibilities of a particular individual within an organization. Checkout clerks in grocery stores have the responsibility to collect cash from customers but cannot accept certain types of checks; they must call a manager for that decision. A division manager may have the responsibility to set prices on products but not the responsibility to borrow money through issuing debt. The responsibility to issue debt is usually retained by the president or the board of directors. The organizational chart in Figure 1.2 represents the structure in a traditional firm. This type of organizational chart frequently is used to provide a hierarchy of responsibilities. As firms adopt advanced manufacturing technologies, they often develop alternative organizational structures and charts that reflect these new management approaches.

Performance Measures

An organization must also motivate individuals to perform their duties in a manner consistent with its goals. Individuals have their own goals, which are not necessarily congruent with those of the organization. To motivate individuals within it, the organization must have a system for measuring performance and rewarding individuals. **Performance measures** are direct or indirect measures of output by individuals or groups of individuals within the organization. Performance measures for a salesperson could include total sales and customer satisfaction based on a survey of customers. Performance measures for a manufacturing unit could include the number of units produced, their cost, and the percentage of defective units.

Rewards

Performance measures are extremely important because rewards are generally based on them. Rewards for individuals within organizations include wages and

Figure 1.2   Partial Organizational Chart of a Corporation

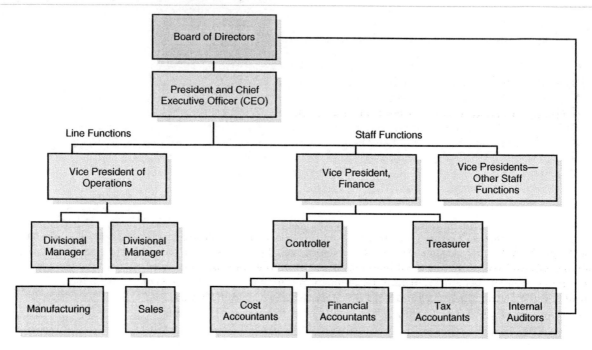

bonuses, prestige and increased responsibilities, promotions, and job security. Because rewards are based on performance measures, individuals and groups are motivated to act to influence the performance measures. Therefore, the performance measures influence the direction of individual and group efforts within the organization. A poor choice of performance measures can lead to conflicts within the organization and derail efforts to achieve its goals. For example, measuring the performance of a college president based on the number of students attending the college will encourage the president to allow ill-prepared students to enter the college, which will reduce the quality of the educational experience for other students.

Decision Making within an Organization

Historically, only individuals at the top of the organizational chart made decisions for the organization; the remaining employees simply did what they were told. Organizations, however, have now recognized that most individuals within them have knowledge that can be useful for decision making. Factory employees often have better knowledge of the manufacturing process than do their superiors. Salespeople usually know their customers better than the sales manager does. To take advantage of this specialized knowledge, organizations have given these employees more responsibilities. This delegation of responsibilities is known as *worker empowerment* or *decentralization*.

    The two general types of decisions that members of the organization must make are planning decisions and control decisions.

**Planning
Decisions**

Planning Decisions

To accomplish the organization's goals, managers must make decisions on what tasks should be performed and how to complete them. **Planning decisions** occur at all levels of the organization. Long-term planning decisions tend to be made by the top-level managers; short-term planning decisions tend to be made by individuals with less responsibility. The president of the organization is likely to make decisions on what product lines to offer and long-term financing. For example, the president of Amazon.com decided to sell audio CDs and videos online in addition to books. Once that decision was made, division managers at Amazon.com determined the specific CDs and videos to sell. Lower-level managers at Amazon.com made other decisions on warehousing, selling, and purchasing procedures.

Planning decisions revolve around activities in the value chain. These activities include the choice and design of products or services to be provided, the activities necessary to make and deliver the products and services, and other customer service choices. But managers make other types of planning decisions.

Control Decisions

Control Decisions

Managing, motivating, and monitoring individuals within the organization is called *control*. **Control decisions** encourage members of the organization to work for the goals of the organization. Due to diverse individual preferences, organizational goals and those of individual members usually do not coincide. For example, the goal of the organization may be to maximize profits. Maximization of profits, however, may mean more hours of overtime for employees, which may not be in the best interest of the employees.

The organizational design and the assignment of responsibilities help to control decisions of members of the organization. For example, a purchasing manager is constrained to follow specific rules in making a purchase and can make purchases above a specified amount only with a superior's approval.

Control decisions also encompass the choice of performance measures and a reward system, which are used to motivate members of the organization.

Organizations also control members through monitoring. Monitoring includes the direct observation of members of the organization to verify that they are performing their duties correctly. For example, telemarketing companies routinely record all telephone conversations or have supervisors randomly monitor calls. Monitoring could also be performed indirectly by observing an individual's output. For instance, monitoring carpenters may include observing the quantity and quality of their output. Reports from monitoring become part of the performance measurement system.

Framework for Organizational Change

The first three sections of this chapter are summarized in the framework for organizational change in Figure 1.1. In the framework, technological change, globalization, and customer needs are all external forces that affect an organization. The organization must adapt to these forces by developing a strategy for creating customer value. These strategies include developing innovative products or services, providing superior quality, or generating products and services at a lower cost.

To implement the strategy, the organization must make both planning and control decisions. Planning decisions are choices of activities that will add value to the customer (value chain). These activities include designing, making, and delivering products and services and providing additional customer services. These decisions should be consistent with the organization's chosen strategy.

To ensure that the strategy is implemented as planned, control decisions must also be made. These control decisions include the assignment of responsibilities within the organization and the selection of performance measures and compensation packages.

MP3.com was incorporated in 1998 and had an initial public offering (IPO) in which it sold shares to the general public in 1999. The company developed a computer file format that allowed it to make music files smaller. Its current technology allows the customer to download a song in about 4 minutes and an entire CD in about 40 minutes using standard telephone lines. Customers can go to its Web site (   ) to download and sample music and purchase CDs. Advertising on the Web site is another source of revenue.

An analysis of MP3.com indicates that it relies on a new technology to create an innovative service: a customer base of young adults who are the largest purchasers of music and are comfortable using the Internet. MP3.com must be concerned, however, about competition. Although the company has the advantage of being one of the first in the market, other competitors will soon enter with improved technology. MP3.com is trying to grow as quickly as possible and create brand awareness and loyalty to discourage competitors. To grow rapidly, the company doesn't charge for its download technology and allows customers to sample music at no cost.

The role of management accounting in implementing this strategy is to measure, analyze, and communicate the costs and benefits of the different services offered by the company. This process is very difficult because most of the costs are occurring now with potential benefits to follow in the future. In one three-month period in 1999, the company reported a net loss of $19,869,290 with revenues of only $4,051,399.

Management accounting also assists in establishing a system of assigning responsibilities, measuring performance, and compensating employees. The company uses growth-oriented performance measures, which are consistent with its current strategy. MP3.com uses the following performance measures: numbers of daily unique visitors to the Web site, estimated Web pages viewed per month, and number of songs and artists on the Web site. Much employee compensation is in the form of stock options, which also encourages employees to make the company grow.

With appropriate planning and control decisions, the organization will create value for customers. If customers find value in what the organization offers, the organization can succeed and the various stakeholders of the organization will receive value from their investment in the organization.

The framework for organizational change is the basis for analyzing organizations. Each chapter contains a business analysis feature (MP3.com in this chapter) that relates the organization's strategic choices to planning and control implementation decisions. Management accounting supports and directs the planning and control implementation decisions while recognizing the organization's strategic choices. More specifically, these analyses address the:

Strategic Level

* What opportunities and threats exist in the business environment with respect to technological change, globalization, and customer needs?
* What are the organization's strengths and weaknesses in creating customer value through innovative products/services, quality, and/or low cost?

Implementation Level

* What activities should be implemented to achieve the strategy and create organizational value?
* How should the organization assign responsibilities, measure performance, and compensate employees to motivate them to make decisions consistent with the strategy?

The framework for organizational change is also used to integrate management accounting topics in this book. The role of accounting in the framework is described in the next section.

ConceptReview

1. Why do organizations form?
2. What are the three basic processes of an organization's structure?
3. How do planning and control decisions help achieve an organization's strategy?

COMPACT DISC STORES
(Continued)

Diane realizes that she has not had time to carefully consider the organizational structure of Compact Disc Stores. She begins by examining the responsibilities that she has delegated. Presently, managers control the daily operations of their respective stores in the suburbs and make their own inventory decisions because Diane believes that the managers have a better understanding of the preferences of their own customers. She currently uses total sales as a performance measure and frequently visits the suburban stores to verify that appropriate shelf space is reserved for local recording artists. The reward system for the managers, however, is not based on any performance measure. They are paid $25,000 whether sales are high or low. Diane decides that a bonus based on sales will provide additional incentives for the managers.

To develop operations and sales on the Web site, Diane must hire another manager who has the requisite technical expertise. This manager will be evaluated on both the number of visits to the site and total sales. Diane also must consider the possible impact of her Internet business on sales in her current locations. Perhaps there is a way to include this possibility in the revised organizational structure.

ROLE OF ACCOUNTING IN THE FRAMEWORK FOR ORGANIZATIONAL CHANGE

Accounting plays an integral part in assisting an organization to achieve its goals. In addition, the importance of accounting in the development of economies has recently been recognized. Developing economies are finding that transparency in organizations is critical to external investment and growth. Transparency is achieved through accounting/ control processes that provide assurances that the organization and the economy are operating appropriately.

Accounting traditionally identifies events affecting the organization and measures and communicates those effects in monetary terms. For example, the purchase of a building by an organization is measured by the cash outlay for it. A sale on credit is identified as a receivable for the organization and is measured in terms of the money owed to it. Since the events are all measured in a common monetary unit, such as the U.S. dollar or the Mexican peso, the accounting systems aggregate the effect of different events and make comparisons. Accumulated accounting data are communicated in accounting reports for managers of the organization and users outside the organization.

The role of management accounting in today's organization goes well beyond recording the dollar amounts of past events. The ability to satisfy user needs, especially by providing forward-looking information, is necessary. To fulfill this role, specifically the information demands of managers and external users, management accountants must ensure that the accounting system encompasses nonfinancial information such as production data, consumer demand forecasts, customer satisfaction statistics, service calls, and industry benchmarks. By integrating financial and nonfinancial data, the accounting system can provide more comprehensive information to better serve its users.

Different parties (such as investors, lenders, and customers) use accounting information related to the organization. Figure 1.3 describes the different roles of an organization's accounting system. Management accounting involves the use of accounting information by managers to help achieve the organization's goals. Managers receive this information in the form of reports such as sales reports, inventory reports, budgets, and monthly operating reports. Management accounting provides information for two general functions: making planning decisions and making control decisions. Accounting allows for better planning decisions by increasing management's knowledge of the problem. Managers use accounting for control decisions by influencing members of the organization to make decisions that are consistent with the organizational goals. Preferred characteristics of management accounting include accurate measures of multiple inputs and outputs of the organization, timeliness, identification of responsibility, and the capacity to be forward looking.

LO 4 Explain the critical role played by management accounting in making planning and control decisions to help managers create organizational value.

Figure 1.3

The Accounting System
Serves Different Purposes

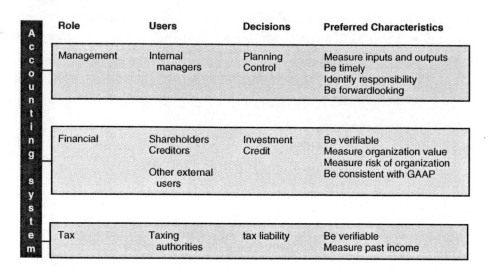

	Role	Users	Decisions	Preferred Characteristics
A c c o u n t i n g s y s t e m	Management	Internal managers	Planning Control	Measure inputs and outputs Be timely Identify responsibility Be forwardlooking
	Financial	Shareholders Creditors Other external users	Investment Credit	Be verifiable Measure organization value Measure risk of organization Be consistent with GAAP
	Tax	Taxing authorities	tax liability	Be verifiable Measure past income

The accounting system must also meet the requirements of constituents outside the organization. **Financial accounting** is used to report to investors, creditors, and other interested parties outside the organization. These parties are primarily interested in information for making investment and credit decisions. Preferred characteristics of financial accounting include verifiability, measures of organizational value, measures of risk to the organization, and consistency with financial reporting regulations, known as *generally accepted accounting procedures (GAAP)*.

Tax accounting is used to calculate income taxes and report to government taxing authorities, such as the Internal Revenue Service (IRS) in the United States or Revenue Canada. Taxing authorities prefer accounting to be verifiable and to measure past income consistent with tax regulations.

Financial reporting and income tax reports are not the primary focus of this book. Nonetheless, reporting to external parties cannot be ignored in management accounting, especially when numbers from the accounting system are used both for external reporting and for planning and control decisions.

Use of Accounting for Making Planning Decisions

**Planning
Decisions**

Planning decisions are made to help an organization achieve its goals. Increased knowledge about the impact of a decision on the organization allows managers to make more informed choices. For example, the sales forecast is used to determine the amount of product to be manufactured. Information from a customer survey can lead to a more accurate sales forecast and to better production decisions.

Management accounting is not the only source of information to improve decision making. Information about the political, legal, and competitive environment also leads to better decisions within an organization. The advantage of management accounting information is the conversion of events into a common unit of measure, the monetary unit. Conversion of events into dollars allows managers to compare the impact of various decisions on the organization. The decision to adopt advanced manufacturing technologies or to continue manual operations can be analyzed by converting both events into dollar outlays and comparing the dollar outlays of each alternative. Other nonfinancial information also may be useful, such as the impact of different alternatives on the welfare of employees. New manufacturing methods may improve or harm employee welfare, especially if adoption leads to the need for fewer workers.

The manner in which management accounting is used to improve planning decisions depends on the organization's strategy. The initial Chapters Two through Five of this book focus on accounting methods that support planning decisions.

Use of Accounting for Making Control Decisions

**Control
Decisions**

Management accounting assists in making control decisions by helping align the interests of the organization's members with its goals. The members are motivated to achieve organizational goals through a reward system. Rewards are based on achieving sufficiently high performance measures, some of which are based on accounting numbers. For example, the manager of each division is commonly evaluated based on the division's accounting profits. Nonaccounting performance measures and direct observation (monitoring) of members are also used to evaluate and reward the members. Management accounting reports often include nonaccounting measures of performance such as customer satisfaction and product defect rates.

Management accounting also helps to assign responsibilities to control members of the organization. Limits on actions by managers frequently are based on accounting numbers. For example, a salesperson may have the right to grant credit to a customer only up to $1,000. The communication of this limit on responsibilities often occurs through management accounting documents such as the budget.

Designing a system to align the interests of the members of the organization with the goals of the organization is not an easy task. Chapters Six and Seven focus on control issues, and Chapters Eight through Fourteen consider the combined use of management accounting for making planning and control decisions.

Emergence of Management Accounting

Management accounting has emerged in parallel with the adaptation of the organization to its environment. While management accounting procedures can be traced to medieval times, the Industrial Revolution marked a turning point in their development. The Industrial Revolution and subsequent decades brought changes in the nature of organizations that required new methods for planning and control. For example, in the eighteenth century, Josiah Wedgwood was motivated by dynamic economic and market conditions to reexamine his business methods. He began to use cost data to calculate production expenses, evaluate economies of scale, and control worker performance at his pottery works. In the nineteenth century, management accounting became more important as firms confronted environmental factors little different from those they face today: technological change, competition, and customer needs. Technological change, such as improved communications and transportation networks, shortened operating cycles and decision-making horizons. Technological innovations intensified competition as customers grew accustomed to the availability of cheaper mass-produced goods. Organizations were increasing the scale and scope of their operations. Prior to 1800, most business firms were small and operated by family members. The shift from the owner-manager, who could directly observe organizational activities, to the salaried manager required different management methods. Previously the owner or family member had made almost all of the decisions, but in this shift, decision making was delegated to employees. Motivation became a concern as firms dealt with the differing interests of shareholders, managers, and workers.[5]

Many of today's management accounting techniques were fine-tuned in the period from 1825 to 1925 with the growth of large organizations.[6] Textile mills in the early nineteenth century grew by combining the multiple processes of making

---

[5] J. R. Edwards and E. Newell, "The Development of Industrial Cost and Management Accounting before 1850: A Survey of the Evidence," *Business History* 33, no. 1 (1991), pp. 35–57; and C. S. McWatters, "Management Accounting and the Calvin Company," *Accounting, Business and Financial History* 5, no. 1 (1995), pp. 39–70.

[6] S. Paul Garner, *Evolution of Cost Accounting to 1925* (Montgomery, Ala.: University of Alabama Press, 1954); and A. D. Chandler, *The Visible Hand* (Cambridge, Mass.: Harvard University Press, 1977).

cloth (spinning the thread, dying, weaving, etc.). These large firms developed systems to measure the cost per yard or per pound for the separate manufacturing processes. These data allowed managers to compare the cost of conducting a process inside the firm with the cost of purchasing the process from external vendors. Similarly, the railroads of the 1850s–1870s developed cost systems that reported cost per ton-mile and operating expenses per dollar of revenue. These measures were a first step in improving operating efficiencies. In the early 1900s, Andrew Carnegie (at what was to become U.S. Steel) devised a cost system that reported detailed unit cost figures for material and labor on a daily and weekly basis. This system allowed senior managers to maintain tight controls on operations and gave them accurate and timely information on marginal costs for pricing decisions. Merchandisers such as Marshall Field's and Sears, Roebuck developed gross-margin (revenues less cost of good sold) and stock-turn ratios (sales divided by inventory) to measure and evaluate performance. Manufacturing companies such as Du Pont Powder Company and General Motors also devised innovative performance measures to control their growing organizations.

In the period 1925–1975, management accounting was heavily influenced by external considerations. Income taxes and financial accounting requirements (e.g., those of the Financial Accounting Standards Board) took precedence over management accounting.

Since 1975, the impact of rapid technological change, globalization, and customer needs has caused managers to question whether earlier (pre-1975) management accounting procedures are still appropriate. In order to succeed, the organization must implement an appropriate strategy supported by an appropriate management accounting system. Therefore, changes in management accounting reflect the firm's strategic efforts to create organizational value.

The history of management accounting illustrates its emergence in response to changing organizational circumstances. Management accounting provides information for planning decisions and control. It is useful for assigning responsibilities, measuring performance, and determining rewards for individuals within the organization. As other parts of the organizational structure adapt and change, it is not surprising that management accounting evolves in a parallel and consistent fashion.

Concept**Review**

1. What are the differences between management accounting and financial accounting?
2. How does management accounting support planning decisions?
3. How is management accounting used for control decisions?
4. What has caused management accounting procedures to evolve over time?

**COMPACT
DISC STORES**
(Continued)

Diane has not paid much attention to the accounting system of Compact Disc Stores. When she started the first store, she purchased software for her personal computer to record expenditures and cash receipts. At the end of the year, she hired a CPA to generate financial statements and fill out income tax forms. The financial statements are sent to Janice Nishimura, her partner, and the bank that made the loan. As long as sales were strong, Diane did not worry about using the accounting system for managing the stores. But sales have declined, and Diane is thinking about how she can make better decisions. In particular, she must decide how to operate her new Web site to make it profitable.

TRADE-OFFS IN USING ACCOUNTING FOR MULTIPLE PURPOSES

Figure 1.3 describes a single accounting system that generates accounting numbers for multiple purposes. But one accounting system is unlikely to be appropriate for all the different decisions that internal and external users of accounting must make. For example, a manager might like to know the cost of developing and maintaining the organization's Web page versus hiring an external Webmaster, but a creditor would want to know the impact of the method on cash flows available to pay interest.

A single accounting system will not provide appropriate information for all decisions; therefore, trade-offs must be made among the different roles for accounting. This theme of trade-offs among different uses of accounting information is referred to throughout this book. The following sections provide examples of these trade-offs.

LO 5 Identify the trade-offs that exist in using information for making planning and control decisions and for external reporting.

Trade-Off between Making Planning and Control Decisions

Managers generally have specialized information that is useful for making planning decisions. To make the best planning decision, the person with the best information about a choice should make the decision. But there is the problem of motivating the individual to make decisions consistent with the organization's goals. For example, a computer specialist may be the best-informed individual on the relative qualities of different computers. If the computer specialist is given the responsibility to purchase a computer for the organization, she may choose the most powerful and expensive computer available. Having the most expensive computer may not be in the organization's best interest if it has a better use for cash elsewhere.

Instead of delegating responsibility to the manager with specialized knowledge, the organization could request the manager to communicate the specialized knowledge to higher-level managers, who would make decisions using the transferred information. But the communicated information could also be used to evaluate the manager with the specialized knowledge. Knowing that any information a manager communicates can be used for evaluation might cause the manager to alter the information and make it less useful for making planning decisions. For example, a telecommunications manager might know how to modify the existing computer network to improve response time. This information would be useful for upper management in making investment decisions for a new network. However, the telecommunications manager is evaluated based on network response time. The manager can modify the network to achieve response-time goals more easily, but upper management's knowledge of this modification would eventually lead to higher expectations about the telecommunications manager's performance. The use of information to reward the telecommunications manager may inhibit the manager in communicating information useful for planning decisions.

Trade-Off between Making Planning Decisions and External Reporting

External reporting is prepared for users outside the organization. Current regulations set forth by financial accounting, tax, and securities regulators in many countries, including Canada and the United States, specify the use of historical costs to report the value of most organizational assets. The *historical cost* of an object is its acquisition price or the value of resources used to acquire the object. For example, land purchased 10 years ago for $70,000 may now have a market value of $200,000, but the land is still recorded at $70,000 in the financial reports. No gain due to the increase in market value is recognized in financial or tax reports until the land is sold.

An advantage of using historical costs is their objective nature. They depend less on the subjective judgment of managers because they reflect actual transactions. Outside investors, creditors, and taxing authorities generally prefer accounting numbers that are not susceptible to manipulation by managers. Nonetheless, historical costs are not necessarily the costs that managers should use for decision making within the organization.

Managers of organizations often use estimates of future costs in making planning decisions. Historical costs are a good estimate of future costs only if the economic, competitive, and operational environments have remained the same. For example, the historical cost of a gold watch is not a very good estimate for making another gold watch if the cost of gold has changed. Therefore, financially reported (historical cost) numbers should be used with care for planning because they can lead to inappropriate decisions.

Trade-Off between Making Control Decisions and External Reporting

If a financial report based on historical costs is the only available method of evaluating managers, managers will work to affect the financial report. Maximizing profit based on historical costs may not be consistent, however, with the shareholder goal of maximizing shareholder value. For example, research and development (R&D) expenditures, which increase the value of the organization, are considered an immediate expense under U.S. and Canadian GAAP and reduce present profit figures. By cutting R&D, managers increase current profit at the expense of future profits. If the R&D activity creates value for customers and shareholders in the long run, the focus on short-term financial reports may conflict with long-term strategies.

To achieve the organization's goals through control, performance measures should be closely associated with those goals. Financial reports based on historical costs may not be closely linked to the organization's goals and could lead to dysfunctional behavior by its members.

Multiple Accounting Systems

Implementing multiple accounting systems could resolve the trade-offs existing among the various uses of an accounting system. Separate accounting systems could be established for making planning and control decisions and for external reporting. The problem with this solution is the cost of establishing multiple systems. Many small organizations have the resources for only a single accounting system. Regulators and banks often require financial reports; therefore, the financial accounting system may be the only accounting system available within an organization. Large organizations, however, might have two or more accounting systems for different purposes.

The results produced by multiple accounting systems can sometimes be confusing. With multiple accounting systems, items may be reported at different costs. One accounting system might report that a particular division made profits of $6.2 million and another accounting system might report its profits at $5.8 million. Managers will be forced to spend time reconciling the differences. Remember the old proverb: "A man with one watch knows what time it is. A man with two watches is never sure."

An accounting system limited to monetary measures is not the only source of information to assist in making planning and control decisions. Planning decisions are likely to be based, at least partially, on nonmonetary factors. For example, planning decisions to achieve goals such as employee satisfaction would use employee surveys as an information source. Control decisions could be based on nonmonetary performance measures such as the percentage of defective units produced.

This book recognizes that most organizations do not have separate accounting systems for different purposes, and trade-offs will exist in using accounting numbers for different types of decisions. The trade-off between making planning and control decisions is a primary focus of this book.

Concept**Review**

1. Why does the use of accounting numbers for both planning and control decisions lead to trade-offs?
2. Why might historical costs from financial reports be inappropriate for making planning decisions?
3. Why might the profit number in financial reports be inappropriate for evaluating managers?

Diane Johnson wants to estimate future cash flows to determine whether she can expand Compact Disc Stores to the Internet without going to the bank. These plans require accurate estimates of future sales, but she is worried that the store managers will provide her with low estimates of future sales if she rewards them based on sales or profits. The managers will want to establish a low benchmark so that they can easily achieve bonuses for high sales and earnings.

In deciding how to expand to the Internet, Diane must estimate the cost of creating a Web site. Because she has never attempted such a project, her current financial accounting system provides no information on necessary expenditures involved in selling on the Internet. Therefore, the financial accounting reports are not relevant. She must acquire more data about Web site design to make the decision.

Diane realizes that her strategies would be more successful if strong links existed between these goals and the performance measurement and reward system. She decides that an initial step would be to compensate her store managers based on the accounting profit generated from their respective stores. But her music store managers are young and looking for other employment opportunities. She is worried that they are not concerned about the long-term interests of Compact Disc Stores. She recently visited one of the stores in the suburbs and found customers grumbling about the lack of employees to provide customer service. When she approached the manager about this problem, he responded that he had cut the number of sales positions to reduce costs and improve profits. Diane is worried that customers will not return to any of the Compact Disc Stores if they are disappointed with service at this suburban store. Therefore, she decides to perform customer surveys as an additional performance measure to be used jointly with accounting profit to reward the managers.

COMPACT DISC STORES
(Continued)

You decide

TYPES OF MANAGEMENT ACCOUNTANTS

Management accountants are responsible for the accounting system within organizations. An accounting system should be designed to assist in making planning and control decisions and in financial and tax reporting. The management

LO 6 Identify the roles of different types of management accountants.

accounting function in small organizations is normally performed by a book-keeper who records transactions. An outside accountant often assists in preparing financial statements and tax returns. The emphasis on financial reporting means that managers may not have relevant information easily available for planning purposes. Control decisions are unlikely to be as important because the manager making these decisions is likely to be the owner.

In large organizations, the **controller** is normally assigned the responsibilities of a management accountant. The controller assists managers in making decisions and reports to the president or chief executive officer (CEO). The controller is delegated responsibility for the communication and implementation of an organization's accounting policies and procedures and acts as both consultant to and evaluator of other parts of the organization. The controller may also have assistant controllers who carry out specialized accounting and reporting duties. The functions of the controller are distinct from those of the treasurer, who deals primarily with financial concerns such as investments, financing, banking, and credit policy. Controllers do more than just compile information; they frequently serve as members of strategic planning teams and act as interpreters and advisors. Controllers are expected to add value to the management process.[7]

In large corporations, the controller often reports to the vice president of finance rather than to the CEO (see Figure 1.2). Large corporations also have an internal audit department, which is involved with the organization's control system. This department's role is to ensure that financial and operating assets are used efficiently and appropriately to achieve organizational objectives. The **internal auditor** monitors the various divisions and departments of the corporation to determine whether prescribed operational procedures are being followed. To maintain its independence and profile, the internal audit department often reports directly to the CEO and the board of directors.

ETHICS AND PROFESSIONAL MANAGEMENT ACCOUNTING ORGANIZATIONS

LO 7 Recognize the role of judgment and ethics in making management accounting choices.

Management accountants apply professional judgment in deciding how to establish and operate accounting systems within an organization. The potential trade-offs that exist because of the multiple uses of accounting systems make the management accountant's judgment critical. The management accountant frequently confronts decisions that affect the welfare of people inside and outside the organization. The process of determining standards and procedures for dealing with judgmental decisions affecting other people is known as **ethics.**

Ethics does not give a specific answer to a problem but suggests a process to deal with it. When faced with an ethical dilemma, the management accountant should gather sufficient information. Conflicts often disappear when sufficient information is obtained. The management accountant should then determine how stakeholders are affected. Too often crises arise when the effect on some individual or group is forgotten or ignored.

For example, suppose a controller finds inventory items that are outdated by newer models. The old inventory items can be sold only below their historic cost. Their sale or write-down will cause a reported loss on the accounting statements and will harm the chances of the division's employees for obtaining a bonus. The controller could simply ignore the old inventory; however, there is a cost to storing the goods. Although recognition of the loss associated with the old inventory may harm the current employees, other parties would be harmed by continuing to ignore it. The owners would have to continue to pay storage costs, and bonuses of future employees may be affected if the loss is postponed. Once the impact on

[7] S. Harrison, "Not Just Bean Counters Anymore," *Management Accounting,* March 1993, pp. 29–32.

all the parties is examined, the controller will have more information to make a judgment.

A code of ethics assists the management accountant in making judgment decisions. Organizations frequently have a code of ethics that deals with standard problems facing the management accountant. This code of ethics reinforces the organization's control system to reduce the risk of unacceptable behavior. Organizations also develop their own ethical commitments and standards that reflect their operating environment and culture. Moreover, ethical standards will differ across countries, and the management accountant must be alert to the possibility that such differences may result in ethical dilemmas. An ethics control system provides guidance in decision making and a framework for accountability.[8]

BellSouth recognized that workers faced increasingly ambiguous situations in their work environment and consequently developed an infrastructure to assist employees to use high ethical standards. In particular, the company created training exercises, communication processes, and systems to promote ethics. The establishment of ethical standards in an organization is important for helping members make appropriate choices.[9]

Various professional bodies of management accountants also have a code of ethics. For example, the Institute of Management Accountants (IMA) has prescribed the following set of ethical standards:

1. Competence. Management accountants should be professionally competent to perform their duties of providing relevant and reliable information in accordance with relevant laws, regulations, and technical standards.

2. Confidentiality. Management accountants should refrain from disclosing confidential information or using confidential information to their own advantage.

3. Integrity. Management accountants should avoid (a) conflicts of interest by refusing compromising gifts and favors, (b) subversion of organizational objectives, (c) communication of biased information, and (d) activities that could discredit the profession.

4. Objectivity. Management accountants should communicate information fairly and objectively and disclose all relevant information.

This code of ethics is not sufficient to solve all ethical problems, but is provides some direction for the management accountant. In the case of the controller who found the old inventory, the integrity section of the code of ethics suggests that the decision to recognize the loss immediately is consistent with the communication of unbiased information. The current employees, however, should not be held responsible for the loss because old inventory reflects a decision made in prior years to produce extra inventory.

In a global market, and with a trend to delegate decision making to lower levels of the organization, organizations often implement ethics programs to ensure that employees understand how ethics relates to the organization's core strategies. Management accountants provide advice and support for the implementation of ethical policies and strategies, especially given their role in decision making and control.[10]

The IMA and the Society of Management Accountants of Canada (SMAC) administer programs that qualify certified management accountants (CMAs).

---

[8] The Society of Management Accountants of Canada has a number of sources to provide guidance on codes of ethics and ethics strategies. See *Management Accounting Issues Paper 13*, "Codes of Ethics, Practice and Conduct," 1977; *Management Accounting Guideline 46*, "Implementing Ethics Strategies within Organizations," 1998; *Management Accounting Handbook*, Standard 6200, Ethics Control Systems, 1999.

[9] S. Harrison, "The Most Natural Thing to Do," *Management Accounting*, March 1995, pp. 22–26.

[10] The Society of Management Accountants of Canada, *Management Accounting Guideline 46*, 1998.

Applicants must pass examinations in management accounting and in the related fields of economics, finance, financial accounting, organizational behavior, and decision analysis. The SMAC and IMA also work with international partners to foster the profession's role in the global marketplace.

Concept**Review**

1. Describe the roles of controllers and internal auditors in organizations.

2. Why should management accountants have a code of ethics?

SUMMARY

1 **Explain how technological change, globalization, and customer needs can affect an organization and its management accounting system.** Technological change offers opportunities for new products and services and more efficient methods of operations. Globalization forces organizations to be more concerned about their customers and operating efficiently. Customer needs continually change. Organizations and their management accounting systems must adapt to these changes.

2 **Identify strategies for achieving customer value.** Customer value can be achieved through innovative product/service design, quality, and low cost.

3 **Describe features of organizations that promote decisions to achieve their goals.** To achieve their goals, organizations must assign responsibilities, measure performance, and compensate their members.

4 **Explain the critical role played by management accounting in making planning and control decisions to help managers create organizational value.** Management accounting improves planning decisions by providing decision makers with more information to make better decisions. Management accounting also supports control decisions by assisting in the assignment of

responsibilities and establishing performance measures to motivate individuals.

5 **Identify the trade-offs that exist in using information for making planning and control decisions and for external reporting.** Using the same accounting system for making planning and control decisions and for external reporting leads to trade-offs. Employees will bias information used for planning purposes if the information is also used as a benchmark for measuring performance. External reports will similarly be affected if also used to evaluate performance.

6 **Identify the roles of different types of management accountants.** Controllers are responsible for the accounting systems within the organization. Internal auditors monitor members of the organization to determine whether prescribed procedures are being followed.

7 **Recognize the role of judgment and ethics in making management accounting choices.** The management accountant must use judgment in resolving trade-offs arising from different uses of accounting information. This judgment should recognize the effect of decisions on all involved parties. A code of ethics assists the management accountant in making decisions.

KEY TERMS

computer-assisted design (CAD)   A system that uses computers for designing new products. *(p. 5)*

computer-aided manufacturing (CAM)   Making products by using programmable robots to assist in production. *(p. 5)*

computer-integrated manufacturing (CIM)   A manufacturing plant with all its systems linked by computer. *(p. 5)*

control decisions   Use of information to influence members of the organization to make decisions that are consistent with organizational goals. *(p. 15)*

controller   The person within an organization responsible for the accounting system. *(p. 24)*

ethics   The process of determining standards and procedures for dealing with judgmental decisions affecting other people. *(p. 24)*

financial accounting   The accounting system used to report to investors, creditors, and other interested parties outside the organization. *(p. 17)*

globalization   The integration of national economies into a single international economy. *(p. 6)*

internal auditor   A person within the organization who monitors various divisions and departments of the organization to determine whether prescribed operations procedures are being followed. *(p. 24)*

just-in-time (JIT) processes Provision of products and services only when they are needed. *(p. 7)*

management accounting The accounting system used within the organization to help the organization achieve its goals. *(p. 4)*

non–value-added activities Activities in an organization that do not benefit its customers. *(p. 8)*

performance measures Direct or indirect measures of actions of individuals or groups of individuals within the organization. *(p. 13)*

planning decisions The selection of activities to help the organization attain its goals. *(p. 14)*

tax accounting The accounting system used to calculate taxable income and report to government taxing authorities. *(p. 18)*

stakeholders Parties affected by an organization. *(p. 13)*

total quality management (TQM) A philosophy of continually lowering costs and improving the provision of services and products to customers. *(p. 8)*

value chain The sequence of critical organizational processes to satisfy customers of the organization. *(p. 8)*

ANALYSIS AND INTERPRETATION PROBLEMS

The owner of a small software company felt his accounting system was useless. He stated, "Accounting systems generate only historical costs. Historical costs are useless in my business because everything changes so rapidly."

a. Are historical costs useless in rapidly changing environments?

b. Should accounting systems be limited to historical costs?

AIP 1.1
Use of Accounting for Making Planning Decisions
(LO 4)

A finance professor and a marketing professor were recently comparing notes on their perceptions of corporations. The finance professor claimed that the goal of a corporation should be to maximize the value to the shareholders. The marketing professor claimed that the goal of a corporation should be to satisfy customers. What are the similarities and differences in these two goals?

AIP 1.2
Goals of a Corporation
(LO 2)

The controller of a small private university is complaining about the amount of work that she is required to do at the beginning of each month. The president of the university requires the controller to submit a monthly report by the fifth day of the following month. The monthly report contains pages of financial data from operations. The controller was heard saying, "Why does the president need all this information? He probably doesn't read half of the report. He's an old English professor and probably doesn't know the difference between a cost and a revenue."

a. What is the probable role of the monthly report?

b. What is the controller's responsibility with respect to a president who doesn't know much accounting?

AIP 1.3
Accounting and Control
(LO 4,6)

A large diversified company hired a recent accounting graduate as an internal auditor. He was thrilled by this opportunity. The company trained him to provide assistance to the managers of the various divisions in achieving the goals of the organization. He would be able to learn about many different aspects of the business in the role of an internal auditor as he rotated among the various divisions. The internal auditor position seemed to be an ideal position that would lead to early advancement in the company. His first outing to a division, however, was not particularly successful. The managers of the division barely tolerated his criticism of their operating processes. Instead of being perceived as a person helping the organization achieve its goals, he was shunned by the divisional managers.

a. Why were the divisional managers not appreciative of the internal auditor?

b. How could the organization improve the role of the internal auditor?

AIP 1.4
Control and Internal Auditors
(LO 6)

The president of the company has come to the controller at the end of the fiscal year. She says, "We've had a pretty bad year. Sales have been off, but I think we'll do better next year. Can you do something about the annual financial report to make us look a little better and get us through until next year. Otherwise, I might get fired."

a. What can the controller do to make the annual financial report look better?

b. What other factors should the controller consider in responding to the president?

AIP 1.5
Financial Reporting and Ethics
(LO 7)

AIP 1.6
One Cost System Isn't Enough
(LO 5)

Robert S. Kaplan in "One Cost System Isn't Enough" (*Harvard Business Review*, January–February 1988, pp. 61–66) states:

> No single system can adequately answer the demands made by diverse functions of cost systems. While companies can use one method to capture all their detailed transactions data, the processing of this information for diverse purposes and audiences demands separate, customized development. Companies that try to satisfy all the needs for cost information with a single system have discovered they can't perform important managerial functions adequately. Moreover, systems that work well for one company may fail in a different environment. Each company has to design methods that make sense for its particular products and processes.
>
> Of course, an argument for expanding the number of cost systems conflicts with a strongly ingrained financial culture to have only one measurement system for everyone.

Critically evaluate the preceding quote.

AIP 1.7
Tax Reporting and Accounting Systems
(LO 5)

Tax laws in Japan tie taxable income directly to the financial statements' reported income. A Japanese firm's tax liability is the net income as reported to shareholders multiplied by the tax rate. In contrast, with a few exceptions, Canadian and U.S. firms can use different accounting procedures for calculating net income for shareholders (financial reporting) and income for calculating taxes.

Given these differences in the tax laws between, for example, those for Canada and the United States and those for Japan, what effect would you expect these institutional differences in tax laws to have on internal accounting and reporting? Why is it essential for management accountants to keep aware of and comment on tax policy and its effects?

AIP 1.8
Planning Decisions and Financial Reporting
(LO 5)

The controller is complaining to his friend about the crazy requests that come from the top managers. "The CEO has requested that I calculate product costs to include research and development and selling costs. Doesn't she know that according to GAAP, research and development and selling expenditures are expensed during the period incurred and are not product costs?"

Evaluate the controller's comments.

AIP 1.9
Role of the Divisional Controller
(LO 6)

Arjohn Corporation is a multidivisional firm. Each division has a manager responsible for division operations. A controller is assigned to each division by the corporate controller's office. The division's controller manages its accounting system and provides financial analysis for the division's management. The division manager evaluates the division controller's performance and makes recommendations for salary increases and promotions. However, the final responsibility for promotion evaluation and salary increases rests with the corporate controller. Each division of Arjohn is responsible for product design, sales, pricing, operating costs and expenses, and profits. However, corporate management exercises tight control over the financial operations of the divisions. For example, corporate management must approve all capital expenditures above a very modest amount. The method of financial reporting from the division to corporate headquarters provides further evidence of the degree of financial control. Each division's manager and controller submit to corporate headquarters a separate and independent commentary on the financial results of the division. The corporate management maintains that the division controller's function is to provide an independent view of the division's operations.

Arjohn Corporation's dual reporting systems for decisions may create problems for the division controller.

a. Identify and discuss the factors that make the division controller's role difficult in this type of situation.

b. Discuss the effect of the dual reporting relationship on the motivation of the division controller.

(CMA adapted)

AIP 1.10
Responsibilities, Information, and Performance Measures
(LO 3)

Steve Johnson sells baskets for a wholesaler to retail shops. Retail shops like to have 30 days to pay after receipt of the goods. Unfortunately, retail shops often have financial difficulties and fail to make timely payments and in some cases make no payments at all. Steve's manager, who has never visited the retail shops, makes the decision whether to require collection on delivery (COD) or allow the store to pay in 30 days. Forcing the store to make payment on delivery often deters the shop from making a purchase. Steve, who visits each store, argues that he should have the right to make the decision on allowing for payment within 30 days.

a. How would the wholesaler benefit from Steve making the decision to allow for payment within 30 days?

b. What types of performance measures should be used for Steve if he is not given the responsibility to allow for payment within 30 days?

c. What types of performance measures should be used for Steve if he is given the responsibility to allow for payment within 30 days?

d. Should Steve be evaluated on increased sales or the level of uncollectible accounts receivable? What are the trade-offs between these two measures?

Jim Jensen has opened a small business making handcrafted guitars. His guitars sell for around $4,000 each, and he sells only about 40 each year. When warned about potential competition from a producer in another country, Jim said, "I'm not worried about competition from abroad. Although my guitars are very expensive, I work hard to satisfy my customers. My guitars have an exclusive name that customers are willing to pay for. I will never be a low-cost producer."

AIP 1.11
Global Competition
(LO 1)

Should Jim worry about global competition and change his business?

Managers' decisions can be categorized as either planning or control. Label each of the following manager activities as either a planning decision or a control decision.

AIP 1.12
Role of Managers
(LO 3)

a. Choosing a price for a product.

b. Explaining to an employee how to operate a machine.

c. Deciding which supplier of a part to use.

d. Congratulating the engineering department for a wonderful design.

e. Planning a building site for a new factory.

f. Asking an employee to provide service to a customer.

g. Creating a new process for manufacturing.

h. Deciding how to finance a new project.

i. Keeping track of the hours worked by the employees.

The owner of a jewelry store has just heard about TQM as a way of managing. The owner sees no reason to invest any further in TQM. As she told a friend, "TQM may be relevant for some of the cheap jewelry shops in town, but I sell only the highest quality diamonds and jewelry. I am already the top-quality jewelry retailer in town. TQM has nothing further to offer me."

AIP 1.13
Total Quality Management (TQM)
(LO 1)

Evaluate the comments of the jewelry store owner.

CAM welding machines can be programmed to make different types of welds. Software is inserted into the machine to change the welding pattern. Kipling Box Company makes steel boxes that require only one type of weld. The president of the company is trying to decide whether the company should invest in a CAM welding machine.

AIP 1.14
Computer-Aided Manufacturing (CAM)
(LO 1)

What are the advantages and disadvantages of investing in the CAM welding machine?

A hospital administrator has just read a book about JIT. She believes that JIT is a good idea for manufacturing companies, but doesn't think that it would be of much use to a service organization.

AIP 1.15
Just In Time (JIT)
(LO 1)

Describe how JIT could be used in a hospital.

A *Wall Street Journal* article indicated that top-level managers do not understand CIM.[11] Only about 20% of the conversions to CIM began with top-level managers, the push for it usually begins with shop-floor engineers.

AIP 1.16
Computer-Integrated Manufacturing (CIM)
(LO 1)

What are the advantages of implementing a change from the top versus the bottom of the organization?

---

[11] *The Wall Street Journal*, April 20, 1995, A 1:5.

AIP 1.17
International and Domestic Differences
(LO 1)

A manager of a fashion designer and manufacturer in Montreal was heard to say, "I don't understand all the fuss about studying international business. Canada has multiple languages and cultures. Inflation is like changing exchange rates; both raise comparability problems. We have operations all across Canada and have to deal with multiple taxing authorities. Since we've been successful in Canada, I have no doubt we will be successful internationally."

How would you respond to this manager?

EXTENDED ANALYSIS AND INTERPRETATION PROBLEMS

AIP 1.18
Ethical Behavior

FulRange Inc. produces complex printed circuits for stereo amplifiers. The circuits are sold primarily to major component manufacturers, and any production overruns are sold to small manufacturers at a substantial discount. The small-manufacturer market segment appears very profitable because the basic operating budget assigns all fixed production expenses to the major manufacturers, the only predictable market.

A common product defect that occurs in production is a "drift" caused by failure to maintain precise heat levels during the production process. Drift rejects from the 100% testing program can be reworked to acceptable levels. However, after a recent analysis of customer complaints, Scott Richardson, the cost accountant, and the quality control engineer have ascertained that normal rework does not bring the circuits up to standard. Sampling shows that about one-half of the reworked circuits will fail after extended, high-volume amplifier operation. The incidence of failure in the reworked circuits is projected to be about 10% over one to five years of operation.

Unfortunately, there is no way to determine which reworked circuits will fail because testing does not detect this problem. The rework process could be changed to correct the problem, but the cost/benefit analysis for the suggested change indicates that it is not feasible. FulRange's marketing analyst has indicated that if the problem is not corrected, it will significantly affect the company's reputation and customer satisfaction. Consequently, the board of directors would interpret this problem as having serious negative implications on the company's profitability.

Richardson has included the circuit failure and rework problem in his report that has been prepared for the upcoming quarterly meeting of the board of directors. Because of the potential adverse economic impact, Richardson has followed a long-standing practice of highlighting this information.

After reviewing the reports to be presented, the plant manager and his staff are upset and indicate to the controller that he should control his people better. "We can't upset the board with this kind of material. Tell Richardson to tone that down. Maybe we can get it by this meeting and have some time to work on it. People who buy those cheap systems and play them that loud shouldn't expect them to last forever."

The controller calls Richardson into his office and says, "Scott, you'll have to bury this one. The probable failure of reworks can be referred to briefly in the oral presentation, but it should not be mentioned or highlighted in the advance material mailed to the board."

Richardson feels strongly that the board will be misinformed on a potentially serious loss of income if he follows the controller's orders. Richardson discusses the problem with the quality control engineer, who simply remarks, "That's your problem, Scott."

a. Discuss the ethical considerations that Scott Richardson should recognize in deciding how to proceed in this matter.

b. Explain what ethical responsibilities should be accepted in this situation by each of the following: controller, quality control engineer, and plant manager and staff.

c. What should Richardson do in this situation? Why?

(CMA adapted)

AIP 1.19
Strategies, Organizational Goals, and Management Accounting

In 1993, Wayne Albo found an opportunity to enter the record-store business. Albo, a Canadian chartered accountant (CA) and specialist in mergers and acquisitions, was also an experienced business evaluator. Through his Calcorp Group of companies, he dealt with clients who had businesses that they were looking to sell or expand. As a result, Albo was on a first-name basis with numerous entrepreneurs. That year, a friend called Albo with a proposition. One of his clients had died suddenly, leaving behind a chain of record stores. The individual had not planned for any successors to carry on the business. The 13 stores were in small cities and had sales of about $4 million (CDN) per year. Although Albo was making a good living as a consultant, the position was generating cash flow, not equity. He decided to take the plunge and enter into the record-store market.

Albo could see the potential for profits. Record stores in smaller cities did not face the same amount of competition as did stores in Montreal, Toronto, and Vancouver. Second, the customers were generally older than those in the teen-driven big city market. Thus, customers had more disposable income, and demand was more stable. Finally, some of the 13 stores were exclusive sites in smaller shopping malls; these permitted higher profit margins.

Once Albo became the owner of a record-store chain, numerous opportunities arose. A&A, another record chain, went bankrupt; Albo picked up a dozen new locations from those stores. When the owner of National Record Stores in Winnipeg died, Albo (with the help of Working Ventures, a labor-sponsored investment fund) purchased the chain of 35 stores, along with its wholesale division, warehouse, and experienced administrative staff. With Working Ventures as an equity partner and cash flow generated from his existing stores, Albo began a nationwide buying spree. He purchased a chain of 17 stores owned by Top Forty in Edmonton in 1996, and then 80 stores run by Rock Entertainment in North Bay.

Albo could see that technology was changing rapidly. He believed that Web-based record stores soon would be his competitors. Although his own company, Ave Entertainment, did not have the necessary expertise or experience to enter that market, Albo knew of two young entrepreneurs, David Cubitt and Bill Birss, who did. In 1989, Cubitt and Birss had started a mail-order catalog business in the basement of a suburban home. With their mail-order marketing, they had brought a huge selection and competitive pricing, usually reserved for urban centers, to rural communities. They later introduced the "warehouse outlet" concept to the music industry. Their next step was to launch a Web site, under their name CDPlus [www.cd-plus.com]. This Web site enabled them to put their 65,000-title catalog online. The Web site also featured interviews, articles, reviews, and links to artist Web pages.

Through a share swap, Albo acquired the bricks-and-mortar stores, the Web site, and the CDPlus name. In the summer of 1999, Albo brought in Leo Sienna, a veteran of the food distribution business, as president and CEO of CDPlus. The bricks-and-mortar locations provided millions of dollars of inventory to online shoppers with a quick turnaround time. In addition, a decade of experience in record sales was transferred to the online market. CDPlus's strategy was to add value to the customer through a large selection, competitive pricing, and favorable exchange rates for U.S. customers. The Internet opened global markets to the "100% Canadian" company.

By the end of 1999, CDPlus.com Inc. had 150 stores across Canada, generated more than $150 million (CDN) in sales per year, and was a publicly traded company [TSE: CDW]. CDPlus had added partnerships with ZapYou.com [video games] and CD Warehouse Inc. [NASDAQ: CDWI]. Any Webmaster could become a CDPlus Partner by placing CDPlus's banner on her own Web site. She would earn a 5% commission on every sale originating from her site. CDPlus would do all the work—processing the order, shipping the product, and handling the customer service and billings. CDPlus also offered a wholesaling service through its operations in Burnaby, B.C.

Wayne Albo was to remain the chairman and controlling shareholder of CDPlus. He still would spend half of his time at Calcorp. Albo planned to continue seeking new opportunities.

a. Refer to Figure 1.1. Using this organizational framework, outline why and how CDPlus adapted its strategies to its environment to achieve customer value.

b. What is the role of management accounting in supporting the firm's strategy to create organizational value? In discussing this question, consider both the financial and nonfinancial information that CDPlus would find useful.

Sources: Terrence Belford, "Note-by-Note Progression Creates Musical Chain," *The National Post*, October 20, 1999.

www.cd-plus.com/cdstore/shop/about.asp
www.cd-plus.com/partners/benefits.asp
www.cd-plus.com/shop/press.asp
www.cd-plus.com/shop/wholesale.asp

Chapter **Two**

Measuring and Analyzing Activity Costs

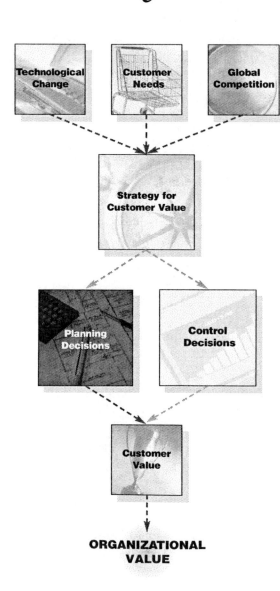

JONES AND MCLEAN, CERTIFIED PUBLIC ACCOUNTANTS

The firm of Jones and McLean, Certified Public Accountants (CPAs), provides consulting, auditing, and tax services for its clients. As a small firm, Jones and McLean competes on the basis of customized services at reasonable cost. Its reputation is important and results from providing

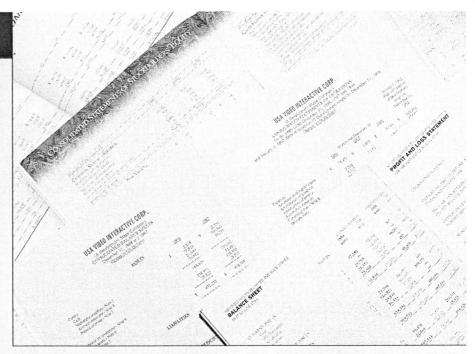

quality services to high-profile clients, primarily corporations. The clients' annual financial reports are audited by Jones and McLean to determine whether the financial statements are not misleading and follow generally accepted accounting principles. In performing the audit, the firm checks the accuracy of the financial statements by examining items such as receivables, inventory, and fixed assets and their corresponding documentation. Much of this work is performed just after the completion of the client's fiscal year, which is often December 31. Therefore, January and February are very busy audit months.

The firm also completes tax returns for its clients. Tax returns should be sent to the Internal Revenue Service two and one-half months after the end of the fiscal year for corporate clients and three and one-half months for individual clients. Extensions can be requested, but the firm prefers to submit all tax returns on a timely basis. Therefore, January, February, March, and the first part of April are busy months for taxes at Jones and McLean.

The consulting services provided by Jones and McLean include advice on management information systems, product development, and executive compensation. Clients demand consulting services more evenly throughout the year compared to the demand for audit and tax services.

The firm consists of 10 CPAs: two partners (Ed Jones and Mary McLean), two managers, and six professional staff. All the CPAs can perform audits, prepare tax returns, and provide consulting services, but at least one partner must check the work for each client. The support staff includes five secretaries.

The two managers and six professional staff members receive annual salaries with no overtime pay. The CPAs generally incur considerable overtime during the first four months of the year and take longer vacations during other times to compensate for the overtime. The support staff is paid on an hourly basis with a 40% increase for overtime. The support staff generally works one hour for every two hours of work by CPAs. Other costs of operating the office include rent, utilities, computing equipment, copiers, and office supplies. Once all revenues and expenses for the year are finalized and the yearly profit is determined, the partners share the net profit according to the terms of their partnership agreement.

Jones and McLean has been asked to audit the local municipality, Grove City. Like most cities in the United States, Grove City's fiscal year ends June 30, so much of the audit work must be done in July and August. The initial audit of the municipality will require more CPA time than subsequent audits because the firm would have to learn about Grove City's accounting systems. Audits are awarded on a competitive basis. Based on the fees paid in previous years and the bids of competing firms, city officials have told Jones and McLean that the city will pay a maximum of $10,000 for the audit services. Jones and McLean must decide if the $10,000 fee is sufficient to accept the audit. The revenue figure of $10,000 is a known factor, but the partners need information about the costs to determine whether the audit contract would be profitable.

MAKING PLANNING DECISIONS

Planning Decisions

Chapter One described the dual roles of management accounting in providing information for making planning and control decisions to create organizational value. This chapter focuses on making planning decisions, which are both long term and short term in nature. These decisions are linked to the organization's strategy and value chain. Typical planning decisions made within an organization include these:

What customers should the organization target and satisfy?

What products or services should the organization provide?

What activities should be used to provide the products or services?

What method should be used to price products or services?

How should the organization finance its operations?

The criteria for making these decisions depend on the organization's strategic mission. The aspects of a decision that will help the organization to achieve its goals are called *benefits*. For example, the strategic mission of the La Leche League is to promote breast-feeding. A direct mailing of information on breast-feeding to pregnant women would be consistent with La Leche's strategic goal and considered a benefit. Benefits, however, are seldom achieved without a cost. The cost of a decision is the amount of organizational resources used to achieve a benefit. The cost of the promotional campaign by the La Leche League is the cost of researching, writing, printing, and mailing the information on breast-feeding.

Decisions should be made after a careful analysis of benefits and costs. The benefits and costs to the organization may be different, however, from the benefits and costs to the manager within the organization who is making the decision. As stated in Chapter One, managers may have goals different from the organization and may tend to make the decision that leads to the greatest net benefit to themselves. The problem of control is to motivate the managers to align their individual goals with the organizational goals. Control problems are discussed in Chapter Six. In Chapters Two through Five, the goals of the managers and the organization are assumed to be the same.

The decision to use billboard advertising to promote the mission of a drug-free society requires careful analysis of the benefits and costs. The benefits of this decision are nonmonetary in nature, difficult to quantify, and obtained if the campaign results in reduced drug use. The costs include the organizational resources consumed to research, develop, and launch an effective advertising campaign.

ELLER

It makes you respond to "hey stupid" ten seconds slower.

Using Cost/Benefit Analysis

Cost/benefit analysis is the process of analyzing alternative decisions to determine which decision has the greatest expected benefit relative to its cost. We all informally use cost/benefit analysis in making day-to-day decisions. For example, a student may need to decide whether to ride a bicycle or drive a car to school. The benefit of riding a bicycle is more exercise; the cost is a longer commute time and possibly the need to take a shower after arriving at school. The benefit of driving a car is a faster commute time; the cost is the payment of parking fees or fines and the cost to operate the car. There are also some uncertainties. For example, the probability of rain, an accident, or a traffic jam should affect the expected benefits and costs of traveling to work. To make a decision, a person identifies, measures, and compares the expected benefits and costs of each alternative and chooses the alternative with the greatest net benefit (total benefits less total costs). Managers should use cost/benefit analysis to make planning decisions, but the benefits and costs are not always easily identified and measured.

One method of avoiding the measurement of all the benefits and costs of each alternative is to compare only those costs and benefits that differ among the alternative decisions. The difference in benefits is known as the **differential benefit,** and the difference in costs is known as the **differential cost.** A comparison of the differential benefits and costs leads to the same decision as a comparison of all the benefits and costs because the remaining costs and benefits do not affect the decision. For example, in 1997 Barnes & Noble had to decide whether to launch its own Web site (www.BarnesandNoble.com). This move was a possible strategic response to the success of Book Stacks Unlimited (www.book-stacks.com) and Amazon.com. The differential benefits of launching the Web site were the increased sales from Internet traffic and the improved quality of customer information gathered from the Web. The differential costs of launching the Web site were the costs of building it, hiring extra staff to maintain it, purchasing new computer hardware and software, and expanding warehouses to meet the additional demand from Internet customers. Barnes & Noble should have launched the Web site if the differential benefit exceeded the differential cost. The remaining benefits and costs generated by Barnes & Noble were irrelevant to the Web site decision since they were the same whether it decided to launch the Web site or not.[1]

LO 1 Use differential costs and benefits to assist in cost/benefit analysis.

Numerical Example 2.1

The manager of Kemp Sports must decide whether to rent only mechanical or only manual stringing machines for the tennis rackets that it manufacturers. One operator can string 60 rackets per hour using a mechanical stringer; one operator can string 10 rackets per hour using a manual stringing machine. The rental cost for a mechanical stringing machine is $100 per hour and for a manual stringing machine is $10 per hour. The cost of electricity for a mechanical stringer is $8 per hour, and labor cost is $9 per hour. Kemp must produce 120 tennis rackets per hour to meet customer demand. To produce 120 rackets, either 2 mechanical or 12 manual machines are required. The other manufacturing processes are not affected by the choice of stringing machines.

Solution

Because the rest of Kemp Sports is not affected by the choice of stringing machine and the revenues will be the same with a sufficient number of stringing machines (2 mechanical or 12 manual), the decision hinges on the differential costs of the two types of machines. The differential costs to string 120 tennis rackets per hour for each type of machine are as follows:

---

[1] Harvard Business School, "Leadership Online: Barnes & Noble vs. Amazon.com (A)," Case 9-798-063, rev. December 4, 1998.

Type of Cost	Manual Method	Mechanical Method	Difference
Rent	(12)($10) = $120	(2)($100) = $200	−$80
Labor	(12)($9) = 108	(2)($9) = 18	+90
Electricity		(2)($8) = 16	−16
Totals	$228	$234	−$6

The manual method results in lower costs and is the preferred choice. This decision, however, overlooks possible qualitative costs and benefits of this choice, such as the effect on quality and employee morale.

Even with differential costs and benefits, not all costs and benefits can be easily identified and measured when performing cost/benefit analysis.

Problems in Identifying and Measuring Benefits

The benefits of making a particular decision depend on the organization's goals. The achievement of some goals, however, is not easily identified and measured. For example, most car dealerships have the goal of customer satisfaction. When you purchase a new car, you receive a survey from the dealership asking if you were satisfied with your new car and the services provided. Since many buyers never return these surveys, the measurement of customer satisfaction is not necessarily accurate.

Benefits to organizations are often measured in terms of cash inflows. The cash inflow from a decision is not always known, however, and often must be estimated. For example, the benefit of introducing a new product is measured based on marketing estimates of future sales. These cash inflows occur in the future; therefore, some uncertainty in measurement exists. Also, cash flows from different time periods should be adjusted for the time value of money before they are accumulated. The time value of money is discussed in Chapter Thirteen.

Not all benefits of a decision have immediate monetary implications. Some benefits, such as learning and training, a better work environment, and increased worker satisfaction, are difficult to identify and measure in terms of dollars, but they have monetary consequences in later years.

Global
Competition

Daimler-Benz recently purchased Chrysler to become DaimlerChrysler. In making that decision, the executives of Daimler-Benz attempted to measure the benefits of owning Chrysler. Some of the benefits are obvious; for example, Chrysler has been a successful car manufacturer in the United States. Other benefits, however, are less direct. By owning Chrysler, Daimler-Benz has access to additional markets and a more diverse portfolio of cars to sell customers. Daimler-Benz also believed that owning Chrysler would give it a competitive advantage over rivals, but these benefits are more difficult to measure.

Problems in Identifying and Measuring Costs

Costs result from the use of organizational resources. Costs are easy to identify and measure when cash is the resource being used. For example, the purchase price of a new laptop computer is easily identified and measured in monetary terms. Some costs, however, do not have immediate or obvious monetary implications. For example, requiring employees to work overtime may adversely affect employee morale and have long-term cost implications.

Measuring the cost of using noncash resources is also a problem. For example, what is the cost of using raw materials in inventory? Possible answers include the purchase price (historical cost), the current market price, and the future replacement cost. What is the cost of using the existing labor pool or the existing facilities?

Once again, there are numerous possible answers. The next section introduces the concept of opportunity cost to answer these questions.

Opportunity Costs

Using an organization's resource, whether the resource is cash, inventory, buildings, or employee time, is a cost to the organization. It is a cost because once the resource is used for one purpose, it cannot be used for another purpose. If cash is spent to buy a machine, it cannot be used to hire a new employee. If a building is used to house the assembly division, the marketing department cannot use it nor can it be sold to another party. An employee who is designing a product cannot be cleaning the plant at the same time. *Cost* is defined as the use of resources. The measurement of costs is based on the forgone opportunities of using those resources for other purposes. The forgone opportunity of using a resource is the **opportunity cost.**

LO 2   Identify and measure opportunity costs for making planning decisions.

You use opportunity costs to make decisions every day. For example, the opportunity cost of accepting a job is forgoing the opportunity to do something else with your time. If your best alternative to working is playing golf, the opportunity cost of working is the forgone opportunity to play golf. If the opportunity to play golf has a value greater than the benefits of working, you will choose to play golf. Another example, is the opportunity cost of attending an early morning class. The forgone opportunity is being able to sleep later. The opportunity cost of taking in a movie is the forgone opportunity of using the time and money for another activity. In each case, a decision to use a resource for one purpose prevents the resource from being used for another purpose.

The concept of opportunity cost is consistent with cost/benefit analysis. Opportunity costs provide a means of measuring the cost of a particular decision. The costs of each alternative decision should be identified and measured in terms of the forgone opportunity of using the resources for other purposes.

Measuring Opportunity Costs

The forgone opportunity of using a resource is the opportunity cost to an organization. If a decision involves the use of many different resources, the opportunity cost of using each should be measured in monetary terms. The opportunity cost for each resource is then added and the total opportunity costs are compared with the benefits derived from the decision.

Cash is an organizational resource that is frequently expended to perform different activities. It is used to purchase materials, hire employees, and pay utility bills. Any proposed activity that requires the outlay of cash is incurring an opportunity cost since cash could be used for many other purposes. The measurement of the opportunity cost of using cash in the short run, however, is simply the face value of the cash expended. For example, if a proposed activity requires the purchase of $100 of bolts, the opportunity cost is $100.

Measuring the opportunity cost of using noncash resources is slightly more complicated. To measure the opportunity cost, the next best use of the resource should be identified. Forgone opportunities of using a resource include selling the resource or using it for another activity. Generally, however, a similar resource can be purchased, so the use of the resource does not necessarily prevent the other activities from occurring. For example, raw materials can be replaced through additional purchases, more machines and buildings can be bought, and more employees can be hired.

If the next best use of the resource is to sell it, the sales price of the resource is the opportunity cost of using it. For example, suppose you are debating whether to keep this book as a reference after the course is over. The opportunity cost of keeping the book is the resale price you would receive at the used bookstore.

If the use of the resource means that additional resources must be purchased for other activities, the cost of replacing the resources is the opportunity cost. For a new-car dealership, the forgone opportunity of selling a car is the inability to sell the same car to another customer. The new-car dealership can, however, buy another car from the manufacture; therefore, the opportunity cost of selling a new car is the cost to acquire another car from the manufacturer.

In general, the opportunity cost of using a noncash resource is either its sales price or its replacement cost. Under the unusual circumstance when a resource cannot be replaced and is critical for another activity, the loss in value to the organization of not being able to perform the other activity is the opportunity cost. For example, the time of an employee who has specialized knowledge of the organization's computer network is limited and cannot be replaced easily by hiring another employee. If the employee has no free time, assigning the employee to one activity prevents the employee from performing some other activity. The opportunity cost to the organization of using the employee's time is the loss in value caused by the employee not being able to undertake the other activity.

The following numerical examples illustrate the identification and measurement of opportunity costs.

Numerical Example 2.2

Doris Wheaton has 10 bags of cement in her garage. Each bag cost $4 last year when purchased. The store now sells each bag for $5 per bag but does not take returns. A neighbor told Doris he would buy the cement from her for $3 per bag if she doesn't want them. Doris is considering using the cement to make a patio.

a. If Doris uses the 10 bags of cement to make her patio and has no other use for them, what is the opportunity cost of using the cement?

b. If Doris must also rebuild her front steps (which requires 20 bags of cement), what is the opportunity cost of using the cement for the patio?

Solution

a. If Doris has no other use for the cement, the next best alternative to using the cement for the patio is to sell it. She can sell each bag to her neighbor for $3, or a total of $30. Therefore, the opportunity cost of using the cement is $30.

b. Using the cement for the patio means that the cement must be replaced to make the front steps. The replacement cost at $5 per bag for 10 bags, or $50, is the opportunity cost of using the 10 bags of cement for the patio.

Numerical Example 2.3

A copy center has hired a permanent employee to operate a copy machine for large jobs. This employee is paid $7 per hour whether or not copy jobs must be performed. Temporary help can be hired for $8 per hour.

a. What is the opportunity cost per hour of using the permanent employee to copy a job if there is no other work for the employee to perform?

b. What is the opportunity cost per hour of using the permanent employee if the employee could be working on another copy job that would generate a value of $6 per hour of work?

c. What is the opportunity cost per hour of using the permanent employee if the employee could be working on another copy job that would generate a value of $10 per hour of work?

Solution

a. If there is no alternative use of the employee's time, the opportunity cost of using the employee is $0 per hour.

b. The cost of hiring a temporary employee ($8/hour) is higher than the increased value of performing the other work ($6/hour). Therefore, the organization will not hire the temporary employee. Using the permanent employee prevents the employee from performing the other work and generating a value of $6 per hour. Under these circumstances, the opportunity cost of using the employee is $6 per hour.

c. Since the cost of hiring a temporary employee ($8/hour) is less than the increased value of performing the other work ($10/hour), the organization will hire the temporary employee if the permanent employee does not have time. Therefore, using the permanent employee on another activity causes the copy center to hire a temporary employee. The opportunity cost of using the permanent employee is the cost of hiring a temporary employee, or $8 per hour.

Numerical Example   2.4

An importer rents a building for storage at a cost of $1,000 per month. Presently, the importer occupies only half of the building space. She could sublet the remaining space for $300 per month. She is also considering importing a new line of products that would use the remaining space. What is the opportunity cost of using the building to add the new line of products?

Solution

The opportunity cost is the forgone opportunity to sublet the remaining space, or $300 per month.

Numerical Example   2.5

Your firm registered the Internet Web address (URL) www.work.com. For $300 per year, your firm has the exclusive right to use this URL. You plan to start a Web site that lists job openings and expect this business to generate revenues of $120,000 per year and expenses of $30,000 per year. Before starting the business, another company offers to buy your Web site URL for $110,000 per year.
a.   What "cost" does the accounting system assign to the Web site URL?
b.   What is the opportunity cost of the URL?

Solution

a.   The accounting system assigns a cost of $300 per year to the Web site URL.
b.   If you start the business, the opportunity cost of the URL is the $110,000 you forgo by not selling it.

The identification and measurement of opportunity costs may appear cumbersome and difficult, but *opportunity costs are the appropriate costs for making planning decisions.* In most cases, the opportunity cost of using a resource is either its purchase price or its selling price. In a competitive market with full information and no transaction costs, purchase and selling prices converge to the market price or value of the resource. Therefore, the market price of a resource is a reasonable approximation of the opportunity cost of using the resource. The following section describes sunk or historical costs, which are generally poorer approximations of opportunity cost.

**Planning
Decisions**

Sunk/Historical Costs

Sunk costs are costs that have already been incurred and cannot be changed no matter what action is taken. Because sunk costs were incurred in the past, they are the same for all possible alternatives in the present and the future. Therefore, sunk costs are irrelevant for cost/benefit analysis. Ironically, we often find ourselves including sunk costs when making decisions. For example, many people use the purchase price originally paid for their home to determine the listing price when they decide to sell. Other people stay to the last inning of a baseball game to "get their money's worth," even though the weather has become miserable and the home team is down by 10 runs.

The historical cost of a resource reflects its cost at the time of its acquisition. When a resource is acquired, the historical cost is usually a close approximation of the opportunity cost because it reflects the market value at that time. Except for somewhat arbitrary write-downs (depreciation and amortization), however, the historical cost of the resource remains the same as long as the organization holds it. The historical cost does not change with changes in market value. The historical cost of a resource becomes a sunk cost following its purchase.

LO 3   Ignore sunk costs for making planning decisions.

As discussed in Chapter One, financial reporting to outside investors is based on historical costs. Most internal accounting reports also use historical costs. The popularity of historical cost accounting reports might appear surprising. Although the historical cost approximates the opportunity cost of a resource at the time of purchase, the historical cost is a sunk cost subsequent to the purchase and should *not* be used for planning purposes. Given potential deviations between historical costs and opportunity costs, there is reason to question why historical cost accounting has survived. In the last century, regulations may have been partly responsible for its survival. Financial reporting requirements around the world are based on historical costs. The demand for opportunity costs (market values) by external parties for making planning decisions (e.g., investment decisions) might, however, have some effect on regulations.

Another reason for the continued popularity of historical costs is their use for control decisions, as discussed in Chapter One. Verifying the actions of managers is an important part of control. Historical costs may be more useful than opportunity costs for control because they reveal the past actions of managers. These costs are easily verifiable and less subject to managerial discretion. These features are important when performance is being measured by historical costs. Thus, historical cost data can be utilized to motivate and reward managers.

Historical costs are used in some situations to make planning decisions. Historical costs or simple adjustments to these figures might be reasonable approximations of opportunity costs. If the environment does not change very much from the time of the resource acquisition, the historical cost might remain a close approximation of the opportunity cost. Using rules of thumb to approximate opportunity costs, such as increasing historical costs by expected price inflation, also might be effective.

The problem for managers is to determine when to use historical cost numbers as reasonable approximations and when to expend additional effort to determine the opportunity costs, which are more closely approximated by the market value.

Numerical Example 2.6

Paul Wong is struggling to assemble a wooden chair. He has spent five hours on the process and estimates that at this rate, he will complete the assembly in two more hours. Joan Jiminez walks into the room and informs Paul that he is doing it the hard way. She describes a simpler method that will take only one hour to disassemble the work Paul has performed over the last five hours and assemble the chair completely. What should Paul do?

Solution

Paul should follow Joan's advice because the remaining time to completion is less. The five hours of work that he has performed is a sunk cost.

Concept**Review**

1. How does the use of differential costs and benefits help in performing cost/benefit analysis?
2. Why are some costs and benefits difficult to measure?
3. What should be considered in determining the opportunity cost of using a resource?
4. Why should sunk costs be ignored for planning purposes?

JONES AND MCLEAN, CERTIFIED PUBLIC ACCOUNTANTS
(Continued)

The firm of Jones and McLean has two alternatives concerning the offer to audit Grove City: (1) accept it or (2) reject it. Ed Jones and Mary McLean will presumably make the decision that most benefits the firm, but they may not agree completely on the goals of the firm. In the summer, Ed prefers to fish while Mary needs to earn extra money to pay for her daughter's college expenses. This type of conflict is a control problem. It may be partially resolved by adjusting the partners' method of sharing the profits that the firm generates and by altering their respective workloads. In this chapter, we assume that Ed and Mary both want to increase the firm's long-term profitability.

To Jones and McLean, the immediate cash benefit of auditing Grove City is the $10,000 fee. But there could be other benefits that are less obvious. For example, by auditing Grove City, the firm could be in the position to acquire other municipal audits. The learning that will occur in auditing Grove City could be applied to these other municipalities. Accepting the audit also provides the firm the option to continue to audit Grove City in the future. If another CPA firm audits Grove City this year, Jones and McLean is not likely to have the opportunity to do its audit in the near future. The firm's reputation also would be enhanced by having Grove City as a client.

In deciding whether to accept or reject the Grove City audit, Ed and Mary should determine the opportunity costs of using materials, labor, and facilities and ignore sunk costs. The materials such as forms and paper will all be replaced, so the replacement cost should be used for the opportunity cost. The seasonal nature of the auditing business means that the firm has excess labor and capacity during the summer months. The opportunity cost of using the CPAs, who are paid an annual salary, would be reduced employee morale from lost free time. Their annual salaries, however, are sunk costs. The support staff is paid on an hourly basis, so any increased support staff hours from the audit of Grove City creates an opportunity cost equal to the additional hours times the wage rate, or 1.4 times the wage rate if overtime is incurred. Overtime may be avoided by hiring temporary help. The costs of the facility appear to be sunk costs. The rent has already been paid and the equipment has already been purchased. There will be some costs to learning how to do the municipal audit. There also may be a slight increase in utilities if the Grove City audit is accepted. If Jones and McLean accepts the Grove city audit engagement, the firm forgoes the opportunity to accept other contracts that might prove more profitable.

Control Decisions

BENEFIT AND COST OF INFORMATION

Cost/benefit analysis, as described in this chapter, applies to all types of planning decisions. One planning decision is whether to choose to gather additional information before making another planning decision. The manager may ask for another accounting report or a marketing survey. How should the manager make the decision to obtain further information? Once again, a cost/benefit analysis is appropriate. If the benefit of further information is greater than the cost, the additional information should be produced or purchased. The problem is measuring the cost and benefit of the information.

LO 4   Use cost/benefit analysis to make information choices.

The cost of more information includes the cost of acquiring, modifying, communicating, and analyzing the information. Resources, including cash and employee time, are used in the process. Each of these resources has an opportunity cost.

The benefit of information comes from improved decisions. If reading *The Wall Street Journal* (*WSJ*) leads to better investment decisions, then the *WSJ* has a benefit. If reading it does not change any decisions, then it has no benefit as an information system. The differential benefit of new information is the difference between the expected benefit of making a decision with the new information and the expected benefit of making the decision with existing information. For instance, you can choose an MBA program without further information. But information on the quality and nature of alternative MBA programs would be beneficial in deciding which MBA program matches your preferences.

Consider, for example, Karen Hwang, who is selecting an MBA school for the upcoming year. Karen believes that an MBA degree will increase her future career opportunities and her salary. She has been accepted by two universities, Kings and Eastern. The universities charge similar tuition fees. However, the two MBA programs differ on other dimensions. Kings offers its program over 16 months; Eastern requires two years of full-time study. The faculty reputation, class size, and placement services are other areas in which they differ. Karen prefers small classes, but she considers faculty reputation and placement services to be more important. Therefore, she will make her choice based on an analysis of these two factors. Karen does not have much time to decide or much money for an extensive search. She plans to visit the Web sites of both universities to seek this information because an Internet search is low cost and timely.

The particular decision being made also affects the benefit of additional information. A weather report is unlikely to have much value in selecting an investment, but is likely to improve the choice of whether to have a picnic or when to plant a field of corn. In doing a cost/benefit analysis for information choice, the decision context must be known. Information that improves more than one decision is likely to be more valuable. Firms that choose to purchase only one management accounting system should select the system that provides the greatest benefit for a large number of decisions. The ability of a management accounting system to satisfy the demands of many users increases its benefit.

Numerical Example 2.7

A pharmaceutical firm is about to mix a batch of a drug. There is a one-in-five chance that the batch will fail due to bacterial contamination. This risk can be reduced to one in seven if a $5,000 diagnostic test is performed first. If the batch is started but scrapped due to the bacterial contamination, the firm loses $25,000. Should the firm spend the $5,000 on the test?

Solution

If the firm doesn't spend the $5,000 to gather information about the presence of the bacteria, the expected loss is $0.20(-\$25,000) + 0.80(\$0)$, or $-\$5,000$. If the firm spends the $5,000, the expected loss is $0.1429(-\$25,000 - \$5,000) + 0.8571(-\$5,000)$, or $-\$8,573$. The expected loss when the test is undertaken is greater than the expected loss of not performing it. Therefore, the test should not be performed because the expected benefit from gathering this additional information exceeds the expected cost.

JONES AND MCLEAN, CERTIFIED PUBLIC ACCOUNTANTS
(Continued)

The firm of Jones and McLean has the option to gather more information before deciding whether to audit Grove City. Additional study may provide more accurate estimates of hourly requirements for the audit and a better measure of its cost. Although it would be preferable to obtain information from other firms that have experience with government audits, competitors are not willing to divulge this confidential information. Instead, Jones and McLean could examine its previous audit work to estimate the cost. The firm could then project the audit cost by developing different estimates and weighting the probability of each. These different estimates also could outline the worst-case and best-case scenarios to assist the partners in assessing the uncertainties involved. Additional study will be costly, however, and should not be performed if the results won't affect the decision. More information should be obtained only if the expected benefits of an improved decision are greater than the cost of the information.

Concept**Review**

1. What is the cost of information?

2. What is the benefit of information?

ACTIVITY COSTS AND THE RATE OF OUTPUT

An organization's operation can be divided into *activities*. these activities are the tasks the organization performs to help achieve its goals. Activities may include designing products, accounting, purchasing materials, hiring employees, making product parts, and responding to customer queries. In Chapter One, specific activities that added to customer value were identified as the value chain of an organization. By adopting an appropriate strategy for customer value and activities linked to this strategy, the needs of customers can be met and organizational value created.

LO 5 Determine how activity costs vary with the rate of output.

Activities are units of work within the organization that are the subject of cost/benefit analysis. An organization must decide whether to engage in a particular activity and, if it decides to do so, it must determine how to do it. For example, an organization must decide whether to advertise a certain product on television or on the Internet or not at all.

Making planning decisions with respect to activities requires knowledge about their benefits and costs. The following sections examine the cost characteristics of activities. Activities use a variety of resources and are, therefore, costly to perform. In general, the cost of an activity is related to the intensity of its performance. For example, surveying 20 customers is more costly than surveying 10. The relation between an activity's costs and its rate of output (e.g., the number of customers surveyed) can be described by stages. These stages include the costs of initiating the activities, performing them at normal rates, and their capacity. Our focus here is on the rate of output; Chapter Three illustrates additional ways to capture activity costs.

Costs of Initiating Activities

Certain costs must be incurred before an activity can begin. These start-up costs may include purchasing materials, machines, and facilities; hiring of employees; and designing and planning the activity. For example, a typical activity performed by an organization is the payment of wages to employees. The activity must be designed to record hours worked, determine deductions, and distribute paychecks. Employees in the payroll department must be hired and trained to perform the activity, and equipment must be purchased. These start-up efforts must occur even if the organization has only a few employees to pay. Therefore, the cost per payroll check issued could be very high if only a few payroll checks are issued.

In summary, the cost per output of an activity is generally quite high for the first few units of output. This high cost per unit reflects the start-up costs of initiating activities.

Costs of Activities at Normal Rates

Once an activity has been designed, sufficient equipment has been purchased, training has been completed, and employees have learned to perform it, the activity achieves a normal rate of operation. In the example of the payroll activity, considerable costs are incurred to initiate it, but once several payroll checks have been processed and issued, considerable learning has taken place. At that point, payroll checks most likely can be issued more efficiently. The cost per additional payroll check issued probably becomes relatively small.

Costs of Activities When Exceeding Capacity

Activities are constrained by the size of the facility, equipment, or employees. **Capacity** is a measure of the constraints on activities. Capacity constraints for a manufacturer include the physical size of the facility, the number of machine hours available, and employee time. When an activity's rate of output reaches capacity, the activity no longer operates efficiently. Additional costs arise because limitations in facility size cause congestion. Extra equipment might have to be purchased, or existing equipment might become overused, resulting in additional maintenance costs. Employees might have to be paid overtime. An organization can increase its capacity for an activity, but the cost of buying a new facility or hiring and training a new set of employees might be high, especially if the firm must act quickly. Therefore, the cost of additional output when exceeding capacity is higher than under normal operations.

Graphical Analysis of Activity Costs and the Rate of Output

The common characteristics of how costs change with increased output of an activity during a period of time are graphed in Figure 2.1. The curve represents the total cost of the activity at different rates of output. Total activity costs might rise sharply at low rates of output (point A) because of start-up costs. Activity costs then increase moderately under normal operating rates (point B). When output rates near capacity (point C), total costs begin to rise sharply again due to congestion and other capacity-related costs.

Marginal and Average Costs

LO 6　Calculate marginal and average costs.

The **marginal cost** of an activity is the cost to produce one more unit of output, given the existing rate of output. The marginal cost of the activity is the slope of the total cost curve in Figure 2.1 at each rate of output. The steeper the slope, the higher the marginal cost. The marginal cost is highest at very low output rates (point A) and output rates near capacity (point C). The marginal cost is lowest at normal operations (point B) between these extreme rates of output.

Figure 2.1

Nonlinear Cost Curve

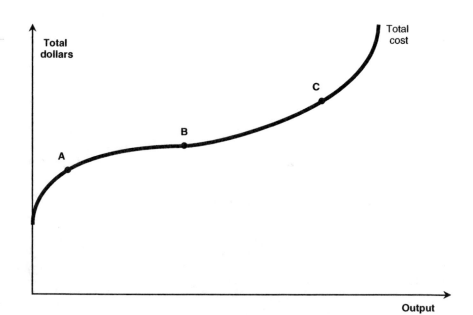

The marginal cost is useful in making decisions about small changes in output rates of activities. Given a particular rate of output, the marginal cost represents the cost of another unit of activity output or the cost savings of one less unit of activity output. In the case of the payroll activity, the marginal cost is the cost of issuing one more payroll check (or the cost savings of issuing one less payroll check), given a specified level of payroll checks being issued.

The **average cost** per unit of activity is calculated by dividing the total activity costs by the number of units of output. For the pattern of total costs in Figure 2.1, the average cost per unit is very high at low levels of output but declines as output increases. The average cost per unit increases only as output nears capacity.

Organizations commonly calculate the average cost per unit. For example, a firm might calculate the average cost of issuing a payroll check by summing all costs related to payroll and dividing by the number of payroll checks issued. This figure does not reflect the cost of issuing additional payroll checks because it includes the initial start-up costs that do not affect the cost of additional ones. Therefore, the average cost should not be used in decisions to make small adjustments to the rate of output.

Numerical Example 2.8

Beechcraft Aircraft Refinishing specializes in refurbishing small aircraft. The company estimates the following total costs for painting aircraft in one month:

Number of Aircraft	Total Cost
10	$100,000
20	150,000
30	190,000
40	220,000
50	250,000
60	280,000
70	320,000
80	370,000
90	470,000
100	600,000

a.   What are the marginal cost and the average cost for each level of output of the painting activity?

b.   The company is currently painting 80 aircraft per month. A small regional airline would like to bring in 10 aircraft for painting this month and is willing to spend $90,000 for the paint job. Should Beechcraft accept this additional job?

Solution

a.

Number of Units	Total Cost	Marginal Cost	Average Cost
10	$100,000	$100,000	$10,000
20	150,000	50,000	7,500
30	190,000	40,000	6,333
40	220,000	30,000	5,500
50	250,000	30,000	5,000
60.	280,000	30,000	4,667
70	320,000	40,000	4,571
80	370,000	50,000	4,625
90	470,000	100,000	5,222
100	600,000	130,000	6,000

b.   The company should not accept the offer because the marginal cost of painting 10 additional aircraft is $100,000. The average cost of $5,222 should not be used for this decision.

Concept**Review**

1. Why are opportunity costs of making the first few units of a product or providing a service likely to be relatively high?

2. Why should capacity be a factor in determining opportunity costs?

3. What type of decisions should use marginal costs?

4. Why is the average cost inappropriate for some decisions?

JONES AND MCLEAN, CERTIFIED PUBLIC ACCOUNTANTS

(Continued)

Before auditing Grove City, the firm of Jones and McLean must learn about government audit requirements and acquaint itself with Grove City's accounting system. These start-up costs make the audit of Grove City more costly than had the firm already performed municipal audits.

If Jones and McLean tried to audit too many municipalities, however, the firm could find itself nearing capacity in terms of office space and support personnel. Increased congestion and delays would impose costs on the other services the firm provides. These congestion costs would be a cost of accepting too many municipal audits.

APPROXIMATIONS OF ACTIVITY COSTS

LO 7 Approximate activity costs using variable and fixed costs.

Activity costs are not always easy to estimate. The activity cost curve in Figure 2.1 requires estimates of the opportunity cost of using resources to perform the activity at different levels of output. Because such estimates are difficult to measure, managers often use approximations. One approximation is to use the market value of resources for the opportunity cost. Chapter Three examines activity costs in terms of whether they are associated directly or indirectly with an activity. In addition, total activity costs can be approximated using fixed and variable costs.

Fixed Costs

An approximation of Figure 2.1 using straight lines is provided in Figure 2.2. The approximation assumes that there is a cost to set up and start operations called a

Figure 2.2

Fixed and Variable Cost Approximation of Activity Costs

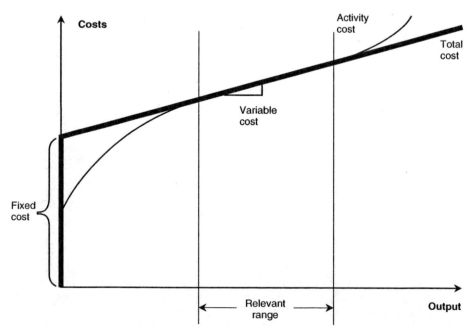

fixed cost (intersection of the cost axis in Figure 2.2). Fixed costs, which do not change with the rate of output, include the cost of using the facilities, purchasing machines, hiring and training employees, and using other resources that do not change with the rate of output.

Variable Costs

Once an activity's fixed costs are incurred, additional operational costs are necessary to produce output for the activity. The costs that increase with the rate of output are called **variable costs.** In Figure 2.2, the linear representation of total activity costs assumes that the variable cost of each additional unit is constant over all rates of output. The **variable cost per unit** is the slope of the line in Figure 2.2. Variable costs include the cost of using additional labor, materials, and other resources to increase the output of the activity.

Relevant Range

In Figure 2.2, the straight line is the fixed and variable cost approximation of the total activity costs. The line most closely approximates the activity costs in the range of normal operations. This range is called the **relevant range;** it encompasses the rates of output where the combined fixed and variable costs are close approximations of the total activity costs. The slopes of the total activity cost curve and the fixed and variable cost curve are about the same; therefore, the variable cost per unit is a close approximation of the marginal cost. In the relevant range, the variable cost can be used to estimate the cost of additional units of output of the activity.

For output quantities below the relevant range of output, the total fixed and variable costs tend to overestimate activity costs. The fixed and variable cost curve is flatter than the activity cost curve, implying that the variable cost per unit underestimates the marginal cost below the relevant range. Therefore, the marginal cost of the first few units of output tends to be higher than the variable cost. Above the relevant range, the total fixed and variable costs tend to underestimate the total activity costs. Once again, the fixed and variable cost curve is flatter than the activity cost curve, implying that the variable cost per output unit underestimates the marginal cost above the relevant range. The marginal cost is greater than the variable cost as the rate of output approaches capacity.

The total costs in terms of variable and fixed costs can be described by the following equation:

Total activity costs = Fixed costs + Variable costs

or

$$\text{Total activity costs} = \text{Fixed costs} + \left(\begin{matrix} \text{Variable cost} \\ \text{per unit of output} \end{matrix} \right)\left(\begin{matrix} \text{Number of} \\ \text{units of output} \end{matrix} \right)$$

Numerical Example 2.9

Jackson Company makes computers. One activity in assembling the computer is to test it before it leaves the factory. The company estimates that the annual fixed costs to purchase testing equipment, provide space for it in the factory, and train employees to use it total $100,000. The variable costs of labor and electricity to do the testing are $10 per unit. What are total expected costs if the company tests 5,000 computers per year? What are total expected costs if the company tests 7,000 computers per year?

Solution

The total expected cost to test 5,000 computers per year is the sum of fixed costs ($100,000) and variable costs (($10/test)(5,000 tests) = $50,000), or $150,000. Total expected testing costs if Jackson Company tests 7,000 computers per year is the sum of fixed costs ($100,000) and variable costs (($10/test)(7,000 tests) = $70,000), or $170,000.

Concept**Review**

1. How does a fixed cost change with the rate of output?

2. What do variable costs approximate?

JONES AND MCLEAN, CERTIFIED PUBLIC ACCOUNTANTS

(Continued)

You decide

For Jones and McLean, the fixed cost of performing a municipal audit is learning the governmental regulations on auditing municipalities and the accounting systems of municipalities. The partners estimate these fixed costs to equal $5,000. The $5,000 will be sunk, and hence irrelevant, when determining the cost to perform additional municipal audits in the future.

The firm estimates variable costs in terms of CPA time. These variable costs include the cost of using supplies and secretarial help and the cost of motivating the CPAs to work during the summer. The partners estimate that the variable cost per hour of CPA time for all these costs is $60/hour. They also estimate that the Grove City audit will require 100 hours of CPA time. Therefore, the total estimated cost of auditing Grove City is $5,000 + (100 hours)($60/hour), or $11,000.

If Jones and McLean performs only one municipal audit (Grove City) this year, the $10,000 revenue wouldn't cover the $11,000 cost of performing the audit. If Jones and McLean performs more municipal audits this year, however, most of the fixed costs related to doing municipal audits would already have been incurred. Therefore, Jones and McLean must decide whether to seek to audit more municipalities than Grove City.

The firm also must consider the option to audit Grove City next year. If some of the fixed costs of auditing Grove City this year will not be incurred next year, the trade-off between losing money this year and making money in subsequent years should be compared. The partners should read Chapter Thirteen on discounting future cash flows to make this type of comparison.

ESTIMATION OF ACTIVITY COSTS THROUGH THE IDENTIFICATION OF VARIABLE AND FIXED COSTS

Fixed and variable costs can be used to estimate an activity's total cost. The problem with estimating activity costs through fixed and variable costs is estimating the fixed and variable cost per unit. The following sections describe two methods: the account classification and the high/low method. The Appendix of this chapter describes a method using regression analysis.

Estimating Variable and Fixed Costs through Account Classification

LO 8   Use the account classification and high/low methods to estimate variable and fixed costs.

Accounting aggregates costs within different categories called *accounts*. For example, all maintenance costs may be aggregated within a single account, and all electricity costs may be aggregated within a single account. The costs in these accounts are treated as if they were all the same and had predictable relations with the output of different activities. For example, the costs in the electricity account are assumed to be similar and have predictable relations with different activities such as accounting and machining. In the case of accounting, the major use of electricity is for lighting. The cost of electricity for lighting is not likely to change much with the output of the accounting department, which could be described in terms of the

Figure 2.3   Classifying Accounts as Fixed and Variable

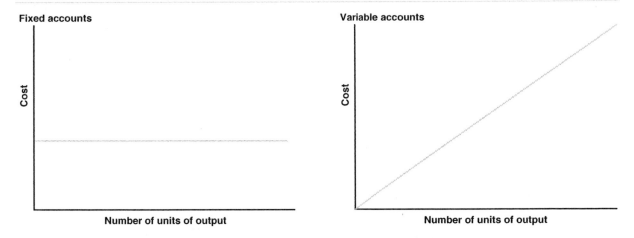

number of transactions recorded or hours of work performed by accountants. Under these circumstances, the cost of electricity is considered *fixed* with respect to accounting. In the case of machining, the major use of electricity is the operation of the machines. The more the machines operate, the more electricity they use. The cost of electricity for machining is likely to change with the change in output of machining, which could be described in terms of machine hours or number of units machined. Under these circumstances, the cost of electricity would be considered *variable* with respect to machining.

The **account classification method** assumes that each cost account associated with the activity of interest can be identified as either fixed or variable with respect to the output of the activity. If the costs of an account do not change with the output level, the account is classified as fixed. If the costs of an account increase proportionally with the units of output of an activity, the account is classified as variable. Figure 2.3 demonstrates the fixed and variable relation.

In reality, very few cost accounts can be described as either exactly variable or exactly fixed with respect to an activity. Costs generally have some of both characteristics and tend to curve instead of being linear as they are in Figure 2.3. The account classification method, however, requires the identification of cost accounts as either fixed or variable.

Once the cost accounts are classified as fixed or variable, all costs in each category are aggregated. The total costs of the fixed cost accounts are the activity's fixed costs. The total costs of the variable cost accounts are divided by the expected units of output of the activity to determine the variable cost per unit.

Knowing the fixed costs and variable costs per unit of an activity provides the ability to estimate costs given different levels of activity output. Each additional unit of output should increase costs by the variable cost per unit until capacity constraints become a factor.

Numerical Example   2.10

Topper Restaurant is trying to estimate the cost of providing a meal using the account classification method. The manager estimates the following costs for serving 20,000 meals during the next year:

Food	$40,000
Service help	80,000
Supervisory help	60,000
Facility rental	50,000
Equipment	10,000

a. What are the fixed costs and the variable costs per unit?

b. What are the estimated costs for preparing 30,000 meals?

Solution

a. Supervisory help, facility rental, and equipment are all fixed costs. Service help may be fixed or variable; food is variable. If service help is fixed, fixed and variable costs are calculated as follows:

Fixed Costs		Variable Costs	
Service Help	$ 80,000	Food	$40,000
Supervisory help	60,000		
Facility rental	50,000		
Equipment	10,000		
Total	$200,000	Total	$40,000

Variable cost/meal = $40,000/20,000 = $2/meal

b. If 30,000 meals are prepared, the estimated costs include fixed costs of $200,000 and variable costs of ($2)(30,000), or total costs of $260,000.

Using the High/Low Method to Fit Historical Cost Data

LO 8 Use the account classification and high/low methods to estimate variable and fixed costs.

Attempting to classify accounts as fixed or variable and to estimate the future cost of each account requires considerable judgment, and errors are possible. Another method of estimating the variable and fixed costs is to consider the activity's past costs. The analysis of past costs provides an approximation of estimated fixed and variable costs if the following conditions hold:

1. *Past costs reasonably approximate future costs.* If operational procedures and prices have not changed too much, past costs should closely approximate future costs.

2. *Several periods of past cost data at different output levels exist.* If the activity is new or recently developed, the analysis of past data will not work.

3. *The future output level is within the range of the past data.* If more units of output of the activity are expected in the future than in the past, the past data will not reveal potential capacity constraints.

4. *The costs of each activity can be identified separately.* All costs can be traced to the activity.

If these conditions are satisfied, a graphical analysis of past costs and output levels will provide an estimate of the fixed and variable costs of the activity. Figure 2.4 shows a graph of historical costs and the output level for many different periods. The pattern of data points indicates a positive relation between the activity's output and its total cost. The problem is to find a line that can closely approximate the data.

One method of drawing the line is to connect the points representing the highest and lowest output of the activity. This is called the **high/low method** and is represented by the line in Figure 2.4. The slope of the line is the variable cost per unit, and the intersection on the y-axis (zero output of the activity) is the fixed cost.

To estimate the variable cost per unit and fixed cost mathematically, the highest and lowest points can be used to determine the equation of the line. The estimated variable cost per unit is the difference between the total activity cost at the highest output level and the total activity cost at the lowest output level *divided by* the difference between the highest output level and the lowest output level. The estimated fixed cost is calculated by *subtracting* the per unit variable costs times the lowest output level from the total activity costs at the lowest output level. The

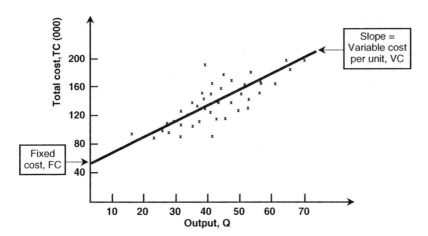

Figure 2.4

Estimating Fixed and
Variable Costs

fixed cost also can be estimated by using the difference between the total activity
costs at the highest output level and the per unit variable cost times the highest
output level. Either method generates the same estimate.

In Figure 2.4, the lowest output level is 18 units with an activity cost of $90.
The highest output level is 69 units with an activity cost of $200. The variable cost
per unit is as follows:

$$\frac{\text{Difference in costs}}{\text{Difference in output}} = \frac{(\$200 - \$90)}{(69 - 18)} = \$2.16/\text{unit}$$

The fixed cost is determined as follows:

$$\begin{pmatrix}\text{Total cost at}\\ \text{the lowest output}\end{pmatrix} - \begin{pmatrix}\text{Variable cost}\\ \text{per unit}\end{pmatrix}\begin{pmatrix}\text{Lowest}\\ \text{output level}\end{pmatrix} = \$90 - (\$2.16/\text{unit})(18\text{ units})$$
$$= \$51$$

Or

$$\begin{pmatrix}\text{Total cost at}\\ \text{the highest output}\end{pmatrix} - \begin{pmatrix}\text{Variable cost}\\ \text{per unit}\end{pmatrix}\begin{pmatrix}\text{Highest}\\ \text{output level}\end{pmatrix} = \$200 - (\$2.16/\text{unit})(69\text{ units})$$
$$= \$51$$

The accuracy of activity cost estimates based on historical costs depends on
whether the economic and operating conditions of the past will continue into the
future. Estimating costs outside the range of historic output is also a concern. In Figure 2.4, the historic output level was between 18 and 69 units. The cost of making
80 units may be much higher than indicated by the line in Figure 2.4. The maximum
output may be 69 units, with any further production requiring increased capacity.

Numerical Example **2.11**

Slugger Company makes wooden baseball bats. The company has used the same manufacturing procedures for
years, and the prices of the wood and labor have remained relatively constant. The following data are historical costs
of making the bats:

Year	Number of Bats Produced	Historical Costs
1994	10,000	$110,000
1995	13,000	120,000
1996	11,000	105,000
1997	15,000	125,000
1998	17,000	125,000
1999	13,000	115,000
2000	16,000	130,000

Business**Analysis**

The Internet has made many question the necessity of traditional brokerage houses that have bricks-and-mortar operations. Online trading has led many established firms to provide innovative pricing strategies to ensure that their services continue to meet customer needs. One critical question for brokerage houses and stock exchanges is how to estimate the opportunity cost of using existing facilities to develop a successful strategy to achieve organizational value.

In 1975, the U.S. brokerage industry was deregulated. Prior to 1975, commissions on stock trades were set and were non-negotiable. Once exempt from fee regulation, stock brokers were free to set their own commission prices. The industry could then compete to add customer value through offering a lower-cost service. Discount brokerage houses such as Charles Schwab became popular. Savvy investors who didn't want the advice and research provided by the major brokerage firms could execute trades with much lower commission fees. In 1994 with the arrival of Internet, trading volume increased while average trading commissions dropped by approximately 50%. With the Internet, firms began offering free trades or cash bonuses to lure clients. Price competition combined with heavy advertising meant losses for many online trading firms. Brokerage houses now have global reach. Canada's TD Bank leverages its knowledge of discount brokerage to promote its U.S. Waterhouse division to traders who demand reliability, low commissions, and the ability to maintain a well-diversified portfolio through access to research services.

    With Internet trading, new competitors such as E*Trade and Ameritrade, operate entirely online. Each company competes by developing new methods of trading, accessing accounts, and providing research online. Quality in terms of accurate trade execution and confidentiality is another way to add customer value. Differences in services and quality, however, are difficult to maintain because other companies can

a. Estimate the variable cost per bat and the fixed costs using the high/low method.

b. Using the estimates of fixed and variable costs, estimate total costs if planned production is 14,000 bats.

Solution

a. The lowest output was in 1994 and the highest output was in 1998. Using those two data points, the variable cost per bat is determined as:

$$(\$125{,}000 - \$110{,}000)/(17{,}000 - 10{,}000) = \$2.14 \text{ per bat}$$

The fixed cost per bat using the 1994 data follows:

$$\$110{,}000 - (\$2.14 \text{ per bat})(10{,}000 \text{ bats}) = \$88{,}600$$

or using the 1998 data:

$$\$125{,}000 - (\$2.14 \text{ per bat})(17{,}000 \text{ bats}) = \$88{,}620$$

The difference in the calculation of the fixed costs when using the lowest and highest outputs is due to rounding error.

b. The estimated costs of 14,000 bats are the fixed costs of $88,600 plus the variable costs of ($2.14/bat)(14,000 bats), or $29,960. Therefore, total estimated costs are $88,600 + $29,960 or $118,560.

In this chapter, fixed and variable costs have been defined as costs that are fixed or vary with the rate of output of an activity. An activity is the building block of the organization, which performs a variety of activities to create products and provide services that add customer value. In Chapter Five, we will see that the cost of products and services also can be viewed through the framework of fixed and variable costs. Fixed costs are those incurred to start making units of the product or service. The variable cost per unit is the cost of making another unit of the product or service.

Concept**Review**

1. How is account classification used to estimate fixed and variable costs?
2. How is the high/low method used to estimate fixed and variable costs?

SUMMARY

1 **Use differential costs and benefits to assist in cost/benefit analysis.** Differential analysis identifies the costs and benefits that vary across alternative decisions. Only differential costs and benefits are relevant for decisions because all other factors are the same for each possible decision.

2 **Identify and measure opportunity costs for making planning decisions.** *Opportunity cost* is defined in terms of alternative uses of a resource. The size of the forgone opportunity of using the resource is the measure of the opportunity cost.

3 **Ignore sunk costs for making planning decisions.** *Sunk costs* are costs that have already been incurred and are not relevant for planning decisions.

4 **Use cost/benefit analysis to make information choices.**
Additional information should be gathered if the benefit of improved decision making is greater than the cost of the information.

5 **Determine how activity costs vary with the rate of output.**
The cost of the first few units of an activity's output tends to be quite high. At normal production levels, the cost of additional units of activity tends to be lower. When the activity nears capacity, the cost of additional units of activity output tends to be higher.

6 **Calculate marginal and average costs.** The *marginal cost* is the cost of one more unit of output, which is the slope of the total cost curve. The *average cost* is the total cost of the activity divided by the number of units of output.

7 **Approximate activity costs using variable and fixed costs.**
Approximating costs by fixed and variable costs assumes that initiating the activity has a cost, which is the fixed cost. Subsequent units of the activity output are assumed to cost the same amount per unit, which is the variable cost per unit.

8 **Use the account classification and high/low methods to estimate variable and fixed costs.** The account classification method identifies fixed and variable costs by categorizing different cost accounts. The high/low method uses the past highest and lowest output data points to estimate fixed and variable costs.

9 **Use regression to estimate variable and fixed costs. (Appendix)**
Regression analysis uses historic outputs and costs to estimate fixed and variable costs.

KEY TERMS

account classification method   The estimation of activity costs through identifying whether a cost account is fixed or variable. *(p. 49)*

average cost   The total cost of production divided by the number of units produced. *(p. 45)*

capacity   A measure of the constraints on an organization's operation. *(p. 44)*

cost/benefit analysis   The process of making decisions by comparing the costs and benefits of alternative choices. *(p. 35)*

differential benefit   The difference in the benefits of two alternative decisions. *(p. 35)*

differential cost   The difference in the cost of two alternative decisions. *(p. 35)*

fixed cost   The cost of initiating production, which does not vary with the number of units produced. *(p. 47)*

high/low method   The estimation of fixed and variable costs using the highest and lowest output data points in the past. *(p. 50)*

quickly duplicate those efforts. For example, the entry of American Express into the brokerage industry, with its offer of free trading and extensive asset management services, has increased pressure on commission revenue. Despite the downward trend in revenues, it is likely that new firms will enter the online market, given the low barriers to entry.

Technological Change

Merrill Lynch, a full-service brokerage house started in 1914, offers multiple services including financial planning, investment banking, foreign exchange trading, insurance, investment research, and trade execution. With 60,000 employees in branch offices in 43 countries, it is one of the dominant players in the brokerage market. Online brokerage houses, however, have begun eating into Merrill Lynch's market share, so the company has entered the online trading competition. Discount brokers such as Charles Schwab also moved to the Internet once customers began to shift away from its proprietary online service.

Strategy for Customer Value

E*Trade, Ameritrade, and Merrill Lynch all attempt to add customer value through different pricing strategies. E*Trade has a sliding scale with the more trades executed per month, the lower the cost per trade (currently ranging from $14.95 to $4.96 per trade). Ameritrade offers all trade executions at a fixed commission rate (currently $8 per trade). Merrill Lynch provides free trade execution, as well as (financial advice, reports, and banking privileges), for a fixed annual fee (currently as low as $1,500, depending on the client's assets held with Merrill Lynch). Each of these pricing strategies is designed to add value to different types of customers. Organizational value, however, also must be achieved. What variable and fixed cost structures for stock trade execution are likely to exist in these companies to be consistent with their pricing strategy? How will the changes in the structure of commission fees affect the ability of both old and new competitors to implement a successful strategy in the long run?

Source: P. Kedrosky, "Free Online Trading Will Wreck Your Broker," *The National Post*, November 20, 1999, p. D8.

www.americanexpress.com

www.ameritrade.com

www.etrade.com

www.ml.com

www.schwab.com

www.waterhouse.com

marginal cost   The additional cost of producing one more unit given a certain level of output . *(p. 44)*

opportunity cost   The cost of a forgone opportunity of using a resource for another purpose. *(p. 37)*

relevant range   The range of output levels over which variable costs are reasonable approximations of opportunity costs. *(p. 47)*

sunk cost   A cost that has already been incurred and cannot be changed. *(p. 39)*

variable cost   The variable cost per unit times the number of units produced. *(p. 47)*

variable cost per unit   An approximation of the marginal cost using fixed and variable costs. *(p. 47)*

APPENDIX

Using Regression to Estimate Fixed and Variable Costs

LO 9   Use regression to esti- mate variable and fixed costs.

The high/low method is described in the chapter as a method to estimate fixed and variable costs. As noted, this method may result in poor estimates if the high and low points represent extreme or unusual levels of operating activity. A statistical method of drawing a line, called *regression*, is more accurate. Regression analysis identifies a line that minimizes the summation of the squared deviations of all historical cost data points from the regression line.

The following data from Numerical Example 2.11 are used to demonstrate fitting a line with regression analysis.

Year	Number of Bats Produced	Historical Costs
1994	10,000	$110,000
1995	13,000	120,000
1996	11,000	105,000
1997	15,000	125,000
1998	17,000	125,000
1999	13,000	115,000
2000	16,000	130,000

These data must be inputted into a software package that performs regression analysis. The historical costs are the dependent variable or the variable to be estimated. The number of bats is the independent variable or the variable that will be used to estimate costs. The output of any regression software program looks like the following:

	Coefficient	Standard Error of Coefficient	*t*-Ratio
Constant	75,611	9,161	8.25
Number of bats	3.165	0.6648	4.76
Adjusted $R^2 = 0.783$			

The estimate of the constant coefficient is an estimate of fixed costs equal to $75,611. The coefficient on the number of bats is the variable cost per bat equal to $3.165. The remaining information of the output indicates how well the regression line represents the historical costs for different levels of output.

The adjusted R^2 is a measure of how well the number of bats explains the costs. If all the plotted points in Figure 2.5 were aligned in a straight line, knowing the number of bats would determine the costs. If the regression line closely represents the cost data, then the adjusted R^2 approaches 1.0. The adjusted R^2 of 0.783 is quite high, indicating that the regression line is a close approximation of the historical cost data for different levels of output. An adjusted R^2 of zero indicates that there is no association between the number of bats and costs. An adjusted R^2 near

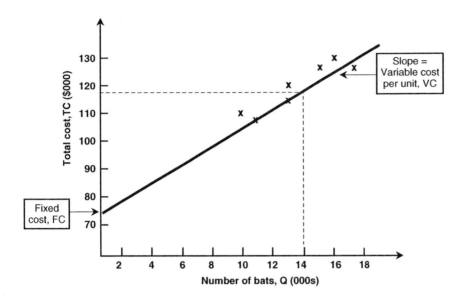

Figure 2.5

Estimating Fixed and
Variable Costs Slugger
Company, 1994–2000

zero indicates that the measures of the variable cost per unit and the fixed costs are not very accurate.

The standard errors of the coefficient indicate how confident we should be in the estimates of the fixed cost and variable cost per unit. In general, there is approximately a 95% chance that the true fixed cost estimate and the true variable cost per unit are within 2 standard errors of their estimates. Therefore, there is a 95% probability that the true fixed cost is within the range of $75,611 + (2)($9,161), or $93,933 and $75,611 − (2)($9,161), or $57,289. The variable cost per unit is within $3.165 + (2)($.6648), or $4.4946 and $3.165 − (2)($.6648), or $1.8354.

The *t*-ratio can be used to determine the probability that the fixed cost and variable cost per unit are different from zero. This information is not particularly useful in this situation because we would expect those costs to be greater than zero.

The estimated fixed cost and per unit variable cost allow for the estimation of costs given planned production. If planned production next year is 14,000 bats, the expected costs given the regression line are as follows:

Fixed costs	$ 75,611
Variable costs ($3.165/bat)(14,000 bats)	44,310
Total estimated costs	$119,921

Although regression uses more historical cost data than the high/low method, it is susceptible to similar problems. In particular, regression assumes that the process that generated the historical costs is the same process that will be used in the estimation period.

Regression is valid for estimating costs only within production levels experienced in the past. For example, the previous range of bats produced was 10,000 to 17,000. Estimates of costs of producing more than 17,000 bats may be influenced by capacity constraints. Regression analysis, however, assumes that variable costs per unit are constant at all levels of output and does not recognize capacity constraints. It also assumes that the relation between costs and levels of output is a straight line.

As a result of these problems, regression analysis is not commonly used to estimate the fixed cost and the variable cost per unit, but it could be used for other purposes. For example, regression could be used to identify cost drivers. In this case, the activity costs are the dependent variable; different potential cost drivers

Figure 2.6   Total Costs of Hiring Personnel as a Function of Number of Personnel and Total Assets

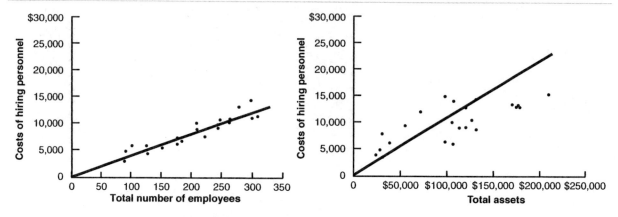

could be tried as the independent variable. The cost driver with the closest association (highest R^2) with the activity cost is the cost driver used by the organization for that activity. For example, Figure 2.6 provides graphs describing the relation between the costs of hiring personnel and two different possible cost drivers, total number of personnel and total assets. The total number of personnel is more closely associated with the cost of hiring personnel and has a higher adjusted R^2. Therefore, the total number of personnel provides a more accurate cost driver for tracing the indirect costs of hiring personnel to different cost objects.

SELF-STUDY PROBLEM I

Identifying Opportunity Costs

Western University (WU) is contemplating dropping all athletic scholarships, which average $10,000 per student annually. Because of budget cutbacks, the administration believes that WU cannot afford athletic scholarships. The Athletic Department is arguing that the cost of dropping them will be high and that they play an important part in WU's strategy to attract star athletes. Fielding competitive teams is known to generate donor revenues and publicity. Without the scholarships, the athletic teams will no longer be competitive, and the school might be dropped from the Big 17 Conference. Ticket revenues are estimated to drop by 10 to 20%. Alumni will not provide as many donations; currently, they give several million dollars per year to WU, and these funds help the University to offset cutbacks in government funding. Since many of the athletes are on partial scholarships, WU also might lose the remaining tuition. The average tuition fees are $20,000 per year. WU will get less publicity, especially in the sports pages of newspapers and on television.

What are the benefits and opportunity costs of providing athletic scholarships?

Solution

The Athletic Department's arguments reveal the benefits of having athletic scholarships, especially as part of WU's strategy to attract star players. Having a competitive team is one way to attract donors and publicity. These benefits, however, are difficult to measure. For example, donations and ticket revenues are likely to be higher with more competitive teams. Athletes on partial scholarships also pay some tuition. Publicity probably will be higher, but the value of that publicity is difficult to measure. The value of being in a particular athletic conference depends on the quality of the other institutions in it. Being in the Ivy League, for example, gives those institutions a certain amount of prestige, which is difficult to value.

These benefits should be offset against the opportunity costs of having athletic scholarships. What are the forgone opportunities of providing scholarships? The opportunity cost of any cash payments to athletes for books, housing, and food can be measured directly, but most of the scholarship involves waiving tuition and providing free education to the athletes. The opportunity cost depends on whether providing free education prevents a tuition-paying student from attending WU. If the University is at capacity and the athlete takes the place of a tuition-paying student, the forgone opportunity is the lost tuition, which is $20,000 per student. If WU is not at capacity, the forgone opportunity is the marginal cost (approximated by the variable cost) of educating an additional student. The variable cost of educating a student (additional materials, grading, etc.) might not be very high because most costs at a university (such as faculty and staff salaries) are fixed.

SELF-STUDY PROBLEM II

Frank Choi, the president of Trace Products, understands product costs, but he believes that estimating opportunity costs for his gold ore processing plant is difficult. Instead, he tells his controller to worry only about fixed and variable costs. The controller estimates that the variable cost of processing gold ore is $1,000 per ton of gold ore. The fixed costs are $50,000.

Approximating Opportunity Costs with Variable and Fixed Costs

a. What is the estimated cost of processing 60 tons of gold ore?
b. What is the danger of approximating activity costs with variable and fixed costs?

Solution

a. The estimated cost of processing 60 tons of gold ore is

(60 tons)($1,000/ton) + $50,000 = $110,000

b. The danger of estimating opportunity costs with variable and fixed costs is being outside the relevant range. In the relevant range, the estimates from variable and fixed costs should be fairly close to the opportunity cost. If output levels are extremely low or near capacity, however, the fixed and variable cost estimate tends to differ from the opportunity cost.

NUMERICAL EXERCISES

A yard maintenance owner has a request to cut and trim a yard. If the owner does the job himself, he estimates that it will take 3 hours to complete. If he calls a temporary worker to do the job, it will take 4 hours to complete. In either case, the transportation costs and the wear on the machinery should cost $5 for the job. The owner values his time at $10 per hour and pays the temporary worker $6 per hour.
    Should the owner do the job himself or have a temporary worker do the job?

NE 2.1
Cost/Benefit Analysis and Differential Costs
(LO 1)

Raw materials on hand originally cost $4 per pound. They can be replaced for $6 per pound and can be sold for $5 per pound.

a. What is the opportunity cost of using the raw materials if they will not be replaced?
b. What is the opportunity cost of using the raw materials if they can also be used in another product?

NE 2.2
Opportunity Costs and Sunk Costs
(LO 2,3)

What is the opportunity cost of an employee's time if she is paid $12/hour, can't be replaced, and could be generating $4 of profit on another project?

NE 2.3
Opportunity Costs
(LO 2)

Determine the marginal and average costs for the following data. Also identify start-up costs and capacity constraints.

NE 2.4
Opportunity Costs and Rates of Output
(LO 5,6)

Number of Units	Total Costs
1	$ 25
2	40
3	52
4	62
5	72
6	82
7	100
8	130

NE 2.5
Activity Costs
(LO 7)

The fixed cost of trucking a load of potatoes is $50, and the variable cost is $0.50 per mile. What is the estimated cost of trucking a load of potatoes 500 miles?

NE 2.6
Fixed and Variable Costs
(LO 7)

A manufacturer of skis has determined that the fixed cost of making skis is $1,000,000 and the variable cost is $100 per pair of skis. During normal operations, the firm plans to make 20,000 pairs of skis.

a. What is the expected cost of making 20,000 pairs of skis?
b. What are the expected costs of making 30,000 pairs of skis?
c. Why might the variable and fixed costs be poor predictors of costs when 30,000 pairs of skis are made?

NE 2.7
Fixed, Variable, and Average Costs
(LO 6,7)

Midwest University is trying to decide whether to admit an additional 100 students. Tuition is $5,000 per year. The controller has determined the following schedule of costs to educate students:

Number of Students	Total Costs
4,000	$30,000,000
4,100	30,300,000
4,200	30,600,000
4,300	30,900,000

The current enrollment is 4,200 students. The president of the University has calculated the cost per student in the following manner: $30,600,000/4,200 students = $7,286 per student. The president wonders why Midwest should accept more students if the tuition is only $5,000.

a. What is wrong with the president's calculation?
b. What are the fixed and variable costs of operating Midwest University?

NE 2.8
Fixed and Variable Costs
(LO 7)

Chen Industries is planning to build a computer chip factory to make 10,000 chips per month. The company has two different options in manufacturing the chips. A CAM approach will cause fixed costs to equal $1,000,000 per month with variable costs of $20 per chip. A more manual approach will cause fixed costs of $500,000 per month and variable costs of $50 per chip.
Which method should the company use to minimize costs?

NE 2.9
Opportunity Costs
(LO 2,3)

Shanti Debi must decide whether to make a fence around her garden or pay someone $300 to make the fence for her, which includes all materials and labor. If Shanti makes the fence, she could use some leftover fencing materials from a previous job. Those materials cost $60, but she can't sell them and has no other use for them. In addition, she would have to buy materials for $100. Shanti estimates that she would spend 15 hours purchasing the materials and putting up the fence. If she doesn't make the fence, she could spend the time playing tennis. She values her tennis-playing time at $10 per hour.
Should Shanti make the fence or pay someone else to make it?

NE 2.10
Opportunity Costs
(LO 2)

Ken Morrow is returning from a thrilling accounting class. As he passes the student union building, he thinks about visiting the video game room. For $5, he can play the video games for 1 hour. The best alternative to playing video games is to study for the accounting exam. One more hour of studying should raise his grade from a B+ to an A−. The higher grade would give Ken an opportunity to get a higher-paying job. He estimates that the higher grade is worth about $200 in job opportunities.
What is the opportunity cost of playing the video games for an hour?

NE 2.11
Variable and Fixed Costs
(LO 7)

The school newspaper editor estimates that the fixed cost of an edition is $10,000. The variable cost is $0.03 per copy.

a. What is the projected cost of an edition if 3,000 copies are produced?
b. What is the projected cost of an edition if 5,000 copies are produced?

NUMERICAL PROBLEMS

A grocery store is deciding how to use a particular space. One option is to put in a leased freezer and sell ice cream bars. The ice cream should generate annual revenues of $10,000 but will reduce revenues from other ice cream sales by $2,000 annually. The freezer leases for $1,000 per year, the electricity for the freezer should cost $500 per year, and the cost of the ice cream bars will be $5,000 per year. The other option is to rent shelving for $500 per year and sell bakery items. The revenues from the bakery items should be $7,000 per year, and their cost should be $3,000. The bakery items should not cause any other loss of revenue. Other revenues and costs are the same for the two options.

What should the grocery store do with the space?

NP 2.1
Differential Costs and Revenues
(LO 1)

Darien Industries operates a cafeteria for its employees. The operation of the cafeteria requires fixed costs of $4,700 per month and variable costs of 40% of sales. Cafeteria sales are currently averaging $12,000 per month.

Darien has an opportunity to replace the cafeteria with vending machines. Gross customer spending at the vending machines is estimated to be 40% higher than current sales because the machines are available at all hours. By replacing the cafeteria with vending machines, Darien would receive 16% of the gross customer spending and avoid all cafeteria costs.

A decision by Darien Industries to replace the cafeteria with vending machines will result in an operating income monthly increase (decrease) of how much?

(CMA adapted)

NP 2.2
Differential, Variable, and Fixed Costs
(LO 1,7)

A hardware store is considering opening on Sunday. The differential cost of paying for salespeople and utilities is $1,000 per Sunday. Sales on Sunday are expected to be $10,000. The sales price of an item is determined by taking the purchase price of the item and adding 20%.

a. If sales on Sunday do not affect sales the rest of the week, should the hardware store open on Sundays if the goal is to increase profit?

b. Should the hardware store open on Sundays if 60% of the sales would have occurred on other days of the week at the hardware store?

NP 2.3
Differential Costs and Revenues
(LO 1)

JP Max is a department store carrying a large and varied stock of merchandise. Management is considering leasing part of its floor space for $72 per square foot per year to an outside jewelry company that would sell merchandise. Two areas are being considered: 1,000 square feet in home appliances and 1,100 square feet in televisions. The annual department profits were $64,000 for appliances and $82,000 for televisions.

Considering all the relevant factors, which department should be leased and why?

NP 2.4
Opportunity Cost of Space
(LO 2)

Emrich Processing is a small processor of custom stainless steel parts. Customers send new and used stainless steel parts to Emrich for cleaning in various acid baths to remove small imperfections or films on the surface. These parts are used in a variety of applications, ranging from nuclear reactors to chemical and medical functions. Depending on the foreign substance to be removed, Emrich chooses the acid-bath mixture and process.

Such chemical cleaning operations require highly skilled technicians to handle the dangerous acids. Environmental Protection Agency (EPA) and Occupational Safety and Health Administration (OSHA) regulations are closely followed. Treatment of the part with other chemicals in the proper chemical bath results in a benign waste solution, which can be disposed of via the city sewer system.

On May 12, Emrich ordered a 50-liter drum of a specialty acid known as GX-100 for use in a May 15 job. It used 25 of the 50 liters in the drum. The 50 liters cost $1,000. GX-100 has a shelf life of 30 days after the drum is opened before it becomes unstable and must be discarded. Because of the hazardous nature of GX-100 and the other chemicals that it uses, Emrich works closely with Environ Disposal, a company specializing in the disposal of hazardous wastes. When it ordered the GX-100, Emrich anticipated no other orders in the May–June time period that could use the remaining 25 liters of GX-100. Knowing it would have 25 liters remaining, it built $1,000 into the cost of the job to cover the cost of the GX-100 plus an additional $400 to cover the cost of having Environ dispose of the remaining 25 liters.

NP 2.5
Opportunity Cost of Using Materials
(LO 2,3)

On June 1, a customer called and asked for a bid for a rush job to be completed on June 5. This job will use 25 liters of GX-100. Emrich is preparing to bid on this order.

What cost amount for the GX-100 must be considered in preparing the bid? Justify your answer.

NP 2.6
Opportunity Cost of Using Display Space
(LO 2)

Home Auto Parts is a large retail auto-parts store selling the full range of auto parts and supplies for do-it-yourself auto-repair enthusiasts. Annual store sales are $5 million. The store is arranged with three prime displays: front door, checkout counters, and end of aisles. These display areas receive the most customer traffic and contain special stands that display the merchandise with attractive eye-catching posters. Each display area is set up at the beginning of the week and runs for one week. Three items are scheduled next week for special display areas: Texcan Oil, windshield wiper blades, and floor mats. The following table provides information for the three promotional areas scheduled to run next week:

	End of Aisles	Front Door	Cash Register
Item	Texcan Oil	Wiper blades	Floor mats
Sales price	69¢/can	$9.99	$22.99
Projected weekly volume	5,000	200	70
Unit cost	62¢	$7.99	$17.49

Past experience indicates that virtually all display-area sales are made by impulse buyers. To increase customer traffic to the store, the special display items are not advertised. The display items purchased don't reduce the sales of similar items in the store because people attracted to the displays didn't enter the store to buy these items. The display items are extra purchases by consumers attracted by the exhibits.

After the preceding table is prepared but before the store manager sets up the display areas, the distributor for Armadillo car wax visits the store. Her firm wants its car wax in one of the three display areas and is prepared to offer the product at a unit cost of $2.50. At a retail price of $2.90, management expects to sell 800 units during the week if the wax is on special display.

a. Home Auto has not yet purchased any of the promotion items for next week. Should management substitute the Armadillo car wax for one of the three planned promotion displays? If so, which one?

b. A common practice in retailing is for the manufacturer to give free units to a retail store to secure desirable promotion space or shelf space. The Armadillo distributor decides to sweeten the offer by giving Home Auto 50 free units of car wax if it places the Armadillo wax on display. Does your answer to (a) change?

NP 2.7
Opportunity Cost of Time
(LO 2)

Indo Corporation is considering leasing a private jet to fly between its corporate offices in Rochester, New York, and its main plant in Tucson, Arizona. The commercial carrier has one flight leaving Rochester each morning and one returning flight departing Tucson in the afternoon. Ten executives take this seven-hour (one-way) trip every day, and 10 make the return flight each day. A recent study showed that business travelers are unable to work while traveling. The average salary (including fringe benefits) of an executive is $200,000. On average, they work 2,500 hours per year. Round-trip airfare on the commercial carrier averages $500.

Two alternative private jets are available for leasing. The following table summarizes various operating statistics for the two jets:

Model	Number of Seats	One-Way Flight Time	Total Daily Operating Cost
Lx-0100	10	6 hrs.	$5,100
Lx-0200	7	4 hrs.	5,200

The leased plane will duplicate the existing commercial carrier's scheduled departure times. The LX-0200 can not make more than one round trip a day.

Which alternative air transportation should the firm undertake? (Show calculations.)

Allan Brothers Company has designed a machine for sorting apples that is able to detect bruises on an apple. Bruised apples are used for making applesauce. The apples without defects are shipped to grocery stores. Managers at Allan Brothers are uncertain of the demand for these sorting machines but have estimated the following total costs of making different numbers of the machines:

NP 2.8
Marginal and Average Costs
(LO 5,6)

Number	Total Costs
1	$100,000
2	150,000
3	190,000
4	220,000
5	250,000
6	280,000
7	340,000
8	400,000
9	500,000

a. Prepare a table showing how the marginal cost of sorting machines varies with the number of machines manufactured.
b. Why does the marginal cost increase after six machines?
c. What is the average cost of making five sorting machines?
d. If the sorting machine can be sold for $70,000, how many machines should be produced?

For parts (a) and (b), draw a graph that depicts how costs vary with volume. Completely label each graph and axis.

NP 2.9
Cost Behavior Patterns
(LO 5)

a. The Medford plant operates 40 hours per week. Management can vary the number of workers; currently, 200 workers are being paid $10 per hour. The plant is near capacity. To increase output, a second shift of 40 hours per week is being considered. To attract workers to the second shift, a 20% wage premium will be offered. Plot total labor costs as a function of labor hours per week.
b. The Dallas plant has a contract with Texas Gas Company to purchase up to 150 million cubic feet of natural gas monthly for a flat fee of $1.5 million. Additional gas can be purchased for $0.0175 per cubic foot. The Dallas plant manufactures aluminum cans; producing 1,000 cans requires 10 cubic feet of gas. Plot total gas costs as a function of can production.

MedView's brochure refers to a new radiology imaging system that the firm rents for $18,000 per month. A "scan" refers to one imaging session that is billed at $475 per scan. Each scan requires giving the patient a chemical injection and exposing and developing an X-ray negative. MedView claims that 45 scans per month are sufficient to cover the cost of renting the machine plus any additional variable costs.
    What variable cost per scan is MedView assuming in calculating the 45 scans per month amount?

NP 2.10
Variable and Fixed Costs
(LO 7)

First Church has been asked to operate a homeless shelter in part of its facility. To manage the shelter, the church would have to hire a full-time employee for $1,200/month. In addition, the church would have to purchase $400 of supplies/month for the people using the shelter. The church currently rents the space that would be used by the shelter for wedding parties. It averages about five wedding parties per month that pay rent of $200 per party. Utilities are normally $1,000 per month. With the homeless shelter, the utilities will increase to $1,300 month.
    What is the opportunity cost to the church of operating a homeless shelter?

NP 2.11
Opportunity Costs
(LO 2,3)

A university with an enrollment of 5,000 students has a capacity for 6,000 students. The fixed cost of operating the school is $1,000,000 per month; the variable cost is $100 per student per month.

NP 2.12
Average, Variable, and Fixed Costs
(LO 6,7)

a. What is the average cost per student of operating the university for 5,000 students?
b. What is the cost of adding 50 more students?

NP 2.13
Average, Variable, and Fixed Costs
(LO 6,7)

A soccer ball manufacturer plans to make 100,000 balls per year. The following annual costs are estimated:

Utilities	$ 10,000
Machines	50,000
Administration	100,000
Marketing	120,000
Labor	200,000
Materials	150,000
Total	$630,000

Labor and materials are variable costs. The remaining costs are fixed.

a. What are the annual fixed costs of making soccer balls?
b. What is the variable cost per soccer ball?
c. What is the average cost per ball?
d. If the manufacturer is operating normally and not near capacity, what is the expected cost of making 1,000 more balls?

NP 2.14
Fixed and Variable Costs
(LO 7)

The university athletic department has been asked to host a professional basketball game at the campus sports center. The athletic director must estimate the opportunity cost of holding the event at the sports center. The only other event scheduled for the sports center that evening is a fencing match that would not have generated any additional costs or revenues. The fencing match can be held at the local high school gym, but its rental cost is $200. The athletic director estimates that the professional basketball game will require 20 hours of labor to prepare the building. Cleanup depends on the number of spectators. The athletic director estimates the time of cleanup to equal 2 minutes per spectator. The labor would be hired especially for the basketball game and would cost $8 per hour. Utilities will increase by $500 if the basketball game is held at the sports center. The professional basketball team would cover all other costs.

a. What is the variable cost of having one more spectator?
b. What is the opportunity cost of allowing the professional basketball team to use the sports center if 10,000 spectators are expected?
c. What is the opportunity cost of allowing the professional basketball team to use the sports center if 12,000 spectators are expected?

NP 2.15
Estimations with Fixed and Variable Costs
(LO 7)

Based on the last few years of operations (when he made between 1,000 and 15,000 units), Bill Jones calculated that the fixed cost of making his sole product is $400,000 and the variable cost per unit is $200.

a. If Jones expects to make 18,000 units, what is his expected cost in the next year using the fixed and variable costs?
b. What are two dangers of using the fixed and per unit variable cost, as calculated, to estimate next year's costs?

NP 2.16
Variable and Fixed Costs Estimated through Account Classification
(LO 8)

Beadco Company sells necklaces of beads and is trying to determine the costs of working with each supplier. One supplier of ceramic beads operates in Kenya. During the year, the supplier is expected to sell Beadco 1,000,000 beads for $0.10/bead. The year's supply of beads is normally sent in a container, which costs $5,000 to ship to the company in New York. With 1,000,000 beads, the container is only half full. There would be no additional freight charges if the container were full. To make the order with the Kenyan company, Beadco must send a purchasing agent to Kenya. The cost of the trip including the salary of the purchasing agent is $10,000. The processing of the purchase order also requires the use of 20 hours of personnel time, which includes time spent by the accountant and the treasurer. The average cost per hour for these personnel is $50. When the beads arrive, each bead must be inspected for quality and breakage. An inspector who is paid $20/hour can inspect 1,000 beads per hour.

a. What is the fixed cost per bead of working with the Kenyan supplier if 1,000,000 beads are purchased?

b. What is the variable cost per bead purchased from the Kenyan supplier?

c. If 1,500,000 beads were purchased, what would be the total costs of purchasing from the Kenyan supplier?

A tennis ball manufacturer is noted for making all its tennis balls exactly the same way. The manufacturer is less certain, however, about its costs. The manufacturer hasn't changed its operating methods in the last 10 years, and the cost of labor and raw materials has remained about the same. The manufacturer has had the following costs and output during the last 10 years:

NP 2.17
Variable and Fixed Costs Identified Using the High/Low Method
(LO 8)

Year	Costs	Number of Balls
1992	$20,000,000	50,000,000
1993	25,000,000	75,000,000
1994	30,000,000	105,000,000
1995	28,000,000	100,000,000
1996	32,000,000	110,000,000
1997	23,000,000	80,000,000
1998	35,000,000	120,000,000
1999	31,000,000	115,000,000
2000	36,000,000	118,000,000
2001	22,000,000	90,000,000

a. Plot these data.

b. Identify the highest and lowest output levels.

c. Using the high/low method, estimate the fixed costs of making tennis balls.

d. What are the variable costs per ball?

e. If the manufacturer expects to make 112,000,000 balls, what are the expected costs in the coming year?

f. Why would it be more difficult to estimate the expected costs if the manufacturer expects to make 150,000,000 balls?

Use the data in NP 2.17.
  Estimate the fixed and variable costs per unit.

NP 2.18
Use of Regression to Estimate Fixed and Variable Costs
(LO 9)

A Christmas tree retailer is trying to estimate demand for Christmas trees before ordering inventory for the season. The retailer purchases the trees from the supplier for $10 and sells them for $25. Fixed costs of operating the Christmas tree lot are $100. Based on prior experience, the retailer estimates that there is a 0.5 probability that 80 trees can be sold and a 0.5 probability that 100 trees can be sold. Any unsold trees must be discarded at a cost of $2 each.

NP 2.19
Sales Estimation
(LO 4,7)

a. Should the retailer order 80 or 100 trees to maximize the expected profit?

b. How would a survey that provides more precise demand for Christmas trees add value to the retailer?

A bus manufacturer estimates that the variable cost per unit of making five or fewer buses per month is $150,000 per bus. The variable cost per unit of making 6 to 25 buses per month is $100,000. Also, the variable cost per unit of making more than 25 buses per month is $200,000. There are no fixed costs using this method of analyzing costs.

NP 2.20
Variable Costs Changed with Rate of Output
(LO 5,7)

a. How does each level of output relate to the concepts of start-up costs and capacity?

b. What is the estimate of fixed costs at the normal level of operations?

ANALYSIS AND INTERPRETATION PROBLEMS

AIP 2.1
Variable and Fixed Costs
(LO 7)

Fast Photo operates four film-development labs in upstate New York. The four labs are identical: They employ the same production technology, process the same mix of films, and buy raw materials from the same companies at the same prices. Wage rates are also the same at the four plants. In reviewing operating results for November, the newly hired assistant controller, Matt Paige, became quite confused over the numbers:

	Plant A	Plant B	Plant C	Plant D
Number of rolls processed	50,000	55,000	60,000	65,000
Revenues ($000s)	$500	$550	$600	$650
Less:				
Variable costs	(195)	(242)	(298)	(352)
Fixed costs	(300)	(300)	(300)	(300)
Profit (Loss)	$ 5	$ 8	$ 2	$ (2)

On further study, Matt learned that each plant had fixed overhead of $300,000. He remembered from his management accounting class that as volume increases, average fixed cost per unit falls. Because plant D had much lower average fixed costs per roll than plants A and B, Matt expected plant D to be more profitable than plants A and B, but the numbers show just the opposite.

Write a concise but clear memo to Matt that will resolve his confusion.

AIP 2.2
Opportunity Costs and Executive Stock Options
(LO 2)

Reporting the findings of a survey on corporate directors' compensation, a large public accounting firm remarked, "Since there are usually greater growth rates in smaller companies, stock options offer directors a good chance at investment appreciation at no cost to the company."

The following example describes a stock option. Suppose that one three-year stock option is granted to a director at today's stock price of $10. Then, at any time over the next three years, the director can buy one share of stock from the company at $10. If next year the stock rises to $14, the director can exercise the option by paying $10 to the company and receiving one share of stock, which then can be sold in the market for $14, thereby realizing a $4 gain.

Critically evaluate the *quoted* sentence.

AIP 2.3
Opportunity Costs of Using Inventory
(LO 2)

After the Iraqi invasion of Kuwait in August 1990, the world price of crude oil doubled to more than $30 per barrel in anticipation of reduced supply. Immediately, the oil companies raised the retail price of refined oil products even though these products were produced from oil purchased at the earlier, lower prices. The media charged the oil companies with profiteering and price gouging, and politicians promised immediate investigations.

Critically evaluate the charge that the oil companies profited from the Iraqi invasion. What advice would you offer the oil companies?

AIP 2.4
Differential Costs of a New Product
(LO 1)

Indurin Company manufactures Syndex, a popular drug for headaches. Recently, Indurin has been subject to increased competitive pressure as other pharmaceutical firms have developed and marketed new products. The president of Indurin is considering the introduction of Syndex Plus, a new drug targeted to consumers who prefer extra-strength medications. The president wants a prediction of the additional profit that this new drug will generate. In his management accounting course, he learned that he should compare incremental revenues with incremental costs. He has determined that the total expected sales of Syndex Plus equals incremental revenues because there were no previous sales of Syndex Plus. The incremental costs are the additional costs necessary to make Syndex Plus. Extra space and labor are available; therefore, these costs are expected to be very low.

When asked to compute the expected costs, the controller asked, "What about the effect of introducing Syndex Plus on the sales of Syndex?" The president replied, "Irrelevant! The decision to introduce a new product should be based only on a comparison of incremental costs and revenues."

Evaluate the president's decision rule.

The Itagi Computer Company based in Japan is considering building a CD-ROM manufacturing facility in North America. Itagi is concerned about the safety and well-being of its employees and wants to locate in a community with good schools. The company also wants the manufacturing plant to be profitable and is looking for subsidies from potential communities. Subsidies are often used as an effective way to entice new businesses to locate in the region and create jobs for citizens. Many communities, especially those with high unemployment, use this strategic incentive.

AIP 2.5
Opportunity Cost of Attracting Industry
(LO 2)

Wellville has not been very well since the shoe factory left town. City officials have been working on a deal to encourage Itagi to locate in Wellville. Itagi officials have identified a 20-acre undeveloped site. The city has agreed tentatively to buy the site for Itagi at a cost of $50,000. As another incentive, the city will not require Itagi to pay any property taxes on the factory for the first five years of operation, which will save Itagi $3,000,000 in taxes over the five years. This deal was leaked to the local newspaper. The headline the next day was "Wellville Gives Away $3,000,000+ to Japanese Company."

a.   Does the headline accurately describe the deal with Itagi?
b.   What are the relevant costs and benefits of making this deal to the citizens of Wellville?

The Government Accounting Office (GAO) has costed recent excursions by the U.S. military into other countries. The calculation is based on the cost of paying and supplying personnel, moving material and personnel to the problem area, depreciating equipment, and using armaments. Newspaper accounts indicate that some of these actions provided training for personnel and experimentation for new technologies. Some older armament was used without any intention of replacement.

AIP 2.6
Opportunity Cost of Using Military Forces
(LO 2,3)

How would you calculate the opportunity cost of using military forces?

Maverick Productions organizes rock concerts. Last year, the company rented the local high school football stadium for a rock concert that included the Rolling Rocks. The concert was a big success, and Maverick made $10,000 on it. This year, Maverick is planning to bring the Rolling Rocks back to town for another concert. The company plans to rent the university football stadium, which is larger, and plans to use the same ticket agency and vendors. Maverick has detailed accounting records of the revenues and costs of the previous Rolling Rocks concert and would like to use these accounting records to make plans for the concert this year.

AIP 2.7
Historical Costs Approximating Opportunity Costs
(LO 2)

a.   What are some of the advantages and disadvantages of using the past concert accounting records to estimate the costs and benefits of the concert this year?
b.   Are there ways to adjust the past accounting records to make them better predictors of costs and benefits?

A paper manufacturer believes that he needs better information on the quality of paper that the plant is producing. He is considering purchasing a scanning machine that would identify defects in the paper as it is being produced. The scanner would have to be operated full time by an employee.

AIP 2.8
Cost/Benefit Analysis of Information
(LO 4)

What factors should the manufacturer consider in determining the costs and benefits of the scanning machine?

The city water department is responsible for supplying water to the city. Water is pumped from deep wells to reservoirs, chlorine is added, and the water is piped to the different customers in the city. The pumps operate only when the reservoirs decline to a certain level. The reservoirs are located on the highest part of the city, so gravity can be used to establish water pressure for the city users. Pipes frequently break due to age, so the water department maintains a maintenance department. The water department has the following accounts to record costs:

AIP 2.9
Classification of Costs As Fixed and Variable
(LO 7)

Maintenance	Rent	Salaries of top managers
Power (for the pumps)	Billings and collection	Chemicals

If liters of water consumed by the city are treated as the water department's output, describe each of the accounts as either fixed or variable. How would you describe each of these accounts if customer services or production activities were used as the cost objectives?

AIP 2.10

Processes Performed by an Organization

(LO 2,4)

The Department of Accounting of the University of New North Wales, which is responsible for teaching accounting classes at the University, is analyzing what it does. The purpose of the analysis is to operate more efficiently and allocate responsibilities among the professors. The Accounting Department is also thinking about hiring an administrator to perform certain activities that don't require the specific skills of the professors.

a. What general activities does an Accounting Department perform?

b. What activities could an administrator instead of a professor perform?

c. How could the costs of the different activities be measured?

AIP 2.11

Estimating Costs Using Past Data

(LO 9)

A business consulting firm recently has begun to make Web pages for 10 of its clients. The firm foresees considerable future demand for Web page construction but is uncertain whether it can compete in this area. To compete successfully, the consulting firm must be a low-cost producer of Web pages. The firm decides to gather extensive cost data for each of the 10 jobs that is has already completed. The firm also knows the number of Web pages produced for each client.

a. How can regression be used to estimate variable and fixed costs of constructing Web pages?

b. What insights about how the firm can compete in the construction of Web pages do estimates of the variable and fixed costs provide?

c. What problems exist in using the data to estimate variable and fixed costs?

AIP 2.12

Cost Estimation with Varying Levels of Output

(LO 5,6)

Fantastic Software Company offers assistance to users of its software via the telephone. The customer-assistance activity is located in one room with space and telephone lines for five technicians who can give advice over the telephone. Each technician can handle up to 20 calls per day.

a. Describe the cost structure of the customer-assistance activity, if calls handled per day is the measure of output.

b. What is the nature of the marginal costs?

AIP 2.13

University Tuition Benefits

(LO 2)

The following is from a recent *Wall Street Journal* article:

> Joseph Mercurio has two children at Boston University, which now charges $21,970 per year for tuition. But he doesn't worry about the cost, because his employer picks up the tab.
>
> That perquisite is even better than it first appears, because it is tax-free. He estimates he would have to earn $80,000 in pretax income to cover his kids' tuition. "It's a benefit of enormous value to me," he says.
>
> So how does he get such an unusual perk? He is executive vice president at Boston University, one of hundreds of colleges and universities that subsidize the cost of education for employees' children and sometimes spouses.
>
> Colleges have long argued they need the benefit to retain and recruit valuable employees who might otherwise be lured to competing institutions or more lucrative jobs in the private sector.
>
> It cost the University of Pennsylvania $7 million last year to send employees' children to Penn and other schools. For Stanford University, the bill is at least $4.5 million, up from $3.5 million four years ago.
>
> Some schools are now discussing cuts in their benefit programs.
>
> To make up an expected $1 million annual decline in federal subsidies, Case Western recently cut its tuition benefit for employee children who attend its graduate schools to 50% from 100%.
>
> *Source:* Steve Stecklow, "How Can You Beat High Cost of College? Become a Professor," *The Wall Street Journal*, April 15, 1997, p. A1.

a. Critically evaluate the statement, "It cost the University of Pennsylvania $7 million last year to send employees' children to Penn and other schools."

b. Do you think that Case Western made a wise decision to cut its tuition benefits for employee children?

EXTENDED ANALYSIS AND INTERPRETATION PROBLEM

Steve Martinez was saddened when he heard of the death of his uncle and was shocked when he learned that he had inherited a 1,000 acre ranch in Wyoming called Windy Acres. The ranch had a house, bunkroom for help, and a barn. The inheritance also included 500 head of cattle. When Steve arrived in Wyoming to check on his inheritance, he found the buildings and fences in need of repair. The manager of the ranch greeted Steve with a hand-shake and the financial statement from the end of the most recent fiscal year, which was about three months ago. The accounting report included only a balance sheet and an income statement:

AIP 2.14
Opportunity Costs

WINDY ACRES
Balance Sheet
12/31/00

Assets		Liabilities	
Cash	$ 2,000	Mortgage	$200,000
Equipment	100,000	**Owner's Equity**	
Buildings	184,000		
Accumulated depreciation	(52,000)	Owner's Share	34,000
Total assets	$234,000	Total liabilities & equities	$234,000

WINDY ACRES
Income Statement
Year of 2000

Sale of cattle	$ 50,000
Cost of supplies	(10,000)
Manager's salary	(15,000)
Depreciation	(10,000)
Interest on mortgage	(20,000)
Net loss	$ (5,000)

Steve looked a little worried after seeing the financial statements. He was relieved, however, when he noticed that the cattle were not on the balance sheet. "Well, at least there's some additional value on this ranch that isn't recorded in the financial statements," he said.

The manager replied, "We decided not to report the cattle as an asset because the number varies throughout the year and we're never sure exactly how many cattle are out there. I'd like to keep working for you, but my feeling is that you should sell this place. A neighbor is willing to buy it for $300,000. I think it is a good offer and you should accept it."

Steve Martinez is reluctant to accept the offer without further investigation of the operations of Windy Acres.

a. How does the offer to buy Windy Acres provide a benchmark for Steve?

b. How should Steve use the balance sheet and income statement to value Windy Acres?

c. If Steve decides to continue operating Windy Acres as a cattle ranch, how should he decide on the appropriate number of cattle to raise?

Chapter**Three**

Measuring and Analyzing Product Costs

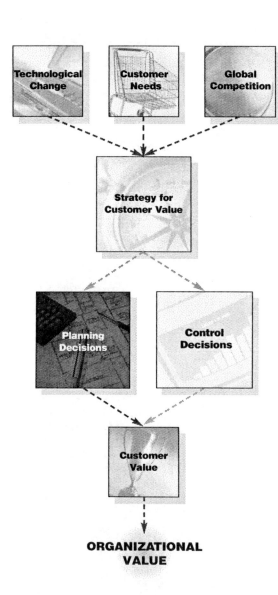

LEARNING OBJECTIVES

1 Treat products as cost objects for making product mix and pricing decisions.

2 Identify activities of the organization related to its different products and services.

3 Estimate the direct costs of a product or service.

4 Identify different levels of indirect product costs.

5 Trace indirect product costs using a cost driver.

6 Use activity-based costing to estimate the cost of a product or service.

7 Recognize the advantages and problems of using activity-based costing.

8 Estimate product costs using a single cost driver.

9 Use product costs for financial reporting. (Appendix)

SNAKE SKATEBOARDS

Snake Skateboards has been operating for five years. It has two products: a flat skateboard sold to large discount chains and a molded skateboard sold to specialty shops. The company has been successful in recent years with the popularity of skateboarding, but its management must make some decisions about changing the prod-

ucts manufactured, the prices of products, the processes of manufacturing, suppliers, and customers.

A skateboard is constructed much like plywood. Thin layers of wood veneer are glued together with the grain of the wood of adjacent layers going in opposite directions. This alternating pattern gives the skateboard strength and some flexibility. The layers of wood veneer of the flat skateboard are glued and squeezed together using a flat press. Because 10 flat skateboards can be pressed at once, they are normally produced in batches of 10. The molded skateboards are pressed in individual molds. There are five molds, so the molded skateboards are made in batches of five. The molded skateboards also have a layer of plastic glued to their bottom to allow them to slide when the rounded bottom comes in contact with rough surfaces. Both types of skateboards use the same polyurethane wheels and axle assemblies, which are purchased from another company and attached at Snake Skateboards. The flat skateboards are painted a single color; the molded skateboards are multicolored with a variety of designs.

Snake Skateboards is owned by Jeff Williams, who also manages the company and designs new products. Jeff has hired four managers for each department: administration, purchasing, production, and marketing. The cost accounting system has separate accounts for the cost of operating each department and the cost of materials and labor used to make the skateboards. He has projected the following costs for next year given the assumption that the company will produce and sell 50,000 flat skateboards and 5,000 molded skateboards.

Materials	$ 60,000
Labor	300,000
Administrative	90,000
Purchasing	50,000
Production (excluding labor and materials)	210,000
Marketing	100,000
Total expected costs	$810,000

Snake Skateboards has competitors that make similar skateboards. They sell flat skateboards to large discount stores for $15 and molded skateboards to specialty shops for $25. Projected revenues for Snake Skateboards at those prices follow:

Flat skateboards (50,000 units at $15/unit)	$750,000
Molded skateboards (5,000 units at $25/unit)	125,000
Total expected revenues	$875,000

ESTIMATING PRODUCT COSTS FOR PLANNING DECISIONS

LO 1   Treat products as cost objects for making product mix and pricing decisions.

Planning Decisions

To make planning decisions, the costs and benefits of different decisions must be estimated. For example, the decision to purchase a computing system for an organization is based on the estimated costs and benefits associated with each computing system considered. The comparison of estimated costs with estimated benefits helps managers identify the best choice for the organization. Management accounting assists in this process by estimating the benefits and costs associated with each decision.

The first step in the cost estimation process is to decide what item of the organization to cost. The item to be costed, called the **cost object,** depends on the decision being made. The primary cost objects described in this chapter are the products or services provided by the organization, but cost objects may also include its subunits, customers, suppliers, and time periods. Each of these cost objects is related to different planning decisions. The cost of using suppliers and the cost of customers are described in the next chapter. The cost of subunits in organizations is important in evaluating managers of the subunit and is discussed in Chapter Seven. Cost associated with a time period is a subject covered in financial accounting.

The cost of using resources to provide a product or service is called the **product or service cost.** For example, the cost of developing, writing, and producing a computer game, which is the cost object, is the product cost of the computer game. For simplification purposes, the term *product cost* is used in this book for both product and service costs. The procedures for estimating service costs are the same as the procedures for estimating product costs.

Estimating the cost of a product or service is very useful in making decisions about what products or services to provide and determining a price for those products and services. The overall objective is the creation of organizational value by providing products and services at a price to meet customer needs. These planning decisions can be improved with better estimates of product costs.

McDonald's customers in Paris face menu choices different from those of its customers in Melbourne. Around the globe, McDonald's selects a mix of products that caters to local tastes and food preferences. Management uses revenue and cost data to determine whether a menu item is profitable, or perhaps should be offered in other market locations.

Product Mix Decision

The role of managers in an organization is to help it achieve its goals. Most organizational goals, from satisfying customers to generating a profit for its owners, are related to the products and services that it provides. Managers must decide which products and services add both customer and organizational value. Customer value occurs if the price of the product is less than the benefits the customer derives from the product. Organizational value occurs if the price of the product is higher than the product cost.

An organization is usually established to provide a certain product or service. As it evolves, it frequently offers other products and services. For example, a bakery may start by making bread but later might decide to branch into pastries. Microsoft started by writing operating systems but now offers a wide variety of software. An organization's product mix continually evolves as new opportunities arise and competitive pressures affect existing products and services.

The choice of what products and services to offer is known as the **product mix decision.** For example, McDonald's must decide what types of food to offer in its restaurants. Not all McDonald's restaurants have the same product mix. For example, the menus in McDonald's in Southeast Asia include milk shakes made from the durian, a popular fruit in that part of the world.

The product cost provides managers information useful in making the product mix decision. The organization with a higher product cost for a particular product is at a competitive disadvantage. If a computer chip manufacturer makes a chip that costs $500, the firm is at a competitive disadvantage if a competitor currently makes a comparable chip for $400. AT&T dropped its personal computer line because it was not competitive in the personal computer market. AT&T continues to be a major supplier of long-distance services and has expanded into other areas of communication technology in which it has a competitive advantage.

An organization must continually analyze its existing and new products or services to determine whether it has a comparative advantage in offering those products and services. For example, an organization may identify a service that it can provide at a low cost because it has special skills. Microsoft has personnel who have an intimate knowledge of the Windows operating system that allowed it to integrate an Internet browser into Windows at a low cost. A low-cost provider of services has a comparative advantage over its competitors and is likely to include that service in its service mix. On the other hand, a high-cost provider is unlikely to continue to include that product or service in its mix unless offering the product provides other benefits.

The ultimate decision on choosing a product mix is based on comparing a product's benefits with the costs of providing it. If the benefits exceed the costs, the organization includes the product in its product mix. The product's benefits are usually measured in terms of revenues generated from sales, but an organization also must consider other benefits of having it. For example, having a particular item in a product mix may be important to the sales of other products. Car dealerships want a wide variety of products to give customers a comprehensive selection. If car dealerships limit their inventory to only the most profitable models, customers would be less likely to shop there. Often offering multiple products provides cost advantages. With economies of scope, an organization can offer two products more cheaply than two separate organizations offering one product each. The benefits of having a product are also related to the organization's employees. Dropping a product from the product mix can mean laying off employees. Managers must continually deal with ethical issues related to the welfare of employees and owners of the organization. Most of the problems and examples in this book focus on revenues as the primary benefit of having a product or service, but other intangible benefits should be considered.

Pricing Decision

Part of the product mix decision is based on the demand for the product or service. If the price of the product or service is too high, consumers will not buy it. If the price is too low, making and selling the product will reduce the value of the

Global Competition

Strategy for Customer Value

Customer Value

organization. Determining the price of a product or service is another important planning decision managers must make.

As we will see in Chapters Four and Five, the pricing decision is complicated and affected by customer value and competition. A product cost also is used to help make pricing decisions; it serves as a lower boundary in making a pricing decision. If products and services are sold below their cost, the organization's value will decline.

Concept**Review**

1. What is a cost object?

2. How does the product cost help support the product mix decision?

SNAKE SKATEBOARDS
(Continued)

Jeff Williams is considering a change in Snake Skateboards' product mix and prices. Currently, about 91% of its skateboards are flat and 9% are molded. The current prices for these skateboards reflect prices of competitors, but Jeff believes that by lowering the price, he can sell more skateboards. Before making these decisions, however, he must determine the cost of each type of skateboard. If the cost of one of the skateboards is higher than the competitors' prices, Jeff should drop that skateboard from the product mix. If the cost of one of the skateboards is less than the competitors' prices, he has some flexibility to reduce the price of that skateboard to increase sales. The present accounting system, however, gives no indication of the cost of either type of skateboard, and Jeff is not sure that the company is currently operating very efficiently. Knowing the costs of his products allows him to reduce them further by cutting non–value-added activities. Before he can identify cost-cutting opportunities, however, he must gain a better understanding of the operating activities in his company.

ACTIVITIES AND PRODUCT COSTS

LO 2   Identify activities of the organization related to its different products and services.

An organization performs a variety of activities. These activities are the building blocks of an organization's effort to provide products and services. In deciding which products and services to offer, managers also must decide on the series of activities necessary to provide those products and services. For example, manufacturing organizations must make decisions on design, engineering, acquisition of raw materials, use of personnel, manufacturing processes, inventory warehousing, transportation, marketing, and customer service. American Express analyzed the service of transferring funds. Figure 3.1 illustrates the various activities in providing this service.[1] For example, in designing its Blue Card, American Express first identified opportunities to attract young, technosophisticated consumers. It developed this card by combining low-cost credit with secure online shopping. The Blue Card provides American Express with an evolving product for which it could develop new features and services, such as online financial planning, before offering them to existing customers of its other

---

[1]D. Carlson and S. M. Young, "Activity-Based Total Quality Management at American Express," *Journal of Cost Management*, Spring 1993, pp. 48–58.

Figure 3.1 Activity Hierarchy of Transferring Funds

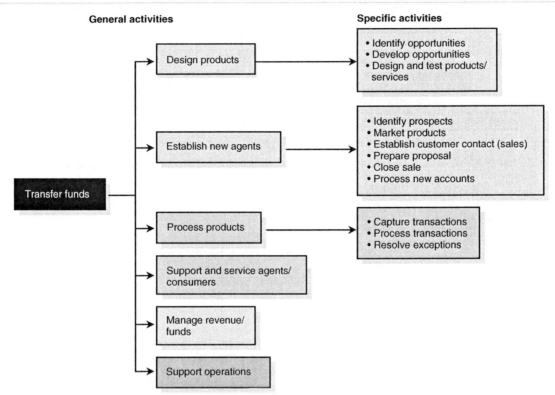

Source: From D. Carlson and S. M. Young, "Activity-Based Total Quality Management at American Express," *Journal of Cost Management,* Spring 1993, pp. 48–58.

charge and credit cards. In addition, the Blue Card can be expanded quickly to its small business customers once consumer acceptance of the product concept is established.[2]

Activities consume resources, such as materials and employee time, and therefore cause costs. Since activities create the products or services that an organization provides, activity costs are the basis for estimating product costs. For example, word processing is an activity in a law firm that is part of the cost of providing legal services.

A simple approach to estimating a product's cost is to aggregate all activity costs associated with that particular product. A problem arises, however, when an activity supports multiple products. For example, the janitorial services in a factory support all the products the factory makes. To estimate the individual product costs, some method for separating costs among the products that the activity supports must be used. This chapter describes methods of tracing activity costs into product costs.

To simplify the tracing process, activities are separated into those that support only one product and those that support multiple products. Activities that are associated with only one product generate costs that are **direct product costs.** Direct product costs can be easily traced from the activity to a single product. Indirect product costs occur because activities support more than one product and cannot be traced easily to a single product. Before we consider methods of tracing activity costs into product costs, we examine some characteristics of direct and indirect product costs.

[2]*Business Week* Online, November 8, 1999, and www.americanexpress.com.

SNAKE SKATEBOARDS (Continued)	The accounting system of Snake Skateboards presently identifies costs by departments (administration, purchasing, production, and marketing). Although these departments represent general activities in the organization, Jeff needs more information about subactivities. For example, the production activity is composed of the following subactivities: warehousing and handling raw materials, cutting, gluing, setting up molds, painting, and assembly. Of these subactivities, warehousing and handling raw materials and setting up molds are identified as non–value-added. Therefore, Jeff should focus his cost-cutting efforts on those activities, but he is still not sure of the costs of each.

DIRECT PRODUCT COSTS

LO 3 Estimate the direct costs of a product or service.

Activities that are associated with only one product create direct product costs. There is no problem tracing those activity costs to a particular product, but they still must be measured. Direct product costs are commonly associated with the use of either material resources or labor. Categorizing direct product costs as material or labor allows managers to analyze the components of the product cost.

Materials used to make a product are called **direct materials.** Direct materials may also be referred to as *raw materials.* The labor used to make the product or to provide a service is also a direct cost of the product or service, and is called **direct labor.** For example, the direct cost of making an oak chair includes the cost of direct materials (the oak and finish used to make it) and the cost of direct labor (the labor used to cut, sand, assemble, and finish the chair). Most service organizations, such as law firms, have direct labor costs but few direct material costs.

Although direct product costs can be traced easily to the product, the management accountant still needs assistance in estimating direct costs. If the product or service has been provided previously, the historical cost usually is of some use in estimating future direct costs, but the management accountant should consult with engineers, suppliers, and personnel managers for information on estimating direct costs.

To determine the cost of direct materials, the management accountant must obtain a list of the raw materials and parts required to make the product. Engineers normally provide this information in a manufacturing plant. Then purchase prices must be obtained for each material and part. The management accountant can estimate direct material prices by surveying suppliers and asking for bids for certain items. For example, to estimate the direct material costs of building a house, a contractor must identify all materials necessary to build it. The contractor then goes to suppliers to determine the price of each item. The estimated direct material cost of the house is determined by multiplying the number of each piece of material in the house by its respective price.

To estimate the cost of direct labor, engineers and other experts are usually consulted to determine the hours of labor necessary to complete the product or provide the service. If the product or service is currently being offered, the labor time required can be measured directly. Adjustments should be made, however, for improvement through learning. Normally, the first time that products are made or services provided requires longer direct labor time. Once the employees have gained experience, the labor operations can be performed more quickly. The cost of direct labor also requires estimates of labor rates, usually provided by a personnel manager in a large organization.

Numerical Example **3.1**

To determine the direct cost of making a hamburger, a restaurant uses the following estimates:

Item	Quantity per Hamburger	Purchase Price
Meat	0.25 lb.	$1.60/lb.
Bun	1	$1.20/dozen
Catsup	0.5 oz.	$0.04/oz.
Pickles	0.5 oz.	$0.06/oz.
Labor	1 minute	$6/hour

Calculate the direct cost of making a hamburger.

Solution

The direct cost is determined by multiplying the number of the different items necessary to make a hamburger by the respective price of each. There is some question about whether the cook's labor is a direct cost of making a hamburger. If the cook also prepares other food at the same time, the labor is an indirect cost of making a hamburger.

Item	Quantity per Hamburger	×	Purchase Price	=	Cost
Meat	0.25 lb.		$1.60/lb.		$0.40
Bun	1		$1.20/dozen		0.10
Catsup	0.5 oz.		$0.04/oz.		0.02
Pickles	0.5 oz.		$0.06/oz.		0.03
Labor	1 minute		$6/hour		0.10
Total direct cost/hamburger					$0.65

 concept**Review**

1. What is the difference between direct and indirect product costs?
2. How are direct product costs commonly classified?
3. Describe methods of estimating direct product and service costs.

Jeff Williams of Snake Skateboards estimates the direct materials and direct labor of the two types of skateboards. The direct materials include the thin sheets of wood veneer, glue, polyurethane, wheels, and axle assemblies. The molded skateboards also require a plastic sheet. To estimate the cost of these direct materials, Jeff obtains price information from the various suppliers for the coming year. Each skateboard requires two sets of wheels and axles. The amount of the remaining materials per skateboard is more difficult to estimate. Jeff examines use of the sheets of wood veneer, sheets of plastic, and the glue in the previous year. By using more experienced employees who cut the veneer more carefully, Jeff figures he can reduce scrap and spoiled units. However, more experienced employees raise labor costs. These improvements should reduce the amount of materials per skateboard by 5%. Jeff decides that estimating glue costs per skateboard is too difficult and decides to treat it as part of indirect production costs.

To estimate direct labor costs, Jeff uses the wage rates on the recently signed labor contract. To determine the amount of time necessary to make each type of skateboard, he uses a stopwatch to time workers. Assuming that learning will take place, he estimates that the time to complete a skateboard in the coming year will be 7% less than his current observations.

SNAKE SKATEBOARDS
(Continued)

The calculation for direct materials after incorporating the scrap improvements follow:

Materials	Quantity	Price	Cost
Flat Skateboard			
Wood veneer	10 sq. ft./unit	$0.02/sq. ft.	$ 0.20/unit
Wheel assemblies	2/unit	$0.44 apiece	$ 0.88/unit
Total direct materials			$ 1.08/unit
Direct labor	0.5 hours/unit	$10/hr.	$ 5.00/unit
Total direct costs			$ 6.08/unit
Molded Skateboard			
Wood veneer	10 sq. ft./unit	$0.02/sq. ft.	$ 0.20/unit
Wheel assemblies	2/unit	$0.44 a piece	$ 0.88/unit
Plastic layer	1/unit	$0.12 a piece	$ 0.12/unit
Total direct materials			$ 1.20/unit
Direct labor	1 hour/unit	$10/hr.	$10.00/unit
			$11.20/unit

Jeff compares these direct costs with his competitors' prices of $15 for the flat skateboard and $25 for the molded skateboard. In both cases, the direct costs are less than the competitors' prices, so there is no immediate indication of a need to drop a product. There may even be an opportunity to lower prices and still make a profit. But Jeff knows that the direct costs are only part of the picture and that he must also estimate the indirect costs of his products.

INDIRECT PRODUCT COSTS

L0 4 Identify different levels of indirect product costs.

Indirect product costs occur because some organizational activities support multiple products. Indirect product costs are also called **overhead costs.** Since indirect product costs cannot be easily traced to specific products or services, their estimation is likely to be more difficult and uncertain than the estimation of direct product costs.

Accounting reports to external parties cannot be relied on when estimating indirect product costs. These reports are based on generally accepted accounting principles (GAAP) and treat some indirect costs, such as research and development and marketing costs, as period costs rather than product costs. The rationale for treating these costs as period costs is the difficulty in measuring the future benefits of those activities, yet research and development and marketing are part of the cost of developing and delivering a product to a customer. In addition, the external accounting reports are based on historic costs, which may not be good estimates of future indirect costs. The Appendix discusses these issues more fully.

To estimate the indirect costs of products, the management accountant must have a good understanding of the organization's operations. Knowing how different activities in the organization interact to create products allows the manager to more accurately trace indirect costs to products. To simplify the analysis of the organization's different activities, indirect product costs are divided into four types: unit level, batch level, product level, and facility level.

Unit-Level Costs

Unit-level costs are indirect product costs that vary according to the number of units of a product or service produced. Certain activities and their associated costs increase with the number of units produced. The cost to use a machine is an example of indirect unit-level costs. The cost of operating a machine increases with the number of units produced because of wear on the machine parts. These indirect costs are proportional to the number of units of all products produced. The costs are indirect because the machine is used to make more than one product.

Batch-Level Costs

Products are often created in batches. A **batch** consists of multiple units of the same product that are processed together. As a batch moves through a manufacturing plant, adjustments to machinery, called *set-ups,* must be made to make the particular product in the batch. Services are also performed in batches. A UPS truckload could be considered a batch of packages to be delivered to different customers. Costs associated with batches are called **batch-level costs;** they are fixed with respect to the number of units in the batch up to capacity limits but vary with the number of batches. An example of an activity that generates primarily a batch-level cost is an airplane flight. Many costs of an airplane flight do not vary with the number of passengers; the cost of the flight crew and the plane are fixed with respect to the number of passengers up to the seating capacity of the plane. The cost of meals, however, is a unit-level cost since it varies with the number of passengers.

Manufacturing also is frequently performed in batches to reduce the need to reset machines continually for different products. Once machines are set up for a batch run, multiple units can be manufactured without additional set-up costs. The set-up activity to run the batch and its corresponding cost are common to all the units in the batch. The cost of the set-up activity is fixed with respect to the number of units in the batch.

Product-Level Costs

Some activities benefit products as a whole rather than individual units or batches of a product or service. For example, engineering and design efforts are common to all units of a particular product. Once the design and engineering activities have been completed for a particular product or service, no more of these costs are incurred in making more units or batches. Costs that are common to all units of a product are called **product-level costs.**

Product-level costs are fixed with respect to the number of units and batches produced but vary with the number of products. In the case of engineering and design activities, each new product incurs additional costs, so engineering and design costs vary with the number of products. In the case of airlines, creating flight service between different cities is a new product. The costs of obtaining gates and ticket counter space and of establishing ticketing, baggage, and gate operations are product-level costs.

Facility-Level Costs

Some activities are not related to any products or services, so their costs cannot be directly traced to a particular product or service. For example, the cost of the building housing a manufacturing plant cannot be traced to the many different products made within the facility, nor is the plant manager's salary associated with any particular unit, batch, or product. Costs that cannot be identified with a particular unit, batch, or product are called **facility-level costs.** Facility-level costs are fixed with respect to the number of units, batches, and products or services produced and are common to multiple products or services. Facility-level costs vary, however, with the size and number of facilities. In the airline industry, the cost of maintaining and operating the airline reservation system is a facility-level cost. These costs do not vary with the number of different services between cities that the airline offers.

Recognizing whether an indirect cost is a unit-, batch-, product-, or facility-level cost is important in understanding the relationship between indirect costs and products and services. Activity-based costing, described later in this chapter, uses the level of indirect costs to trace indirect costs to products and services.

Concept**Review**

1. What are indirect product costs?

2. Explain how indirect product costs are classified as unit, batch, product, and facility level.

SNAKE SKATEBOARDS
(Continued)

Jeff Williams categorizes the indirect costs of Snake Skateboards as follows:

Support Function	Level	Amount
Administrative	Facility	$ 90,000
Purchasing	Batch	50,000
Production		
Warehousing and handling	Batch	18,000
Cutting	Unit	50,000
Gluing	Unit	10,000
Setting-up molds	Batch	55,000
Painting	Unit	35,000
Assembly	Unit	42,000
Marketing	Product	100,000
Total		$450,000

This categorization indicates that tracing indirect costs to the two types of skateboards is complicated. Splitting the indirect costs among the flat and molded skateboards should recognize each of these levels of indirect costs.

INDIRECT COSTS TRACED USING A COST DRIVER

LO 5 Trace indirect product costs using a cost driver.

Although tracing indirect costs to different products appears to be problematic, a careful analysis of the activities that cause the indirect costs can provide some direction. Indirect product costs occur because an organization performs an activity related to multiple products. This activity is triggered by some event called a **cost driver.** A cost driver is the cause of an activity's cost. For example, purchasing raw materials is an activity for many products. Purchasing costs occur because purchase orders must be processed. Therefore, a cost driver for purchasing costs could be the number of purchase orders. The more purchase orders that a product generates, the more purchasing costs it causes. The purchasing costs can therefore be traced to the different products based on how much of the cost driver (purchase orders) each product uses.

Part of the cost of long-distance services is the cost to ensure that the service is always available. Maintaining and repairing telephone lines are facility-level costs that telecommunications firms like AT&T incur, but which customers might not appreciate. Management accountants at AT&T and at other similar firms perform the task of developing an accurate and reliable way to incorporate this facility-level cost into the service rates charged to individual customers.

The procedure for tracing activity costs to different products through cost drivers is described in the following steps:

1. Identify the activities that generate indirect product costs.
2. Estimate the cost of the activities.
3. Select a cost driver for each activity.
4. Estimate the cost-driver usage by all products.
5. Calculate a cost-driver application rate.
6. Apply activity costs to each product.

Identify the Activities That Generate Indirect Product Costs

The procedure for tracing activity costs to different products begins with identifying organizational activities that cause indirect costs. Indirect costs do not just happen; something causes them, and the management accountant must identify the activities that cause them. Some activities, such as engineering and marketing, causing indirect costs provide value to the customer. These activities are on the value chain. Other activities, which provide little value to the customer, such as moving products within the organization and setting up machines, are called *non–value-added activities*.

Identifying activities within the organization that cause indirect product costs requires considerable knowledge of the organization. Management accountants cannot provide good estimates of product costs from the security of their office. They must observe all activities related to the product or service and be aware of all operations and how they interact.

Business Analysis

Before the break-up of AT&T, the long-distance telephone market was regulated. Public boards set rates at levels sufficient to cover the cost of the telephone service and provide profit for AT&T. AT&T controlled almost all access to telephones in the United States, and there was very little domestic competition. Subsequent to the deregulation of long-distance services, companies such as MCI and Sprint entered the market. With the advent of wireless telephone service and the potential for Internet and television cable providers to enter the market, the long-distance telephone industry has become one of the most competitive in the world. Even with many large mergers, global competition remains intense as is evident around dinnertime when companies often make sales calls.

The cost of providing a long-distance telephone call plays an important role in the turmoil surrounding the long-distance telephone market. Almost all of AT&T's long-distance telephone services are facility- or product-level activities that include the establishment and maintenance of satellite and trunk lines, research and development, and sales activities. Billing services could be considered at the batch level if service to each customer is perceived as a batch. There are essentially no cost activities at the unit level except payment to the local telephone companies (the Baby Bells) for the use of their lines. Therefore, the marginal cost of providing one more long-distance telephone call for an existing customer is very small as long as the network has sufficient capacity. If the system is very busy, an additional call can delay other calls, reducing the customer's value of AT&T's service.

This product cost structure and the intense competition provide some interesting problems for AT&T in making pricing and other strategic decisions. What are some creative ways for AT&T to compete on price? What types of acquisitions could help solidify AT&T's position in the long-distance market?

Technological Change

Estimate the Costs of the Activities

Once the activities are identified, the costs associated with each activity are estimated. These costs should include employee time and materials consumed by the activity as well as utility and rental costs.

If purchasing is identified as an organizational activity causing indirect costs, all costs associated with it are identified and estimated. Those costs would include the wages of those working in the purchasing activity and the costs of their supplies, travel to visit suppliers, computers, telephone and other utilities, and the space used by purchasing. All of these costs would be aggregated and treated as the cost of the purchasing activity.

Select a Cost Driver for Each Activity

After identifying the activities and estimating their costs, a cost driver is chosen for each activity. As explained earlier, a cost driver causes or "drives" the costs of an activity. The choice of the cost driver should recognize whether the activity causes unit-level, batch-level, product-level, or facility-level costs. The cost drivers for unit-level costs vary with the number of units, such as direct labor hours, cost of raw materials, or simply the number of units. Cost drivers for batch-level costs vary with the number of batches, such as the number of purchase orders (for batches of parts), the time to reset machines for new batches, or simply the number of batches. Cost drivers for product-level costs reflect the proportion of the activity dedicated to the different products. For example, the number of design hours could be used to determine design costs and product-level costs could be divided equally among all of the products. Choosing cost drivers for facility-level costs is more problematic because these costs seldom vary according to the product activity.

Cost drivers are ideal tracers of indirect activity costs when the usage of the cost driver is proportional to the activity costs. When proportionality exists between cost-driver usage and an activity's costs, each unit of the cost driver used causes the same activity cost. Proportionality assumes that there are no fixed costs. Figure 3.2 depicts a proportional relationship. Implicitly, this relation assumes that all indirect costs are variable with respect to the chosen cost driver.

Estimate the Cost-Driver Usage by All Products

Indirect product costs are generated by activities that support more than one product. These activity costs are traced to the different products based on their usage of the activity's cost driver. The more a particular product uses the cost driver, more activity costs are traced to the product. The problem is determining the cost of using a single unit of the cost driver. The cost of using a single unit of the cost driver is estimated by dividing the total activity costs by the total usage of the cost driver by all products, as demonstrated in the next section. Therefore, an estimate of the cost-driver usage by all products must be made. For example, if the number of purchase orders is selected

Figure 3.2

Proportionality of Cost-Driver Usage and Activity Costs

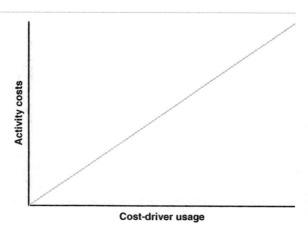

as a cost driver for purchasing costs, the total number of purchase orders to be used by all products must be estimated.

Calculate a Cost-Driver Application Rate

The **cost-driver application rate** is used to trace activity costs to different products. To determine the cost-driver application rate for each activity, its estimated costs are divided by the total estimated usage of their respective cost driver. The ratio provides an estimate of the cost of using one unit of the cost driver.

For example, assume that the total estimated purchasing cost for all products is $1,000,000 and the total estimated number of purchase orders, the cost driver, is 20,000. Then the cost-driver application rate for a purchase order is $1,000,000/ 20,000 purchase orders, or $50/purchase order. Each purchase order is estimated to cost $50.

Apply Activity Costs to Each Product

Once a cost-driver application rate for an activity is calculated, the activity costs are traced based on the usage of the cost driver by each product and service. The cost-driver application rate is multiplied by the cost-driver usage of each product.

If a cost-driver application rate is estimated to be $50 per purchase order, a product estimated to use 10 purchase orders will be assessed ($50/purchase order)(10 purchase orders), or $500. The $500 becomes part of the product cost.

Numerical Example 3.2

A sunglasses company manufactures three different products (Euro, Aussie, and Salsa) that use the same assembly line. To change production from one product to another, the machines on the assembly line must be reset, an activity estimated to cost $400,000 during the year. The number of resets estimated for each product are 50 for Euro, 200 for Aussie, and 150 for Salsa. If the number of resets is the cost driver of the resetting activity, how should the resetting costs be traced to the three products?

Solution

The estimated resetting activity cost is $400,000. The number of resets is chosen as the cost driver. The estimated total cost-driver usage is 50 + 200 + 150, or 400 resets. The cost-driver application rate is $400,000/400 resets, or $1,000 per reset. The resetting activity costs traced to the different sunglasses follow:

Product	Estimated Resets	Application Rate	Traced Costs
Euro	50	$1,000/Reset	$ 50,000
Aussie	200	1,000/Reset	200,000
Salsa	150	1,000/Reset	150,000
Total	400		$400,000

More resetting costs are traced to the Euro model, since it uses more of the cost driver.

Concept**Review**

1. What are the six steps in tracing indirect costs to products?
2. What is the preferred relationship between cost-driver usage and activity costs?

ACTIVITY-BASED COSTING

Most firms are finding that indirect product costs have become a higher proportion of their total product costs. In fact, the indirect product costs for many organizations

LO 6   Use activity-based costing to estimate the cost of a product or service.

**Technological
Change**

are more than 50% of total costs. Automation and computing systems have increased the indirect costs of many organizations and, in many cases, have replaced direct labor. As the proportion of indirect costs to direct costs increases, firms have begun to take a closer look at how indirect costs are related to their different products. Without an accurate tracing of indirect costs to products, organizations are likely to make poor product mix and pricing decisions.

Indirect product costs occur because activities often support more than one product. The previous section outlines the procedure for tracing the cost of a single activity to different products. That procedure can be duplicated for other activities within the organization. Tracing the costs of different activities to products is the basis of **activity-based costing (ABC).** By analyzing its activities and how they relate to different products, an organization can more accurately estimate its product costs. More accurate product costs can lead to better product mix and pricing decisions.

ABC is a procedure to trace costs from activities to products, which is the focus of this chapter. Additionally, the analysis of activities and their costs can lead to better decisions about cost-reduction opportunities, more efficient supplier relations, and more focus on added value to the customer. These issues are discussed in Chapter Four in the section on activity-based management.

In this section, ABC is used to trace all activity costs to the different products. Of course, activities that are dedicated to only one product involve no tracing difficulties since they generate direct product costs. Tracing indirect product costs is more problematic, however. The previous section outlined six steps to trace costs of activities that support multiple products. To complete the product cost estimation process, those steps must be followed for each activity. The estimated cost of a product is the sum of the direct product costs and the indirect product costs traced from the various activities.

Numerical Example 3.3

A tree nursery is considering a change of product mix in its inventory. The manager wants to estimate the product cost of different types of trees. There are no activities that lead to direct costs. Indirect costs are identified and estimated for the following activities: watering, repotting (transferring trees to larger pots), and administration. Total estimated annual costs for each activity, the cost driver for each activity, and the expected annual usage of each cost driver are as follows:

Activity	Estimated Costs	Cost Driver	Estimated Usage of Cost Driver
Watering	$100,000	Number of trees	500,000
Repotting	200,000	Number of repots	200,000
Administration	150,000	Number of different types of trees	500

a. What is the application rate for each activity?

b. Given the choice of cost driver, at what level is each activity: unit, batch, product, or facility?

c. What are the estimated costs of 100 weeping birches, each of which requires one repotting each year?

Solution

a. The application rate for each activity is calculated by dividing the activity 's estimated costs by the estimated usage of its respective cost driver:

Activity		Application Rate
Watering	$100,000/500,000	$0.20/Tree
Repotting	$200,000/200,000	$1.00/Repot
Administration	$150,000/500	$300/Type of tree

b. Both watering and repotting are unit-level activities since their cost drivers vary according to the number of units. Administration is treated as a product-level activity because each product receives the same indirect costs.

c. The indirect costs traced to the 100 weeping birches follow:

Activity	Application Rate	Weeping Birch Usage	Weeping Birch Costs
Watering	$0.20/Tree	100	$ 20.00
Repotting	$1.00/Repot	100	100.00
Administration	$300/Type of tree	1	300.00
Total of annual indirect costs			$420.00

The estimated cost per willow tree is $420/100 weeping birch trees, or $4.20/tree.

Numerical Example 3.4

An online retailer of sports equipment is attempting to determine the cost of the products that it sells over the Internet. The company buys its products directly from manufacturers in batches and stores them at a central warehouse. The products are shipped to the consumer via UPS. The company incurs additional costs resulting from advertising to encourage consumers to visit its Web site, designing the Web site, purchasing, and general administration. The costs of the different activities and cost-driver usage are as follows:

Activity	Activity Cost	Cost Driver	Total Usage of Cost Driver
Warehousing	$1,000,000	Average cost of inventory	$ 2,000,000
Shipping	3,000,000	Direct material (DM) cost	$30,000,000
Advertising	5,000,000	?	
Web site			
General design	1,000,000	?	
Product related	4,000,000	Number of Web pages	8,000 pages
Purchasing	2,000,000	Number of purchase orders	5,000 purchase orders
General admin.	1,000,000	?	

In addition to these activity costs, the company purchases $30,000,000 of products for resale.

a. Why are there question marks for the cost driver for certain activities?

b. What level of costs (unit, batch, or product) are generated by warehousing, shipping, Web site product-related, and purchasing activities?

c. What are the cost-driver application rates for these activities?

d. To determine the profitability of selling basketballs on the Internet, the company wants to estimate their total product cost. It plans to buy $500,000 of basketballs for resale. On average, the warehouse will hold $100,000 of basketballs in inventory. Basketballs require 20 pages on the Internet and 10 purchase orders. What is the total estimated cost of selling basketballs?

Solution

a. The activities with question marks are not related to any particular product and could be considered facility-level costs. Tracing these costs may cause misleading product costs because they probably do not vary with additional products. They are not included in the following analysis but must be considered part of the organization's total cost.

b. Warehousing costs vary with the value of the inventory in the warehouse, so these would be unit-level costs. Shipping costs vary with direct material costs and would also be unit level. Product-related Web page costs vary with the number of different products and are product level. Purchasing costs are performed in batches and are batch-level costs.

c.

Activity		Application Rate
Warehousing	($1,000,000/$2,000,000)	50% of average inventory $
Shipping	($3,000,000/$30,000,000)	10% of DM cost
Web site		
Product related	($4,000,000/8,000)	$500/Page
Purchasing	($2,000,000/5,000)	$400/Purchase

d.

Activity	Application Rate	Basketball Usage	Cost
Warehousing	50% of avg. inventory $	$100,000	$ 50,000
Shipping	10% of DM cost	$500,000	50,000
Web site			
Product related	$500/Page	20 pages	10,000
Purchasing	$400/Purchase	10 purchases	4,000
Direct cost of basketballs			500,000
Total cost of basketballs			$614,000

The estimated total cost of selling basketballs via the Internet is $614,000.

Advantages of ABC

LO 7 Recognize the advantages and problems of using activity-based costing.

ABC seeks to improve tracing indirect costs to products by recognizing the different levels of activities that lead to indirect product costs. Because each activity has its own cost driver, ABC can capture some of the complexity of indirect product costs.

ABC is most beneficial in estimating accurate product costs for organizations with multiple products and services. If a firm has only one product or service, there is no problem in tracing its costs.

ABC is also more beneficial for firms where products and services use overhead activities in different ways. If some of an organization's products require considerable engineering time and others require considerable machine time, these products use overhead activities differently. Also, high- and low-volume products tend to use overhead activities differently, especially if there are batch-level and product-level costs.

ABC is especially useful to organizations with a high percentage of indirect product costs. When a large percentage of product costs are indirect, accurately tracing them to products becomes more important.

ABC's usefulness in making planning decisions is not limited to providing accurate product costs. It also assists managers in finding opportunities to reduce costs. The identification of activities that cause costs often reveals activities that do not add value. Identifying these non–value-added activities provide opportunities to reduce costs.

Planning Decisions

ABC can provide useful information as to how the different overhead activities relate to the rest of the organization. **Activity-based management** is the process of managing the various organizational activities to allow the organization to operate more efficiently. ABC is part of activity-based management, which is covered in Chapter Four.

Installing an ABC system requires considerable knowledge about how the different overhead activities are related to products. The process of implementing ABC forces members to analyze and understand their organization better. This knowledge will be beneficial in making other planning decisions.

Problems with ABC

Although ABC has many advantages, it is not without some problems, nor does it always achieve a particularly accurate estimate of the cost of making a product. The accuracy of ABC depends on identifying and estimating the costs of the activities as well as the relation between the cost driver to the costs of the activity. If cost-driver usage is not proportional to the cost of the activity, inaccurate estimates will occur. Cost-driver usage will not be proportional to activity costs if some of the activity costs are fixed with respect to the cost driver. For example, a company may decide to purchase an expensive testing machine to inspect different products. Inspection is an activity and the number of inspections could be used as the cost driver. The cost of the machine, however, is fixed with respect to the number of inspections.

LO 7 Recognize the advantages and problems of using activity-based costing.

If activity costs have a fixed component with respect to the cost driver, ABC ignores the difference between an activity's fixed and variable costs. In this case, the application rate reflects both the activity's fixed and variable costs and will not accurately reflect the cost of its additional use.

ABC cannot resolve the problem of what to do with facility-level costs. These costs do not lend themselves to tracing to different products since they are fixed with respect to the number of products.

ABC is also costly to implement. Many measurements and observations must be made to implement it and may have control effects. For example, if engineering hours are used to trace engineering costs to products, engineering hours will be more carefully controlled. Therefore, both planning and control decisions should be considered jointly in determining whether to adopt ABC.

Control Decisions

Concept**Review**

1. How are product costs estimated using activity-based costing?
2. What are the advantages and disadvantages of activity-based costing?

Jeff Williams wants to estimate Snake Skateboards' product costs under ABC. The following indirect cost activities and cost drivers are identified. Also, activity costs, cost-driver usage, and application rates are estimated.

SNAKE SKATEBOARDS
(Continued)

Activity	Cost Driver	Costs	Cost Driver Usage	Application Rate
Administration	Direct labor hours	$ 90,000	30,000	$3/DLH
Purchasing	Number of orders	50,000	100	$500/Order
Warehousing	Number of deliveries	18,000	150	$120/Delivery
Cutting	Machine hours	50,000	5,000	$10/Machine hour
Gluing	Labor hours of gluing	10,000	5,000	$2/Gluing hour
Setting up	Number of set-ups	55,000	6,000	$9.17/Set-up
Painting	Gallons of paint	35,000	1,000	$35/Gallon
Assembly	Hours to assemble	42,000	10,500	$4/Hour
Marketing	Customer visits	100,000	80	$1,250/Visit

Tracing indirect costs to each product depends on the expected usage of the cost drivers by the two products. The indirect costs traced to each product are as follows:

Activity	Application Rate	Usage by Flat Skateboards	Applied to Flat Skateboards	Usage by Molded Skateboards	Applied to Molded Skateboards
Administration	$3/DLH	25,000	$ 75,000	5,000	$ 15,000
Purchasing	$500/Purchase	30	15,000	70	35,000
Warehousing	$120/Delivery	50	6,000	100	12,000
Cutting	$10/Machine hour	4,000	40,000	1,000	10,000
Gluing	$2/Gluing hour	4,500	9,000	500	1,000
Setting up	$9.17/Set-up	5,000	45,833	1,000	9,167
Painting	$35/Gallon	500	17,500	500	17,500
Assembly	$4/Hour	8,000	32,000	2,500	10,000
Marketing	$1,250/visit	40	50,000	40	50,000
Total			$290,333		$159,667

The indirect cost per unit using ABC with these cost drivers follows:

Flat skateboards	$290,333/50,000 units	$ 5.81/unit
Molded skateboards	159,667/5,000 units	$31.93/unit

With direct costs, the estimated costs of making each product is

	Direct Materials	Direct Labor	Indirect Costs	Cost per Unit
Flat skateboards	$1.08	$ 5.00	$ 5.81	$11.89
Molded skateboards	1.20	10.00	31.93	43.13

Using these product costs, the molded skateboard that sells for $25 looks like a big loser. Jeff should not eliminate the molded skateboards from the product mix, however, without further investigation. The ABC method applied facility-level costs that are common to both flat and molded skateboards; these costs will not necessarily be avoided by dropping the molded skateboards. The opportunity cost of making molded skateboards should consider the alternative use of the facilities if those skateboards are no longer made. In addition, some of the indirect costs may be sunk; that is, they will be incurred whether molded skateboards are made or not. These sunk costs should be ignored in making the product mix decision.

INDIRECT PRODUCT COSTS TRACED USING A SINGLE COST DRIVER

LO 8   Estimate product costs using a single cost driver.

Under ABC, each activity that generates an indirect product cost should have its own cost driver to trace its costs to the different products. By tracing an activity's indirect costs to different products and services, an organization can make more informed decisions, such as pricing and product mix decisions. If these planning decisions are not sensitive to the accuracy of the estimate of indirect product costs, using a single cost driver to trace all indirect product costs is often sufficient. For example, an organization is unlikely to be as concerned about tracing indirect costs to its products and services when these costs represent only a small percentage of total costs. Large discount retail stores, such as Wal-Mart, have very large direct costs to purchase merchandise. The indirect costs tend to be relatively small when compared to the direct costs, so the method of applying indirect product costs is not so important. Many professional services also have a cost structure dominated by direct costs; for example, the costs in accounting and legal firms are primarily for professional personnel whose work can be traced directly to a particular client or service, such as an audit or legal case. Once again, the relatively small proportion of indirect costs makes the application procedure less important.

The benefits of ABC do not always outweigh its costs; therefore, many organizations still use one cost driver to trace all indirect product costs to the different products. The following steps describe the tracing process using a single cost driver. The process is the same as for ABC except all the indirect costs are pooled together and only one cost driver is used.

Identify and Estimate All Indirect Product Costs

Before indirect product costs can be traced, they first must be identified and estimated. The costs of all activities that support multiple products are included. Direct product costs are measured separately. As mentioned earlier, in financial reporting to external parties, some indirect costs, such as research and development and marketing, are not traced to products and services. For making planning decisions, however, the cost of all indirect resources used by a product or service should be identified and estimated.

Identify a Cost Driver to Apply Indirect Costs and Estimate the Cost Driver's Usage for All Products and Services

Once the total indirect product costs have been estimated, a single cost driver must be chosen that reflects the cause of the indirect costs. This cost driver could be related to the process of making the product or providing the service. For example, the number of direct labor hours used for each product or service is a possible cost driver as is some physical characteristic of the product or service such as the number of parts. As with ABC, the cost-driver usage should approximate the cost of using the indirect resources. This link will be more tenuous since all indirect costs are pooled together and it is unlikely that one cost driver can be found that is proportional to all indirect costs.

The cost driver should be easily measurable because, once chosen, its amount used by each product or service must be estimated. This estimate is the sum of the estimated usage of the cost driver by each of the organization's products and services. For example, if the number of machine hours is the cost driver, the number of machine hours used by all of the organization's products and services must be estimated.

Calculate the Application Rate

Once a single cost driver has been identified to trace indirect costs to different products or services, the application rate is calculated by dividing the total estimated indirect costs by the total estimated usage of the cost driver across all products or services. For example, suppose the estimated indirect costs for a car repair shop are $50,000 for 2,500 repair jobs. The management accountant could apply them equally to each repair job by using an application rate of $50,000/2,500 repair jobs, or $20 per repair job. That procedure would not recognize, however, that some repair jobs are simple and that their indirect cost is lower than the indirect cost of more complex repairs. If the number of direct labor hours, cost of parts added, or number of hours in the shop are used as cost drivers to apply indirect costs, the indirect cost of working on a car may be more closely approximated. If direct labor hours are used to apply indirect costs and the 2,500 service jobs require an estimated 5,000 direct labor hours, the application rate would be $50,000/5,000 direct labor hours, or $10 per direct labor hour.

Apply Indirect Costs to the Various Products and Services

Once the application rate has been calculated, the estimated indirect costs are traced to the different products and services based on the estimated usage of the cost driver. In the car repair shop example, an application rate of $10 per direct labor hour is estimated. A repair job that requires 5 direct labor hours has $50 of estimated indirect costs, or $10 per direct labor hour (the application rate) times 5 direct labor hours (the cost driver).

Each product or service will receive a portion of the indirect costs based on the estimated usage of the cost driver by that product or service. This procedure separates all expected indirect costs to the products and service.

Numerical Example | **3.5**

The Cascade Cleaning Service in Fallbrook, Canada, provides cleaning services for commercial buildings. The company cleans three different buildings:

	Square Meters	Estimated Hours of Cleaning Time
Anderson Office Building	100,000	8,000
Carla's Pizza	10,000	6,000
City Hall	90,000	6,000
Total	200,000	20,000

Cascade Cleaning Service has the following estimated indirect costs:

Supplies	$ 50,000
Administration	50,000
Total	$100,000

Apply these indirect costs to the different buildings using both square meters and estimated hours of cleaning time. Which application procedure is better?

Solution

If square meters are used, the application rate is $100,000/200,000 square meters, or $0.50 per square meter. Using this application rate, the application of estimated indirect costs follows:

	Square Meters	Application Rate	Estimated Indirect Costs
Anderson Office Building	100,000	$0.50	$ 50,000
Carla's Pizza	10,000	0.50	5,000
City Hall	90,000	0.50	45,000
Total applied costs			$100,000

If estimated hours of cleaning are used, the application rate is $100,000/20,000 hours, or $5 per hour of cleaning. Using this application rate, the application of estimated indirect costs follows:

	Estimated Hours	Application Rate	Estimated Indirect Costs
Anderson Office Building	8,000	$5	$ 40,000
Carla's Pizza	6,000	5	30,000
City Hall	6,000	5	30,000
Total applied costs			$100,000

There is insufficient evidence to determine which application procedure is better. The goal is to apply indirect costs to approximate the costs of using the indirect resources. The cost of using supplies is probably more closely associated with the hours of cleaning time, although the cost of floor wax could be more closely associated with the square meters of floor space. The administrative cost may be fixed and common to all the cleaning jobs and does not represent a cost of providing a specific cleaning job. The administrative costs would have to be analyzed more carefully to determine whether they represent costs of individual cleaning jobs. If they do not, the administrative costs should not be applied to the different cleaning jobs to estimate indirect costs.

Skateboarders compare and select different models in terms of style, features, and price. Market forces require manufacturers to set selling prices based on those of competitors, customer demand, and their own costs. The final cost of a skateboard is the total of the direct costs and the numerous indirect costs that must be traced to products using cost drivers.

Concept**Review**

1. How are indirect product costs traced to different products and services using a single cost driver?

2. What are some problems in tracing indirect product costs using a single cost driver?

Snake Skateboards could trace indirect costs by using many different types of single cost drivers. Two possible cost drivers are the number of units and the number of direct labor hours. The total indirect costs are estimated to be $450,000. The number of units is estimated to be 50,000 of flat boards and 5,000 of molded boards, or a total of 55,000 units. Therefore, the application rate by number of units equals $450,000/55,000 unit, or about $8.181818 per unit. With this application rate, the indirect costs are traced in the following manner:

SNAKE SKATEBOARDS
(Continued)

	Number of Units	Application Rate	Traced Costs
Flat skateboards	50,000	$8.181818	$409,091
Molded skateboards	5,000	8.181818	40,909
Total traced costs			$450,000

You decide

Based on this tracing of indirect costs, the estimated cost per unit of the two types of skateboards is as follows:

	Direct Materials	Direct Labor	Indirect Costs	Cost per Unit
Flat skateboards	$1.08	$ 5.00	$8.18	$14.26
Molded skateboards	1.20	10.00	8.18	19.38

Snake Skateboard could also apply indirect costs using the estimated number of direct labor hours. Each flat skateboard uses an estimated 0.5 hour of direct labor and each molded skateboard uses an estimated 1.0 hour of direct labor. A total of (0.5 hours/unit)(50,000 units), or 25,000 hours, is expected to be used for the flat skateboard and (1 hour/unit) (5,000 units), or 5,000 hours, is expected to be used for the molded skateboard. Therefore, a total of 25,000 hours + 5,000 hours, or 30,000 direct labor hours, are expected to be used. The application rate is $450,000/30,000 hours, or $15/hour. Using this application rate, the indirect costs are applied in the following manner:

	Units	Number of Hours	Application Rate	Traced Costs	Traced Costs per Unit
Flat skateboards	50,000	25,000	$15	$375,000	$ 7.50
Molded skateboards	5,000	5,000	15	75,000	15.00
Total traced costs				$450,000	

Based on this tracing of indirect costs, the estimated cost per unit of the two types of skateboards is as follows:

	Direct Materials	Direct Labor	Indirect Costs	Cost per Unit
Flat skateboards	$1.08	$ 5.00	$ 7.50	$13.58
Molded skateboards	1.20	10.00	15.00	26.20

Jeff is very confused by these results. Using the number of units to trace indirect costs indicates that both the flat skateboard with a $15 sales price and the molded skateboard with a sales price of $25 are profitable. After this analysis, Jeff is suspicious of using a single cost driver to trace indirect costs. In fact, his analysis of the unit-, batch-, product-, and facility-level costs indicates that a single cost driver will not trace indirect costs accurately.

SUMMARY

1 **Treat products as cost objects for making product mix and pricing decisions.** Estimating the cost of a product allows managers to estimate the product's profitability and whether to include that product in the product mix.

2 **Identify activities of the organization related to its different products and services.** The organization's activities are either directly or indirectly linked to its different products and services.

3 **Estimate the direct costs of a product or service.**
Direct product and service costs are divided into direct labor and direct materials. Estimates of direct labor costs can be made by estimating the labor time required to make a product or provide a service and multiplying that labor time by the estimated wage rate of laborers. The direct material cost is estimated by determining the necessary parts and materials and multiplying by their respective prices. The labor rates and price of materials are intended to approximate the opportunity cost of using the labor and materials.

4 **Identify different levels of indirect product costs.**
Indirect product costs are unit level if they vary by the number of units, batch level if they vary by the number of batches, product level if they vary by the number of products, and facility level if they vary by the number and size of facilities.

5 **Trace indirect product costs using a cost driver.**
Indirect costs are traced to products using the following steps: (1) identifying activities, (2) estimating the cost of activities, (3) selecting the cost driver for each activity, (4) estimating the total usage of the cost driver, (5) calculating the cost-driver application rates, (6) and applying indirect activity costs based on usage of the cost drivers.

6 **Use activity-based costing to estimate the cost of a product or service.** Activity-based costing identifies activities that cause indirect costs and cost drivers that can be used to trace those activity costs to different products and services. An application rate is calculated for each cost driver to apply the indirect costs.

7 **Recognize the advantages and problems of using activity-based costing.** Activity-based costing recognizes that indirect costs vary with different levels of operations. Indirect costs also have different causes, and appropriate cost drivers are chosen to reflect these differences. Activity-based costing does not adjust for fixed opportunity costs and presumes that indirect costs vary with the usage of the cost driver.

8 **Estimate product costs using a single cost driver.** With a single cost driver, all indirect product costs are lumped together to calculate an application rate. All indirect product costs then are traced based on the usage of the single cost driver.

9 **Use product costs for financial reporting. (Appendix)**
Product costs in financial reports are dictated by generally accepted accounting principles (GAAP). Whether a cost is a period or a product cost for financial reporting purposes potentially influences shareholder wealth, management compensation, and taxes.

KEY TERMS

activity-based costing (ABC)   A process of identifying activities that cause indirect costs and choosing cost drivers to apply those indirect costs for different products and services. *(p. 82)*

activity-based management   A process of managing the different overhead activities to allow the organization to operate more efficiently. *(p. 84)*

batch   Multiple units of the same product that are processed together. *(p. 77)*

batch-level costs   Indirect costs associated with the number of batches of a particular product or service. *(p. 77)*

cost driver   The cause of the cost of an activity. *(p. 78)*

cost-driver application rate   The ratio of the total activity cost divided by the total expected usage of the activity's cost driver. *(p. 81)*

cost object   An item to be costed for decision-making purposes. *(p. 70)*

cost of goods sold   The historical cost of products sold as reported in the income statement. *(p. 92)*

direct labor   Labor costs that can be identified with a specific product or service. *(p. 74)*

direct materials   Parts and raw materials used to make a product. *(p. 74)*

direct product costs   Costs that can be directly traced to a specific product. *(p. 73)*

facility-level costs   Indirect costs that are common to multiple products and services. *(p. 77)*

indirect product costs   Costs associated with more than one product. *(p. 76)*

overhead costs   Indirect costs of products or services. *(p. 76)*

period costs   Costs associated with periods of time, rather than products, for reporting to external parties. *(p. 92)*

product or service cost   The forgone opportunity of using resources to provide a product or service. *(p. 70)*

product-level costs   Costs associated with a product but not with a particular unit or batch of the product. *(p. 77)*

product mix decision   A decision on the types and proportions of products and services to offer. *(p. 71)*

unit-level costs   The costs associated with individual units of a product or service. *(p. 77)*

APPENDIX

Product Costs and Financial Reporting

LO 9 Use product costs for financial reporting.

As mentioned earlier, the product costs reported in financial reports are not necessarily the product costs that are estimated through ABC or other methods for management decisions. Managers are concerned about all costs related to the product from research and development to customer service. Financial reporting practices dictated by generally accepted accounting principles (GAAP) in Canada and the United States, for example, require that certain costs be treated as a cost of the period rather than of a product. **Period costs** or expenses are assigned to the period of time in which they were incurred. Research and development, marketing, and general administrative costs are period costs rather than product costs for financial reporting purposes. They become expenses of the period in which they occurred.

An additional expense of the period is the cost of the products sold during the period. The product cost of products sold is called **cost of goods sold.** The product cost of products not sold is treated as an asset and is called *inventory.* Inventory costs become cost of goods sold only when the inventory is sold.

A major financial reporting issue is to determine whether a cost is a period cost or a product cost. If a particular cost is determined to be a period cost, it must be expensed immediately. If it is a product cost, it becomes an expense of the period in which the product is sold, which could be in subsequent years. Managers often have preferences on whether to treat a particular cost as a period or product cost for financial reporting purposes because of the potential influence of financial reports on shareholder wealth, management compensation, and taxes. For internal planning decisions, however, managers prefer a product cost estimate that encompasses all aspects of making and delivering the product or service.

The typical company's income statement begins with revenues, which reflect the sales of the period. The cost of goods sold and other period expenses are then deducted from the revenues to determine income.

Numerical Example 3.6

Pebble Bookstore opened on January 1, 2000. During the year, the bookstore paid $500,000 to purchase the books and $50,000 of freight charges to deliver them. Over the year, the book store had the following other costs, which are treated as period costs:

Rent	$12,000
Advertising	30,000
Salaries	80,000

Pebble Bookstore had revenues of $800,000 during 2000 and had 20% of its books unsold at the end of the year. Prepare an income statement for the bookstore for 2000.

Solution

The freight charges are treated as product costs, so total product costs during the year are $550,000. Since 80% of the books are sold during the year, the cost of goods sold is (80%)($550,000), or $440,000. The remaining product costs (20%)($550,000), or $110,000, remain as an inventory asset. The period costs are completely expensed during 2000.

PEBBLE BOOKSTORE Income Statement Year of 2000	
Revenues	$800,000
Cost of goods sold	(440,000)
Rent	(12,000)
Advertising	(30,000)
Salaries	(80,000)
Net income	$238,000

Financial reports treat time periods as the cost object. Revenues identified through the revenue recognition principle and expenses identified through the matching principle are traced to different time periods. Using the period of time as the cost object is not consistent with any specific internal planning decisions. The increased value or income the organization achieves during a particular time period can be estimated by tracing costs and revenues to that particular period. This measure provides information to external users about the value of debt and ownership shares of the organization as well as information used by owners to evaluate senior managers. For internal purposes a measure of period income gives an indication of how well the existing organizational strategy is working. A loss during a period may indicate that the organization needs to reexamine its strategy.

ORGANIZATIONAL VALUE

SELF-STUDY PROBLEM

Your company, Day-Glo Painting, has just finished its first year of operation. During the first year, you painted the exterior of 20 houses in pink with purple trim. Although the first few homeowners were unsure about the colors and threatened to sue the company, the pink and purple houses are now becoming a fad. The income statement for the company during the first year follows:

DAY-GLO PAINTING Year of 2000	
Revenues	$120,000
Direct labor ($20/hour)	(75,000)
Paint	(20,000)
Rental of painting equipment	(5,000)
General administration	(10,000)
Profit	$ 10,000

The direct labor of painting and the cost of paint vary with the square meters of surface area painted. During the year, the company painted 400,000 square meters of surface. In addition, direct labor, but no significant paint, is used to paint the trim around doors and windows. Painting trim takes an hour per 20 meters. During 2000, the company painted 40,000 meters of trim.

The second year is just beginning. The time and cost of labor, the cost of paint per liter, and the cost of rental and general administration are expected to be the same in the second year. Day-Glo Painting is bidding to paint a house that has 25,000 square meters of surface area and 3,000 meters of trim.

a.   What is the cost of paint per square meter of surface?
b.   What is the cost of direct labor per meter of trim?

c. What is the cost of direct labor per square meter of surface?

d. What is the rental and administration cost of painting the house?

e. What is the total cost of painting the house?

Solution

a. The cost of paint per square meter of surface is:

Cost = $20,000   Sq. meters = 400,000
Cost/sq. meter = $20,000/400,000 sq. meters = $0.05/sq. meter

b. The cost of direct labor per meter of trim is:

Cost per hour of labor = $20/hour. Meters of trim per hour = 20 meters/hour
Cost per meter of trim = ($20/hour)/(20 meters/hour) = $1 per meter

c. The cost of direct labor per square meter of surface is:

Total direct labor hours used in 2000: ($75,000)/($20 per hour)	3,750
Direct labor hours used for trim: (40,000 meters)/(20 meters/hour)	(2,000)
Direct labor hours used for painting 400,000 sq. meters of surface	1,750
Direct labor cost of painting 400,000 sq. meters of surface (1,750 hours)($20/hour)	$35,000

Cost per square meter = $35,000/400,000 sq. meters = $0.0875/sq. meter

d. The rental and administration costs of painting the house are the indirect costs to the painting of a particular house. It is not clear what the opportunity cost is of using these resources.

e. The total cost of painting the house is:
The total direct costs are:

Painting surface:	
Paint ($0.05/sq. meter)(25,000 sq. meters)	$1,250
Labor ($0.0875/sq. meter)(25,000 sq. meters)	2,187
Painting trim:	
Labor ($1/meter)(3,000 meters)	3,000
Total direct costs	$6,437

The indirect costs are not obvious.

NUMERICAL EXERCISES

NE 3.1
Direct and Indirect Costs of Activities
(LO 2, 3, 5)

City Athletic Club estimates the cost of its three departments: aquatics, court sports, aerobics/weight room. These departments had the following direct costs:

Aquatics: $200,000
Court sports: $100,000
Aerobics/Weight room: $100,000

In addition, estimated indirect costs for all three departments related to locker rooms and central administration costs were $200,000. These costs tend to be proportional to the department costs.

What are the total costs of each of the departments?

NE 3.2
Product Costs and Financial Reporting
(Appendix)

Wilby Wright buys model airplanes for $1 each and sells them for $2 each. In addition, the firm incurs administration expenses that are treated as a period expense. Wilby Wright began operations in 1999.

What is the income for 1999, 2000, and 2001 given the following data?

Year	Units Sold	Units Purchased	Administration Expenses
1999	10,000	12,000	$ 5,000
2000	25,000	30,000	10,000
2001	30,000	35,000	12,000

What are the direct costs of a baseball that requires $0.20 of leather, $0.01 of string, and 5 minutes of labor at $6 per hour?

NE 3.3
Direct Product Costs
(LO 3)

The total expected overhead of a machine shop is $200,000. The overhead is traced using machine hours as a cost driver. The estimated machine hours for all products are 10,000 hours.
  How much overhead is traced to a product that requires 20 machine hours?

NE 3.4
Single Cost Driver Used to Trace Indirect Costs
(LO 5)

Novex Corporation wants to trace costs to its customers through ABC. The following activities and costs are traced using cost drivers:

NE 3.5
Activity-Based Costing Used to Trace Indirect Costs
(LO 6)

Activity	Expected Cost	Cost Driver	Expected Use of Cost Driver
Advertising	$200,000	Sales	$2,000,000
Customer service	80,000	Number of calls	10,000
Accounting	140,000	Number of customers	2,000

2,800

  What is the indirect cost of a customer who buys $20,000 of Novex's products and makes 20 calls to customer service?

A farmer has an extra plot of ground for growing vegetables. The farmer has the choice of planting carrots or onions. The plot would produce 500 kilograms of carrots or 1,000 kilograms of onions. The carrots sell for $0.17/kilogram and the onions sell for $0.11/kilogram. The carrot seeds cost $10 and the onion sets (similar to seeds) cost $40. Both carrots and onions require $50 of labor for tilling, weeding, and harvesting.
  What should the farmer plant on the acre?

NE 3.6
Costs for Product Mix Decisions
(LO 1)

A new hardware store buys $340,000 of inventory during the year. The store sells all items for 40% more than their costs. At the end of the year, the cost of inventory not yet sold was $40,000. The payments to the inventory suppliers are considered product costs, but all other costs are treated as period costs. Those costs include $15,000 for rent, $6,000 for utilities, and $60,000 for salaries.
  What is the income for the period?

NE 3.7
Costs Associated with Periods
(Appendix)

Wooden Chair Company makes maple and oak chairs. The board-foot cost of maple is $0.80 and of oak is $1.00. A board-foot is 1 foot square and an inch thick. The controller of Wooden Chair Company estimates that both maple and oak chairs use 10 board-feet of wood. The cutting, assembling, and finishing of each type of chair require 3 direct labor hours. Labor costs are $8 per hour.
  What are the direct product costs of each type of chair?

NE 3.8
Estimation of Direct Product Costs
(LO 3)

A chartered accountant firm is estimating the direct service costs of performing an audit. The firm estimates that the audit will require 5 partner hours, 20 manager hours, and 50 assistant hours. The estimated opportunity costs of using these people are $150 for partners, $80 for managers, and $40 for assistants.
  What is the direct service cost of performing the audit?

NE 3.9
Estimation of Direct Service Costs
(LO 3)

Suppose that engineering is identified as a product-level, indirect cost activity and the number of hours engineers devote to each product is used as a cost driver. Engineering costs are $100,000. Product A uses 700 hours and product B uses 300 hours for a total of 1,000 engineering hours. There are only two products.
  What is the application rate for engineering costs? How is this rate applied to products A and B?

NE 3.10
Estimation of Application Rates
(LO 4)

NE 3.11
Estimation of Indirect Product Costs Using a Single Cost Driver
(LO 5, 8)

A sheet metal wholesaler purchases sheet metal and cuts and bends it to customer specifications. The cutting and bending require the use of large, expensive machines. Since most of the indirect costs are related to these machines, the manager of the company decides to apply indirect costs based on the number of machine hours required to meet customer specifications. The manager estimates that total indirect costs for the next period will be $100,000 and the machines will be used a total of 2,000 hours.

a. What is the application rate for indirect costs?
b. What is the applied indirect cost of a job that requires four hours of machine time?

NUMERICAL PROBLEMS

NP 3.1
Product Mix Decision
(LO 1)

Bob Jitters, owner of Virtual Buzz Coffee House, is in a quandary. Many customers have expressed disappointment that Virtual Buzz does not serve espresso hot chocolate. Currently, it serves both espresso and hot chocolate separately but not together. The espresso sells for $0.75 per shot and costs $0.40 to make. The hot chocolate sells for $1.75 per mug and costs $0.50 to make. If Bob were to make espresso hot chocolate, he would sell it for $2.50, but it would cost $1.40 per mug to make. Monthly sales of espresso and hot chocolate are currently 3,000 shots and 300 mugs, respectively. Based on customer responses, Bob estimates that he could sell 500 mugs of the espresso hot chocolate per month, but his sales of hot chocolate would be cut in half. He does not believe that his other beverage sales will be affected.

Should Bob add espresso hot chocolate to his product mix?

NP 3.2
Relation of Costs to Time Periods
(Appendix)

Master Artworks buys and sells paintings. During March, the company had the following paintings (with their costs) in inventory. Some of the paintings have been sold and the sales price is also reported.

Painting	Cost	Sales Price
Van Goof	$30,000	$50,000
Rembranch	20,000	Not sold
Angelomichael	10,000	40,000
Gogone	25,000	Not sold
Monnay	13,000	10,000
Picatto	3,000	7,000

Master Artworks also has the following period costs during March: rent, $3,000; salaries, $10,000; utilities, $1,000; insurance, $500.

What is the income for Master Artworks during March?

NP 3.3
Estimation of Direct Service Costs
(LO 3)

Southwest Bank provides house loans for the region. Customers seeking a loan to buy a house initially talk to a loan officer who gathers the appropriate information. The bank then hires a local appraiser to evaluate the home. The customer information and appraisal information then are sent to a vice president of the bank to make the final decision on the loan. If both the bank and the customer agree on the conditions of the home loan, the bank sends its lawyer to the closing on the sale of the house with the appropriate documents. Once the bank loan is implemented, a loan maintenance officer receives and records the monthly payments and sends the checks on to the treasurer, who deposits them in the bank. The average time spent on a house loan by each of these employees and their hourly wages are as follows:

Employee	Time (hours)	Wage Rate/Hour
Loan officer	2.0*	$15
Appraiser	3.0*	40
Vice president	0.5*	80
Lawyer	2.0*	70
Loan maintenance officer	4.0/year	20
Treasurer	1.0/year	30

*Occurs only in the first year of the loan.

a. The vice president makes a decision about making the loan. The work by the loan officer and appraiser has already been completed. What is the cost of a loan application that has been turned down?

b. If the loan is accepted, the remaining labor costs are incurred. What is the average direct labor cost of an accepted loan the first year?

c. What is the average direct labor cost of an accepted loan the second year?

A car repair shop applies overhead to different service jobs using direct labor hours. The manager estimates that total indirect costs will be $30,000 and total direct labor hours will be 2,000.

NP 3.4
Estimation of Indirect Service Costs Using a Single Cost Driver
(LO 4)

a. What is the application rate for indirect costs?

b. If a service job requires 5 direct labor hours, how much of indirect costs will be applied to it?

c. If direct labor costs $10 per hour, what is the total service cost of a job that requires 6 direct labor hours and $100 of parts?

Collins Sheet Metal Shop is considering adding a metal dry box for rafts to its product mix. The metal box requires 20 square feet of ⅛-inch aluminum. The cost of the aluminum sheet metal is $5 per square foot. Direct labor on the box is estimated to be 5 hours at $10/hour. The following activities, their cost drivers, and application rates are expected to be used in making the new box:

NP 3.5
Activity-Based Costing
(LO 6)

Activity	Cost Driver	Application Rate	Usage per Dry Box
Bending	Number of bends	$0.20/bend	20 bends
Drilling	Number of holes	$0.10/hole	30 holes
Welding	Number of inches	$0.30/inch	100 inches
Marketing	Number of products	$50/product	Marketed as 1 product
Accounting	Number of sales	$5/sale	Sold individually

← per unit (Box)

← per 10 units (Boxes)
 per unit (Box)

Collins Sheet Metal is making 10 of these dry boxes.
   What is the expected cost per dry box?

A tennis racquet manufacturer makes several types of racquets. At the start of the year, the manufacturer estimates overhead to equal $4 million. The overhead is applied to tennis racquets based on direct labor dollars, which are estimated to be $2 million in the coming year. Direct material costs are estimated to be $3 million.

NP 3.6
Estimation of Product Costs
(LO 8)

a. What is the application rate for the manufacturer?

b. What is the product cost of a batch of 1,000 racquets that use 200 direct labor hours at $10 per hour and $5,000 of direct materials?

A manufacturing firm has the following expected overhead costs, cost drivers, and cost-drive usage:

NP 3.7
Multiple Cost Drivers
(LO 6)

Overhead Item	Cost Driver	Expected Cost	Expected Cost-Driver Usage
President's salary	Number of products	$100,000	100 products
Personnel Dept.	Direct labor hours	80,000	8,000 hours
Machine set-ups	Number of batches	50,000	250 batches

   What is the indirect cost of a product that uses 100 direct labor hours and requires 5 batches to make 100 units?

First Eastern Bank is a large, multibranch bank offering a wide variety of commercial and retail banking services. Eastern determines the cost of its services to provide information for a variety of decisions.

NP 3.8
Cost of a Bank Service
(LO 2, 6)

One set of services is a retail loan operation providing residential mortgages, car loans, and student college loans. At a branch bank, an applicant files a loan application. The branch manager is responsible for completing the loan application. From there, the loan application is sent to the loan-processing department where the applicant's prior credit history is checked. This department recommends whether to approve the loan or not based on the applicant's credit history and current financial situation. This recommendation is forwarded to the loan committee of senior lending officers who review the file and make a final decision. Thus, making a loan involves three bank departments: a branch that takes the application, the loan-processing department, and a loan committee.

Mr. and Mrs. Jones visit the West Street branch and file an application for a residential mortgage. The following information about each stage of processing the Joneses' loan application is available:

* *West Street Branch Bank.* The branch manager spends one hour taking the application. She spends 1,000 hours per year of her total time taking loan applications and the remainder of her time providing other direct services to customers. Total overhead in the West Street Branch is budgeted to be $259,000, excluding the manager's salary, and is traced to direct customer services using the branch manager's time spent providing direct customer services. The branch manager's annual salary is $42,600.

* *Loan-Processing Department.* The loan-processing department budgets its total overhead for the year to be $800,000, which is traced to loans processed using direct labor hours. Budgeted direct labor hours for the year are 40,000. Direct labor hours in the processing department cost $18 per direct labor hour. The Joneses' loan requires 5 direct labor hours in the loan-processing department.

* *Loan Committee.* Ten senior bank executives make up the loan committee, which meets 52 times per year, all day every Wednesday, to approve all loans. The average salary and benefits of each member of the loan committee total $104,000. The loan committee spends 15 minutes reviewing the Joneses' loan application before approving it.

For costing purposes, all employees are assumed to work 8-hour days, 5 days per week, 52 weeks per year.

Calculate the total cost of taking the Joneses' application, processing it, and approving it.

NP 3.9

Product Cost with Multiple Cost Drivers

(LO 4, 5, 6)

Neptune Corporation is planning to make 1,000 units of toy planets, which use $1 of raw materials per unit and 10 minutes of direct labor at $12 per hour. The manufacture of the 1,000 planets also uses the following overhead cost drivers:

Cost Driver	Application Rate	Usage in Making Toy Planets
Machine hours	$20/Machine hour	100 machine hours
Number of set-ups	$200/Set-up	3 set-ups
Raw material cost	$0.20/$1 of raw materials	$1,000 of raw materials
Number of products	$4,000/Product	1 product

a. Describe each of the cost drivers as representing a unit-level, batch-level, product-level, or facility-level cost.

   Machine hours _____   Number of set-ups _____

   Raw materials cost _____   Number of products _____

b. What is the average cost per unit for making toy planets?

NP 3.10

Comparison of Single Cost Drivers to ABC

(LO 6, 7, 8)

A road contractor has been using kilometers of road constructed as a cost driver. Based on last year's costs, he estimates that he can build a kilometer of road for $3 million. The county has recently asked him for an estimate to build 20 kilometers of road.

Before making his bid based on his $3-million-per-kilometer estimate, he goes to his accountant for advice. The accountant has analyzed last year's costs much differently. She has divided last year's costs into different activities and chosen a cost driver and measured its usage last year. Her estimates follow:

Activity	Costs (000,000)	Cost Driver	Cost Driver Usage	
Surveying	$ 10	Hours	200,000 hours	50/hr
Excavating	200	Tons of earth moved	2,000,000 tons	100/ton
Bridges	120	Number of bridges	60 bridges	2,000,000/Bridge
Grading	80	Number of kilometers	200 kilometers	400,000 Klm
Gravel	30	Tons of gravel	750,000 tons	40/ton
Paving	160	Number of kilometers	200 kilometers	800,000/Klm

The costs from last year appear to be good estimates of costs for the coming year.

The 20 kilometers of county road up for bid will require 30,000 hours of surveying, 300,000 tons of earth to be moved, 10 bridges, 20 kilometers of grading and paving, and 80,000 tons of gravel.

a. Allowing for a 10% profit, what should the road contractor's bid be using the $3-million-per-kilometer cost driver?

b. What is wrong with using kilometers as a cost driver?

c. Allowing for a 10% profit, what should the road contractor's bid be using the multiple cost drivers suggested by the accountant?

During the last 10 months, Arcade Corporation has had the following indirect costs. It is trying to determine a good cost driver for the indirect costs. The usage of two potential cost drivers, direct labor hours and machine hours, has been recorded over the last 10 months.

NP 3.11
Use of Regression to Choose Cost Drivers
(LO 5)

Month	Indirect Costs	Direct Labor Hours	Machine Hours
1	$3,200,000	5,000	3,000
2	3,600,000	5,100	3,400
3	3,800,000	5,400	3,500
4	3,500,000	5,200	3,300
5	2,800,000	5,000	2,900
6	4,000,000	5,500	4,000
7	3,500,000	5,100	3,400
8	3,700,000	5,400	3,800
9	4,200,000	5,700	4,200
10	2,500,000	4,500	2,600

Which cost driver is most closely associated with the indirect costs?

A CPA firm treats its secretarial pool as an indirect cost for its three major services: auditing, tax, and consulting. The estimated costs of the secretarial pool are $300,000 for the year. The firm is considering the following cost drivers with the corresponding usage by each service.

NP 3.12
Activity Costs Traced to Products
(LO 5)

Cost Driver	Auditing	Tax	Consulting
Number of telephone calls	800 calls	100 calls	100 calls
Dollars of revenue	$4 M	$4 M	$4 M
Hours working on projects	4,000 hours	4,000 hours	2,000 hours

a. Which cost driver appears to most accurately reflect the costs of the secretarial pool?

b. How are the secretarial pool costs traced using each cost driver?

c. Why might the CPA firm decide to use a cost driver other than the one that most accurately reflects the costs of the secretarial pool?

A dialysis clinic offers two services, hemiodialysis (HD) and peridoneal dialysis (PD). HD requires patients to come to the clinic three times a week to receive treatment. PD allows patients to administer their own treatment daily in their own homes. The profit analysis of the two services follows:

NP 3.13
Activity-Based Costing
(LO 6)

	Total	HD	PD
Revenues			
Total revenue	$3,006,775	$1,860,287	$1,146,488
Analyzed service costs			
Standard supplies	664,900	512,619	152,281
Episodic supplies	310,695	98,680	212,015
General overhead	785,825		
Unanalyzed service costs			
Durable equipment	137,046	116,489	20,557
Nursing services	883,280	750,788	132,492

Activity analysis of the general overhead indicated the following costs, cost drivers, and their usage:

Activity	Costs	Cost Driver	HD Usage	PD Usage
Facility costs	$233,226	Square footage	18,900	11,100
Support staff	354,682	Number of patients	102	62
Communications	157,219	Number of treatments	14,343	20,624
Utilities	40,698	Kilowatt usage	563,295	99,405
Total	$785,825			

What is the profitability of the two services under ABC? Calculate the average cost per treatment using ABC.

Source: "Applying ABC to Healthcare," *Management Accounting,* February 1997.

ANALYSIS AND INTERPRETATION PROBLEMS

AIP 3.1
Product Mix Decision
(LO 1)

Jen and Barry's Ice Cream is a small company that makes its own ice cream and sells ice cream cones and cartons of ice cream in a retail space. The company has been known for its 23 flavors of ice cream. The owner of the firm, however, is thinking of adding a 24th flavor, Chocolate Highway. Chocolate Highway is a mixture of chocolate ice cream, macadamia nuts, and chunks of white chocolate. The company currently makes chocolate ice cream, but none of its other products uses macadamia nuts or white chocolate.

What costs should be considered in deciding whether to add Chocolate Highway to Jen and Barry's product mix?

AIP 3.2
Identification of Direct Costs of a Service Organization
(LO 3)

Avant Airlines is attempting to estimate the direct cost of flying a passenger from Austin, Texas, to Los Angeles, California. The direct cost estimation is the initial step in determining a new pricing strategy for the firm. A careful examination of operations, however, indicates that very few costs can be traced directly to a specific passenger on a flight.

Identify the direct costs of servicing an airline passenger. Explain how they could be measured.

AIP 3.3
Level of Indirect Costs
(LO 4)

Describe the following activities as producing unit-level, batch-level, product-level, or facility-level costs.

a. Sending truckloads of products to customers.
b. Providing data processing services for the office.
c. Operating a machine to make products.
d. Setting up machines to make different products.
e. Applying for patents on products.
f. Accounting for sales transactions.

_____ **a.** ABC is likely to benefit multiproduct firms more than single-product firms.

_____ **b.** A move from a single unit-based cost driver to ABC is likely to shift overhead from low-volume products to high-volume products.

_____ **c.** ABC improves the ability to trace direct costs to products.

_____ **d.** With ABC, all cost drivers should be correlated with the number of units of output.

_____ **e.** The application rate per cost driver is normally calculated at the end of the period.

AIP 3.4
Activity-Based Costing
(LO 6, 7)
True or False

A railroad company is trying to decide how to charge its customers for carrying freight. A manager suggests the following would be a good measure on which to base the price: Multiply the weight in kilograms times the distance traveled in kilometers.

a. What types of customers is the railroad company likely to lose to other transport companies if it decides to charge customers based on the manager's suggestion?

b. Suggest a pricing system for freight based on the concept of activity-based costing.

AIP 3.5
Levels of Indirect Costs
(LO 4)

In an article in *The Wall Street Journal*, Thai Airlines announced that it was reducing costs by reducing the different types of airplanes that it flies from 15 to 5 and was reducing the number of different types of airplane engines that it would use. The company was not planning to reduce the number of airplanes in its fleet but only the composition of the fleet.

a. How does the reduction in the different types of planes and engines lead to cost reductions?

b. How does this action relate to the different levels of indirect costs?

Source: The Wall Street Journal, February 27, 1995, B 8B:5.

AIP 3.6
Cost Reduction
(LO 4)

The City of Progress is considering a reimbursement fee to recover costs of its fire department when the local court finds the parties responsible for a fire guilty of gross negligence. If the program is successful, the city might extend the program to all emergency services and be able to reduce the local property tax levy. The city currently uses labor hours to trace costs to different services. The cost per labor hour is determined as follows:

AIP 3.7
Costs of Providing a Service
(LO 3, 8)

Annual salaries and benefits (12,480 hours)	$225,000
Education and training	50,000
Property and liability insurance	40,000
Depreciation of building and equipment	65,000
Operating supplies	25,000
Utilities	20,000
Total annual costs	$425,000

Cost per labor hour = $425,000/12,480 = $34.05/Labor hour

The fire department currently performs many services including (1) fire fighting, (2) medical assistance, (3) hazardous waste removal, (4) rescuing pets, (5) search and rescue, (6) community service at local schools and the senior citizen center, (7) training, and (8) maintenance of equipment. The latter three activities account for more than 80 percent of the annual labor hours.

Is the $34.05/labor hour fee an accurate measure of the cost of fighting fires due to gross negligence?

A fast-food restaurant is trying to determine the cost of its two services, counter service/eat in and drive through/take out. Describe the typical activities associated with a fast-food restaurant.

Which activities are common to both services and which activities are related to only one?

AIP 3.8
Activities Related to Products
(LO 2)

AIP 3.9
Activity-Based Costing
(LO 7)

Critically discuss the following quotation:

> ABC (activity-based cost) information, by itself, does not invoke actions and decisions leading to improved profits and operating performance. . . . For ABC systems to be effective, everyone in the company—from top management to operating personnel—must view them as cost management tools rather than as accounting tools. To achieve this objective, the accounting or finance department must relinquish ownership of these systems to the users. If accounting or finance fails to understand this key point, then ABC is unlikely to succeed. . . . While traditional systems are the property of accounting and are used to support the financial accounting process, successful ABC systems are owned by the functions and are designed to support the needs of cost management, not financial accounting. The result is a reduction in the role of accounting in the management of costs. Most companies that implement ABC systems run them in parallel to their financial accounting systems. Parallel systems remove the risk of compromising the cost management capabilities of ABC to accommodate financial accounting rules and regulations.

Source: Robin Cooper, "Look Out, Management Accountants," *Management Accounting*, May 1996, pp. 20–21.

EXTENDED ANALYSIS AND INTERPRETATION PROBLEM

AIP 3.10
Pilot Plant

Bion Company has an R&D building which is shared by three R&D groups: High Voltage, Medium Voltage, and Low Voltage. Adjacent to the R&D building is Pilot Plant, a small-scale production facility designed for limited runs of experimental and commercial products. The three groups rely on Pilot Plant to produce samples of their formulations.

At Pilot Plant, sample sizes vary from about 1,000 kilograms to 10,000 kilograms. The R&D groups, including Pilot Plant, are run as cost centers. Pilot Plant also accepts special production runs for external customers that are too small for a regular plant. Pilot Plant consists of three combination blending/extruding machines, which produce pellets of compounded material. Unlike large commercial compounding machines, which can operate 24 hours per day, these machines are run for approximately 2,700 hours a year. In the past, Pilot Plant costed its jobs based on direct materials, variable machine time, and allocated overhead. Overhead is allocated by machine time. A single plantwide machine rate is calculated pooling all three machines. The overhead pool includes plant fixed costs plus the labor cost of the pilot plant.

Approximately 20% of the machine technicians' time is spent performing general cleanup and maintenance. Before each job, machine time is calculated by a computer program, which outputs feed rate and set-up parameters. Each product is scheduled to a specific machine based on its formulation. The cost schedule of each machine follows. Capacity represents the historical annual average capacity.

	Cleanup (hours/batch)	Capacity (kg./yr.)	Variable Cost ($/hr.)	Technicians
Machine 1	4	250,000	25	2
Machine 2	6	250,000	25	2
Machine 3	8	500,000	50	1
Fixed costs $200,000/yr.				
Labor costs				
1 manager @ $ 45,000/yr.				
6 technicians @ $ 30,000/yr.				

While formulations vary considerably, 90% of the blends are either resin or flame-retardant magnesium hydroxide. These bulky materials normally are ordered one to two weeks ahead of time and take up much of the floor space. The additives are quite standard and are kept in stock. Weigh-ups and general set-up are time consuming and vary from job to job; a formulation that requires seven additives takes considerably more time to prepare than a similar run with two additives. Time spent on set-up has not been tracked, but it is a simple matter for the technician to include these numbers with the run report. One of the technicians is not assigned to a particular machine but is responsible for arranging stock on the floor. Technicians work 2,000 hours per year. The manager spends most of his time scheduling runs and attending to administrative work.

In a typical job, total weigh-up time is the amount of labor time required to locate, prepare, and mix the direct materials prior to inserting them in the machine.

Job #71302

Composition and Direct Cost

Sample run 5,000 kg.:	90%	NCPE-0600, Resin	$0.10/kg.
	8%	Kisuma, Flame Retardant	$0.12/kg.
	2%	Compound Z, Anti-Oxidant	$0.14/kg.

| Run on Machine 1 | 250 kg. per hr. for 20 hours |
| Total Weigh-Up Time | 16 technician hours |

a. Calculate the cost of the sample run as charged to Low Voltage group.
b. What is wrong with this system? Construct an alternative costing system and describe its benefits.
c. Recalculate the cost of this run using this new system.

Source: B. Graham, R. Mardsen, J. Quinn, P. Leparulo, N. Ahmed, and J. Vallandingham.

Chapter**Four**

Managing Activities

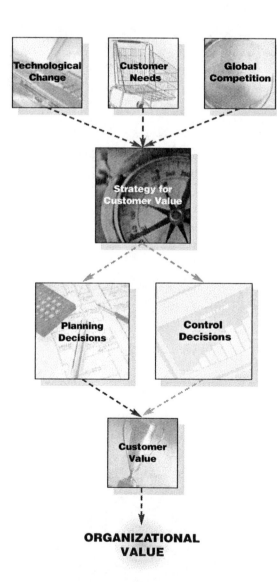

DELL COMPUTER CORPORATION

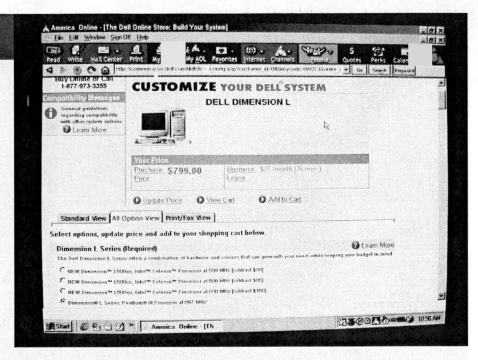

As the individual behind Dell Computer Corporation, Michael Dell is recognized for his vigilance in keeping the company focused on the customer. Dell designs, develops, manufactures, markets, services, and supports a wide range of computer systems, including desktops, notebooks, and network servers. From its base in Round Rock, Texas, Dell conducts operations worldwide through wholly owned subsidiaries. Its products are sold in more than 140 countries. Dell has experienced many changes in its business and market since it began operations in 1984, when it operated from a bedroom in a university dormitory. Sales have gone from $6 million in its first year to almost $30 billion.

The implementation of the appropriate strategy is necessary to achieve organizational goals, but many external factors also affect Dell's business success. These factors include the general economic and business environment, the level of demand for computers, and the level and intensity of competition in the computer industry. In an era of global markets and technological change, Dell has attempted to keep pace with changing customer needs. For example, while many firms are just beginning to confront the challenges of e-commerce, Dell reacted swiftly to the Internet; it introduced online shopping in 1995, well before many competitors were aware of the opportunity.

Technological Change

STRATEGIC DECISIONS

**Strategy for
Customer Value**

Customer Value

The two groups of planning decisions are strategic and short term. Strategic decisions have long-term implications and go beyond the confines of the organization to determine how it should operate in a global economy. Strategies must consider the organization's strengths and weaknesses and how it can take advantage of market opportunities. These market opportunities occur when an organization can add greater customer value than competing organizations can. Strategic decisions are normally made by the organization's leaders to provide focus and direction. This chapter focuses on strategic decisions and their management accounting implications.

Members of an organization must also make shorter-term planning decisions. Every day, managers must decide how many units of different products to make, how to use scarce resources, and how to modify activities to make the organization operate more efficiently. With short-term planning decisions, most of the organization's resources are fixed. In the short term, the organization is not able to change the capacity of its facilities. Therefore, managers must make decisions based on using the existing space. Short-term decisions are also required to adapt to minor changes in market conditions. Chapter Five is devoted to short-term planning decisions.

For a strategy to be successful, an organization must continually adapt to customer needs and do so better than its competitors do. In Chapter One, the critical success factors were defined as innovative product/service design, high-quality products and services, and low-cost production. Each of these strategies offers an opportunity to compete, but an organization must identify its comparative advantages before selecting a strategy.

Organizations that choose to compete through innovative product and service design must excel at understanding their customers through marketing efforts. The organizations must be creative and fast moving to meet their customers' changing needs. Excelling in design and engineering is critical. Changes in technology often open windows of opportunity, so organizations that compete through innovation are usually on the cutting edge of the technological revolution. Nokia, the world leader in cellular telephones, keeps ahead of the competition by offering the latest technology. Nokia's strategy is to introduce new products yearly, such as its move into Web-surfing smart telephones, preempting other market players.

Organizations that choose to compete through the delivery of high-quality products and services must excel in manufacturing and the delivery of customer services. When customers contract with an organization, they expect products and/or services with specific characteristics. The delivery of products and services that do not meet those expectations will cause customers to look for other suppliers. Alternatively, if customers can rely consistently on an organization to deliver products and services that conform to their expectations, customers gain considerable value from repeat purchases from the organization. Amazon.com, the Wal-Mart of the Internet, strives to meet customer expectations by using technology to determine customer needs and to make these products readily available. Success is measured in terms of repeat customers who represent about 70% of Amazon.com's sales.

Organizations that choose to compete through low-cost production excel through efficient operations. These organizations achieve lower production costs by carefully analyzing the different activities that they perform. Amazon.com also competes by providing low-cost goods and services. Compared to its rival, Barnes & Noble, Amazon.com offers lower prices as a result of lower investment in fixed costs, such as warehouses.[1] Much of the remaining chapter examines ways to reduce costs by analyzing activities.

---

[1]*BusinessWeek Online,* "The e.biz 25," September 27, 1999, and "A New Era of Bright Hopes and Terrible Fears," October 4, 1999.

1. How do strategic decisions differ from short-term decisions?

2. What are the critical success factors that add customer value?

Dell's value chain is customer focused. Its goal is to deliver the best customer experience through direct, comprehensive customer relationships, cooperative research and development with technology partners, custom-built computer systems, and service and support programs tailored to customer needs.

    Dell's value chain begins with the initial product design. Direct customer relationships provide Dell with a flow of information about its customers' plans and requirements. This market intelligence enables Dell to weigh customer needs against the company's products and services. The design stage incorporates this customer information to better understand end users' needs and to deliver high-quality computer products and services tailored to meet those needs.

DELL COMPUTER CORPORATION
(Continued)

ACTIVITY-BASED MANAGEMENT AND THE VALUE CHAIN

In Chapter Three, activities were analyzed to determine product costs. Activity-based costing (ABC) was originally developed because traditional methods appeared to be providing misleading product costs. ABC provides an alternative way to trace costs to products that, in some cases, leads to very different product costs. Better product cost information alters either product prices or the product mix.

In Japan, ABC has not been well received. Japanese managers work in a highly competitive environment and cannot change the prices of their products. Their goal is to be the low-cost producer. In their view, ABC is just another way to trace costs without obtaining any insights on how to reduce costs. For ABC to become more useful in these Japanese companies, it must be expanded and integrated with the strategy of low-cost production.

Activity-based management (ABM) extends ABC by analyzing the management of activities instead of simply retracing the costs of activities. The goal of ABM is to provide value to the customer and provide profit to the shareholders. ABM connects ABC to the organization's strategy.

ABM achieves its twin goals of achieving customer value and providing shareholder value primarily by analyzing activities along the value chain. The value chain identifies those activities that affect the value received by a customer from purchasing the organization's products or services. As discussed in Chapter One, those activities that add value to the customer are called *value-added activities,* which are described in an organization's value chain. The value chain for the production of a motion picture would be as follows:

> Writing the script → The actors → Designing sets and costumes →
> Shooting the film → Editing → Delivering the film to theaters

Each activity in the value chain is critical to the value derived by a customer viewing the film.

Another example of a value chain is for the manufacturer of oak chairs:

> Design → Acquisition of materials → Cutting → Sanding → Assembly →
> Finishing → Marketing → Distribution → Customer service

L0 2 Use activity-based management to reduce the organization's costs without affecting customer value.

ORGANIZATIONAL VALUE

Customer Value

**Planning
Decisions**

Each of these activities is critical to making the oak chair and satisfying the customer.

Service organizations would likely have different types of value chains. For example, a university might have a value chain similar to the following:

Research and development → Teaching →
Student services → Placement → Alumni relations

Research and development includes activities such as developing curriculum, making teaching plans, and acquiring knowledge for use in the classroom. Teaching is the activity of communication and discovery in the classroom. Student services include other learning activities and advising. Placement involves helping students find employment. The alumni relations function maintains communications with alumni. Each of these activities adds value to the student but is part of the cost of the students' education.

Organizations also perform activities that are not on the value chain called *non–value-added activities*. Discussed earlier, non–value-added activities have no effect on customer value. For example, customer value is not affected if products are moved from the manufacturing floor to inventory, if products remain in inventory for any length of time, or if machines are set up for a production run. In addition, many administrative activities have no direct effect on customer satisfaction. Each of these activities has a cost without providing any direct benefit to the customer. Therefore, the identification and measurement of non–value-added activities give some indication of cost-saving opportunities for an organization.

Activity-based management implies a cross-functional approach to management rather than managing the functional areas such as manufacturing, engineering, finance, and customer service separately. Activities tend to be performed by employees of multifunctional groups. Activity analysis and the search for cost-reduction opportunities require input from employees of different functional areas. The use of multifunctional teams provides a means to foster information sharing and is consistent with ABM.

An analysis of activities through ABM should also lead to a comparison of how other organizations perform those activities. An organization should look at the "best practices" of other organizations to establish a benchmark for evaluating its own practices. If a particular activity can be performed better and at a lower cost by another organization, there may be an opportunity to outsource that activity. **Outsourcing** is a decision to pay some other organization to perform certain activities. The decision to outsource an activity is based on the cost of performing the activity in-house versus the cost of paying another organization to perform it. Publishing companies, for example, may outsource editing and printing. Universities often outsource food service and bookstores. Organizations that outsource essentially all of their activities are called *virtual organizations*. Omnicom Group is a virtual organization that provides communications services to clients by acting primarily as a facilitator between the client and the service provider rather than undertaking the work itself.

The outsourcing decision should also consider quality and timely delivery. If outsourcing an activity means reduced quality control or late deliveries, the organization should reconsider its decision. Many U.S. companies outsource certain activities to organizations in other countries because of lower costs. However, if lower costs are accompanied by reduced quality and slow delivery, these companies might be better off performing the activity in-house.

Outsourcing is also associated with an ethical dilemma. An example of this conflict is the 1998 strike at General Motors (GM). Workers at the Flint Metal Center and Delphi Flint East plants went on strike because GM continued to outsource jobs to Mexico, Thailand, and South America. Union leaders accused GM of breaking its social contract with U.S. workers to provide good-paying, secure jobs. Alternatively, GM stated that its plants needed to be more efficient to compete with nonunionized plants operated by foreign firms, such as those in Japan and Europe. Greater efficiency would create value for shareholders and help GM to remain competitive. After seven weeks, the strike was resolved when GM promised to invest in new equipment and keep the plants open. In 1996, two other GM plants had struck over the outsourcing issue. That strike was settled when GM agreed to update a brake factory in the United States to make it more competitive, but GM maintained the right to outsource in the future if it was cost effective.[2]

Global Competition

Numerical Example | **4.1**

An Internet retailer of home furnishings purchases furniture from different manufacturers. The furniture is shipped to the company headquarters in Kansas City, where it is stored until sold. The furniture is then shipped to the customer using the company's truck fleet. The activities, their costs, and the cost of best practices for the different activities follow:

Activity	Cost	Cost of Best Competitor
Purchasing	$5,000,000	$6,000,000
Shipping to Kansas City	3,000,000	2,000,000
Receiving	500,000	600,000
Warehousing	2,000,000	2,000,000
Web page maintenance	800,000	600,000
Order processing	4,000,000	4,500,000
Shipping to customer	3,000,000	2,000,000

What activities are potential sources of cost savings?

Solution

Three of the activities are not on the value chain. Shipping to Kansas City, receiving the furniture, and warehousing don't add value to the customer. Those activities could be replaced by having the manufacturers ship directly to the customer. Therefore, the activity of shipping to the customer using its own fleet should be reexamined. Purchasing and order processing appear to be operating efficiently when compared to the cost of the best competitor, but Web page maintenance is a potential source of cost savings either through improvement or outsourcing.

Concept**Review**

1. How does activity-based management help an organization?

2. How can the analysis of activities lead to outsourcing?

---

[2] http://cnnfn.com/hotstories/companies/9806/15/gm_a/; http://www.n-jcenter.com/1998/Jun/15/BIZ2.htm.

**DELL
COMPUTER
CORPORATION**
(Continued)

After the design has been completed, the next link in Dell's value chain is the actual production of the computer system. Production of computer systems on demand allows customers to "design" the system to include the features and capabilities to match their specific requirements. Via the Internet or telephone, customers can configure the system that best matches their preferences at a price that represents fair value.

Once the computer is produced, the next stage is its delivery to the customer. Courier service delivers the product right to the customer's doorstep. The direct relationship continues after the sale as dedicated account teams of sales, customer service, and technical personnel continue to support the customer's technology objectives.

Since Dell operates in a highly competitive industry with short product life cycles, it must eliminate activities that do not create customer and organizational value. Internal as well as external factors affect Dell's performance and must be carefully monitored. One method used to monitor and create organizational value is activity-based analysis and management.

For instance, Dell must effectively manage periodic product transitions and component availability and develop new products based on new or evolving technologies and the market's acceptance of those products. Inventory control is necessary because Dell must balance its inventory levels to minimize excess stock. The risk of obsolescence also is high when product life cycles are short. Finally, activities are performed by individuals, and Dell must continue to improve its infrastructure (including personnel and systems) to keep pace with the growth in its overall business activities.

Dell analyzes its various activities to determine which are essential to create shareholder and customer value. Some activities, such as carrying inventory, do not add value and possibly could be eliminated. Their elimination might reduce costs and improve the company's bottom line.

At Dell, short product life cycles see models quickly replaced by new ones offering more features, often at less cost. Inventory management is critical to ensure that customers obtain the computer that meets their needs and to minimize the risk of obsolete products. ABM is one tool that Dell uses to reduce or eliminate non-value-added activities such as carrying excess inventory, and to determine which activities are essential to create customer and shareholder value.

COST REDUCTION

Cost reduction must be continually on the minds of managers of organizations. Low-cost production is one of the primary ways that organizations compete in a global economy. With strong competitive pressures, organizations have very little control over prices. Therefore, an important way to improve profit is to decrease costs.

Activity-based management is one approach to reducing costs. The identification and reduction of non–value-added activities can increase profits by lowering costs. Outsourcing certain activities is another way to reduce costs.

In the next two sections, two other cost reduction approaches are examined: product life cycle and target costing.

Product Life Cycle

A strategic approach to making product mix and pricing decisions and looking for cost reduction opportunities requires a broad perspective of the product and the way it adds value to the customer. The **product life cycle** describes all stages of supplying a product or service from its initial conception to the satisfaction of the last customer and the product's removal from the marketplace. The product life cycle recognizes that product costs are more than just the costs of making the product. An organization incurs considerable costs related to a product before the first unit is made and it incurs them after the product is sold because of delivery costs and customer service. These costs are incurred over the whole life of the product, which may be as short as a month or as long as 50 years. Computers and other electronic equipment tend to have very short product lives since new innovations quickly cause existing products to become outdated. Other products such as corn flakes have been around for many years and are still popular.

LO 3   Make trade-offs in the product life cycle to reduce overall product costs.

Planning Decisions

The product life cycle begins with the initial planning and proposal stage. Organizational activities at this stage include marketing surveys to determine customer demand, analysis of demographics to evaluate customer characteristics, analysis of competitors, and evaluation of the organization's strengths and weaknesses.

When a proposal is accepted, the product or service is designed and engineered. During the design and engineering process, comparisons are made with leading competitors' products and services, a process called **benchmarking.** The design stage is usually extremely important to the success of the product or service. Although the design and engineering activities themselves may not be very costly, the design and engineering stage predetermines the major cost of providing the product or service. Once the design is completed, most of the necessary raw materials, manufacturing activities, and labor requirements have been determined.

Production is the stage of manufacturing a product or providing services. Most product and service costs are incurred at this stage. Activities during the production stage include acquiring resources, setting up machines to manufacture the product, assembling the product, and providing the product or service to the customer.

Once production begins, the organization must engage in distribution and customer service activities. It does not end its relationship with the customer at the time of the sale. An organization should monitor customer satisfaction and obtain information on ways to improve the product or service. It should also support customers who are dissatisfied with the product or service through warranties and repairs to faulty products.

Each of these stages contains activities that are costly to perform. If the product life cycle is likely to be very long, a useful exercise in analyzing the cost of a new product is to estimate the costs of the different stages over the product's life. Occasionally companies forget to recognize the costs of initiating the product and of customer service in estimating the cost of a product. Table 4.1 presents costs that occur over the product's life.

The costs at the later stages are heavily influenced by the decisions made during the earlier stages. The planning and design stages commit the organization to most of the costs of providing a product or service. For example, the design stage determines the type of materials necessary to make the product. Unless the organization can find a cheaper supplier of materials, their cost is determined when the

Table 4.1

Costs of Different Stages in Different Years of the Product Life

Stage	2000	2001	2002	2003	2004	Totals
Design	$100,000	$ 50,000				$ 150,000
Marketing	20,000	40,000	$100,000	$ 30,000	$ 10,000	200,000
Engineering	80,000	100,000	10,000	10,000		200,000
Production		100,000	800,000	700,000	100,000	1,700,000
Customer service			30,000	40,000	50,000	120,000
Total product cost						$2,370,000

Figure 4.1

Product Life Cycle and Costs

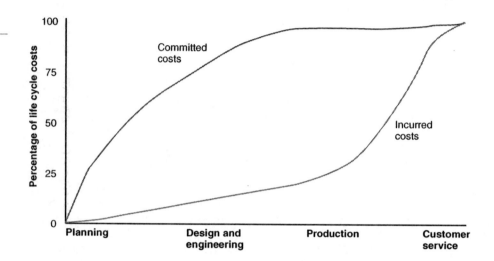

product is designed. The cash outlays to buy the materials, however, are delayed until the production stage begins. Figure 4.1 is a graph identifying the stages when product costs are committed and when cash outlays are made.

Since many product and service costs are predetermined during the earlier stages of the product life cycle, management accountants should be involved in these stages. If they become involved only during the production stage, their opportunities to influence the product or service cost through cost-savings decisions are limited.

Typical decisions related to the product life cycle involve trade-offs among the different product life cycle stages. For example, more effort and cost during the planning stage can reduce customer service costs; a well-planned product is more likely to satisfy customer demand and less likely to cause customer complaints and returned merchandise. Design and engineering efforts also can reduce production costs. Boeing has spent considerable time and effort using three-dimensional designs for its aircraft; these three-dimensional designs are costly to prepare but reduce production costs because potential problems in the production stage can be identified much more easily than with two-dimensional designs.

The cost of the product to the customer does

Skiers seeking the exhilaration of the perfect ski run are known to upgrade their gear with the most recent equipment. Ski manufacturers expend significant costs to develop and market the latest designs. The expected benefits of the incremental costs of a new model or material are the expected incremental revenues from being the first mover with the latest trend to enhance the ski experience.

not end with its purchase. The customer incurs costs to operate, maintain, and dispose of the product. Therefore, the seller can add value to the customer by making the product less costly to operate, maintain, and dispose of. Trade-offs yielding overall cost reductions may involve reduced costs to the customer after purchasing the product. Most tire shops are willing to accept used tires because their proper disposal is costly for individual customers. The United States has only recently become aware of the high disposal costs of some used products, such as the spent fuel rods of nuclear reactors. In Canada and some European countries, disposal costs are explicitly included in the cost of various products.

Customer Value

Numerical Example **4.2**

FastSki is in the process of designing and engineering a new snow ski. Although the current design is acceptable, FastSki is considering new design and engineering efforts that would cost $100,000 and reduce the cost of making a pair of skis by $11. FastSki expects to make and sell 10,000 pairs of this new ski in the coming year. Should it spend the $100,000 to improve the design?

Solution

Spending $100,000 in the design stage will save ($11/pair)(10,000 pairs), or $110,000 in the production stage in the coming year. If production continues beyond the coming year, even more production savings will occur. Therefore, the extra designing and engineering benefit FastSki.

Target Costing

Target costing is a strategic management process for reducing costs at the early stages of product planning and design. It is a common practice in Japan where markets are extremely competitive. The market determines the price of products and there is little opportunity for the individual organizations to set prices. Therefore, controlling costs is extremely important.

With target costing, a product opportunity is identified first. The product opportunity is a description of all of the product's functional characteristics. For example, a new car's functional characteristics include engine size, wheelbase dimensions, interior, and electronic components. At the same time, a price is identified that would make that product competitive. The product opportunity and the necessary functional characteristics are then turned over to the design and engineering department to determine whether the product can be made at a sufficiently low cost to provide a profit for the organization.

Target costing considers all product costs in the product life cycle; its goal is to reduce the total product cost. The target costing process requires a multifunctional team effort because trade-offs in cost reduction may be necessary; the organization does not want cost reduction in one area to be offset by cost increases in another. Using a concurrent design process, team members can share their knowledge of design, marketing, manufacturing, and purchasing so that the final product meets customer specifications. This approach provides opportunities for cost reduction at the design stage since the requirements of the entire product life cycle are recognized then. Target costing reduces the risk inherent in a sequential design process in which one stage, such as manufacturing and marketing, can reject a product because factors were overlooked at an earlier step.[3]

More than 30 years ago, Toyota was one of the first companies to use target costing. Members of its sales division, who are closest to the customers and understand their preferences, identify cars with characteristics that are particularly attractive to customers. For example, dual-side air bags are a component that most customers expect in the cars they buy. The sales staff establishes a price (say, $31,000) for such a car, and estimates the amount of sales for that model. Next, a

LO 4 Use target costing to select viable products and reduce product cost.

Planning Decisions

---

[3]Society of Management Accountants of Canada, *Management Accountants Handbook*, Section 6080.

profit per car (say, $1,000) is chosen to provide the necessary return to undertake the investment. A target cost ($31,000 − $1,000 = $30,000) is then determined to give Toyota the necessary profit. The company then seeks a design that will allow it to reduce costs without losing the functional characteristics. For example, the design team may find ways to redesign the manufacturing process or decrease the number of model-specific parts to reduce costs without affecting customer value. The target cost frequently is less than the initial cost estimate. The design is reworked and milestones are established to reach the target cost. Target costing has allowed Toyota to reduce costs but still manufacture a high-quality car.

Numerical Example 4.3

Targa International's marketing department has identified a new e-mail pager for which customers are willing to pay $300. Required features are an LCD screen, a keyboard, and a roller-wheel mouse. Targa's normal margin is 20% of the sales price. What is the e-mail pager's target cost?

Solution

The margin is (0.20)($300), or $60. Therefore, the target cost is $300 − $60, or $240. Targa must design an e-mail pager that can be produced at a maximum cost of $240. If it cannot do so, it will not be competitive in this market.

Concept**Review**

1. How does an analysis of the product life cycle lead to lower costs?
2. What part of the product life cycle is extremely important in reducing costs using target costing?

DELL COMPUTER CORPORATION
(Continued)

While Dell doesn't compete primarily on price, a key way to increase profits is to reduce costs, especially those related to non–value-added activities. As mentioned, customers don't receive value from inventory handling and storage, nor do they wish to bear the cost of obsolescent products. Therefore, building computers on demand translates into lower space requirements for inventory and lower investments in working capital.

This approach appears to be the model for sure success, yet this has not always been the case. At the end of the 1980s, Dell's sales and net income were growing at impressive rates. However, there was a downside to such rapid growth. To meet the increasing demand for its products, Dell purchased as many 256K memory chips as possible. Prices for memory chips were at their peak but then decreased significantly. One reason for the price drop was the market introduction of 1 megabyte memory chips. Suddenly, Dell found itself with a surplus of expensive, obsolete chips.

Dell was forced to sell off the inventory, which decreased earnings. To compensate for the drop in earnings, it raised its prices. Its growth rate decreased, and its expansion into new countries lost some momentum. After this experience, Dell analyzed its inventory and purchasing activities and adapted them to improve its inventory turnover and to utilize forecasting more effectively to reduce its overall cost of doing business.

Another way to reduce costs relates to Dell's direct customer relationship. This approach allows Dell to reduce the non–value-added costs of wholesale and retail networks. Dell's strategy differs from those of other computer firms, such as Gateway, that compete by using both direct sales and retail networks.

Outsourcing is another way to reduce costs. If Dell can outsource a product or service to an external supplier at a lower cost, it can eliminate one activity and concentrate on those that create organizational value. For example, the components in a Dell computer are produced by outside suppliers who deliver the parts as required. Outsourcing reduces the risk of carrying inventory and helps to reduce costs.

Outsourcing also allows firms to focus on what they do best. For example, in late 1999, Dell and IBM announced an agreement to make IBM Global Services a strategic provider of computer-related services to Dell customers. The arrangement joins the complementary capabilities of a world leader in direct computer systems and of the largest provider of information technology services. In early 2000, Dell began to offer its U.S. corporate, government, and education customers a variety of installation and on-site warranty services from IBM Global Services for Dell's products with later expansion to international markets. Outsourcing services to IBM allows Dell to offer its customers more information technology choices while it concentrates on value-added activities. The result should be better value for customers, which in turn should lead to improved organizational value for Dell.

SUPPLY CHAIN MANAGEMENT AND COSTS

Supply chain management focuses on the management of relations with other organizations. Each organization is a link in a supply chain. Products and services flow into the organization from external suppliers and flow out to customers.

Efficient interactions among different organizations in the supply chain have a substantial impact on reducing costs. The cost of parts and services from external suppliers is becoming a higher percentage of total costs as organizations choose to outsource many of their activities. If an organization is looking for ways to reduce costs, interactions with suppliers is an obvious source given the proportion of costs related to suppliers.

Supplier and consumer organizations interact in many ways. Traditionally, consumer organizations request bids for parts and services from supplier organizations; in fact, most governmental organizations are required to go through a bidding process in selecting a supplier. The qualified supplier who submits the lowest bid is awarded the contract. The danger of this procedure, however, is that the lowest bidder may not always result in the lowest cost when other costs are considered.

Planning Decisions

Estimating the Cost of a Supplier

Suppliers affect an organization's costs in many different ways. The timeliness of the delivery of the parts or services affects costs; a late delivery can shut down an organization, which is an extremely expensive event. The packaging of parts or products from suppliers also has an impact on costs. Some packaging is difficult to dismantle and dispose. Ideally, organizations prefer that the supplier package its parts or products so they are ready for immediate use without requiring unpacking and warehousing or disposing of packaging.

The quality, of the supplier's products or services also affects an organization's costs. Even if an organization can return defective parts, the cost of inspecting them and handling those with defects can be large. A high-quality part is much

LO 5   Estimate the costs of using different suppliers.

easier to assemble and can reduce customer service costs because of reduced customer complaints.

Suppliers also affect purchasing costs. An organization incurs purchasing costs because its purchase agents must contact and communicate with suppliers. Purchasing department staff must write purchase orders, and accountants must record transactions with suppliers and maintain supplier accounts. Accounts payable staff must prepare invoices for payment. Checks need to be issued, frequently requiring the approval and signature of the organization's treasurer. Some suppliers require more purchasing costs than do other suppliers.

Treating the supplier as a cost object can help identify whether it is truly a low-cost supplier. To determine the cost of a supplier, the costs related to delivery, inspection, warehousing, quality, and purchasing must be added to the purchase price of the part or service. Activity costs through the use of cost drivers can be traced to different suppliers.

Numerical Example 4.4

Tip Top Computer Company is looking for suppliers of modems to ship with its computers. The company needs 10,000 modems and has requested bids from suppliers. Tip Top recognizes that the cost of the modems goes beyond their purchase price. Some suppliers require more contact with the purchasing department, which costs the company $50 per contact. The suppliers also have different expected defect rates. Tip Top inspects all incoming modems and discovers about 60% of the defective units. These defective units are returned to the supplier at a cost of $40 per modem. The undiscovered defective modems are sent to customers. When the customer discovers the defect, the cost to the company to replace the defect and provide the additional customer service is $200 per modem. The bids, expected purchase contacts, and defect rates for the suppliers follow:

Supplier	Bid per Modem	Purchase Contacts	Percentage of Defects
A	$20.00	50	1.00%
B	19.50	40	2.00
C	20.50	80	0.50

Which supplier is least costly?

Solution

The number of defects discovered through inspection and by customers is as follows:

Supplier	Total Defects	Discovered through Inspection	Discovered by Customers
A	(0.01)(10,000) = 100	(0.6)(100) = 60	(0.4)(100) = 40
B	(0.02)(10,000) = 200	(0.6)(200) = 120	(0.4)(200) = 80
C	(0.005)(10,000) = 50	(0.6)(50) = 30	(0.4)(50) = 20

To estimate the supplier costs, multiply the bid per modem by 10,000 to determine the cost of each modem; the number of purchase contacts by $50 to determine their cost; the number of defects discovered through inspection by $40 to determine the cost of returns; and the number of defects discovered by customers by $200 to determine the cost of customer complaints.

Supplier	Cost of Modems	Purchase Contacts	Returns	Customer Complaints	Total Cost
A	$200,000	$2,500	$2,400	$ 8,000	$212,900
B	195,000	2,000	4,800	16,000	217,800
C	205,000	4,000	1,200	4,000	214,200

Supplier B has the lowest purchase cost, and Supplier C has the lowest defect rate, but Supplier A has the lowest total overall costs.

Working with Suppliers to Reduce Costs

At first glance, a natural tension appears to exist between a supplier and a purchasing organization. Any change in the price of a part or service reduces one party's profit and increases the other party's profit. Alternatively, the purchasing organization is the customer of the supplier, which should be looking for ways to add value to its customers.

LO 6   Use supply chain management to operate more efficiently and reduce costs.

As noted in the previous section, the cost of a supplier is not determined solely by the price of the part or service purchased. Customers also receive value from innovative features and the quality of the product or service. To improve on the features and quality of the product or service supplied, the supplier must have knowledge of the customer's operations and expectations. Cooperation, therefore, is the key to successful relationships between suppliers and customers.

Suppliers can reduce customers' costs by linking their computer systems through electronic data interchange (EDI). When the customer's computer detects a need for more inventory, it sends a message directly to the supplier's computer. The supplier can then replenish the inventory without the order process. Wal-Mart uses EDI extensively to reduce its costs of ordering inventory. Business-to-business e-commerce allows organizations to interact over the Internet. Cisco Systems handles the majority of its orders via the Internet and has its products delivered directly to customers. FreeMarkets Inc. links suppliers and customers through online purchasing auctions. These auctions decrease purchase time and cost and allow firms to monitor product availability on a global basis. Global marketplaces often increase quality since firms must compete on both quality and cost dimensions to retain their place in these online exchanges.

Receiving, inspecting, warehousing, purchasing, and dealing with defective parts are also costs of working with suppliers. Each of these costs can be reduced through cooperation with the supplier. For example, the supplier can work with the customer to determine the appropriate packaging and delivery locations to reduce receiving costs. If the supplier can guarantee quality levels, the customer can eliminate costs, associated with inspection costs and defects. The customer's purchasing costs, which increase with multiple transactions and interactions with the supplier, can be reduced through long-term relations with suppliers that eliminate the start-up costs of working with a new supplier.

Warehousing costs can be very high for organizations with considerable inventory. Inventory levels and therefore warehousing costs can be reduced through closer links to suppliers. Suppliers who have information about their customers' inventory levels can make timely deliveries to meet customer needs without inundating their customers with excessive inventory. Suppliers of grocery stores use EDI and e-commerce to connect to the store's inventory information system so the grocery store shelves can be replenished in a timely manner.

If an organization operates a just-in-time (JIT) system, its suppliers must have knowledge of the orders it receives. The suppliers must deliver parts and services on demand because a JIT organization has minimal inventory on hand.

Business Analysis

Many older, brick-and-mortar retailers have lost sales to Internet companies. The additional cost of warehouses, stores, and inventory makes competing with Internet companies very difficult. Office Depot, however, has found success in selling through both stores and the Internet. Having stores throughout its sales region actually reduces the cost of the products sold on the Internet.

Office Depot is a retailer of office supplies through 750 superstores and 30 warehouses. The company has both individual and corporate clients. When Web-based retailing became a reality, Office Depot recognized an opportunity to add value to customers by reducing costs. The most obvious reduction in costs was related to the order-taking process. Office Depot estimates that orders taken via the Internet cost 1% of the sales amount while orders taken over the telephone cost 2% of sales. The company also reduced purchasing costs for its clients by installing customized Web pages for 37,000 corporate customers. Under the new system, purchase order costs (including ordering and paying the invoice) have been reduced per order from $100 to less than $25.

Office Depot also has been able to use its vast warehouse system to reduce transportation costs through its extensive local distribution network. Office Depot's size gives it considerable purchasing power when dealing with its suppliers. All of these cost reductions translate into lower product costs for customers and has made the company the leader in Internet sales of office supplies.

How does the operation of both retail stores and Internet sales sites affect the pricing decision? How should sales prices be affected by activities that reduce Office Depot's cost of delivery and its clients' purchasing costs?

Source: Business Week, September 27, 1999.

The discussion of supplier relationships illustrates the importance of interorganizational information systems. For suppliers to serve their customers appropriately, they need to have real-time access to their customers' inventory records. Sharing inventory information with suppliers via EDI and business-to-business e-commerce is common practice.

Concept**Review**

1. What activities add to the cost of working with a supplier?
2. How can an organization work with its suppliers to reduce costs?

DELL COMPUTER CORPORATION
(Continued)

Like its competitors, Dell seeks to gain competitive advantage through supply chain management. By maintaining strong links with suppliers, Dell also develops cooperative, meaningful relationships with the world's most advanced technology companies. Working with these companies, Dell's engineers manage quality, integrate technologies, and design and manage system architecture. The goal is to deliver the right technology to its customers in a competitive time frame.

Supply chain management and build-to-order manufacturing processes enable Dell to work with its suppliers to create customer value. These activities allow Dell to rapidly incorporate new technologies and components into its product offerings. Supply chain management is enhanced through electronic links to its top suppliers. The results of these efforts contribute to a return on investment that is roughly four times that of its nearest rival.

CUSTOMER RELATIONSHIPS AND PROFITABILITY

LO 7   Estimate customer profitability.

The supply chain focuses on an organization's relationships with both suppliers and customers. The previous section described relationships with suppliers, but those with customers also provide opportunities to reduce cost and add value to customers. To add value, organizations must know their customers and be able to identify the most profitable ones.

In the past, most organizations believed that any customer was a good customer. However, organizations now evaluate their customers and are finding that some are not so profitable as others. How do customers differ? Some buy more than others; some customers are farther away and require higher delivery costs. Some customers are chronic complainers or demand additional customer service. To evaluate customers, an organization should treat them as cost objects. Customer-related costs are compared with the benefits of having the customer; in some cases, the cost is higher than the benefit. For example, insurance companies often find that drivers with a history of accidents tend to create costs that are higher than the premiums that they pay. In this case, the insurance company can refuse to provide insurance for those high-risk drivers or increase their premiums.

ORGANIZATIONAL VALUE

Some organizations attempt to educate customers to make them more profitable. For example, golf courses try to educate golfers on appropriate behavior on the course. Slow play and damage to greens can be costly, so most golf courses have rangers on the course to encourage faster play and respect of the course.

A cost/benefit analysis of customers is useful in identifying unprofitable customers and should reveal the type of customer that is the most profitable. When the preferred type of customer is identified, marketing efforts can be focused on that group. For example, banks have found that extensive users of their credit cards are very profitable. Therefore, banks put considerable effort into recruiting new credit card holders.

Numerical Example 4.5

Janice Wilson, a contractor, purchases 1,000 windows annually from Clear Windows, a window manufacturer, for $120,000. The product cost of $80 per window includes the cost of designing and manufacturing the windows but doesn't include transportation or customer service. The cost to Clear Windows for delivering the 1,000 windows to Janice is $10,000. Employees at Clear Windows spend 80 hours a year taking orders, answering questions, and offering other assistance for Janice. The cost of using employee time is $20 per hour. What is the annual net benefit to Clear Windows of having Janice Wilson as a customer?

Solution

The benefit of having Janice Wilson as a customer is the revenue generated from sales, or $120,000. The costs include the following:

Cost of goods sold (1,000 windows)($80/window)	$ 80,000
Cost of transportation	10,000
Cost of service ($20/hour)(80 hours)	1,600
Total costs	$91,600

The net benefit is the benefit ($120,000) less the cost ($91,600), or $28,400.

With customers providing differential net benefits to it, an organization may want to consider differential pricing. For example, customers purchasing large amounts of the product are likely to be more profitable. The organization could give price discounts for large purchases. The next section examines the pricing decision for an organization.

Concept**Review**

1. What types of customers are most expensive?
2. How can an organization work with customers to make them more profitable?

As Michael Dell noted, "From the start, our entire business . . . was oriented around listening to the customer, responding to the customer, and delivering what the customer wanted. Our direct relationship—first through telephone calls, then through face-to-face interactions, and now through the Internet—has enabled us to benefit from real-time input from real customers regarding product and service requirements, products on the market, and future products they would like to see developed. . . . While other companies had to guess which products their customers wanted, because they built them in advance of taking the order, we knew—because our customers told us before we built the product."

Customers are good, but profitable ones are better. Dell has used its customer knowledge to analyze customer needs and to determine what they value and are willing to pay for. Direct customer contact allows Dell to maintain, monitor, and update its database of information about customers and their current and future product and service needs. This information can be used to shape future product offerings and after-sales service activities.

DELL COMPUTER CORPORATION
(Continued)

Service and support activities are designed to fit specific customer requirements. Dell offers a broad range of activities through its own technical personnel and its direct management of specialized service suppliers. These services range from telephone support to on-site customer-dedicated systems engineers.

PRICING AND CUSTOMER VALUE

Customer Value

An important strategic planning decision for an organization is the pricing of its products and services. The pricing decision is complicated and requires knowledge of customers, present and potential competitors, and product costs.

Knowledge of potential customers is probably the most important and difficult aspect of the pricing decision. The products and services offered by the organization are intended to add customer value. Some customers, however, receive more value from the products and services than others do. For example, the value of an airplane ticket from Denver to Miami is much higher to a businessperson going to Miami for an important meeting than it is to someone who is considering a Florida vacation. Customers purchase the product or service only if the value derived is greater than the purchase price.

An organization cannot make pricing decisions without considering its competition, both existing and potential. In a global economy, new competition can arise quickly and set lower prices because of lower labor or material costs. E-commerce reduces barriers to entry by providing global access to markets.

The product cost also is an important element in the pricing decision and serves as a lower boundary for the pricing decision. Products sold below their cost reduce organizational value.

Pricing to Maximize Organizational Value

LO 8   Make pricing decisions that maximize organizational value.

A business organization's primary goal is to create value. Therefore, identifying the price of a product that will maximize its value is important. To determine the price that maximizes value, a manager must know the quantity demanded for the product or service at different prices. The quantity demanded at a given price reflects how many consumers derive value greater than the price. In general, the quantity demanded rises if the price is lowered. Alternatively, fewer customers will purchase the product or service if the price is raised. The following schedule of quantities and prices for kayaks is an example of changing demand with changing prices:

Kayaks Sold	×	Price per Unit	=	Total Revenues
100		$900		$ 90,000
150		800		120,000
200		700		140,000
300		600		180,000
400		500		200,000
480		400		192,000
600		300		180,000

Notice that the number of units that can be sold increases with a decrease in price.

Table 4.2

Revenues, Costs, and Value Added

Kayaks Sold	Price	Total Revenues	−	Total Costs	=	Added Value
100	$900	$ 90,000		$ 80,000		$ 10,000
150	800	120,000		95,000		25,000
200	700	140,000		110,000		30,000
300	600	180,000		140,000		40,000
400	500	200,000		170,000		30,000
480	400	192,000		194,000		−2,000
600	300	180,000		230,000		−50,000

It is unlikely that this kayaker spends his time on the water thinking about marginal costs and revenues. Most firms also do not estimate the marginal cost and revenue of each additional unit. While the purchaser faces one price for an individual kayak, the firm does not set the price on a unit-by-unit basis, but rather estimates costs and revenues for different incremental levels of production and sales.

The maximum revenues are generated when a price of $500 per kayak is set and 400 kayaks are sold. But choosing the price that maximizes revenue does not necessarily maximize value. The product cost at different levels of output must also be estimated. If the variable cost per unit and fixed costs can be identified and measured, total costs at different levels of output are easy to estimate. In the kayak example, suppose that the fixed cost of making them is $50,000 and the variable cost is $300 per kayak. Table 4.2 presents the total revenues, total costs, and value added from making and selling different numbers of kayaks.

Producing 300 kayaks and selling them for $600 per unit creates the highest value added for the organization. The choice of making 300 kayaks can also be made using incremental costs and incremental revenues. The **incremental costs** and revenues are the additional costs and revenues of making more units of a product or service. The incremental revenue of increasing production from 200 kayaks to 300 kayaks is $180,000 − $140,000, or $40,000; the incremental cost is $140,000 − $110,000, or $30,000. Therefore, making 300 kayaks is preferred to making 200. The incremental revenue of increasing production from 300 kayaks to 400 kayaks is $200,000 − $180,000, or $20,000; the incremental cost is $170,000 − $140,000, or $30,000. Therefore, moving below a price of $600 with the production of 300 kayaks causes incremental costs to be higher than incremental revenues and is not preferred.

Economic theory states that the price and quantity should be chosen so that the marginal cost equals the marginal revenue. To determine the marginal cost and marginal revenue, however, total revenues and total costs for each unit must be estimated. Estimating revenues requires precise knowledge of consumers and competitors. Revenue estimates tend to be rough approximations and usually are not made on a unit-by-unit basis. In the kayak example, revenues and costs are estimated at price increments of $100 instead of a unit-by-unit basis. Therefore, incremental costs and revenues are compared instead of marginal costs and revenues. Incremental costs never equal incremental revenues in the kayak example, but they are closest around the price of $600 and the output of 300 kayaks.

ORGANIZATIONAL VALUE

Numerical Example **4.6**

NetLaw networks computers in law firms. The hardware, software, and other variable costs are $100,000 per installation. The fixed costs of operating NetLaw are $1,000,000. NetLaw's president estimates the following levels of sales given different prices:

Price	Expected Sales
$150,000	50
175,000	44
200,000	30
225,000	20

What price per installation should be set by the president to maximize NetLaw's value?

Solution

The revenues and costs for the different levels of production are as follows:

Price	Expected Sales	Total Revenues	Total Costs	Added Value
$150,000	50	$7,500,000	$6,000,000	$1,500,000
175,000	44	7,700,000	5,400,000	2,300,000
200,000	30	6,000,000	4,000,000	2,000,000
225,000	20	4,500,000	3,000,000	1,500,000

Installing 44 network systems for $175,000 each is the preferred strategy.

Pricing in a Competitive Environment

Organizations that choose to compete by offering innovative products or services have a more difficult pricing decision because no price for the new product or service exists. Competitors have not yet duplicated the product or service, which provides the organization some leeway in setting prices. Once competition enters the market, however, the organization has a much more difficult time differentiating its product from competing products. Flexibility in price setting is reduced since customers will switch to a competitor's product if it is priced lower.

With strong competition, a product's price becomes squeezed between its cost and the lowest price of a competitor. Therefore, the competitive advantage shifts to the lowest-cost producer. Organizations that produce at a high cost must consider eliminating the product from its product mix.

Numerical Example 4.7

A textile manufacturer can make the following products: slacks, jeans, shirts, dresses, and socks. The product costs of each item and competitor prices follow:

Product	Product Cost	Competitor Price
Slacks	$10	$15
Jeans	9	8
Shirts	6	9
Dresses	13	20
Socks	2	1

a. What products should be in the manufacturer's product mix?

b. What is the possible range of prices at which the textile manufacturer could offer the products in the product mix?

Solution

a. The textile manufacturer should not make products with a product cost higher than the competitor's price. Therefore, the company should make only slacks, shirts, and dresses.

b. The possible prices should range between the product cost and the competitor's price. Therefore, the prices should be in the following ranges:

Product	Price Range
Slacks	$10–15
Shirts	$ 6– 9
Dresses	$13–20

Cost-Based Pricing

The financial benefits of estimating customer value and the corresponding demand at different prices and then choosing prices to maximize organizational value appear obvious. Many businesses, however, use only costs to make pricing decisions. A recent study reported that approximately 70% of the U.S. businesses surveyed continued to use cost-based pricing.[4]

Cost-based pricing generally uses the average product cost as the base. A percentage is added to the product cost to cover period costs not included in the average product cost and to provide a profit. Some businesses, such as grocery stores, use very low percentage markups over the product cost. Other businesses, such as fine jewelry stores, set prices two or more times higher than their product costs. The choice of the mark-up percentage is based on the relative size of nonproduct costs, the ability to sell the product quickly, and the way competitors are pricing their products.

LO 9   Explain why some organizations use cost-based pricing.

Numerical Example 4.8

A grocery store marks up all items 10%. The cost of a 15-pound turkey is $20. At what price should it be sold?

Solution

The turkey should be sold at (1 + 0.10)($20), or $22.

Setting prices based on the product cost without considering customer value and demand could put businesses at a competitive disadvantage. An analysis of both product costs and the demand for products at different prices is necessary to maximize profit. The following reasons are often given for pricing based only on product costs: (1) difficulty in estimating customer value and therefore demand at different prices, (2) contracts and regulations, (3) long-term customer goodwill, and (4) discouraging competition. Each of these reasons is discussed in the following sections.

Difficulty in Estimating Customer Value

Many businesses have a difficult time estimating customer value and therefore demand for their product or service. The product or service could be new so the marketing group can provide little insight on customer demand. The product or service may have numerous competitors whose reaction to a pricing decision is uncertain. A decision to lower prices may be followed by a similar decision by competitors and may not lead to increased sales. These types of complications make demand estimation very difficult and point out the importance of knowing the customer and competitors well.

After the deregulation of long-distance telephone services, Bell Canada attempted to maintain its market share of long-distance subscribers by reducing its price on its various long-distance services in response to the low rates and special incentives being offered by discount suppliers. However, Bell Canada's action and

Customer Value

[4]E. Shim and E. F. Sudit, "How Manufacturers Price Products," *Management Accounting*, February 1995, pp. 37–39.

that of competitors, such as Sprint Canada, triggered a reduction in rates by all long-distance service suppliers. With all suppliers reducing rates, there was no clear winner in terms of gains in market share. The suppliers, including Bell Canada, were simply selling their services at reduced prices, causing lower profits. All long-distance service firms began to raise rates, for example, by placing limits on "free" calling time with no major changes in market share. This example indicates the dilemma of estimating customer demand for a product at different prices.

Contracts and Regulations

Sometimes sales contracts are based on product costs. For example, a company may agree to build a hydroelectric dam for its costs plus 15%. Contracts with the defense department for complicated equipment commonly base price on product costs. Cost-based contracts often are used when the cost of the product is difficult to estimate before production begins. For example, estimating the costs of a new commercial jet is difficult because much of the technology is untested. By not determining the price until completion, the supplier of the product or service is not forced to bear the risk of uncertain costs. The purchaser agrees to bear the risk by reimbursing the costs plus a certain amount for profit.

Regulated industries, such as utilities, also use cost-based pricing. Utilities are often monopolies, which have no competitors and therefore could set very high prices if they are not regulated. Regulatory boards allow these utilities to sell their service for a price that recovers the cost of the service and provides enough for a reasonable profit for the owners.

Long-Term Customer Goodwill

Temporary reductions in supply or increases in demand allow organizations to set a much higher price than normal. For example, a shortage of gasoline in the 1970s allowed retailers to set very high prices for gasoline. Increased demand for basketball tickets during a winning season allows a university to charge a higher price for them. Organizations with these temporary opportunities do not always adjust their prices to take advantage of excess demand because they recognize that at least some customers will not return to a business that raised prices during a shortage. Newly opened restaurants do not generally charge higher prices than competitors; they recognize instead the greater need for return customers to remain profitable once their novelty has faded. A long-term strategy that ignores short-run opportunities to raise prices may create the most value for the organization.

Discouraging Competition

Global Competition

An organization has flexibility in pricing a unique product or service. Customers do not have the opportunity to shift to a similar product if the price is set too high. If the organization attempts to take advantage of the uniqueness of the product or service by setting a relatively high price, new competitors will quickly introduce similar products and services to share in the success. However, setting a lower price with only a small mark-up on the product cost will discourage competitors from making similar products or services.

Cost as a Lower Boundary for Price

Pricing decisions should consider both the demand for and the costs of providing a product or service. If demand is difficult to estimate, however, the product or service cost offers a lower boundary in making the pricing decision. Pricing a product below its cost reduces the value of the organization. The two exceptions to this rule are lead-loss pricing and predatory pricing. **Lead-loss pricing** is a strategy of selling a particular product at a price below its cost to lure customers with the hope of selling other products. **Predatory pricing** is a strategy of selling a product at a price below its cost to drive out competition. Once competition is eliminated, the organization raises its prices to capture the benefits of being the sole product supplier. Predatory pricing is illegal in many countries. Organizations cannot set prices below costs to eliminate competition.

Concept**Review**

1. What is the economic rule for selecting a price to maximize value?
2. How does a competitive environment affect the pricing decision?
3. Why is the product cost sometimes used as a base for pricing?

The intensity of competition in the computer industry results in pricing pressures and the need to respond quickly to customer needs. Dell is not considered to be the lowest-cost provider of computer systems. Instead, its flexible pricing strategy provides customers with the ability to create the system that matches their needs and their pocketbook. For example, different customers have different needs and preferences; they consider some features necessary and others, such as the best sound speakers to listen to CDs while surfing the Internet, as optional or an indulgence. When building their computers, customers can trade off certain features to arrive at an acceptable price. In addition, Dell's just-in-time system translates into less inventory risk and the ability to change prices quickly as market conditions dictate.

Striving to create customer value by providing what customers want, when and where they want it, ensures the emphasis of activities that add value. The direct sales approach also eliminates the need to support an extensive network of wholesale and retail dealers, thereby avoiding typical dealer mark-ups. This strategy makes it easier for Dell to adapt to the marketplace and to offer more competitive pricing.

Sources: M. Dell with Catherine Fredman, *Direct from Dell: Strategies That Revolutionized an Industry* (New York: Harper-Collins Publishers, Inc., 1999); http://www.webevents.broadcast.com/dell/announce092799/press_release.html; lhttp://www.fastcompany.com/nc/001/012.html, by Scott Kirsner, "The Customer Experience"; Dell Form 10-K, 1998.

DELL COMPUTER CORPORATION
(Continued)

You decide

SUMMARY

1 Select a competitive strategy for an organization. The critical success factors to compete and to increase customer value include offering innovative products and services, high-quality products and services, and low costs.

2 Use activity-based management to reduce an organization's costs without affecting customer value. Activity-based management identifies the non–value-added activities as areas for potential cost reduction.

3 Make trade-offs in the product life cycle to reduce overall product costs. Most costs of a product are predetermined by its design. Improved design

can reduce the cost of manufacturing, delivering, maintaining, and disposing of the product.

4 Use target costing to select viable products and reduce product cost. Target costing identifies the product opportunity first. Then a multifunctional team determines whether and how the organization can offer the product and still make a profit.

5 Estimate the costs of using different suppliers. The cost of a supplier includes the costs of late delivery, inspections, unpacking, warehousing, purchasing, and quality.

6 Use supply chain management to operate more efficiently and reduce costs. Supply chain management focuses on relations with both suppliers and customers. Cooperating and sharing information with both of these groups can reduce costs for all parties.

7   **Estimate customer profitability.** The cost of a customer includes the cost of the product or service sold plus the cost of customer service, freight charges, and collection. These costs should be compared with the revenues from that customer to determine customer profitability.

8   **Make pricing decisions that maximize organizational value.** Organizational value is maximized when prices and quantity of output are chosen at the output level at which the marginal cost equals the marginal revenue.

9   **Explain why some organizations use cost-based pricing.** Cost-based pricing may be used when customer value is difficult to estimate, contracts and price regulations are based on costs, and long-term customer goodwill and competition are factors.

KEY TERMS

benchmarking   The process of comparing an organization's products and activities with those of other organizations to determine best practices. *(p. 111)*

incremental costs   The additional costs of making more units of a product or service. *(p. 121)*

lead-loss pricing   A strategy of selling a particular product at a price below its cost to lure customers with the hope of selling other products. *(p. 124)*

outsourcing   A decision to pay some other organization to perform certain activities. *(p. 108)*

predatory pricing   A strategy of selling a product at a price below its cost to drive out competition. *(p. 124)*

product life cycle   The stages of supplying a product or service from its initial conception to the satisfaction of the last customer and the product's withdrawal from the marketplace. *(p. 111)*

supply chain management   Management of relations with other organizations. *(p. 115)*

target costing   A strategic management process beginning with the identification of a market opportunity and the design of a product or service to meet the market opportunity and make a profit for the organization. *(p. 113)*

SELF-STUDY PROBLEM

Part A

The Kadok Company's design team has recently developed a new product concept: a digital camera for children. The president of the company thinks that it is a good product idea, but she is unsure about how to proceed. She realizes that the decision to begin production of the digital camera depends on competition, customers, suppliers, and the capabilities of Kadok Company. Describe steps that the company should take before committing to production of the digital camera.

Part B

Suppose the Kadok Company has decided to begin production of 100,000 digital cameras for children. The company must decide on a supplier for the plastic case of the camera. Polly Plastics has provided Kadok with a bid of $2 for each case. Kadok has used Polly Plastics in the past and has never had problems with either defects or timing delays. Rainbow Plastics is a new company, which has not previously supplied Kadok. A discussion with other customers of Rainbow Plastics indicates that a 0.1% defect rate should be expected. Rainbow Plastics has entered a bid of $1.50 per case. Each defect is expected to cost Kadok $50 in inspection and return costs. In addition, Kadok will have to spend $20,000 to station an employee at Rainbow Plastics to ensure timely delivery. Which supplier should Kadok use?

Solution

Part A

Competition: Kadok Company must determine if other companies have or are in a position to make digital cameras that can be operated by children. If other companies are already producing digital cameras for children, a close analysis of those products yields critical information. Competition may not come solely from other manufacturers of digital cameras. Although film cameras don't have all of the functions available in digital cameras, their lower prices and simplicity make them attractive.

Customers: A study of potential use of digital cameras by children is also a critical component of the decision to produce. How big is the market? What camera functions are of value to children? What design features make a camera easier to handle by children? What are children (or their parents) willing to pay for a digital camera?

Suppliers: Kadok Company should work closely with its suppliers to determine the feasibility and design of the digital camera. Suppliers can provide design ideas and cost estimates.

Capabilities of Kadok: The existing and potential competition in digital cameras in conjunction with the capabilities of Kadok will help determine the strategy for Kadok. If digital cameras already exist, Kadok can only become a product innovator if it designs a camera with new functions that add value to the customers. If Kadok has a reputation among customers as a high quality manufacturer of cameras, Kadok could enter the market as a high quality producer with good customer service. A third alternative is to become the low cost producer of digital cameras for children. This strategy would require efficient manufacturing processes.

Bottom line: To be successful in this market, Kadok must be able to produce a digital camera that adds sufficient value to customers to cover the cost of production and provide some return to the owners.

Part B

The cost of using Polly Plastics is determined by the bid price ($2/camera case). Total costs are (100,000 cameras)($2/camera) = $200,000.

The cost of using Rainbow Plastics must also include costs of defects and the cost of maintaining timely delivery. Total costs are (100,000 cameras)($1.50/camera) + (0.001 defects/camera)(100,000 cameras)($50/defect) + $20,000 = $175,000.

Based on this analysis, Rainbow Plastics is the low cost bidder. Kadok Company, however, must consider some other costs and benefits of suppliers. Because Kadok has never used Rainbow Plastics, there are start-up costs of interacting with new suppliers. Billing systems and delivery logistics must be established. More suppliers increase the complexity of an organization and, therefore, the costs. Long-term supplier relationships can reduce costs through support in designing and costing new products. Kadok should look closely before deciding to use a new supplier.

NUMERICAL EXERCISES

Applegate Farms is currently selling 100 dozen eggs monthly to Jiffy Super Market for $0.50 per dozen. The manager at Applegate Farms estimates that the cost of feeding and caring for the chickens and collecting the eggs is $0.30 per dozen. Applegate Farms makes four deliveries a month to Jiffy Super Market, which is located 5 kilometers from the farm. The manager of Applegate Farms estimates that the cost per kilometer for the truck and driver is $0.50.

Assuming that no other costs are associated with selling to Jiffy Super Market, what is the monthly profit generated by Applegate Farms from selling eggs to it?

NE 4.1
Customer Profitability
(LO 7)

Benson Shoe Company makes 100,000 pairs of shoes each year. The company has fixed costs of $200,000 per year and variable costs of $10 per pair of shoes. The company would like to have earnings 20% higher than total costs.

What price should the company charge?

NE 4.2
Pricing
(LO 9)

OnAir makes cellular telephones and currently has plans to manufacture the AZZ01 model. By redesigning the case at a cost of $95,000, it estimates that it can cut the number of returned defective units in half. OnAir expects to sell 300,000 AZZ01s in the first year. The company expects that 2% of AZZ01s will require warranty work if the case isn't redesigned. The cost of repairing and returning a defective telephone is $33.50.

Should OnAir redesign the case of the AZZ01?

NE 4.3
Trade-Offs in the Product
Life Cycle to Reduce Costs
(LO 3)

OnAir, a maker of cellular telephones, currently plans to manufacture the TEL99 model. By redesigning the telephone's motherboard at a cost of $495,000, OnAir estimates that it can cut the telephone's production cost by $0.72 per unit. It expects to sell 220,000 TEL99s in the first year.

Should OnAir redesign the TEL99's motherboard?

NE 4.4
Trade-Offs in the Product
Life Cycle to Reduce Costs
(LO 3)

Based on customer demand and competition, a car manufacturer has decided to offer a 100,000-kilometer warranty on all parts. Using current parts and production standards, the warranty will cost the company $100,000,000 per year. Using parts that last longer will cost $40,000,000 per year more but will reduce the warranty costs to $55,000,000 annually.

Should the company use longer-lived parts?

NE 4.5
Product Life Cycle Costs
(LO 3)

NE 4.6
Target Costing
(LO 4)

Jamestown Company has identified customers willing to buy stopwatches with specific characteristics for $20 each. Jamestown wants a 20% profit margin on anything it makes and sells.
    What is the target cost to achieve the 20% profit margin on the stopwatches?

NE 4.7
Estimation of Customer Profitability
(LO 7)

Alpaca Products imports Peruvian sweaters and sells them wholesale. Costcor is a large retailer with 50 different warehouse stores in the Pacific Northwest. Alpaca normally purchases sweaters for $5 each and ships them to the United States via boat for $0.50 each. Alpaca normally sells each sweater for $10, but Costcor is considering the purchase of 1,000 sweaters and wants the price reduced to $8. Costcor also wants the 1,000 sweaters delivered in a month. Alpaca will have to air freight the shipment for $1,000. Costcor also expects Alpaca to put Costcor labels on the sweaters and ship them directly to the warehouse stores. Labeling will require 20 hours of labor at $10/hour, and shipping will cost $0.40 per sweater.
    What is the profit to Alpaca of having Costcor as a customer?

NE 4.8
Estimation of the Cost of Different Suppliers
(LO 5)

Warpco has asked for bids for making 1,000 mechanical arms. Hand Company has bid $10 each, and Elbow Company has bid $11. If Warpco accepts Hand Company's offer, it must send a manager to Hand Company at a cost of $800 to check on the quality of production. Warpco also must test each mechanical arm delivered from Hand Company at a cost of $0.40 each. Warpco has already worked with Elbow Company and would not need quality checks on its mechanical arms.
    Which supplier should Warpco use?

NE 4.9
Use of Product Life Cycle for Planning Decisions
(LO 3)

A nursery has the choice of planting trees in the ground or in pots prior to sale. The pots cost $5 each. Potted trees must be watered 100 times a year, but trees planted in the ground must be watered only 25 times a year. Each watering costs $0.05 in water and labor. When sold, the trees planted in the ground must be dug up with a backhoe. The total cost of digging up each tree and putting its roots in a burlap sack is $10. The average time between planting and sale for a tree is two years.
    Should the nursery use pots?

NE 4.10
Use of Product Life Cycle to Reduce Costs
(LO 3)

Xeron Computer company is considering a design change that would reduce the weight of its desktop computer by 2 kilograms. This design change would cost $300,000 to implement for all computers sold. The cost saving from this change is the reduced shipping cost. The company expects to sell 500,000 more of these computers. The shipping cost is approximately $1 per kilogram.
    What should Xeron Computer do?

NE 4.11
Cost-Based Pricing
(LO 9)

A bank loans money at 8% annually. It generates cash by selling certificates of deposit (CDs). One-year CDs are sold in denominations of $1,000, $10,000, and $100,000. The processing cost of selling a CD is $50 for all denominations.
    What interest rate should the bank offer its customers for each denomination if it wants to limit its costs to 7% net of processing costs?

NUMERICAL PROBLEMS

NP 4.1
Estimation of Costs Related to Suppliers
(LO 5)

A car manufacturer has decided to outsource 20,000 car seats. It asks three manufacturers of car seats (Fast Co., Slow Co., and Steady Co.) to bid on them. They have made the following bids:

	Fast Co.	Slow Co.	Steady Co.
Bid per seat	$100	$90	$105

The car manufacturer has more information on the suppliers as a result of previous business with them. Each supplier's probability of having a late delivery and a defect is different. The car manufacturer uses a JIT system, so a late delivery causes the plant to shut down at a cost of $15,000. Defects are returned to the supplier, but the cost of dealing with the defect is $80 each. The number of defects and late deliveries expected from each manufacturer for the 20,000-seat order follow:

	Fast Co.	Slow Co.	Steady Co.
Number of defects	300	100	20
Number of late deliveries	10	25	0

Which supplier of car seats should the manufacturer use?

Home Town Bank has two types of individual customers who make demand deposits: college students and regular customers. The bank charges college students $0.10 per check, but regular customers get free checking service. The bank earns 10% on the customer deposits by lending money to other clients and pays the customers 5% on deposits. Each type of customer costs the bank $20 in terms of accounting and mailing. The average college student deposit in Home Town Bank is $300; regular customers have average deposits of $1,000. College students write an average of 100 checks per year.

Which type of customer is more profitable for the bank?

NP 4.2
Costs and Revenues Related to Customers
(LO 7)

After an extensive cost/benefit analysis, Mercy General Hospital has decided to outsource its ambulance operations to a private company. The administration has narrowed its decision to two companies that meet the initial bid specifications. Hell's Bell's Company submitted a bid of $50,000 per year plus $30 per hour of actual emergency service. Just-in-Time Company submitted a bid of $100,000 per year plus $25 per hour of actual emergency service. Based on previous experience and trends, the administration expects between 12,500 and 15,000 hours of emergency service work during the next year.

NP 4.3
Estimation of Cost of Suppliers
(LO 5)

a. What is the range of costs for the two ambulance services?
b. What other criteria should Mercy General consider in this decision?

Measer Enterprises produces standardized telephone keypads. The firm operates in a highly competitive market in which the keypads are sold for $4.50 each. Due to the nature of the production technology, the firm can produce only between 10,000 and 13,000 units per month in fixed increments of 1,000 units. Measer has the following cost structure:

NP 4.4
Optimal Output Levels
(LO 8)

	Rate of Production and Sales (000 units) ($ in 000s)			
	10,000	11,000	12,000	13,000
Factory cost, variable	$37,000	$40,800	$44,600	$48,400
Factory cost, fixed	9,000	9,000	9,000	9,000
Selling cost, variable	6,000	6,600	7,400	8,200
Administration, fixed	6,000	6,000	6,000	6,000
Total	$58,000	$62,400	$67,000	$71,600
Average unit cost	$5.80	$5.67	$5.58	$5.51

At what output level should the firm operate?

Four Stars Entertainment is trying to decide what price to charge customers to enter its new amusement park. The cost of operating the park is fixed at $300,000 per day. All rides are free with the price of admission. The expected daily attendance depends on the daily admission fee. Management makes the following estimates:

NP 4.5
Pricing
(LO 8)

Individual Admission Fee	Expected Attendance
$10	20,000
20	15,000
30	12,000
40	10,000
50	7,000

a. What is the marginal cost of another individual attending the amusement park?

b. What price should Four Stars Entertainment charge for admission to maximize profit?

NP 4.6
Management of the Supply Chain to Reduce Costs
(LO 6)

FloorCare manufactures, packages, and sells floor wax to hospitals. Truckloads of chemicals are delivered to FloorCare, which then mixes and packages the floor wax in containers of various sizes. FloorCare maintains an average daily inventory of $500,000 of one chemical, X7666, that is used in all floor waxes. This amount represents one-half month's supply. At the beginning of each month, the current supplier delivers $1 million of X7666 (200,000 liters) to FloorCare. The cost of in-bound freight (paid by FloorCare) is $2,300. To finance its inventory (including in-bound freight), FloorCare borrows money from the bank at 18% per year.

A new supplier proposes to make daily just-in-time deliveries of X7666 for $5.03 per liter, which includes the in-bound freight paid by the new supplier. The quality of X7666 from the new supplier is equivalent to that of the current supplier. The average daily inventory of X7666 with the new supplier's JIT deliveries is 5,000 liters.

a. Should FloorCare switch to the new supplier?

b. What other factors should FloorCare consider before switching to the new supplier?

NP 4.7
Cost-Based Pricing
(LO 9)

A grocery store makes pricing decisions based on cost of the products. All other costs are fixed at $800,000 per year. The average cost of inventory at the store is $1,000,000. The inventory turns over eight times a year.

a. If prices are set at 12% above cost, what is the profit of the grocery store for the year?

b. What is the profit of the grocery store if turnover increases to 10 times per year and prices remain at 12% above costs?

c. What price mark-up is necessary for the company to have a $300,000 profit if inventory turnover occurs eight times per year?

ANALYSIS AND INTERPRETATION PROBLEMS

AIP 4.1
Target Costing and Product Mix
(LO 4)

The Peter Paint Company makes water- and oil-based paints for houses. Recently, the firm has been investigating other opportunities. One possibility is producing finger paints for children. Finger paints are considerably different than house paints since they must be designed and produced to be easily washable. The marketing people at Peter Paint believe that there is an opportunity to enter this new market. They estimate that the company could sell 1 million units of finger paints annually for $1 per unit.

How should Peter Paint use this information in making a decision about adding finger paints to its product mix?

AIP 4.2
Pricing Decision
(LO 8)

Internetco offers a wireless connection to the Internet in Portland, Oregon. The connection is achieved with a remote modem that sends and receives signals through a network of antenna located throughout the city, which has already been established. The customer simply buys the remote modem from the company and then pays a monthly fee for the service. Internetco is attempting to decide what price to charge for the service.

What factors should Internetco consider in making the pricing decision?

AIP 4.3
Value Chain
(LO 2)

FastBike Company manufactures bicycles and is trying to identify which overhead activities are value added and which overhead activities are non-value-added. Describe each of the following activities as value added or non-value-added:

Engineering and designing the bicycle.
Storing the finished bicycles.
Moving the raw materials from the warehouse to the assembly area.
Assembling wheels to the frame.
Providing customer service.

AIP 4.4
Estimation of Customer Profitability
(LO 7)

A bank spends considerable time in evaluating loan applicants for houses, cars, and business reasons. The loan officers must analyze these requests to decide which applicants should be granted a loan.

a. How does the process of evaluating a loan request relate to a cost/benefit analysis of customers?

b. Rather than just making a decision to deny or grant a loan application, what other options do loan officers have in dealing with loan applicants?

In recent years, U.S. businesses have found that providing health insurance for employees is very costly. One approach to containing these costs is the use of a health maintenance organization (HMO). An HMO agrees to cover the health costs of an organization's employees. In return, the organization pays a premium of a certain amount per employee. The HMO then contracts with doctors to provide the health services. Choosing an HMO has been a real dilemma for organizations, however; some questionable suppliers have entered this market and have offered services, been paid the premiums, and then failed to provide the health services. In these cases, the organization still must cover the health expenses. Therefore, the HMO that provides the lowest bid is not necessarily the lowest cost supplier of health services for employees.

AIP 4.5
Decisions Made with Respect to Suppliers
(LO 5)

a. What other factors should the organization consider in choosing an HMO than the bid price?

b. What are other ways of contracting with HMOs to ensure quality health service for employees?

The following article appeared in *The Wall Street Journal* on December 18, 1990:

AIP 4.6
Pricing Services
(LO 8)

> Big brokerage firms, responding to the deep slump in stock-trading volume, are hitting investors with a round of commission increases. Merrill Lynch & Co., the nation's biggest brokerage firm, will raise by 5% the commission rates it charges individuals to buy or sell stocks on any order over $5,000. . . . It is the firm's first commission boost in 4¼ years, and the first for trades over $10,000 in 12 years. (There will be no change in commissions for trades under $5,000.)
>
> Merrill also will boost its handling charges, which cover the cost of processing and mailing transactions statements, to $4.85 a transaction from $2.35. . . . John Steffens, Merrill's executive vice president in charge of private-client businesses, said the firm has been considering raising commissions and fees for some time. "We think [the increases] are justified based on a whole series of things, including postal-rate increases."
>
> "The deterioration in [trading] volumes has pressured a lot of firms to raise commissions to cover their infrastructure costs," said Dean Eberling, a securities industry analyst.
>
> Earlier this year other brokerage houses, including discount firms, raised commissions and fees.

Discuss the issues raised in this article.

The U.S. government often purchases items from suppliers using cost-plus contracts. In the past, the government reimbursed the suppliers for their costs and paid an additional percentage for profit, but many problems were associated with this procedure. Finally, the government established the Cost Accounting Standards Board to identify acceptable accounting practices in determining the cost of a product.

AIP 4.7
Cost Accounting Standards Board
(LO 9)

a. Explain why the U.S. government uses cost-plus contracts.

b. Explain why the government was having problems with the cost-plus contracts.

c. How could the Cost Accounting Standards Board help to alleviate these problems?

Your company makes computer mouse pads. The annual fixed costs are $50,000, and the variable cost per unit is $1. The company president has asked you to choose a price for the mouse pads. A careful study of the competition indicates that a price between $3 and $5 would be appropriate. The president, however, wants to use a cost-based pricing system. She suggests a price that is 100% higher than the average cost. You return to your office thinking that this type of pricing will be simple, but then you become confused in calculating the average cost and the corresponding price.

AIP 4.8
Pricing Based on Cost
(LO 9)

a. What information is missing to calculate the average cost?

b. What is the relationship between a price based on average cost and the amount produced?

c. What is the danger of using any type of cost to determine the price?

AIP 4.9
Choice of Competitive Strategies
(LO 1)

For each of the companies listed, identify competitive strategy using the following categories:

a. Innovative product/service design.
b. High-quality products and services.
c. Low-cost production.

 1. Apple Computer
_____ 2. Wal-Mart
_____ 3. Dell Computer
_____ 4. Mobil Oil service stations
_____ 5. Ritz-Carlton hotels
_____ 6. Nokia cell phones
_____ 7. EBay.com
_____ 8. Southwest Airlines and America West Airlines

AIP 4.10
Identification of Non–Value-Added Activities
(LO 2)

Which of the following activities of a manufacturer don't add value?

a. Purchasing raw materials for production.
b. Inspecting incoming raw materials when received.
c. Shipping completed products to customers.
d. Preparing the machines for production.
e. Producing products on the machine.
f. Cleaning out the machine after production.
g. Scrapping products during production.
h. Storing partially completed products in warehouse until the next machining operation.
i. Inspecting the quality of finished products.

AIP 4.11
Activity-Based Management and Cost Reduction
(LO 2)

A fast-food chain has produced a series of cost benchmarks for various activities within its restaurants. The local franchise of the fast-food chain has made the following cost comparisons for the different activities:

Activity	Local Franchise Cost	Food Chain Benchmark
Cooking	$0.50/Meal	$0.52/Meal
Taking orders and serving	$0.30/Meal	$0.25/Meal
Cleaning	$0.05/Sq. meter	$0.05/Sq. meter
Storage	$0.10/$1 of inventory	$0.11/$1 of inventory
Administration	$7,000/Month	$6,500/Month

On what activities should the local franchise focus its attention to cut costs?

AIP 4.12
Product Life Cycle Costs and Activity-Based Costing
(LO 2, 3)

Manitou Company is trying to reduce its costs to remain competitive. It uses ABC: One of the overhead activities is purchasing. The cost driver for purchasing is number of parts. Based on ABC, Manitou's product designers have decided to reduce the number of parts for each product to reduce costs. For example, a tool manufactured by the company previously was composed of 45 parts but after redesign contained only 40 parts.
    Is this approach to cost savings successful?

AIP 4.13
Pricing and Activity-Based Costing
(LO 1, 2, 9)

Mittelberg Paper Company purchases large rolls of paper from manufacturers. The company then cuts and packages the paper to meet the demand of small printing companies. The company uses ABC to determine the cost of the product and then charges the printing companies an additional 20% for profit. The price calculation for a recent order is as follows:

Activity	Application Rate	Usage of Cost Driver	Cost
Cutting	$5/Cut	30 cuts	$ 150
Packaging	$1/Package	200 packages	200
Storing	$0.60/Package	200 packages	120
Delivery	$4/Kilometer	10 kilometers	40
Administration	$40/Order	1 order	40
Total activity costs			$ 540
Raw materials			300
Total cost			$ 840
Profit (0.20)($840)			168
Price			$1,008

The customer is not happy with the price and threatens to change suppliers.

How should Mittelberg Company reexamine its activities, relation with its customer, and pricing process?

The pricing practices of major oil companies in the United States are coming under close scrutiny. The companies claim that they use cost-based pricing in charging their retail outlets for gasoline. The retail outlets then pass on the costs of the gasoline to the customers. The reason for the scrutiny is that the price of gasoline varies considerably across the United States. Even within the state of California, the price of the same brand of gasoline can vary up to 40% with consumers in Northern California paying much higher prices than those in Southern California do.

AIP 4.14
Cost-Based Pricing
(LO 9)

a.   Why do oil companies claim to use cost-based pricing?
b.   What information would be critical to verify that costs are the basis for price deviations around the United States?

General home-building contractors contract with a person desiring a new home to construct the house according to the architect's specifications at a set price and by a specific date. The price may change if the purchaser of the new home alters the specifications, or if contingencies occur because of unforeseen difficulties (such as dense rock excavation that wasn't apparent until the foundation was dug). The delivery date of the finished home also may change based on agreement between the purchaser and the contractor. If the buyer is under some urgency to move into the house, the contract may include penalties if the house isn't completed on time. In summary, the reward to the general contractor is conditional on building the house to specifications at a sufficiently low cost and on time.

AIP 4.15
Supply Chain Management
(LO 6)

The general contractor usually subcontracts parts of the building to specialists such as excavators, electricians, and plumbers. These subcontractors have significant influence over the cost of the project and how quickly it is completed. Therefore, the reward structure of the general contractor depends on its relations with subcontractors.

What are various methods of working with and managing subcontractors that will help make the general contractor profitable in the long run?

EXTENDED ANALYSIS AND INTERPRETATION PROBLEM

Johnson Industry is a manufacturer of heavy equipment used in road building, forestry, and construction. Although the company has been successful in these areas, the company is looking to expand into other businesses. Farm equipment is considered a possibility. In particular, the company has designed a combine for harvesting wheat. The combine uses a rubber track rather than wheels as a means of locomotion. The rubber track has the advantage of less pressure on the soil and, therefore, less compaction of the soil. The track also has better traction on especially hilly fields. The track-driven combines, however, are more difficult to transport over long distances on highways.

AIP 4.16
Strategy and Pricing

There are six varieties of wheat grown in the United States, but they can generally be categorized as either winter or spring wheat. Winter wheat is planted in the late fall and harvested in the spring. Spring wheat is planted in the spring and harvested in the summer. The following table describes the number of bushels of wheat grown in the top 10 states in 1996.

State	Number of Bushels (Millions)
North Dakota	393
Kansas	255
Montana	190
Washington	183
South Dakota	130
Idaho	117
Minnesota	104
Oklahoma	93
Colorado	76
Nebraska	73

The management of Johnson Industry estimates 5,000 new combines are sold each year in the United States for the harvesting of wheat. The management has developed the following analyses of the competition and potential customers.

Analysis of Competition: There are currently two other major competitors that have lines of combines. Jones Farm Equipment Company works through agriculture cooperatives and provides a low-cost line of combines with prices ranging from $150,000 to $250,000. Their combines have less capacity, power, and longevity than the product designed by Johnson Industry. The combines are normally serviced through the cooperatives.

Jordan Manufacturing produces a line of combines comparable to the combine designed by Johnson Industry in terms of capacity, power, and longevity. Their combines, however, do not currently have tracks although there are rumors that they are thinking of such a product. Jordan Manufacturing has an extensive network of dealership and service units throughout the wheat growing areas. Their combines have prices between $200,000 and $300,000.

Customer Analysis: There are three major groups of customers for wheat combines: (1) traveling crews that move from farm to farm to harvest wheat, (2) large agribusiness farms, and (3) smaller privately owned farms. The travelling crews need combines that are easily transportable. The agribusiness farms and privately owned farms purchase combines for use on their own farms. The agribusiness farms tend to buy a combine almost every year and self-service their fleet of combines. The travelling crews must replace their combines every three to four years and depend on local dealerships to service their combines. Smaller farmers may buy a new combine every 10 years and also require local dealerships for service. Each group of customers purchases about the same number of combines each year.

The purchase of a combine is a big investment for all of the customers. They are all very knowledgeable about the different functions of the combine. They value capacity, power, and longevity and are also concerned about the comfort of the cab. They have heard about Johnson Industry's track-driven combine and are curious about how well it will function.

In addition to the functionality of the combine, the travelling crews and smaller farmers value service. If a combine breaks down during harvest, it is critical that it be fixed immediately. There is a very short window when the harvest can occur. A combine that is out of service for a week can mean the loss of the whole crop.

Johnson Industry has also performed an analysis of its strengths and weaknesses. Its major strength is its reputation for good quality products in other heavy industries. It has an extensive set of dealerships located in states with large construction projects and growth in the housing industry. Johnson Industry's major weakness is a lack of knowledge of the agriculture business. Although farmers recognize the Johnson name, they are uncertain about the ability of the company to offer farm equipment with the appropriate functions and service. Johnson Industry does not have any overseas experience.

Johnson Industry estimates that the variable cost of making its combine will be about $150,000 per combine. Advertising and fixed construction costs are estimated to be $20 million annually. Service units will be self-sufficient if they are located in close proximity to a minimum of 40 Johnson combines.

a. Describe a plausible strategy for Johnson Industry for the production and sales of its combine.

b. Describe a pricing strategy for the combine.

c. Given the pricing strategy in part (b), what percentage of the market must be captured annually to make a profit?

Chapter**Five**

Short-Term Decisions and Constraints

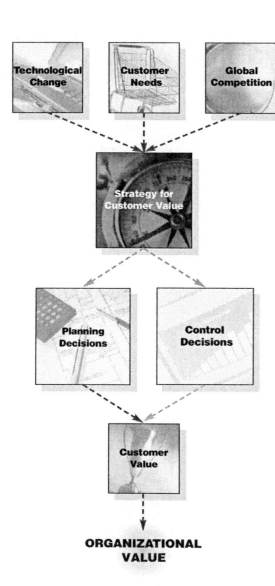

Technological Change

Customer Needs

Global Competition

Strategy for Customer Value

Planning Decisions

Control Decisions

Customer Value

ORGANIZATIONAL VALUE

TOAD HALL BED AND BREAKFAST

In 1880, a wealthy Boston Banker built Toad Hall as a summer home on the shore of a scenic lake in the White Mountains of New Hampshire. Toad Hall is not a small lake cottage. The main house has six bedrooms, and the property has a caretaker house. Toad Hall has remained in the family for several generations, but the current generation can no longer afford the upkeep of such a large vacation property. The family has put the property up for sale for $700,000.

Susan and Ed White live in New York City and have always dreamed of an escape to the country. After reading the advertisement for Toad Hall, they decided to rent a car and drive to New Hampshire to take a look. They were thrilled with the beautiful redwood interior and thought that Toad Hall would make a wonderful bed and breakfast inn. They contacted a local contractor to determine the cost of converting Toad Hall into a bed and breakfast. The contractor estimated that an additional $300,000 would be required to convert the main house into a bed and breakfast with six bedrooms, each with its own bathroom. The Whites figure that they could live in the caretaker house if they bought Toad Hall.

Before purchasing Toad Hall, the Whites make the following estimates of the costs of operating it as a bed and breakfast inn:

Interest on mortgage of $800,000 at 10% (with a down payment of $200,000 on the purchase and the remodeling)	$80,000 per year
Insurance	5,000 per year
Property taxes	10,000 per year
Utilities and maintenance	8,000 per year + $5 daily per rented room
Breakfast ($3/person, 2 people per room)	$6 daily per rented room
Maid service	$15 daily per rented room

After completing this list of costs, the Whites are unsure of how to use them to make a decision.

Susan and Ed check with local bed and breakfast owners and learn that their prices range from $75 to $150 per room. The Whites are aware that the higher the price they charge for rooms, the fewer rooms they will rent.

SHORT-TERM PLANNING DECISIONS

LO 1 Explain how short-term decisions differ from strategic decisions.

Planning Decisions

Strategic planning decisions, such as opening a chain of stores, have long-run implications for the organization. Strategic decisions involve analysis of the strengths and weaknesses of the organization and affect the way it can compete in a global economy. Organizations make strategic planning decisions infrequently. For example, strategic planning often is tied to the budgeting process, which commonly occurs on an annual basis.

Alternatively, short-term planning decisions must be made on a daily basis. Managers make frequent decisions on production, price discounts, use of resources, and modifications of activities. Minor changes in the product mix or price also might be made in the short run.

The defining characteristic of a short-term planning decision is the inability to change the organization's capacity. New factories cannot be constructed in a few days, weeks, or even months. Moreover, entirely new product lines cannot be designed and implemented in the short term. With short-term decisions, managers are limited to the use of existing long-term assets, such as buildings and equipment.

Managers make planning decisions by considering the incremental effect of those decisions. Consideration of incremental effects is appropriate in the short term because much of the environment is fixed and will not be influenced by the decision.

To capture the incremental approach of short-term planning decisions, costs are divided into fixed and variable amounts. Fixed costs reflect the cost of the existing capacity of the activity or product. On the one hand, if the fixed costs have already been incurred, they are sunk and therefore are not relevant to the short-term planning decision. For example, property taxes are paid annually. Once paid, they are sunk until they are due next year. Variable costs, on the other hand, reflect incremental changes and become an important decision variable. This chapter examines short-term management decisions with fixed costs and constraints.

Concept**Review**

1. How do short-term decisions differ from strategic decisions?
2. Why are fixed and variable costs important in making short-term decisions?

TOAD HALL
(Continued)

Susan and Ed estimate that their variable costs are $26 per room:

Utilities and maintenance	$ 5
Breakfast ($3/person, 2 people per room)	6
Maid service	15
Total variable costs	$26/room

COST-VOLUME-PROFIT ANALYSIS

LO 2 Estimate profit and break-even quantities using cost-volume-profit analysis.

Planning Decisions

Cost-volume-profit (CVP) analysis is a method that examines a product's profitability at different sales volumes. As more units of the product are sold, both revenues and costs increase. CVP estimates the change in profit with a change in units sold. It makes certain assumptions about revenues and product costs to simplify the analysis.

The first assumption is the separation of product costs into fixed and variable. Therefore,

Total product costs = Variable costs + Fixed costs
$$(VC/\text{Unit})(Q) + FC$$

Where

VC = Variable cost per unit

Q = Number of units produced and sold

FC = Fixed costs

By assuming that the total product costs are either fixed or variable, capacity constraints are not recognized. The variable cost per unit is assumed to be constant over all levels of production. For example, suppose a cellular telephone costs $10 a month plus $0.08 per minute. The telephone's fixed cost is $10 and its variable cost is $0.08 per minute.

The second assumption is that all units of the product sell for the same price. Every customer pays the same price for the product, and the price remains the same no matter how many units are sold. The revenues generated from the sale of the product, therefore, are calculated as follows:

Revenues = (P)(Q)

Where

P = Sales price per unit

Under CVP, profit from the product is simply the revenues less the costs and can be determined as follows:

Profit = Revenues − Variable costs − Fixed costs

Using the previous assumptions, the profit equation for CVP analysis can be written as follows:

Profit = (P)(Q) − (VC/Unit)(Q) − FC

Rearranging the profit equation yields

Profit = (P − VC/Unit)(Q) − FC

The sales price per unit minus the variable cost per unit is called the **contribution margin per unit,** which is the increase in profit caused by making and selling one additional unit of the product or service. The fixed costs do not change as additional units are made. For example, if the contribution margin of making a car is $5,000, selling 100 more cars will increase profit by ($5,000)(100), or $500,000. Through the contribution margin per unit, CVP analysis is particularly useful in estimating the short-term profit impact of selling more or fewer units.

Numerical Example   5.1

The variable cost of making a pager is estimated to be $10. The monthly fixed costs to operate the facility are $100,000. Each pager sells for $25. What is the expected profit of producing and selling 10,000 pagers? What would be the additional profit of producing and selling 1,000 more pagers?

Solution

If 10,000 pagers are produced and sold,

Profit = (P − VC)(Q) − FC = ($25 − $10)(10,000) − $100,000 = $50,000

The profit from making 11,000 pagers follows:

Profit = (P − VC)(Q) − FC = ($25 − $10)(11,000) − $100,000 = $65,000

Therefore, the additional profit from selling 1,000 additional pagers is $65,000 − $50,000, or $15,000. The additional profit from these additional sales can also be estimated by multiplying the per unit contribution margin times the additional quantity:

Profit = (P − VC)(Q) = ($25 − $10)(1,000) = $15,000

TOAD HALL
(Continued)

Susan and Ed have reevaluated their original cost numbers. They realize that the opportunity cost of purchasing and remodeling Toad Hall should include not only the interest payment on the mortgage but also the forgone interest earned on the $200,000 down payment. If that forgone interest is also at a 10% rate, the opportunity cost of investing $1,000,000 in Toad Hall is $100,000 per year. Therefore, the following are the fixed costs per year of operating Toad Hall as a bed and breakfast:

Opportunity cost of purchasing and remodeling	$100,000
Insurance	5,000
Property taxes	10,000
Utilities and maintenance	8,000
Total fixed costs	$123,000

Variable costs per room rented per day, or room-day, follow:

Utilities and maintenance	$ 5
Breakfast	6
Maid service	15
Variable cost per room-day	$26

As an initial estimate of profit, Susan and Ed assume that they can rent rooms at $80 per night and operate at half of the capacity of Toad Hall. Toad Hall's capacity would be (365 days per year) (6 rooms), or 2,190 room-days. Half of that capacity would be 2,190/2, or 1,095 room-days. With variable costs of $26 per room-day, the expected profit is as follows:

$$(P - VC)Q - FC = (\$80 - \$26)(1{,}095) - \$123{,}000 = -\$63{,}870$$

Susan and Ed are quite discouraged by this estimate.

Break-Even Analysis

CVP analysis also can be used for making planning decisions with longer time horizons. In planning for an investment in a new product, information about the number of units that must be sold to break even or have zero profit is useful. If the organization cannot hope to sell enough units of the new product to break even, then it should not make the investment. **Break-even analysis** determines the sales level in units at which zero profit is achieved. Using variable and fixed costs to approximate product costs, the equation solves for the number of units at which profit equals zero:

Hot-dog vendors face uncertain demand, weather, and competition from other sidewalk stands. Vendors must calculate how many sales are required to be profitable and have enough hot dogs ready to meet demand, while not preparing too many. CVP analysis is one tool that provides a quick way to evaluate different combinations of sales prices, quantities, and costs.

$$0 = (P - VC)(Q) - FC$$
$$FC = (P - VC)(Q)$$
$$FC/(P - VC) = Q$$

The break-even quantity is simply the fixed costs divided by the contribution margin per unit. The Appendix to this chapter outlines additional approaches to calculate the break-even quantity.

Numerical Example 5.2

Laura Gonzalez is a hot dog vendor. She must pay $100 per day to rent her cart and sells her hot dogs for $1. The variable costs of making the hot dog are $0.20 per hot dog. How many hot dogs must Laura sell per day to break even?

Solution

The break-even quantity is

$FC/(P - VC) = \$100/(\$1 - \$0.20) = 125$ hot dogs

Break-even analysis also can be used to determine prices or target costs that are sufficient to cause zero profit. For example, the break-even equation can be solved for the price per unit:

$0 = (P - VC)(Q) - FC$
$P = (FC/Q) + VC$

Numerical Example 5.3

A contractor can build 20 condominiums a year with a fixed cost of $1 million and a variable cost per condo of $50,000. At what price must the contractor sell the condos to break even?

Solution

$P = (FC/Q) + VC = (\$1,000,000/20) + \$50,000 = \$100,000/\text{Condo}$

TOAD HALL
(Continued)

Ed and Susan clearly are not thrilled with their initial profit estimate. So instead of estimating profit given the expected number of room rentals, they decide instead to estimate how many rooms must be rented to break even. They keep their initial cost estimates of $123,000 of fixed costs and $26 of variable costs per room per room-day. They also assume that the daily room rental rate will remain at $80 per room. The break-even number is as follows:

$FC/(P - VC) = \$123,000/(\$80 - \$26) = 2,278$ room-days

This result is even more discouraging since the break-even number is higher than Toad Hall's capacity, which is 2,190 room-days.

The Whites then decide to try to estimate a daily rental rate that will allow them to break even given a 50% occupancy rate (1,095 room-days).

$P = (FC/Q) + VC$
Rental rate $= (\$123,000/1,095) + \$26 = \$138$ per room-day

This rental rate is within the range of rental rates charged by competitor bed and breakfast inns, but it provides no profit for Ed and Susan. They decide to use a $150 per room-day rate in their remaining calculations, which is the highest charged by any competitor in the area.

Achieving a Specified Profit

The profit equation also can be used to determine the necessary amount of a product or service that must be produced and sold to achieve a specified target profit. Instead of setting the profit equal to zero, the profit can be set at a specified amount and the profit equation can be used to solve for the required number of units produced and sold:

$$\text{Profit} = (P - VC)(Q) - FC$$
$$\text{Profit} + FC = (P - VC)(Q)$$
$$(\text{Profit} + FC)/(P - VC) = Q$$

The necessary number to achieve a certain profit is the sum of the profit and fixed costs divided by the contribution margin per unit.

Most firms are interested in the cash flow available after paying income taxes. An extension of CVP analysis provides the number of units that must be sold to achieve a specified after-tax profit. The Appendix outlines the calculation of the necessary quantity to produce and sell to achieve a certain after-tax profit.

Numerical Example 5.4

Suppose that Laura Gonzalez, the hot dog vendor who pays $100 per day to rent her cart, wants to make a $60 profit a day. She sells hot dogs for $1 and the variable costs of making the hot dog are $0.20 per hot dog. How many hot dogs must Laura sell per day to have a profit of $60?

Solution

The necessary quantity to have a profit of $60 is as follows:

$$(\text{Profit} + FC)/(P - VC) = (\$60 + \$100)/(\$1 - \$0.20) = 200 \text{ hot dogs}$$

TOAD HALL
(Continued)

Susan and Ed realize that they cannot live on zero profit. To estimate an acceptable profit, they examine their existing annual profit from working at their jobs in New York City. Presently their joint salaries total $100,000, but they pay $45,000 per year for their apartment. By living in the caretaker house at Toad Hall, they will not have to pay rent, so the net forgone profit of buying Toad Hall is $55,000. The Whites also value the intangibles of living in the country to be $25,000 per year. Therefore, they believe that they would need a profit of at least $30,000 annually from Toad Hall to make the investment comparable to their existing situation. The number of room-days that must be rented to achieve a $30,000 profit, if a daily rental rate of $150 is used, follows:

$$(\text{Profit} + FC)/(P - VC) = (\$30,000 + \$123,000)/(\$150 - \$26) = 1,234 \text{ room-days}$$

Although this number is well below the total capacity of 2,190, Susan and Ed are not sure that they can rent that many rooms, especially at a daily rate of $150 per room.

Graph of CVP Analysis

CVP analysis can be represented easily by a graph. Figure 5.1 demonstrates "hot dog vendor" Laura Gonzalez's CVP problem. The total cost line is in the same form as the variable and fixed cost approximation of opportunity costs in Chapter Two. The hot dog vendor's fixed cost of $100 is the intercept of the vertical axis. The variable cost of $0.20 per hot dog is the slope of the total cost line. The total

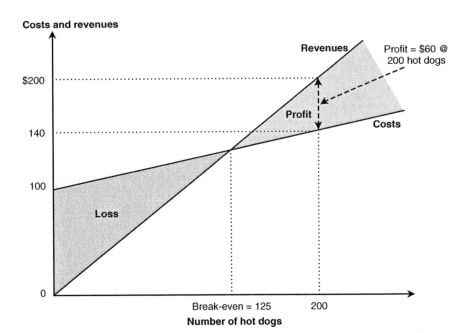

Figure 5.1

Cost Structure for a Hot Dog Vendor

revenue line is a straight line that extends from the origin. The slope of the total revenue line is equal to the sales price of $1 per unit.

The break-even point occurs when total costs equal total revenues, which occurs where the two lines intersect. The shaded area to the left of the break-even number represents the expected loss if fewer hot dogs are produced and sold. The shaded area to the right of the break-even number represents the expected profit if more hot dogs are produced and sold. From Numerical Example 5.4, we see that producing and selling 200 hot dogs a day achieves a $60 profit.

CVP Analysis and Opportunity Costs

CVP analysis is used for planning purposes; therefore, the opportunity costs are the appropriate costs to measure. The cost of using noncash resources to make the product should reflect the alternative use of that resource. Also, if the investment being considered involves the long-term use of cash, the planning decision should recognize that there is an opportunity cost of using cash. If cash is borrowed, the interest expense should be included in the analysis as a fixed cost of the product. If the organization has available cash for a long-term investment in a product, the investment prevents the organization from receiving interest on the cash. That forgone interest is an opportunity cost. Therefore, CVP analysis should include the interest expense of borrowed cash plus the forgone interest of available cash used to make the investment.

Numerical Example 5.5

Paul McDonald is thinking about buying a farm that costs $400,000. He can borrow $300,000 for the purchase at 10% interest but must use $100,000 of his own cash for the remainder. What is the annual cost of financing the investment in the farm?

Solution

External financial reports in the form of an income statement would recognize only the 10% interest on the loan (0.10)($300,000), or $30,000, annually. For CVP analysis, however, there is a forgone opportunity of using the $100,000 cash to buy the farm. If the cash had earned 10%, the cost of financing for CVP analysis is (0.10)($400,000), or $40,000, annually.

Problems with CVP Analysis

CVP analysis is simple to use. It approximates activity costs using fixed and variable costs while the sales price and variable cost per unit are assumed constant over all levels of output. These simplifications allow us to estimate profit by looking at the difference between two straight lines, as in Figure 5.1. Most likely, however, cost and revenue estimates are only reasonable approximations within a small range of output levels.

Approximating Costs with Fixed and Variable Costs

In Chapter Two, we learned that fixed and variable costs only approximate costs in an intermediate range of outputs. That range is the *relevant range*. At low levels of output, product costs are likely to be less than the sum of fixed plus variable costs. Also, as an organization nears capacity, its product costs are likely to be higher than fixed plus variable costs. Therefore, CVP analysis should not be used at low levels of output or at output levels near capacity.

Assuming a Constant Sales Price

In most markets, if you want to sell more units, you must lower your sales price. Assuming that you can sell very large amounts at a constant price is unrealistic. CVP analysis has no explicit assumption of a constraint in production or sales. The assumption of a constant sales price is probably accurate only over a narrow range of output levels. For example, Nike can sell only a certain number of sneakers at $100 per pair; if it wants to sell more, it must lower the price.

Determining Optimal Quantities and Prices

CVP analysis assumes that straight lines can represent costs and revenues. Therefore, the choices of quantity and price in CVP analysis are not determined by setting marginal cost equal to marginal revenue. As drawn in Figure 5.1, the marginal revenue (the slope of the revenue line) is always greater than the marginal cost (the slope of the cost line). The slopes of the two lines are not equal at any level of output. CVP analysis suggests that profit is maximized when an infinite number of units is produced. This result is absurd given capacity constraints and the need to make price concessions to sell more units.

CVP Analysis and the Time Value of Money

CVP analysis is a one-period model. During a period of time, the revenues and costs are estimated for different levels of output. Products may have a life cycle of many years, however; to accommodate a longer product-life cycle, an assumption could be

For most goods, including high-end athletic shoes, a lower price is needed to increase sales. This basic law of supply and demand highlights one limitation of CVP analysis – the assumption of a constant sales price. Even firms that offer the latest fashion trend face constraints in terms of sales and production levels.

made that each intermediate time period is identical in terms of revenues and costs. If revenues and costs differ for different intermediate time periods, some method of trading off profit from different periods of time must be used. Large capital investments to make the product may adversely affect profit early in the product life cycle but may improve it in the latter stages of the product life cycle. Chapter Thirteen describes such a method to deal with multiple periods and to recognize the time value of money.

CVP Analysis and Multiple Products

CVP analysis assumes that the fixed and variable costs of each product can be identified separately. However, most organizations provide multiple products, and some costs frequently are common to these products. For example, a cellular telephone manufacturer produces numerous models ranging from inexpensive, simple telephones to expensive, complex units. Under these circumstances, CVP analysis is not a very good planning tool unless the multiple products can be considered as a "basket" of goods. The basket would contain a certain proportion of all the different goods provided by the organization and would be treated as a single good.

For instance, a company that makes and sells bicycles and tricycles could consider its basket of products to be two bicycles and one tricycle. The price of the basket is the sales price of two bicycles and one tricycle. The cost of the basket includes the fixed costs of the company plus two times the variable cost of the bicycle plus the variable cost of the tricycle. CVP analysis then could be used for the basket of goods because there is a single basket price and a single fixed and variable cost for the basket. This procedure works, however, only if the proportions of different products in the basket remain constant for all levels of output.

Numerical Example 5.6

A company is considering buying a factory that assembles personal computers and laser printers. The factory is expected to make and sell twice as many personal computers as laser printers. The factory has annual fixed costs, such as property taxes and insurance, of $20 million that are not identified with either the personal computers or the laser printers. The sales price and variable cost per unit of the personal computer are $1,000 and $400, respectively. The sales price and variable cost per unit of the laser printer are $800 and $300, respectively. How many units of personal computers and laser printers must be sold to break even?

Solution

To solve this problem, a basket of both goods must be established. The products are made and sold in a 2-to-1 proportion; therefore, the basket should contain two personal computers and one laser printer. The sales revenue of this basket is (2)($1,000/personal computer) + (1)($800/laser printer), or $2,800. The variable cost of this basket is (2)($400/personal computer) + (1)($300/laser printer), or $1,100. The break-even quantity of this basket is calculated as follows:

($20,000,000)/($2,800 − $1,100) = 11,765 baskets

The 11,765 baskets are equivalent to 23,530 personal computers and 11,765 laser printers.

The limitations of CVP analysis described in this section indicate that it should be used with care. CVP analysis has the advantage of being simple but should be used only as a rough planning tool. It provides a manager with a low-cost approximation of the profit effect of an investment. Whether a manager wants to analyze the investment further depends on the cost of that analysis and the potential benefits of more accurate information.

Concept**Review**

1. What is the basic profit equation for CVP analysis?
2. What is the purpose of performing break-even analysis?
3. What are the major assumptions of CVP analysis?
4. How does CVP analysis work with multiple products?

PRICING DECISIONS IN THE SHORT TERM

LO 4 Make short-term pricing decisions considering variable cost and capacity.

Planning Decisions

Chapter Four described strategic pricing issues. Managers must, however, often make short-term pricing decisions. For example, a customer might request a discount on the price of a product or might give the organization a "take-it-or-leave-it" offer to purchase a product. Customers are constantly pitting one supplier against another to get the best price. How do managers decide on a price when customers threaten to go to a competitor?

In Chapter Four, the product cost was described as the lower boundary for a pricing decision. The product cost includes all direct and indirect costs of designing, making, and selling the product. To be profitable in the long term, the revenues generated from the sale of the product must be higher than the cost of all of the activities associated with the product. In the short term, however, some of the product costs are fixed, and the variable cost per unit is the best estimate of the cost of making another unit of the product. Therefore, the result of any sales price higher than the per unit variable cost is a positive contribution margin and provides higher profit for the organization.

Using the variable product cost as a base for pricing all units will lead to a loss if fixed costs cannot be covered by revenue. On the one hand, an organization should not use the variable product cost for a short-term pricing decision if production is at capacity and all the units can be sold at a higher price. On the other hand, if the organization has excess capacity and a one-time opportunity to sell additional units to a customer at a price above the variable cost, the transaction will increase organizational value.

Numerical Example 5.7

It is late at night and a customer arrives at a motel on the interstate. The customer has only $30 dollars and tells the motel manager that he will take a room for $30; otherwise, he will sleep in his car at the next rest stop. The normal price of a room for the night is $70, but the motel is only 30% full and very few new customers are expected. The variable cost of renting the room including linen, maid service, and utilities is $20. The fixed cost of operating the motel is $1,000,000 per year. Should the motel manager take the customer's offer and rent the room for $30?

Solution

Given that the motel has excess capacity and will lose this customer if this one-time offer is refused, the motel manager should accept the offer. The contribution margin of the additional room rental is $30 − $20, or $10.

Concept**Review**

1. What cost should be considered in making a short-term pricing decision?
2. How does capacity affect the short-term pricing decision?

TOAD HALL
(Continued)

Ed is confused about using the variable cost to make a pricing decision. He asks Susan, "Do you mean that if a customer arrives late at night and we have empty rooms that will not be filled, we should be willing to rent a room for as low as $26? Nobody rents rooms for that low a price. We'll lose money."

Susan replies, "The variable cost of renting one more room is $26. If we can rent it for $30, we make $4 more than if we don't rent it at all."

Ed still is not convinced. He provides another argument for not renting at such a low price: "What if we rent a room to someone earlier in the day for $100 and then rent a room for $30 to a late arrival? What happens if they have breakfast together and discover the price difference? Would the person paying the higher rent be upset?"

PRODUCT MIX DECISIONS

Chapter Four described strategic issues surrounding the selection of products to offer. An organization should offer a product mix that reflects its competitive advantage, whether it is innovation, quality, or low-cost production. Modifications to the strategic product mix decision must be made given short-term changes in the market. For example, an organization might temporarily eliminate a product from its product mix because of a short-term price decline. In this section, the following short-term decisions are examined: (1) to add a product or service, (2) to drop a product or service, (3) to make or buy a product or service, (4) to process a product further, and (5) to promote a product or service. The analysis in each case examines the incremental impact of the decision on the organization's profit.

Decision to Add a Product or Service

When a product or service is added to an existing product mix, both costs and revenues are affected. Costs generally increase because additional inputs such as direct labor and direct material are necessary to make the new product or provide the new service. Indirect costs also may increase if additional indirect resources, such as supervisory costs and utilities, are used to make or provide the new product or service.

An additional product also affects revenues. Revenues from selling the new product are added to the revenues of the existing products, but the new product might affect the revenues of the existing products. A new product might be an accessory of an existing product and increase that product's sales. For example, designing new software for an existing computer should increase sales for both the computer and the software. A new product might also be a substitute for an existing product and replace its sales. For example, an improved laundry detergent probably would reduce the sales of the firm's existing laundry detergents.

The decision to add a new product should be based on a comparison of the incremental costs and incremental revenues. If incremental revenues are higher than incremental costs, the new product should be added. For example, if Laura Gonzalez, the hot dog vendor, is considering the sale of soft drinks, she should consider only incremental costs such as the cost of a refrigeration unit and the cost of purchasing the soft drinks. Incremental revenues should include not only the sale of soft drinks but also the effect on hot dog sales. If incremental revenues are higher than incremental costs, Laura also should sell soft drinks.

Business Analysis

Ryanair is a low-cost air carrier based in Dublin, Ireland. As in North America, deregulation of the airline industry in Ireland has brought increased competition and more choice for passengers. One way in which airlines measure their operating performance is revenue per seat. Cheap fares decrease revenues, but operating their aircraft more efficiently may offset this loss. Ryanair focuses on the market segment seeking discount fares—passengers who are willing to trade off convenience and amenities for cost. Initially, Ryanair used only one type of aircraft which allowed it to increase the efficiency of its maintenance and servicing and to shorten its turnaround time at airports. Other cost-cutting measures are selling sandwiches and using fewer flight attendants per flight. Ryanair also operates from smaller airports that are less frequented and less costly. This strategy makes it possible for Ryanair to offer lower fares based on its lower operating cost.

The larger airlines might pose a threat to Ryanair if they decide to compete in this market segment. Larger firms, such as British Airways, find, however, that the low-cost-low-service approach hasn't been as successful for them as for the smaller airlines, which sell seats at a price near marginal cost. Inexpensive economy fares are costly in terms of decreased yield per seat. The industry also suffers from increased price pressure as a result of excess capacity. Business passengers are more lucrative since they are less sensitive to price and are more willing to pay for convenience and flexibility.

Ryanair also must deal with higher airport fees charged by government authorities and the renewal of its fleet of aircraft. Economic factors need to be monitored closely because Ryanair passengers tend to be tourists, not businesspeople.

How might Ryanair and other low-cost carriers establish airfares? What threats do such pricing strategies face? Why can some airlines offer low fares and be profitable while other airlines find this approach not to be feasible? How might an airline such as Ryanair use break-even analysis to determine whether it should provide fewer or more flights in a specific market?

Source: The Economist, November 13, 1999, p. 72.

Numerical Example 5.8

The owner of a professional football team and a football stadium is considering renting the facility to a professional baseball team. The baseball team would need the stadium for 80 games and would be willing to pay rent of $20,000 per game. The football stadium, which originally cost $20 million to build, can be converted from football to baseball and baseball to football at a cost of $40,000 per conversion. The cost of cleanup and maintenance

LO 5 Make decisions to add or drop products or services.

Football stadiums are expensive to build, but these costs are sunk once spent. As well, football stadiums are often empty due to short playing seasons, motivating owners to seek additional uses, such as rock concerts and other sports. Converting a stadium for other purposes can be costly and time consuming; thus the decision to do so requires a careful evaluation of the incremental costs and benefits of each opportunity.

due to each baseball game is estimated to be $15,000. Given the overlap of the football and baseball season, the stadium would have to be converted eight times each year. Should the owner of the professional football team rent the stadium to the baseball team?

Solution

The incremental revenues are (80)($20,000), or $1,600,000. The incremental costs are (8 conversions)($40,000/conversion) + ($15,000/game)(80 games), or $1,520,000.

The incremental revenues are higher than the incremental costs, so the football team owner should rent to the baseball team. The cost to build the stadium is sunk and irrelevant to the decision.

TOAD HALL
(Continued)

Ed and Susan are considering adding dinner service to the other services that they would offer at Toad Hall. This service would be available to guests and the public by reservation. The kitchen and dining room are already available, but there is a $100,000 remodeling cost to make the kitchen meet health codes. Other incremental costs would include food, beverages, and a cook. The incremental cost of providing 5,000 dinner meals annually is estimated to be $150,000. The average meal price is estimated to be $40. In addition, having a dinner service should increase room rentals (at $150 per room) by 200.

Given this information, Sue and Ed calculate the additional profit that the dinner service will generate:

Incremental revenues	
Meals ($40)(5,000)	$200,000
Additional room rental revenues ($150)(200)	30,000
Total incremental revenues	$230,000
Incremental costs	
Interest forgone in remodeling kitchen ($100,000)(10%)	$ 10,000
Food, beverages, and cook	150,000
Variable room costs ($26)(200)	5,200
Total incremental costs	$165,200
Excess of incremental revenues over incremental costs	$ 64,800

These additional estimated profits make the purchase of Toad Hall much more appealing.

Decision to Drop a Product or Service

Not all products and services are a success. Even previously successful ones may no longer be popular with customers. At some point, management must decide when to drop these products or services. This decision depends on a careful comparison of incremental costs with incremental revenues.

The product cost is not always known, however, and is often approximated using historical direct and indirect costs. The indirect costs are traced to the product through some cost driver. These indirect costs include overhead items, such as the supervisor's salary, that may not disappear if a product is dropped. In other words, not all of the estimated product costs are avoidable if a product is eliminated. A manager should identify the **avoidable product or service costs** in making a decision to drop a product or service. If avoidable costs are higher than the incremental revenue of a product, it should be dropped from the product mix.

Numerical Example 5.9

Based on the following information, a plastic pipe manufacturer is considering dropping a pipe that handles high pressure from its product mix:

Revenues from high-pressure pipe	$100,000
Costs from high-pressure pipe	
Direct material	(30,000)
Direct labor	(50,000)
Allocated overhead	(30,000)
Loss from high-pressure pipe	($ 10,000)

What factors should the manufacturer consider before dropping this product?

Solution

Direct costs are generally avoidable, but the allocated overhead might not be. If only half of the allocated overhead ($15,000) were avoidable, then revenues ($100,000) would be higher than avoidable costs ($95,000). Another factor to consider is any alternative use of the space, labor, and machines presently devoted to making the high-pressure pipe. If there is an alternative use of those resources, managers should consider the profit forgone from those alternative uses as part of the opportunity cost of making the high-pressure pipe. Managers also should consider the effect of dropping the high-pressure pipe on the demand for its other products.

Decision to Make or Buy a Product or Service

Boeing Company produces commercial airplanes. Boeing imports most airplane parts from companies all over the world and then assembles the airplanes in the United States (primarily near Seattle, Washington). Why does Boeing choose not to make the various parts itself? Many companies have decided not to do their own payroll or tax accounting but hire other companies to perform those functions. Why are they reluctant to do their own payroll and tax accounting?

LO 6 Determine whether to make or buy a product or service.

Organizations must determine what they can do themselves and what they should pay other organizations to do. This outsourcing decision was described in Chapter Four. This decision should be based on a comparison of the costs of providing the product or service in-house with the cost of purchasing it from an external supplier. If the cost to purchase the product or service is lower than the cost to provide it within the organization, the organization should outsource.

The problem once again is identifying the costs. If the product or service is currently provided in-house, identification of avoidable costs is important. Indirect costs traced or allocated to a product or service are not always avoidable if an organization decides to use an outside supplier. Alternatively, if an outside supplier is currently providing the product, the incremental costs of providing the product in-house should be identified when considering in-house production.

Make-or-buy decisions involve factors other than immediate cost implications. Using outside suppliers gives an organization less control over quality and timely delivery. However, outside suppliers often have the expertise and equipment to provide the product at a lower cost than the organization can.

Some organizations have taken outsourcing (the use of outside suppliers) to an extreme. Sun Microsystems, a maker of computer workstations, concentrates on hardware and software design. Every other process is outsourced. The employees of the company never touch its top-selling products.[1]

Decision to Process a Service or Product Further

L0 7 Determine whether to process or promote a product or service further.

Another decision related to the product mix is whether to process a product further and sell a more refined product. For example, wooden furniture may be sold stained or painted or not stained or painted. A restaurant may choose to serve food in a buffet style or have a server deliver it to the table. The decision to process further is based on a comparison of the incremental costs and incremental revenues of further processing. If the incremental revenues are higher than the incremental costs, the product should be processed further.

Numerical Example 5.10

A department store is deciding whether to sell bicycles assembled or unassembled. It can purchase an unassembled bicycle for $100 and sell it unassembled for $200. To assemble a bicycle requires 30 minutes of labor time at a labor cost of $16 per hour. If the department store assembles the bicycle, it sells it for $210. Should the department store sell the bicycle assembled or unassembled?

Solution

The incremental revenues are $210 − $200, or $10. The incremental costs are the cost of assembly, or (1/2 hour)($16 per hour), or $8. The incremental revenues are higher than the incremental costs, so the store should assemble the bicycle. Note that the department store's purchase cost of $100 is irrelevant to the decision. Once it purchases the unassembled bicycle, the $100 is a sunk cost.

TOAD HALL
(Continued)

Susan and Ed have thought of another way to make the Toad Hall Bed and Breakfast more profitable. Instead of making breakfast and dinner for guests, they could have the meals catered. By using a catering service, they could save $100,000 in remodeling costs because the kitchen wouldn't have to be changed to satisfy health code requirements as well as the costs of a cook. The $3 breakfast cost per person would also be saved. A caterer would supply breakfasts for $5 each and dinners for $30 each. Dinners would still be sold for $40 each and breakfast would be included as part of the rental rate of the room. The Whites assume that 2,500 breakfasts and 5,000 dinners would be served annually.

Incremental annual costs of providing breakfast and dinner (not catered) are as follows:

Breakfasts ($3)(2,500)	$ 7,500
Dinners (food and cook)	150,000
Interest forgone in remodeling kitchen ($100,000)(10%)	10,000
Total incremental costs	$167,500

Catering costs are estimated as follows:

Breakfasts ($5)(2,500)	$ 12,500
Dinners ($30)(5,000)	150,000
Total catering costs	$162,500

Catering the breakfasts and dinners will save $167,500 − $162,500, or $5,000 per year. The Whites are not sure, however, whether the catering company is reliable, so they decide not to use it.

---

[1] R. Drtina, "The Outsourcing Decision," *Management Accounting*, March 1994, pp. 56–62.

Decision to Promote a Product or Service

The decision to promote a product or service also is based on a comparison of incremental costs and incremental revenues. In the case of advertising, the incremental revenues are the additional sales generated by the advertising. The incremental costs are the costs of the additional advertising and of making the additional units. If the incremental revenues are higher than the incremental costs, the advertising campaign should proceed.

L0 7   Determine whether to process or promote a product or service further.

Another promotion decision for an organization is persuading a customer to buy one of its products instead of another. For example, which car on the lot of a new car dealership would the owner want the customer to buy? Why type of ticket does the manager of a baseball team want a fan to purchase? Of course, the organization wants to sell the product that generates the most profit. The contribution margin per unit is the profit from selling one more unit of a product if the organization is operating below capacity. The product with the highest contribution margin per unit will generate the most profit if sold. For most car manufacturers, higher-priced cars with luxury options have the higher contribution margin per unit. Therefore, most car salespeople push customers to buy more expensive cars.

Numerical Example   5.11

A company manufactures three types of lawn tractors in separate plants. Their costs and prices are as follows:

Type of Tractor	Fixed Costs	Variable Cost per Unit	Price per Unit
MB-2000	$10,000,000	$ 500	$ 800
MB-2400	30,000,000	700	1,300
MB-2800	40,000,000	1,000	1,500

Assume that all three divisions are operating below capacity. If a customer decides to buy one of these three tractors, which model should the company promote?

Solution

The contribution margins per unit of the three types of tractors follow:

Type of Tractor	Contribution Margin per Unit
MB-2000	$300
MB-2400	600
MB-2800	500

The MB-2400 has the highest contribution margin per unit and is the tractor that the company prefers to sell. The fixed costs are irrelevant in this decision.

Concept Review

1. What types of costs should be considered to make a decision to add a product?
2. Why are avoidable costs used to make a decision to drop a product?
3. Why do some organizations decide to buy products rather than make the products in-house?
4. How should an organization decide whether to process a product further?
5. What types of products do organizations prefer to sell?

PRODUCT MIX DECISIONS WITH CONSTRAINTS

Short-term decisions are influenced by the existence of capacity constraints. If organizations are operating below capacity, the variable cost approximates the

Planning Decisions

LO 8 Decide which products and services to provide when there is a constraint in the production process.

marginal cost of making further units of different products. The use of the excess capacity should be directed toward making and selling more of the product with the highest contribution margin per unit. If there is a capacity constraint that affects multiple products or services, however, the problem becomes more complex. For example, suppose that a machine used to process more than one product is operating at capacity. If the organization has some flexibility in determining which product should use the machine more frequently, how should the organization make that decision?

The product with the highest contribution margin per unit is not necessarily the one that should have priority on a machine that is a constrained resource. Instead, the organization should determine which product yields the highest contribution margin per use of the machine. If a product with a high per unit contribution margin requires considerable machine time, the contribution margin per use of the machine is low. Another product might have a low contribution margin per unit but can be processed quickly and therefore has a high contribution margin per use of the machine. The following example demonstrates this relationship.

Product	CM*/Unit	Units/Machine Hour	CM/Machine Hour
A	$8	3	$24
B	3	10	30

* CM represents the contribution margin.

In this example, using the machine to manufacture B, the lower contribution margin product, results in a higher contribution margin per machine hour. The machine is the constraint in the production process for both products A and B; therefore, the organization wants to use the machine in the most profitable manner. Giving product B a higher priority creates a higher profit for the organization, assuming it can sell as many units of B as it can produce.

Numerical Example 5.12

William Chang, CPA, is a sole proprietor who does corporate, partnership, and individual tax returns. He is constrained by his time, which is his only cost. On average, the revenues and time required for different types of tax returns are as follows:

Type of Tax Return	Time in Hours	Revenue per Tax Return
Corporate	20	$2,000
Partnership	10	1,200
Individual	5	400

Which type of tax return should William prepare if he has plenty of opportunities to do all three types of tax returns?

Solution

Since variable costs are zero (other than the opportunity cost of William's time), the contribution margin of doing each type of tax return equals the revenue. The contribution margin per use of the scarce resource (an hour of William's time) for each type of tax return is determined as follows:

Tax Return	Contribution Margin per Hour
Corporate	$100/Hour
Partnership	120/Hour
Individual	80/Hour

The partnership tax return has the highest contribution margin per hour of William's time and is the preferred tax return to prepare.

Identifying the product that yields the highest contribution margin per use of a scarce resource requires simple calculations. If more than one constraint exists (such as a constraint on both machine time and labor time), the problem is much more difficult to solve. A procedure called *linear programming* can be used to choose a product mix that maximizes the contribution margin given more than one constraint. This procedure is studied in operations management and advanced management accounting classes.

TOAD HALL
(Continued)

The primary constraint in operating Toad Hall is space. Susan and Ed could use one of the bedrooms as a private dining room in addition to the main dining room. This choice should be based on the comparison of the contribution margins from alternative uses of the bedroom: room rental versus private dining room. This bedroom would be the last rented. The Whites estimate that they can rent it 100 days of the year with a contribution margin of $124 at a $150 rate per night. The total contribution margin from rental is (100)($124), or $12,400. The Whites estimate that they can sell 1,100 more dinners in a private dining room with a contribution margin per dinner of $10 if catered. The total contribution margin from using the room as a private dining room is (1,100)($10), or $11,000. Therefore, the Whites decide not to use the bedroom as a private dining room.

Following this analysis, Susan and Ed decide to purchase Toad Hall. With the extra $74,800 in profit from adding the dinner service, they can operate the remaining parts of the bed and breakfast at a loss of $34,800 and still achieve a total profit of $30,000. Also, if the bed and breakfast is not financially successful, they assume that they can sell Toad Hall to another gullible couple wanting to leave the city.

You decide

THEORY OF CONSTRAINTS

In the book *The Goal*, Eliyahu Goldratt reinforces the importance of identifying constraints within an organization. This process of identifying and managing constraints is called the **theory of constraints.**

In describing opportunity costs and the rate of output, we noted that the marginal cost of making a product increases as capacity is reached. Not all processes within an organization, however, have the same capacity. For example, the steps to make plywood include debarking, heating, and cutting the logs into veneer (thin layers of wood); cutting the veneer into sheets, sorting it, drying it, and layering and gluing it; and trimming the plywood, and sanding and patching it. Each if these steps likely has a different capacity. In terms of tons of wood product processed per day, a particular plywood factory has the following constraints:

Planning Decisions

Process	Tons of Wood Product per Day
Debarking log	300,000
Heating log	200,000
Cutting log into veneer	100,000
Cutting veneer	150,000
Sorting veneer	120,000
Drying veneer	130,000
Layering and gluing veneer	150,000
Trimming plywood	250,000
Sanding and patching plywood	300,000

LO 9   Identify and manage a
bottleneck to maximize
output.

Cutting the log into veneer has the lowest capacity and is called the **bottleneck**. Bottlenecks usually can be identified, even if the capacity of the different processes is unknown, because work-in-process (unfinished inventory) accumulates prior to the bottleneck process. The bottleneck deserves the primary attention of management because it inhibits the flow of the production process. Care should be taken that the bottleneck process operate as many hours as possible. Maintenance of the bottleneck process is extremely important and methods of increasing its capacity should be considered. By increasing the capacity of the bottleneck process, the organization can produce more units of its product or service. If those additional units can be sold at a price above the variable cost per unit, then the organization can increase its profit.

Dealing with bottlenecks is a continuous process. Suppose that the plywood factory purchases another lathe to cut logs into veneer. This additional lathe increases the capacity of cutting logs to 200,000 tons per day, so cutting them into veneer is no longer the bottleneck. Therefore, sorting veneer becomes the bottleneck at 120,000 tons per day. The sorting of veneer then becomes the primary focus of management attention.

The theory of constraints also has control implications. Employees often are rewarded based on the output of the particular process that they control. The more output that they can produce, the more they are rewarded. In an organization with processes that have different capacities, this reward system can lead to dysfunctional behavior. Employees do not benefit the organization by creating more output if they are operating a process that is not a bottleneck. Increasing the output of a nonbottleneck process simply increases work-in-process but does not lead to more finished units. More finished units can be made only by increasing the output of the bottleneck process. The excess work-in-process actually can be costly to the organization since it causes congestion and uses resources. The just-in-time production method, described in Chapter Twelve, deals with the problem of excess work-in-process.

Concept**Review**

1. If a capacity constraint affects multiple products, which product should have priority?
2. How should an organization manage a bottleneck?

SUMMARY

1 Explain how short-term decisions differ from strategic decisions. Strategic decisions involve long-term planning with the opportunity to change the existing resources of the organization; short-term decisions assume that most of the organization's resources cannot be changed.

2 Estimate profit and break-even quantities using cost-volume-profit analysis. The break-even quantity is the level of output that generates zero profit and can be estimated by dividing the fixed costs by the contribution margin per unit. The output level necessary to achieve a specified profit is the sum of the profit and fixed costs divided by the contribution margin per unit.

3 Identify limitations of cost-volume-profit analysis. Cost-volume-profit analysis assumes that costs can be approximated with fixed and variable costs, and assumes a constant sales price. It cannot be used to determine optimal levels of output and price, nor does it consider the time value of money.

4 Make short-term pricing decisions considering variable cost and capacity. If an organization is operating below capacity, the marginal cost is approximated by the variable cost. Therefore, in the short term, the variable cost should be considered as the lower boundary in making a pricing decision.

5 Make decisions to add or drop products or services. Products or services should be added if the incremental revenues are higher than the incremental costs. Products and services should be dropped if the lost revenues are lower than the avoidable costs.

6 **Determine whether to make or buy a product or service.** A product or service should be purchased instead of produced if the purchase price is lower than the cost of making it.

7 **Determine whether to process or promote a product or service further.** A product or service should be processed further if the incremental revenue is higher than the incremental cost. Managers that are maximizing profit prefer to sell products with higher contribution margins if the organization is operating below capacity.

8 **Decide which products and services to provide when there is a constraint in the production process.** A

manager attempting to maximize profit will choose to produce more of the product or service with the highest contribution margin per use of the scarce resource.

9 **Identify and manage a bottleneck to maximize output.** A bottleneck is the limiting factor of the operating rate of an organization. It should be managed so that it is operating at its capacity, and ways to relax the bottleneck process should be considered.

10 **Use extensions of cost-volume-profit analysis to make planning decisions. (Appendix)** Break-even quantities can be expressed in terms of sales. Cost-volume-profit analysis assists in the operating leverage decision and can be used to estimate after-tax profit.

KEY TERMS

avoidable product and service costs Costs that are no longer incurred if a product or service is dropped. *(p. 149)*

bottleneck The process of an organization that has the least capacity. *(p. 154)*

break-even analysis The process of identifying the number of units that must be sold to achieve zero profit. *(p. 140)*

contribution margin per unit The sales price minus the variable cost per unit. *(p. 139)*

contribution margin ratio The ratio of the contribution margin to sales revenues. *(p. 155)*

cost-volume-profit (CVP) analysis The process of estimating profit assuming fixed and variable costs and a constant price over all rates of output. *(p. 138)*

operating leverage A measure of an organization's cost structure calculated as the ratio of its fixed costs to its total costs. *(p. 157)*

theory of constraints A process of identifying and managing constraints in making products. *(p. 153)*

APPENDIX
Additional Aspects of CVP Analysis

This Appendix describes some extensions of CVP analysis that can be used to make various planning decisions. As noted in the chapter, CVP often provides an initial analysis to determine whether further study is warranted.

LO 10 Use extensions of cost-volume-profit analysis to make planning decisions.

Examining the Contribution Margin Ratio

The **contribution margin ratio** is the ratio of the contribution margin to sales revenues, generally expressed as a percentage. This ratio can be used to examine the impact of changes in sales revenues, fixed costs, and the break-even quantity. For example, a firm has sales revenues of $200,000 and variable costs of $80,000. Its contribution margin is $200,000 − $80,000, or $120,000. The contribution margin ratio is $120,000/$200,000, or 60%. If revenues increase by 10% or $20,000, the corresponding increase in the contribution margin is 60% of $20,000, or $12,000. Similarly, if sales decline by 20%, the impact on the contribution margin is a decrease of 60% of $40,000, or $24,000. Examining the contribution margin ratio provides a quick analysis of the effect of fluctuations in sales revenues on profits.

The contribution margin ratio has other applications. For instance, it provides a means to determine the break-even point when cost and revenue data are not

Planning Decisions

available on a per unit basis. The approach is similar to the break-even quantity in units but substitutes the contribution margin ratio for the per unit contribution margin in the break-even formula.

Numerical Example 5.13

A firm has fixed costs of $1 million and variable costs of $750,000. Its current sales revenues are $2,000,000. At what level of sales will the firm break even?

Solution

The firm's contribution margin is $2,000,000 − $750,000, or $1,250,000. The contribution margin ratio is $1,250,000/$2,000,000, or 62.5%. The break-even quantity, expressed in terms of sales revenues, is as follows:

$$FC/(\text{CM ratio}) = \$1,000,000/0.625 = \$1,600,000$$

Most firms offer a basket of goods or a number of products in a product line. In these situations, the contribution margin ratio represents the average contribution margin ratio of this basket of goods. It then can be used to determine the overall sales revenues required to break even.

Numerical Example 5.14

Alpha Company sells a basket of goods whose current sales revenues are $150,000. The total variable costs are $82,500 and total fixed costs are $35,000. At what level of sales will the firm break even?

Solution

The firm's contribution margin is $150,000 − $82,500, or $67,500. The contribution margin ratio is $67,500/$150,000, or 45%. The break-even quantity in terms of sales revenues is as follows:

$$FC/(\text{CM ratio}) = \$35,000/0.45 = \$77,778$$

The section on cost-volume-profit analysis in the chapter described the use of CVP with multiple products. In that section, the sales price and variable cost of each product were known. If we knew instead the contribution margin ratio of each product, we could determine the break-even quantity in terms of sales revenues.

Numerical Example 5.15

Delta Company manufactures and sell three products, X, Y, and Z, in its basket of goods. The contribution margin ratios are 45%, 35%, and 50% respectively. The basket of goods is composed of 10% of X, 30% of Y, and 60% of Z. The total variable costs are $82,500, and fixed costs are $35,000. At what level of sales will the firm break even?

Solution

The weighted-average contribution margin is (0.10)(0.45) + (0.30)(0.35) + (0.60)(0.50), or 0.45. The break-even quantity in terms of sales revenues is as follows:

$$FC/(\text{CM ratio}) = \$35,000/0.45 = \$77,778$$

This break-even quantity assumes that there is no change in the product mix.

The contribution margin ratio is a useful tool for determining the increase in sales revenues required to cover higher fixed expenses, such as an increase in property taxes or administrative expenditures. It also can be used to compute the additional sales revenues necessary to provide an increase in the desired target profit. The next section outlines an extension of CVP analysis based on the knowledge of an organization's cost structure.

Analyzing Operating Leverage

Knowledge of the fixed and variable components of an organization's cost structure is useful planning information, especially for designing changes to the product mix or marketing campaigns or examining the effect of short-term fluctuations in operating levels. The ratio of fixed costs to total costs is known as **operating leverage.** The higher the organization's fixed costs, the higher is its risk. This high leverage means that small percentage changes in sales volume translate into large percentage changes in net cash flow and profit. Firms with low operating leverage (a low ratio of fixed costs to total costs) have less variability in cash flows and profits. These firms are less risky than their competitors whose cost structures have a higher proportion of fixed costs.

Firms with high operating leverage experience higher net income when sales exceed the break-even point. When sales fall below the break-even point, the impact on net income is correspondingly greater. Firms with low operating leverage experience less impact on net income when cash flows exceed or fall below the break-even level. To summarize, high operating leverage magnifies the effect of percentage changes in sales revenues, whereas low operating leverage reduces this impact.

Operating leverage is inversely related to variable costs: the higher the organization's variable costs, the lower its operating leverage. In the short term, a firm cannot alter its cost structure significantly. However, it might be able to substitute variable costs for fixed costs to reduce its operating leverage. For example, a firm might outsource activities to convert certain fixed costs into variable costs, thereby reducing its operating risk. The degree of operating leverage is one indication of an organization's ability to withstand short-term declines in sales.

Consider two firms, LeBas and LeHaut. The following is a summary of the firms' revenues and costs:

	LeBas	LeHaut
Sales revenues	$10,000	$10,000
Variable costs	5,000	2,500
Fixed costs	2,000	5,000
Net income	$ 3,000	$ 2,500

LeBas's operating leverage is $2,000/$7,000, or 0.2857. LeHaut's operating leverage is $5,000/$7,500, or 0.6667. Thus, LeHaut is more highly leveraged compared to LeBas. If sales increase or decrease by a given percentage, the impact on LeHaut's net income will be greater than the impact on LeBas's net income. To illustrate, let's examine a drop in sales of 30%:

	LeBas	LeHaut
Sales revenues	$7,000	$7,000
Variable costs	3,500	1,750
Fixed costs	2,000	5,000
Net income	$ 1,500	$ 250

When sales decrease by 30%, LeBas's net income falls by 50%, whereas that of LeHaut drops by 90%. Hence, LeBas's cost structure, which contains a lower percentage of fixed costs, cushions the impact of decreases in the firm's operating level. This cushion has a corresponding effect when sales increase. LeBas experiences a smaller percentage increase in net income for a percentage increase in sales revenues compared to that which LeHaut experiences.

Achieving a Specified After-Tax Profit

This section describes how to modify the cost-volume-profit formulas in the chapter to include taxes. Not-for-profit organizations do not have to pay income taxes, but other organizations do. The amount of the tax paid depends on the taxable income and the income tax rates. The profit calculated using variable and fixed costs to approximate product costs does not necessarily equal taxable income. For example, depreciation is often calculated differently for tax purposes and financial reporting purposes. In this section, we assume that the profit determined by the variable and fixed costs is also the taxable income; a constant tax rate (t) is used to calculate taxes. Under these circumstances, the after-tax profit is calculated as follows:

$$[(P - VC/\text{Unit})(Q) - FC](1 - t)$$

To determine the number of units necessary to achieve a specified after-tax profit, the formula can be rearranged to solve for Q:

$$\text{After-Tax profit}/(1 - t) = (P - VC/\text{Unit})(Q) - FC$$
$$[\text{After-Tax profit}/(1 - t)] + FC = (P - VC/\text{Unit})(Q)$$
$$[(\text{After-Tax profit}/(1 - t)) + FC] \div (P - VC/\text{Unit}) = Q$$

Laura Gonzalez, the hot dog vendor in the chapter, had fixed costs of $100 per day, variable costs of $0.20 per hot dog, and a price of $1.00 per hot dog. If she has a tax rate of 30% and wants to have a profit after taxes of $50 per day, how many hot dogs must she sell? Using the preceding equation, we determine the following:

$$[(\text{After-Tax profit}/(1 - t)) + FC]/(P - VC/\text{Unit}) =$$
$$[(\$50/(1 - 0.3)) + \$100]/(\$1.00 - \$0.20) = 215 \text{ hot dogs}$$

How many hot dogs must Laura sell to break even (after-tax profit = $0)?

$$[(\$0/(1 - 0.3)) + \$100]/(\$1.00 - \$0.20) = 125 \text{ hot dogs}$$

Notice that this is the same number of hot dogs when taxes are ignored. Taxes are paid only when there are profits. At break-even, there are no profits and, hence, no taxes.

SELF-STUDY PROBLEM

Small Bike Company is the idea of Charles Johnson. He has designed a portable bicycle that can be disassembled easily and placed in a suitcase. He is thinking about implementing the idea and going into production. Charles estimates that the fixed costs of producing between 1,000 and 3,000 portable bicycles will be $50,000 annually. In addition, the variable cost per portable bicycle is estimated to be $40. Charles could outsource the suitcase production, which would reduce the fixed costs to $40,000 annually and the variable costs to $35 per bicycle. If the company makes fewer than 2,000 portable bicycles, there would be excess capacity to make an additional 1,000 regular bicycles. There would be no additional fixed costs, and the variable costs would be $60 per regular bicycle. There is no other use for the space.

a. Charles would like to make $60,000 annually on this venture. If he makes and sells 3,000 portable bicycles (with the suitcase), what price should he charge for each portable bicycle?

b. If Charles decides to charge $80 per portable bicycle while making the suitcase, what is the break-even number of portable bicycles?

c. If Charles makes 2,500 portable bicycles, should he consider buying the suitcases from an outside supplier at a price per suitcase of $10?

d. If Charles makes and sells only 2,000 portable bicycles because of limited demand, what is the minimum selling price that he should consider for 1,000 regular bicycles built with the excess capacity?

Solution

a.   Profit = (Price per unit − Variable cost per unit)(Number of units) − Fixed cost

$60,000 = (Price per unit − $40)(3,000) − $50,000

Price per unit = $76.67

b. Break-even quantity = Fixed cost/(Price per unit − Variable cost per unit)

Break-even quantity = $50,000/($80 − $40) = 1,250 portable bicycles

c. Avoidable costs if the suitcase is not made in-house:

Reduction in fixed costs ($50,000 − $40,000)	$10,000
Reduction in variable costs (2,500 units)($40 − $35)	12,500
Total avoidable costs	$22,500
Cost of purchasing suitcases ($10)(2,500)	$25,000

Therefore, the suitcases should be made in-house.

d. The regular bicycles do not add to the fixed costs; therefore, the variable cost per unit establishes the lower boundary for pricing them. As long as the price is higher than the variable cost of $60, the company has a positive contribution margin from the regular bicycles.

NUMERICAL EXERCISES

A taxi driver must pay $100 per day for taxi rental, insurance, and licenses. Gas and maintenance costs are $0.15 per kilometer. The taxi driver charges $0.50 per kilometer and travels 50 kilometers per day without customers.

NE 5.1
Break-Even Analysis
(LO 2)

a. Not counting tips, how many kilometers must the taxi driver carry customers to break even?

b. How many kilometers must the taxi driver carry customers to make $50 plus tips?

A company's product has a fixed cost of $400,000 and a variable cost of $100 per unit. The company has been making 10,000 units and selling them for $200 per unit. There is excess capacity in the factory and a buyer has asked to buy 1,000 units for $120 apiece.
    What should the company do?

NE 5.2
Short-Term Pricing Decisions
(LO 4)

A company makes a product with a fixed cost of $400,000 and a variable cost of $100 per unit. The sales price is $200 per unit.
    What is the break-even point for the product? How many units must be made and sold to make $50,000 profit?

NE 5.3
Cost-Volume-Profit Analysis
(LO 2)

What is the break-even price when a company expects to sell 5,000 units, the fixed costs are $50,000, and the variable costs are $30 per unit?

NE 5.4
Cost-Volume-Profit Analysis
(LO 2)

Multiplex store sells televisions for $500 and stereo systems for $800. The variable costs of televisions and stereos are $300 and $600, respectively. The common fixed costs of operating the store are $100,000 per year. The store expects to sell two televisions for every one stereo system.
    What is the break-even point per year?

NE 5.5
Estimation of Break-Even Quantity
(LO 2,10)

NE 5.6
Product Mix Decisions
(LO 5)

A hair salon is now providing haircuts for men and is considering offering shaving as an additional service. The salon plans to charge $10 for a shave with half going to the beautician as a commission. The additional equipment for shaving will cost $10,000 per year. The salon expects to provide 3,000 shaves during the year. The beauticians work on a 50% commission. The additional shaves will result in 300 fewer haircuts due to capacity constraints. Each haircut generates a contribution margin of $10.

Should the salon add shaving to its service mix?

NE 5.7
Product Mix Decisions
(LO 5)

A company has $600,000 in fixed costs. A product that sells for $50 and has a variable cost of $40 is a candidate for being dropped from the product mix. The company estimates that all variable costs and 10% of the fixed costs are avoidable. If the company continues to provide the product, sales should be 5,000 units.

Should the company drop the product?

NE 5.8
Decision to Promote a Product
(LO 7)

A lawn and garden store has two types of lawn tractors for sale. Tractor A sells for $5,000 and costs $3,000 to purchase. Tractor B sells for $4,000 and costs $1,500 to purchase. The fixed costs of operating the lawn tractor sales area are $100,000 per year.

Which tractor should the salespeople try to get the customers to buy if the customer is going to buy one?

NE 5.9
Product Mix Decisions with Constraints
(LO 8)

Products A, B, and C have contribution margins per unit of $10, $8, and $6, respectively. Each product is processed by the same machine, which has a capacity of 100 hours a week. The processing times on this machine for products A, B, and C are 10 minutes, 6 minutes, and 4 minutes, respectively.

Which product should have priority on the machine if all of the products can be sold?

NUMERICAL PROBLEMS

NP 5.1
Addition of a New Service
(LO 8)

Beechwood Paper Company presently sells large rolls of paper weighing 2,000 kilograms to wholesalers for $1,000 each. The wholesalers cut the paper into letter-size paper and package it in 2 kilogram packages and sell them to printers for $2 per package. There is no waste in the cutting process. Beechwood Company currently produces 10 million kilograms of paper annually at a fixed cost of $1 million and a variable cost of $0.30 per kilogram. If Beechwood bypassed the wholesalers and cut its own paper for sale directly to printers, it would have to add equipment and personnel that would increase incremental fixed costs annually to $3 million. Incremental variable costs would be $0.10 per kilogram.

Should Beechwood cut its own paper and bypass the wholesalers?

NP 5.2
Cost-Volume-Profit Analysis
(LO 2)

You are considering starting a business selling roller blades. You assume that you will charge a price of $100 per pair. You can purchase roller blades from a manufacturer in China for $20 per pair. Transportation to the United States costs $5 per pair. Administration costs of operating are $1 million and don't vary with the number of roller blades purchased or sold.

How many pairs of roller blades must be purchased and sold to make $100,000 in profit? (Ignore taxes.)

NP 5.3
Product Mix Decision
(LO 5, 8)

A candy shop sells candy with three types of filling: chocolate, cream, and caramel. The candy shop manager is analyzing its product mix through the following product prices and costs:

	Chocolate Filled	Cream Filled	Caramel Filled
Sales price/Kilogram	$3.00	$2.00	$2.50
Direct costs/Kilogram	(1.50)	(0.50)	(1.00)
Variable overhead/Kilogram	(0.60)	(0.50)	(1.00)
Fixed overhead/Kilogram	(0.25)	(0.50)	(1.00)
Profit/Kilogram	$0.65	$0.50	($0.50)

The fixed costs aren't avoidable and are allocated to products based on the number of kilograms of candy produced. They candy shop has excess capacity.

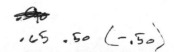

a. Which product should the shop promote if the promotion will result in sales of 100 kilograms more of the promoted type?

b. Should the caramel-filled candy be dropped from the product mix? Explain.

c. How does the product mix problem change if the candy shop is operating at capacity?

With the possibility that the U.S. Congress will relax restrictions on cutting old growth, a local lumber company is considering expanding its facilities. The company believes that it can sell lumber for $0.18/board-foot, which is a measure of lumber. The tax rate for the company is 30%. The company has the following two opportunities:

NP 5.4
Cost-Volume-Profit Analysis
(LO 2, 10)

Build factory A with annual fixed costs of $20 million and variable costs of $0.10/board-foot. This factory has an annual capacity of 500 million board-feet.

Build factory B with annual fixed costs of $10 million and variable costs of $0.12/board-foot. This factory has an annual capacity of 300 million board-feet.

a. What is the break-even point in board-feet for factory A?

b. If the company wants to generate an after-tax profit of $2 million with factory B, how many board-feed would it have to process and sell?

c. If demand for lumber is uncertain, which factory is riskier?

d. At what level of board-feet would the after-tax profit of the two factories be the same?

Leslie Mittelberg is considering the wholesaling of a leather handbag from Kenya. She must travel to Kenya to check on quality and transportation; the trip will cost $3,000. The cost of each handbag is $10. Shipping to the United States can be done through the postal system for $2 per handbag or through a freight company that will ship a container that can hold up to 1,000 handbags for $1,000. However, it will charge $1,000 even if fewer than 1,000 handbags are shipped. Leslie will try to sell the handbags to retailers for $20. Assume there are no other costs and benefits.

NP 5.5
Cost-Volume-Profit Analysis
(LO 2)

a. What is the break-even point if shipping is through the postal system?

b. How many units must be sold if Leslie uses the freight company and wants to have a profit of $1,000?

c. At what output level would the two shipping methods yield the same profit?

d. Suppose a large discount store asks to buy an additional 1,000 handbags beyond normal sales. Which shipping method should be used and what minimum sales price should Leslie consider in selling those 1,000 handbags?

The Rose Bowl sells tickets for $100 per person and has a capacity of 100,000 people. Each person buys on average $20 of food and trinkets. The cost of providing the food, trinkets, guards, ticket salespeople, and cleanup is estimated to be $10 per person. The fixed cost of renting the Rose Bowl and paying the teams is $10,000,000. Television pays $5,000,000 for the right to broadcast the game.

NP 5.6
Cost-Volume-Profit Analysis
(LO 2)

How many tickets must be sold to have a profit of $3,000,000? (Assume no taxes.)

A firm makes telephones that sell for $50 per unit and calculators that sell for $30. The variable cost of making a telephone is $40 per unit and of making a calculator is $18 per unit. The firm has additional manufacturing costs of $2 million.

NP 5.7
Contribution Margin
(LO 5, 8)

a. If the firm sells 100 more units of the calculator, what is the additional profit to the firm?

b. If the firm could sell one more telephone or one more calculator, which product would it prefer to sell?

c. Under what conditions would the firm want to drop the telephones from the product mix?

You are considering the purchase of a hotel with 20 rooms. If you buy it, the fixed costs are expected to be $200,000 per year. The variable costs of renting a room for one night include $20 for maid service and $5 for utilities and other costs. Assume no taxes.

NP 5.8
Cost-Volume-Profit Analysis
(LO 2)

a. If you expect to rent the rooms for $90, how many rooms must you rent during the year to break even?

b. If you want to have a profit of $50,000 and expect to be at 70% of capacity for 365 days of the year, what price per room would you have to charge?

NP 5.9

Decision to Drop Products or Increase Output

(LO 5, 8)

You perform the following profitability analysis on the products that you manufacture:

	Product A	**Product B**	**Product C**
Revenues	$300,000	$800,000	$100,000
Variable costs	200,000	500,000	40,000
Fixed costs	100,000	100,000	100,000
Profit	$ 0	$200,000	($ 40,000)
Number of units made and sold	1,000	10,000	100

Fixed costs are sunk and there is excess capacity.

a. Should product C be dropped? Explain.

b. Which product would provide the most profit if one more unit were sold?

NP 5.10

Contribution Margin and a Single Constraint

(LO 8)

Warehouse Company makes three types of paper (A, B, and C) using the same machine. The fixed overhead costs are allocated to the types of paper by machine hours. The following data are used to calculate the profitability of the three types of paper:

	A	**B**	**C**
Revenues	$900,000	$500,000	$100,000
Variable costs	600,000	300,000	50,000
Fixed costs	200,000	90,000	50,000
Profit	$100,000	$110,000	$ 0
Number of tons	4,000	3,000	500
Machine hours	1,000	450	250

a. If the paper machine were operating below capacity, which type of paper would produce more profit if an additional ton of it can be made and sold?

b. If the paper machine were operating at capacity, which type of paper would the company prefer to make and sell?

NP 5.11

Contribution Margin

(LO 6)

Peluso Company, a manufacturer of snowmobiles, is operating at 70% of plant capacity. Its plant manager is considering manufacturing headlights, which are now being purchased for $11 each (a price that isn't expected to change in the near future). The Peluso plant has the equipment and labor force required to manufacture the headlights. The design engineer estimates that each headlight requires $4 of direct materials and $3 of direct labor. Peluso's plant overhead rate is 200% of direct labor dollars, and 40% of the overhead is fixed cost.

If Peluso Company manufactures the headlights, how much of a gain (loss) for each headlight will result?

(CMA adapted)

NP 5.12

Break-Even Quantity

(LO 2)

You are considering ways to expand an optometry practice and its earnings capacity. Optometrists perform eye exams, prescribe corrective lenses (eyeglasses and contact lenses), and sell corrective lenses. One alternative being explored is to hire an additional optometrist to conduct additional eye exams. The annual cost of the optometrist, including salary, benefits, and payroll taxes is $63,000. You estimate that this individual can conduct two exams per hour at an average price of $45 to the patient. The new optometrist will work 40-hour weeks for 48 weeks per year. However, because of scheduling conflicts, patient no-shows, training, and other downtime, the new optometrist will be able to conduct, bill, and collect only some fraction less than 100% of his or her available examination time.

From past experience, you know that each eye exam drives additional product sales. Each exam might lead to either an eyeglass sale with a net profit (revenue less cost of sales) of $90 (not including the exam fee) or a contact lens sale with a net profit of $65 (not including the exam fee). Of the exams performed, 60% lead to eyeglass sales, 20% lead to contact lens sales, and 20% lead to no sales.

In addition to the optometrist's salary, additional costs to support him or her include these:

Office occupancy costs	$ 1,200/year
Leased equipment	330/year
Office staff	23,000/year

In terms of the percentage of available time, what is the minimum number of examinations that the new optometrist must perform to recover all incremental costs related to his or her hiring?

Outdoor Flower Shop sells the following different types of flowers with their corresponding purchase and selling prices:

NP 5.13
CVP Analysis with Multiple Products
(LO 2)

Type of Flower	Purchase Price per Dozen	Sales Price per Dozen
Roses	$8	$15
Daisies	1	3
Tulips	5	10

The shop tends to sell 50% roses, 20% daisies, and 30% tulips. The fixed costs of operating the shop total $30,000 annually.

How many dozens of each type of flower must the shop sell to break even?

Neptune Car Company is considering opening a new manufacturing plant. The objective is to make 10,000 cars annually at the plant. Its size depends on which car parts Neptune decides to outsource. If all parts are made in-house, the fixed costs are expected to be $100 million and the variable costs are expected to be $4,000 per car. The company is considering outsourcing the engine, drive shaft, and dashboard. If each part is outsourced, Neptune estimates the following reduction in fixed costs and variable costs per car. It also has obtained the following purchase price for each part from an external supplier:

NP 5.14
Make or Buy
(LO 6)

Part	Reduction in Fixed Costs	Reduction in Variable Cost per Unit	Purchase Price
Engine	$20,000,000	$1,000	$1,200
Drive shaft	5,000,000	200	400
Dashboard	6,000,000	300	1,000

a.   Which of the different parts should be outsourced based on the costs and prices?
b.   What other factors should be considered in making the outsourcing decision?

Promo Company has three different products, Ooze, Mud, and Goop, that are used as facial creams and are sold in bottles. Without advertising, these products are expected to have the following revenues and costs:

NP 5.15
Constraints in the Advertising Budget
(LO 7)

Product	Number Sold	Revenues	Variable Costs	Fixed Costs	Profit
Ooze	10,000	$100,000	$30,000	$40,000	$30,000
Mud	20,000	80,000	50,000	10,000	20,000
Goop	30,000	150,000	90,000	10,000	40,000

To attract customers to these wonderful products, the company has established an advertising budget of $10,000, which is sufficient to advertise only one of the products. The marketing group believes that spending the $10,000 to advertise a particular product will increase the number of Ooze, Mud, and Goop sold by 30%, 20%, and 10%, respectively. The company is presently well below capacity.

Which product should Promo Company advertise?

NP 5.16
Maximization of Profit with Constraints
(LO 8)

Judson Company makes widgets and wangles, both of which use a polishing machine as part of production. The widgets and wangles have the following price and cost characteristics:

	Widgets	Wangles
Annual capacity	1,000 units	2,000 units
Price per unit	$50	$100
Variable cost per unit	$20	$50
Annual fixed costs	$10,000	$10,000
Polishing machine hours per unit	1 hour	2 hours

The polishing machine can operate for a total of 3,000 hours during the year.

a. What product mix creates the most profit for Judson Company, given all the constraints?

b. If there were only machine hour constraints, what product mix would create the greatest profit mix for Judson?

NP 5.17
Bottlenecks
(LO 9)

A car manufacturing plant is responsible for assembly. The assembly line begins with the chassis and the following parts are added:

Part	Assembly Time in Minutes
Engine	5
Drive train	4
Electrical system	10
Seats	6
Dashboard	3
Hood, trunk, and side panels	5
Doors	2

a. Under these circumstances, how fast can the assembly line move?

b. Where should the plant place additional effort to increase the speed of the assembly line?

NP 5.18
Break-Even Analysis and Operating Leverage
(LO 2,10)

News.com is a Web site that offers users access to current national and international news stories. News.com doesn't charge users a fee for accessing the site but charges advertisers $0.05 per "hit" to the Web site, which is a user who logs on. The user's e-mail address is also provided to the advertiser.

News.com is considering two alternate internet service providers (ISPs), NetCom and Globalink, that will link News.com's computer system to the Internet. These firms are identical in terms of access speeds and number of users able to connect to the site per minute and both are equally reliable. NetCom proposes to charge $3,000 per month plus $0.01 per hit to News.com. Globalink will charge $2,000 per month plus $0.02 per hit. Assume that the only costs that News.com incurs are the ISP's access fees.

a. Calculate the number of hits to its Web site needed to break even if News.com uses NetCom.

b. Calculate the number of hits to its Web site needed to break even if News.com uses Globalink.

c. Which ISP do you recommend News.com use? Explain why.

d. Monthly demand (in terms of number of hits) for News.com is expected to be either 50,000 if the economy is slumping or 150,000 if it is booming, each of which is equally probable. Which ISP should News.com choose and why?

ANALYSIS AND INTERPRETATION PROBLEMS

Eastern University is considering adding 100 undergraduate students, 25 in each entering class, for the next four years. Its president argues that since excess capacity exists in classes, no additional faculty will be required. Thus, the teaching cost of these 100 additional students is zero.

    Comment on the president's argument.

AIP 5.1
Addition of Services
(LO 5)

A timber company is considering how large a wood lot to purchase. The amount of timber on a wood lot is measured in board-feet. The fixed cost of setting up to cut the timber is $20,000, and the variable cost is $0.20 per board-foot. The selling price of the timber, however, keeps fluctuating, and the timber company is uncertain what the selling price per board-foot will be when the timber is cut and sold. The company estimates that the price will be between $0.60 and $1 per board-foot. The expected price is $0.80 per board-foot.

    How can the company perform break-even analysis in terms of size of wood lot with uncertainty about the price of timber?

AIP 5.2
Break-Even Analysis with Uncertainty
(LO 2)

A company is considering the purchase of a grocery store. The company would like to perform CVP analysis, but the store has 5,000 different products. There is also a common fixed cost of operating the grocery store. Each product has a different cost and price, so a "basket" of goods would be extremely difficult to calculate. The store prices each product, however, by writing up its variable costs by 15%.

    How could the company use CVP analysis of the grocery store even with multiple products?

AIP 5.3
Percentage Write-Up for CVP Analysis with Multiple Products
(LO 2, 3,10)

In a *Wall Street Journal* article, Fleer Corporation announced that it would no longer make its own trading cards in-house. Fleer Corporation is primarily known for its sports cards, which are collected and traded by the young and not-so-young. The article stated that the company would focus on marketing, sales, and development. The outsourcing of production was expected to have a slightly positive impact on earnings.

a. How did Fleer make this decision to outsource the production of the trading cards?

b. When a company decides to outsource a process, is an immediate positive impact on earnings always expected?

Source: The Wall Street Journal, November 29, 1995, B 8:2.

AIP 5.4
Make-or-Buy Decision
(LO 6)

An insurance company is primarily devoted to processing claims from insured customers. Processing claims involves analyzing the claim form, telephoning the claimant, visually inspecting the damages, and writing a check to the claimant. The president of the company has just heard about the theory of constraints, which he thinks is an interesting theory but applicable only to manufacturing companies. Therefore, he believes that the theory of constraints isn't relevant to his firm.

a. Can an insurance company such as this one have bottlenecks?

b. How should the insurance company manage its process under the theory of constraints?

AIP 5.5
Bottlenecks
(LO 9)

The manager of a fast-food hamburger shop was trying to understand the costs of operating the business. First, he divided the costs into fixed and variable. The fixed costs included his salary, the interest on the mortgage, utilities, fixed asset depreciation, and property taxes. The variable costs included wages of cooks and servers, maintenance, and food. He was especially interested in the variable costs because they were more controllable. His business was open from 11 AM to 11 PM, and he calculated the variable costs per revenue dollar for each hour of operation. The following table shows the result of this exercise:

AIP 5.6
Variable Costs and Use of CVP Analysis
(LO 3)

Time	Variable Costs per Revenue Dollar
11AM–12PM	0.57
12PM–1PM	0.65
1PM–2PM	0.58
2PM–3PM	0.75
3PM–4PM	0.66
4PM–5PM	0.60
5PM–6PM	0.57
6PM–7PM	0.68
7PM–8PM	0.58
8PM–9PM	0.70
9PM–10PM	0.75
10PM–11PM	0.85

The 12PM–1PM and 6PM–7PM hours were the busiest.

The manager was confused by the results because he expected the variable cost per revenue dollar to be constant.

a. What is causing the variability in the variable costs per revenue dollar?

b. Is CVP analysis appropriate if the manager wants to determine the profitability of increasing dinnertime sales?

c. Are there any hours during which the hamburger shop should consider closing?

AIP 5.7
Short-Term Pricing
(LO 1, 4)

The late-night receptionist of a hotel was told to lower the price of rooms for potential guests who were reluctant to pay the full price and who were considering going elsewhere. The minimum price to be charged for a room was $40 per night, which was above the variable cost of $25 per night for cleaning and maintenance. The full price for the room was $100 per night.

a. What type of pricing decision rule should the hotel provide the night receptionist when almost all of the rooms are rented and more potential guests might arrive?

b. How does this pricing rule differ from a long-term pricing strategy?

EXTENDED ANALYSIS AND INTERPRETATION PROBLEMS

AIP 5.8
CVP Analysis

Café Noir is a small coffee shop located in the financial district of downtown Toronto. Its owner is considering the purchase of a European espresso machine to preserve her customer base in the market. The café is experiencing increased difficulty competing with large coffee chains such as Second Cup and Starbucks that offer customers a wider variety of specialty coffee beverages. The shop is open Monday to Friday, 50 weeks per year.

The cost of the European machine is $30,000. The selling price of the specialty coffees is $1.50 per cup, and the variable cost per cup is $0.30. (Assume for simplicity that all beverages have on average the same selling price and variable cost.)

a. What is the number of specialty coffee sales per day that must be achieved to break even?

b. Upon further investigation, the owner learns that the new machine requires substantial maintenance, which will increase the variable cost by either $0.20 or $0.40. She is not certain but believes that there is an equal probability of either increase. How would this information affect your answer to part (a)?

c. What other factors should the owner consider before making the final decision to purchase the machine?

Source: "Latte U Brews Jobs," *The Montreal Gazette*, August 31, 1999, pp. A1–2.

AIP 5.9
CVP Analysis and
Incremental Costs and
Benefits

Susan Whyte sells watercolor paintings at the Queenstown market. She currently sells 50 paintings per year. She offers both framed and unframed paintings; framed paintings are offered to lure the impulse buyer who wants a ready-to-hang picture. She estimates that producing her watercolors costs $80 in painting supplies and other variable costs. Framing incurs an additional $100 cost. She sells her paintings for an average price of $300 unframed and $500 framed. Of sales, 40% is framed paintings and the remainder is unframed.

A local gallery has offered to feature Susan's watercolors in its store. The gallery wants exclusive rights to them, so she would have to give up her Queenstown market sales. The gallery also requires unframed paintings because it has its own custom-framing service. It would sell her paintings for $500 each, and Susan would receive 80% of the sales price. The gallery would guarantee sales of 40 paintings per year.

a. Based on the current situation, what is Susan's yearly income from the watercolors?

b. If customers were indifferent as to framed and unframed paintings, should she continue to offer the framed watercolors?

c. Assume that Susan accepted the gallery's offer and that it sold 40 watercolors in the first year. What would have been the effect on her yearly income?

d. In your opinion, would this decision be the correct one?

Excellent Promotions Company promotes concerts. The company has three full-time employees who are responsible for contracting with bands, renting venues for the concert, and advertising it. The cost of operating the office, including the salary of the three full-time employees (but not including advertising and specific concert payments), is $200,000 annually.

AIP 5.10
Concert Promotion

Temporary help is added the day of the concert to assist in security, ticket sales, and cleanup. These employees are added based on the expected ticket sales of the concert. Usually by the day of the concert, the company can estimate ticket sales quite well based on advance ticket sales. These employees are paid $10 per hour and work for an average of 5 hours at each concert. The number of employees that must be hired includes one security employee for each 100 tickets sold, one ticket seller for every 400 tickets sold, and one employee for cleanup for every 200 tickets sold.

Excellent Promotions is considering bringing in a jazz band for a concert. The jazz band wants $20,000 to come and perform. The company can rent a local hall that holds 2,400 concert fans for $5,000. The sales price for each ticket to the concert is expected to be $20. A local food service company is willing to pay the promotions company $500 to sell food and drinks at the concert. The concert advertising budget is expected to be $2,000.

a. How should the salaries of the company's three full-time employees be treated in analyzing the profitability of the concert with the jazz band?

b. The success of this concert depends on the number of ticket sales. What is the break-even point in terms of ticket sales?

c. What is the maximum profit that this concert can generate?

d. Suppose that Excellent Promotions decides to promote the concert. On the day of the concert, no advance tickets have been sold, and there is every indication of a disaster. If the sales price is reduced, the company estimates the following number of people will come:

Ticket Price	Attendees
$20	100
18	200
16	300
14	400
12	450
10	500

What ticket price will provide the greatest profit for the company?

Chapter**Six**

Managing Organizations

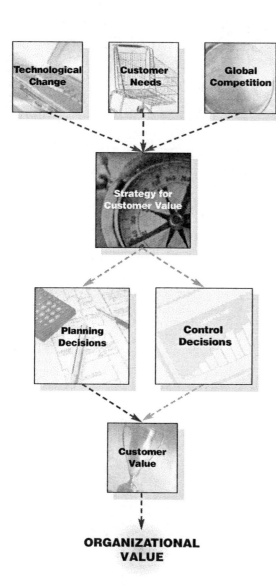

LEARNING OBJECTIVES

1 Balance the assignment of responsibilities, the choice of performance measures, and the compensation based on performance.

2 Link responsibilities with individuals who have the specific knowledge to make decisions.

3 Recognize self-interest in motivating individuals within organizations.

4 Identify the costs and benefits of monitoring members of an organization.

5 Choose performance measures that reveal actions of members of an organization.

6 Design compensation contracts based on performance measures and responsibilities assigned.

7 Design internal control systems by separating the planning process from the control process.

8 Identify control issues within an organization.

MILLER DEPARTMENT STORE

Charles Miller built Miller Department Store in 1950. He still owns the store, but Robin Wheeler is presently its general manager and is responsible for all of its operating decisions. Miller Department Store is in a three-story building in the center of town. It offers a wide selection of goods and competes with specialty shops, and large discount retailers who have moved into malls in the city's suburban areas. Miller Department Store attempts to compete through the quality of its inventory and customer service. The discount retail stores, however, have forced the store to compete with lower prices. In recent years, Miller Department Store has recorded losses, and Robin is considering reorganizing the store to improve management decisions and provide more motivation for employees.

The present organizational chart of the store has Robin on the top as the general manager. Under her are managers representing the accounting department, the purchasing department, the receiving and warehouse department, the marketing department, the maintenance department, and the retail sales department. The accounting department is responsible for recording daily transactions, depositing cash in the bank, paying suppliers and employees, and providing monthly, quarterly, and annual financial statements. The purchasing department works with suppliers and makes all inventory decisions for the store. The receiving and warehouse department is responsible for receiving and inspecting inventory from suppliers. This department also stores the inventory until the retail sales department needs it. The marketing department is responsible for advertising and customer goodwill. The maintenance department is responsible for maintaining and cleaning the facility. The manager of the retail sales department, the largest department, is responsible for hiring salespeople and displaying inventory. Under the manager of retail sales are five assistant managers responsible for managing salespeople in each of the following sales departments: men's clothing, women's clothing, sporting goods, furniture, and toys. All products are priced 50% over their costs.

All employees are paid a fixed salary. There is considerable turnover among the salespeople, reflecting boredom and low salaries. The managers tend to stay with the store for longer periods of time; they appear to prefer the job security of working with Miller Department Store to other entrepreneurial endeavors.

Robin is not sure how to reorganize the store and motivate the employees, but she knows that without a better system, it is unlikely to survive.

FRAMEWORK FOR ORGANIZATIONAL CHANGE REVISITED

LO 1 Balance the assignment of responsibilities, the choice of performance measures, and the compensation based on performance.

Chapter One proposed a framework for change within an organization. This framework is presented here as Figure 6.1. As described in Chapter One, three primary external forces influence an organization: technological change, customer needs, and global competition. To succeed, the organization must develop a competitive strategy by adding customer value through product/service innovation, quality, or low cost. Once a strategy has been chosen, an organization must make a series of planning decisions to add customer value and a series of control decisions to ensure that the planning decisions are consistent with organizational goals and are implemented as planned. If the planning and control decisions are successful, customers will receive value in interacting with the organization, and the value of the organization will increase.

This chapter focuses primarily on control decisions. To adapt and change successfully, an organization must integrate the following procedures that make up its control system:

1. Assigning responsibilities.
2. Measuring performance.
3. Providing compensation for performance.

Figure 6.1

Framework for
Organizational Change

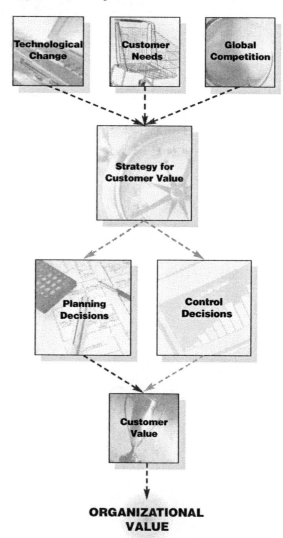

These three procedures are like the legs of a three-legged stool. For the stool to remain level, each of the three legs must match the other two. Similarly, the three procedures that compose the control system of the organization must be coordinated. The performance measurement system must evaluate the manager's performance in areas over which he or she has been assigned responsibilities. Likewise, the reward system must be matched to those areas over which performance is being measured. Although this sounds obvious, what frequently is less obvious is that changes in one system require corresponding changes in the other two.

These procedures will continue to change as the environment in which the business operates also changes. Keeping the three procedures in balance while changing each of them to meet new environmental demands is a challenge for most organizations. They must learn to manage change in the external environment by making complementary changes within the organization.

The internal accounting system is a significant part of performance measurement. Changes in the performance measurement system often are made without regard to the impact of such changes on compensation. Managers making alterations to the accounting system are surprised when the stool no longer remains level because one of the legs has become a different length than the other two. As discussed in earlier chapters, the business environment is constantly changing. Organizations and their management accounting systems also must adapt continually to achieve customer and organizational value.

CONTROL WITHIN AN ORGANIZATION

One role of management accounting is to supply information to assist managers in making better planning decisions. Planning decisions (described in Chapters Two to Five) for products and services (mix and pricing decisions), activities, customers, and suppliers can be improved with additional information. These planning decisions may be either strategic or short term.

**Control
Decisions**

Control is the other major role for management accounting information. Control is the process of getting the organization's members to work toward its goals. Control is achieved by assigning responsibilities to the organization's members and motivating them to act in its best interests. Individuals owning and operating a business by themselves do not have to worry about control. In these cases, the individual is both the owner and only employee; therefore, no assignment and motivation problems exist. As the business grows and the owner hires others to perform some of its functions, these employees must be assigned responsibilities. Not all employees will naturally act in the best interest of the owner. Employees must be motivated through monetary and nonmonetary rewards to act in the owner's best interest. All organizations with more than one member face these control issues.

Control within an organization is not achieved without cost. Assigning responsibilities and motivating, monitoring, and rewarding individuals within the organization require the use of resources such as time, money, and effort. An organization is economically viable only if the benefits of having it are greater than the costs of control within it. If the costs of control exceed the benefits of having the organization, there is pressure for it to divide or disband. Procter and Gamble (P&G) and many other companies have recently downsized to a more manageable size. P&G recognized that it needed to balance quick decision making with centralized control of certain activities. Its wide range of products and brands had to be tailored to local tastes while competing in a global market. P&G's diversity meant that many of its products no longer were building market share.[1] Part of the reason for downsizing is to alleviate control problems when the organization becomes involved in too many diverse activities.

[1] S. Bell, "P&G Forced by Rivals to Change Old Habits," *Marketing,* June 17, 1999.

Management accounting plays an important role in control. In particular, accounting is frequently used to measure performance. Performance measures are the basis for rewarding individuals within the organization. Budgeting (discussed in Chapter Eight) is an important tool in communicating responsibilities, and accountants within the organization play a major role in monitoring the budget.

This chapter and Chapter Seven focus on management accounting and control issues. Chapters Eight through Twelve examine management accounting issues related to both planning decisions and control decisions.

Concept**Review**

1. What are the two internal roles of management accounting?

2. Why do large organizations have greater control problems?

MILLER DEPARTMENT STORE
(Continued)

One option for Robin Wheeler, the general manager, is to eliminate most of the administrative departments and to outsource these activities to external parties. For example, she could contract with other organizations to do the accounting, marketing, maintenance, and receiving and warehousing. With these administrative operations in the hands of specialists in those fields, Robin no longer would have to worry about controlling managers and employees in those departments. Robin could concentrate on what Miller Department Store does best: purchasing and selling.

To successfully divest those administrative functions from the department store and have them performed by outside organizations, Robin must negotiate contracts with the supplying organizations that will satisfy both cost and quality considerations. For example, the cost of purchasing administrative services from other organizations should include the expected cost of resolving contract disputes. The quality of the purchased services should include timely delivery and flexibility. If the external suppliers can provide administrative services at a lower cost without reducing the quality of service, then Robin should consider disbanding some of her administrative departments and purchasing administrative services from other organizations.

KNOWLEDGE AND DECISION MAKING WITHIN AN ORGANIZATION

LO 2 Link responsibilities with individuals who have the specific knowledge to make decisions.

Planning Decisions

A critical part of the organizational structure is the assignment of responsibilities, which determines who is responsible for different facets of the organization. Responsibilities describe any limitations on decisions made by the different individuals within the organization. For example, a checkout clerk in a grocery store is responsible for collecting money from customers but can accept checks only less than $20. The checkout clerk cannot accept checks for more than $20 unless the store manager initials them.

In the case of corporations, shareholders assign responsibilities to a board of directors, who assigns the vast majority of these responsibilities to the chief executive officer (CEO). The board of directors retains the right to replace the CEO and to set the pay for this position. The CEO retains some responsibilities and reassigns the remainder to subordinates. This downward cascading of responsibilities within an organization creates the familiar pyramid shape of organizational hierarchies. Centralization and decentralization revolve around the question of partitioning responsibilities among higher versus lower levels of the organization. Centralized organizations tend to leave most of the responsibilities with their leaders. Decentralized organizations allow lower-level managers and employees to have more responsibilities.

Throughout the remainder of this book, we describe the importance of assigning responsibilities to various subunits and people within the organization. Who or what group of individuals within the organization has the responsibility to set the price, hire workers, accept a new order, or sell an asset? One of the key decisions of managers is whether to retain the responsibility to make a particular decision or to delegate it to someone else. The question of whether the firm is centralized or decentralized is an issue of responsibility assignment. *Worker empowerment* is a term that refers to the assignment of more responsibilities to workers (i.e., decentralization). Coca-Cola Enterprises, the largest Coca-Cola bottler worldwide, attributes its success to the empowerment of its employees. The company recognized the importance of having decisions made at the local level rather than at corporate headquarters in Atlanta, Georgia, and of pushing responsibility to the lower level. Today, Coca-Cola Enterprises is described as a "mean, lean, efficient organization" made up of individuals who have the responsibility to make decisions and know how their decisions affect the bottom line.[2]

The distribution of knowledge throughout the organization is an important issue in the assignment of responsibilities. Individuals have limited capacities to gather and process knowledge, which is costly to acquire, store, and process. Individuals choose to acquire different types of knowledge, allowing some of them to make better decisions in one setting and others to make better decisions in another setting. For example, a computer scientist has specialized knowledge to make informed decisions regarding the operation of computers. The purchasing agent has specialized knowledge about suppliers to make more informed decisions about purchasing items. The authors of management accounting texts have specialized knowledge about management accounting topics but do not possess the same level of knowledge about the books' marketing and distribution.

One solution to the problem of assigning organizational responsibilities is to distribute responsibilities to the individuals with the best knowledge for the particular decision. This solution links knowledge and responsibilities. Linkage occurs when knowledge and the responsibilities related to it reside with the same individual.

Ideally, knowledge and responsibilities should be linked, leading to improved decision making. In some cases, however, an organization may intentionally separate knowledge and responsibilities. Improved decision making from linking knowledge and responsibilities may come at too high a cost to the organization. A manager with the best knowledge of a particular facet of the organization will not necessarily make the decision that is in the organization's best interest. For example, the salesperson in many firms such as an automobile dealership does not have the right to finalize the sales price with the customer, despite having specialized knowledge of the customer's demand. Instead, the sales price is determined

Do you pay for your groceries by cash, check, or credit card? If you choose to pay by check, do you need to wait until the clerk obtains approval? While checkout clerks are delegated the responsibility to handle cash and credit cards, they usually have limits in terms of accepting checks. This system exemplifies the control mechanism that is found in all organizations where responsibilities cascade down the organizational hierarchy.

[2] *Beverage and Industry* 90, no. 1 (January 1999), pp. 16–18.

centrally by the sales manager. Organizations that do not give their sales agents the responsibility to make pricing decisions are concerned that the agents will choose a price that is too low in order to complete the sale. If the salesperson is compensated on a commission basis, the individual will prefer to make a sale, even at a low price, rather than to make no sale at all. The impact of the lower price on commission income might be negligible.

The divergence of individual and organizational goals is the primary reason for not linking responsibilities with the individual who possesses the primary knowledge related to the decision. If the individual with the specialized knowledge is given the responsibility, costly control procedures must be added to ensure that the person's decisions are consistent with the organization's goals.

An alternative to having the person with the specialized knowledge make the decision is to have that individual transfer the knowledge to someone else who has the decision-making responsibility. For example, the president of an organization may want to retain the responsibility for long-term investment decisions but recognizes that other members have better knowledge about customer demand and technical production issues. If the members who possess specialized information on customer demand and production transfer their knowledge to the president, then the president can make an informed decision. If all the relevant knowledge can be transferred, the responsibility and knowledge are once again linked.

One of the key factors in determining the assignment of responsibilities is how the knowledge related to a decision is generated in the firm and how difficult or easy it is to transfer that knowledge. The linkage of knowledge and responsibilities is easier to achieve if knowledge can be easily transferred. For example, knowledge about prices and quantities can be transferred at a low cost. In these cases, the knowledge is transferred to the person with the responsibility to make the decision. Other knowledge is difficult to transfer. Technical knowledge, such as how to design a computer chip, is costly to transfer. Knowledge that changes quickly, such as whether a machine is idle for the next hour, is costly to transfer in time to utilize it. Therefore, the responsibility to schedule the machine is usually transferred to the person with the knowledge; again, the knowledge and responsibilities are linked.

Figure 6.2 demonstrates the relation between responsibilities and knowledge and the role of accounting. In panel A of Figure 6.2, the manager transfers responsibilities to the knowledgeable individual but also creates a control system to motivate and monitor that person who is making decisions. Management

Figure 6.2

Knowledge and
Responsibility

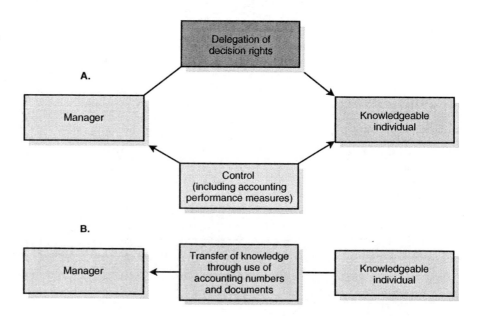

accounting is used to measure the performance of the individual with the responsibility and is important in the control process. In panel B of Figure 6.2, the knowledgeable individual transfers the specialized knowledge to the manager who retains the responsibility. Knowledge is frequently transferred in the form of accounting numbers and documents.

Retailers that do not keep up with fashion trends and preferences often find that customers no longer shop there and spend their fashion dollars in competitors' stores. Keeping up with customer preferences is the responsibility of the purchasing and marketing departments, but the results affect those responsible for retail sales. Retailers need to develop effective ways to ensure that all parts of their operations share the organizational goals of meeting customer needs and of creating organizational value.

Within all organizations, responsibilities must be assigned and knowledge-transfer systems developed. Ultimately, the goal is to link responsibilities and knowledge. As we will see, accounting systems, especially budgets (Chapter Eight) and standard costs (Chapter Fourteen), are important devices for transferring knowledge to individuals with the responsibility to make a decision or giving the responsibility for making the decision to the individual with the knowledge.

Concept**Review**

1. How do responsibilities "cascade" from top-level managers to the rest of the organization's employees?
2. How does the linkage of responsibilities and knowledge benefit an organization?
3. How does the transfer of knowledge allow for knowledge and responsibilities to be linked and still allow for control?

Miller Department Store's manager of retail sales has recently been complaining that he cannot sell the merchandise that the purchasing department is buying. For example, the purchasing department has been purchasing conservative clothing for middle-aged women, but the store's clientele has changed to a younger consumer who is interested in more trendy colors and the latest styles. The manager of retail sales also is complaining about the marketing department, which is always advertising items that are currently out of stock.

Robin Wheeler realizes that she must consider knowledge and responsibilities when she reorganizes the store. One solution is to make the manager of retail sales responsible for purchasing and marketing given his knowledge of customer demand and the store's present inventory.

MILLER DEPARTMENT STORE
(Continued)

MOTIVATION OF INDIVIDUALS TO SUPPORT AN ORGANIZATION'S GOALS

Control is the process of encouraging members of the organization to work for its goals. As stated earlier, individuals have their own goals, which Abraham Maslow describes in terms of satisfying different levels of needs.[3] According to Maslow, an individual first seeks to satisfy physiological needs (food and shelter), followed by

LO 3   Recognize self-interest in motivating individuals within organizations.

---

[3] A. Maslow, *Motivation and Personality* (New York: Harper & Row, 1954).

**Control
Decisions**

safety needs (security), love and belonging (a place within a group), esteem (self-respect), and self-actualization (creative expression). Although research questions the accuracy of this hierarchy, an individual undoubtedly joins an organization to satisfy some of these desires. Any decision made by an individual within an organization would be influenced by his or her personal desires. The organizational control problem is to motivate the organization's individual members to achieve its goals.

The following section begins with the discussion of two important concepts that underlie the organizational control issue:

* Self-interested behavior of individuals.
* Monitoring costs to reduce self-interested behavior.

Once these two concepts have been discussed, two organizational systems are outlined. These two systems are important factors in later chapters and provide for the following:

* Measurement of individual performance.
* Rewards for individual performance through compensation contracts.

The existence of self-interested behavior and monitoring costs makes these two organizational systems necessary.

Self-Interested Behavior

One of the fundamental tenets of economics is that individuals act in self-interest. In making a decision, an individual considers factors that cause personal pleasure or pain such as consumption of resources, social interactions, effort, and recreation. Individuals make cost/benefit trade-offs to maximize personal pleasure and to avoid pain. For example, a person must decide how hard to work. The opportunity cost of working includes the effort required and the inability to do something else. Working also provides the individual with benefits, such as cash and social status.

When joining an organization, the individual perceives that the benefits of joining are greater than the costs. The benefits may be monetary (salary) or nonmonetary (nice working conditions and feelings of power or adulation). The cost of joining includes the time, effort, and opportunity cost of doing something else.

In accepting a new member, an organization must recognize that the individual is influenced by self-interest. The organization must devise a mechanism that motivates the new member to act in its best interest but still provides benefits to the new member in excess of his or her costs. Another mechanism might involve monitoring the individual, especially when the individual's actions are not easily observed.

Monitoring Costs

When the actions of an individual within an organization can be easily observed, motivating the individual to act in the organization's best interest is simple. The individual is assigned a particular task or responsibility and receives benefits only if it is performed. The individual can be observed performing the task; thus, there is no question whether or not to reward the individual. For example, if an employee agrees to sweep floors in a grocery store, the supervisor can easily observe the employee doing this and reward him or her accordingly. The employee will accept and perform the task if the benefits received (for instance, salary and job security) are greater than the cost of its performance.

Not all individuals can be easily observed, however, when performing duties within an organization. For example, door-to-door salespeople normally operate alone and nobody from the organization observes their behavior. When an individual within an organization cannot be observed, there is some doubt as to whether he or she has correctly performed the assigned job. The individual is

LO 4   Identify the costs and benefits of monitoring members of an organization.

influenced by self-interest and, therefore, may not act in the organization's best interest. Salespeople may not exert themselves to make a sale.

One solution to this problem is to monitor members of the organization as they perform their duties, but monitoring takes effort and is costly. **Monitoring costs** are a drain on an organization's resources, but monitoring encourages the individuals who work for it to act in its best interest. Examples of monitoring include the use of supervisors, closed-circuit television, and random observations, which can be very costly in some situations. Traveling salespeople, for example, could be monitored more easily if they worked in two-person teams, but that arrangement would to be overly expensive. An indirect way to monitor a salesperson's performance is to review the person's daily, weekly, or monthly reported sales. Computer technology has increased the ability to undertake these reviews more frequently and at lower cost. Customer surveys about the salesperson's behavior is another monitoring method; many organizations survey their customers to get feedback on their interactions with salespeople.

Accountants within organizations often are asked to monitor the actions of others. The role of internal auditors, for example, includes verifying that different segments of the organization are following its policies.

The existence of self-interested behavior and monitoring costs create a dilemma for the organization in motivating its members. To motivate members, organizations must design two mechanisms: a performance measurement system and a reward system. The next two sections describe these two systems.

Robin Wheeler realizes that most of her time is spent monitoring other individuals at Miller Department Store. She reviews most of the decisions made by the marketing and purchasing departments. In addition, she devotes several hours a day in the retail area of the department store, watching salespeople and making sure the facility looks nice for customers. Robin would like to spend more time on planning decisions, but she is not confident that her managers will perform their duties to her liking if she does not keep her eye on them. She must think of some way to reduce these monitoring costs.

MILLER DEPARTMENT STORE
(Continued)

Measurement of Individual Performance

Performance measures describe how well an individual has performed a task. Although the individual might not be directly observed, performance measures can be used to evaluate and reward his or her performance within an organization. For example, the owner of a home-renovation business might assign a painter to paint a house. It is costly to monitor directly the painter's actions and effort, but the performance can be evaluated by the quality of the paint job. If the paint job is deemed satisfactory, the owner can assume that the painter performed the task as specified and should be rewarded. The quality of the paint job is the performance measure used as a basis to evaluate and reward the painter.

LO 5   Choose performance measures that reveal actions of members of an organization.

Similarly, instructors cannot directly observe how much effort students are exerting in their studies. The instructors use test scores as performance measures to infer whether students have studied and learned the material. The grades based on test scores also are used to motivate students. Students with good grades are frequently rewarded with scholarships, acceptance to graduate school, and better job opportunities.

A good performance measure reveals how well individuals have performed their duties and motivates them to achieve organizational goals. Good performance measures, however, are not always easy to find. Performance measures should reveal the actions of the individual being evaluated, but they can be affected by factors outside that individual's control. For example, salespeople are often evaluated based on sales revenues. Sales are clearly affected by the salespeoples' efforts; however, other factors, such as the state of the economy and the sales potential of the districts to which salespeople are assigned, also affect revenues. Salespeople could perform their duties exactly as the organization expected yet still do poorly in terms of sales results.

In addition to revealing the actions of the individuals within the organization, performance measures should also motivate them to act in its best interest. Performance measures are used to reward individuals so they will attempt to influence the performance measures in a positive way. If the performance measures are not aligned with the organizational goals, they could lead to dysfunctional behavior and failure to achieve those goals.

Performance measures might not be able to isolate the performance of individual members of the organization. Instead, they might reflect the joint output of multiple individuals. If two people are carrying a large awkward box and it slips and falls, which do you blame? Did one of them let it go? Or did it slip out of one person's hands because the other person tripped? If only team effort can be observed, team members have incentives to shirk their responsibilities. Team loyalty, pressure from other team members, and monitoring reduce this shirking but do not eliminate it entirely. For instance, students who work in groups often comment that group-based grades do not measure or distinguish individual performance, allowing some group members to "free ride" on the performance of others. Group pressure alleviates some of the problem. Peer evaluation also attempts to reduce the tendency to free ride, but students often are reluctant to report such behavior.

Cultural differences influence performance measurement significantly since people behave and react to situations differently, depending on the norms of the culture in which they have been raised. A nation's culture is a product of its religious beliefs, history, and economic circumstances; language also is an important dimension. A number of studies have found cultural differences across nations. Dutch passengers are more likely than are Belgians to greet strangers when entering a train. Japanese and Israeli cultures emphasize group (or collective) versus individual orientation, whereas the United States, Canada, and Australia emphasize individualism.[4] Even within the same country, there can be cultural differences, such as the differences in rural versus urban areas. It is important to consider these cultural differences in designing the management control system.

Cultural differences affect management accounting in several ways. The Japanese collective orientation fosters its approach to teams, participative decision making, and quality circles. *Quality circles* are routine meetings of production workers to develop improved manufacturing processes. Team performance measures have been very common in Japan. Social pressure and team loyalty are more likely to overcome the incentive to shirk. In contrast, many U.S. control systems are built around monitoring individual, not collective, contributions. Team-based performance measurement has not proven as popular in the United States as it has elsewhere. An intriguing but currently unanswered question for global organizations is the extent to which successful accounting systems developed in one national culture can be exported to a different national culture.[5] When expanding beyond the United States, Coca-Cola Enterprises recognized the need to adapt to the social conventions, culture, and consumer tastes of other countries. One issue

---

[4] G. Hofstede, *Culture's Consequences: International Differences in Work-Related Values* (London: Sage Publications, 1980). Also see J. Birnberg and C. Snodgrass, "Culture and Control: A Field Study," *Accounting, Organizations & Society* 13 (1988), pp. 447–464.

[5] V. N. Awasthi, C. W. Chow, and A. Wu, "Performance Measure and Resource Expenditure Choices in a Teamwork Environment: The Effects of National Culture," *Management Accounting Research* 9 (1998), pp. 119–138. See also C. Chow, M. Shields, and Y. K. Chan, "The Effects of Management Controls and National Culture on Manufacturing Performance: An Experimental Investigation," *Accounting, Organizations & Society* 16 (1991), pp. 209–226.

that confronted Coca-Cola was whether it could transport the Coca-Cola operating culture, especially its emphasis on empowerment and decentralized decision making, to multinational settings.[6]

There is also some danger in using individual performance measures when individuals must work and support each other in team activities. Individuals might act to boost their personal performance measures while sacrificing team performance measures. The individual might gain on a personal basis from certain activities while team members share any impact on team performance and evaluation. For example, many professional football players receive bonuses if they achieve certain individual statistics. Quarterbacks might be rewarded for the number of pass completions during the season. Therefore, quarterbacks might be motivated to pass more frequently, even when it is risky and to the detriment of the team.

Accounting numbers are frequently used as performance measures. Shareholders use financial accounting reports to evaluate the chief executive officer (CEO). Additional accounting reports highlight the contribution of individual divisions to the organization's overall performance. The CEO uses these reports to evaluate presidents of the divisions. In turn, presidents of divisions use internal accounting reports to evaluate their managers. The quality of these performance measures depends on how closely they reveal the performance of the individual being evaluated and how well they motivate the individual to achieve the organizational goals.

Certain aspects of financial accounting systems exist today because of the demand for performance measures. Historical cost accounting systems are based on actual past transactions. By focusing on past transactions, the historical cost system may reveal the actions of the managers better than accounting systems can based on market value or opportunity cost.

Accounting numbers, however, are not always good performance measures. Accounting numbers are commonly affected by factors that are not under the control of the individual being evaluated and, therefore, do not completely reveal the actions of the individual.

A single performance measure seldom reveals all of an individual's actions in an organization. However, multiple performance measures generally reveal individual actions more accurately. For example, professors use multiple performance measures (test scores, papers, and participation) to evaluate students. Multiple performance measures also are more likely to motivate the individual to achieve organizational goals. Organizations have multiple goals, and managers are expected to make some trade-offs among them. Evaluations based on multiple performance measures are more likely to motivate individuals to make the appropriate trade-offs among the organization's goals.

In an article in the *Harvard Business Review*,[7] R. Kaplan and D. Norton suggest the importance of establishing goals and corresponding performance measures that provide a comprehensive view of the organization. They call this set of measures the **balanced scorecard,** which relates performance measures to the goals of the owners and the satisfaction of customers. These measures also provide information about critical internal processes and how the organization is learning and changing to take advantage of new opportunities. Figure 6.3 illustrates the four interconnected perspectives of the balanced scorecard.

The reasoning behind the balanced scorecard is as follows. An organization exists to create value for its owners/shareholders by providing a financial return commensurate with the risk undertaken. To do so, the organization must create customer value by meeting customer needs for goods and services. This objective is met by ensuring that its internal processes are efficient and high quality. The firm strives to maintain or enhance value-added activities while reducing or eliminating

ORGANIZATIONAL VALUE

---

[6] *Beverage and Industry* 90, no. 1 (January 1999), pp. 16–18.

[7] R. Kaplan and D. Norton, "The Balanced Scorecard—Measures That Drive Performance," *Harvard Business Review,* January–February, 1992, pp. 71–79.

Figure 6.3

Four Perspectives of the
Balanced Scorecard

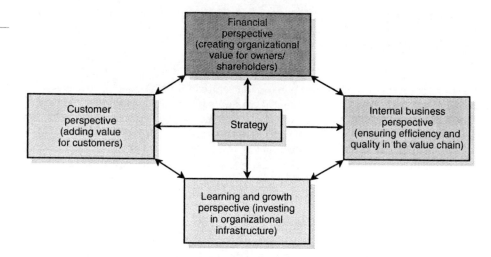

non–value-added activities when possible. The learning and growth perspective emphasizes the provision of adequate training and resources so that people can contribute effectively to organizational goals. The decisions taken in each dimension reflect the firm's overall strategy to compete successfully in its environment.

An overemphasis on one performance measure can lead to an unbalanced scorecard. At Bausch and Lomb, a pharmaceutical firm and supplier of eyeglasses and contact lenses, employees were under extreme pressure to improve earnings, which was being used as a performance measure. To achieve higher profits, managers were forcing their customers, drug stores and variety stores, to accept excess shipments ($75 million) of sunglasses and contact lenses. Complaints from the customers alerted the board of directors to the problem. If Bausch and Lomb had implemented a balanced scorecard with performance measures of customer satisfaction, the problem might not have occurred. Chapter Twelve examines the balanced scorecard in more detail.

MILLER DEPARTMENT STORE
(Continued)

In reorganizing Miller Department Store, Robin has not thought of performance measures. She knows that the owner, Charles Miller, expects her to operate the store at a profit, so one of her performance measures is profit. She has not established any performance measures for her managers, however. What performance measures indicate that her managers have performed their duties as expected? Before choosing these measures, she must reconsider the responsibilities that she has given to each manager.

Robin makes the following table of responsibilities and possible performance measures:

Manager	Responsibilities	Performance Measure
Accounting	Recording transactions, making deposits, paying suppliers, making accounting reports	Timeliness of reports
Purchasing	Making inventory decisions	Sales and inventory
Receiving and warehousing	Receiving and storing inventory	Inventory spoilage
Marketing	Advertising and monitoring customer goodwill	Customer complaints
Maintenance	Maintaining and cleaning facility	Cleanliness of floors
Retail sales	Managing salespeople, making inventory displays	Sales

Rewards for Individual Performance through Compensation Contracts

An individual joins an organization to achieve higher personal benefits relative to personal costs. Benefits are distributed to individual members of the organization based on implicit or explicit contracts. A *contract* is an agreement between two parties to exchange products, services, or cash. Most employee contracts are agreements between an organization and an employee stating that the organization will pay the employee for his or her services. Salaries and bonuses, a company car, and a corner office are some of the compensation that employees can receive from the organization. More generally, an organization can be viewed as a set of contracts among organizational members that identify the assignment of responsibilities, the performance measures to evaluate the members, and the way the benefits generated by the organization are shared. Members who perform their specified duties and make good decisions, as revealed by the performance measures, will be rewarded.

If a performance measure is chosen to evaluate and reward an individual, the individual will perform in such a way as to influence the performance measure. In other words, what you measure is what you get. Therefore, the performance measure should not only reveal the individual's action but also be consistent with organizational goals. For example, a goal of a health-care facility is to provide excellent health care. Health-care facilities often use the number of patients seen as a performance measure for doctors. The performance measure reveals many of the doctors' actions, but the doctors have an incentive to spend less time with individual patients to affect the performance measure. Less time with patients can lead to poorer health care, which is inconsistent with the organization's goals.

To motivate members without incurring excessive monitoring costs, the organization must be careful in designing compensation contracts. Compensation through providing rewards is used as a motivational tool. If poor performance measures are chosen, however, individuals within the organization will not act in its best interest.

LO 6 Design compensation contracts based on performance measures and responsibilities assigned.

Concept**Review**

1. What are the costs and benefits to an individual of joining an organization?
2. Why should an organization incur monitoring costs?
3. What is the role of performance measures within an organization?
4. What characterizes a good performance measure?
5. How are compensation and performance measures related?

Once Robin chooses performance measures for each manager of the department store, she considers the reward system. Certainly the present fixed salaries offer little incentive for managers to perform. She decides to give the managers a bonus if they achieve a certain level for their respective performance measures. The bonus scheme does not work exactly as she expects, however. The accounting manager earns her bonus by issuing timely reports, but they have many errors. The purchasing department manager receives his bonus but inventory in the store always seems very low. Spoilage is down and the warehouse manager receives his bonus, but inventory is slow getting from the warehouse to the sales floor. The marketing manager doesn't get her bonus and insists that customer complaints are due to low inventory and impolite salespeople. The maintenance manager gets his bonus by cleaning the floors hourly but does not perform other maintenance; burned-out bulbs are not changed promptly. The manager of retail sales doesn't get his bonus and once again complains about

MILLER DEPARTMENT STORE
(Continued)

not being able to control inventory decisions. Robin realizes that choosing performance measures and compensating managers is more complex than she originally had thought.

SEPARATION OF PLANNING AND CONTROL IN DECISION MAKING

LO 7 Design internal control systems by separating the planning process from the control process.

LO 8 Identify control issues within an organization.

Planning Decisions

Control Decisions

Another method of controlling managers is to separate the responsibilities of planning and control. By using a system of approvals and monitoring, there is less chance that an individual manager will make a decision that harms the organization.

Lower-level managers are seldom given sole responsibility for a decision. Consider how a typical decision to hire a new employee works. First, a lower-level manager requests authorization to add a new position. Higher-level managers review this request. Once the position is authorized, the manager making the request and higher-level managers undertake the recruiting and interviewing processes. Finally, a new employee is hired. After being employed for a period of time, the employee's performance is evaluated. In general, the following steps occur in the decision process: (1) initiation, (2) ratification, (3) implementation, and (4) monitoring.

Initiation is the first step in the decision process and is a planning decision. Individuals identify potential areas of improvement within the organization, such as new products or manufacturing processes. Other examples of initiation are the identification of profitable opportunities and new customers.

Ratification is a decision control process. Individuals with the responsibility to ratify other individuals' suggestions determine whether the suggestion is consistent with the organization's goals. The ratification process is especially important if large sums of money are at issue. For example, large loan requests in banks or large investment decisions in manufacturing organizations must be ratified by higher-level managers.

Implementation is a planning decision process. Individuals are assigned responsibilities to carry out the organization's plans. For example, investments are made and processes are revamped, individuals are hired and fired, and new products are manufactured.

Monitoring is a decision control process. Some individuals in the organization are responsible for monitoring other individuals to be sure that implementation happens as planned. Individuals and projects are evaluated to determine whether they should be maintained or adjustment must be made. The entire decision process is evaluated to determine whether changes should be made in the future.

The four steps of the decision process are illustrated in Figure 6.4. Note that alternating steps involve either a planning decision process or a decision control process; no single individual within the organization should handle sequential steps in the decision process. Often, a different person is responsible for one step. If the organization is small, one person may be responsible for initiation and implementation and another person responsible for ratification and monitoring.

Separating the planning decision process from the decision control process is an important method of maintaining control over the members of the organization. By assigning planning decisions to one set of individuals and control decisions to another set of individuals, there is less chance that individual decisions will stray from those desired by the organization. By separating responsibilities for planning decisions and control decisions, the members of the organization monitor each other.

The U.S. Constitution separates the powers of the various branches of government and operates as a control system. The executive branch makes a spending request, which the legislature approves. The executive branch is then charged with making the expenditure. The judicial branch is the ultimate decision monitor of both the executive and legislative branches.

Planning decision process   **Decision control process**

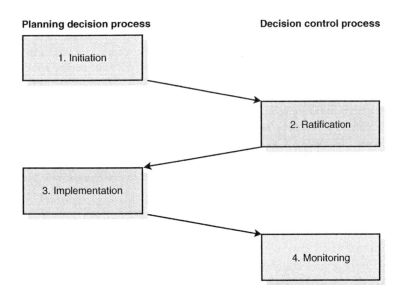

Figure 6.4

Separating Steps of
Decision Process

Most organizations separate planning decisions from control unless it is too costly to do so. For example, managers are often assigned the responsibility to make small purchases (perhaps under $500) without ratification because the costs of separating planning from control exceed the benefits. A major cost of separating planning from control is the cost incurred in delaying a decision. It

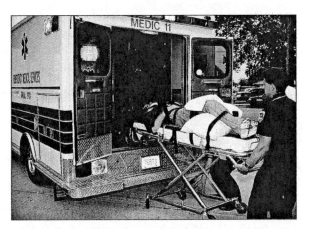

Paramedics frequently deal with emergency situations where urgent decisions must be made. The need for quick thinking and treatment precludes the usual process of contacting doctors to determine the best course of action. Most organizations face similar circumstances in which the benefit of separating the planning and control stages of the decision process is weighed against the cost of delaying a decision.

takes time to receive ratification so opportunities can be lost or adverse consequences can occur. A vivid illustration of delay costs comes from paramedicine. Paramedics operate under standing orders written by a medical control officer. The rules normally allow for little variance. On a noncritical call, the team member makes contact and evaluates the patient. Next, the paramedic calls in to the doctor who gives treatment orders to follow. The paramedic is not assigned the responsibility for certain procedures in these cases. But on a critical call, planning and control are linked to enable paramedics to respond in emergencies during which delays can be catastrophic. The general principle is that the paramedic's authority increases as the critical level of the patient's condition rises. An unwritten rule is that if a treatment is going to be done in the emergency room to help the patient, it should be done on the scene by the team who are trained in these procedures. Therefore, in emergencies, paramedics have the authority to initiate life-saving measures.[8]

Separating responsibilities for different stages of the decision process is not always sufficient to maintain control. Some organizational decisions are inherently difficult to control; for example, an organization's purchasing agent can collude with its suppliers to adversely affect it. The purchasing agent can agree to purchase from a particular supplier based on a bribe, which is called a *kickback.* Recently, former employees at General Motors were charged with taking kickbacks from suppliers selling goods and services to two GM plants. Investigators had

---

[8] Information from an online interview: www.paramedicpages.com.

worked with local law enforcement agencies to track the scheme that had been operating for several years.[9] In 1996, GM changed its ethics codes, including strict policies on gifts, gratuities, and entertainment, to ensure that high ethical standards are maintained.

Separating planning decisions from control is a procedure used in internal control systems. An **internal control system** is a system of checks and balances to verify that transactions are recorded and implemented correctly. An internal control system dissuades employees from committing fraud against the organization by establishing a trail of documents and by using the separation of duties so that employees monitor each other. Internal control systems work well unless employees collude to commit fraud. With collusion, planning and control are no longer separated.

Concept**Review**

1. What are the four steps of the decision process and how are they related to planning and control?
2. Why might an organization want to separate control from planning decisions?

MILLER DEPARTMENT STORE
(Continued)

You decide

In assigning responsibilities, Robin must think about separating planning decisions from control at Miller Department Store. This is especially true in the accounting area. For example, the person who writes the checks to pay the suppliers should not be the same person who authorizes the payment of a bill. If the authorization and check-writing responsibilities are performed by the same individual, that person could potentially write checks to himself or herself. The collection and deposit of cash also should be separated from the accounting for cash deposits. Accountants generally are in control positions and should not be in a position to make planning decisions.

Robin decides that the entire store must be reorganized to give the managers with the detailed knowledge of the customers' desires more responsibility over the merchandise sold in their area. The manager of the women's clothing department is on the floor every day talking to customers about what they are looking to buy, thus acquiring knowledge of their demands. Robin decides to link the responsibility for purchasing and pricing to the five sales departments. The toy sales department manager has the responsibility to purchase and price the toys. The furniture sales manager has the responsibility to buy and price furniture. And so on. To provide incentives for these managers, Robin has decided to offer each manager a fixed salary plus a percentage of his or her department's profits.

The five sales department managers still report to the retail sales manager, Julie Shepard, who is responsible for the profits of all five departments. While each of the five sales managers has the responsibility to make purchases and price them for their departments, Julie still retains the responsibility for ratifying the purchasing and pricing decisions. This ratification ensures that common themes are captured and that the customer faces a consistent set of policies.

Marketing, receiving and warehousing, and purchasing now report to Julie, and their costs are deducted from the sales departments' profits. Most of the purchasing agents are reassigned to work directly under a retail sales department manager, such as the toy or furniture manager. Julie's compen-

---

[9] http://www.treep.com/business/qgm1.htm.

sation consists of a fixed wage plus a percentage of all the five sales departments' profits less the costs of marketing, receiving and warehousing, and purchasing.

Robin still retains the direct authority over the accounting and maintenance departments. Since accounting calculates the profits of the sales departments, it should be separated from the retail sales department. Maintenance works on the entire building, not just the part of the building used by the retail sales department.

Chapter Seven continues to examine control issues in a decentralized organization. Decentralized organizations occur when lower-level managers have increased responsibilities. Any decentralization, however, must be accompanied by a corresponding change in the performance measures and compensation.

SUMMARY

1 **Balance the assignment of responsibilities, the choice of performance measures, and the compensation based on performance.** The assignment of responsibilities, the choice of performance measures, and the compensation system should be consistent with each other and should change simultaneously when the organizational structure changes.

2 **Link responsibilities with individuals who have the specific knowledge to make decisions.** Ideally, responsibility within an organization should reside with the individual with the best information related to that decision or with an individual in a position to receive that information. The responsibilities should be assigned to the person with the knowledge, or the knowledge should be transferred to the person with the responsibility for making the decision. The method chosen depends on the relative costs of transferring responsibilities or the knowledge.

3 **Recognize self-interest in motivating individuals within organizations.** Individuals join organizations and work in them to better their own welfare. The benefits each individual receives from joining the organization must exceed the costs that individual bears. Self-interested individuals do not automatically seek to further the organization's goals unless incentive systems motivate such behavior.

4 **Identify the costs and benefits of monitoring members of an organization.** Monitoring individuals within an organization to determine whether they are properly performing their duties is costly. Someone must observe their behavior or measure the results of their actions. Without some monitoring, however, individuals will not always perform their duties to benefit the organization.

Business Analysis

United Health Group (www.unitedhealthgroup.com), based in Minneapolis, is a diversified health and well-being enterprise. Today it is the second largest health insurer in the United States. One of its major components is the operation of health maintenance organizations (HMOs) with 8.7 million people served by its managed-care units. HMOs have developed in the United States in the last 20 years in response to the increasing cost of health care. Cost-cutting methods included increasing the emphasis on disease prevention through regular checkups and requiring patients to use family doctors or general practitioners as gatekeepers to specialized care. Most HMOs required these family doctors to contact the HMO for authorization when choosing a course of treatment such as hospitalization or minor surgery in the doctor's office.

HMOs have received negative publicity and have angered physicians and patients by withholding authorization from certain treatments that were considered too "experimental" or unnecessary. Recent legislative action has attempted to make HMOs potentially liable for medical malpractice for withholding authorization for certain services.

In 1999, United Health Group announced that it would no longer require doctors to obtain authorization prior to choosing a treatment for a patient. The company said that the cost of ratifying all of the requests was higher than the cost savings of limiting some of the doctor's decisions. How will United Health Group control costs without the authorization procedure?

5 **Choose performance measures that reveal actions of members of an organization.** Performance measures should reveal the actions of the individuals being evaluated and be consistent with the organization's goals. The measures should not be easily manipulated by the individual being evaluated.

6 **Design compensation contracts based on performance measures and responsibilities assigned.** Individuals within an organization should have compensation contracts that motivate them to act in the organization's best interest. The performance rewards should be matched to and coordinated with the performance evaluation system and the responsibilities assigned to the person. All legs of the three-legged stool must match.

7 **Design internal control systems by separating the planning process from the control process.** Responsibilities associated with making planning decisions, such as initiation and implementation, should be separated from responsibilities for control, such as ratification and monitoring.

8 **Identify control issues within an organization.** The purpose of control is to motivate individuals within the organization to act in its best interests.

KEY TERMS

balanced scorecard A set of performance measures that provide a comprehensive view of the organization by recognizing the goals of shareholders and the satisfaction of customers. *(p. 179)*

implementation The step in the decision process that carries out the organization's plans. *(p. 182)*

initiation The step in the decision process that identifies areas of improvement within the organization. *(p. 182)*

internal control system A system of checks and balances within the organization that helps it achieve its goals. *(p. 184)*

monitoring The step in the decision process to make sure that plans are implemented as intended. *(p. 182)*

monitoring cost The cost of observing members of the organization directly or indirectly. *(p. 177)*

performance measure A description of how well an individual has performed a task. *(p. 177)*

ratification The step in the decision process that determines whether a proposal is consistent with the organization's goals. *(p. 182)*

SELF-STUDY PROBLEM

Jennifer Whitsell had worked for men long enough. She was neither promoted nor recognized for her skills, and she was paid less than her male counterparts. Jennifer decided it was time to become her own boss, so she started her own advertising agency. Its primary function was to match organizations that wanted to advertise with media companies. Her agency was paid a percentage of every advertising contract that it arranged.

Jennifer had had such a difficult time as a woman working for men that she attempted to give women plenty of opportunities in her organization. Recently she has had a problem, however; one of her female employees just had a baby and wants a more flexible work schedule. Instead of working from nine to five, Monday through Friday, this woman wants to work some evenings but take off during the afternoons to be with her baby. She also wants to work at home rather than in the office. Jennifer is not sure that allowing for flexible time would work in her company. On the one hand, flexible time and working at home mean that Jennifer would not be able to control her employees very well because she would not be able to observe their activities. What if employees say they are going to work at home but end up playing with their children? On the other hand, she knows that flexible work time will improve morale and may even improve productivity.

How can Jennifer solve this problem?

Solution

Jennifer assumes that she can control her employees only by observing them. There are, however, many other ways to control employees. For example, Jennifer could have employees work in teams. Members of teams tend to control each other. If performance measures are team based, the other team members will be sure that each member does his or her fair share, or they will complain.

Jennifer could also use employee output as a performance measure rather than the number of hours they work. An employee who generates advertising contracts contributes to the advertising agency. The dollar amount of contracts written by an employee could be used as a performance measure, which would indirectly measure the employee's effort and skill. It also is consistent with the goal of maximizing profit for the agency. Number of hours worked is not a very good performance measure because an employee could spend a good deal of time in the office without contributing to the agency.

ANALYSIS AND INTERPRETATION PROBLEMS

Drivers for long-haul (cross-country) moving companies (e.g., Allied Van Lines) are often independent contractors whereas intercity movers are usually company employees.

Why are long-haul drivers often not employees of a company?

AIP 6.1
Monitoring
(LO 4)

Prior to the U.S. Securities Acts of 1933 and 1934, corporations with publicly traded stock were not required to issue financial statements, yet many voluntarily issued income statements and balance sheets.

Discuss the advantages and disadvantages of such voluntary disclosures.

AIP 6.2
Voluntary Disclosure of Performance Measures
(LO 4)

In a bank, the employee interacting with someone seeking a loan does not have the authority to grant the loan.

Why is the employee not given that responsibility?

AIP 6.3
Separation of Duties
(LO 1)

Jen and Barry opened an ice cream shop in Eugene, Oregon. It was a big success, so they decided to open ice cream shops in other cities including Portland, Oregon. They have hired Dante to manage the shop in Portland. Jen and Barry are considering two different sets of performance measures for him. The first would grade him based on the cleanliness of the restaurant and customer service. The second set would use accounting numbers, including the profit of the shop in Portland.

What are the advantages and disadvantages of each set of performance measures?

AIP 6.4
Choice of Performance Measures
(LO 1, 5, 8)

Physicians practicing in Eastern University's hospital have the following compensation agreement. Each doctor bills the patient (or Blue Cross/Blue Shield) for his or her services. The doctor pays for all direct expenses incurred in the clinic including nurses, medical malpractice insurance, secretaries, supplies, and equipment. Each doctor has a stated salary cap (e.g., $100,000). For patient fees collected over the salary cap, the doctor retains 30% of the additional fees less expenses. For example, if a doctor bills and collects $150,000 from patients and pays related expenses of $40,000, the doctor retains $3,000 of the excess net fees [30% of ($150,000 − 40,000 − 100,000)] and Eastern University receives $7,000. If $120,000 of fees are collected and $40,000 of expenses are incurred, the physician's net cash flow is $80,000 and Eastern University receives none of the fees.

Critically evaluate the existing compensation plan and recommend changes.

AIP 6.5
Compensation
(LO 5)

Donald Curtis criticized corporate accounting systems by arguing the following:

AIP 6.6
Performance Measures
(LO 5)

> The SEC, the stock market, and the corporate compensation committees all seem to focus on accrual earnings as the only reliable and fair measure of corporate performance. . . . What's wrong is that the modern American accounting system is a very imperfect measure of corporate performance. (Whether publicly held or not.) The plain fact is that it cannot *technically* do what we are asking it to do with anything like the precision we are expecting. A failure to adequately understand the system's limitations—combined with our penchant for treating things which seem to be quantifiable (such as profit) as more real than things which are difficult to quantify (such as quality of a company's [product])—has, in my view, contributed to serious mismanagement of American business during the last several years.

Critically evaluate the statement in terms of the issues presented in this chapter.

Source: Donald Curtis, "The Modern American Accounting System: Does It Really Measure Corporate Performance?" *The Financial Executive,* January/February 1985, pp. 58–62.

AIP 6.7

Identification of Control Issues

(LO 3, 8)

Mary Sweet has just opened a candy store. It is open from 10 AM to 8 PM each day, which means that Mary must work a minimum of 10 hours a day, seven days a week. In addition to sales, she must spend time on purchasing, paying bills, and cleaning. She quickly decides she needs to hire help. Her first hire is a person to operate the cash register for five days each week. This person also will be responsible for closing the shop on those days so Mary can spend the evenings with her family. While Mary was operating the store by herself, she did not have to worry about control issues. Now that she is hiring another person, she must consider mechanisms to control the new employee.

Describe some control problems that might arise and some mechanisms that Mary could use to help monitor these problems.

AIP 6.8

Linkage of Responsibilities and Knowledge

(LO 2)

A professional football team has both a coach and a general manager. The general manager is usually responsible for the organization's operations and is responsible for selecting team personnel. The coach is responsible for training the team and making decisions on game day. Many coaches have been unhappy with their relationship with the general manager and believe that they should have more responsibilities in choosing the players. Some of the top coaches are now insisting on being both the coach and the general manager.

What are the advantages and disadvantages of separating the duties of the coach and general manager with respect to selecting members of the football team?

AIP 6.9

Monitoring of Computer Use

(LO 4)

Samson Company is an engineering firm that employs many engineers who work individually on different projects. Most of the design work takes place on computers, which are connected by a network. Employees can also surf the Internet through their desktop computers.

The president is concerned about productivity among her engineers. She has acquired software that allows her to monitor each engineer's computer work. At anytime during the day, she can observe on her screen exactly the task on which the different engineers are working. The engineers are quite unhappy with this monitoring process; they believe that it is unethical for the president to be able to access their computers without their knowledge.

Discuss the pros and cons of monitoring by observing the engineers' computer work.

AIP 6.10

Choice of Performance Measures

(LO 5)

The president of Canby Insurance Company has just read an article on the balanced scorecard. A company has a balanced scorecard when it has a set of performance measures that reflect the diverse interests and goals of all the organization's stakeholders (shareholders, customers, employees, and society). Presently, Canby has only one performance measure for the top executives: profit. The board of directors claims that profit as the sole performance measure is sufficient. If customers are satisfied and employees are productive, then the company will be profitable. Any other performance measure will detract from the basic goal of making a profit.

Explain the costs and benefits of having only profit as a performance measure.

AIP 6.11

Performance Measures and Responsibilities

(LO 6)

The new president of Sawtooth Division of Waterhouse Company is complaining about the limitations that the CEO of Waterhouse has placed on him. Sawtooth Division is composed of several logging mills in the Pacific Northwest. These mills were designed to cut large "old-growth" logs. Recent regulation has curtailed the cutting of almost all old-growth forests, and the mills are struggling to find a sufficient supply of logs to operate. The president is being evaluated based on the profit of the logging mills; if things continue the way they are now, a loss is inevitable. The president's main complaint is that he does not have the right to change the logging mills to accommodate smaller logs or move into a secondary wood-products field, such as wood trim or prefabricated houses.

Does Sawtooth Division's president have a reasonable complaint?

AIP 6.12

Performance Measures and Teams

(LO 3, 6, 7)

Royal Motors is a car manufacturer. Until recently, the company operated as an assembly line. The chassis was started at one end of the factory. As it moved through the plant, parts were added until a completed car emerged from the other end of the plant. Henry Ford developed this assembly line approach near the beginning of the twentieth century.

Royal Motors recently has decided to change to a cell manufacturing approach. A cell is composed of a team that completes an entire car in a relatively small area. Workers have multiple skills that allow them to perform many different operations rather than a single operation on an assembly line. Parts are brought to the cell for assembly.

On the assembly line, a worker was evaluated by the performance of a single task. The work performed by the individual workers of the cell-manufacturing team is not as easily identifiable.

How should Royal Motors change performance measures to accommodate cell manufacturing?

Travel Magazine's executive group is very unhappy with its photographer. She had been sent to Tahiti to take some pictures of sunny beaches to entice visitors to Tahiti. Unfortunately, all of her pictures have a grayish tinge to them, making the beaches appear to be rather ordinary. The magazine executives are thinking about replacing the photographer. The photographer believes that it was not her fault that the photographs turned out so poorly. She worked extremely hard, but it rained almost every day while she was in Tahiti.

Why has this conflict developed? Are there ways to resolve it?

AIP 6.13
Outcome versus Input Performance Measures
(LO 5)

The local electric utility receives thousands of checks every day from its customers. The following processes occur in handling them: opening the letters, recording the amount of the check and the customer's account, filling out a deposit slip for the bank, and depositing the checks with the bank.

Describe methods of controlling these processes so that checks are not misplaced or stolen.

AIP 6.14
Separation of Duties
(LO 1)

The manufacturing division manager of a computer chip company had traditionally been evaluated based on costs. As long as he could produce computer chips more cheaply than the previous year, he received his bonus. The initial benchmark for the bonus was established based on the first year of manufacturing a new computer chip. The company recognized, however, that this type of reward system for the manufacturing manager would no longer work. First, the product life of the computer chips was becoming shorter and shorter; some chips were made only for a year. Second, the company had switched to target costing. Its customers would request a computer chip with certain characteristics and at a price that they would be willing to pay. The company's engineers then attempted to design a chip that had all the required features and that could be made cheaply enough to earn a profit. Once the engineers were satisfied that the computer chip had been appropriately designed, the company signed the deal and turned the design over to the manufacturing division manager for production. The target cost based on the engineers' estimate became the benchmark on which the manufacturing manager's bonus was based. If he could produce the new chip below the target cost, he would receive a bonus.

The manufacturing manager did not like this new bonus system; he felt that the target cost was imposed on him and did not consider the problems of producing new chips, especially the learning process.

How could the process of choosing a target cost and using it as a benchmark for the manufacturing division affect the manager's compensation?

AIP 6.15
Target Costs as Benchmarks for Performance Measures
(LO 6)

It was in Deyang in 1969 that I came to know how China's peasants really lived. Each day started with the production team leader allocating jobs. All the peasants had to work, and they each earned a fixed number of "work points" (*gong-fen*) for their day's work. The number of work points accumulated was an important element in the distribution at the end of the year. The peasants got food, fuel, and other daily necessities, plus a tiny sum of cash, from the production team. After the harvest, the production team paid part of it over as tax to the state. Then the rest was divided up. First, a basic quantity was meted out equally to every male, and about a quarter less to every female. Children under three received a half portion.

The remainder of the crop was then distributed according to how many work points each person had earned. Twice a year, the peasants would all assemble to fix the daily work points for each person. No one missed these meetings. In the end, most young and middle-aged men would be allocated ten points a day, and women eight. One or two whom the whole village acknowledged to be exceptionally strong got an extra point. "Class enemies" like the former village landlord and his family got a

AIP 6.16
Performance Measures and Free Riders
(LO 5, 6)

couple points less than the others, in spite of the fact that they worked no less hard and were usually given the toughest jobs.

Since there was little variation from individual to individual of the same gender in terms of daily points, the number of work points accumulated depended mainly on how many days one worked, rather than how one worked.

What predictable behavior do you expect the Chinese agricultural system will generate?

Source: J. Chang, *Wild Swans: Three Daughters of China* (New York: Anchor Books, 1991), pp. 414–415.

AIP 6.17

Performance Measures, Responsibilities, and Self-Interest

(LO 1, 3)

The following quote is from a textbook on organization theory:

> Drawing upon the writing of Maslow, McGregor presented his Theory X–Theory Y dichotomy to describe two differing conceptions of human behavior. Theory X assumptions held that people are inherently lazy, they dislike work, and that they will avoid it whenever possible. Leaders who act on Theory X premises are prone to controlling their subordinates through coercion, punishment, and the use of financial rewards; the use of external controls is necessary, as most human beings are thought to be incapable of self-direction and assuming responsibility. In contrast, Theory Y is based on the assumption that work can be enjoyable and that people will work hard and assume responsibility if they are given the opportunity to achieve personal goals at the same time.

Using the framework presented in the text, critically analyze the Theory X–Theory Y quotation above.

Source: V. K. Narayanan and R. Nath, *Organization Theory: A Strategic Approach* (New York, NY: McGraw-Hill/Irwin, 1993), p. 403.

AIP 6.18

Three-Legged Stool

(LO 1)

Sue Koehler manages a revenue center of a large national manufacturer that sells office furniture to local businesses in Detroit. A revenue center is evaluated on its revenues. Sue has responsibility over pricing. Her compensation is a fixed wage of $23,000 per year plus 2% of her office's total sales.

Critically evaluate the control issues in Sue's revenue center.

AIP 6.19

Compensation and Incentives

(LO 3, 5, 6)

I used to run the company that made Formula 409, the spray cleaner. From modest entrepreneurial beginnings, we'd gone national and shipped the hell out of P&G, Colgate, Drackett, and every other giant that raised its head. From the beginning, I'd employed a simple incentive plan based on "case sales": Every month, every salesman and executive received a bonus check based on how many cases of 409 he'd sold. Even bonuses for the support staff were based on monthly case sales. It was a happy time, with everyone making a lot of money, including me.

We abandoned our monthly case-sales bonus plan and installed an *annual* profit-sharing plan, based on personnel evaluations. It didn't take long for the new plan to produce results.

What do you think happened at this company after it started the annual profit-sharing plan?

Source: Wilson Harrell, "Inspire Action: What Really Motivates Your People to Excel?" *Success,* September 1995.

AIP 6.20

Changes to the Three-Legged Stool

(LO 1)

A *Wall Street Journal* article (December 26, 1996, p. A1) describes a series of changes at the Pratt & Whitney Maine plant that manufactures parts for jet engines. In 1993, it was about to be closed, because of its high operating costs and inefficiencies. A new plant manager overhauled operations. He broadened job descriptions so that inspectors do 15% more work than they did five years ago. A "results-sharing" plan pays hourly workers if the plant exceeds targets such as cost cutting and on-time delivery. Now everyone is looking to cut costs.

Hourly workers also helped design a new pay scheme that is linked to the amount of training a worker has, not seniority. This plan was designed after the plant manager picked

22 factory-floor workers, gave them a conference room, and told them to draft a new pay plan linked to learning.

Shop-floor wages vary between $9 and $19 per hour, with the most money going to people running special cost studies or quality projects, tasks previously held by managers.

This chapter has emphasized the importance of keeping all three legs of the stool in balance. Identify the changes that Pratt & Whitney made to all three legs of the stool at its Maine plant.

EXTENDED ANALYSIS AND INTERPRETATION PROBLEM

Woodhaven Service is a small, independent filling station located in the Woodhaven section of Queens. It has three gasoline pumps and two service bays. The repair facility specializes in automotive maintenance (oil changes, tune ups, etc.) and minor repairs (mufflers, shock absorbers). Woodhaven generally refers customers who require major work (transmission rebuilds, electronics) to shops that are better equipped to handle such repairs. Major repairs are done in-house only when both the customer and the mechanic agree that this would be the best course of action.

AIP 6.21
Woodhaven Service Station

During the 20 years that he has owned Woodhaven Service, Harold Mateen's competence and fairness have built a loyal customer base of neighborhood residents. In fact, demand for his services has been more than he can reasonably meet, yet the repair end of his business is not especially profitable. Most of his competitors earn the lion's share of their profits through repairs, but Harold is making almost all of his money by selling gasoline. If he could make more money on repairs, Woodhaven would be the most successful service station in the area. Harold believes that Woodhaven's weakness in repair profitability is due to the inefficiency of his mechanics. They are paid the industry average of $500 per week. Harold does not think he overpays them, but he feel he is not getting his money's worth.

Harold's son, Andrew, is a philosophy student at Humanities University, where he has learned the Socratic dictum of "to know the Good is to do the Good." Andrew provided his father with a classic text on employee morality, the Reverend Doctor Weisbrotten's *Work Hard on Thine Job and Follow the Righteous Way.* Every morning for two months, Harold, Andrew, and the mechanics devoted one hour to studying this text. Despite many lively and fascinating discussions on the rights and responsibilities of the employee, productivity did not improve one bit. Harold figured he would just have to go out and hire harder-working mechanics.

The failure of the Weisbrotten method did not surprise Lisa, Harold's daughter. A student at Commerce College, she has the training to know that Andrew's methods were bunk. As anyone serious about business knows, the true science of productivity and management of human resources resides in Dr. von Drekken's masterful *Modifying Organizational Behavior through Commitment to a Happy Environment.* Yes, happiness leads to greater productivity! Harold followed the scientific methods to the letter. Despite giving out gold stars, blowing up balloons, and wearing a smiley face button, Lisa's way proved no better than Andrew's did.

Harold thinks that his neighbor, Jack Myers, owner of Honest Jack's Pre-Enjoyed Autorama, might be helpful. After all, one does not become as successful as Jack without much practical knowledge. Or, maybe it is Jack's great radio jingle that does it. However, Jack says:

> It's not the jingle, you idiot! It's the way I pay my guys. Your mechanics make $500 a week no matter what. Why should they put out for you? Who cares about gold stars? My guys—my guys get paid straight commission and nothing more. They do good by me and I do good by them. Otherwise, let 'em starve.
>
> Look, it's real simple. Pay 'em a percentage of the sales for the work they do. If you need to be a nice guy about it, make that percent so that if sales are average, then they make their usual 500 bucks. But if sales are better, they get that percent extra. This way they don't get hurt but got real reason to help you out.

Straight commission, however, seemed a little radical for Harold. What if sales were bad for a week? That would hurt the mechanics.

Harold figured that it would be better to pay each mechanic a guaranteed $300 a week plus a commission rate that would, given an average volume of business, pay them the extra $200 that would bring their wage back to $500. Under this system, the mechanics would be insulated from a bad week, would not be penalized for an average week, and would still have the incentive to attempt to improve sales. Yes, this seemed fairer.

On the other hand, maybe Jack knows only about the used car business, not about business in general. Harold figured that he should look for an incentive pay method more in line with the way things are done in the auto repair business. Perhaps he should pay his mechanics in the same way that his customers pay him—by the job. It is standard practice for service stations to charge customers a flat rate for the labor associated with any job. The number of labor hours for which the customer is charged is generally taken from a manual that outlines expected labor times for specific jobs on specific vehicles. The customer pays for these expected hours regardless of how many actual labor hours are expended on the job. Many shops also pay their mechanics by the job. Harold thinks that this approach makes theoretical sense because it links the mechanic's pay to the labor charges paid by the customer.

a. This problem presents three popular approaches to alleviating control problems. Although certain aspects of each of these methods are consistent with the views presented in the chapter, none of them is likely to succeed. Discuss the similarities and differences between the ideas in the chapter and

    1. Rev. Dr. Weisbrotten's approach.

    2. Dr. von Drekken's approach.

    3. Harold Mateen's idea of hiring "harder-working" mechanics.

b. Discuss the expected general effect at Woodhaven Service of the newly proposed incentive compensation plans. How might they help Woodhaven and, assuming that Harold wants his business to be successful for a long time to come, what major divergent behaviors would be expected under the new compensation proposals? How damaging would you expect these new behaviors to be on a business such as Woodhaven Service? Present a defense of each of the following propositions:

    1. Harold's plan offers less incentive for divergent behavior than Honest Jack's.

    2. Limiting a mechanic's pay by placing an upper bound of $750 per week on his earnings reduces incentives for divergent behavior.

c. Suppose that Harold owned a large auto repair franchise located in a department store in a popular suburban shopping mall. Suppose also that this department store is a heavily promoted, well-known national chain famous for its good values and easy credit. How should Harold's thinking on incentive compensation change? What if Harold did not own the franchise but was the manager of a company-owned outlet?

d. The mechanic who services the car decides what services are warranted. Discuss the costs and benefits of this fact for Woodhaven Service and the independently owned chain store repair shop.

Chapter**Seven**

Decentralized Organizations

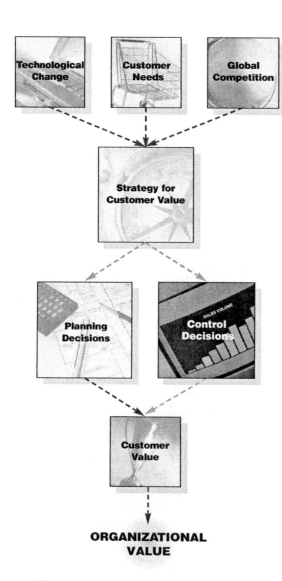

1 Use the controllability principle to choose performance measures for managers.

2 Identify responsibility centers based on the extent of each manager's responsibilities.

3 Choose performance measures for cost, profit, and investment centers.

4 Identify the strengths and weaknesses of using return on investment (ROI) and residual income as performance measures for investment centers.

5 Choose transfer prices to create performance measures that reflect the activities controlled by each manager.

6 Use opportunity costs to choose transfer prices that will lead to decentralized decision making that is best for the organization.

7 Choose transfer prices to minimize taxes and overcome international obstacles.

SHAH MOTORS

Shah Motors is a new- and used-car dealership. Jeremy Shah, its owner and president, makes long-term strategic decisions for the company and supervises the managers of its three departments: new-car sales, used-car sales, and service. Alice Dempster, the new-car sales manager, advises Jeremy on orders for new cars, makes the final pricing decision on sales, is responsible for customer satisfaction, and coordinates the new-car sales staff. The sales staff is paid solely on a commission basis with the opportunity for a few bonuses such as free trips.

Slick Thompson, the used-car sales manager, operates a lot next to the new-car dealership. He must accept the used cars from the new-car dealership that are traded in to purchase a new car. He also purchases inventory directly from wholesalers and people wanting to sell their used cars. Slick makes the final pricing decision and coordinates the used-car sales staff, which is rewarded based on commissions from sales.

Grease Johnson, the service manager, is in charge of the service department, which provides maintenance and repair services for cars. He is responsible for maintaining a parts department and coordinating a service crew, which is paid a fixed salary.

Like most car dealerships, Shah Motors' financial success varies with the economy. When the economy is booming, the new- and used-car sales make the business very profitable. When it is weak, Shah Motors must rely on profits from the service department to survive. Jeremy believes that his company should not be so dependent on the economy and is considering a new compensation scheme for its managers. Presently, the managers receive a fixed salary, but Jeremy believes that some type of bonus scheme might motivate them to work harder to achieve higher profits for the company.

CONTROLLABILITY PRINCIPLE

L0 1 Use the controllability principle to choose performance measures for managers.

Control Decisions

The idea of holding managers responsible for those decisions for which they are given authority is called the **controllability principle. Controllable costs** are costs affected by a manager's decisions. Managers affect controllable costs; therefore, these costs partially reflect the managers' actions. Through the measurement of controllable costs, superiors have information about what decisions managers have made. Therefore, controllable costs are potential performance measures for managers who control those costs. For example, the managers of a manufacturing plant are held responsible for the costs of the plant because they make decisions that affect plant costs.

A single manager generally does not have control over all of an organization's costs. Each manager has responsibilities that are limited by the job description and allow him or her to control only certain costs. Some costs are also affected by the organization's environment and are not controlled by its managers. For example, economic forces that a plant manager cannot control affect the price of raw materials. Uncontrollable costs generally do not reveal his or her actions and are poorer performance measures.

Costs generally cannot be classified as either completely controllable or completely uncontrollable. Figure 7.1 demonstrates that costs are usually influenced by both managerial actions and uncontrollable environmental factors. For example, marina managers who are not held accountable for damage done by hurricanes have less incentive to prepare the marinas for severe storms. Although the managers cannot influence the occurrence of hurricanes, they can influence the costs incurred from their impact. In these cases, the managers should be responsible for the portion of costs that they can control. Holding them accountable for only those costs solely under their control does not provide them with incentives to take actions that can affect the consequences of an uncontrollable event. The feedback loop from the performance measures and rewards in Figure 7.1 demonstrates the influence of the performance measurement system and the reward system on the managers' actions.

Managers prefer to be evaluated based on controllable costs because their rewards will be much more predictable. Managers generally do not want their rewards to be uncertain, and to avoid uncertainty, they do not want performance measures that are affected by factors that they cannot control. Therefore, they prefer controllable performance measures, such as controllable costs.

Some performance measures, however, are partially affected by factors not under the managers' control. In the previous example, hurricanes were not controllable, but they affected costs. Managers would like to eliminate the uncontrollable portion of the costs from their performance measures.

One method of removing uncontrollable factors from a performance measure is to compare performance measures of different managers facing similar circumstances. The use of **relative performance measurement** allows a manager's performance to be judged relative to the performance of a comparison group. The comparison group helps control for random events that affect both the person being evaluated and the comparison group. If the costs of the marina managers are compared with those of other marina managers adversely affected by the hurricane, its uncontrollable effects can be eliminated. Relative performance measurement is also

Figure 7.1

Controllability of Costs

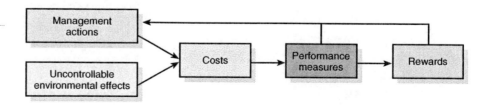

used in assigning course grades. Many instructors "curve" the grades; instead of awarding A's for scores of 94 to 100, the top 15% of the class receives A's. Curving the grades controls for unusually easy or hard exams and is a way of removing some of the risk for students.

Relative performance measures, however do not recognize whether all students or managers performed better or worse than some absolute standard. By comparing individual performances with the performance of others, approximately half of the individuals will always be graded better than average and half will always be graded worse than average. There is no possibility for all individuals to be rated above average even if they performed their duties as specified. Relative performance measures discourage cooperative effort across individuals because they recognize that they will be compared with others.

In summary, each manager of an organization is given certain responsibilities that define the limits of the manager's control. The part of the organization within these limits is under the manager's control. Ideally, managers are evaluated based on performance measures of activities that they also control.

Concept**Review**

1. Why is the controllability principle used in most organizations?

2. What are the advantages and disadvantages of using a relative performance measure?

SHAH MOTORS
(Continued)

To analyze his organization, Jeremy Shaw outlines the responsibilities that he has given his three managers. Before designing the performance measurement and compensation system, he must determine what each manager controls.

Alice Dempster, new-car sales manager, controls the product mix ordered from the factory, price, sales staff, and customer interactions. She does not control the size of new-car inventory and showroom facility, or liabilities of the dealership.

Slick Thompson, used-car sales manager, controls purchasing and the size of inventory, the used-car lot and office, sales staff, and prices of used cars. He does not control the acceptance of used cars from the new-car center or liabilities of the dealership.

Grease Johnson, service department manager, controls the scheduling of maintenance, parts management, and service workers. He does not control billing rates and price of parts, the size of the service shop, or the liabilities of the dealership.

RESPONSIBILITY CENTERS

Organizations are typically composed of subunits. For example, a firm might be organized into functional areas such as marketing, manufacturing, and distribution departments. Another organization is divided into subunits by product or service offered. A university, for example, is divided into colleges that teach different topics. Each of these subunits is commonly subdivided into smaller subunits. For example, manufacturing might be further subdivided into parts manufacturing and assembly, and assembly might be organized according to the product assembled. Colleges are divided into departments and specialized groups within departments. Each of these subunits represents work groups and managers with specific responsibilities.

LO 2 Identify responsibility centers based on the extent of each manager's responsibilities.

Table 7.1

Differences among Cost, Profit, and Investment Centers

Type of Responsibility Center	Responsibilities	Performance Measurement
Cost center (type 1)*	Choose output for a given cost of inputs	Output (maximize given quality constraints)
Cost center (type 2)	Choose input mix to achieve a given output	Cost (minimize given quality constraints)
Profit center	Choose inputs and outputs with a fixed level of investment	Profit (maximize)
Investment center	Choose inputs, outputs, and level of investment	Return on investment, residual income (maximize)

* If output is revenue, this type of center is often referred to as a *revenue center.*

Responsibility accounting is the process of recognizing subunits within the organization, assigning responsibilities to managers of those subunits, and evaluating the performance of those managers. These organizational subunits, called *responsibility centers,* could be a single individual, a department, a functional area such as finance or marketing, or a division. The manager of each responsibility center has different responsibilities and, accordingly, different performance measures. In each case, responsibilities should be linked with the requisite specialized knowledge. Responsibility accounting therefore dictates the design of the performance measurement system of the results from the responsibilities assigned to each manager. For example, if a manager is assigned responsibilities to sell products to customers in New York, performance measurement of this individual should not include sales to customers in Maine. The following sections and Table 7.1 describe different types of responsibility centers.

Cost Centers

A manager's responsibilities dictate the type of responsibility center and imply the appropriate performance measure for him or her. Some managers have more responsibilities than others; those with more responsibilities generally make more complex decisions. Managers with fewer responsibilities have less control over factors that affect the organization's value. A manager's responsibilities are commonly described in terms of the different types of responsibility centers.

Managers of **cost centers** tend to have the fewest responsibilities within an organization. They generally have control over a limited amount of assets but usually have no right to price those assets for sale or to acquire more assets. Managers of an organization's internal service are typically managers of a cost center. Managers of data processing, accounting, personnel, research and development, and manufacturing are usually cost center managers.

Cost centers can operate in two ways. Some of them (type 1 in Table 7.1) are given a fixed amount of resources (a budget). They are told to produce as much output as they can for the given amount of fixed resources. For example, suppose the manager of a sales department has a fixed budget for sales staff and advertising. This manager is evaluated based on the amount of sales generated with the fixed budget. The cost center manager usually has authority to change the mix of inputs so long as the unit stays within the budget constraint. The sales cost center manager can substitute between sales staff and advertising as long as the total cost stays within the budget.

The performance measures for the manager of a type 1 cost center are the amount and quality of the output. Producing a large number of units without controlling for quality is not in the organization's best interest. Thus, quality must be monitored. The danger also exists that an output performance measure will

L0 3   Choose performance measures for cost, profit, and investment centers.

motivate the manager to overproduce, which can lead to the imposition of costs on other parts of the organization. For example, the manufacturing manager of a computer plant who makes more computers than can be sold will impose costs on the part of the organization that is responsible for storing the finished inventory.

An alternative cost center arrangement (type 2 in Table 7.1) is the minimization of costs while producing a fixed amount of output. For example, the manager of a metal stamping department is told to produce 10,000 stampings per day of a fixed specification and quality. The manager is evaluated on meeting the production schedule and on reducing the cost of the 10,000 stampings without reducing quality. The performance measure is the total cost necessary to produce the required output. Once again, however, quality must be monitored since the focus on minimizing costs could lead to a lower quality of output.

Neither type of cost center manager has the responsibility to set the price or scale of operations. In both types of cost centers, the manager has the responsibility to change how inputs are combined to produce the output. Performance measures include total costs, amount produced, and quality of output.

SHAH MOTORS
(Continued)

Jeremy considers his managers and what they control. Grease Johnson, the service manager, controls the input mix (service staff and parts) to repair a car but does not control the billing rate or the price of parts. At first glance, the service department appears to operate as a cost center, but Jeremy is not sure how to choose the performance measure for this department. On the one hand, output is limited to the cars needing repair; therefore, using the number of repairs as a performance measure does not appear to be appropriate. On the other hand, Jeremy is worried that using cost as a performance measure will encourage Grease to take shortcuts in making repairs. To circumvent this problem, Jeremy decides to use both costs and customer evaluations as performance measures for Grease.

Profit Centers

Some managers have responsibilities beyond the control of costs through the efficient use of resources. Typically, managers of products are ultimately responsible for both the cost and the pricing of the product. These product managers are described as managers of **profit centers.** They have some control over both revenues and expenses, which are the factors that lead to profit. In addition, managers of restaurants and retail shops are typically treated as profit center managers.

Profit center managers are given a fixed amount of assets (for example, the restaurant or retail shop and its furnishings) and usually have the responsibility for pricing and input mix decisions. They can decide what products to produce, the quality level (given some constraints), and how to market the products. For example, the local branch of a chain of copy centers is treated as a profit center. The branch manager does not have the responsibility to increase the size of the building or to open other local branches. The branch manager can, however, change the mix of services the store offers and is also responsible for marketing those services. The branch manager has the responsibility to price the various services offered because this person has the knowledge of the local competition. If pricing decisions were not assigned to the branch manager, the company could not respond quickly to changes in competitor prices.

The primary performance measure for a profit center is the profit it generates. One of the goals of a profit organization is to generate profit. Therefore, using profit as a performance measure generally motivates the profit center manager to act in the best interest of the entire organization. Profit centers are not always independent of other profit centers within the same organization, however. For

Chain restaurants affect and are affected by the performance of all members of the chain. Customers frequent these restaurants seeking good value, consistent service, and quality. To promote organizational goals, chains often tie managerial performance and rewards to financial and non-financial targets for the individual restaurant and the entire chain.

example, managers of restaurants belonging to the same chain can affect each other's profits. Customers who have a bad experience in one of the chain's restaurants are unlikely to try others in the chain. Therefore, the evaluation of profit center managers commonly uses other performance measures such as quality and customer satisfaction in addition to profits.

Profit center managers have greater responsibilities than do cost center managers. In many cases, several cost centers are grouped together to form a profit center. The managers of the cost centers within the profit center are managed by, and report to, the profit center manager. For example, a manufacturing unit and a sales unit could be separate cost centers within a single profit center. The profit center manager tells the manufacturing manager what to produce and the sales manager how much cash is available to promote and generate sales. The manufacturing and sales managers can choose the mix of resources to accomplish their tasks, but the profit center manager holds the pricing responsibilities. The manufacturing manager is evaluated on costs necessary to produce the required output. The sales manager is evaluated on sales generated from advertising and the efforts of the sales staff. The profit manager is evaluated on the profit of the combined efforts of manufacturing and sales.

SHAH MOTORS
(Continued)

Jeremy believes that the new-car sales division should be treated as a profit center. Alice Dempster, the manager, controls price and the product mix but not the size of the inventory or showroom. Using profit as the sole performance measure for Alice appears, however, to be a little risky for both parties. She is worried that her performance will be affected by changes in the economy. Profits and therefore her reward will be depressed during economic downturns. Jeremy believes that using profits as a sole measure of performance is risky because he is not sure how long Alice will be working for Shah Motors; some competitors have been trying to hire her. Jeremy also is worried that she will act in an unethical manner to entice customers to purchase cars to increase short-term profit. Jeremy decides to use a relative performance measure (profits compared to the industry average) in conjunction with customer surveys to evaluate Alice.

Investment Centers

Some managers have even more responsibilities than managers of a profit center have. Managers of profit centers are limited to the use of a prespecified amount of assets. Managers of **investment centers** have all the responsibilities of a profit center manager in addition to the right to expand or contract the size of operations. Division managers who control multiple product lines are normally considered investment center managers. Investment center managers can request more funds from the central administration to increase capacity, develop new products, and expand into new geographical areas. If these requests are too large or inconsistent with organizational policy, they may have to be ratified by someone in the central administration. Even investment center managers have limits on their responsibilities and some control is imposed on them.

Figure 7.2   Hierarchy of Responsibility Centers

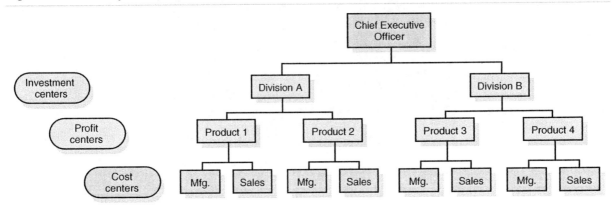

Investment centers usually contain several profit centers. For example, local branches of a copy center organization may be treated as profit centers and regional districts treated as investment centers. Managers of the regional district are responsible for all of the local branches (profit centers) within the district. In addition, managers of the regional district have the responsibility to identify and construct new local branches and to close existing local branches that are not successful.

The choice of responsibility centers through granting responsibilities reflects the organization's hierarchy. The organization is composed of investment centers, which are composed of profits centers, which are composed of cost centers. This hierarchy of responsibility centers is demonstrated in Figure 7.2

Performance measures for investment center managers are more difficult to identify because of the nature of their responsibilities. Although investment managers have the opportunity to expand or contract their investment center, they are generally not responsible for financing the expansions. Cash infusions necessary for expansion usually come from the central administration, which is responsible for issuing debt and stock. Investment center managers generally have control only of assets and short-term liabilities, such as accounts payable. The accounting reports of these investment centers include no interest expenses or dividend payments.

The absence of interest expenses in an investment center means that profit is not a very good performance measure for a center's manager. Investment center managers can generally increase the profit from the assets by increasing the asset size. However, increasing the size of the investment center without recognizing the opportunity cost of having more cash invested in assets (the opportunity cost of capital) can be harmful for the entire organization.

The **opportunity cost of capital** is represented by a percentage return that reflects the forgone opportunity of using the cash. This forgone opportunity could be interest earned by placing the money in a bank account or the cost of borrowing more money to fund other investment opportunities. In the former case, the opportunity cost of capital is the interest rate earned in a bank account. The opportunity cost in the latter case is the interest rate paid to borrow money. Chapter Thirteen provides a more detailed description of the opportunity cost of capital. In this chapter, the opportunity cost of capital is provided. In finance, the opportunity cost of capital must be estimated.

Numerical Example 7.1

The television division of an electronics firm requests $100 million from the central administration to develop, manufacture, and sell a new television model. Central administration borrows the $100 million at 10% interest to provide the cash. The television division invests the $100 million to generate annual profits of $6 million. What is the net effect of these transactions on the profit of the electronics firm?

Consumers demand televisions seemingly customized to their preferences. The decision to introduce a new model requires the analysis of the impact on customer demand and profits, including the cost of additional capital funding. Incremental revenues of new models must cover incremental costs, including the opportunity cost of capital invested.

Solution

The interest expense on the $100 million is $10 million annually. Therefore, the investment in the new television caused a $4 million loss ($6 million profit − $10 million interest expense) to the electronics firm.

Identification of Responsibility Centers

Although cost, profit, and investment centers are identified by the responsibilities of their managers, not all managers fit exactly into one of these categories. For example, manufacturing managers are commonly treated as managers of cost centers, yet these managers typically influence revenues although they do not have responsibilities over pricing. Revenues are influenced by customer satisfaction due to timely delivery and quality. The manufacturing manager does influence timely delivery and quality, so this manager is partially responsible for revenues.

Profit center managers seldom control all aspects of revenues and costs but are usually able to make marginal adjustments to the asset size of the responsibility center. Investment center managers, alternatively, seldom have unlimited authority to increase asset size.

Therefore, identifying the appropriate type of responsibility center is often difficult. Nonetheless, the partitioning of the organization into different types of responsibility centers is important for guiding the choice of performance measures. In particular, it is important to match the performance measures chosen to the responsibilities assigned to the responsibility center.

Concept**Review**

1. What are the two types of cost centers?
2. Why should quality performance measures be used in conjunction with cost as a performance measure for cost centers?
3. What type of responsibilities do profit center managers typically have?
4. Why are performance measures of investment centers difficult to determine?
5. Why is it difficult to classify some responsibility centers?

SHAH MOTORS
(Continued)

Jeremy has given Slick Thompson, the manager of the used-car division, more responsibilities than the rest of the managers. Slick not only can choose the used cars for his inventory (but he must accept trade-ins for new cars from the new-car division) but also can decide on the size of his inventory up to $1 million. When Slick expands his inventory, however, he must obtain the necessary cash from Jeremy. Unfortunately, the profit of the used-car division does not explicitly recognize the opportunity cost of holding the inventory, so Jeremy is worried that Slick will overuse the privilege of buying inventory. If Jeremy uses the profit of the used-car division, which does not recognize the opportunity cost of capital, as a performance measure for Slick, then Slick will choose to have the maximum inventory allowed. More inventory will increase the number of opportunities to make a sale, but Slick would not be penalized for holding excess inventory. Jeremy must find a different performance measure for the used-car division, which he recognizes as an investment center.

ACCOUNTING-BASED PERFORMANCE MEASURES

Managers of responsibility centers are evaluated on the basis of performance measures. Those performance measures should be based on the controllability principle; they may be either accounting based or nonfinancial. Return on investment and residual income/economic value added are accounting-based performance measures commonly used to evaluate managers of investment centers. These performance measures have their own strengths and weaknesses and generally are more effective when used in conjunction with other performance measures.

LO 4 Identify the strengths and weaknesses of using return on investment (ROI) and residual income as performance measures for investment centers.

Control Decisions

Return on Investment (ROI)

The profit (excluding the opportunity cost of capital) generated by an investment center depends on its size; therefore, performance measures should reflect the size of the investment center. The larger the asset size of the investment center, the greater the opportunity cost of having cash wrapped up in its assets. **Return on investment (ROI)** adjusts for size by dividing the profit (excluding interest expense) generated by the investment center, by the total assets of the investment center:

$$\text{ROI} = \frac{\text{Earnings before interest}}{\text{Total assets of the investment}}$$

ROI is the most popular investment center performance measure. It has intuitive appeal since the comparison of ROI to the opportunity cost of capital (the interest rate of borrowing or the dividend rate of stock) provides a benchmark for a center's performance (see box at the top of p. 204).

If the ROI is greater than the opportunity cost of capital, the assets of the investment are increasing the organization's value. An organization that can borrow $1,000 in cash for 10% for a year and then invest the money in assets that generate a 14% annual return on the investment will increase its value. At the end of the year, the organization must repay the loan ($1,000) and the interest ($1,000)(0.10), or a total of $1,100, but the organization has the investment ($1,000) and a return of ($1,000)(0.14), or $1,140. The net gain is $1,140 − $1,100, or $40.

Business Analysis

Like many organizations, Microsoft's bureaucracy was getting in the way of innovation. To retain key personnel and to meet its goals of customer satisfaction and industry leadership, Microsoft decentralized decision making. This approach encourages a climate in which decisions can be made and customer demands met more quickly and effectively.

In spite of 30% annual growth over the life of the company and recently becoming the largest company in the United States in terms of the market value of equity ($414 billion), President Steven Ballmer and CEO William Gates were worried that Microsoft was getting sluggish. One of the biggest problems was the requirement that all major decisions go through Ballmer and Gates. Bureaucratic delays due to five layers of management were causing Microsoft to lose business in the rapidly changing high-technology world. Important managers were leaving the company in frustration.

Steve Ballmer recently instituted Vision 2 as a complete reorganization of Microsoft. Decision making is delegated to the leaders of eight new centers. Ballmer and Gates still approve goals for profitability, customer satisfaction, and industry leadership, but responsibility for making decisions to achieve those goals resides with the leaders of the centers.

Microsoft has been able to decentralize decision making because the new centers are based on customers rather than functional areas that require more central coordination. The new centers and their customer bases are as follows:

Business Productivity: Knowledge workers

Business and Enterprise: Corporate customers

Home and Retail: Home users of computer games

Developer: Corporate programmers

Consumer and Commerce: Web surfers and cybershoppers

Consumer Windows: Home PC users

Sales and Support: Small businesses and Internet service providers

Research: Computer scientists

What type of responsibility centers are these centers likely to be? What are some advantages and disadvantages of organizing Microsoft around types of customers rather than functions or products?

Source: "Remaking Microsoft," *Business Week*, May 17, 1999.

The Du Pont Company ROI Method

In the early 1900s, the E.I. Du Pont de Nemours Powder Company was the leading firm in the manufacture of gun powder and high explosives. Its operations were geographically dispersed, and it would later grow into one of the world's largest chemical companies. To control and evaluate these operations, Du Pont managers, Pierre Du Pont in particular, developed the concept of return on investment.

The financial staff traced the cost and revenues for each product produced. This gave management accurate information of profits, which provided a more precise way of evaluating financial performance. However, they found product-line profits to be an incomplete measure of performance because it did not indicate the rate of return on capital invested. One manager said, "The true test of whether the profit is too great or too small is the rate of return on the money invested in the business and not the percent of profit on the cost."

Developing a rate of return on each segment of business required accurate data on investment in fixed capital. Du Pont undertook a careful valuation of each of its plants, properties, and inventories by product line. These data along with profits allowed management to track ROI by product line. In addition, they decomposed ROI (profits ÷ investment) into its component parts to account specifically for the underlying causes for changes in ROI. The following figure illustrates this decomposition:

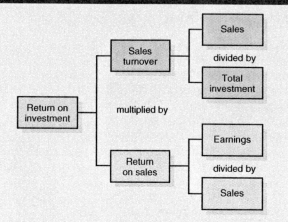

ROI is the product of sales turnover (sales ÷ total investment) and return on sales (earnings ÷ sales). Given these data, managers could determine the causes of a product's change in ROI. Du Pont managers used these data to evaluate new capital appropriations by establishing the policy that there "be no expenditures for additions to the earnings equipment if the same amount of money could be applied to some better purpose in another branch of the company's business."

Source: A. Chandler, *The Visible Hand* (Cambridge, Mass.: Harvard University Press, 1977), pp. 445–49.

Numerical Example 7.2

An investment center of an organization has the following investment opportunities:

Project	Required Investment	Annual Earnings before Interest
A	$500,000	$50,000
B	200,000	10,000
C	100,000	20,000

The opportunity cost of capital to the organization is 8%. What is the ROI of these investment opportunities and which investments would add value to it?

Solution

The ROI is the earnings divided by the investment:

Project	ROI
A	$50,000/$500,000 = 0.10, or 10%
B	$10,000/$200,000 = 0.05, or 5%
C	$20,000/$100,000 = 0.20, or 20%

Projects A and C would add value to the organization. The return on those investments is greater than the opportunity cost of capital of 8%. Project B would not add value because its return on investment is less than the opportunity cost of capital.

Problems with ROI

Although ROI has the advantage of controlling for the size of the investment center, it has problems as a performance measure. These include measurement problems, failure to recognize the risk of the projects, and incentives to underinvest.

ROI is not necessarily a measure of the center's percentage change in markert value for at least two reasons. First, accounting income (the numerator of the ROI) is not a measure of change in the organization's market value. Second, investment (the denominator of the ROI) is not the market value of the center's investment. Traditionally, the income and investment are measured using historical costs, which usually differ from the market value. Accounting depreciation, which is deducted from accounting profits, does not necessarily reflect the change in market value of fixed assets. Investment center managers evaluated on ROI can make inappropriate decisions because of the way ROI is measured. For example, new assets cause higher depreciation expenses and lower profits (the numerator of ROI) and higher net assets (the denominator of ROI). The combined effect reduces the short-term ROI although there may be long-term benefits to purchasing the new assets.

The ROI of an investment center does not explicitly recognize the center's risk. From finance theory, we know that risky investments should have a higher expected return to compensate for the higher risk. Therefore, a manager who generates a large ROI could be investing in riskier assets, which may not be consistent with the organization's goals.

The use of ROI as a performance measure of an investment center also can lead to an underinvestment in assets. Managers might attempt to increase the average ROI by investing only in assets that have ROIs above the current average ROI and forgoing projects with ROIs below the current average ROI. If a project with an ROI above the current average ROI but less than the opportunity cost of capital is chosen, the organization decreases in value. Likewise, rejecting a project with an ROI above its cost of capital but below the average ROI of the investment center reduces the organization's value. To increase the value, a manager should invest in all assets that have returns greater than the opportunity cost of capital rather than projects that raise the investment center's average ROI. For example, suppose an investment center has an average ROI of 20 percent and a cost of capital of 15 percent. A proposed project has an ROI of 18 percent. Although this project lowers the investment center's average ROI, it is still profitable because its return of 18 percent exceeds its cost of capital of 15 percent.

Numerical Example 7.3

An investment center manager is considering four possible investments. The required investment, annual profits (which are approximately equal to cash flows), and ROIs of each investment are as follows:

Project	Required Investment	Annual Earnings	ROI
A	$400,000	$80,000	20%
B	200,000	10,000	5
C	300,000	36,000	12
D	100,000	15,000	15

The investment center is currently generating an ROI of 18% based on $1,000,000 in assets and a profit of $180,000. The company can borrow cash at a 10% annual rate. Which projects will increase the investment center's ROI? Which projects will increase the organization's value?

Solution

Only project A will increase the ROI of the investment center:

($180,000 + $80,000)/($1,000,000 + $400,000) = 18.57%

Projects C and D will also increase the value of the entire organization. The additional profit generated by these projects is greater than the interest expense from borrowing to invest in C (($30,000)(0.10) = $30,000) and D (($100,000)(0.10) = $10,000).

Residual Income/Economic Value Added

To overcome the incentive problems of ROI, such as underinvestment and lack of risk adjustment, some firms use residual income to evaluate performance. **Residual income** is the difference between the investment center's profits and the opportunity cost of using its assets. The opportunity cost of using the assets is the opportunity cost of capital times the market value of the assets. The following equations define the relationship between residual income and ROI:

$$\text{Residual income} = \text{Profits} - (\text{Opportunity cost of capital})(\text{Total assets})$$
$$= (\text{Profits}/\text{Total assets})(\text{Total assets}) - (\text{Opportunity cost of capital})(\text{Total assets})$$
$$= (\text{ROI})(\text{Total assets}) - (\text{Opportunity cost of capital})(\text{Total assets})$$
$$= (\text{ROI} - \text{Opportunity cost of capital})(\text{Total assets})$$

Therefore, the residual income is positive if the ROI is greater than the opportunity cost of capital. A positive residual income number means that the investment center manager has added value to the organization by achieving a higher return on the assets than the cost of using them. If residual income is used as a performance measure, the investment manager invests in all assets that have a positive residual income. There is no underinvestment incentive.

In measuring residual income, the profit figure does not include any interest expense. Interest expense is excluded to avoid double counting the cost of debt. The opportunity cost of capital includes a charge for the cost of debt and equity.

Measuring residual income requires measuring the opportunity cost of capital, which should reflect the risk of the assets in the investment center. Banks are more reluctant to lend money to organizations that invest in high-risk projects; to compensate for the additional risk, they charge a higher interest rate. This problem is discussed in Chapter Thirteen and finance texts. By choosing the opportunity cost of capital to reflect the risk of the assets, there are no incentives to choose high-risk projects just to increase the ROI.

Numerical Example 7.4

A tractor division has profits (not including interest expense) of $20 million and investment (total assets) of $100 million. The division has an opportunity cost of capital of 15%. What is its residual income?

Solution

The residual income is as follows:

$$\$20 \text{ million} - (0.15)(\$100 \text{ million}) = \$5 \text{ million}$$

Residual income is not a perfect performance measure. As with ROI, the profits and total assets are commonly measured using historical costs from the financial reporting system. If the accounting profits vary due to changes in the market value of the assets and the book value of assets is not representative of the market value of the assets, the residual income will not function well as a performance measure. Managers will be trying to maximize accounting residual income, but the owners of the organization would prefer that they increase the organization's market value.

Another perceived problem when using residual income is the comparison and evaluation of performance across investment centers of different sizes. Residual income is an absolute dollar figure and is likely to be higher for larger investment centers. For example, consider the situation of two investment centers, Divisions A and B in Table 7.2.

Division A has a higher ROI, but Division B has a higher residual income because it is larger. Which division's manager is performing better? If both managers have control over the size of their divisions (that is, they are investment centers),

Table 7.2

Comparison of Residual
Income to ROI (thousands
of dollars)

	Division A	Division B
Net assets	$100	$1,000
Net income	30	250
Cost of capital (20%)	20	200
Residual income	10	50
ROI	30%	25%

then the manager of Division B is performing better. Although the manager of Division A is operating efficiently with a smaller amount of net assets, he or she is not able to find as many profitable opportunities as can the manager of Division B. Division B's manager adds more value to the organization and should be rewarded accordingly. Residual income is appropriate for evaluating managers of investment centers of different sizes since the managers have control of the size of the investment center. If the managers do not control size and the division is more like a profit center, then ROI is more appropriate as a relative performance measure for managers of differently sized divisions.

A variant of residual income is the *economic value added (EVA)*,[1] which is calculated in the same manner as residual income, but differences in the general formula are noted in practice. First, EVA makes a series of adjustments to accounting income. For example, research and development costs often are included as assets and amortized over the estimated useful lives of these expenditures. Second, the opportunity cost of capital is calculated as the weighted-average cost of debt and equity. Third, EVA has been linked more frequently to managerial compensation contracts. This linkage increases the manager's risk but creates incentives to maximize organizational value.

Multiple Performance Measures

As in the case of cost and profit centers, the manager of an investment center should not be evaluated by a single performance measure. An organization generally has multiple goals, and a single performance measure will not motivate the manager to consider all of those goals. For example, investment center managers usually are constrained in terms of the quality of products that they can sell and the market niches that they can enter. The reason for these constraints is to prevent these managers from debasing the firm's brand-name capital (the firm's reputation). For example, Eastman Kodak entered the consumer battery market by creating an investment center called Kodak Ultra Technologies. Although Kodak had a reputation for high-quality products, one way for Ultra Technologies managers to meet their profit and ROI targets was to reduce costs by offering products of lower quality than the consumer expected. Over time, consumers came to learn of the lower-than-expected quality of the batteries. Ultra Technologies' managers might have exceeded their short-term target profits, but the market lowered its expectations of quality for all Kodak products. To control this problem, senior Kodak managers put in place

Photographers expect quality pictures. They also want to view them immediately and e-mail them across the globe. Kodak's brand name provides advantages when entering new markets, such as digital photography. In the race for market share, Kodak cannot sacrifice quality; therefore, it uses targets and monitoring to ensure standards are met.

[1] EVA is a registered trademark of Stern Stewart & Company. It is described more fully in B. Stewart, *The Quest for Value* (New York: Harper Business, 1991).

devices to continually monitor the quality of the batteries produced to ensure that they met Kodak's quality standards.[2]

ConceptReview

1. What are the benefits and problems with using ROI as a performance measure?
2. What are the benefits and problems of using residual income as a performance measure?

SHAH MOTORS
(Continued)

Jeremy is considering the use of ROI as a performance measure for Slick Thompson. Jeremy is not concerned with problems in measuring profit and net assets; most of the assets of the used-car division are in the form of used cars. These used cars are normally sold within four months, so book value should not differ much from market value, and the accounting profit of the used-car division should be a close approximation of change in economic value. Jeremy is also not concerned about the risk of the used-car division because the sale of used cars tends to be less sensitive to changes in the economy. He is concerned, however, about the underinvestment problem. He thinks that Slick Thompson may be able to increase ROI by buying and selling only foreign used cars, which generally have a higher profit margin than domestic cars do. Good foreign used cars are hard to find, however, and Slick would operate with a substantially reduced inventory. Jeremy feels that the domestic used-car market is still profitable and does not want Slick to focus on foreign cars. Therefore, he concludes that residual income is a better performance measure because it would encourage Slick to invest in all used cars that have ROIs higher than the opportunity cost of capital. Jeremy uses the interest rate on his debt to approximate the opportunity cost of capital.

TRANSFER PRICING

LO 5   Choose transfer prices to create performance measures that reflect the activities controlled by each manager.

Most organizations contain multiple responsibility centers that can interact in many ways and can create adverse or favorable impacts on other responsibility centers. A manufacturing department's operating efficiency can be affected by the size and timing of the orders that it receives from the marketing department. A purchasing department can affect the manufacturing department's operations by the timing and quality of the raw materials it purchases. The sharing of a newly discovered cost-saving idea or R&D development by one responsibility center with other centers is an example of a favorable interaction. Managing these interactions (eliminating the negative ones and encouraging the positive ones) is critical to the successful partitioning of responsibilities to the organization's different managers. The firm's management accounting system often plays a powerful role in either encouraging or discouraging these interactions. The management accounting system recognizes the interactions of different responsibility centers through **transfer pricing,** a system of pricing products or services transferred within the same organization.

Reasons for Transfer Pricing

Figure 7.3 presents a typical scenario with an internal transfer of a product or service. Division A of an organization purchases raw materials from an external supplier and converts them into an intermediate product used by Division B. Division B converts the intermediate product into a finished product for sale to an external

---

[2] Eventually, Kodak sold the battery business to a group of private investors.

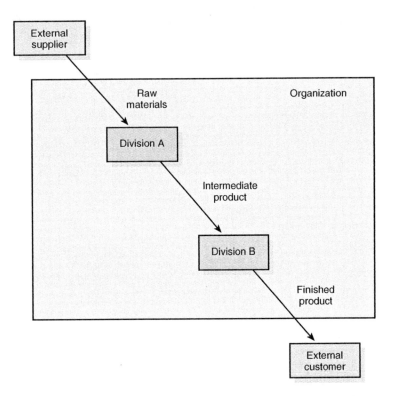

Figure 7.3

The External and Internal
Transfer of Products

customer. The purchase price of the raw materials and the sale price of the finished product are determined by external market forces, although they do not directly affect the "price" of the intermediate product, which is transferred between division within the organization. Therefore, some flexibility exists in setting that internal "price."

When goods or services are transferred from one responsibility center to another, the internal price or transfer price is attached to the units transferred. For example, Chevrolet manufactures an engine that is installed in a Buick. The transfer price in this case is the internal charge that General Motors' Buick Division pays to its Chevrolet Division. The transfer payment may not involve any cash flows between the two divisions, but an accounting entry is made to reflect a cost to Buick and a corresponding revenue to Chevrolet.

Transfer prices are much more prevalent in organizations than most managers realize. Consider the charge that the advertising department receives from the maintenance department for janitorial service, or the monthly charge for telephones, security services, data processing, or legal and personnel services. Most firms distribute the costs of services to the departments that use the services received from another part of the organization. These cost distributions are internal transfer prices.

The three main reasons for transfer pricing within firms are control (incentives and performance measures), decentralized planning decisions, and international/tax reasons. All of these factors should be considered in setting transfer prices. Table 7.3 outlines four common transfer pricing methods, which are discussed in the following sections in terms of control and planning. The choice of one method over another usually reflects a compromise in terms of its effectiveness for control versus planning purposes.

Transfer Pricing for Control

Transfer prices are used for control purposes in a decentralized organization. As discussed in Chapter Six, decentralization involves transferring certain responsibilities to subordinates, which is accomplished by partitioning the organization

**Control
Decisions**

Table 7.3

Summary of Transfer
Pricing Methods

Method	Advantages	Disadvantages
Market based	Approximates opportunity cost if competitive market exists	May not have external market for intermediate goods Excludes effects of internal transaction costs on transfer price
Variable cost	Approximates opportunity cost if fixed costs are sunk	Does not allow the selling division to recover fixed costs Provides incentive for selling division to convert fixed costs to variable costs
Full cost	Reduces disputes because the figure is objective Is simple to compute because it parallels accounting system figures Mimics opportunity cost if division is operating at capacity	Overstates opportunity cost if excess capacity exists
Negotiated	Maintains managerial autonomy Preserves upper management time	Is time consuming and relies on negotiation skills of divisional managers May not be the optimal price for the firm as a whole Can lead to conflicts among responsibility centers

into responsibility centers and by designing performance measurement and compensation systems for the responsibility centers. Firms create profit and investment centers primarily to link specialized knowledge and responsibilities and to increase the motivation for local managers. Moreover, profit centers also improve response time, conserve central management's time, and facilitate training of local managers.

Measuring the performance of profit or investment centers requires the use of transfer prices when one profit or investment center transfers goods or services to another unit. Transfer-pricing systems should reflect the controllability principle by assigning costs to the responsibility center managers responsible for the costs. Transfer prices should lead to performance measures that discriminate between good and bad managers. In other words, managers of responsibility centers should not be rewarded or penalized by transfer prices that are affected by the performance of managers of other responsibility centers. For example, the manager of an engineering department should not be able to charge the manager of the production department for cost overruns due to mistakes the engineering department made.

Numerical Example 7.5

The parts division of an organization sells parts to the assembly division of the same organization. The cost of providing the parts to the parts division is $10 per unit. At a cost of $4 per unit, the assembly division assembles the parts purchased from the parts division and sells the assembled product to another organization for $23 per unit.

a. What is the profit per unit of the two divisions if the transfer price is $12 per unit?

b. What is the profit per unit of the two divisions if the cost of $10 per unit to the parts department is used as the transfer price?

c. If the parts department operates inefficiently and the cost of parts rises to $11 per unit and that cost is used as the transfer price, what is the profit of the two divisions?

d. What is wrong with the solution in part (c)?

Solution

a. If the transfer price is $12 per unit, the profit per unit of the two divisions is as follows:

Parts Division		Assembly Division	
Revenue per unit	$12	Revenue per unit	$23
Cost per unit	10	Parts cost per unit	12
Profit per unit	$ 2	Assembly costs	4
		Profit per unit	$ 7

b. If the transfer price is $10 per unit, the profit of the two division is as follows:

Parts Division		Assembly Division	
Revenue per unit	$10	Revenue per unit	$23
Cost per unit	10	Parts cost per unit	10
Profit per unit	$ 0	Assembly costs	4
		Profit per unit	$ 9

Notice that the higher transfer price shifts profit from the assembly division to the parts division. With each transfer price, the total profit of both division is $9 per unit.

c. If the transfer price is $11 per unit due to inefficiencies in the parts division, the profit of the two division is as follows:

Parts Division		Assembly Division	
Revenue per unit	$11	Revenue per unit	$23
Cost per unit	11	Parts cost per unit	11
Profit per unit	$ 0	Assembly costs	4
		Profit per unit	$ 8

d. The additional cost of $1 per unit due to inefficiencies in the parts division does not affect its profit but adversely affects the assembly division's profit. The parts division is responsible for the extra $1 per unit cost; therefore, the performance measure of the parts division, not the assembly division, should reflect that responsibility.

Transfer Pricing for Decentralized Planning Purposes

Managers also use transfer prices for decentralized planning purposes. In a decentralized organization, managers of responsibility centers make certain input and output decisions. For some inputs and outputs, however, the managers may not have the right to go outside the organization. For example, the manager of the Buick Division of General Motors is required to purchase engines from the Chevrolet Division but does not have the right to go to DaimlerChrysler or Ford to purchase engines. Under these circumstances, a transfer price does not affect the choice of the supplier or buyer, but it influences the level of output of both divisions. For example, if the transfer price is too high, the internal buyer tends to purchase less of the internally supplied service or product than would be optimal for the entire organization. The problem is choosing a transfer price that leads to decentralized decisions consistent with the entire organization's goals.

Planning Decisions

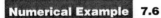 **Numerical Example** **7.6**

A company that makes large earth-moving machines has a parts division and an assembly division. The parts division supplies the assembly division a set of parts that it assembles and sells. The sales price per machine declines because the demand for it is sensitive to the final selling price. The following are the costs and company revenues for different levels of output:

Output per Week	Parts Division Costs	Assembly Division Costs	Selling Price per Unit	Total Revenues	Company Profits
1	$100,000	$ 50,000	$200,000	$200,000	$50,000
2	180,000	100,000	170,000	340,000	60,000
3	240,000	150,000	160,000	480,000	90,000

What problems will the company encounter if it uses a transfer price of $100,000 per set of parts and allows the assembly division manager to make the choice of how many sets of parts to assemble? The assembly division manager is evaluated on the division's profits.

Solution

With a transfer price of $100,000, the following are the profits of the assembly division:

Output per Week	Cost of Parts	Assembly Division Costs	Total Revenues	Assembly Division Profit
1	$100,000	$ 50,000	$200,000	$50,000
2	200,000	100,000	340,000	40,000
3	300,000	150,000	480,000	30,000

The assembly division's profits are highest when it assembles one set of parts per week. The division's manager, therefore, will choose to assemble one set although the company's profit would be maximized if it made and assembled three sets of parts.

Managers of some responsibility centers are given the opportunity to buy or sell outside the organization although there is an internal supplier of its inputs or an internal buyer of its outputs. Allowing managers to go outside the organization forces the responsibility centers within the organization to compete with outside suppliers and buyers. Competitive markets provide the discipline to encourage the efficient operation of responsibility centers; inefficient responsibility centers will not survive under these circumstances. Once again, the transfer pricing system should be designed to motivate managers to make input and output decisions that are consistent with the organization's goals, such as maximizing profits.

To motivate managers to make decentralized input and output decisions (choices of quantity, supplier, and customer) consistent with maximizing the entire organization's profit, the transfer price should be set equal to the opportunity cost of providing the product or service being transferred. If there is insufficient capacity to sell both inside and outside the firm, this opportunity cost is composed of the opportunity cost of using raw materials, labor, and the facilities along with the forgone profit of not being able to sell the product or service to an outside party. Cash outlays, alternative uses of the material, labor, facilities, and forgone profit should be considered in establishing the transfer price. The opportunity cost of providing the product or service may be difficult to estimate; therefore the following sections describe some useful heuristics for doing so.

LO 6 Use opportunity costs to choose transfer prices that will lead to decentralized decision making that is best for the organization.

Existence of a Competitive Market for the Intermediate Product or Service

Suppose that a competitive market exists for the product or service being transferred between the two responsibility centers. The center providing the product or

Global Competition

service could sell it to someone outside the organization, and the center using the product or service could purchase it from an outside supplier. The sale to an outside buyer or the purchase from an outside seller would be at a market price determined by competitive forces.

The general rule of transfer pricing is to use the external market price of the intermediate product or service if a competitive market exists. The market price approximates the opportunity cost of providing the product or service and is equal to the cost of making the product or service plus the forgone profit of not selling it to an outside party.

In some cases, the external market price does not exactly equal the opportunity cost of providing the intermediate product or service. Sometimes additional opportunity costs of dealing with external customers exist. For example, external customers may require more negotiating and accounting effort to complete the deal. Additional transaction and customer service costs may be incurred when dealing with an external customer. Therefore, the opportunity cost of selling to external customers is the market price less these additional costs, which should be reflected in the transfer price. A transfer price below the market price encourages the internal customer to purchase the intermediate product and allows the company to avoid the costs of dealing with the external customer.

Numerical Example 7.7

The restaurant division of a hotel provides a catering service for the hotel's convention center. It charges outside organizations $20 per person for catering. To cater outside events, however, the restaurant incurs additional costs of $1 per person, which include the cost of transporting and reheating the food. What transfer price should be used between the restaurant division and the convention center to encourage decentralized decision making that will maximize profit for the hotel?

Solution

The transfer price should be the market price of $20 less the additional transaction and contracting costs of $1, or $19 per person. The restaurant is indifferent at that transfer price between catering internally or externally. The $19 transfer price encourages the convention center to buy from the restaurant division. Otherwise, the convention center would have to pay a price of about $20, reflecting additional costs if it purchases from an outside supplier.

Producing internally (even though less expensive external markets exist) may also make sense if timeliness of supply and quality control are important. When these factors are included in the analysis, the external market may no longer be less expensive. The market price should be adjusted for these other factors to determine the transfer price.

Sometimes an internal supplier of a service or product cannot compete with external suppliers, even after adjusting for transportation costs, quality, and timely delivery. Under these circumstances, the internal supplier is forced to improve efficiency or shift to providing other services or products.

Numerical Example 7.8

Kali Company has two divisions. Each year the paper division makes 10,000 tons of paper that costs $1,000 per ton. It can either sell all of the paper in the market for $1,500 per ton or transfer all of it to Kali's printing division which converts it into gift wrap at an additional cost of $4,000 per ton. The gift wrap can be sold for $5,200 per ton.

a. What is the company's profit if the paper is transferred to the printing division?

b. What is the company's profit if the paper is sold in the market and the printing division is closed?

c. How does the use of the market price as the transfer price cause managers of the division to achieve the highest profit for the company?

Solution

a. The profit of the company if the paper is transferred to the printing division follows:

Revenues (10,000 tons)($5,200/ton)	$52,000,000
Paper costs (10,000 tons)($1,000/ton)	(10,000,000)
Printing costs (10,000 tons)($4,000/ton)	(40,000,000)
Profit	$ 2,000,000

b. The profit of the company if the paper is sold in the market and the printing division is closed is as follows:

Revenues (10,000 tons)($1,500/ton)	$ 5,000,000
Paper costs (10,000 tons)($1,000/ton)	(10,000,000)
Profit	$ 5,000,000

c. If the market price of $1,500 is used as the transfer price, the printing division's costs ($1,500/ton + $4,000/ton) will be higher than its revenues ($5,200/ton). Rather than operating at a loss, the manager can close the printing division or look for a more profitable opportunity. This example assumes that the costs of the two divisions are opportunity costs and reflect alternative uses of the inputs to the process.

No Competitive Market Exists for the Intermediate Product or Service

If no external market exists for the intermediate product or service, there is no alternative to selling it to another buyer. The intermediate service or product can be sold only internally. There is no forgone profit opportunity, and the opportunity cost is limited to the cost of using the raw materials, labor, and facilities to supply the product or service. The cost of each input should be considered in terms of cash outlays and alternative uses of the assets. For example, if the existing facilities have already been purchased and there is no alternative use of them, the opportunity cost of using them is limited to the incremental costs of operating them. Opportunity costs are approximated by the variable cost if the fixed costs are sunk. If fixed costs are sunk and included in the transfer price, the responsibility center that is purchasing tends to purchase less of the intermediate product or service than is best for the entire organization.

Numerical Example 7.9

The CD-ROM division of a large computer company manufactures and sells CD players to the company's laptop division. The variable cost to the CD-ROM division to provide the product is $100 per unit and the fixed sunk cost is $50 per unit. The CD-ROM division has excess capacity and no alternative use for it. At an additional variable cost of $60 per unit, the laptop division modifies the product purchased from the CD-ROM division and then sells the modified product to another computer firm for $180 per unit. What is the contribution margin per unit for the organization if the transfer price is the variable cost? What happens if the full cost is used as the transfer price?

Solution

If the variable cost of the CD-ROM division ($100) is used as the transfer price, CD-ROM's contribution margin is $100 − $100, or $0. The laptop division's contribution margin is $180 − $100 − $60, or $20 per unit. The contribution margin of the entire firm is $20 per unit. The transfer price based on the full cost of the CD-ROM division is the sum of the fixed cost ($50) and variable cost ($100), or $150. If the full cost of $150 is used as the transfer price, the CD-ROM's contribution margin is $150 − $100, or $50. The laptop division's contribution margin is $180 − $150 − $60, or $−30. Under these circumstances the laptop division manager receives $50 less in contribution margin compared to the amount received when the variable cost is used as the transfer price. Therefore, the manager would not want to purchase CD-ROM players from the CD-ROM division. The manager receives $0 in contribution margin by not selling modified CD-ROM players rather than purchasing them from the CD-ROM division. This amount ($0) is higher than the loss in contribution margin ($−30) that the manager receives when the transfer price is full cost. The entire organization would lose the chance of earning a $20 contribution margin per unit.

Numerical Example 7.9 makes an important point. Think of the firm's total profit as a pie. The choice among transfer-pricing methods changes not only how the pie is divided among the profit or investment centers but also the size of the pie to be divided. Many managers think that changing transfer-pricing methods merely shifts income among responsibility centers (as illustrated in Numerical Example 7.5) and that except for relative performance evaluation, nothing else is affected. Unfortunately, this is not true. The level of the firm's output and its overall profitability may change with different transfer prices.

One problem with using the variable cost as a transfer price is that the selling responsibility center does not recover its fixed costs. If *all* of the selling division's output is transferred internally, the only revenue that the seller receives is variable cost, and its fixed costs are not recovered. Thus, sellers show losses and appear to be losing money. One solution is to treat the selling division as a cost center or as part of the purchasing division.

Any transfer-pricing scheme that involves calculating variable costs creates incentives for selling division managers to classify costs as variable. Classifying costs into variable and fixed is somewhat arbitrary; thus, managers in the selling and buying divisions and senior managers waste their time debating the nature of costs. Moreover, the selling division manager has incentives to convert a dollar of fixed costs into more than a dollar of variable costs although this reduces the firm's value. For example, the selling division may choose to replace a $1 fixed machine cost with a $2 variable labor cost. The buying division not the selling division pays the extra cost, and the selling division is relieved of the burden of the fixed cost.

To avoid wasteful disputes that distract them from making operating and strategic decisions, operating managers often adopt simple, objective transfer-pricing rules such as full accounting cost. Since full cost is the sum of fixed and variable cost, it cannot be changed by simply reclassifying a "fixed" cost as a "variable" cost. Using a full cost transfer price results in better *control* by reducing the producer division's incentives to reclassify fixed costs as variable costs. Full cost transfer pricing comes at a price, however: *decision making* is poorer because the buying unit purchases too few units. Thus, the trade-off between *making planning decisions* and *control* is observed again.

To improve decentralized planning decisions, the transfer price should equal the opportunity cost of providing the intermediate product or service. If the selling responsibility center is operating at capacity and has alternative uses of that capacity, the opportunity cost of providing a product or service should include the forgone profit of using the facility for some other purpose. Although the fixed cost of using the facility does not change with the number of units produced, it is often a close approximation of the forgone profit of using the facility. Under these circumstances, the full cost (including variable and fixed costs) is a reasonable approximation of the opportunity cost.

To summarize the discussion of transfer pricing, firms decentralize and form responsibility centers to take advantage of the division manager's specialized knowledge of local conditions. Responsibility center managers are given responsibilities to make certain local decisions and are held responsible for the center's performance. Transfer-pricing systems offer desirable mechanisms for permitting local managers to exploit specialized information that they possess about local opportunities.

Table 7.4 describes the appropriate transfer prices for decentralized planning decisions. In each case, the transfer price is intended to equal the opportunity cost of providing the intermediate product or service.

Table 7.4

Transfer Prices for
Decentralized Planning
Decisions

Circumstance	Transfer Price
Market price exists	Market price
No market price exists; supplying division has no alternative use of capacity	Variable cost
No market price exists; supplying division has alternative use of capacity	Full cost*

* The full cost is intended to be a rough approximation of the forgone opportunity of
using the facilities of the supplying division to do something else.

Choice of Transfer Prices: Making Control and Planning Decisions

Accounting numbers are often used in setting internal transfer prices. The conflict between planning decisions and control decisions discussed in Chapter One also applies to transfer prices. In setting the transfer price that maximizes firm value, a compromise between transfer pricing for planning decisions and control often must be made. The transfer price that most accurately measures the opportunity cost to the organization of transferring one more unit internally might not be the transfer-pricing method that motivates internal managers to maximize the organization's value. For example, if the transfer-pricing method that most accurately measures the opportunity cost of units transferred also requires managers producing the units to reveal privately held and hard-to-verify knowledge of their costs, then these managers have much discretion over the transfer prices. If these prices are important in rewarding managers, the producing managers can distort the system to their benefit and to the detriment of maximizing firm profits. Alternatively, a transfer-pricing scheme which less accurately measures opportunity cost but is less subject to managerial discretion might produce a higher firm value than a transfer-pricing scheme that more closely mimics opportunity costs.

Another control problem arises when actual costs are used as a transfer price. The selling responsibility center manager does not have an incentive to control costs since any increase in cost is passed on to the buying responsibility center through the transfer price. The buying center's manager is penalized for the inefficiencies of the selling center. To overcome this problem, an estimated cost should be used as the transfer price instead of the actual cost. Any variation of the actual cost from the estimated cost is attributed to the manager of the selling center.

In some organizations managers of the selling and buying responsibility centers negotiate transfer prices. Negotiation is time consuming, however, and leads to conflicts among responsibility centers. Divisional performance measurement becomes sensitive to the relative negotiating skills of the two managers. Negotiated transfer prices are more successful when managers have a fall-back position, such as an external market for the intermediate product. In this case, the external market acts as a check on opportunistic management behavior.

Given the many different factors that influence the choice of transfer prices, it is not surprising that different organizations choose different transfer-pricing methods. Table 7.3 summarized the advantages and disadvantages of the various transfer-pricing methods, and Table 7.5 reports a survey of transfer-pricing methods used by Fortune 500 companies. Cost-based transfer pricing is more prevalent than are market-based methods for domestic transfers, whereas market-based transfers are more prevalent than are cost-based transfers for international transactions. The higher use of market price as a transfer price for international transfers presumably is due to tax regulations in many countries that frequently require the use of market price as the transfer price for calculating income taxes.

Pricing Methods	Domestic Transfer Prices (% of total)	International Transfer Prices (% of total)
Cost-based transfer prices	46.2	41.4
Market-based transfer prices	36.7	45.9
Negotiated prices	16.6	12.7
Other	0.5	0.0
Total—all methods	100.0	100.0

Table 7.5

Comparison between the Transfer-Pricing Methods Used by Fortune 500 Companies in 1990

Source: R. Tang, "Transfer Pricing in the 1990s," *Management Accounting,* February 1992, p. 25.

Concept**Review**

1. How should transfer pricing be used to improve decision control?

2. How should transfer prices be chosen to improve decentralized planning decisions?

SHAH MOTORS
(Continued)

The three divisions of Shah Motors have considerable interactions. Both the new- and used-car divisions use the service department to make final preparations of cars sold. All divisions use the accounting services of the central administration. The primary interaction that is causing problems at Shah Motors is the transfer of used cars from the new-car division to the used-car division. Alice Dempster, the new-car sales manager, gives very generous trade-in allowances to new car buyers. She would like to pass these costs on to the used-car division, but Slick Thompson claims that he would operate at a loss if he had to buy them at their inflated trade-in price. Under present policy, Slick must buy all used cars the new-car division receives. To solve this problem, Jeremy decides to use published lists of used-car prices as the transfer price. If Alice decides to give a trade-in allowance greater than the list price of the used car, she will have to bear the cost.

At the end of the year, Jeremy decides to calculate the profit of each of the three departments of his company. He allocates his central administration costs, which are mostly interest costs at 10% annually, to the three managers based on total sales. Transfers of trade-ins from the new-car department to the used-car department occur at a list price published by an outside source.

	New-Car Sales	Used-Car Sales	Service Dept.
Revenues	$ 8,000,000	$2,000,000	$1,500,000
Sale of trade-ins	1,000,000		
Total revenues	$ 9,000,000	$2,000,000	$1,500,000
Controllable costs	(5,000,000)	(700,000)	(1,200,000)
Cost of trade-ins		(1,000,000)	
Profit before allocation	$ 4,000,000	$ 300,000	$ 300,000
Allocated administration costs	(2,160,000)	(480,000)	($ 360,000)
Profit/loss	$ 1,840,000	($ 180,000)	($ 60,000)
Average net assets	$20,000,000	$1,900,000	$ 300,000

Alice Dempster is most pleased with this segment reporting. She is evaluated based on profit, and the new-car sales department shows a profit of $1,840,000.

Slick Thompson is not happy with the profit analysis of the segments. He is supposed to be evaluated based on residual income, but the profit calculated in the segment reports includes interest charges allocated from central administration. Slick argues that the residual income of his department is the profit before the allocation of administration costs less the opportunity cost of capital or $300,000 − (0.10)($1,900,000), or $110,000.

Grease Johnson is also unhappy with the analysis. He has provided good-quality service at a low cost. He has no control over the pricing of his department's services, and the allocated administrative costs appear excessive given that they are primarily interest costs and the net assets of his department are relatively small.

Jeremy agrees with most of his managers' arguments. He is still concerned, however, about the allocation of administration costs to the different departments. If he cannot cover those costs with profits from the different departments, his business will incur a loss. Jeremy decides that he should read Chapter Nine on allocating costs.

You decide

INTERNATIONAL TRANSFER-PRICING ISSUES

LO 7   Choose transfer prices to minimize taxes and overcome international obstacles.

Planning Decisions

ORGANIZATIONAL VALUE

In a purely domestic firm, the choice of the "best" transfer price involves considering the effect of transfer pricing on the selling and buying divisions' incentives. If the price set is too high, the buyer purchases too few units. Alternatively, if the price set is too low, the seller produces too few units. Transfer pricing, which is already a complicated choice problem, becomes even more complicated for a multinational organization. Internal incentives aside, domestic and foreign taxes and political considerations are affected. The following sections outline some of the more important international aspects of transfer pricing.

Tax Minimization

If a multinational company transfers products between two countries with different corporate income tax rates, the multinational will try to set a transfer price to minimize its total tax liability in the two countries. One way to do this is to recognize more of the profits in the country with the lower tax rate. If the country of the supplying division has the lower tax rate, a higher transfer price shifts profit to the supply division and lowers after-tax profit. If the country of the purchasing division has the lower tax rate, a lower transfer price shifts profit to the purchasing division and lowers after-tax profit.

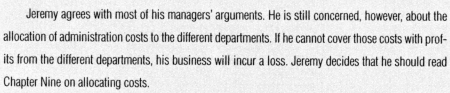

Numerical Example   **7.10**

Suppose Pepsi ships 5,000 units of syrup from the United States to a foreign country subsidiary that adds carbonated water and cans and sells the mixture. Suppose the U.S. income tax rate is 40% and the foreign country's tax rate is 20%. The cost to manufacture and ship the syrup is $14 per unit. It costs the foreign subsidiary $10 per unit to add the water, can, and sell the drink for $80 per unit. The following table summarizes the tax rates, final sales price, operating costs, and units transferred. To simplify the example, the foreign country's sales have been converted to U.S. dollars.

	United States	**Foreign Subsidiary**
Tax rate	40%	20%
Units transferred and sold	5,000	5,000
Incremental costs per unit	$14	$10
Incremental costs	$70,000	$50,000
Selling price per unit		$80
Revenue from final sales		$400,000

Suppose Pepsi can select a per unit transfer price of $16 or $18. Which should it select?

Solution

The following table calculates Pepsi's total tax liability if the syrup is transferred at $16 per unit.

	United States	**Foreign Subsidiary**	**Total**
Revenue from transferring syrup @ $16	$80,000		
Revenue from final sales		$400,000	
Cost of syrup transferred		80,000	
Incremental costs	70,000	50,000	
Income before taxes	$10,000	$270,000	
Taxes	$ 4,000	$ 54,000	$58,000

The preceding table indicates that Pepsi's total tax liability is $58,000 if the transfer price is set at $16 per unit. The following table shows that the total tax liability rises to $60,000 if the transfer price is set at $18 per unit.

	United States	**Foreign Subsidiary**	**Total**
Revenue from transferring syrup @ $18	$90,000		
Revenue from final sales		$400,000	
Cost of syrup transferred		90,000	
Incremental costs	70,000	50,000	
Income before taxes	$20,000	$260,000	
Taxes	$ 8,000	$ 52,000	$60,000

Pepsi's taxes are higher with the $18 transfer price because profits are shifted out of the low-tax foreign subsidiary to the high-tax U.S. parent.

Transfer pricing is an effective way for multinational organizations to shift taxes to lower-income tax jurisdictions. Therefore, government officials closely monitor firms' transfer-pricing methods. For example, in an important case, the U.S. Tax Court found Ciba-Geigy Corporation deficient for more than $50 million in taxes for transfer-pricing arrangements between its U.S. subsidiary and Swiss parent. Transfer-pricing cases such as this one are time consuming and expensive. The *Ciba-Geigy* case was filed in the late 1980s and covered transactions dating from the 1960s.[3] Tax authorities in both the importing and exporting countries scrutinize the transfer-pricing schemes used. Moreover, numerous tax treaties exist between countries that specify the general transfer-pricing methods that companies in the two countries covered by the treaty can use when conducting business. In general, these treaties specify the use of the market price as the transfer price. Thus, while firms have some discretion in setting transfer prices, they are constrained by existing tax laws and treaties.

---

[3] A summary of legal cases dealing with transfer pricing can be found at www.transferpricing.com.

Decentralized Organizations

Global Competition

Globalization affects transfer pricing as firms organize themselves across borders to maintain their international competitiveness. Increasing trade in services and via the Internet makes determining where a transaction has taken place more difficult. Some countries, such as those in the European Union, are examining the benefits of increased harmonization of taxes to reduce the cost of scrutinizing transfer-pricing mechanisms. Tax harmonization also would reduce firms' non–value-added activities devoted to transfer-pricing and taxation disputes.

Political Considerations

Taxes and tariffs are important considerations in setting transfer prices of goods shipped among multinational subsidiaries. Political considerations also can influence the transfer-pricing decision; if the local government is threatening to expropriate the assets of high-profit, foreign-owned companies, these companies may want to choose high transfer prices to reduce the apparent profitability of their operations. This action might reduce the attractiveness of seizing the foreign-controlled company to the government. Also, high transfer prices, which lower reported profits, might forestall entry by local competitors. For example, the U.S. government investigated the sales of crude oil purchased in Saudi Arabia by major oil firms. Despite claims of tax deficiencies amounting to several million dollars, the courts ruled that the firms had complied with price restrictions imposed by the Saudi Arabian government. If the firms had not complied, an important source of crude oil could have been blocked and firms' assets confiscated.

Governments frequently engage in tax competition, offering lower tax rates to lure firms to locate in their jurisdictions. Studies have found that firms increasingly are influenced by these taxation policies and choose to locate where taxation is lowest.[4]

Trade-Offs with Planning and Control Decisions

As discussed earlier, domestic organizations try to set transfer prices for performance evaluation purposes to encourage the buying and selling divisions to exchange the number of units that maximize the organization's overall profits. However, in multinational firms, income taxes and political considerations force managers to choose a transfer price that trades off planning for taxes and political purposes with control. One solution is to choose a transfer price that partially satisfies planning and control functions within the multinational but is optimal for neither purpose. If multinationals choose transfer prices solely to minimize taxes, they must devise alternative measures of performance to motivate managers of the foreign subsidiaries. Instead of relying on accounting profits affected by transfer prices to measure and reward the performance of its subsidiary managers, organizations might want to use revenues, production costs, and market share.

If income taxes and political considerations have a significant effect on the choice of transfer-pricing methods, organizations may change their structure. Some firms may become more centralized because they cannot rely on transfer prices to create appropriate decentralized incentives.

---

[4] "The Mystery of the Vanishing Taxpayer" and "Gimme Shelter" in "Survey: Globalisation and Tax," *The Economist,* January 29, 2000, pp. 1–22.

ConceptReview

1. For a product transferred between two subsidiaries of a multinational firm operating in two foreign countries, how would you set the transfer price to minimize the combined income tax liability?
2. How do international taxation and political considerations affect multinational organizations' decision management and control systems?

SUMMARY

1 **Use the controllability principle to choose performance measures for managers.** Managers should be evaluated based on the activities that they control. Performance measures should reflect those controllable activities.

2 **Identify responsibility centers based on the extent of each manager's responsibilities.** Managers who have responsibilities over only the input mix of their activities are managers of cost centers. Managers who have responsibilities over only the input and output mix of their activities are managers of profit centers. Managers who have the additional responsibilities to change the size of their responsibility center are managers of investment centers.

3 **Choose performance measures for cost, profit, and investment centers.** Managers should be evaluated by multiple performance measures to control for quality and other organizational goals. For cost centers, the primary accounting performance measure is cost: for profit centers, profit; and for investment centers, ROI or residual income.

4 **Identify the strengths and weaknesses of using return on investment (ROI) and residual income as performance measures for investment centers.** ROI provides a return measure that controls for size and is comparable to other return measures. However, the measurement of ROI can be difficult and does not explicitly correct for differences in risk. ROI also can lead to underinvestment. The residual income measure, however, corrects for the underinvestment problem but requires an estimate of the opportunity cost of capital.

5 **Choose transfer prices to create performance measures that reflect the activities controlled by each manager.** Transfer prices are used to charge responsibility centers for products or services that they receive from other responsibility centers within the same organization. The transfer price should be chosen so that each party to the internal transaction is rewarded or penalized for the activities that they control.

6 **Use opportunity costs to choose transfer prices that will lead to decentralized decision making that is best for the organization.** To allow decentralized managers to make the most profitable input and output decisions for the entire organization, the transfer price should reflect the opportunity cost. If a market price exists for the intermediate product or service, the market price, adjusted for transaction and contracting costs, is the appropriate transfer price. If no market exists for the intermediate product, the opportunity cost depends on alternative use of raw materials, labor, and facilities.

7 **Choose transfer prices to minimize taxes and overcome international obstacles.** Income can be transferred among countries through the use of transfer prices. Besides transfer pricing, political considerations also might affect the income of organizational units in different countries.

KEY TERMS

controllable costs Costs affected by a particular manager's decisions. *(p. 196)*

controllability principle The concept that holds managers responsible for only those decisions over which they have authority. *(p. 196)*

cost centers Areas of responsibility within the organization in which responsibilities are limited to maximizing output given a certain level of cost or minimizing cost given a certain level of output. *(p. 198)*

investment centers Areas of responsibility within the organization in which responsibilities include choices affecting costs, revenues, and the amount invested in the center. *(p. 200)*

opportunity cost of capital The forgone opportunity of using cash for another purpose, such as earning interest in a bank account. *(p. 201)*

profit centers Areas of responsibility within the organization in which responsibilities include choices affecting costs and revenues but not size of investment. *(p. 199)*

222   Decentralized Organizations

relative performance measure   A device that judges performance relative to how some comparison group performed. *(p. 196)*

residual income   A performance measure for investment centers that subtracts the opportunity cost of the investment from the income (excluding interest expense) generated by the assets of the investment. *(p. 206)*

responsibility accounting   The process of recognizing subunits within the organization, assigning

responsibilities to managers in those subunits, and evaluating the performance of those managers. *(p. 198)*

return on investment (ROI)   A performance measure calculated by dividing the income (excluding interest expense) from an investment by the size of the investment. *(p. 203)*

transfer pricing   A system of pricing products and services transferred from one responsibility center to another within the same organization. *(p. 208)*

SELF-STUDY PROBLEM

Tam Burger has opened more than 200 stores within the past five years, 80% of which are franchised (independently owned). Two of the company-operated units, Northside and Southside, are among the fastest-growing stores. Both are considering expanding their menus to include pizza. Installation of the necessary ovens and purchase of the necessary equipment would cost $180,000 per store. The current investment in the Northside store totals $890,000; its revenues are $1,100,500, and expenses are $924,420. Expansion of Northside's menu should increase profits by $30,600. The current investment in the Southside store totals $1,740,000, its revenues are $1,760,800, and expenses are $1,496,680. Adding pizza to Southside's menu should increase its profits by $30,600.

Tam Burger evaluates its managers based on return on investment. Managers of individual stores have responsibilities over the pizza expansion.

a.   Calculate the return on investment for both stores using current numbers for the expansion project and for the stores after expansion.

b.   Assuming a 14% cost of capital, calculate residual income for both stores before and after the potential expansion.

c.   Will the Tam Burger stores choose to expand? How would your answer change if the stores were franchised units and owned by value-maximizing investors?

Solution

a.   Return on investment before and after the pizza expansion:

	Northside	Southside
ROI before pizza		
Revenue	$1,100,500	$1,760,800
Expenses	924,420	1,496,680
Net income	$ 176,080	$ 264,120
Assets	890,000	1,740,000
ROI	19.78%	15.18%
ROI of pizza only		
Increased profits from pizza	$ 30,600	$ 30,600
Expansion cost	180,000	180,000
ROI of project	17.00%	17.00%
ROI after pizza		
Total income	$ 206,680	$ 294,720
Total assets	1,070,000	1,920,000
Total ROI	19.32%	15.35%

b.   Residual income before and after the pizza expansion:

Cost of capital	Northside 14.00%	Southside 14.00%
Residual income before pizza		
Net income	$176,080	$264,120
Assets × 14%	124,600	243,600
Residual income	$ 51,480	$ 20,520
Residual income of pizza only		
Increased profits from pizza	$ 30,600	$ 30,600
Less: 14% × Expansion cost	(25,200)	(25,200)
Residual income	$ 5,400	$ 5,400
Residual income after pizza		
Net income	$206,680	$294,720
14% × Assets	149,800	268,800
Residual income	$ 56,880	$ 25,920

c. The two units currently have different ROIs. The smaller Northside store is earning an ROI of just under 20%; the larger Southside store is earning an ROI of just over 15%. Since the ROI of the project is 17%, adding the project to the Northside store lowers its average ROI while adding the project to the Southside store raises its average ROI. Therefore, the Northside manager will not want to add pizza to the menu since its average ROI would drop as a result. The Southside manager, however, would want to add it since the store's ROI would subsequently rise.

    If the stores were franchised units, the owners definitely would expand. The ROI of the pizza is higher than the cost of capital. Thus, a positive residual income for the project is ensured. As long as the residual income is positive, any franchise owner would jump at the opportunity. Franchise owners would not care whether the store's average ROI dropped as long as the residual income increased.

NUMERICAL EXERCISES

An organization's investment center has the following opportunities:

NE 7.1
ROI and Investment Centers
(LO 4)

Project	Required Investment	Annual Earnings before Interest
X	$250,000	$12,500
Y	100,000	15,000
Z	50,000	10,000

The opportunity cost of capital of the organization is 8%.
    What is the ROI of these investment opportunities? Which investment would add value to the organization?

A manager's division has $10,000,000 in assets and no debt. Its profit is $500,000 for the year, and the cost of capital is 8%.
    What is the division's ROI? What is its residual income? How is it performing?

NE 7.2
ROI and Residual Income
(LO 4)

The ROI of three potential investments is 20%, 15%, and 10%, respectively. The cost of capital is 12%, and the ROI of existing assets is 18%.
    Which investment(s) will the manager choose if he or she is evaluated based on ROI? Which investment(s) will increase the value of the organization?

NE 7.3
Selection of Performance Measures
(LO 4)

NE 7.4
Choice of Transfer Prices for Planning and Control
(LO 5)

Division A makes 100 units of a product for a fixed cost of $200 and a variable cost of $5 per unit. Division B of the same company purchases the product from Division A, adds $3 per unit, and sells it to an outside buyer for $13 per unit.

What is the profit of the two divisions with respect to this product if the transfer price is $8 per unit?

NE 7.5
Choice of Transfer Prices
(LO 5)

Division A makes 100 units of a product for a fixed cost of $200 and a variable cost of $5 per unit. Division B of the same company purchases the product from Division A, adds $3 per unit, and sells the product to an outside buyer for $13 per unit. Division A can sell the 100 units of the intermediate product to an outside buyer for $11 per unit.

What should be the transfer price? What decentralized decision does Division B reach? Show why this is the correct decision for the entire organization.

NE 7.6
Selection of Transfer Prices
(LO 5)

Division A makes 100 units of a product for a fixed cost of $200 and a variable cost of $5 per unit. Division B of the same company purchases the product from Division A, adds $3 per unit, and sells the product to an outside buyer for $9 per unit. There is no other buyer for the intermediate product, and the fixed cost is sunk.

What happens if the full cost is used as the transfer price? What happens if the variable cost is used as the transfer price?

NE 7.7
Residual Income
(LO 4)

The computer division of Acme Inc. has profits (not including interest expense) of $15 million and investment (total assets) of $120 million. The division has an opportunity cost of capital of 10%.

What is the division's residual income?

NE 7.8
Transfer Prices and Decentralized Decision Making
(LO 6)

Food services at Eastern University provides meal services to Eastern's conference facility. It also provides catering to off-campus organizations at an average cost of $30 per person. Off-campus events require additional services to transport staff, food, and equipment to these locations. The cost of these services is $4 per person.

What transfer price should be used between Eastern's conference facility and food services to encourage decentralized decision making that will best benefit the university?

NE 7.9
ROI and Residual Income
(LO 4)

The following data summarize the operating performance of your company's wholly owned Canadian subsidiary for 1999–2001, in millions of dollars. The opportunity cost of capital for this subsidiary is 10%.

	1999	2000	2001
Subsidiary net income	$ 14.0	$ 14.3	$ 14.4
Total assets in subsidiary	125.0	130.0	135.0

Calculate the ROI and residual income of the subsidiary for each year.

NE 7.10
Transfer Prices and Divisional Profit
(LO 5)

A chair manufacturer has two divisions, framing and upholstering. The per chair costs for framing are $100, and for upholstering are $200. The company makes 5,000 chairs each year, which are sold for $500.

a. What is the profit of each division if the transfer price is $150?
b. What is the profit of each division if the transfer price is $200?

NUMERICAL PROBLEMS

NP 7.1
ROI and Residual Income
(LO 4)

The following investment opportunities are available to an investment center manager:

Project	Investment	Annual Earnings
A	$800,000	$90,000
B	100,000	20,000
C	300,000	25,000
D	400,000	60,000

a. If the investment manager were currently making a return on investment of 16%, which project(s) should be pursued?

b. If the cost of capital is 10% and the annual earnings approximate cash flows excluding finance charges, which project(s) should be chosen?

c. Suppose that only one project can be chosen and the annual earnings approximate cash flows excluding finance charges. Which project should be chosen?

Suppose that a division of a company is treated as an investment center. Its manager is currently obtaining an ROI of 15% from existing assets of $1 million. The cost of capital (corporate discount rate) is 10%. The division manager has the option of choosing among the following projects, which are independent of existing operations and the other alternative projects:

NP 7.2
ROI and Residual Income
(LO 4)

Project	Investment	ROI
A	$100,000	14%
B	400,000	20
C	200,000	14
D	300,000	12
E	500,000	8

a. Given the current investment in existing assets, in which additional projects should the division manager invest if the objective is to maximize ROI?

b. Which projects have a negative residual income?

c. Using this example, explain why underinvestment is a problem when using ROI for evaluation purposes.

Alpha Division of Carlson Company manufactures product X at a variable cost of $40 per unit. Alpha's fixed costs, which are sunk, are $20 per unit. The market price of X is $70 per unit. Carlson's Beta Division uses product X to make Y. The variable costs to convert X to Y are $20 per unit and the fixed costs, which are sunk, are $10 per unit. Product Y sells for $80 per unit.

NP 7.3
Transfer Prices
(LO 6)

a. What transfer price of X causes divisional managers to make decentralized decisions that maximize Carlson Company's profit if each division is treated as a profit center?

b. Given the transfer price from part (a), what should Beta Division's manager do?

c. Suppose there is no market price for product X. What transfer price should be used for decentralized decision making?

d. If there is no market for product X, are Beta Division's operations profitable?

Scoff Division of World-Wide Paint currently is losing money; therefore, senior management is considering selling or closing it. Scoff's only product, an intermediate chemical called Binder, is used principally by the firm's Latex Division. If Scoff is sold, Latex Division can purchase ample quantities of Binder in the market at sufficiently high quality levels to meet its requirements. World-Wide requires all of its divisions to supply product to other World-Wide divisions before servicing the external market.

NP 7.4
Decision to Drop a Division
(LO 6)

Scoff's statement of operations for the last quarter follows:

SCOFF DIVISION
Profit/Loss Last Quarter
($ thousands)

Revenues		
Inside	$200	
Outside	75	$275
Operating expenses		
Variable costs	$260	
Fixed costs	15	
Alloated corporate overhead	40	315
Net income (loss) before taxes		($40)

Note the following:

1. World-Wide Paint has the policy of transferring all products internally at variable cost. In Scoff's case, variable cost is 80% of the market price.
2. All of Scoff's fixed costs are avoidable cash flows if it is closed or sold.
3. Of the allocated corporate overhead, 10% is caused by the presence of Scoff and will be avoided if Scoff is closed or sold.

Should the Scoff Division be sold?

NP 7.5
ROI Using Market Values
(LO 4)

Your firm uses ROI to evaluate investment centers and is considering changing the valuation basis of assets from historical cost to current value. The historical cost of the asset is updated using a price index to approximate replacement value. For example, a metal-fabrication press, which bends and shapes metal, was bought seven years ago for $522,000. The company will add 19% to this cost, representing the change in the wholesale price index over the seven years. This new, higher cost figure is depreciated using the straight-line method over the same 12-year assumed life (no salvage value).

a. Calculate depreciation expense and book value of the metal press based upon both historical cost and the change in the wholesale price index.
b. In general, what is the effect on ROI of changing valuation bases from historical cost to current values?
c. The manager of the investment center with the metal press is considering replacing the press, which is becoming obsolete. Will the manager's incentives to replace the metal press change if the firm shifts from historical cost valuation to the proposed price-level adjusted historical cost valuation?

(*Contributors:* L. Harrington, R. Lewis, P. Siviy, and S. Spector.)

NP 7.6
Transfer Price and Capacity
(LO 6)

Microelectronics is a large electronics firm with multiple divisions. Its circuit board division manufactures circuit boards, which it sells externally and internally. Its phone division assembles cellular telephones and sells them to external customers. Both divisions are evaluated as profit centers. The firm has the policy of transferring all internal products at market price.

The sales price of cellular telephones is $400, and the external market price for the cellular telephone circuit board is $200. The outlay cost for the phone division to complete a telephone (not including the cost of the circuit board) is $250. The variable cost of the circuit board is $130.

a. Will the phone division purchase the circuit boards from the circuit board division? (Show calculations.)
b. Suppose the circuit board division, which has the capacity to manufacture 15,000 boards, is currently manufacturing and selling externally 10,000 per month. From the standpoint of Microelectronics, should it manufacture and transfer 3,000 additional boards internally?
c. Discuss what transfer price should be set for part (b).
d. List the three most important assumptions underlying your analysis in parts (b) and (c).

NP 7.7
Transfer Price and Capacity
(LO 6)

Jefferson Company has two divisions: Jefferson Bottles and Jefferson Juice. Jefferson Bottles makes glass containers, which it sells to Jefferson Juice and other companies. It has a capacity of 10 million bottles a year. Jefferson Juice currently has a capacity of 3 million bottles per year. Jefferson Bottles has a fixed cost of $100,000 per year and a variable cost of $0.01/bottle. Jefferson Bottles can currently sell all of its output at $0.03/bottle.

a. What should Jefferson Bottles charge Jefferson Juice for bottles so that both divisions make appropriate decentralized planning decisions?
b. If Jefferson Bottles can sell only 5 million bottles to outside buyers, what should Jefferson Bottles charge Jefferson Juice for bottles so that both divisions make appropriate decentralized planning decisions?

NP 7.8
Planning Decisions and Transfer Price
(LO 6)

A hotel company is divided into two divisions: construction and management. The construction division builds the hotels, and the management division operates them. The construction division borrows money to cover the cost of construction and charges the management division an annual price per room to use the hotel. The construction division uses the transfer price to make the annual debt payments.

The estimated costs of both divisions and the estimated revenues for the management division for different number of rooms follow:

Number of Rooms	Construction Division Annual Debt Costs	Management Division Annual Costs	Management Division Annual Revenues
150	$2,000,000	$10,000,000	$15,000,000
200	2,400,000	11,000,000	16,500,000
250	2,600,000	12,000,000	18,000,000
300	2,700,000	13,000,000	18,500,000

a. What number of rooms in the new hotel maximizes the hotel company's value?
b. If the transfer price is set at $15,000 per year per room, what is the profit for each division?
c. What number of rooms will the management division choose if the transfer price is $15,000 per year per room?
d. Why is this transfer price not working for the company?

Alaskan Fishing Company operates five trawlers (fishing boats) out of Juneau, Alaska. The boats are of different sizes and incur different operating expenses during the year. The following table describes the operating data and value of each boat:

NP 7.9
ROI and Residual Income
(LO 4)

	Boats				
	A	B	C	D	E
Revenues	$5,500,000	$8,300,000	$10,400,000	$12,800,000	$20,400,000
Annual expenses	3,800,000	8,200,000	9,100,000	9,900,000	18,900,000
Income	$1,700,000	$ 100,000	$ 1,300,000	$ 2,900,000	$ 1,500,000
Book value	$ 0	$5,200,000	$ 6,100,000	$ 5,200,000	$ 8,300,000
Market value	5,000,000	6,200,000	8,000,000	10,000,000	15,000,000

The cost of capital for the company is 10%.

a. What is the ROI of each boat using the book value of the investment in it?
b. What is the ROI of each boat using the market value of the investment in it?
c. What is the residual income of each boat using its book value?
d. What is the residual income of each boat using its market value?
e. Which trawler had the best year?

A soft drink company has three bottling plants throughout the country. Bottling occurs at the regional level because of the high cost of transporting bottled soft drinks. The parent company supplies each plant with the syrup. The bottling plants combine the syrup with carbonated soda to make and bottle the soft drinks, which then are sent to regional grocery stores

The bottling plants are treated as cost centers, and their managers are evaluated based on minimizing the cost per soft drink bottled and delivered. Each bottling plant uses the same equipment, but some produce more bottles because of different demand levels. The costs and output for each bottling plant are as follows:

NP 7.10
Performance Measures for Cost Centers
(LO 1, 2, 3)

	A	B	C
Units produced	10,000,000	20,000,000	30,000,000
Variable costs	$ 200,000	$ 450,000	$ 650,000
Fixed costs	1,000,000	1,000,000	1,000,000

a. Estimate the average cost per unit for each plant.
b. Why would the manager of plant A be unhappy using average cost as the performance measure?

228   *Decentralized Organizations*

c. What alternative performance measure would make the manager of plant A happier?
d. Under what circumstances might the average cost be a better performance measure?

NP 7.11
ROI and Residual Income
(LO 4)

Swan Systems develops and manufactures under-the-sink residential water filtration units that remove chlorine and other chemicals from drinking water. This Dutch company has successfully expanded sales of its units in the European market for the past 12 years. Six years ago, Swan started a U.S. manufacturing and marketing division and three years ago an Australian manufacturing and marketing division. The following are summary operating data for the last fiscal:

SWAN SYSTEMS				
Summary of Operations				
Last Fiscal Year				
(millions of Dutch guilders)				
	Australia	**Netherlands**	**United States**	**Total**
Sales	50	55	75	180
Divisional expenses	38	33	58	129
Net income	12	22	17	51

Senior management is in the process of evaluating the relative performance of each division. While the Netherlands division is the largest and generates the most profit, it also has the largest asset investment, as indicated by the following:

SWAN SYSTEMS				
Miscellaneous Operating Data				
Last Fiscal Year				
(millions of Dutch guilders)				
	Australia	**Netherlands**	**United States**	**Total**
Divisional net assets	80	195	131	406
Allocated corporate overhead*	4	4	6	14
Cost of capital	8.0%	8.0%	8.0%	

* Allocated based on divisional sales revenue.

After careful consideration, senior management has decided to examine the relative performance of the three divisions using several alternative measures of performance: ROI (measured by net assets, or total assets less liabilities), residual income (net income less the cost of capital times net assets), and both of these measures after subtracting allocated corporate overhead from divisional income. The cost of capital in each division is estimated to be the same (8%). (Assume that this 8% estimate is accurate.)

There has been much debate about whether corporate overhead should be allocated to the divisions and subtracted from divisional income. Senior management has decided to allocate back to each division the portion of corporate overhead that is incurred to support and manage it. The allocated corporate overhead items include worldwide marketing, legal expenses, accounting, and administration. Sales revenue has been selected as the allocation base. It is simple to use and best represents the cause-and-effect relationship between the divisions and the generation of corporate overhead.

a. Calculate ROI and residual income (1) before any corporate overhead allocations and (2) after corporate overhead allocations for each division.
b. Discuss the differences among the various performance measures.
c. Based on the data presented in the case, evaluate the relative performance of the three operating divisions. Which division do you think performed the best and which performed the worst?

NP 7.12
International Transfer Pricing and Taxes
(LO 7)

Phipps manufactures circuit boards in its Low Division located in a country with a 30% income tax rate. Low Division transfers them to High Division located in a country with a 40% income tax rate. An import duty of 15% of the transfer price is paid on all imported products; it is not deductible in computing taxable income. The circuit boards' full cost is

$1,000; variable cost is $700. High Division sells them for $1,200. The tax authorities in both countries allow firms to base their transfer prices on either variable cost or full cost.

Analyze the effect of full cost and variable cost transfer-pricing methods on Phipps's cash flows.

Multi-National Enterprises (MNE) operates in two countries, X and Y, with tax rates of 40% and 10%, respectively. Production costs are exactly the same in each country. The following summarizes the operating data for the two subsidiaries. (All data have been converted to dollars to simplify the example.)

NP 7.13
International Taxation
(LO 7)

	Subsidiary in Country X	Subsidiary in Country Y
Tax rate	40%	10%
Units sold	100	200
Unit cost	$10	$10
Selling price per unit	$20	$20

a. If each operating unit of MNE produces and sells only in its local country, is treated as a separate company, and pays taxes only in the country of its operations, what is MNE's total tax bill?

b. Suppose that MNE's subsidiary in country Y manufactures all the output sold in both countries. It ships the output to the subsidiary in country X that sells the product. The transfer price is set at $20. There are no costs of shipping the units from Y to X. If each country taxes only those profits that occur within its jurisdiction, recalculate MNE's total tax liability.

c. Now suppose that the subsidiary in country X manufactures all the output sold in both countries. It ships the output to the subsidiary in country Y that sells the product. Again, there are no costs of shipping the units from Y to X. If each country taxes only those profits that occur within its jurisdiction, what transfer price must be set to minimize MNE's total tax liability?

A company has two divisions, Division A in Mexico and Division B in Canada. Division A makes a product at a cost of $3 per unit that it transfers to Division B. At an additional cost of $1 per unit, Division B sells the product to outside customers for $8 per unit. During the year, 100,000 units are produced, transferred, and sold. Assume that the tax rate in Canada is 30% and that the tax rate in Mexico is 40%.

What is the total tax liability of the company if the transfer price is $5 per unit?

NP 7.14
International Transfer Prices
(LO 7)

ANALYSIS AND INTERPRETATION PROBLEMS

Maple Way Golf Course is a private club owned by its members. It has the following managers and organizational structure:

AIP 7.1
Responsibility Centers
(LO 1, 2, 3)

Eric Olson: General manager; responsible for all operations of the golf course and other facilities (swimming pool, restaurant, golf shop).

Jennifer Jones: Manager of the golf course; responsible for its maintenance.

Edwin Moses: Manager of the restaurant.

Mabel Smith: Head golf professional; responsible for golf lessons, the golf shop, and reserving times for starting golfers on the course.

Wanda Itami: Manager of the swimming pool and family recreational activities.

Jake Reece: Manager of golf carts rented to golfers.

Describe each manager in terms of being responsible for a cost, profit, or investment center. Provide possible performance measures for each manager.

Bookmark Company uses cost-based transfer pricing to transfer books from the publication division to its bookstores. The transfer price is based on a budget established at the beginning of the year. At the end of the year, the publication division had a cost overrun, and its manager wants to charge the bookstores for the extra costs. Under which of the following cases does the publication manager have a valid argument?

AIP 7.2
Transfer Prices
(LO 5)

a. The cost overruns were due to equipment failure.

b. The cost overruns were due to rush orders from the bookstores.

c. The cost overruns were due to the return of defective books.

d. The cost overruns were due to lower demand for books than expected.

AIP 7.3

Evaluation of a New Product with ROI

(LO 4)

A Canadian wholesaler of Mexican crafts is considering importing rugs handwoven in southern Mexico using natural dyes. The rugs cost an average $250 Canadian including transportation and handling. The wholesaler plans to sell them in Canada for $300 Canadian. Therefore, the profit per rug should be $50 Canadian. The wholesaler's cost of capital is 10% annually. The wholesaler estimates an ROI on the project of ($50)/$250, or 20%. The residual income is estimated to be $50 − (0.10)($250), or $25 Canadian per rug.

What is wrong with the use of ROI and residual income in this analysis?

AIP 7.4

Responsibility Centers

(LO 2)

News Inc. owns five newspaper stands for which it purchases the newspapers. Each stand has a manager responsible for ordering newspapers each day. Any newspapers not sold at the end of the day are thrown away.

Describe how the newspaper stands might operate as cost centers, profit centers, and investment centers. Outline the advantages and disadvantages of each type of responsibility center.

AIP 7.5

Salespeople as Profit Centers

(LO 2)

Memories Company sells cosmetics door-to-door. The company has traditionally paid its salespeople a commission based on total sales, but it is considering making each salesperson a profit center.

How would making each salesperson a profit center affect his or her behavior?

AIP 7.6

Influences on the ROI Measure

(LO 4)

The president of a company is trying to improve his firm's ROI. He asks a consultant for assistance. The consultant tells the president that he must increase either his profit margin (income/sales) or asset turnover (sales/assets). The president complains that every time he tries to increase his profit margin, the asset turnover goes down.

Evaluate the consultant's advice and the president's complaint.

AIP 7.7

ROI and Throughput

(LO 4)

A popular book claims that manufacturing managers should always work to improve throughput (the time from starting the manufacturing process to the time of sale).

How is this philosophy related to ROI?

AIP 7.8

Transfer Prices

(LO 6)

Peaceful Valley Company owns both hotels and manufacturing companies. One hotel has a convention center, which is leased to various groups. The manufacturing companies want to use the convention center for a training session.

What conditions should affect the choice of the transfer price?

AIP 7.9

Transfer Prices and Change from a Cost to a Profit Center

(LO 2, 5)

Northern Blue Company has manufacturing plants and retail shops. The retail shops purchase products from the manufacturing plants. Currently, the manufacturing plants are operated as cost centers and supply only the retail shops. The retail shops operate as profit centers. The transfer price is cost based. The president of the company is considering an increase in manufacturing capacity that will allow sales to customers outside the organization. She plans to make the manufacturing plants profit centers.

Why are the managers of the retail shops unhappy with these new plans?

AIP 7.10

ROI and Other Performance Measures

(LO 4)

Brownside Company is highly decentralized. Its divisions can issue their own debt, but they must pay their own interest. The manager of Park Division, who is evaluated based on ROI, has borrowed a considerable amount of money from the bank for expansion. A large interest expense on that debt is lowering the division's income. Brownside Company's president calculates Park's ROI by using the net income, which includes the interest expense, and dividing this figure by the total assets of the division.

Why does the manager of the Park Division believe this ROI measure is inappropriate? Suggest alternative performance measures.

AIP 7.11

Transfer Price

(LO 6)

U.S. Pumps is a multidivisional firm that manufactures and installs chemical piping and pump systems. Its valve division makes a single standardized valve. The valve division and installation division currently are involved in a transfer-pricing dispute. Last year, half of the valve division's output was sold to the installation division for $40 and the remaining half was sold to outsiders for $60.

The existing transfer price of $40 per pump has been set through a negotiation process between the two divisions and with the involvement of senior management. The installation division has received a bid from an outside value manufacturer to supply it with an equivalent valve for $35 each.

The valve division's manager has argued that if it is forced to meet the external price of $35, it will lose money on internal sales.

The operating data for the last year for the valve division follow:

VALVE DIVISION Operating Statement Last Year		
	To Installation Division	**To Outside**
Sales	20,000 @ $40 $800,000	20,000 @ $60 $1,200,000
Variable costs	@ $30 (600,000)	(600,000)
Fixed costs	(135,000)	(135,000)
Gross margin	$ 65,000	$ 465,000

Analyze the situation and recommend a course of action. What should the installation division managers do? What should the valve division managers do? In your opinion, what should U.S. Pumps' senior managers do?

AIP 7.12
Transfer Prices
(LO 5, 6)

Lewis is a large manufacturer of office equipment including copiers. Its electronics division, which is a cost center, currently sells circuit boards to other divisions exclusively. Lewis has a policy that internal transfers are to be priced at full cost (fixed + variable). Thirty percent of the cost of a board is considered fixed.

The electronics division is currently operating at 75% of capacity. Given this excess capacity, it is seeking opportunities to sell boards to outside firms. Its policy on non-Lewis sales states that each job must cover full cost and a minimum 10% profit. The electronics division management will be measured on the ability to make the minimum profit on any non-Lewis contracts accepted.

Copy products, another Lewis division, recently reached an agreement with Siviy, a non-Lewis firm, to assemble subsystems for a copier. Copy products has selected Siviy based on Siviy's low labor cost. The subsystem that Siviy will assemble requires circuit boards. Copy products has stipulated that Siviy must purchase the circuit boards from the electronics division because of electronics' high quality and dependability. Electronics is anxious to accept this new work from copy because it will increase electronics' workload by 15%.

In negotiating a contract price with Siviy, copy products needs to consider the cost of the circuit boards from electronics. The financial analyst from copy products assumes that electronics will sell the circuit boards to Siviy at full cost (the same as the internal transfer price). Electronics is considering adding the minimum 10% profit margin to its full cost and transferring at that price to Siviy.

Develop and discuss at least three options that may be used to establish the transfer price between the electronics division and Siviy. Discuss the advantages and disadvantages of each.

AIP 7.13
Transfer Prices and Contracts
(LO 5)

To induce utilities to award contracts to Westinghouse Electric to build nuclear reactors, Westinghouse contracted to supply uranium to these utilities at an average price of $9.50 over a 20-year period. In 1966, Westinghouse disclosed the following in its annual report:

Westinghouse Electric Corporation has entered into a number of long-term contractual agreements to sell up to 80 million tons of uranium to utility companies to encourage nuclear reactor construction and to secure sales of uranium. The contracts are optional to the purchasers at a fixed price. The average contract price is approximately $9.50 per pound, and the current market price is $8.00 per pound. We cannot reasonably estimate the amount of purchases that will be made under these agreements because of the optional nature of the contracts.

By 1976, the market price of uranium was more than $40 per pound. Westinghouse was unable to meet its commitments and was faced with a potential loss of $2.275 billion, which was more than six times the company's net income in 1976.

In 1976, a new manager of the Westinghouse Uranium Supply Division (USD) was hired. This division was responsible for the acquisition and sales of uranium to utilities, both those that had Westinghouse reactors and those with competitor reactors. USD purchased raw uranium in world markets and then processed it into nuclear reactor fuel cells. This division was evaluated as a profit center. The new manager argued that a number of long-term supply agreements were signed before he joined Westinghouse; thus, USD's revenues on these old contracts should have been measured using the current market price rather than the original contract price.

a. How should Uranium Supply Division's performance have been measured?

b. State commissions regulate public utilities in the United States, including those with nuclear power–generating plants. State regulatory commissions set the utilities' prices for electricity based on cost plus a "fair return on capital." Cost is based on transaction prices. Given the facts in the problem, how should managers of public utilities with Westinghouse Electric contracts behave, given the difference in the contract price of $9.50 per pound of uranium and a current market price of $44.50?

AIP 7.14
Transfer Price from Shared Service
(LO 6)

Susan Willard, the CEO of Troy Industrial Designs (TID), has called a meeting to evaluate the present method of charging the two offices at Washington and Rochester for the shared services of the Creative Design Group (CGD). She wants to discuss the present cost allocation system and suggest a better one.

TID is a reputable firm in the industrial design sector. It bids for design contracts from different firms. If successful, it either makes prototypes based on the client's blueprints, designs new products from existing designs, or draws designs for a product that the client has in mind. For the use of TID designs or products it designs, TID charges clients a fixed figure on completion of the job and 1% of sales accruing to the client every year for the first seven years.

The two TID offices are run independently by different managers and are profit centers. Each manager assigns account executives to individual accounts. The account executives are paid a fixed salary, but a large part of their compensation is their bonus, which is based on the revenues accruing from the jobs that they manage. On receiving a job, the account executive informs George Scott, the head of CDG. They meet with the client and decide on a plan, detailing the job, expected time to complete it, and other specific factors. The account executive then waits for the final design before informing the client and discussing it. As soon as a job is finished, the account executive prepares a detailed report explaining the work done, the number of designers employed for it, the number of hours worked on it, the amount billed to the client, and any follow-up. Design is a one-time job and it seldom requires follow-up time. Account executives are responsible for any follow-up on their jobs. If the client comes back with another project, it is treated as a separate job.

TID centralized the design departments of the two offices to take advantage of the designers' specialized knowledge. Although CDG is only five years old, it employs the best talent and uses the latest technology. This strategy has had a positive impact on customers; therefore, TID has grown rapidly in the past few years. The two offices have great confidence in CDG and use it for all their design needs. The rapid growth has caused top management to rethink the cost procedures and other organizational aspects of the business.

CDG is totally responsible for designing the job. It interacts with the client only at the design stage; all other aspects of the job are performed by the appropriate account executive. CDG works in small teams, each of which is led by a supervisor who reports to George on a day-to-day basis. George is evaluated on the excess of revenues collected from the two offices over the costs of his department. The cost charged to each office is decided before CDG takes the design job. Before the client is brought in for the discussion, the account executive and George decide what fees CDG will charge the office for the services. Revenues for CDG come from the predetermined fees charged to the two offices.

Susan suggests that CDG should provide its services free of charge. Under this proposal, George would receive a fixed salary and a bonus based on overall firm profits (i.e., a percentage of the combined profits of the two offices). She believes that as the cost of the department is finally consolidated with those of the firm, there should be no allocation of costs for the department. Removal of the transfer price will help reduce the work of the accounts department and help streamline it to cope with the rapid growth of the firm. Susan says that the firm is committed to designing the best products and that cost allocations really do not matter.

Will the resources of CDG be efficiently utilized under the new plan? Why? What are the merits and demerits of the existing arrangement? Is the proposed plan better than the existing arrangement? Why?

Celtex is a large, successful, decentralized specialty chemical producer. It is organized into five independent investment centers, each of which is free to buy products either inside or outside the firm and is judged on residual income. Most of each division's sales is to external customers. Celtex has the general reputation of being one of the top two or three companies in each of its markets.

Don Horigan, president of synthetic chemicals (synchem) division, and Paula Juris, president of consumer products division, are embroiled in a dispute. It all began two years ago when Paula asked Don to modify a synthetic chemical for a new household cleaner. In return, synchem would be reimbursed for out-of-pocket costs. After spending considerable time perfecting the chemical, Paula solicited competitive bids from Don and some outside firms. Ultimately, she awarded the contract to an outside firm that was the low bidder. This decision angered Don, who expected his bid to receive special consideration because he had developed the new chemical at cost and the outside vendors took advantage of his R&D.

The current conflict has to do with synchem's production of chemical Q47, a standard product, for consumer products. Due to an economic slowdown, all synthetic chemical producers have excess capacity. Synchem was asked to bid on supplying Q47 for consumer products, which is moving into a new, experimental product line for which Q47 is a key ingredient. While the magnitude of the order is small relative to synchem's total business, the price of Q47 is very important in determining the profitability of the experimental line. Don bid $3.20 per gallon. Meas Chemicals, an outside firm, bid $3.00. Paula is angry because she knows that Don's bid contains a substantial amount of fixed overhead and profit. Synchem buys the base raw material, Q4, from organic chemicals division of Celtex for $1.00 per gallon. Organic chemicals' out-of-pocket costs (i.e., variable costs) are 80% of the selling price. Synchem then further processes Q4 into Q47, incurring additional variable costs of $1.75 per gallon. Allocated fixed overhead adds another $0.30 per gallon.

Don argues that he has $3.05 of cost in each gallon of Q47. If he sells the product for anything less than $3.20, he is undermining his recent attempts to get his salespeople to stop cutting their bids and start quoting full-cost prices. Don has been trying to enhance the quality of the business that he is getting. He fears that if he is forced to make Q47 for consumer products, all of his effort in the last few months would be for naught. He argues that he gave away the store once to consumer products and he will not do it again. He questions, "How can senior managers expect me to return a positive residual income if I am forced to put in bids that do not recover full cost?"

In a chance meeting at the airport with Debra Donak, senior vice president of Celtex, Paula describes the situation and asks her to intervene. Paula believes that Don is trying to get even after their earlier clash, arguing that the success of his new product venture depends on being able to secure a stable, high-quality source of supply of Q47 at low cost.

a. Prepare a statement outlining the cash flows to Celtex of the two alternative sources of supply for Q47.

b. What advice would you give to Debra Donak?

In a *Wall Street Journal* article, General Motors announced a reorganization to "designate individuals who will be accountable for the development of new cars and light trucks." The newly created post of vehicle-line manager was established to "make sure new products get to market quickly and efficiently." Also, the position of brand manager was established for "making sure each individual model has a consistent and well-defined image in consumers' eyes."

a. Based on their responsibilities, would you classify the vehicle-line manager and the brand manager as managers of cost, profit, or investment centers?

b. What are possible performance measures for these two types of managers?

(*Source: The Wall Street Journal*, October 20, 1995, p. B 4:3.)

Monsanto is a worldwide chemical company. In the 1980s, it noticed that in certain foreign markets sales were declining. The local managers in these markets were asked to increase their advertising and marketing expenditures to try to stem the decline. Accounting reports of advertising and marketing expenditures in these markets indicated that these expenditures were declining. Monsanto had the accounting practice of converting all foreign currencies into U.S. dollars before reporting the foreign results to U.S. senior managers. The dollar had been strengthening against the local currencies in the foreign markets. When asked why they had not increased these expenditures, the foreign managers were confused and said they had increased the expenditures. Explain the apparent inconsistency between the foreign managers and the accounting reports used by the senior U.S. managers.

AIP 7.15
Transfer Prices in a Competitive Market
(LO 6)

AIP 7.16
Identification of Responsibility Centers
(LO 1, 2)

AIP 7.17
Exchange Rates and Performance Evaluation
(LO 7)

AIP 7.18
Transfer Prices and Responsibility Centers
(LO 2, 5, 6)

US Copiers manufactures a full line of copiers including desktop models. Its Small Copier Division (SCD) manufactures desktop copiers and sells them in the United States. A typical model has a retail price of less than $500. An integral part in the copier is the toner cartridge that contains the black powder used to create the image on the paper. The cartridge can be used for about 10,000 pages and then must be replaced. The typical owner of an SCD copier purchases four replacement cartridges over the life of the copier.

SCD buys the initial toner cartridges provided with the copier from Toner Division (TD) of US Copiers. TD sells subsequent replacement cartridges to distributors who sell them to U.S. retail stores. Toner cartridges sell to the end consumer for $50. TD sells the toners to distributors for about 70% of the final retail price paid by the consumer. TD's manager argues that its market price of $35 (70% × $50) is the price SCD should pay TD for each toner cartridge transferred.

a. Why does US Copiers manufacture both copiers and toner cartridges? Why do separate firms not exist that specialize in either copiers or toner cartridges, as Intel specializes in making computer chips and Gateway specializes in assembling computers and selling PCs?

b. You work for SCD's president. Write a memo to your boss outlining the salient issues that she should raise in discussing the price SCD should pay TD for toner cartridges included in SCD copiers.

AIP 7.19
ROI and Economic Value Added (EVA)
(LO 4)

General Motors' CFO, Michael Losh, converted GM's performance measure for compensation from net income to return on investment, calculated as return on assets (ROA). In explaining the move he said,

> ROA was a logical next step because all those other measures generally have focused on the income statement. Moving to ROA means that we're going to focus not only on the income statement, but on the balance sheet and effective utilization of the assets and liabilities that are on the balance sheet as well.
>
> ROA is a better measure for us than EVA. . . . EVA is simpler conceptually, because it automatically builds on growth, whereas with this approach we know that we've got to have growth as an overlying objective. EVA is more comprehensive. And that has a certain appeal to me. But, given our situation, particularly in our North American operations, it just would not have been the right measure.
>
> ROA works for us and EVA doesn't because our operations have to deal with those two different kinds of starting points. Within GM, in our North American operations, you've got a classic turnaround situation, and in our international operations, you've got a classic growth situation. You can apply ROA to both; you can't apply EVA to both.

a. Explain how ROA focuses on both the income statement and the balance sheet.
b. Explain why EVA is more "comprehensive" than ROA.
c. Do you agree with Mr. Losh's statement that "you can apply ROA to both; you can't apply EVA to both"? Explain.

AIP 7.20
Transfer Prices and External Market Opportunities
(LO 6)

KCG is a division of Metro Stores (a large retail firm) that designs and maintains Web sites for its individual stores. It also sells its services outside the firm to other retail stores. KCG, a profit center, has two Web designers, each of whom earns $4,000 per month, who do not have an assignment for the next month. The Dallas Metro store wants its Web site updated, which will require two designers one month each to complete the project.

a. How much should the Dallas metro store be charged for KCG's services?
b. Suppose that KCG expects that the two designers will be assigned to work on an outside job that will generate revenues of $15,000. What should the Dallas Metro store be charged?

EXTENDED ANALYSIS AND INTERPRETATION PROBLEMS

AIP 7.21
IBM Data Center for Eastman Kodak

In 1989, IBM and Kodak entered into an agreement by which IBM would build and operate a data processing center in Rochester, New York, which consolidated five Kodak data centers into one. Of the five original data centers, three were at separate sites in Rochester, one was in Colorado, and the fifth was in Canada. More than three hundred data processing Kodak employees became IBM employees. Originally, IBM purchased Kodak-owned IBM computer equipment and moved into the IBM data center. IBM augmented this equipment with a significant amount of new equipment (both IBM and non-IBM products).

Kodak pays an annual fee to IBM based on the amount of computing services that it receives (e.g., lines printed, amount of disk space). The IBM data center pays all labor costs, occupancy costs, and costs of all software and hardware acquired. The IBM data center is evaluated based on profits and the satisfaction of Kodak consumers.

Prior to the IBM–Kodak agreement, excess capacity in the mainframe business had increased price competition. A third-party vendor bid to operate Kodak's five data centers at substantial cost savings to Kodak. One source of the savings came from the vendor's use of less expensive computers, which are plug-compatible with IBM's machines. IBM made a competitive counteroffer, which it won, to keep the Kodak account and to run the data center.

Kodak views this contract as being very important because it can get out of the business of operating computers and focus management attention on more strategic issues, such as the design and maintenance of its applications software directed at its core businesses. These application computer programs run at the data center and include billing, payroll, accounts payable and receivable, cost accounting, and manufacturing production control and scheduling.

IBM considers the data center an important test case for its other large corporate clients, which are looking to move away from IBM hardware to plug-compatible mainframe clones. If IBM can successfully operate this data center for Kodak, it opens an important market of other large Fortune 100 companies. IBM has the expertise in centralizing and standardizing different data centers into one using a common set of operating standards. There are economies of scale in corporate computing. Also, operating data centers allows IBM to learn about large corporate-client computing, to develop new software and hardware, and to test new products before they are released.

One key issue that arises is the internal transfer price that the IBM data center pays for the IBM hardware and software that it "purchases" from other IBM divisions. This transfer price does not affect the price Kodak pays to IBM. Suppose that a hypothetical IBM mainframe A606, which sells for $3 million, is installed in the Kodak data center. The variable cost of this machine is $1 million and its full manufactured cost, including fixed and variable costs (unit manufactured cost) is $1.6 million. Moreover, IBM's total selling, general, and administrative costs are 30% of revenue, of which half (15%) varies directly with revenue. The comparable plug-compatible machine to the A606 sells for $1.9 million. The other IBM divisions, which provide goods and services to the data center, have profit responsibilities.

a. What factors should IBM consider when developing the transfer-pricing rule used to charge the data center for IBM products installed in the data center?

b. Given the limited information in the case, what transfer-pricing rule would you suggest that IBM adopt for its products installed in the data center? Using your transfer-pricing rule, what price should be charged for the hypothetical A606 mainframe?

PortCo Products is a divisionalized furniture manufacturer. The divisions are autonomous segments, each of which is responsible for its own sales, costs of operations, working capital management, and equipment acquisition. Each division serves a different market in the furniture industry. The markets and products of the division are so different that there have never been any transfers between them.

**AIP 7.22
PortCo Products**

Commercial division manufactures equipment and furniture that is purchased by the restaurant industry. The division plans to introduce a new line of counter and chair units that feature a cushioned seat for the counter chairs. John Kline, the commercial division's manager, has discussed the manufacturing of the cushioned seat with Russ Fiegel of the office division. They both believe a cushioned seat currently made by the office division for use on its deluxe office stool could be modified for use on the new counter chair. Consequently, John has asked Russ for a price for 100-unit lots of the cushioned seat. The following conversation took place about the price to be charged for the cushioned seats.

FIEGEL: John, we can make the necessary modifications to the cushioned seat easily. The raw materials used in your seat are slightly different and should cost about 10% more than those used in our deluxe office stool. However, the labor time should be the same because the seat fabrication operation basically is the same. I would price the seat at our regular rate—full cost plus 30% markup.

KLINE: That's higher than I expected, Russ. I was thinking that a good price would be your variable manufacturing costs. After all, your capacity costs will be incurred regardless of this job.

FIEGEL: John, I'm at capacity. By making the cushioned seats for you, I'll have to cut my production of deluxe office stools. Of course, I can increase my production of economy office stools. The labor time freed by not having to fabricate the frame or assemble the deluxe stool can be shifted to the frame fabrication and assembly of the economy office stool. And you will save the cost of the framing raw materials. However, I am constrained in terms of the number of hours I have for cushion fabrication. Fortunately, I can switch my labor force between these two models of stools without any loss of efficiency. As you know, overtime is not a feasible alternative in our community. I'd like to sell it to you at variable cost, but I have excess demand for both products. I don't mind changing my product mix to the economy model if I get a good return on the seats I make for you. Here are my budgeted costs for the two stools and a schedule of my manufacturing overhead. [See the following budgeted costs and overhead schedule.]

KLINE: I guess I see your point, Russ, but I don't want to price myself out of the market. Maybe we should talk to corporate to see if they can give us any guidance.

OFFICE DIVISION Budgeted Costs and Prices				
	Deluxe Office Stool			**Economy Office Stool**
Raw materials				
Framing	$8.15			$ 9.76
Cushioned seat				
Padding	2.40			—
Vinyl	4.00			—
Molded seat (purchased)	—			6.00
Direct labor				
Frame fabrication (0.5 × $7.50/DLH)*	3.75		(0.5 × $7.50/DLH)	3.75
Cushion fabrication (0.5 × $7.50/DLH)	3.75			—
Assembly (0.5 × $7.50/DLH)†	3.75		(0.3 × $7.50/DLH)	2.25
Manufacturing				
Overhead (1.5DLH × $12.80/DLH)	19.20		(0.8DLH × $12.80/DLH)	10.24
Total standard cost	$45.00			$32.00
Selling price (30% markup)	$58.50			$41.60

* DLH = direct labor hours.

† Attaching seats to frame and attaching rubber feet.

OFFICE DIVISION Manufacturing Overhead Budget		
Overhead Item	**Nature**	**Amount**
Supplies	Variable—at current market prices	$ 420,000
Indirect labor	Variable	375,000
Supervision	Nonvariable	250,000
Power	Use varies with activity; rates are fixed	180,000
Heat and light	Nonvariable—light is fixed regardless of production while heat/air conditioning varies with fuel charges	140,000
Property taxes and insurance taxes	Nonvariable—any change in amounts/rates is independent of production	200,000
Depreciation	Fixed dollar total	1,700,000
Employee benefits	20% of supervision, direct and indirect labor	575,000
Total overhead		$3,840,000
Capacity in DLH		÷ 300,000
Overhead rate/DLH		$ 12.80

a. John Kline and Russ Fiegel did ask PortCo corporate management for guidance on an appropriate transfer price. Corporate management suggested that they consider using a transfer price based on opportunity cost. Calculate a transfer price for the cushioned seat based on variable manufacturing cost plus forgone profits.

b. Which alternative transfer-pricing system—full cost, variable manufacturing cost, or opportunity cost—would be better as the underlying concept for an intracompany transfer-pricing policy? Explain your answer.

(CMA adapted)

AIP 7.23
Royal Resort and Casino

Royal Resort and Casino (RRC), a publicly traded company, caters to affluent customers seeking plush surroundings, high-quality food and entertainment, and all the "glitz" associated with the best resorts and casinos. RRC consists of three divisions: hotel, gaming, and entertainment. The hotel division manages the reservation system and lodging operations. Gaming consists of operations, security, and junkets; junkets offer complimentary airfare, lodging, and entertainment at RRC for customers known to wager large sums. The entertainment division consists of restaurants, lounges, catering, and shows. It books lounge shows and top-name entertainment in the theater. Many people attending the shows and eating in the restaurants stay at RRC, but customers staying at other hotels and casinos in the area also frequent RRC's shows, restaurants, and gaming operations. The following disaggregates RRC's total EVA of $12 million into an EVA for each division:

ROYAL RESORT AND CASINO EVA by Division (millions $)				
	Entertainment	**Hotel**	**Gaming**	**Total**
Adjusted accounting profits	$ 5	$ 10	$30	$ 45
Invested capital	$40	$120	$60	$220
Weighted-average cost of capital	15%	15%	15%	15%
EVA	($1)	($8)	$21	$12

Based on an analysis of similar companies, it is determined that each division has the same weighted-average cost of capital of 15%.

Across town from RRC is a city block with three separate businesses: Big Horseshoe Slots & Casino, Nell's Lounge and Grill, and Sunnyside Motel. These businesses serve a lower-income clientele.

a. Why does RRC operate as a single firm, whereas Big Horseshoe Slots & Casino, Nell's Lounge and Grill, and Sunnyside Motel operate as three separate firms?

b. Describe some of the interdependencies that likely exist across RRC's three divisions.

c. Describe some of the internal administrative devices, accounting-based measures, and/or organizational structures that senior managers at RRC can use to control the interdependencies that you described in (a).

d. Critically evaluate each of the "solutions" that you proposed in (c).

Chapter**Eight**

Budgeting

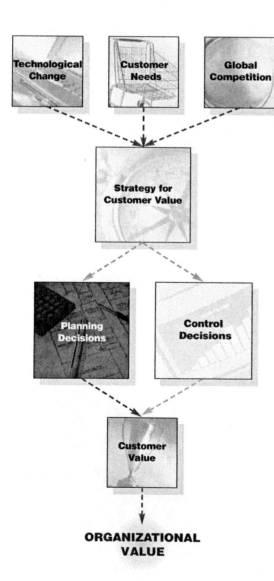

MAPLEDALE CHILD CENTER

Mapledale Child Center (MCC) is a not-for-profit organization that provides day care and kindergarten education to the children of the Mapledale housing subdivision of Tucson, Arizona. MCC rents space in a neighborhood building, where both the day care and kindergarten programs are housed with MCC's administrative offices.

The day care program is for children between six months and five years of age. MCC charges $500 monthly per child for eight hours of day care every weekday. MCC's day care program is open 12 months of the year. A licensed staff of counselors provides a structured set of activities tailored to the age of the children; one counselor is required for every five children. The day care center has a capacity of 50 children.

The kindergarten is four hours per day, either morning or afternoon, for nine months. Each session has a capacity of 75 children and costs $360 per month per child. MC needs one kindergarten teacher for every 10 children. A nurse is always on staff for both the kindergarten and the day care programs.

A 10-member board of directors oversees and supervises MCC's operations. The board hires the manager of the day care center, the manager of the kindergarten, and the office manager. The managers of the day care and kindergarten programs hire their staffs, plan their programs, and are responsible for the financial operations of the programs. The office manager supervises a secretary and bookkeeper who prepare the monthly bills for the users of the facility and the monthly financial reports for the board of directors, purchase the supplies, and are responsible for collecting and disbursing funds.

MCC's fiscal year is from July 1 to June 30; prior to its beginning, the office manager asks the day care and kindergarten managers to prepare budgets to plan for the coming fiscal year. MCC cannot spend more than its revenue, so the budgeting process is very important for planning for the new school year. While not profit-driven, MCC strives to create value for parents by providing quality programs. This strategy ensures that organizational value is created in terms of MCC's continued attractiveness and viability as an educator.

PURPOSE OF BUDGETS

Organizations develop strategies as a basis to compete in their operating environment. **Budgets** are a key component of the organization's planning and control system, providing the mechanism to translate organizational goals into financial terms. More specifically, budgets are forecasts of future revenues and expenditures. Once established, budgets provide a control tool to ensure that organizational members work to achieve the goals that create value. **Budgeting** is the process of gathering information to assist in making those forecasts; it is a very costly process. Managers often spend up to 20% of their time on budgeting. Its popularity, however, indicates that its perceived benefits are greater than its costs.

The benefits of budgeting result from making planning and control decisions. For planning purposes, the budgeting process generates and communicates information to improve coordination. The budgeting process is the initial step to implement change in an organization in response to changes in its environment and customer needs. The control benefits of budgets include assigning of responsibilities and scarce resources, providing goals to motivate managers, and establishing performance measures to reward managers.

Budgeting for Planning Decisions

LO 1   Use budgeting for planning purposes.

Planning Decisions

Budgets play an integral role in making planning decisions. One purpose of budgeting is to transfer information to the individuals within the organization making decisions. Managers near the top of an organization's hierarchy must make major, long-term planning decisions, yet some of the information necessary to make those decisions is located with managers lower in the hierarchy. To improve major, long-term decisions, the information located lower in the hierarchy must be transferred to top-level management. The budgeting process attempts to fulfill this role by encouraging the "bottom-up" flow of information. An example of the bottom-up flow of information in the budgeting process is the collection of expenditure requests by the central administration of a university from the various departments. The head of each department knows that department's needs, which are communicated to the central administration through the budgeting process.

Lower-level managers of the organization also must make decisions. To improve their decisions, these managers could use information located with top-level managers. Top-level managers have aggregated information from the various parts of the organization and the outside environment. To allow lower-level managers to make both more informed decisions and decisions that are coordinated with other managers within the organization, top-level management must communicate its information and plans from the "top down." For example, the top managers of a bottle-manufacturing firm must communicate production requirements to the managers of the different manufacturing facilities. The top-level managers have information on global demand for bottles and use this information to determine production requirements for each of the manufacturing facilities.

Budgeting for Control

LO 2   Use budgeting for control purposes

Control Decisions

Budgets also play an important role in control. The budget is often used to assign responsibilities by allocating resources to different managers. Giving a manager an advertising budget of $800,000 authorizes that manager to consume $800,000 of the firm's resources on advertising. The level of responsibility given to the manager determines how the $800,000 on advertising can be spent. If he or she has the confidence of the top-level managers and specialized knowledge of advertising, the budget might give the advertising manager the flexibility to choose how to spend the $800,000. If he or she is new and does not have specialized knowledge, the budget might also specify how the $800,000 is to be spent. For example, it might stipulate spending $500,000 on radio advertisements and $300,000 on newspaper advertisements. With more constraints in the budget, a manager has fewer opportunities to make decisions.

The numbers in the budget are also used as goals to motivate organizational members. Budgeted numbers become targets for managers. For example, the manager of a factory making tennis racquets is allocated $700,000 to make 10,000 racquets; the 10,000 racquets represent a goal for the manager, who is expected to work hard and manage well to achieve that goal.

Once the budget is set, it becomes the target by which performance is evaluated and rewarded. In setting the budget, some experts argue that the budget should be "tight" but achievable. If budget goals are too easily achieved, they provide little incentive to expend extra effort. If budgets are unachievable, they provide little motivation. The motivation to achieve budgeted numbers results from rewards. If budgeted numbers are achieved, the manager is rewarded with bonuses or other privileges. The manager of the tennis racquet factory strives to achieve the goal of manufacturing 10,000 racquets for $700,000, knowing that rewards are based on achieving the budget.

The difference between a budgeted performance measure and an actual performance measure is called the **variance.** An **unfavorable variance** occurs when actual costs exceed the budgeted costs, or actual revenues are less than budgeted revenues. A **favorable variance** occurs when actual costs are less than the budgeted costs, or actual revenues are higher than budgeted revenues. Variances are commonly calculated in monthly reports to identify how successfully an organization is achieving its goals. Large favorable or unfavorable variances are commonly investigated to determine the reason for them and to correct any problems that may exist.

Tennis stars, like the Williams sisters, expect much of themselves and their equipment. A faulty racquet could be the difference between a win and runner-up status. Racquet manufacturers must meet exacting quality and cost standards. Their marketing managers face similar demands, often seeking exclusive contracts with pros to enhance product image.

 **8.1**

Ayala Telecom has the following budgeted and actual results for the month of July:

AYALA TELECOM Budgeted and Actual Income for July		
	Budgeted	**Actual**
Revenues	$450,000	$453,000
Cost of goods sold	(235,000)	(248,000)
General administration	(80,000)	(132,000)
Selling expenses	(100,000)	(90,000)
Profit	$ 35,000	($ 17,000)

Calculate the variances for each of the items in the monthly report and describe them as favorable or unfavorable. What item appears to warrant investigation?

Solution

The variances are the difference between the budgeted and actual amounts:

AYALA TELECOM			
Budgeted and Actual Income for July			
	Budgeted	**Actual**	**Variance**
Revenues	$450,000	$453,000	$ 3,000 F
Cost of goods sold	(235,000)	(248,000)	13,000 U
General administration	(80,000)	(132,000)	52,000 U
Selling expenses	(100,000)	(90,000)	10,000 F
Profit	$ 35,000	($ 17,000)	$52,000 U

The actual general administration expense account is much different than expected and has the largest variance. Large unfavorable variances are generally the focus of an investigation if the cause is unknown. The other accounts have smaller variances but also might be investigated.

Organizations should modify the budgeting process to meet their special planning and control needs. The HON Company, the nation's largest maker of mid-priced office furniture, operates in a very volatile industry. Annual budgets for the company do not provide meaningful targets because of changing demand for its product. To adapt to a rapidly changing environment, the HON Company makes new budgets every three months. By continuously updating budgets every three months, the firm is able to meet its two strategic objectives: ongoing new product and service development and rapid continuous improvement.[1]

MAPLEDALE CHILD CENTER (Continued)

MCC's budget translates its strategy into specific activities and programs and forms the basis for their control. Budgeting is extremely important for MCC. Initially, the budget is used to estimate the total enrollment and revenues available, which MCC used to determine how many teachers to hire. The budget also specifies how much the managers of the day care and kindergarten programs and the office manager can spend on educational and office supplies. A larger budget for educational and office supplies gives the managers more responsibilities. No bonuses are based on the budget, but having greater resources makes teaching easier and more rewarding.

CONFLICT BETWEEN PLANNING AND CONTROL

LO 3 Identify the conflicts that exist between planning and control in the budgeting process.

A budgeting system serves two principal purposes, planning and control. In making planning decisions, budgets communicate specialized knowledge from one part of the organization to another. For making control decisions, budgets serve as benchmarks for performance measurement systems. The budget becomes the benchmark against which to judge actual performance. Because budgets serve several purposes, trade-offs must be made when designing or changing a budgeting system. If too much emphasis is placed on the budget as a performance benchmark, managers with the specialized knowledge might stop disclosing accurate forecasts of future events for planning decisions and tend to report budget figures that make benchmarks easier to achieve.

[1] R. Drtina, S. Hoeger, and J. Schaub, "Continuous Budgeting at the HON Company," *Management Accounting*, January 1996, pp. 20–24.

The trade-off between planning and control decisions is a particularly severe problem in marketing. Salespeople usually have specialized knowledge of future sales. This information is important in setting future production plans, such as how many units to manufacture. If budgeted sales are used to evaluate salespeople at the end of the year, they have an incentive to underforecast future sales, thus improving their performance evaluation. However, production plans then will be too low, and the firm will incur costs due to its inability to plan the most efficient production schedules.

Planning Decisions

To manage the conflict between making planning and control decisions, many organizations put the chief executive officer (CEO) in charge of the budgeting process. While the actual collection of data and the preparation of the budget are the formal responsibility of the chief financial officer or controller, the president or CEO has the final responsibility. The CEO has immediate control for numerous reasons. First, this signals the importance of the budgeting process. Second, resolving disagreements among departments requires making trade-offs, and the CEO, who has the overall view of the whole firm, is best able to make them.

Control Decisions

In addition to placing the CEO in charge of the budgeting process, many firms also use a budget committee. Such a committee consists of the major functional executives (vice presidents of sales, manufacturing, finance, and human resources) with the CEO as chairperson. The budget committee facilitates the exchange of specialized knowledge and the achievement of consensus in establishing a budget.

The budget is an informal set of contracts between the various units of the organization. By accepting the budget, the organization's managers agree to perform the responsibilities assigned and to abide by the limitations it specifies.

Most budgets are set in a negotiation process involving lower- and higher-level managers. Lower-level managers have incentives to set easier targets to guarantee that they will meet the budget and be favorably rewarded; higher-level managers have incentives to set more difficult targets to motivate the lower-level managers to exert additional effort. The conflict between making planning decisions and control is often viewed as a trade-off between bottom-up versus top-down budgeting. Bottom-up budgets are submitted by lower levels of the organization to higher levels and usually imply better information for planning decisions. An example of a bottom-up budget is the submission by the field sales offices of their forecasts for the next year to the marketing department. A top-down budget would be the central marketing department's use of aggregate data on sales trends to forecast sales for the entire firm and then disaggregating this firmwide budget into field office targets. This top-down budget provides greater control.

A bottom-up budget process, in which the person ultimately held responsible for meeting the target makes the initial budget forecast, is called **participative budgeting.** Participation enhances the motivation of the lower-level participants by motivating them to accept the targets.

The extent to which a budget is bottom up or top down ultimately depends on where the knowledge is located. If it is with the field salespeople, the responsibility to set the budget should be linked with the knowledge and placed in the field. If the central marketing organization has better knowledge, a top-down budget is likely to prove better. Which budgeting scheme provides better motivation depends, in the final analysis, on how the performance measurement and reward systems are designed.

In a survey of 98 large U.S. companies, firms indicated that they used participative budgeting more frequently when lower-level managers had specialized knowledge.[2] Moreover, participative budgeting is more frequently used when managers' rewards are based on their performance against the budget. This evidence

[2] M. Shields and S. Young, "Antecedents and Consequences of Participative Budgeting: Evidence on the Effects of Asymmetrical Information," *Journal of Management Accounting Research*, 1993, pp. 265–80.

is consistent with budgets and performance reward systems being designed to link responsibilities and specialized knowledge.

Concept**Review**

1. What are the planning benefits of budgeting?
2. What are the control benefits of budgeting?
3. How do planning and control issues lead to conflict in the budgeting process?

MAPLEDALE CHILD CENTER
(Continued)

The managers of the day care and kindergarten programs are responsible for estimating how many children will attend their programs next year because they are closer to the parents of the children than is the board of directors and, therefore, they have the specialized knowledge to make that estimate. But the managers have a dilemma. They know that their estimated enrollment numbers will be used to allocate space, teachers, and supplies to their respective programs. The higher the estimated enrollment, the greater the resources that they will receive. Recognizing this conflict, the board of directors decides to do its own survey of the community to verify the estimates of the program managers.

HOW BUDGETING HELPS RESOLVE ORGANIZATIONAL PROBLEMS

Budgeting systems are an administrative device used to resolve organizational problems. In particular, these systems help link knowledge with the responsibility to make planning decisions and distribute responsibilities and measure and reward performance for control. This section further describes the economics of various budgeting devices, such as short-term versus long-term budgets, line-item budgets, budget lapsing, flexible budgets, and incremental versus zero-base budgets.

Short-Term versus Long-Term Budgets

L0 4   Describe the benefits of having both short-term and long-term budgets.

Most organizations have annual budgeting processes. Starting in the prior year, organizations develop detailed plans of how many units of each product they expect to sell in the next year, at what prices, the cost of such sales, and the financing necessary for operations. These budgets then become the internal "contracts" for each responsibility center (cost, profit, and investment center) within the firm. These annual budgets are *short term* in the sense that they project only one year at a time. But most firms also project 2, 5, and sometimes 10 years in advance. These *long-term* budgets are a key feature of the organization's strategic planning process.

Strategic planning, described in Chapter Four, is the process by which managers select the firm's overall objectives and the tactics to achieve those objectives. Strategic planning is primarily concerned with ways the organization can add customer value and respond to competitors. For example, Eastman Kodak faces the strategic question of how to respond to the electronic imaging market. Making this decision requires specialized knowledge of the various technologies on which Kodak and other market participants compete in addition to knowledge of the demand for various future products.

Long-term budgets, like short-term budgets, encourage managers with specialized knowledge to communicate their forecasts of future expected events. Such long-term budgets contain forecasts of large asset acquisitions (and financing plans) for the manufacturing and distribution systems required to implement the strategy. Research and development budgets are long-term plans of the multiyear spending

Strategy for Customer Value

required to acquire and develop the technologies to implement the strategies.

In short-term budgets, important estimates include the quantities produced and sold and the prices. All parts of the organization must accept these estimates. In long-term budgets, important assumptions involve the choice of markets and the technologies to be acquired.

Planning Decisions

A typical firm integrates the short- and long-term budgeting process into a single process. As next year's budget is being developed, a five-year budget is also produced. Year 1 of the five-year plan is next year's budget. Years 2 and 3 are fairly detailed, and year 2 becomes the base on which to establish next year's one-year budget. Years 4 and 5 are less detailed but incorporate new market opportunities. Each year, the five-year budget is rolled forward one year, and the process begins anew.

The short-term (annual) budget involves both planning and control functions; thus, a trade-off between these two functions arises. Long-term budgets are rarely used as a control (performance evaluation) device. Rather, long-term budgets are used primarily for planning. Five- and ten-year budgets force managers to think about strategy and to communicate their specialized knowledge of potential future markets and technologies. Thus, long-term budgets have much less conflict between planning and control since much less emphasis is placed on using the long-term budget as a performance measurement tool.

Long-term budgets also reduce managers' focus on short-term performance. Without long-term budgets, managers have an incentive to cut expenditures, such as maintenance, advertising, and R&D, in order to improve short-term performance. Alternatively, managers might seek to balance short-term budgets at the expense of the firm's long-term viability. Budgets that span five years increase the likelihood that top management and/or the board of directors are informed of the long-term trade-offs that are being taken to accomplish short-term goals.

Line-Item Budgets

Line-item budgets refer to budgets that authorize the manager to spend only up to the specified amount on each line item. For example, consider Table 8.1.

LO 5 Explain the responsibility implications of a line-item budget.

In this budget, the manager is authorized to spend $12,000 on office supplies for the year. If the supplies can be purchased for $11,000, the manager with a line-item budget is not able to spend the $1,000 savings on any other category (such as additional office equipment) without prior approval; therefore, the manager has less incentive to look for savings. Moreover, if next year's line item is reduced by the amount of the savings, managers have even less incentive to search for savings.

The benefit of a line-item budget is the imposition of control on the manager. Managers responsible for line-item

---

*Business **Analysis***

Ericsson, a worldwide leader in telecommunications, is headquartered in Sweden. It operates in more than 140 countries and has more than 100,000 employees. Ericsson's strategy is focused on the customer and the need to react constantly to market trends. Rapid changes in technology, such as the shift to wireless communications, the Internet, and the demand by customers for total solutions, have required Ericsson to adapt not only its products but also its organizational structure. In a highly competitive industry where market dominance is difficult to attain and sustain, Ericsson initially had been slow to ensure that its operations enhanced customer value. Recently, however, Ericsson reorganized to gain the requisite flexibility to be competitive in this dynamic environment. The reorganization has eliminated several levels of management and introduced management teams centered on business segments and market regions. Ericsson also has adopted a more entrepreneurial strategy with greater decentralization of decision making to its operating segments. Business segments, established by customer category, handle product range and customer responsibilities. Product units work with several business units to take advantage of potential synergies and to create organizational value through efficient use of resources.

In parallel with its reorganization, Ericsson changed its accounting system. It eliminated its use of annual budgets, replacing them with a system of rolling (continuously updated) financial plans and forecasts. The focus is on activities and how cost centers consume financial resources on various activities. Along with these rolling financial forecasts, Ericsson reports quarterly operating profit and sales per business segment. Increased local responsibility also has been given for financial transactions and spending. Ericsson has broadened its reporting to include a series of key performance indicators (KPIs) that provide nonfinancial measures on customers, finance, employees, internal efficiency, and innovation. The forecasts and KPIs form the basis for performance evaluation of the business units, with each unit agreeing to specific targets.

How has the organizational structure at Ericsson adapted to changes in its environment and its strategy? Why has Ericsson's management accounting system been required to evolve with these changes? What risks and trade-offs exist in Ericsson's new reporting system? What are some possible measures that Ericsson might use to track its key performance indicators?

Source: www.ericsson.se; www.ericsson.com/infocenter.

Table 8.1

Line-Item Budget Example

Line Item	Amount
Salaries	$185,000
Office supplies	12,000
Office equipment	3,000
Postage	1,900
Maintenance	350
Utilities	1,200
Rent	900
Total	$204,350

Control Decisions

budgets cannot reduce spending on one item and divert the savings to items that enhance their own welfare. By maintaining tighter control over how much is spent on particular items, the organization reduces the possibility that management action is inconsistent with organizational goals.

Line-item budgets are quite prevalent in government organizations such as municipalities and states. They also are used in some corporations but with fewer restrictions. Line-item budgets provide an extreme form of control. The manager does not have the responsibility to substitute resources among line items as circumstances change, which require special approval from a higher level in the organization, such as the city council.

Line-item budgets illustrate how the budgeting system partitions responsibilities, thereby controlling behavior. A survey of 120 large publicly traded firms found that among units reporting directly to the CEO, 22% cannot substitute among line items, 24% can substitute if they receive authorization, and 26% can make substitutions within prespecified limits.[3] The remaining 28% can make substitutions if they improve the unit's financial objective. These findings suggest that even at fairly high levels in for-profit firms, line-item budgets are prevalent.

Budget Lapsing

LO 6 Identify the costs and benefits of budget lapsing.

Another common feature in budgeting is **budget lapsing.** If budgets lapse, funds that have not been spent at year-end do not carry over to the next year. Budget lapsing creates incentives for managers to spend their entire budget. Not only do they lose the benefits from the unspent funds, but they might have the next year's budget reduced by the amount of the underspending.

Budgets that lapse provide tighter controls on managers than budgets that do not lapse. If budgets do not lapse, managers have the opportunity to choose when to make expenditures. When budgets lapse, managers can make the expenditure only in the current year.

Control Decisions

The disadvantage of lapsing budgets is less efficient operations. Managers devote substantial time at the end of the year ensuring that their budget is fully expended. This action is taken, even if it means buying items of lower value (and of a higher cost) than those that would be purchased if the budget carried over to the next fiscal year. Often, these end-of-year purchases cause the firm to incur substantial warehousing costs to hold the extra purchases. In one example, a Navy ship officer purchased an 18-month supply of paper to spend his remaining budget. The paper weighed so much that it had to be stored evenly around the ship to make sure the ship did not tilt to one side. Managers cannot adjust to changing operating conditions during the year if budgets lapse. For example, if managers have expended all of their budget authority and the opportunity to make a bargain purchase arises, they cannot "borrow" against next year's budget without getting special permission.

Without budget lapsing, managers could build up substantial balances in their budgets. Toward the end of their careers with the firm, these managers then would be tempted to make large expenditures of perquisites. For example, they could take their staff to Hawaii for a "training retreat." Budget lapsing also prevents risk-averse managers from "saving" their budget for a rainy day. If it were optimal for a manager to spend a certain amount of money on a particular activity

---

[3] A. Christie, M. Joye, and R. Watts, "Organization of the Firm: Some Survey Results," working paper, University of Rochester, 1993.

Table 8.2

Flexible Budget for Concert

	Formula	Ticket Sales		
		3,000	**4,000**	**5,000**
Revenues	$18N*	$54,000	$72,000	$90,000
Band	$20,000 + 0.15($18N)	(28,100)	(30,800)	(33,500)
Auditorium	$5,000 + 0.05($18N)	(7,700)	(8,600)	(9,500)
Security	$80(N/200)	(1,200)	(1,600)	(2,000)
Other costs	$28,000	(28,000)	(28,000)	(28,000)
Profit/(loss)		($11,000)	$ 3,000	$17,000

* N is the number of tickets sold.

such as advertising, then saving part of that amount as a contingency fund would reduce the organization's value. Budget lapsing is one way to prevent the occurrence of these control problems.

Static versus Flexible Budgets

All of the examples in this chapter have described **static budgets,** which do not vary with volume; each line item is a fixed amount. In contrast, a **flexible budget** is stated as a function of some volume measure and can be adjusted for changes in volume. Flexible budgets and static budgets provide different incentives.

LO 7 Develop flexible budgets and identify when flexible budgeting should be used instead of static budgeting.

As an example of flexible budgeting, consider the case of a concert for which a band is hired for $20,000 plus 15% of the gate receipts. The auditorium is rented for $5,000 plus 5% of the gate receipts. Security guards costing $80 apiece are hired, one for every 200 people. Advertising, insurance, and other fixed costs are $28,000. Ticket prices are $18 each. A flexible budget for the concert is presented in Table 8.2.

Each line item in the budget is stated in terms of how it varies with volume, or ticket sales in this case. Then a budget is prepared at different volume levels. At ticket sales of 3,000, an $11,000 loss is projected. At sales of 4,000 and 5,000 tickets, $3,000 and $17,000 of profit are forecasted, respectively.

The major reason for using flexible rather than static budgets is to better gauge the actual performance of a person or venture after controlling for volume effects, assuming, of course, that the individual being evaluated is not responsible for the volume changes. For example, consider the following illustration. After the concert, which 5,000 persons attended, the actual cost of the auditorium was $9,900. The budget for the auditorium is automatically increased to $9,500 as the result of the 5,000 ticket sales, and the manager is not held responsible for volume changes. However, the manager is held responsible for the $400 unfavorable variance between the actual charge of $9,900 and $9,500. In evaluating the manager's performance, the cause of the variance should be investigated. For example, if the $400 had been caused by damage to the auditorium, would additional security guards have prevented it?

Control Decisions

When should a firm or department use a static budget and when should it use a flexible budget? Volume fluctuations in static budgets are passed through and show up in the difference between actual and budgeted numbers. Thus, static budgets force managers to be responsible for volume fluctuations. If the manager has some control over volume or its consequences, then he or she should use a static budget as the benchmark to gauge performance. Flexible budgets, which adjust for volume effects, do not pass volume fluctuations through and do not show up in the difference between actual and budgeted numbers. Flexible budgets do not force managers to be responsible for volume fluctuations. Therefore, if the manager does not have any control over volume, he or she should use a flexible budget as the benchmark to gauge performance. Flexible budgets reduce the risk that volume changes are borne by managers.

Of 219 publicly traded U.S. firms, 48% indicated that they use flexible budgets for manufacturing costs, but only 27% used flexible budgets for distribution, marketing, R&D, or general and administrative expenses.[4] These data suggest that flexible budgets are widely used in manufacturing where volume measures are readily available and many costs vary with volume.

Numerical Example 8.2

Duffy Bicycle Company, maker of mountain bikes, establishes a flexible annual budget. The company sells its bikes for $200 each. Its fixed manufacturing costs are budgeted to be $2 million, and its variable manufacturing costs are budgeted to be $80 per bike. Selling and administrative costs are expected to be fixed and are budgeted to be $1 million. There is no beginning and ending inventory.

a. Make a budget for income for the company assuming the manufacture and sale of 20,000, 30,000, and 40,000 bikes.

b. The company actually produced and sold 34,000 bikes. Actual revenues are $6,500,000, actual variable costs are $2,500,000, actual fixed manufacturing costs are $2,100,000, and actual selling and administrative costs are $950,000. What are the variances of each of these accounts and the profit variance?

Solution

a.

<table>
<tr><th colspan="4">DUFFY BICYCLE COMPANY
Budgeted Income</th></tr>
<tr><th></th><th colspan="3">Number of Bicycles Manufactured and Sold</th></tr>
<tr><th></th><th>20,000</th><th>30,000</th><th>40,000</th></tr>
<tr><td>Revenues ($\times$ $200)</td><td>$4,000,000</td><td>$6,000,000</td><td>$8,000,000</td></tr>
<tr><td>Variable costs ($\times$ $80)</td><td>(1,600,000)</td><td>(2,400,000)</td><td>(3,200,000)</td></tr>
<tr><td>Fixed manufacturing</td><td>(2,000,000)</td><td>(2,000,000)</td><td>(2,000,000)</td></tr>
<tr><td>Selling and administration</td><td>(1,000,000)</td><td>(1,000,000)</td><td>(1,000,000)</td></tr>
<tr><td>Profit/(loss)</td><td>($ 600,000)</td><td>$ 600,000</td><td>$1,800,000</td></tr>
</table>

b. If 34,000 bikes are produced and sold, the budgeted revenues and costs, actual revenues and costs, and variances are as follows:

	Budgeted	Actual	Variance
Revenues (34,000 $\times$ $200)	$6,800,000	$6,500,000	$300,000 U
Variable costs (34,000 $\times$ $80)	(2,720,000)	(2,500,000)	220,000 F
Fixed manufacturing	(2,000,000)	(2,100,000)	100,000 U
Selling and administration	(1,000,000)	(950,000)	50,000 F
Budgeted profit	$1,080,000	$ 950,000	$130,000 U

The unfavorable variance results from lower-than-expected prices and higher-than-expected fixed manufacturing costs.

Incremental versus Zero-Base Budgets

LO 8   Explain the costs and benefits of using zero-base budgeting.

Most organizations construct next year's budget by starting with the current year's budget and then adjusting each line item for expected price and volume changes. Each manager submits a budget for next year by making incremental

---

[4] W. Cress and J. Pettijohn, "A Survey of Budget-Related Planning and Control Policies and Procedures," *Journal of Accounting Education* 3 (Fall 1985), pp. 65–66.

changes in each line item. For example, the line item in next year's budget for purchases is calculated by increasing last year's purchases for inflation and including any incremental purchases resulting from volume changes and new programs. Only detailed explanations to justify the increments are submitted or reviewed. These **incremental budgets** are reviewed and changed at higher levels in the organization, but usually only the incremental changes are examined in detail. The base/core budget (i.e., last year's base budget) is taken as given.

Planning Decisions

Under **zero-base budgeting,** senior management mandates that each line item in total must be justified and reviewed each year. Each line item is reset to *zero* each year. Departments must defend their entire expenditures each year, not just the changes. In a zero-base budget review, the following questions are usually asked: Should this activity be provided? What will happen if the activity is eliminated? At what quality/quantity level should the activity be provided? Can the activity be provided in some alternative way, such as hiring an outside firm to provide the goods or service? How much are other, similar companies spending on this activity (benchmarking)?

In principle, zero-base budgeting (ZBB) motivates managers to maximize firm value by identifying and eliminating expenditures whose total costs exceed total benefits. Under incremental budgeting, which adds incremental changes to the base budget, incremental expenditures are deleted when their costs exceed their benefits. However, inefficient base budgets often continue to exist.

In practice, ZBB is infrequently used. It is supposed to overcome traditional, incremental budgeting, but ZBB likely deteriorates into incremental budgeting. Each year under ZBB, the same justifications as those used the previous year are typically submitted and adjusted for incremental changes. Since the volume of detailed reports in the organization is substantially larger under ZBB than under incremental budgeting, higher-level managers tend to focus on the changes from last year anyway. The focus on budgetary changes is especially true if managers have been with the organization for a number of years and already know the "base-" level budgets.

ZBB is most useful and common with changes in top-level management. New managers do not have the specialized knowledge incorporated in the base budgets and they bring changes in strategy. Prior budgets are no longer as relevant when each line item requires justification in light of these changing goals and strategies. However, ZBB is substantially more costly to conduct and is unlikely to continue once management has gained knowledge of operations and the budgets have encompassed the new goals.

Concept**Review**

1. How do short- and long-term budgets relate to planning and control?
2. How do line-item budgets affect a manager's responsibilities?
3. What are the costs and benefits of budget lapsing?
4. How do the responsibilities of the manager influence the choice between static and flexible budgets?
5. Under what conditions is zero-base budgeting useful?

The board of directors of MCC is primarily concerned about the annual budget. The purchase of a building is the only strategic issue that the board is examining. This long-term decision will be based primarily on demand for day care and kindergartens in the Mapledale area. Long-term demand for MCC day care and kindergarten is a function of the cost, perceived quality of care and instruction, competition from other day care providers, and the future demographics of the Mapledale subdivision.

MAPLEDALE CHILD CENTER
(Continued)

Information on these factors is located with the board of directors, which is responsible for making this decision. Therefore, the budgeting process is not necessary to communicate the information.

The managers of the day care and kindergarten programs are relatively new, so the board of directors has decided to use a line-item budget. This budget relieves the managers of the decision on how to spend the money allocated to the programs. The board also uses a lapsing budget, so the novice program managers need not make decisions on the periods in which to spend resources.

A static budget is developed based on the original projection of enrollment. The program managers are responsible for the quality of their programs, which is the determining factor in whether parents keep their children at MCC. Any lost revenue from dropouts during the year is the responsibility of the program managers, so flexible budgeting would provide the wrong incentives.

MCC's board of directors has had greater longevity than the program managers. This continuity brings considerable experience in budgeting for MCC. In addition, the operational procedures of MCC have not changed much over the years, so the board has budget and accounting data from past years that it can use to prepare the new budget. Therefore, MCC uses an incremental approach to budgeting.

COMPREHENSIVE MASTER BUDGET ILLUSTRATION

LO 9 Create a master budget for an organization including sales, production, administration, capital investment, and financial budgets.

The previous sections described the basic concepts that must be considered in budgeting. This section describes how to construct a **master budget,** which integrates the estimates from each department to predict production requirements, financing, cash flows, and financial statements at the end of the period. The master budget serves as a guide and benchmark for the entire organization.

To prevent the example from becoming overwhelming with respect to the amount of data, a simple firm, NaturApples, an apple processor, is used. This example describes how various parts of the organization develop their budgets. It illustrates the importance of coordinating the volume of activity across the different parts of the organization and how budgets are then combined for the firm as a whole.

For apple processors, the fall harvest begins a lengthy and complex cycle. The budgeting process is similar. In both cases, each stage depends upon the inputs from the previous one. Bad data like bad apples can disrupt the entire budget process; therefore, most firms retain budget responsibility at executive levels.

Description of the Firm: NaturApples

NaturApples processes apples into two products, applesauce and apple pie filling. Apples purchased from local growers are processed and packed in tin cans as either applesauce or pie filling. Principal markets are institutional buyers, such as hospitals, public schools, military bases, and universities. NaturApples' market is regional and is serviced by four salespeople who make direct calls on customers in a four-state area.

The firm is organized into two departments, production and marketing. A vice president who reports directly to the president heads each department. In addition, a vice president of finance is responsible for all financial aspects of the firm, including collecting data and preparing budgets. The three vice presidents and the president compose NaturApples' executive committee, which oversees the budgeting process.

Independent farmers in the region grow the apples. Once harvested, they are purchased through the efforts of the vice president of finance and are stored either in coolers at NaturApples or in third-party warehouses until NaturApples can process them.

The processing plant operates for nine months of the year; in October, it begins operations after a three-month shutdown. Workers first thoroughly clean and inspect all the processing equipment. The apples begin arriving in the middle of October and by the end of November, all of the apple harvest is in warehouses or started in production. By June, all apples have been processed, and the plant shuts down for July, August, and September. NaturApples has a fiscal year starting October 1 and ending September 30.

For both products, applesauce and pie filling, the production process begins by inspecting, washing, peeling, and coring the apples. Next, the apples are either mashed for applesauce or diced for pie filling. The apples then are combined with other ingredients, such as spices and chemical stabilizers, and cooked in vats. Both products are immediately canned on a single canning line in 5-pound tins and packed in cases of 12 cans. At this point, the product has a two-year shelf life and is stored until a customer order is received.

Overview of the Budgeting Process

The budgeting process begins the first of December, 10 months before the start of the next fiscal year. The president and the vice president of finance forecast the next year's crop harvest, which will determine the purchase cost of apples. The vice president of marketing begins forecasting next year's sales of applesauce and pie filling. Likewise, the production vice president forecasts production costs and capacity. Every two months for the next 10 months, these marketing, processing, and apple procurement forecasts and budgets are revised in light of new information. All three vice presidents and the president then meet for a morning to discuss their revisions. On August 1, the executive committee adopts the final master budget for the next fiscal year, which begins October 1, and then takes it to the board of directors for final approval. The executive committee also meets weekly to review current year operations as compared to budget and discuss other operational issues. Figure 8.1 is a schematic diagram that illustrates the relationships among the component budgets of NaturApples' master budget. The final product of the master budget is the budgeted income statement, budgeted balance sheet, and budgeted cash flows at the bottom of Figure 8.1. All other budgets provide the supporting detail, including the various key planning assumptions underlying the master budget.

The budgeting process should yield budgets that are internally consistent. For example, the amount of apples purchased should be equated to the amount processed into sauce and pie filling. To maintain consistency, a sequential and simultaneous process, similar to the one in Figure 8.1, is commonly used. The budgeting process normally begins with a sales estimate, which depends on the price of the product. Sales quantities and prices should be chosen to maximize profits. The sales estimate also must consider production costs, which depend on the availability and cost of raw materials (apples), direct labor, and overhead. Thus, the sales budget, the production budget, and the apple procurement should be considered jointly.

The production budget includes raw materials, direct labor, and factory overhead budgets, which jointly affect the estimated cost of goods sold. Not all expenditures are treated as part of the cost of goods sold, however; selling and administrative expenditures are treated as expenses in financial reporting and are budgeted separately.

Figure 8.1

Budgeting Process for
NaturApples

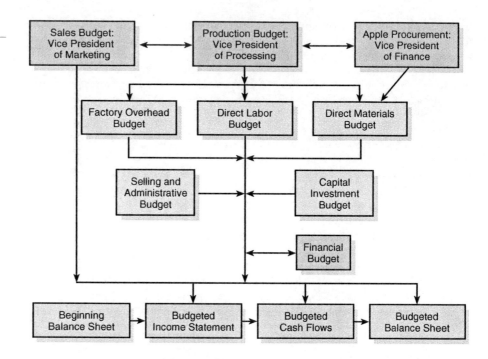

The production budget also is used to determine whether new property, plant, or equipment must be purchased to provide sufficient capacity to meet production requirements. The capital investment budget reflects the estimated purchase of property, plant, and equipment for the next fiscal year.

Capital expenditures require cash. If cash is not available from operations, the firm may have to borrow to make large purchases. The financial budget is used to plan for borrowing, issuing stock, and making interest and dividend payments.

The individual budgets for sales, production, capital investments, and so forth are used to estimate financial statements at the end of the fiscal year. The estimated income statement and cash flow statement are used to adjust the beginning balance sheet to form an estimated ending balance sheet. The remainder of this section illustrates the preparation of these various component budgets and the estimated financial statements.

Table 8.3 is the estimated balance sheet for the beginning of the fiscal year. The beginning balance sheet is estimated because the budget is determined before the end of the previous fiscal year. The beginning balance sheet represents the starting point for operations in the upcoming fiscal year.

Sales Budget

The sales (revenue) budget is generally created with the help of the marketing department. Its employees usually have more information about the nature of potential customers. Moreover, they can provide insights on the relationship between the selling price and the amount that customers will purchase. The production department also must be involved in setting the sales budget because cost information is important in setting prices.

At NaturApples, the executive committee agrees on an estimate of next year's sales and prices based on information from the marketing and production departments. The sales budget for the next fiscal year appears in Table 8.4. The executive committee agrees that that the firm should be able to sell 140,000 cases of sauce at $68 per case and 60,000 cases of pie filling at $53. After months of exploring alternative price and quantity assumptions, these numbers and prices were finalized. In particular, the budgeted prices and numbers represent the managers'

Table 8.3

NATURAPPLES
Expected Beginning Balance Sheet
October 1, 2001

Assets

Cash		$ 100,000
Accounts receivable		200,000
Inventory		
Sauce (13,500 cases)($58/case)	$783,000	
Pie filling (2,500 cases)($48/case)	120,000	903,000
Property, plant, and equipment (net)		2,300,000
		$3,503,000

Liabilities and Stockholders' Equity

Accounts payable		$ 100,000
Long-term debt		1,000,000
Stockholders' equity		2,403,000
		$3,503,000

Table 8.4

NATURAPPLES
Sales Budget
For Fiscal Year Beginning October 1, 2001

	Budgeted Cases	Budgeted Price/Case	Budgeted Revenue
Sauce	140,000	$68	$ 9,520,000
Pie filling	60,000	53	3,180,000
Total			$12,700,000

best judgment of the amount at which marginal cost and marginal revenue are equal. Presumably, higher prices (and thus lower sales) or lower prices (and higher sales) will both result in lower profits than the combinations presented in Table 8.4.

Production Budget

The second major component of the master budget is the production budget. The production volume is chosen based on the following equation:

Beginning inventory + Production = Sales + Desired ending inventory

or

Production = Sales + Desired ending inventory − Beginning inventory

The total units in beginning inventory plus the units produced during the fiscal year must be either sold or placed in ending inventory. Any units scrapped are considered part of production.

Numerical Example 8.3

BB Company manufactures baseballs. In the next year, the company expects to sell 20,000. It has 2,000 baseballs in its beginning inventory and wants to have 1,000 in ending inventory. How many baseballs should the company plan to manufacture?

Solution

Production = Sales + Ending inventory − Beginning inventory
         = 20,000 + 1,000 − 2,000 = 19,000

Table 8.5

			NATURAPPLES Number of Cases to Be Produced October 1, 2001–September 30, 2002			
Product	**Sales**	**+ Ending Inventory**	**–**	**Beginning Inventory**	**=**	**Production**
Sauce	140,000	5,000		13,500		131,500
Pie filling	60,000	1,000		2,500		58,500

To solve for the number of units to produce at NaturApples, sales estimates from the sales budget in Table 8.4 are used. In addition, the beginning inventory from the expected beginning balance sheet in Table 8.3 must be estimated and a desired ending inventory position must be projected. Table 8.5 presents the estimated units to be produced given a desired ending inventory level of 5,000 cases of sauce and 1,000 cases of pie filling. This ending inventory amount should cover expected sales in October before production begins for the next fiscal year.

The budgeted number of units to be produced during the year is used as a basis for estimating the required amounts of direct materials, direct labor, and factory overhead. This information is usually derived through discussions with the individual in charge of operations. For NaturApples, 50 pounds of apples and 0.60 hours of direct labor are necessary to make a case of sauce. To make a case of pie filling, 40 pounds of apples and 0.50 direct labor hours are necessary. The cost of apples is estimated to be $0.40 per pound, and the cost of direct labor is estimated to be $10 per hour. Factory overhead is estimated to occur at the rate of $2 for every $1 of direct labor. Table 8.6 is the production budget for NaturApples and includes the raw materials, direct labor, and factory overhead budget.

The production budget in Table 8.6 determines that 8,915,000 pounds of apples must be purchased to achieve the production target. If spoilage is a problem, more apples must be obtained to cover expected spoilage. The production budget also provides an estimate of the direct labor requirements; to meet production targets, the company should plan on 108,150 hours of direct labor. The production budget also estimates the cost of apples, direct labor, and overhead. The overhead depreciation expense is identified separately because depreciation does not involve the use of cash. This point is important to recognize for cash flow planning purposes.

The production budget in Table 8.6 is an annual budget. The company may also want to have monthly production budgets, which are useful for planning cash flows and material and labor requirements, especially when production is cyclical, as in the case of NaturApples.

Selling and Administration Budget

Selling and administrative expenses are treated as period expenses for financial reporting purposes although some of these costs can be traced to products. The generation of estimated (end-of-year) financial statements is one of the functions of the budgeting process. Therefore, selling and administrative expenses frequently are identified separately.

The selling and administration budget for NaturApples in Table 8.7 contains the remaining operating expenses, including the costs of the marketing department, finance, trucking, and the president's office. The total of all these administrative costs is $1.19 million.

Capital Investment Budget

The capital investment budget is used for planned purchases of major property, plant, and equipment. These purchases generally appear as fixed assets on the

Table 8.6

NATURAPPLES
Production Budget
October 1, 2001–September 30, 2002

Raw Materials

Product	Pounds per Case	×	Cases	=	Pounds	×	Cost per Pound	=	Cost
Sauce	50		131,500		6,575,000		$0.40		$2,630,000
Pie filling	40		58,500		2,340,000		0.40		936,000
Total					8,915,000				$3,566,000

Direct Labor

Product	Hours per Case	×	Cases	=	Hours	×	Cost per Hour	=	Cost
Sauce	0.60		131,500		78,900		$10		$ 789,000
Pie filling	0.50		58,500		29,250		10		292,500
Total					108,150				$1,081,500

Overhead

Product	Direct Labor Cost	×	Overhead per Direct Labor Dollar	=	Cost
Sauce	$789,000		$2		$1,578,000
Pie filling	292,500		2		585,000
Total					$2,163,000*

Product Costs

Product	Total Product Cost (Materials + Labor + Overhead)	÷	Cases	=	Cost per Case
Sauce	$4,997,000		131,500		$38
Pie filling	1,813,500		58,500		31
Total	$6,810,500				

* Includes $400,000 of depreciation expense.

balance sheet but could include research and development (R&D) expenditures for a new product. R&D spending would be expensed for financial reporting purposes.

In the process of establishing the production budget, NaturApples' executive committee recognizes that additional coring and dicing machines must be purchased to increase capacity. The capital investment budget in Table 8.8 includes the expected purchase price of the two machines.

Table 8.7

NATURAPPLES
Selling and Administration Budget
For Fiscal Year Beginning October 1, 2001

Selling & administrative areas	
Marketing	$ 470,000
Finance	160,000
Trucking	380,000
President's office	180,000
Total selling & administration	$1,190,000

Financial Budget

One reason for budgeting is to ensure that ample cash is available for operations and major purchases. If cash shortages are expected, the organization must plan to borrow money to cover the shortages. The financial budget is used to plan for borrowing cash and to record planned interest expense, retirement of debt, issuance of stock, and the payment of dividends.

Table 8.8

NATURAPPLES Capital Investment Budget October 1, 2001–September 30, 2002		
Capital Investment Project	**Purchase Date**	**Cost**
Coring machine	10/5/01	$ 40,000
Dicing machine	10/5/01	80,000
Total		$120,000

Table 8.9

NATURAPPLES Financial Budget October 1, 2001–September 30, 2002		
Financial Transactions	**Date**	**Amount**
Loan from bank	10/5/01	$ 100,000
Repayment of bank loan	4/5/02	(100,000)
Retirement of long-term debt	6/1/02	(200,000)
Payment of interest	12/31/01	(50,000)
Payment of interest	6/30/02	(50,000)
Payment of dividends	9/30/02	(2,000,000)
Net cash flow from financial transactions		($2,300,000)

Numerical Example 8.4

At the beginning of the month, Trevor Book Store has cash of $1,000 and accounts receivable of $4,000. This month, the book store manager plans to collect 80% of the beginning accounts receivable, make sales of $8,000 ($5,000 in cash and $3,000 on account due next month), and make payments of $12,000 to book publishers. How much must the book store borrow this month?

Solution

Beginning cash balance	$ 1,000
Collection of receivables (0.80 × $4,000)	3,200
Cash sales	5,000
Payments to publishers	(12,000)
Ending cash balance without financing	($ 2,800)

The manager must borrow at least $2,800 to cover the cash shortfall.

NaturApples must purchase both the coring and dicing machines early during the fiscal year. Given that the beginning cash balance is insufficient to cover this purchase, the company must borrow an additional $100,000 from the bank. Near the end of the fiscal year, however, NaturApples should have enough cash to pay off the loan, retire an additional $200,000 of long-term debt, and pay shareholders $2,000,000 in dividends. In addition, the executive committee estimates that interest costs during the fiscal year will be $100,000. This information is provided in the financial budget in Table 8.9.

Budgeted Financial Statements

Budgeted financial statements are the end product of the budgeting process. In a for-profit organization, these statements include the budgeted income statement, the budgeted cash flow statement, and the budgeted balance sheet. These bud-

Table 8.10

NATURAPPLES
Budgeted Income Statement
October 1, 2001–September 30, 2002

Revenues (sales budget)			$12,700,000
Cost of goods sold			
Beginning inventory (beg. balance sheet)		$ 903,000	
+ Production costs ((production budget)		6,810,500	
− Ending inventory (production budget)			
Sauce ($38/case))(5,000 cases)	$190,000		
Pie filling ($1/case)(1,000 cases)	31,000	(221,000)	(7,492,500)
Gross margin			$ 5,207,500
Selling and administrative expenses (sell. & admin. budget)			(1,190,000)
Interest expense (financial budget)			(100,000)
Net income before taxes			$ 3,917,500
Income taxes ($3,917,500 × 0.40)			(1,567,000)
Net income			$ 2,350,500
Beginning stockholders' equity (beg. balance sheet)			$ 2,403,000
+ Net income (from above)			2,350,500
− Dividends (financial budget)			(2,000,000)
Ending stockholders' equity			$ 2,753,500

geted financial statements provide a picture of the organization's financial condition at the end of the budget period if events happen according to plan.

Budgeted Income Statement

Most elements in the budgeted income statement come from parts of the prior budgets. The cost of goods sold is the one part of the budgeted income statement that remains to be estimated. This estimate depends on the accounting method used to record the flow of inventory costs. The first-in, first-out (FIFO) method assumes that the products sold are from the beginning inventory and early production and that the products most recently made are in ending inventory. Other inventory costing methods include last-in, first-out (LIFO) and average costing. These methods are explained further in the Appendix to Chapter Ten and in financial accounting textbooks.

NaturApples employs the FIFO method, so the estimated cost of ending inventory is determined using the most recent product costs ($38 per case for sauce and $31 per case for pie filling).

Tax planning is also part of the budgeting process. For the next fiscal year, NaturApples plans to pay 40% of its net income in taxes. Table 8.10 contains the budgeted income statement for NaturApples. The numbers in the statement come from the previous budgets.

Budgeted Cash Flow Statement

The budgeting of cash flows is extremely important to an organization. Running out of cash is inconvenient and can lead to bankruptcy although the organization may be profitable. Simply stated, accounting profit is not the same as cash on hand. Therefore, monthly budgeted cash flow statements should be prepared to avoid cash shortfalls.

Cash flow statements identify cash flows from operations, capital investments, and financial transactions. These transactions are captured in the sales, production, selling and administration, capital investment, and financial budgets.

In addition, the collection of accounts receivable and the payment of accounts payable influence cash flows. Hastening the collection of receivables and postponing the payment of payables can have a positive short-term effect on cash flows. However, such behavior may not be consistent with the organization's goals. For example, rather than billing customers 30 days later, requiring them to pay cash may reduce total sales. For the purpose of annual budgeting, cash flow effects can be determined by estimating ending balances in the receivables and payables accounts and calculating the change in those balances from the beginning of the year. Decreases in accounts receivable and increases in accounts payable mean more cash available. Increases in accounts receivable and decreases in accounts payable mean less cash available.

Numerical Example 8.5

Kreuger Corporation had beginning accounts receivable and accounts payable balances of $20,000 and $10,000, respectively. The corporation estimates that ending balances for accounts receivable and accounts payable will be $30,000 and $5,000, respectively. What are the cash flow implications?

Solution

Change in accounts receivable: $30,000 − $20,000 = $10,000

    The increase of $10,000 implies a $10,000 decline in cash available.

Change in accounts payable: $5,000 − $10,000 = − $5,000

    The decrease of $5,000 implies a $5,000 decline in cash available.

The combined effect is a $15,000 decline in cash available.

The executive committee at NaturApples estimates that accounts receivables at the end of the next fiscal year will be $300,000 and accounts payable will be $150,000. The budgeted cash flow statement is presented in Table 8.11.

Table 8.11

NATURAPPLES Budgeted Cash Flow Statement October 1, 2001–September 30, 2002		
Cash flows from operations		
Income (income statement)		$2,350,500
Depreciation (income statement)		400,000
		$2,750,500
Change in accounts receivable		
Ending accounts receivable (predicted)	$ 300,000	
Beginning accounts receivable (beg. bal. sheet)	(200,000)	(100,000)
Change in inventory		
Ending inventory (predicted)	$ 221,000	
Beginning inventory (beg. bal. sheet)	(903,000)	682,000
Change in accounts payable		
Ending accounts payable (predicted)	$ 150,000	
Beginining accounts payable (beg. bal. sheet)	(100,000)	50,000
Total cash flows from operations		$3,382,500
Cash flows for capital investments (cap. inv. budget)		
Purchase of coring machine	($ 40,000)	
Purchase of dicing machine	(80,000)	(120,000)
Cash flows for financial transactions (financing budget)*		
Loan from bank	$ 100,000	
Repayment of bank loan	(100,000)	
Retirement of long-term debt	(200,000)	
Payment of dividends	(2,000,000)	(2,200,000)
Change in cash balance		$1,062,500
Beginning cash balance		100,000
Ending cash balance		$1,162,500

* The interest is already included in the net income.

Table 8.12

NATURAPPLES
Budgeted Balance Sheet
September 30, 2002

Assets

Cash (cash flow statement)		$1,162,500
Accounts receivable (predicted)		300,000
Inventory (predicted)		
Sauce ($38/case)(5,000 cases)	$ 190,000	
Pie filling ($31/case)(1,000 cases)	31,000	221,000
Property, plant, and equipment (net)		
Beginning balance (beg. bal. sheet)	$2,300,000	
Capital investments (cap. inv. budget)	120,000	
Depreciation (income statement)	(400,000)	2,020,000
		$3,703,500

Liabilities and Stockholders' Equity

Accounts payable (predicted)	$ 150,000	
Long-term debt		
Beginning balance (beg. bal. sheet)	1,000,000	
Retirement (financing budget)	(200,000)	800,000
Stockholders' equity (income statement)		2,753,500
		$3,703,500

Budgeted Balance Sheet

The budgeting process begins with a beginning balance sheet. These beginning balances are adjusted for expected events during the coming fiscal year; the adjusted balances of each account comprise the budgeted balance sheet for the end of the fiscal year. The budgeted balance sheet for NaturApples is shown in Table 8.12.

The budgeted financial statements (income, cash flow, and balance sheet) are called **pro forma financial statements,** which predict how financial statements will look in the future if the expected events occur. Financial statements are used to measure performance; thus, managers are very concerned about the pro forma

LO 10   Create pro forma financial statements based on data from the sales, production, administration, capital investment, and financial budgets.

Not-for-profits, such as day-care centers, must budget carefully. They require reliable estimates of revenues and expenditures, generally linked to the quantity and quality of services. While not operating to make a profit, not-for-profits must cover all costs and maintain adequate cash flow. Budgets also should be tied to strategy in order that cost concerns do not supplant strategic objectives, resulting in a failure to create value for stakeholders.

financial statements. If the organization's top managers do not like the pro forma financial statements that result from the budgeting process, they will ask its members to repeat the process using different strategies and assumptions. This process continues until the pro forma financial statements are improved or top management is convinced that better alternative plans do not exist.

Concept**Review**

1. What is normally the first step in the master budget process?
2. How are estimated sales and inventory levels used to estimate production requirements?
3. Why is a financial budget necessary?
4. What are pro forma financial statements?

MAPLEDALE CHILD CENTER
(Continued)

MCC's board of directors has asked the two program managers to estimate the number of children who will attend their programs next year. The day care program manager estimates an average of 40 children every month, and the kindergarten program manager estimates 60 children for the morning session and 50 children for the afternoon session. These estimates are consistent with the survey performed by the board of directors. The revenue budget for MCC follows:

Program	Children	Price/Month	Months	Revenues
Day care	40	$500	12	$240,000
Kindergarten	110	360	9	356,400
Total revenues				$596,400

MCC's production budget encompasses the operations of its two programs. Given the enrollment estimates, the day care program manager is given the right to hire eight full-time teachers. The kindergarten program manager is given the right to hire five and one-half full-time instructors (five for both morning and afternoon, and one for just the morning). The expected annual cost of hiring a day care counselor is $18,000 and of hiring a kindergarten teacher is $20,000 for nine months. Resources for educational supplies are allotted to the programs based on the estimated number of registrations per year; the current rate is $400 for each child. The following budget also includes the program managers' salaries.

Day care program	
Program manager	$ 20,000
Counselors (8 × $18,000)	144,000
Educational supplies ($400 × 40)	16,000
Total	$180,000
Kindergarten program	
Program manager	$ 20,000
Instructors (5.5 × $20,000)	110,000
Educational supplies ($400 × 110)	44,000
Total	$174,000
Total program costs	$354,000

MCC also has a selling and administrative budget that includes advertising, rent, insurance, and the salaries of the office manager, secretary, and bookkeeper:

Selling and administrative budget	
Advertising	$ 10,000
Rent	100,000
Insurance	20,000
Salaries	50,000
Total	$180,000

MCC's board of directors decides that the coming year is a good time to update the computer equipment in the office and the classrooms. The planned expenditure is $50,000. MCC is a not-for-profit organization, which typically does not have income statements. MCC operates strictly on a cash basis and does not record payables and receivables. Fixed assets, such as computers, are treated as cash expenditures rather than being recognized as assets. MCC is a service organization and has no inventory. Any leftover supplies from one period are considered immaterial. Therefore, MCC is concerned only about its cash flows and the beginning and ending cash balances.

MCC has an estimated beginning cash balance of $10,000. The following cash flow statement is used to estimate the ending cash balance:

Beginning cash balance	$ 10,000
Estimated revenues	596,400
Program costs	(354,000)
Selling and administrative costs	(180,000)
Capital investments (computers)	(50,000)
Ending cash balance	$ 22,400

You decide

SUMMARY

1   **Use budgeting for planning purposes.** Budgeting facilitates the flow of information from the bottom up for general planning and from the top down for coordination.

2   **Use budgeting for control purposes.** The budget is used to allocate responsibilities to different members of the organization and to establish performance measures, which are used to reward managers.

3   **Identify the conflicts that exist between planning and control in the budgeting process.** The flow of information in the budgeting process might be inhibited or biased because the information used for planning is often the same information used for performance evaluation.

4   **Describe the benefits of having both short-term and long-term budgets.** Long-term budgets are used for

long-term planning. Short-term budgets are used for both planning and control.

5   **Explain the responsibility implications of a line-item budget.** Line-item budgets constrain responsibilities by limiting managers' ability to shift resources from one use to another.

6   **Identify the costs and benefits of budget lapsing.** Budget lapsing constrains the manager to expend resources in the budget period. This policy provides increased control; however, managers are not able to use their specialized information to make more efficient decisions and frequently are motivated to consume excess resources during the budgeted period.

7   **Develop flexible budgets and identify when flexible budgeting should be used instead of static budgeting.** Flexible budgeting adjusts for volume effects. If the manager cannot control volume, the flexible budget provides more appropriate numbers for evaluating the manager.

8 **Explain the cost and benefits of using zero-base budgeting.** Zero-base budgeting (ZBB) is costly because each line item in total must be justified. The benefit of ZBB is the additional flow of information that might be useful to new managers and might lead to more efficient use of resources.

9 **Create a master budget for an organization including sales, production, administration, capital investment, and financial budgets.** The master budget is a plan for a certain period that includes expected sales, operating costs (production and administration), major investments, and methods to finance those investments.

10 **Create pro forma financial statements based on data from the sales, production, administration, capital investment, and financial budgets.** The pro forma statements include the budgeted income statement, the budgeted cash flow statement, and the budgeted balance sheet.

11 **Use spreadsheets to analyze monthly cash flows. (Appendix)** Monthly cash flow analysis is extremely important to determine whether a cash shortage might occur in a given month. If a cash shortage is expected, the organization can plan to find some financing to allow it to pay its bills and continue to operate. Spreadsheets offer a means of determining the sensitivity of cash flows to the budget estimates.

KEY TERMS

budget lapsing Concept that budgets for one period cannot be used to make expenditures in subsequent periods. *(p. 246)*

budgeting Process of gathering information to assist in making forecasts. *(p. 240)*

budgets Forecasts of future revenues and expenditures. *(p. 240)*

flexible budgets Budgets that adjust to some measure of volume. *(p. 247)*

favorable variance The amount by which budgeted costs are greater than actual costs, or budgeted revenues are less than actual revenues. *(p. 241)*

incremental budgets Budgets that use last year's budget as a base to make future ones. *(p. 249)*

master budget A document that integrates all the estimates from the different departments to establish guidelines and benchmarks for the whole organization. *(p. 250)*

participative budgeting The preparation of the initial budget forecast by eliciting opinions from those managers responsible for meeting the budget targets. *(p. 243)*

pro forma financial statements Financial statements based on forecasted data. *(p. 259)*

static budgets Budgets that do not adjust for volume. *(p. 247)*

strategic planning The process by which managers select the firm's overall objectives and tactics to achieve those objectives. *(p. 244)*

unfavorable variance The amount by which budgeted costs are less than actual costs, or budgeted revenues are greater than actual revenues. *(p. 241)*

variance The difference between a budgeted and an actual number. *(p. 241)*

zero-base budgeting A budgeting process by which each line item in total must be justified and reviewed each year. *(p. 249)*

APPENDIX

Monthly Cash Flow Estimates and Spreadsheets

LO 11 Use spreadsheets to analyze monthly cash flows.

One of the most important aspects of budgeting is to be sure that the organization has sufficient cash. Many growing organizations tend to underestimate the amount of cash that they need. Cash is obviously needed for purchasing long-term assets and production purposes. However, it is also needed as the result of increases in inventory and other current assets. Accounts receivable, for example, tend to increase as sales increase. The organization must wait to be paid cash for sales made on credit, sometimes the customer never pays the organization for its purchases.

An organization must estimate future cash flows carefully. If the cash balance becomes negative, the organization will not be able to pay its own bills. As stated earlier, a cash shortfall can force a profitable organization into bankruptcy. Therefore, monthly budget predictions of cash flows are extremely important to avert an unexpected cash shortfall. If an organization can predict a cash shortfall early enough, it can alter its plans to conserve cash, or it can plan to borrow cash.

Most events affecting future cash flows are not completely predictable. Sales, collection of accounts receivable, and production costs are all difficult to predict, yet unpredictability does not mean that budgets for cash flows should not be made. Instead of making a single cash flow budget, the organization should make multiple ones given different scenarios. These different scenarios reflect various estimates about sales and other events affecting cash flows. For example, cash flows could be estimated assuming a monthly increase in sales of 1% per month and 2% per month. By changing the estimate of the monthly growth in sales, a manager can consider the sensitivity of cash flows to sales estimates and can obtain a range of plausible cash flow estimates by varying the estimates of the different events affecting cash flows.

Analyzing the sensitivity of cash flows to different estimates can be costly if managers must go through all procedures of the master budget by hand for each different estimate. Spreadsheets offer a quick means of analyzing data that have specific relations. Once a spreadsheet is set up with the raw data and the functional relations, it is quite simple to change some of the parameters and obtain a new solution. In the case of cash flows, the relations among the different events have been outlined in the master budget and can be placed in spreadsheet form for analysis. Spreadsheets provide an efficient means to obtain cash flow estimates for multiple scenarios, and they allow for simple updates of future monthly cash flows once the outcomes of earlier months are known.

The example in Table 8A.1 illustrates the functional relations that can be captured through spreadsheet analysis. The monthly cash-budgeting process begins with estimates of monthly sales. The purchase of inventory sold occurs two months prior to the sales month, but the bills for those purchases are paid in the month prior to the sale. There is a 30% profit margin on sales. Other costs are estimated and paid in the month incurred. Large cash investments are identified separately. Sales are assumed to be composed of 20% cash sales, 50% credit sales that are collected in the following month, and 30% credit sales that are collected in the second month following the sales transaction. Only sales, purchases, and the accounts that affect cash flows and the cash balances are reported in this example. A typical spreadsheet analysis would have multiple worksheets that are interrelated and could generate all of the pro forma financial statements. The subscripts on the functional relations represent the month relative to month t.

The monthly cash flow analysis in Table 8A.1 indicates that the organization will have cash problems in May and June, primarily because of a cash investment

Table 8A.1   Monthly Cash Flow Budget

Account	Functional Relationship	January	February	March	April	May	June
Sales	Estimated	$10,000	$20,000	$25,000	$15,000	$10,000	$20,000
Purchases	$(0.70)(Sales_{t+2})$	17,500	10,500	7,000	14,000	21,000	15,000
Cash flow effects							
Cash sales	$(0.20)(Sales_t)$	$ 2,000	$ 4,000	$ 5,000	$ 3,000	$ 2,000	$ 4,000
Collection of credit sales	$(0.50)(Sales_{t-1})+$ $(0.30)(Sales_{t-2})$	10,000	10,000	13,000	18,500	15,000	12,500
Inventory payment	$Purchases_{t-1}$	(14,000)	(17,500)	(10,500)	(7,000)	(14,000)	(21,000)
Other costs	Estimated	(2,000)	(3,000)	(2,000)	(1,500)	(3,000)	(2,000)
Large cash investments	Estimated					(20,000)	
Net cash flows	$Cash\ sales_t + Collections_t$ $-\ Payments_t - Other\ costs_t$ $-\ Investments_t$	(4,000)	(6,500)	(5,500)	13,000	(20,000)	(6,500)
Beg. cash balance	$End.\ cash\ balance_{t-1}$	20,000	16,000	9,500	4,000	17,000	(3,000)
End. cash balance	$Beg.\ cash\ balance_t +$ $Net\ cash\ flows_t$	16,000	9,500	4,000	17,000	(3,000)	(9,500)

Table 8A.2   Monthly Cash Flow Budget with Additional April Sale

Account	Functional Relationship	January	February	March	April	May	June
Sales	Estimated	$10,000	$20,000	$25,000	**$40,000**	$10,000	$20,000
Purchases	$(0.70)(Sales_{t+2})$	17,500	**28,000**	7,000	14,000	21,000	15,000
Cash flow effects							
Cash sales	$(0.20)(Sales_t)$	$ 2,000	$ 4,000	$ 5,000	**$ 8,000**	$ 2,000	$ 4,000
Collection of credit sales	$(0.50)(Sales_{t-1}) +$	10,000	10,000	13,000	18,500	**27,500**	**17,000**
	$(0.30)(Sales_{t-2})$						
Inventory payment	$Purchases_{t-1}$	(14,000)	(17,500)	**(28,000)**	(7,000)	(14,000)	(21,000)
Other costs	Estimated	(2,000)	(3,000)	(2,000)	(1,500)	(3,000)	(2,000)
Large cash investments	Estimated					(20,000)	
Net cash flows	$Cash\ sales_t + Collections_t$	(4,000)	(6,500)	**(12,000)**	**18,000**	**(7,500)**	**(2,000)**
	$- Payments_t - Other\ costs_t$						
	$- Investments_t$						
Beg. cash balance	$End.\ cash\ balance_{t-1}$	20,000	16,000	9,500	**(2,500)**	15,500	8,000
End. cash balance	$Beg.\ cash\ balance_t +$	16,000	9,500	**(2,500)**	**15,500**	**8,000**	**6,000**
	$Net\ cash\ flows_t$						

of $20,000 in fixed assets. If these estimates are accurate, the organization will have to borrow money in May or reconsider the large cash investment.

The numbers in Table 8A.1 are estimates or functions of estimates. No certainty exists that they actually will occur. Suppose that in April an additional sale of $25,000 is possible. Spreadsheet analysis can accommodate this adjustment by simply increasing the April sales estimate of $15,000 by $25,000 to $40,000. Table 8A.2 illustrates the effects of this change on other accounts in bold print.

The additional sale in Table 8A.2 actually causes a cash shortage during an earlier month (March) when the organization will be forced to borrow money. This shortage occurs because the organization must purchase the inventory before selling it. The additional sale, however, provides sufficient cash flows in May and June to allow for the $20,000 large cash investment.

SELF-STUDY PROBLEM

Joseph Chang, president of Changware Company, has developed a software program for accounting for drugstores. The firm's competitive strategy is to meet customer needs in the drugstore market by providing quality software. In the first year, sales were far greater than expected, and Joseph hired additional marketing and customer service personnel. In addition, Joseph must keep up with the competition, so he has added more software engineers and programmers to create new software. This hiring increase has caused him to rent larger facilities. Although Changware appears to be successful, Joseph has cash flow problems with all the expansion activities. He believes that it is time to make a budget.

a. Describe the planning and control implications of the budgeting process for Changware.
b. Should Changware emphasize short- or long-term budgets? Explain.
c. Should Changware use line-item budgets, budget lapsing, flexible budgets, or zero-base budgets? Explain.

Solution

a. Changware needs a budget for two reasons, planning and control. The company is in a state of growth and change. Rapid growth is requiring the use of additional cash, and Joseph Chang must plan to ensure that the company has sufficient cash. He must estimate cash inflows from sales and the collection of accounts receivable to determine whether sufficient cash is available to fund the expansion. If cash inflows from operations are insufficient, Joseph will have to investigate alternative methods of financing, such as bank loans or issuing stock.

The growth in Changware also means that the firm will become more decentralized and require more control efforts. Joseph will not be able to make all the decisions. The budget serves as a means to communicate organizational goals to other members of the organization and to establish performance expectations. The budget also serves as a benchmark for rewarding individuals within the organization.

b. Changware's budget should probably emphasize short-term planning and control. Organizational change and the volatile nature of the software industry make long-term budgets less valuable. The creation of organizational value depends on Changware's ability to adapt quickly to changes in technology and the drugstore market.

c. Ordinarily, the addition of many new employees would suggest the use of a line-item budget, yet flexibility is extremely important in an industry with an average product life of about 18 months. A line-item budget might constrain the organization too much.

Budget lapsing probably will not be appropriate because the development of new software may take more than a year. Changware would not want to restrict funding to fiscal years. The company is more likely to budget for a project rather than for a period of time.

Flexible budgets are appropriate if the responsible parties cannot control the sales volume. The software-manufacturing unit is unlikely to have much control over volume, so flexible budgeting would be appropriate for that unit.

Zero-base budgeting is likely to be appropriate for the company, especially given that this is its first budget. Even subsequent budgets are not likely to be incremental because of the volatile nature of the business and the continual cycle of new products.

NUMERICAL EXERCISES

Shocker Company's sales budget shows quarterly sales for the next year as follows:

NE 8.1
Estimation of Production
(LO 1)

Quarter 1	10,000 units
Quarter 2	8,000 units
Quarter 3	12,000 units
Quarter 4	14,000 units

Company policy is to have a finished goods inventory at the end of each quarter equal to 20% of the next quarter's sales.

Compute budgeted production for the second quarter of the next year.

(CMA adapted)

Candice Candy Company expects to sell 100,000 cases of chocolate bars during the next year. Budgeted costs per case are $150 for direct materials, $120 for direct labor, and $75 for manufacturing overhead (all variable). Candice Company begins the year with 40,000 cases of finished goods on hand and wants to end the year with 10,000 cases of finished goods inventory.

Compute the budgeted manufacturing costs of Candice Candy Company for the next year.

NE 8.2
Computation of Budgeted Manufacturing Costs
(LO 1)

A chair manufacturer has established the following flexible budget for the month.

NE 8.3
Flexible Budgets
(LO 7)

	Units Produced and Sold		
	1,000	**1,500**	**2,000**
Sales	$10,000	$15,000	$20,000
Variable costs	(5,000)	(7,500)	(10,000)
Fixed costs	(2,000)	(2,000)	(2,000)
Profit	$ 3,000	$ 5,500	$ 8,000

a. What is the sales price per chair?

b. What is the expected profit if 1,600 chairs are made?

NE 8.4
Flexible Budget
(LO 7)

Tubbs Company has established the following flexible budget for the coming month:

Units produced	10,000	11,000	12,000
Total costs	$30,000	$32,000	$34,000

a. What is the variable cost per unit?
b. What is the fixed cost?

NE 8.5
Estimation of Cash Collections and Accounts Receivable
(LO 11)

Wolski Company expects sales in July to be $100,000. Of total sales, 20% are anticipated to be cash with the remaining to be collected in August. Accounts receivable at the beginning of July total $70,000, which will be collected in July.

a. How much cash is expected to be collected in July from accounts receivable and cash sales?
b. What is the expected ending balance of accounts receivable in July?

NE 8.6
Variance Analysis
(LO 2)

A company had the following budgeted and actual results during the year:

	Budgeted	Actual
Revenues	$200,000	$210,000
Cost of goods sold	(100,000)	(75,000)
General administration	(20,000)	(18,000)
Selling expenses	(50,000)	(85,000)
Profit	$ 30,000	$ 32,000

Perform a variance analysis and identify variances that should be investigated.

NE 8.7
Flexible Budgets
(LO 1)

A company that makes multiple products uses direct labor hours to measure activity. The following are expected: variable costs of $40 per direct labor hour, revenues of $60 per direct labor hour, fixed manufacturing costs of $200,000, and fixed selling and administrative costs of $100,000.

Make a flexible budget for 20,000, 30,000, and 40,000 direct labor hours.

NE 8.8
Estimation of Production Requirements
(LO 9)

A company plans to sell 5,000 units. It has beginning inventory equal to 500 units and plans to have 800 units in ending inventory.

How many units must it produce?

NE 8.9
Estimation of Direct Materials
(LO 9)

A company makes a product that requires 3 kilograms of raw material A and 5 meters of wire per unit. The cost of raw material A is $10 per kilogram; the cost of the wire is $1 per meter. The company has 100 kilograms of raw material A in beginning inventory and would like to have 200 kilograms in ending inventory. There are 200 meters of wire in beginning inventory, and the company would like to have 500 meters in ending inventory.

What is the cost of purchasing raw materials during the period if 1,000 units must be produced?

NE 8.10
Estimation of Cash Collections and Accounts Receivable
(LO 11)

A company plans to have sales of $20,000 in January, $30,000 in February, and $40,000 in March. Cash sales are expected to be 20% of the total with the remaining sales to be on account and collected the month after the sales. Accounts receivable total $25,000 at the beginning of January.

How much cash from sales and the collection of accounts receivable is expected in January, February, and March?

A company has the following beginning and expected ending balances:

NE 8.11
Estimation of Cash Flows
(LO 11)

	Beginning	Ending
Accounts receivable	$40,000	$30,000
Inventory	60,000	80,000
Accounts payable	20,000	35,000
Wages payable	10,000	12,000

What are the cash effects of these changes in the balances?

NUMERICAL PROBLEMS

The annual cost of goods sold for a company is expected to be $82,000. The beginning inventory balance is $25,000, and the ending inventory balance is expected to be $21,000. All purchases are on credit. The beginning and ending balances for accounts payable are expected to be $11,000 and $8,000, respectively.

What is the amount of cash payments made to pay accounts payable?

NP 8.1
Estimation of Cash Payments for Inventory
(LO 1)

Topper Restaurant uses a flexible budget to estimate profit for each month. The restaurant expects to charge $15 per meal on average. Some costs are assumed to vary with the number of meals served, so it estimates a variable cost of $5 per meal served. The restaurant also has monthly fixed costs of $10,000.

Prepare a monthly flexible budget of total revenue, costs, and profit, given 1,000, 1,500, and 2,000 meals served.

NP 8.2
Flexible Budget
(LO 7)

Fancy Umbrella Company makes beach umbrellas. The production process requires 3 square meters of plastic sheeting and a metal pole. The plastic sheeting costs $0.50 per square meter and each metal pole costs $1.00. At the beginning of the month, the company has 5,000 square meters of plastic and 1,000 poles in raw materials inventory. The preferred raw material amount at the end of the month is 3,000 square meters of plastic sheeting and 600 poles. At the beginning of the month, the company has 300 finished umbrellas in inventory. It plans to have 200 finished umbrellas at the end of the month. Sales in the coming month are expected to be 5,000 umbrellas.

NP 8.3
Estimation of Production Costs
(LO 1)

a. How many umbrellas must the company produce to meet demand and have sufficient ending inventory?
b. What is the cost of materials that must be purchased?

Humdrum Company is worried about cash flows. The company has $1,000 in cash at the start of February. January's total sales were $20,000, and total sales in February are expected to be $30,000. Sales are 30% cash sales and 70% sales on account collected in the following month. Production costs in February are expected to be $25,000, all of which must be paid during February. The company would also like to buy equipment that costs $10,000.

How much will the company have to borrow to have $800 in cash at the end of February?

NP 8.4
Estimation of Cash Requirements
(LO 11)

Birdie Company makes badminton racquets. Beginning inventory for the coming year is 1,000 racquets. The company expects to sell 10,000 racquets during the year and wants to have 800 racquets in inventory at the end of the year.

How many racquets must the company produce during the year to meet demand and to have sufficient inventory at the end of the year?

NP 8.5
Production Requirements
(LO 1)

NP 8.6
Pro Forma Financial Statements
(LO 9, 10)

Gold Bay Hotel is developing a master budget and pro forma financial statements for 2002. The beginning balance sheet for the fiscal year 2002 is estimated to be as follows:

GOLD BAY HOTEL			
Estimated Balance Sheet			
January 1, 2002			
Cash	$ 20,000	Accounts payable	$ 20,000
Accounts receivable	30,000	Note payable	500,000
Facilities	3,010,000	Capital stock	100,000
Accumulated dep.	(1,100,000)	Retained earnings	1,340,000
Total assets	$1,960,000	Total equities	$1,960,000

During the year, the hotel expects to rent 30,000 rooms. Rooms rent for an average of $90 per night. Additionally, the hotel expects to sell 40,000 meals at an average price of $20 per meal. The variable cost per room rented is $30, and the variable cost per meal is $8. The fixed costs, excluding depreciation, are projected to be $2,000,000. Depreciation is expected to be $500,000. The hotel also plans to refurbish the kitchen at a cost of $200,000, which is capitalized (included in the facilities account). Interest on the notes payable is expected to be $50,000, and $100,000 of the notes payable will be retired during the year. The ending accounts receivable balance is projected to be $40,000, and the ending accounts payable balance is expected to be $30,000.

Prepare pro forma financial statements for the end of the year.

NP 8.7
Estimation of Direct Materials Purchase
(LO 1)

Jung Corporation's budget calls for the following production:

Quarter 1	45,000 units
Quarter 2	38,000 units
Quarter 3	34,000 units
Quarter 4	48,000 units

Each unit of product requires 3 kilograms of direct material. The company's policy is to begin each quarter with an inventory of direct materials equal to 30% of that quarter's direct material requirements.

Compute budgeted direct materials purchases for the third quarter.

(CMA adapted)

NP 8.8
Variance Analysis
(LO 2)

August Company's budget for July called for producing and selling 5,000 units at $8 each. Actual units produced and sold totaled 5,200, yielding revenue of $42,120. Variable costs per unit were budgeted at $3 and fixed costs were budgeted at $2 per unit. Actual variable costs were $3.30 per unit and fixed costs totaled $12,000.

a. Prepare a variance report for July operations comparing actual and budgeted revenues and costs.

b. Write a short memo analyzing performance in July.

NP 8.9
Monthly Estimates of Cash Flows
(LO 11)

Corner Hardware Store is developing a budget to estimate monthly cash balances in the near future. At the end of December, the cash balance is $6,000, and the accounts payable balance is $30,000 (reflecting December's purchases of inventory). Corner Hardware Store expects $40,000 in sales in January and an increase in sales of 2% per month over the next six months. All sales are on a cash basis. Inventory purchases and sales are expected to rise at the same rate. Inventory purchases are paid in the month following the purchase. Other monthly cash outflows are expected to be $10,000 per month.

a. How much money will the store have to borrow to pay $20,000 for a new computer system in May?

b. How much will the store have to borrow to pay $20,000 for a new computer system in May if sales and purchases are expected to increase by 5% per month?

Quality Auto Parts Wholesaler, which maintains an inventory of car parts to supply local car repair shops, is making cash flow estimates for the coming year. The monthly inventory purchases are sufficient to cover sales for a two-month period, but the bills for those purchases are paid in the month prior to their sale. There is a 20% profit margin on sales. Other costs are $2,000 per month paid in the month incurred. Sales are assumed to be composed of 10% cash sales, 70% credit sales collected in the following month, and 20% credit sales collected in the second month following the sales transaction. The cash balance at the beginning of March is $5,000. Expected sales by month are as follows:

NP 8.10
Monthly Estimates of Cash Flows
(LO 11)

Account	January	February	March	April	May	June	July	August
Sales	$10,000	$12,000	$10,000	$20,000	$25,000	$15,000	$10,000	$20,000

a. What will be the cash balances for the end of March, April, May, and June?

b. Will the company have to borrow money during the months March through June?

c. Would the firm have to borrow cash if June sales were expected to be $50,000 instead of $15,000?

Toronto Eye Company (TEC) makes reading glasses. Its expected beginning balance sheet on January 1, 2002, follows:

NP 8.11
Master Budget and Pro Forma Statements
(LO 9, 10)

TORONTO EYE COMPANY
Expected Beginning Balance Sheet
January 1, 2002

Assets

Cash	$ 80,000
Accounts receivable	50,000
Inventory (6,000 units at $6/unit)	36,000
Property, plant, and equipment (net)	100,000
	$266,000

Liabilities and Shareholders' Equity

Accounts payable	$100,000
Long-term debt	100,000
Shareholders' equity	66,000
	$266,000

During 2002, TEC expects to sell 100,000 units (reading glasses) for $12 each. They are sold on account, and the accounts receivable balance is expected to be $100,000 on December 31, 2002. The firm expects to have 10,000 reading glasses in inventory on that date.

TEC has no raw materials inventory. Instead, it purchases raw materials only when needed immediately for the assembly of reading glasses at its Toronto facility. The cost of the materials is $6/unit. The raw materials are bought on account, and the company expects the accounts payable balance on December 31, 2002, to be $120,000.

Labor and overhead are treated as period expenses. The average direct labor for each pair of reading glasses is expected to be $2/unit. The overhead is fixed and is projected to be $200,000 for the year. Depreciation of $20,000 is included in fixed overhead. The remaining overhead requires cash payments.

During 2002, TEC plans to buy $50,000 in property, plant, and equipment and to issue $20,000 more in long-term debt. The interest on the long-term debt for 2002 is expected to be $12,000. The firm expects to pay $10,000 in dividends in 2002.

Prepare a master budget and pro forma statements for TEC for December 31, 2002.

Adrian Power manufactures small power supplies for car stereos. The company uses flexible budgeting techniques to deal with the seasonal and cyclical nature of the business. The accounting department provided the following data on budgeted manufacturing costs for the month of January 2001:

NP 8.12
Flexible Budgets
(LO 7)

270   *Budgeting*

ADRIAN POWER Planned Level of Production January 2001	
Budgeted production (in units)	14,000
Variable costs (vary with production)	
Direct materials	$140,000
Direct labor	224,000
Indirect labor	21,000
Indirect materials	10,500
Maintenance	6,300
Fixed costs	
Supervision	24,700
Other (depreciation, taxes, etc.)	83,500
Total plant costs	$510,000

The following summarizes actual operations for January 2001:

ADRIAN POWER Actual Operations January 2001	
Actual production (in units)	15,400
Actual costs incurred	
Direct materials	$142,400
Direct labor	259,800
Indirect labor	27,900
Indirect materials	12,200
Maintenance	9,800
Fixed costs	
Supervision	28,000
Other (depreciation, taxes, etc.)	83,500
Total plant costs	$563,600

a.   Prepare a report comparing the actual operating results to the flexible budget.

b.   Write a short memorandum analyzing the report prepared in part (a). What likely managerial implications do you draw from this report? (What are the numbers telling you?)

NP 8.13
Budget for a Takeover
(LO 1)

You are working for a firm that specializes in mergers and takeovers, and your job is to analyze potential acquisitions. You are assigned to evaluate a possible merger between NE and Upstate Airlines. These two carriers are competing in the upstate-downstate New York markets of Rochester, Albany, Syracuse, and New York City. Excess capacity currently exists in these two airlines. Your boss thinks that a merger of the two airlines, accompanied by canceling some redundant flights and raising some fares, could create the "synergy" necessary to make a positive return on the acquisition. Your boss asks you to provide her with an estimate of the first year's cost savings that would result from a combination of NE and Upstate Airlines. You assemble the following operating data on the two airlines:

	NE Airlines	**Upstate Airlines**
Passenger miles flown	72 million	80 million
Average price per passenger mile	25¢	25¢
Number of jets	3	4
Operating labor costs	$5 million	$6 million
Corporate office expense	$2 million	$2 million
Landing and parking fees*	$0.75 million	$1 million

* These fees are proportional to the number of jets in the fleet.

Both airlines are using the same type of jet. The annual operating costs and lease payment (including fuel, maintenance, licenses, and insurance) are $3 million per jet. After analyzing the various markets served, you determine that a combination of the two airlines would result in the following operating data: average price can be increased 10%, some duplicate flights can be canceled, and combined corporate office expenses can be cut by $1 million. The combination of the higher prices and reduced frequency of flights is expected to cut demand by 6%. The existing flights have enough excess capacity to support a reduction in the fleet size of the combined airline by one jet.

Each firm's operating labor costs are proportional to the number of jets in the fleet. You assume that the combined firm will have operating labor costs per jet equal to that currently incurred by NE. However, Upstate Airlines' labor union contract specifies that employees with five or more years of service with the airline cannot be laid off in the event of a merger. Therefore, only some of the labor cost savings that could have been achieved by reducing the fleet to six jets will be achieved. An additional $0.5 million of labor cost will be incurred as a result of the existing Upstate labor contract.

Prepare an analysis comparing the current profitability of the two airlines as independent firms with a combined firm using the planning assumptions stated. Recommend a course of action, outlining other factors to consider in terms of the airlines' strategies and operating environment.

NP 8.14
Flexible Budgets
(LO 7)

Golf World is a 1,000-room luxury resort with swimming pools, tennis courts, three golf courses, and many other resort amenities.

The head golf course superintendent, Sandy Green, is responsible for all golf course maintenance and conditioning. Sandy also has the final say as to whether a particular course is open or closed due to weather conditions and whether players can rent motorized riding golf carts for use on a particular section of the course. If the course is very wet, the golf carts will damage the turf, which her maintenance crew will have to repair. Since Sandy is out on the course every morning supervising the maintenance crews, she knows the condition of the courses.

Wiley Grimes is in charge of the golf cart rentals. His crew maintains the golf cart fleet of over more than 200 cars, cleaning them, putting oil and gas in them, and repairing minor damage. He also is responsible for leasing the carts from the manufacturer, including the terms of the lease, the number of carts to lease, and the choice of the cart vendor. When guests arrive at the golf course to play, they pay greens fees to play and a cart fee if they wish to use a cart.

Wiley and Sandy manage separate profit centers. The golf cart's profit center revenues are composed of the fees collected from the cart rental. The revenues for the golf course profit center are from the greens fees collected. In reviewing the results from April, golf cart operating profits were only 49% of budget. Wiley argued that the poor results were due to the unusually heavy rains in April. He complained that the course was closed to golf carts for several days. Although only a few areas of the course were wet, the ground crew was too busy to rope off these areas from carts so that the entire course was closed to carts.

To better analyze the performance of the golf cart profit center, the controller's office has implemented a flexible budget based on the number of cart rentals:

	Static Budget	Actual Results	Variance from Static Budget	Flexible Budget	Variance from Flexible Budget
			GOLF WORLD Golf Cart Profit Center Operating Results April		
Number of cart rentals	6000	4000	2000	4000	0
Revenues (@$25/car)	$150,000	$100,000	$50,000 U	$100,000	0
Labor (fixed cost)	7,000	7,200	200 U	7,000	200 U
Gas & oil (@$1/rental)	6,000	4,900	1,100 F	4,000	900 U
Cart lease (fixed cost)	40,000	40,000	0	40,000	0
Operating profit	$ 97,000	$ 47,900	$49,100 U	$ 49,000	$1,100 U

a. Evaluate the performance of the golf cart profit center for the month of April.

b. What are the advantages and disadvantages of the controller's new budgeting system?

c. What additional recommendations would you make regarding the operations of Golf World?

NP 8.15
Flexible Budgeting
(LO 7)

Wielson Company employs flexible budgeting techniques to evaluate the performance of several of its activities. The selling-expense flexible budgets for three representative monthly activity levels follow:

WIELSON COMPANY Representative Monthly Flexible Budgets for Selling Expenses			
Activity measures			
Unit sales volume	400,000	425,000	450,000
Dollar sales volume	$10,000,000	$10,625,000	$11,250,000
Number of orders	4,000	4,250	4,500
Number of salespersons	75	75	75
Monthly expenses			
Advertising and promotion	$1,200,000	$1,200,000	$1,200,000
Administrative salaries	57,000	57,000	57,000
Sales salaries	75,000	75,000	75,000
Sales commissions	200,000	212,500	225,000
Salesperson travel	170,000	175,000	180,000
Total selling expenses	$1,702,000	$1,719,500	$1,737,000

The following assumptions were used to develop the selling-expense flexible budgets:

*   The average size of Wielson's sales force during the year was planned to be 75 people.
*   Salespeople are paid a monthly salary plus commissions on gross dollar sales.
*   The travel costs are best characterized as a step-variable cost. The fixed portion is related to the number of salespersons; the variable portion fluctuates with gross dollar sales.

A sales force of 80 people generated a total of 4,300 orders, resulting in a sales volume of 420,000 units during November. The gross dollar sales amounted to $10.9 million. The selling expenses incurred for November were as follows:

Advertising and promotion	$1,350,000
Administrative salaries	57,000
Sales salaries	80,000
Sales commissions	218,000
Salesperson travel	185,000
Total	$1,890,000

Prepare a selling expense report for November that Wielson Company can use to evaluate its control over selling expenses. The report should have a line for each selling expense item showing the appropriate budgeted amount, the actual selling expense, and the monthly dollar variation.

(CMA adapted)

NP 8.16
Flexible Budgets
(LO 7)

The coating department of a parts-manufacturing department coats various parts with an antirust zinc-based material. The parts to be processed are loaded into baskets, and then the baskets pass through a coating machine that sprays the zinc material on the parts. Next, the machine heats the parts to ensure that the coating bonds properly. All parts being coated are assigned a cost for the coating department based on the number of hours that the parts spend in a coating machine. Prior to the beginning of the year, cost categories are accumulated by department (including the coating department). These cost categories are classified as being either fixed or variable, and then a flexible budget for the department is constructed. Given an estimate of machine hours for the next year, the coating department's projected cost per machine hour is computed.

Data for the last three operating years follows. Expected coating machine hours for 2001 are 16,000 hours.

COATING DEPARTMENT Operating Data			
	1998	**1999**	**2000**
Machine hours	12,500	8,400	15,200
Coating materials	$ 51,375	$ 34,440	$ 62,624
Engineering support	27,962	34,295	31,300
Maintenance	35,850	35,930	36,200
Occupancy costs (square meters)	27,502	28,904	27,105
Operator labor	115,750	78,372	147,288
Supervision	46,500	47,430	49,327
Utilities	12,875	8,820	16,112
Total costs	$317,814	$268,191	$369,956

a. Estimate the coating department's flexible budget for 2001. Explicitly state and justify the assumptions used in deriving your estimates.

b. Calculate the coating department's cost per machine hour for 2001.

Construct a master budget using the following data:

NP 8.17
Preparation of a Master Budget
(LO 9)

COMPANY C Beginning Balance Sheet January 1, 2001			
Cash	$1,000	Accounts payable	$1,200
Accounts receivable	500	Notes payable	3,000
Raw materials	800		
Finished goods	3,000	Capital stock at par	100
Prop., plant, & eqpt.	5,000	Additional paid in	1,000
Accumulated Dep.	(1,000)	Retained earnings	4,000
	$9,300		$9,300

The following events are expected to happen during 2001:

- Sale of 2,000 units at $10 per unit.
- Cost of each unit equal to $3 in raw materials and $2 in direct labor.
- Manufacturing overhead equal to $3/unit, which includes $1/unit of depreciation.
- The cost/unit is the same as last year.
- Purchase equipment for $1,000.
- Payment of interest of $300.
- Retire notes payable of $500.
- Expected selling and administrative expenses of $400.
- Final expected balances: Accounts Receivable, $600; Raw Materials, $900; Finished Goods, $2,400; Accounts Payable, $1,500.

ANALYSIS AND INTERPRETATION PROBLEMS

Professors at Southeastern University are given a budget of $2,000 per year for travel and research purposes. Presently, the university allows the professors to carry over unused balances from one year to the next. The university is considering a new policy of having the $2,000 lapse from year to year.

AIP 8.1
Budget Lapsing
(LO 6)

What are the advantages and disadvantages of having the travel and research budget lapse?

AIP 8.2

Different Types of Budget

(LO 4, 5, 6, 7, 8)

Sticky Company makes a glue used to make the layers of wood veneer adhere to make plywood. The glue-making process has been used for many years, and the customers are satisfied with the product. Sticky Company has had very low turnover of personnel, and the president and all of the managers have been with the firm for many years. Although the company appears stable today, plywood prices are rising, and the construction industry is beginning to switch to chipboard, a cheaper product. Chipboard uses a different glue than the product made by Sticky Company.

Given the present condition of Sticky Company, should it use long-term budgets, line-item budgets, budget lapsing, flexible budgets, or zero-base budgeting?

AIP 8.3

Long-Term Budgets

(LO 4)

The sales manager of T Corporation is complaining about the budget process. He notes, "Each year the central administration asks for expected sales in each of the next three years. The first year's budget is used to determine production amounts and establish benchmarks for measuring performance, and rewarding employees. The second and third year budgets, however, seem to be forgotten. Next year, management asks us again for expected sales in each of the next three years. Why does management not simply use last year's forecast, or only ask us to make sales forecasts for one year ahead?"

Does the sales manager have a legitimate complaint?

AIP 8.4

Budgets and Performance Evaluation

(LO 3)

I've given a good deal of thought to this issue of how companies . . . go about negotiating objectives with their different business units. The typical process in such cases is that once the parent negotiates a budget with a unit, the budget then becomes the basis for the bonus. And they are also typically structured such that the bonus kicks in when, say, 80% of the budgeted performance is achieved; and the maximum bonus is earned, when management reaches, say, 120% of the budgeted level. There is thus virtually no downside and very limited upside.

Now, because the budget is negotiated between management and headquarters, there is a circularity about the whole process that makes the resulting standards almost meaningless. Because the budget is intended to reflect what management thinks it can accomplish—presumably without extraordinary effort and major changes in the status quo—the adoption of the budget as a standard is unlikely to motivate exceptional performance, especially since the upside is so limited. Instead it is likely to produce cautious budgets and mediocre performance.

So, because of the perverse incentives built into the budgeting process itself, I think it's important for a company to break the connection between the budget and planning process on the one hand and the bonus systems on the other hand. The bonuses should be based upon absolute performance standards that are not subject to negotiation.

Critically evaluate the preceding quotation.

Source: G. Bennett Stewart III, "CEO Roundtable on Corporate Structure and Management Incentives," *Journal of Applied Corporate Finance,* Fall 1990, p. 27.

AIP 8.5

Zero-Base Budgeting

(LO 8)

Rogers Petersen and Cabots are two of the five largest investment banks in the United States. Last year, a major scandal at Cabots involved the manipulation of some auctions for government bonds. A number of senior partners at Cabots were charged with price fixing in the government bond market. The ensuing investigation led four of the eight managing directors (the highest-ranking officials at Cabots) to resign. A new senior managing director was brought in from outside to run the firm. This individual recruited three outside managing directors to replace the one who had resigned. There was then a thorough "house cleaning." In the following six months, 15 additional partners and more than 40 senior managers left Cabots and were replaced, usually with people from outside the firm.

Rogers Petersen has had no such scandal and almost all of its senior executives have been with the firm for all of their careers.

a. Describe zero-base budgeting (ZBB).

b. Which firm, Rogers Petersen or Cabots, is more likely to be using ZBB and why?

A *Fortune* magazine article included the following statements:

> Budgets, say experts, control the wrong things, like head count, and miss the right ones, such as quality, customer service—and even profits. Worse, they erect walls between the various parts of the company and between a company and its customers.
>
> When you're controlled by a budget, you're not controlling the business.
>
> Reliance on budgets is the fundamental flaw in American management. That's because they assume that everything important can be translated into this quarter's or this year's dollars, and that you can manage the business by managing the money. Wrong. Just because a budget was not overspent doesn't mean it was well spent.
>
> For tracking where the money goes, budgets are dandy. They become iniquitous when they are made to do more—when the budget becomes management's main tool to gauge performance. Managers do incredibly stupid things to make budget, especially if incentive pay is at stake. They woo marginal customers. They cut prices too deeply.
>
> The worst failure of budgets is what they don't measure. Budgets show what you spend on customer service, but not what value customers put on it.

Critically evaluate the article.

Source: "Why Budgets Are Bad for Business," *Fortune*, June 4, 1990.

AIP 8.6
Problems with Budgets
(LO 1, 2)

In March, a devastating ice storm struck Monroe County, causing millions of dollars of damage. Mathews & Peat (M&P), a large horticultural nursery, was hard hit. As a result of the storm, $653,000 of additional labor and maintenance costs were incurred to clean up the nursery, remove and replace damaged plants, repair fencing, and replace glass broken when nearby tree limbs fell on some of the greenhouses.

M&P is a wholly owned subsidiary of Agro Inc., an international agricultural conglomerate. The manager of M&P, Rolando Dye, is reviewing its operating performance for the year of the ice storm. The results for the year as compared to budget follow:

AIP 8.7
Responsibility for an Unusual Event
(LO 2)

MATHEWS & PEAT
Summary of Operating Results
For the Year 2000
(thousands of dollars)

	Actual Results	Budgeted Results	Actual as % of Budget
Revenues	$32,149	$31,682	101%
Less			
Labor	13,152	12,621	104
Materials	8,631	8,139	106
Occupancy costs*	4,234	4,236	100
Depreciation	2,687	2,675	100
Interest	1,875	1,895	99
Total expenses	30,579	29,566	103%
Operating profits	$ 1,570	$ 2,116	74%

* Includes property taxes, utilities, maintenance, and repairs of buildings, etc.

After thinking about how to present M&P's performance for the year, Rolando decides to break out the costs of the ice storm from the individual items affected by it and report the storm separately. The total cost of the ice storm of $653,000 consists of additional labor costs of $320,000, additional materials of $220,000, and additional occupancy costs of $113,000. These amounts are net of the insurance payments received due to the storm. The alternative performance statement follows:

MATHEWS & PEAT			
Summary of Operating Results			
For the Year 2000			
(thousands of dollars)			
	Actual Results	**Budgeted Results**	**Actual as % of Budget**
Revenues	$32,149	$31,682	101%
Less			
Labor	12,832	12,621	102
Materials	8,411	8,139	103
Occupancy costs	4,121	4,236	97
Depreciation	2,687	2,675	100
Interest	1,875	1,895	99
Total expenses	29,926	29,566	101%
Operating profits before ice storm costs	2,223	2,116	105%
Ice storm costs	653	0	
Operating profits after ice storm costs	$ 1,570	$ 2,116	74%

a. Put yourself in Rolando's position. Write a short, concise cover memo for the second operating statement to summarize the essential points that you want to communicate to your superiors.

b. Critically evaluate the differences between the two performance reports as presented.

AIP 8.8
Lapsing and Multiyear Budgets
(LO 4, 6)

Robin Jones, manager of market planning for Viral Products of IAIP Pharmaceutical Co., is responsible for advertising a class of products. She has designed a three-year marketing plan to increase the market share of her product class involving a major increase in magazine advertising. She has met with an advertising agency that has designed a three-year advertising campaign involving 12 separate ads that build on a common theme. Each advertisement will run in medical magazines for three consecutive months and then will be followed with the next ad in the sequence. Up to five different medical journals will carry the ad campaign. Direct-mail campaigns and direct-sales promotional material will be designed to follow the theme of the ad currently appearing. The following data summarize the cost of the campaign:

	Year 1	Year 2	Year 3	Total
Number of ads	4	4	4	12
Number of magazines	5	5	4	
Cost per ad	$ 6,000	$ 6,200	$ 6,500	
Advertising cost	$120,000	$124,000	$104,000	$348,000

The firm's normal policy is to budget each year as a separate entity without carrying forward unspent funds. Robin is requesting that, instead of approving only the budget for next year (Year 1 in the table), the entire three-year project be budgeted. This approval would allow her to move forward with the campaign and would give her the freedom to apply any unspent funds in one year to the next year or to use them in another part of the campaign. She argues that the advertising campaign is an integrated project stretching over three years and should be either approved or rejected in its entirety.

Critically evaluate Robin's request and make a recommendation as to whether a three-year budget should be approved per her proposal. For purposes of your answer, assume that the advertising campaign is expected to be a profitable project.

You are working in the office of the vice president of administration at International Telecon (IT) as a senior financial planner. IT is a Fortune 500 firm with sales approaching $1 billion. IT provides long-distance satellite communications around the world. Deregulation of telecommunications in Europe has intensified worldwide competition. It also has increased pressures inside IT to reduce costs to allow lower prices without cutting profit margins.

IT is divided into several profit and cost centers. Each profit center is further organized as a series of cost centers. Each profit and cost center follows IT policy regarding submitting budgets to IT's vice president of administration and then is held responsible for meeting the budget. The vice president of administration described IT's financial control, budgeting, and reporting system as "pretty much a standard, state-of-the-art approach, where we hold our people accountable for producing what they forecast."

Your boss has assigned you the task of analyzing firmwide supplies expenditures with the goal of reducing waste and lowering expenditures. Supplies include all consumables ranging from pencils and paper to electronic subcomponents and parts that cost less than $1,000. Long-lived assets that cost under $1,000 (or the equivalent dollar amount in the domestic currency for foreign purchases) are *not* capitalized (and then depreciated) but are categorized as "supplies" and written off as an expense in the month purchased.

You first gather the operating data for the entire firm for supplies and payroll data for the past 36 months. The payroll data are used to help you predict how much supplies should be used. You divide each month's payroll and supplies amount by revenues in that month to control for volume and seasonal fluctuations. The following graph plots the two data series:

AIP 8.9
Budget Effects of Purchasing Patterns
(LO 1, 2, 3, 6)

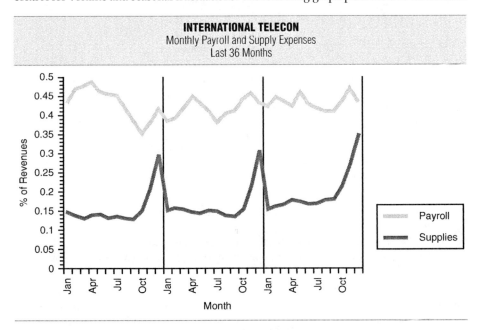

Payroll fluctuates between 35 to 48% of sales, and supplies fluctuate between 13 to 34% of sales. The graph shows the last three years for supplies and payroll; the vertical lines in the graph divide the fiscal years. For financial and budgeting purposes, IT is on a calendar-year (January to December) fiscal year.

In addition to focusing on consolidated firmwide spending, you prepare disaggregated graphs like the one above but at the cost and profit center levels. The overall patterns observed in the consolidated graphs are repeated in general in the disaggregated graphs.

a.   Analyze the behavior over time of supplies expenditures for IT. What is the likely reason for the observed patterns in supplies?
b.   Given your analysis in part (a), what corrective action might you consider proposing? What are its costs and benefits?

Panarude Airfreight is an international air-freight hauler with more than 75 jet aircraft operating in the United States and the Pacific Rim. The firm is headquartered in Melbourne, Australia, and is organized into five geographic areas: Australia, Japan, Taiwan, the United States, and Korea. Supporting these areas are several centralized, corporate function

AIP 8.10
Adjustment of Budgets and Effect on Behavior
(LO 1, 2, 3, 6)

services (cost centers): human resources, data processing, fleet acquisition and maintenance, and telecommunications. Each responsibility center has a budget negotiated at the beginning of the year with the vice president of finance. Any unspent funds at year-end do not carry over to the next fiscal year. The firm is on a January-to-December fiscal year.

After reviewing the month-to-month variances, Panarude senior management had become concerned about the large increases in spending occurring in the last three months of each fiscal year. In particular, in the first nine months of the year, expenditure accounts typically had shown favorable variances (actual spending was less than budget) and in the last three months, unfavorable variances had been the norm. In an attempt to smooth out these spending patterns, each responsibility center now is reviewed at the end of each calendar quarter, and any unspent funds can be deleted from the budget for the remainder of the year. For example, the budget and actual spending in the Telecommunications Department for the first quarter of 2001 are as follows:

	PANARUDE AIRFREIGHT Telecommunications Department 2001 First Quarter Budget and Actual Spending (Australian dollars)					
	Monthly Budget	**Cumulative Budget**	**Actual Spending**	**Cumulative Spending**	**Monthly Variance**	**Cumulative Variance**
Jan.	$110,000	$110,000	$104,000	$104,000	$6,000 F	$6,000 F
Feb.	95,000	205,000	97,000	201,000	2,000 U	4,000 F
Mar.	115,000	320,000	112,000	313,000	3,000 F	7,000 F

At the end of the first quarter, Telecommunications' total annual budget for 2001 can be reduced by $7,000, the total budget underrun in the first quarter. The remaining nine monthly budgets for Telecommunications are reduced by $778 ($7,000 ÷ 9). If at the end of the second quarter, Telecommunications' budget shows an unfavorable variance of say $8,000 (after reducing the original budget for the first quarter's underrun), management of Telecommunications is held responsible for the entire $8,000 unfavorable variance. The first-quarter's underrun is *not* restored. If the second quarter's budget variance is also favorable, the remaining six monthly budgets are reduced again by one-sixth of the second quarter's favorable budget variance.

a. What behaviors would this budgeting scheme engender in the responsibility center managers?

b. Compare the advantages and disadvantages of the previous budget regime in which any end-of-year budget surpluses do not carry over to the next fiscal year to the system of quarterly budget adjustments described here.

AIP 8.11
Analyzing Variances
(LO 2)

Old Rosebud is a Kentucky horse farm that specializes in boarding thoroughbred breeding mares and their foals. Customers bring their breeding mares to Old Rosebud for delivery of their foals and after-birth care of the mare and foal. Recently, there has been a substantial decline in thoroughbred breeding as a result of changes in the tax laws. Due to these changes in the market for thoroughbred boarding, profits in the industry have declined.

Old Rosebud prepared a master budget for 2000 by splitting costs into variable and fixed. The budget for 2000 was prepared before the extent of the downturn was fully recognized. Exhibit AIP 8.11 on the next page compares the actual results to the budget for 2000.

Evaluate Rosebud Farms' operating performance based on the variances in the table.

EXTENDED ANALYSIS AND INTERPRETATION PROBLEMS

AIP 8.12
Budgets and Cost Centers

Eastern University publishes and distributes more than 100,000 copies of its *Official Bulletin on Undergraduate Studies* to prospective students, high school guidance counselors, faculty and staff of the University, and other interested parties. This 250-page catalog with four-color pictures is one of the primary marketing devices for the University's undergraduate programs. High school seniors expressing interest in attending the University receive the

OLD ROSEBUD FARMS
Income Statement
For Year Ended December 31, 2000

	Budget Formula (per mare per day)	Actual	Master Budget	Variance
Number of mares		52	60	8
Number of boarding days		18,980	21,900	2,920
Revenues	$25.00	$379,600	$547,400	$167,900 U
Less variable expenses				
Feed & supplies	5.00	104,390	109,500	5,110 F
Veterinary fees	3.00	58,838	65,700	6,862 F
Blacksmith fees	0.30	6,074	6,570	496 F
Total variable expenses	$ 8.30	$169,302	$181,770	$ 12,468 F
Contribution margin	$16.70	$210,298	$365,730	$155,432 U
Less fixed expenses				
Depreciation & insurance		$ 56,000	$ 56,000	0
Utilities		12,000	14,000	$ 2,000 F
Repairs & maintenance		10,000	11,000	1,000 F
Labor		88,000	96,000	8,000 F
Total fixed expenses		166,000	177,000	11,000 F
Net income		$ 44,298	$188,730	$144,432 U

Note: U (F) denotes an unfavorable (favorable) variance.

Bulletin, along with other information. It lists the various programs of studies, course offerings, and requirements. Each year, it is revised and reprinted as courses and programs change and the photographs are updated to improve it as a recruiting tool. The annual cost of preparing and printing the *Bulletin* is about $1 million, which includes the cost of photographers, nonuniversity graphic designers, typesetting, and printing. This figure excludes the cost of University employees who rewrite the text, proofread the galleys, and manage the entire process.

The Admissions Office and the Public Relations Department share the responsibility of preparing the catalog. The Admissions Office coordinates the collection of the basic data on course and program changes. Many of these are not known until May after the various faculties have met and approved academic program and course changes. These changes are edited and the overall content of the publication is determined based on the Admissions Office's experience with high school applicants. Admissions then sends a draft copy of the catalog to Public Relations, which is responsible for the overall image and publicity of the University and for ensuring that the University publications present a consistent image. Public Relations, using outside graphic designers, marketing specialists, typesetters, and printers whom it has come to know, takes the changes and produces an attractive, high-quality catalog.

The Admissions Office reports to the dean of the Undergraduate College, who reports to the president. The Public Relations Department reports to the vice president of External Affairs, who also reports to the president. The Admissions Office affects the cost of the catalog in terms of the amount of text to be included and how many *Bulletins* must be ordered to satisfy its distribution plan. Public Relations affects the cost by using color photographs, expensive paper and cover materials, and elaborate layouts. Both Admissions and Public Relations affect the cost by not meeting timely production schedules. If copy is returned late or the design is not completed on time, additional charges are incurred for typesetters and printers working overtime to meet the publication schedule. It is critically important to the admissions process that the *Bulletin* be available for distribution in September to high school seniors beginning their college search process.

Admissions and Public Relations are both cost centers. They have been arguing over whether the cost of the *Bulletin* should be in the budget of the Admissions Office or the Public Relations Department.

a. Discuss the advantages and disadvantages of placing the budget for the *Bulletin* in the Public Relations versus the Admissions Office budget.

b. What are some alternative ways to handle the *Bulletin*'s budget?

c. Based on your analysis, what recommendation would you make?

AIP 8.13
Master Budget

Eugene Brewing Company is budgeting for the next year. The following is the company's beginning balance sheet:

EUGENE BREWING COMPANY Balance Sheet January 1, 2001			
Assets		**Liabilities and Equities**	
Cash	$ 10,000	Accounts payable	$ 3,000
Accounts receivable	20,000	Long-term debt	50,000
Inventory	30,000		
Total current assets	$ 60,000	Total liabilities	$ 53,000
Fixed assets	200,000	Common stock at par	$ 10,000
Accumulated depreciation	(90,000)	Additional paid-in	20,000
		Retained earnings	87,000
Total assets	$170,000	Total liabilities and equities	$170,000

The company expects to collect the beginning balance of accounts receivable in January. In general, 30% of the company's sales are on a cash basis. Of the credit sales, 40% are paid in the following month, and 60% are paid in the second month after the sale.

The accounts payable at the beginning of the year must be paid in January. All materials are purchased on credit and paid for in the following month.

The long-term debt has an annual interest rate of 12%. Interest payments of 1% of the principal are made each month. The long-term debt is not due for another five years.

Eugene Brewing Company makes two different types of beer, an ale and a porter. The ale is a lighter beer that requires fewer ingredients than does the darker and heavier porter. The input requirements for a case of beer for each type of beer follow:

For Making Ale		
Material	**Quantity per Case**	**Cost**
Hops	5 lb.	$0.30/lb.
Yeast	1 oz.	0.10/oz.
Sugar	0.5 lb.	0.40/lb.
Bottles	24	0.05/bottle

For Making Porter		
Material	**Quantity per Case**	**Cost**
Hops	10 lb.	$0.30/lb.
Yeast	1 oz.	0.10/oz.
Sugar	0.8 lb.	0.40/lb.
Bottles	24	0.05/bottle

The labor to make a case of beer is the same for each type of beer, 0.20 hours at $10/hour. Labor is paid in the month earned.

Monthly overhead expenses are paid in the month incurred and expected to be as follows:

Electricity	$ 2,000
Indirect labor	20,000
Rent	5,000
Depreciation	2,000

Ale sells for $10 per case, and porter sells for $12 per case. Estimated sales (in cases) for Eugene Brewing follow:

	Ale	Porter
January	3,000	4,000
February	3,000	5,000
March	4,000	3,000
April	2,000	2,000

The beginning inventory includes 2,000 cases of ale and 3,000 cases of porter. The company prefers to have inventory at the end of each month equal to the expected sales in the next month. Eugene Brewing uses a first-in, first-out (FIFO) method of costing inventory.

The company must buy a new bottling machine for $20,000 at the end of January.

a. Estimate cash flows in each of the months.

b. Does the company need to borrow money in any of the months?

c. Make a balance sheet as of the end of March and an income statement for the first three months. Assume that the company borrows cash at an interest rate of 1% per month to make up any shortage of cash.

Chapter**Nine**

Cost Allocations

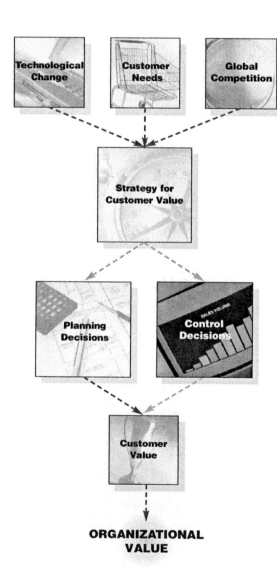

LEARNING OBJECTIVES

1 Describe the relations among common resources, indirect costs, and cost objects.

2 Explain the role of allocating indirect costs for external financial reports, income tax reports, and cost reimbursement.

3 Identify reasons for cost allocation for planning purposes.

4 Identify reasons for cost allocation for control purposes.

5 Describe how the various reasons for cost allocation can create conflict within the organization.

6 Allocate indirect costs using five basic steps.

7 Create segment reports for the organization.

8 Use direct, step-down, and reciprocal methods to allocate costs of service departments that interact. (Appendix)

VALLEY CLINIC

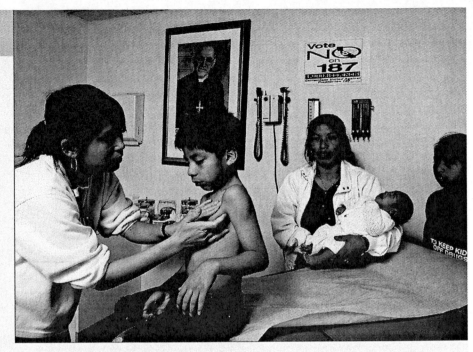

Valley Clinic is composed of a group of family practitioners who provide health-care services to different types of patients. Patients are categorized by the method of pay for services. Some patients come to Valley Clinic through an agreement with a local health maintenance organization (HMO). The HMO has agreed to cover all medical costs of some of the larger area businesses for a fixed fee. The HMO then contracts with Valley Clinic to provide certain basic health-care services and to act as a referral service if the patient needs the attention of a specialist or hospital. The HMO pays Valley Clinic $150 per year for each patient covered by the HMO. Each patient selects a doctor at Valley Clinic as the primary care giver.

Medicare and private insurance plans cover other patients and pay Valley Clinic based on diagnostic-related groups (DRGs), which are specified treatments given to patients, such as setting a fractured bone or providing an annual physical examination. Medicare and insurance companies pay Valley Clinic a certain amount for each DRG provided to a patient covered by those plans. This method is called *fee for service*.

Finally, another group of patients pays its own medical costs. These patients are charged an amount based on the cost of services provided.

Valley Clinic's owners are 12 doctors, each of whom is paid based on the profit he or she generates. The doctors have hired a clinic director, who is responsible for its general operations and management. An accountant, bookkeeper, procurement manager, and secretary provide administrative support to the director. The costs related to this support group are treated as general administration costs. The following departments assist the doctors in performing their duties: X-ray, nurses, and receptionists. In addition, the clinic incurs costs related to the building, such as rent and utilities. Laboratory tests are performed by an outside agency and are billed separately.

Valley Clinic's accountant faces two primary problems: how to determine the cost of services provided by the doctors and how to determine the profit generated by each doctor. In addition, the accountant is concerned about how to report the general administration costs, the building costs, and the costs related to the departments that support the doctors.

283

ALLOCATING INDIRECT COSTS

L0 1 Describe the relations among common resources, indirect costs, and cost objects.

Cost allocation is the process of assigning indirect costs to cost objects. **Cost objects** include products, activities, subunits of the organization, customers, suppliers, and time periods. For example, cost objects in a hospital could include a patient, the pediatrics department, or the first quarter of the fiscal year. Each of these cost objects has direct and indirect costs associated with it. Direct costs occur when resources are used for only one cost object. For example, raw materials are used by a specific product and are considered direct costs of the product. The product is the cost object. Indirect costs, however, result from the use of resources by multiple cost objects. A machine that is used by many products is an indirect cost to those products. The allocation of indirect costs to cost objects is the subject of this chapter.

In Chapter Three, indirect product costs for planning purposes were traced using activity-based costing (ABC). Indirect product costs are part of the cost of providing a product and must be traced or allocated to the different products through the use of cost drivers. The cost drivers are chosen to reflect the cause of the indirect costs. If the product uses the cost driver, indirect costs are traced to the product. Ideally, tracing indirect costs through cost drivers reflects the cost of using the indirect resources.

Choosing cost drivers to trace indirect costs is appropriate if the purpose is to make a planning decision with respect to the cost object. However, indirect costs are allocated to cost objects for reasons other than making planning decisions. This chapter also examines the allocation of indirect costs for control and external reporting purposes. Allocating indirect costs through cost drivers is not necessarily best for the organization when control and external reporting issues are considered. While ABC can be worthwhile, other indirect cost allocation mechanisms often prove more beneficial in motivating managers or influencing users of external accounting reports. The choice of the cost allocation method is subjective, and ethical considerations must be made. Cost allocations for control purposes can adversely affect certain managers and benefit others. Cost allocation methods for external reporting are often chosen to minimize the organization's tax liability.

The subjective nature of indirect cost allocations makes the process one of the most controversial in accounting. Inappropriate cost allocation mechanisms can lead to poor planning decisions, demoralized managers, and unhappy customers. In spite of the potential problems associated with cost allocation, its use is prevalent in organizations. For example, personnel department costs are an indirect cost to other departments and are commonly allocated to those departments. Hospitals allocate the indirect costs of shared medical equipment among the departments that utilize it. Computer center costs are allocated among the computer users within the organization. The depreciation of manufacturing facilities is allocated among the products manufactured there.

For instance, Du Pont Canada allocates the cost of its engineering services to its manufacturing operations on a per hour basis for actual services delivered. The users are charged only for work received. However, these users also pay for the overhead and administrative costs of engineering services in approximate proportion to the business units' usage of these services. These overhead and administrative costs are more difficult to trace. Conflicts over cost allocations could arise between the different user groups and between the users and engineering services due to the ambiguous nature of these costs.

The widespread use of cost allocation implies that many benefits also result from the practice. However, an organization should clearly identify why costs are being allocated and the effect of those cost allocations on management behavior. Each cost allocation has planning, control, and external reporting implications. An organization often must make trade-offs among these considerations in choosing an allocation method.

ConceptReview

1. What are some examples of cost allocation?

2. What is the relation between common resources and cost objects?

Valley Clinic's general administration, building, and other departments (X-ray, nurses, and reception-ists) support the doctors. All these departments are indirect resources for the doctors and are used by all the doctors and many of the patients. The doctors and the patients are the cost objects or recipients of the allocated indirect costs from the indirect resources. A method must be chosen to allocate these indirect costs.

VALLEY CLINIC
(Continued)

REASONS FOR ALLOCATING INDIRECT COSTS

Most organizations use cost allocation, but the allocation of indirect costs remains controversial. One example is the allocation of indirect costs to responsibility centers controlled by managers. The controllability principle based on responsibility accounting suggests that managers should be held responsible for costs that they can control. Yet the allocation of indirect costs is often a distribution of costs to managers who have little or no control over those costs. Managers in many organizations complain bitterly about the allocation of certain indirect costs. While managers usually do not have complete control of indirect costs, they often partially affect the use of the indirect resource. For example, a production department that expands its number of workers places greater demands on the human resources department, which ultimately must expand or provide less service to the other departments.

The allocation of some indirect costs to products is also controversial. In Chapter Five, the pricing decision that maximized profits was determined through the use of marginal costs. A product cost that includes allocated fixed costs does not appear to be a likely representation of the marginal cost of making a product.

Given the contentious nature of the allocation of indirect costs, its use must provide some benefits. These benefits fall into three categories: (1) satisfying external requirements, (2) planning purposes, and (3) control purposes. These benefits are discussed in the following sections.

Satisfying External Requirements

Not all management accounting decisions are based on internal demand for information for making planning decisions and control. Organizations often have responsibilities to provide certain information to outside parties. For example, shareholders of corporations have the right to receive financial reports from it. Profit organizations must file tax returns to governmental bodies and not-for-profit organizations must file informational returns. Some contracts between different organizations specify that the costs incurred by one organization will be reimbursed by the other organization. Therefore, cost information must be communicated from one organization to the other.

Allocated indirect costs play an important role in each of these settings. In some cases, the method of allocating indirect costs is specified. In other cases, the

L0 2 Explain the role of allocating indirect costs for external financial reports, income tax reports, and cost reimbursement.

allocation of indirect costs provides opportunities for an organization to achieve some financial objective, such as reducing taxes. The following sections describe each setting and the corresponding cost allocation requirements and opportunities.

Financial Reports to Shareholders

The compilation of financial reports to shareholders is based on regulations from bodies such as the Financial Accounting Standards Board (FASB), the Securities and Exchange Commission (SEC), and other authoritative professional bodies such as the American Institute of Certified Public Accountants (AICPA) in the United States and the Canadian Institute of Chartered Accountants (CICA) in Canada. Rules from the FASB, SEC, and others do not cover all aspects of financial reporting. Moreover, financial accounting and taxation rules followed in one country are not necessarily the same as those followed in other countries. When rules from the regulatory bodies do not specify the appropriate accounting method, past accounting practices provide guidelines. Rules from the regulatory bodies and guidelines based on past accounting practices compose generally accepted accounting principles (GAAP).

The allocation of indirect manufacturing costs to products is a financial accounting procedure that has become part of GAAP as a result of past practice. Traditionally, indirect manufacturing costs, but not indirect selling and administrative overhead costs, have been allocated to products. In most wholesale, retail, and service organizations, no indirect costs are allocated to the product or service for financial reporting purposes.

The method used to allocate indirect manufacturing costs to products affects the calculation of profit. Indirect manufacturing costs that are allocated to products become part of the inventory cost and remain an asset until the product is sold. The allocation of indirect manufacturing costs to products that remain in ending inventory affects the current period's financially reported profits.

Numerical Example 9.1

A sports equipment manufacturer makes two types of balls: soccer balls and basketballs. It has no beginning inventory and during the year makes 20,000 soccer balls and 40,000 basketballs. The year's indirect manufacturing costs are $100,000. During the year, all the soccer balls and 30,000 of the basketballs are sold. The company is considering two possible methods of allocating indirect manufacturing costs: (1) to allocate $80,000 to the soccer balls and $20,000 to the basketballs or (2) to allocate $40,000 to the soccer balls and $60,000 to the basketballs. Which method causes a higher reported profit this period?

Solution

The number of unsold basketballs is 10,000/40,000, or 25%. Therefore, indirect manufacturing costs associated with the unsold basketballs remain an asset; they are not a deduction from income. Under the first method, 25% of the manufacturing overhead of $20,000, or $5,000, is not deducted from income in the current period. Under the second method, 25% of $60,000, or $15,000, is not deducted. Therefore, the second method causes reported profits to be $15,000 − $5,000, or $10,000 higher.

The pressure increases to allocate indirect costs to influence externally reported income if management compensation is based on that income number. Top-level managers frequently have bonuses tied to externally reported income, so they are concerned about how indirect manufacturing costs are allocated. There are constraints, however, in the allocation of costs for external reports; for example, the allocation method must follow GAAP. Importantly, managers cannot change the method of allocation without agreement from the external auditors.[1]

---

[1]When the units in inventory are sold, the indirect costs allocated to them are charged to income. Thus, managers cannot continually increase earnings by allocating excessive indirect costs to units in inventory without building inventories.

Reporting of Taxable Income

Tax accounting rules require inventory to be stated at cost, including an appropriate amount for indirect manufacturing costs. For example, inventory includes not only direct labor and direct material but also a fraction of factory depreciation, property taxes, and the salaries of its security guards. As in the case of external financial reports, the allocation of these indirect manufacturing costs among products can influence the calculation of taxable income.

The owners of an organization would like to allocate costs in a manner that reduces taxable income. The lower the taxable income, the lower are its tax payments. The methods of allocating indirect costs, however, are constrained by the rulings of the taxing authority.

Cost Reimbursement Contracts

Cost reimbursement is another reason for cost allocation. Government cost-based contracts and medical reimbursements for costs give rise to cost allocations. The U.S. Department of Defense purchases billions of dollars a year under cost-plus contracts. This type of contract states that the customer will compensate the supplier for the cost of the product or service plus some amount or percentage to provide the supplier a profit. For example, a security surveillance system contract may state that the supplier will be paid for the cost of the system plus a 10% markup to allow the supplier to make a profit.

Cost reimbursement contracts frequently are used when the product or service is unique and the cost of making it or providing it is uncertain. With uncertain costs, suppliers may be unwilling to offer the product or service. By promising to reimburse costs, the customer removes the risk of uncertain costs from the supplier. The customer, however, must worry about incentives for the supplier to control costs. A supplier that knows that all costs will be reimbursed is probably not as careful to control costs. For example, in 1999, the Japanese National Space Development Agency revamped its rocket program. The cost of Japanese rocket models was several times more than were those of foreign competitors. In order to contain costs, the agency allowed competition from foreign suppliers for components such as rocket engines.

Global Competition

Indirect cost allocation is a controversial part of cost reimbursement. If a supplier makes multiple products and sells some on a cost reimbursement basis, the supplier prefers to allocate as many indirect costs as possible to the products that are reimbursed based on cost. The allocation of more indirect costs to products subject to cost reimbursement translates into greater revenues for the organization.

Numerical Example 9.2

A Web page design firm has two types of clients, those that request a cost-plus 20% contract and those that request a fixed fee of $20,000 for design services. The firm completes 50 Web designs of each type during the year. The average direct costs of each design total $10,000. Indirect costs for the firm total $500,000. The first method of allocating indirect costs assigns $200,000 to the cost-plus designs and $300,000 to the fixed-fee designs. The second method allocates $400,000 to cost-plus designs and $100,000 to fixed-fee designs. Which method provides a higher profit for the Web page design firm?

Solution

The reported cost for the cost-plus designs under the first method follows:

Direct costs (50)($10,000)	$500,000
Indirect costs	200,000
Total	$700,000

The total profit of both the cost-plus and fixed-fee contracts using the first method of allocating indirect costs is calculated as follows:

Revenues	
Cost-plus ($700,000)(1.20)	$ 840,000
Fixed-fee (50)($20,000)	1,000,000
Total	$1,840,000
Costs	
Direct (100)($10,000)	1,000,000
Indirect	500,000
Net income	$ 340,000

The reported cost for the cost-plus designs under the second method is calculated as follows:

Direct costs (50)($10,000)	$500,000
Indirect costs	400,000
Total	$900,000

The total income of both the cost-plus and fixed-fee contracts using the second method of allocating indirect costs is determined as follows:

Revenues	
Cost-plus ($900,000)(1.20)	$1,080,000
Fixed-fee (50)($20,000)	1,000,000
Total	$2,080,000
Costs	
Direct (100)($10,000)	1,000,000
Indirect	500,000
Net income	$ 580,000

The second method provides a higher income because more reimbursable indirect costs are allocated to the cost-plus designs.

The allocation of indirect costs is a critical aspect of cost reimbursement contracts; therefore, the contracts should specify the allowable cost allocation methods. To help regulate cost allocations by suppliers of U.S. government agencies, the U.S. federal government established the Cost Accounting Standards Board (CASB). It issues standards covering the broad areas of cost measurement, cost assignment to accounting periods, and cost allocation within an accounting period. Suppliers of U.S. government agencies with cost-plus contracts must follow the accounting procedures specified by the CASB.

In addition to defense contractors, the revenues of public utilities, such as electric and gas companies, are tied to reported costs. Public utilities are often granted exclusive monopolies over service territories by their respective government authorities. In return for the monopoly, the government regulates the prices that the utility can charge its customers. In many cases, the regulated prices are based on reported costs, including allocated costs. In public-utility regulation, the major issue is deciding how to allocate the indirect costs of capacity, such as those of the electricity-generating plant, among the different classes of users (residential versus business customers). Cost allocation is the preeminent issue in many public-utility rate-setting cases.

In 1998 in Canada, the Ontario government decided to deregulate the electricity market and eliminate the monopoly of the public utility, Ontario Hydro. After more than 90 years, the market was opened to competition from independent companies. The government established a number of firms to replace its public utility. Two of these were Ontario Hydro Services, which was given responsibility for the existing transmission network, and Ontario Power Generation, which assumed control of the existing power-generating facilities. The government faced many technical and administrative challenges in the process of opening the market to competition by the end of 2000.

One critical issue was how to determine market rates in a deregulated retail and wholesale market given the existence of these two large firms. The independent firms needed assurance that they would have fair access to the transmission network and the power-generating facilities at competitive prices. A mechanism also was required to prevent Ontario Hydro Services and Ontario Power Generation from overcharging the independent companies by allocating an unfair proportion of their own operating costs to the new market entrants. To mitigate these potential abuses, the government established a Market Power Negotiation Agreement with short-, medium-, and long-term measures to regulate prices, to cap revenues, and to reduce the capacity of Ontario Power Generation. These steps included disposing of some of its assets. The government expected the new system to enhance competition by increasing the number of suppliers. Deregulated firms would create value for customers through a wider selection of energy services, options, and reduced prices.[2]

Customer Value

Different Accounting Systems for External and Internal Purposes

Using a single cost allocation method for external financial reports, tax reporting, and cost reimbursement can lead to conflicts. Management may want to choose cost allocation methods that increase present income to receive bonuses; owners may want to choose methods that reduce present income for tax purposes. In addition, increasing revenues through cost reimbursement may lead to a different cost allocation scheme. One solution is to have different accounting systems for each purpose.

In a similar fashion, the cost allocation methods used for external reports need not affect the choice of cost allocation methods for internal purposes. One reason for using a single accounting system is to reduce accounting costs since having multiple accounting systems is more costly. The disadvantage of having a single accounting system is the conflict that might arise from using the system for different purposes. These conflicts in external reporting can lead to lost revenues and higher income taxes. Losses from using a single accounting system within the organization occur due to the conflict between planning and control. These issues are discussed in the next two sections.

Concept**Review**

1. How is cost allocation used with external financial and tax reporting?
2. How do cost reimbursement contracts influence cost allocations?

Valley Clinic is not a manufacturing concern with inventory, so it has no cost allocation problems in terms of manufactured products for financial reporting or income tax reporting. It does, however, charge the self-paying patients based on the cost of services provided. In this case, the patient is the ultimate cost object, and general administration and other service costs are allocated to the different

VALLEY CLINIC
(Continued)

---

[2]Detailed information about the deregulation of the power market is available at www.ohsc.com and www.ontariopowergeneration.com.

patients. Given that the revenues generated from other patients are either fixed (HMO patients) or based on predetermined rates for the services provided (Medicare and insurance companies), Valley Clinic would like to allocate as many indirect costs to the self-paying patients as is ethically possible. Self-paying patients are charged for the allocated and direct costs of services that they use; however, they are not restricted to coming to Valley Clinic, so there are other limits on what they can be charged. For example, should self-paying patients be charged for the cost of supplying services to individuals who do not pay their medical bills? In choosing cost allocation methods for patients, Valley Clinic must offset the cost of disgruntled, self-paying patients and the benefit of additional short-term revenue. A strategy of increasing revenue in the short run by charging self-paying patients more can lead to a long-run loss in revenue if those patients decide to go to other clinics.

Cost Allocation for Planning Purposes

LO 3   Identify reasons for cost allocation for planning purposes.

Planning Decisions

Information for planning purposes is used to make better decisions through increased understanding of the problem. The allocation of indirect costs can provide managers information that allows them to make better decisions. For example, the allocation of indirect costs provides a better measure of the cost of providing a product or service. The allocation of indirect costs also is a communication mechanism to let managers know how their actions are affecting costs in the rest of the organization.

Estimation of the Cost of Products and Services

Managers must make planning decisions related to products and services. In particular, managers make pricing and product-mix decisions, which should be based on the cost of providing those products and services. The allocation of indirect costs to products improves planning decisions if the allocated indirect costs represent the opportunity costs of providing those products and services.

The allocated indirect costs do not necessarily equate to the opportunity cost of using a resource. For external reporting purposes, all indirect manufacturing costs are allocated to products. However, the use of facilities for which no better alternatives exist does not constitute an opportunity cost. The cost of the facility allocated to products for external reporting purposes, therefore, does not necessarily reflect an opportunity cost of making the product. The estimation of the opportunity cost of the indirect resource requires a clear understanding of how a product or service uses the indirect resource and of its alternative uses.

Communication of Costs to Improve Planning Decisions

The allocated indirect costs also serve as a communication device to inform managers of the cost of their actions to the entire organization. When managers use

A "green thumb" takes pleasure in gardening, but also in the enjoyment that the colorful blooms bring to passersby. The view is free, and requires no gardening effort on the viewers' part. A positive externality results, as the gardener receives no direct compensation and cannot charge for the view.

internal resources or services, they impose costs on other parts of the organization. For example, most universities offer advising services to all students, the cost of which is allocated to the different colleges within the university based on the number of students in each. The allocated cost is intended to represent the cost of advising additional students. If a college accepts more students, the latter will use the advising services, and the advising office must hire more advisors. Otherwise, the quality of student advising declines. By allocating the cost of advising services to the different colleges, the university is communicating to the college deans the cost of providing these services. With this additional information, the deans can make better decisions about admission levels.

Managers are not always aware of some of the costs (or benefits) that they impose on other parts of the organization. In many cases, these costs or benefits are imposed on others without either their consent or direct compensation. These costs or benefits are called **externalities.** Externalities are usually considered in a social context. For example, pollution is a negative externality or cost imposed on others. Automobile exhaust pollutes the air, yet drivers do not pay for the pollution costs that their driving imposes on others (except via gasoline taxes), nor are the consumers of polluted air paid directly for the polluted air they breathe. Education contains a positive externality because people derive benefits from having more educated citizens with whom to interact. Well-tended gardens of private homes create positive externalities by providing a pleasant view for passersby and increasing the property values of neighboring homes.

Externalities pervade organizations. Improvements in tracking materials in the supply room provide positive externalities to the manufacturing department, as material requisitions can be met more quickly. Hiring another salesperson imposes negative externalities on the human resource department and other departments that provide services to employees. Adding a new product or service can impose either positive or negative externalities on other products or services of the same organization. The communication of the costs or benefits of externalities through the allocation of indirect costs allows managers to make more informed decisions. The problem with externalities, however, is that they are difficult to identify and measure. Therefore, allocated costs often are a proxy for the cost of an externality.

Concept**Review**

1. What type of cost should cost allocations approximate if they are used for planning purposes?
2. How are cost allocations used to resolve externality issues?

Cost Allocation for Control Reasons

Motivation and control are likely explanations for the prevalence of cost allocations within organizations. Cost allocations control managers through the allocation of resources and the effect of cost allocations on performance measures. Cost allocations also allow managers to monitor each other. The way in which indirect costs are allocated affects managers' behavior. Therefore, the choice of the allocation method is a tool for controlling managers.

LO 4   Identify reasons for cost allocation for control purposes.

Control Decisions

Cost Allocations and the Allocation of Resources

The allocation of costs in some organizations coincides with the allocation of resources. For example, universities may shift resources from one college to another by allocating more general administrative costs to one than another. The allocated costs are like a tax that is imposed on each college. The university president constrains the deans of the colleges by allocating costs to them and forcing them to pay a higher tax. Funds are distributed to the deans after the allocated general administration costs have been deducted.

Cost Allocations and Performance Measures

LO 5   Describe how the various reasons for cost allocation can create conflict within the organization.

Responsibility centers are evaluated, at least partially, based on accounting numbers. Costs, profit, and return on investment (ROI) are performance measures commonly used to evaluate managers. These accounting numbers are influenced by the allocation of indirect costs from resources used by multiple responsibility centers. For example, suppose that the marketing department's costs are allocated to the various responsibility centers that benefit from marketing; these costs become part of the performance measures of the managers of the other responsibility centers.

As discussed in Chapter Six, performance measures ideally should reveal the actions of the manager being evaluated. As discussed earlier, the controllability principle is based on the theory that managers should be evaluated on costs that they can control. Therefore, the allocation of indirect costs to responsibility centers for the purpose of measuring performance should occur only if the manager has some control over either the cause of the indirect costs or how they are allocated to the responsibility center. For example, if general administrative costs over which a manager has no control are arbitrarily allocated to that individual, her or his performance measures will be affected and the manager will be rightfully upset.

However, an organization may choose to allocate uncontrollable indirect costs using methods that managers can affect. In doing so, the organization can motivate managers to achieve certain organizational goals. For example, suppose an organization would like to reduce the number of employees; its president chooses to allocate the uncontrollable general administrative costs based on the number of employees in each responsibility center. To reduce the amount of general administrative costs allocated to their responsibility centers, the managers reduce the number of their employees. Therefore, the allocation of general administrative costs motivates managers to achieve the organization's goals even though a reduction in employees may not affect general administrative costs.

Cost allocations act as a tax system; therefore, the organization uses the allocation of general administrative costs to tax the hiring of employees. As in any tax system, individuals modify their behavior to reduce the taxes that are imposed on them. If a characteristic of the responsibility center, such as the number of employees, is used to allocate indirect costs, that characteristic is taxed, and the manager will choose to use less of it. If multiple characteristics are used to allocate indirect costs, the manager of the responsibility center will use less of the heavily taxed characteristics and more of those that are taxed less or not at all.

Cost allocations change behavior within organizations. By imposing taxes on certain characteristics used to allocate costs, the organization is motivating managers to reduce those characteristics. The organization should recognize, however, that although taxing certain characteristics may achieve short-term goals, it might lead in the long term to perverse decisions by managers. For example, Tektronix, an electronics manufacturer, used direct labor to allocate indirect costs. Engineers were encouraged to reduce the cost of the products, so they reduced the amount of direct labor required to make new products. Eventually, the manufacturing plant was almost fully automated, but the company's total costs were even higher.

To avoid such perverse behavior, an organization should continually evaluate its cost allocation methods. If the costs of an indirect resource are being allocated at a rate different than the opportunity cost of using that indirect resource, managers will have an incentive to use either too much or too little. In the case of Tektronix, direct labor was taxed at a rate higher than the opportunity cost of using it. This situation led to excessive use of other factors, such as machines, and a correspondingly higher cost of production.

Mutual Monitoring Incentives

The usual method of monitoring behavior within firms is for superiors to monitor subordinates. Monitoring can occur, however, among managers at the same level of the organization. This control, or **mutual monitoring,** can result when cost allocations are made from one responsibility center to another. For instance, suppose that the costs of a computer service department are allocated to other departments. If those allocated costs become too high, other departmental managers will complain and urge the computer service department to cut costs. Managers who have the opportunity to acquire computer services elsewhere will force the computer service department to lower its costs. Otherwise, they will seek other options, such as outsourcing their computer needs. If costs from the computer service department are not allocated to other departments, the other departmental managers will not be concerned about cost control in the computer service department, resulting in less mutual monitoring. The discipline to control costs in the computer service department will have to be imposed by higher-level management.

In order to maintain control of costs and to encourage efficiency of its support services, DuPont Canada allows its manufacturing operations to outsource some services that its own engineering group could provide. Engineering services must be cost competitive and prove that they add value to the customer on other dimensions beyond the cost of those services.

Concept**Review**

1. How can cost allocations affect resources available to managers?
2. How can cost allocations influence the behavior of managers?
3. What is mutual monitoring and how is it influenced by cost allocations?

Cost allocation at Valley Clinic plays an important role in determining the performance measures and rewards of the doctors. As noted, each doctor is rewarded based on the profit that he or she generates for the clinic. Costs that are allocated to the doctors, who are the cost objects under this system, affect the profit associated with each doctor. General administration and other service department costs are allocated to the doctors to determine the profits generated by each. Valley Clinic must be careful in allocating costs to the doctors; they may have an incentive to under- or overuse a service department if costs are allocated by certain methods. Valley Clinic is very concerned about maintaining its reputation for offering top-quality medical service. The clinic does not want the cost allocation scheme to lead doctors to make decisions that could harm that reputation.

VALLEY CLINIC
(Continued)

BASIC STEPS OF COST ALLOCATION

All indirect cost allocation methods are composed of the same series of steps. Chapter Three discussed the steps leading to the tracing of indirect costs through cost drivers to cost objects. The steps described in this section are the same except that the term *allocation base* is used instead of *cost driver*. An **allocation base** is a characteristic of the cost object on which costs are allocated. A cost driver is a type of allocation base; it is the characteristic of the cost object that causes the indirect costs. Cost drivers are important for estimating the cost of a product or other cost object. Allocation bases, however, may be chosen for reasons other than cost estimation, such as control. As described in the previous section, cost allocations can motivate managers to make certain decisions.

LO 6 Allocate indirect costs using five basic steps.

The steps for cost allocation are (1) defining the cost objects, (2) accumulating the indirect costs in cost pools, (3) choosing an allocation base, (4) estimating an application rate, and (5) distributing indirect costs based on usage of the allocation base. Each step is described in the following sections.

Defining the Cost Objects

The organization must decide what departments, products, customers, suppliers, or processes should receive the indirect costs. For example, users of the computer center may be defined as cost objects, or the computer center itself may be chosen as a cost object. The cost object can be a subunit of the organization, such as a cost or profit center. As described in Chapter Three, services and products generated by an organization are treated as cost objects. In each case, the choice of a cost object is based on the desire to obtain cost information about the cost object that is useful for planning purposes or to influence the decisions of managers for control purposes.

ORGANIZATIONAL VALUE

The Center for Substance Abuse Treatment developed a uniform accounting package to provide cost data to manage its operations and to determine program effectiveness and efficiency. An initial step was to develop a cost allocation methodology to combine financial, service, and client data into cost pools and profiles. Its cost allocation system allows the Center to determine the cost by unit of service (e.g., medical examination, counseling, client education, and transportation) and the unit cost per client. Information available to meet external reporting requirements also provides internal management with data to analyze the costs and benefits of different treatment options. Cost data are standardized to enable the Center to measure and evaluate the outcomes of its programs and services.[3]

VALLEY CLINIC (Continued)

Valley Clinic has two cost objects, doctors and patients. The remaining part of this chapter analyzes the allocation of costs to doctors to determine their share of the profit. This allocation of costs also influences doctors' decisions to use common resources. A similar type of analysis, but with a different goal (cost reimbursement), would have to be performed to allocate costs to patients.

Accumulating the Indirect Costs in Cost Pools

The common use of a resource, such as a machine, building, administrative service, or a production or service department, creates indirect costs. Costs associated with these resources are accumulated in **cost pools.** The size of the cost pool depends on how resources are aggregated. For example, each machine could have a separate cost pool, or the costs associated with all the machines could be placed in a single cost pool.

Indirect costs associated with a resource include all the costs that can be traced to the resource. For example, the indirect cost pool associated with the computer department includes direct costs to the department, such as the cost of the hardware, the labor costs of its employees, and computer paper and supplies.

In addition, a cost pool may contain costs that are associated only indirectly with the resource. These indirect costs are allocated to the cost pool from other cost pools that represent commonly shared resources. For example, the maintenance department is a resource that many other departments use. If the computing department uses the maintenance department, the computing department cost pool should contain allocated costs from the maintenance department cost pool.

[3]Information on this accounting system can be found at www.samhsa.gov.

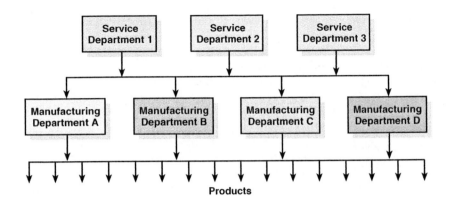

Figure 9.1

Two-Stage Allocation
Procedure

Multi-stage cost allocation occurs when costs are allocated through a series of cost pools. Figure 9.1 is an example of a two-stage allocation procedure. The costs of internal service departments are allocated to production departments that use the internal service departments. Internal service departments include human resources, accounting, maintenance, and computer services. Production department costs then are allocated to the different products that use the different production departments. Production departments, such as assembly departments, are directly associated with the product or service that the organization provides. In this case, the production departments are the intermediate cost objects, and the products and services are the final cost objects.

Valley Clinic chooses the following cost pools for allocating costs to doctors:

VALLEY CLINIC
(Continued)

Cost Pool	Types of Costs
General administration	Salaries of director, accountant, bookkeeper, secretary, supplies, insurance
Building	Rent, cleaning, utilities
X-rays	Technician's salary, X-ray machine, film
Nurses	Salaries
Receptionists	Salaries

Choosing an Allocation Base

An allocation base is a measurement of a characteristic used to distribute indirect costs of a cost pool to cost objects. Each cost pool may have a different allocation base. Under ABC described in Chapter Three, cost drivers are the allocation bases that distribute costs from overhead activity cost pools to different responsibility centers and products. The cost driver chosen through ABC is intended to reflect the usage of the overhead activity. An allocation base, however, need not even be associated with the costs in the cost pools. As noted earlier, for example, a company might choose an allocation base to reduce a particular organizational characteristic. If the number of defects is chosen as the allocation base for general administration costs, managers would be motivated to reduce the number of defects so that fewer costs would be allocated to their responsibility center. The number of defects might not be associated with general administrative costs. Instead, the allocation base is chosen to achieve an organizational goal to reduce

Hitachi first began operations in Japan in 1910 making electric motors. It is now a global giant manufacturing a wide range of electronic products. Its main product lines include consumer goods (HDTVs, VCRs, and DVD players), industrial equipment (construction and power tools), information systems (printers, copiers, and software), materials (wire and cable), and services (transportation and financial). In one of its plants in the consumer division, Hitachi manufactures VCR players. This plant is heavily automated but continues to allocate overhead based on direct labor, even though the managers know that direct labor does not reflect the cause-and-effect relation between overhead and the overhead cost drivers. Hitachi managers continue to use direct labor as the allocation base because they are committed to long-term aggressive automation. Taxing direct labor is a way to reduce direct labor.

Does Hitachi use cost allocation primarily for planning or control purposes? Why would cost allocation for the purpose of accurate product costs be less important in the consumer electronics industry? How does the cost allocation procedure at Hitachi relate to its strategy?

Sources: www.hitachi.co.jp; T. Hiromoto, "Another Hidden Edge: Japanese Management Accounting," *Harvard Business Review*, July–August 1988.

defects. Japanese firms often use simpler allocation systems based on direct labor. Less precision is accepted in order to focus management attention on direct labor, as the latter tends to be a scarce resource.[4]

The choice of the allocation base depends on the goals of the organization. Cost allocations are used internally for two primary purposes, making planning decisions and control. Therefore, no single choice of an allocation base is always right or always wrong. Table 9.1 shows the choice of allocation bases made by 49 U.S. banks to allocate various indirect costs (executive salaries, central office rent or depreciation, advertising and marketing expenses, and data processing and accounting expenses) to responsibility centers. The allocation bases are listed from the most important (frequently used) method to the least important. In general, the most frequently used allocation bases are those that have the greatest association with the cost being allocated. For example, the most important method for allocating executives' salaries is time spent by executives in the responsibility center. Rent is allocated most frequently based on square footage. Advertising and data processing are usually allocated based on the time spent on the responsibility center. The allocation of advertising and marketing expense commonly utilizes the time spent by marketing personnel on center activities as the allocation base.

Table 9.1 also indicates the diversity in the selection of allocation bases. This diversity might be the result of different

Table 9.1

Ranking of Allocation Methods Used by Large U.S. Banks

	Types of Overhead Costs Allocated to Responsibility Centers			
Level of Importance*	Executive Salaries	Central Office Rent or Depreciation	Advertising and Other Marketing Expense	Data Processing and Accounting Expense
1	Time spent by executives	Square footage	Time spent by marketing personnel	Time spent by accountants, etc.
2	Personnel costs	Personnel costs	Number of customers served by the center	Transactions volume
3	Transactions volume	Transactions volume	Other (including "no allocation")	Personnel costs
4	Other (including "no allocation")	Number of customers served by the center	Transactions volume	Other (including "no allocation")
5	Number of customers served by the center	Interest costs	Personnel costs	Number of customers served by the center
6	Interest costs	Other (including "no allocation")	Interest costs	Interest costs
7	Square footage	(Not reported)	Square footage	Square footage

*1 = most, 7 = least important.

Source: M. Gardner and L. Lammers, "Cost Accounting in Large Banks," *Management Accounting*, April 1988, Table 3.

---

[4]K. A. Merchant and M. D. Shields, "When and Why to Measure Costs *Less* Accurately to Improve Decision Making," *Accounting Horizons* 7, no. 2 (June 1993), pp. 76–81.

goals within the sampled banks. Another factor in the choice of allocation base is the ease of measurement. A particular allocation base might be closely associated with an indirect cost but could be difficult and costly to measure. For example, in Table 9.1, the most popular allocation base for executive salaries is the time spent by executives in each responsibility center. To measure this time is a nuisance, however, and some organizations might choose an easier allocation base to measure.

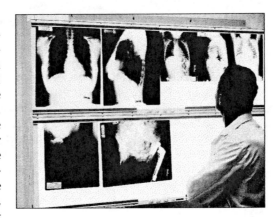

Medical costs are a significant percentage of gross national expenditure in many countries. When doctors and patients do not observe or pay the cost of medical procedures, such as X-rays, they tend to overuse them. Overuse degrades the quality of service and increases costs. Allocation based on the number of patients motivates doctors to utilize the service, but can result in too many X-rays, as the doctor's incremental cost is zero.

In choosing the allocation bases for the cost pools, Valley Clinic wants to motivate the doctors to use common resources efficiently and to provide good service to patients. The following choices are made with those goals in mind:

VALLEY CLINIC
(Continued)

Cost Pool	Allocation Base
General administration	Number of patients
Building	Number of examination rooms
X-rays	Number of X-ray patients
Nurses	Hours used
Receptionists	Number of patients

These choices are based partly on recognizing the cost of using common resources and partly on achieving the goal of good patient care. For example, insurance, a major general administration cost, is closely related to the number of patients that a doctor sees. The number of examination rooms is used as an allocation base to discourage doctors from tying up too many examination rooms while patients wait to see them. Each doctor has the choice of the number of examination rooms to reserve for his or her patients. The number of X-ray patients, rather than the number of X-rays, is used as an allocation base for the X-ray department due to the fixed cost of preparing the patient for a series of X-rays. Moreover, the clinic does not want to skimp on the number of X-rays. Under this system, the incremental cost of another X-ray to the doctor is zero, so doctors will tend to have too many X-rays taken on a particular patient. The use of staff, nurses, and receptionists is a problem in the clinic. The allocation bases tend to encourage doctors to use the reception staff more and the nurses less because the allocated costs of using nurses increases by hour of use. Under this system, however, there is no incremental cost to the doctors of using receptionists to perform another task. Given that the salary of a nurse is higher than that of a receptionist, the clinic prefers to have receptionists do some tasks normally performed by nurses.

Estimating an Application Rate

Once the allocation base for a cost pool has been selected, an application rate is calculated. Normally, the application rate is determined at the beginning of the year, prior to the actual incurrence of the common cost. A predetermined application rate allows for the allocation of costs during the period before common costs are completely measured. The allocated cost information is more timely with predetermined application rates but may not reflect actual costs incurred. The sum of all indirect costs allocated to cost objects with a predetermined application rate does not usually equal the actual indirect costs. This problem is discussed in Chapter Ten. In this section, we assume that management can make accurate estimates of indirect costs and allocation bases. For simplicity, we also assume that no difference exists between allocated indirect costs and actual indirect costs.

The application rate for an allocation base is commonly estimated with the following ratio:

$$\frac{\text{Estimated dollars in the cost pool}}{\text{Estimate total usage of the allocation base}}$$

As an example, suppose that the estimated cost pool of the computer service department for the next period is $400,000. The allocation base is the number of hours that computer service personnel work on projects for different responsibility centers. The managers of the responsibility centers estimate that they will use 5,000 hours of computer service personnel time. Therefore, the application rate is $400,000/5,000 hours, or $80 per hour.

A number of problems are inherent in this application rate. First, cost allocation for planning decisions should be performed to obtain estimates of the cost of using the indirect resource. Some of the estimated computer costs may be sunk if they are estimated using a historical cost system. For example, the cost pool may contain historical cost depreciation rather than the change in market value of a fixed asset (often referred to as *economic depreciation*).

Second, cost pools usually contain fixed costs with respect to the allocation base. For example, some costs of the computer service department do not vary with the number of hours that its personnel work for other departments. The cost of using some of the hardware is likely to be fixed with respect to the number of hours that computer service personnel work. All the computer service costs, however, are allocated as if they varied with the number of hours that its personnel work. After the fixed costs have been incurred, the application rate, which includes both fixed and variable costs, exceeds the variable costs of operating the computer service department. This relation is shown in Figure 9.2 with the cost application curve being steeper than the total cost line. If allocated costs are higher than the

Figure 9.2

Applied and Estimated Costs

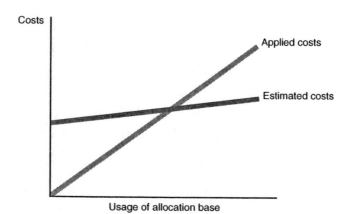

incremental costs of operating the computer service department, managers will tend to use the computer service department less than they should.

Numerical Example 9.3

A motor pool allocates costs to other departments of the same organization based on the number of miles driven in company cars. The motor pool expects to incur annual fixed costs of $200,000 and variable costs of $0.20 per mile driven. Company cars are expected to be driven a total of 800,000 miles. What application rate does the motor pool use? How does that application rate lead to underuse of the motor pool and costly behavior by other departments?

Solution

The application rate is the total expected costs in the motor pool divided by the total expected miles driven:

$$\frac{\$200,000 + (\$0.20/\text{mile})(800,000 \text{ miles})}{800,000 \text{ miles}} = \$0.45/\text{mile}$$

This application rate, however, is higher than the incremental cost of operating an automobile, which is $0.20 per mile. The application rate acts as a transfer price. Therefore, managers in other departments will choose to use other means of transportation if the cost per mile of alternative transportation is less than the application rate of $0.45 per mile for the motor pool. The entire organization would benefit, however, if the motor pool were used whenever the cost of the alternative means of transportation exceeded $0.20 per mile.

Fixed costs in the cost pool also mean that the application rate is affected by total estimated usage of the allocation base. If the cost pool contains only variable costs, a 10% increase in the estimated usage of the allocation base causes a 10% increase in the size of the cost pool. If fixed costs are in the cost pool, however, the size of the cost pool will increase proportionally less than the usage of the allocation base. Therefore, higher estimated usage of the allocation base causes the application rate to be lower. If the estimated usage of the allocation base declines, the application rate becomes higher. In other words, a reduction in the allocation base means that the fixed costs must be spread over fewer units of the allocation base.

Numerical Example 9.4

Use the data in Numerical Example 9.3, except assume that the motor pool expects company cars to be driven a total of 1,000,000 miles. What application rate does the motor pool use?

Solution

The application rate is the total expected costs in the motor pool divided by the total expected miles driven:

$$\frac{\$200,000 + (\$0.20/\text{mile})(1,000,000 \text{ miles})}{1,000,000 \text{ miles}} = \$0.40/\text{mile}$$

This rate is less than the application rate when it is assumed that 800,000 miles will be driven.

With fixed costs in the cost pool, one responsibility center can affect the application rate used to allocate costs to other responsibility centers. In other words, if one department decides not to use an internal service represented by a cost pool, the application rate increases, and the service becomes more costly for other departments. When managers affect the cost allocations to other managers, the controllability principle is violated. Managers prefer application rates that are insulated from the effects of other managers. If the cost pool being allocated includes fixed costs, application rates calculated by the total estimated usage of the allocation base do not insulate managers from the performance of other responsibility centers.

Numerical Example 9.5

Use the data in Numerical Example 9.3. Suppose that one department decides not to use the motor pool because of alternative transportation opportunities, and the total number of miles expected to be driven is reduced to 600,000. What is the effect on the application rate?

Solution

The new application rate follows:

$$\frac{\$200,000 \ + \ (\$0.20/mile)(600,000 \ miles)}{600,000 \ miles} = \$0.53/mile$$

The application rate is higher than the rate of $0.45 per mile in Numerical Example 9.3, as the remaining users of the motor pool must pay a higher share of the fixed costs. The fixed costs of operating the motor pool must be spread over fewer users.

VALLEY CLINIC
(Continued)

The following table is used to calculate application rates at Valley Clinic:

Cost Pool	Expected Costs	Expected Allocation Base	Application Rate
General administration	$500,000	25,000 patients	$20/patient
Building	100,000	20 exam rooms	$5,000/exam room
X-rays	50,000	500 X-ray patients	$100/X-ray patient
Nurses	200,000	12,500 hours	$16/hour
Receptionists	75,000	25,000 patients	$3/patient

Distributing Indirect Costs Based on Usage of the Allocation Base

Once the application rate for the allocation base has been estimated, indirect costs are allocated to cost objects as they use the allocation base. For example, if hours of maintenance is the allocation base of the maintenance department cost pool, maintenance costs are allocated to cost objects when the cost object incurs hours of maintenance.

Numerical Example 9.6

The application rate for maintenance department costs is $20 per hour of service. The following is the usage of the maintenance department by other departments:

Department	Hours
Accounting	50
Sales	80
Manufacturing	200

How much of the maintenance department costs are allocated to these departments?

Solution

Department	Hours	Application Rate	Allocated Costs
Accounting	50	$20	$1,000
Sales	80	20	1,600
Manufacturing	200	20	4,000
Total costs allocated			$6,600

In summary, the cost allocation procedure allows for the assignment of costs from a cost pool to cost objects. Cost objects are identified, costs are accumulated in cost pools, allocation bases are chosen, application rates are calculated, and in-direct costs are allocated. These steps are repeated several times in the case of multi-stage cost allocations. A more difficult problem exists, however, when inter-actions exist between cost pools. As a result, one or more cost pools are the cost ob-jects of other cost pools. For example, suppose that different cost pools represent the accounting and maintenance departments and each department provides ser-vices to the other department. In other words, the accounting department uses the maintenance department, and the maintenance department uses the accounting department. The interaction of service departments leads to a special cost alloca-tion problem. The Appendix of this chapter examines these interactions and their accounting treatment.

Concept**Review**

1. How are cost objects chosen?
2. What is a cost pool?
3. What is the purpose of an allocation base?
4. How is an application rate calculated?
5. How are common costs allocated to multiple cost objects?
6. What is the difference between a cost driver and an allocation base?

Each doctor at the clinic acts as a profit center and is evaluated and rewarded based on the profit that he or she generates. Dr. Kim, a doctor at Valley Clinic, has 4,000 patients who generated total revenues of $400,000 during the year. Forty of her patients used X-rays. Dr. Kim used two patient rooms and 3,000 hours of nurse time. The profit associated with her is determined as follows:

VALLEY CLINIC
(Continued)

Revenues	$400,000			
Costs				
	Cost Pool	**Application Rate**	**Usage**	**Costs Allocated**
	General administration	$20/patient	4,000 patients	$ 80,000
	Building	$5,000/patient room	2 patient rooms	10,000
	X-rays	$100/X-ray patient	40 X-ray patients	4,000
	Nurses	$16/hour	3,000 hours	48,000
	Receptionists	$3/patient	4,000 patients	12,000
	Total costs			$154,000
	Profit			$246,000

The profit of $246,000 generated by Dr. Kim represents her share of the total clinic profit. Notice that the $246,000 profit is Dr. Kim's profit share and her compensation for the medical services that she provided.

You decide

SEGMENT REPORTING

Segment reporting is the process of developing accounting reports for the separate units of the organization. The income of each unit is measured to evaluate its per-formance and that of its managers. The ability to identify profitable and unprofitable segments of the business allows the president of an organization to add or withdraw

LO 7 Create segment reports for the organization.

resources from the segments and to reward the managers appropriately. If internal transfers occur among the units, the management accountant must use transfer prices to calculate each unit's income. The profit of each unit or segment should reflect the sales to other segments within the organization and to external customers.

The income of each segment also includes costs of resources that are used by multiple segments. Therefore, these resource costs must be allocated to the segments. The internal purposes for allocating costs to segments are (1) to communicate information to managers of the different segments and (2) to motivate the managers to make decisions consistent with organizational goals. External reports also use segment reporting. Corporations are required to report the profit of their segments that correspond to different lines of business and geographic areas. For example, Du Pont reports the profit of the following lines of business: agriculture and nutrition, nylon, performance coatings and polymers, pharmaceuticals, pigments and chemicals, polyesters, specialty fibers, specialty polymers, and other businesses. Each line of business is a cost object and a recipient of costs allocated from organizational resources used by other lines of business. Each line of business is also a profit center with both internal and external sales recognized. Du Pont reports the sales by segment and the intersegment transfers to determine its overall financial results.

Companies also must report profits from different geographical areas. Du Pont, for example, identifies profits separately for its North American, Asia Pacific, South American, European, and other geographical areas. This process also involves transfer pricing and the allocation of costs.

External reports include segment reporting to provide external users, such as investors, more information about the profitability of the organization's different components. If segment reports were not included in external reports, investors would not be able to discern whether a highly profitable segment is offsetting an unprofitable one.

Numerical Example **9.7**

Green Corporation makes two products, chemex and citrol. The corporation has two product lines. A separate manager is responsible for each division. The chemex division sells 50 tons of chemex on the open market for $10,000 per ton and transfers 20 tons to the citrol division. The citrol division sells 100 tons of citrol on the open market for $20,000 per ton. Variable costs per ton are $5,000 for chemex division and $8,000 for citrol division, excluding the cost of chemex. Fixed costs are $200,000 for the chemex division and $400,000 for the citrol division. The central administration allocates $100,000 of fixed costs to the chemex division and $500,000 to the citrol division. Calculate the profit of the two divisions, using the market price as the transfer price of chemex.

Solution

	Chemex Division	Citrol Division
Revenues		
Open market sales	$500,000	$2,000,000
Internal sales of chemex	200,000	
Variable costs		
Internal purchase of chemex		(200,000)
Other variable costs	(350,000)	(800,000)
Contribution margin	$350,000	$1,000,000
Fixed costs	(200,000)	(400,000)
Profit before allocated costs	$150,000	$ 600,000
Allocated costs	(100,000)	(500,000)
Divisional profit	$ 50,000	$ 100,000

If all the central administration costs have been allocated, Green Corporation's profit is the sum of the profit of the two divisions, or $150,000.

In Numerical Example 9.7, the allocated costs, fixed costs, and internal sales are reported separately in the segment reports of the two divisions. These costs and sales are highlighted to provide managers increased information for decision making. For example, allocated costs might be eliminated for performance evaluation if they are not controlled by, or affect the behavior of, the divisional manager. Reporting each division's contribution margin allows a manager to ignore fixed costs when making incremental planning decisions. Internal sales should be highlighted to identify interactions among the divisions. These interactions provide important information when considering the elimination of or changes in one of the divisions.

**Control
Decisions**

Segment reporting is just one of the results of the transfer-pricing and cost allocation process; product costs are another result. The next chapter describes different methods of allocating costs to products.

ConceptReview

1. What is the purpose of segment reporting?
2. How do transactions with other units of the organizations affect segment reports?

SUMMARY

Describe the relations among common resources, indirect costs, and cost objects.   Common resources are resources that are used by more than one subunit or product of an organization. Common resources generate indirect costs, which may be allocated to the users of the common resource. The recipients of allocated indirect costs are called *cost objects.*

Explain the role of allocating indirect costs for external financial reports, income tax reports, and cost reimbursement.   For external financial reporting and income tax reports, manufacturing overhead is traditionally allocated to products. Costs allocated to products sold on a cost reimbursement contract provide additional revenues for the organization.

Identify reasons for cost allocation for planning purposes.   If allocated costs provide better estimates of the opportunity cost of providing a product or service, they are valuable for planning purposes. In this case, cost allocations communicate information to managers about the opportunity cost of using common resources.

Identify reasons for cost allocation for control purposes.   Common cost allocation is a method for allocating scarce resources in some organizations. It is also used for external reporting, cost reimbursement, and motivating managers to use common resources in a manner consistent with organizational goals.

Additionally, cost allocation can be used for mutual monitoring.

Describe how the various reasons for cost allocation can create conflict within the organization.   Costs are allocated for external reporting, planning decisions, and control purposes. A single cost allocation system will lead to conflict, as each reason for cost allocation might imply a different allocation method.

Allocate indirect costs using five basic steps.   Indirect costs are allocated by (1) defining the cost objects, (2) accumulating indirect costs in cost pools, (3) choosing an allocation base, (4) estimating an application rate, and (5) distributing indirect costs based on usage of the allocation base by the cost objects.

Create segment reports for the organization.   Segment reports disclose the profit of the organization's subunits. Their profit reflects transfer prices and cost allocation.

Use direct, step-down, and reciprocal methods to allocate costs of service departments that interact. (Appendix)   The direct method ignores any interaction of service departments. The step-down method allocates service department costs in sequence and recognizes some of the interaction of service departments. The reciprocal method solves simultaneous equations (one for each service department) to account for all interactions of service departments.

KEY TERMS

allocation base   A characteristic of the cost object used to distribute indirect costs. *(p. 293)*

cost allocation   The distribution of indirect costs among cost objects. *(p. 284)*

cost object   The subject of interest in determining the cost. *(p. 284)*

cost pool   The accumulation of costs related to an indirect activity. *(p. 294)*

direct method   A method of allocating service department costs that ignores any interaction of the service departments. *(p. 305)*

externality   The effect of a decision on parties other than the contracting parties. *(p. 291)*

multi-stage cost allocation   The process of allocating costs to cost objects followed by the allocation of costs from those cost objects to other cost objects. *(p. 295)*

mutual monitoring   A process of having members of an organization monitor and control each other. *(p. 293)*

reciprocal method   A method of allocating service department costs that recognizes all interactions among the service departments. *(p. 308)*

segment reporting   The process of developing accounting reports for the separate units of an organization. *(p. 301)*

step-down method   A method of allocating service department costs that sequentially allocates the costs of the service departments. *(p. 306)*

APPENDIX

Allocating Costs of Service Departments with Interactions

L0 8   Use direct, step-down, and reciprocal methods to allocate costs of service departments that interact. (Appendix)

In this chapter, cost allocations flow from the cost pools of indirect costs to cost objects. This flow of allocated costs could occur in multiple stages as in Figure 9.1, but costs do not flow back to any cost pools after the costs of that cost pool have been allocated. In other words, costs could be allocated from the computer service department to the accounting department, but accounting costs could not be allocated back to the computer service department. In many organizations, service departments, represented by different cost pools, provide services to each other. The cost pool of each department is a cost object of the other. This interaction leads to a special cost allocation problem. How can costs be allocated from one service department to another and then back again?

With reciprocal service department costs, the service departments are not the ultimate cost objects, although they receive services from each other. In the example in Table 9A.1, the ultimate cost objects are two operating divisions, A and B, which use two service departments, telecommunications and data processing. The two operating divisions are the ultimate recipients of all of the service department costs. Both service departments in Table 9A.1 use the number of hours of their respective services as an allocation base.

Table 9A.1 provides the usage of the service departments by each other and the two operating divisions. Telecommunications consumes 100 hours of its own service internally and 200 hours of data processing services. Data processing consumes 300 hours of its own service internally and 400 hours of telecommunications services. The goal is to assign the costs of the service departments (telecommunications and data processing) to the operating divisions (A and B). Divisions A and B make the final products, and the cost of those products should include the telecommunications and data processing costs.

Suppose the total costs as follows (top of page 305) of the two service departments are to be allocated to Divisions A and B:

Table 9A.1

Hours of Use of Service Departments

	Telecommunications	Data Processing	Division A	Division B	Total
Telecommunications	100	400	400	100	1,000
Data processing	200	300	600	900	2,000

Telecommunications	$200,000
Data processing	150,000
Total costs	$350 000

Service department costs can be allocated to the operating divisions in several ways: direct allocation, step-down allocation, and reciprocal allocation. This Appendix uses the preceding data to illustrate the computations of the various methods and to discuss the advantages and disadvantages of each method.

Direct Allocation Method

The first method for allocating service department costs is direct allocation. The **direct method** ignores all the internal and interactive usage of the service departments. Only the usage of the service departments by the two operating divisions is considered in allocating the costs of the two service departments.

If usage only by the two operating divisions is considered, the application rates are determined by dividing each service department's costs by its total number of hours of service supplied to the two operating divisions. These application rates are calculated in the first panel of Table 9A.2. Once the application rates are estimated, the service department costs are allocated in the second panel of Table 9A.2.

Table 9A.2 demonstrates the allocation of the total service department costs to the two operating divisions. Division A receives a total of $160,000 + $60,000, or $220,000. Division B receives a total of $40,000 + $90,000, or $130,000, from the two service departments.

The direct method of allocating service department costs is simple to perform but ignores the interaction of services by the service departments. This simplification can lead managers to make poor decisions. In particular, ignoring the reciprocal services means that the application rate will not reflect the opportunity cost of using the service department. Managers of the operating divisions will tend to over- or underutilize the service departments, depending on whether the application rate is lower or higher than the opportunity cost of the service department.

Another problem with direct cost allocation is that each service department will overuse the other service departments. Each service department's costs are

**Planning
Decisions**

Table 9A.2

Direct Allocation Method

Calculation of the Application Rates

	Service Department Costs	Total Hours Used by Divisions A and B	Application Rate per Hour
Telecommunications	$200,000	400 + 100 = 500	$200,000/500 = $400
Data processing	150,000	600 + 900 = 1,500	$150,000/1,500 = $100

Allocation of Service Department Costs to Divisions A and B

	Telecommunications			Data Processing		
	Hours Used	Application Rate	Costs Allocated	Hours Used	Application Rate	Costs Allocated
Division A	400	$400/hour	$160,000	600	$100/hour	$ 60,000
Division B	100	400/hour	40,000	900	100/hour	90,000
Total costs			$200,000			$150,000

Control Decisions

allocated only to the operating departments; thus, the service departments view the usage of other service departments as being free. They are not charged for other service departments and therefore have no monetary incentive to limit their usage. Accordingly, other administrative mechanisms must be implemented to control the utilization of each service department by the others. Such controls could include a constraint in the budget limiting the number of hours that can be used among service departments or a priority system in providing services.

Step-Down Allocation Method

The **step-down method** recognizes some of the interaction between service departments but not all of the reciprocal uses. The procedure begins by choosing a service department and allocating all of its costs to the remaining service and operating departments. Then a second service department is chosen and all of its costs (including its allocated costs from the first service department) are allocated to the remaining service and operating departments. This process continues until all service department costs have been allocated. In this way, all service department costs cascade down through the service departments and eventually are allocated to the operating departments.

Figure 9A.1 describes the flow of costs through service and operating departments. Computing costs are allocated to the remaining service departments (accounting and purchasing) and the two operating departments (cutting and assembly). Accounting costs, which now include some allocated computing costs, are allocated to purchasing, cutting, and assembly. Then purchasing costs, which include some computing and accounting costs, are allocated to cutting and assembly. In this manner, all of the service department's costs are allocated to the operating departments. The cost pools of cutting and assembly, which included allocated costs from the internal service departments, then are allocated to the different products to determine product costs.

Using the example in Table 9A.1, assume that the first service department costs to be allocated are telecommunications. Its costs are allocated to data processing and Divisions A and B in the first step-down. In the second step, data processing costs plus its share of telecommunication costs are allocated to Divisions A and B. The step-down method recognizes the use of telecommunications by data processing, but not the use of data processing by telecommunications. Internal use by each service department of its own services is also ignored. The step-down allocation method is demonstrated in Table 9A.3.

The total costs allocated to Divisions A and B ($184,445 + $165,555, or $350,000) equal the original service department costs to be allocated. The costs allocated to each division using the step-down method differ considerably from the costs allocated by the direct method. The difference occurs because some of the interactions are considered.

Figure 9A.1

Flow of Costs Using the Step-Down Method

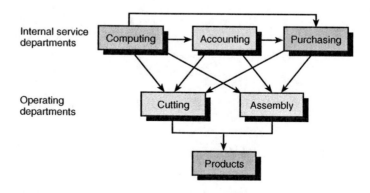

Allocation of Telecommunications to Data Processing and Divisions A and B

Application rate = $200,000/(400 + 400 + 100 hours) = $222.222/hour

To data processing ($222.222/hour)(400 hours)	$ 88,889
To Division A ($222.222/hour)(400 hours)	88,889
To Division B ($222.222/hour)(100 hours)	22,222
Total costs allocated from telecommunications	$200,000

Allocation of Data Processing to Division A and Division B

Costs to be allocated	
Original costs	$150,000
Costs from telecommunications	88,889
Total costs of data processing	$238,889

Application rate = $238,889/(600 + 900 hours) = $159.2593/hour

To Division A ($159.2593)(600 hours)	$ 95,556
To Division B ($159.2593)(900 hours)	143,333
Total data processing costs allocated	$238,889

Total Service Department Costs Allocated to Divisions A and B

	To Division A	To Division B
From telecommunications	$ 88,889	$ 22,222
From data processing	95,556	143,333
Total costs allocated	$184,445	$165,555

Like the direct method, the step-down method also has some problems. One is deciding the order of service departments to be allocated. A general rule of thumb is to allocate first the department that provides the highest level of services to other users in either dollar or percentage terms (or a combination). However, this procedure need not be followed, and the order of the service departments ultimately affects the total costs allocated to the final cost objects. This flexibility might result in conflicts between managers whose departmental allocations depend on the selected order. For example, if data processing were allocated first, the total service department costs allocated to Divisions A and B would be approximately $227,062 and $122,941, respectively.

The order of the service departments also affects their application rates. Service department costs that are allocated early have lower application rates than they do under the direct method, and service department costs that are allocated late have higher application rates than they do under the direct method. For example, the application rates under the direct and step-down methods are as follows:

	Telecommunications	Data Processing
Direct method	$400.00	$100.00
Step-down method		
Telecommunications first	222.22	159.26
Data processing first	435.29	88.24

If these application rates differ from the opportunity costs of using the service departments, managers will tend to use too much or too little of these services. The ordering of the service departments, however, allows the organization to put more weight on certain allocation bases instead of others. By allocating a service department's costs last under the step-down method, the organization is taxing the allocation base of that service department more heavily and discouraging its use.

The Reciprocal Method

The **reciprocal method** of allocating service department costs recognizes all the interactions among service departments. The reciprocal method begins by establishing an equation for each service department; this equation includes the cost of the service department and its proportional use by other service departments and itself. In the example demonstrated in Table 9A.1, telecommunications (TEL) uses 100/1,000, or 0.100, of its own services and 200/2,000, or 0.10, of data processing. Data processing (DP) uses 300/2,000, or 0.15, of its own services and 400/1,000, or 0.40, of telecommunications. These proportions are used to establish the following equations, which represent the "total" cost of operating the service departments. This total cost equals each service department's costs plus a proportion of its own and other service department costs based on its use of the allocation base:

$$TEL = \$200,000 + 0.10(TEL) + 0.10(DP)$$
$$DP = \$150,000 + 0.15(DP) + 0.40(TEL)$$

These two equations have two unknown variables, the cost of telecommunications (TEL) and the cost of data processing (DP). By substituting one equation into the other, TEL and DP can be calculated as $255,172 and $296,552, respectively. These costs are considerably higher than the original costs of the two service departments; they represent costs to be allocated to each other as well as to the ultimate cost objects, Divisions A and B. The proportion of divisional usage of the service department to total usage of the service department is used to allocate costs to Divisions A and B. Table 9A.4 demonstrates this allocation.

The total allocated costs to Divisions A and B ($191,035 + $158,965, or $350,000) equal the original costs of the two service departments, so the reciprocal method is consistent with complete cost allocation. The reciprocal method also recognizes the interaction of service departments. It provides a cost allocation equal to the opportunity cost of using the service department if the costs being allocated are the opportunity costs to operate the service department and vary with the allocation base. If costs other than opportunity costs are being allocated, users of the service department are likely to misuse the service department no matter which method is used for cost allocation. Also, if fixed and variable costs of operating the service department are allocated together, no method of cost allocation will approximate the opportunity cost of using the service department. To take full advantage of the reciprocal method's ability to estimate opportunity costs, only the variable costs in each service department should be allocated using the system of equations. The fixed costs in each service department either should not be allocated or should be allocated based on another allocation base, such as each operating division's planned use of the service department's capacity.

Although the reciprocal method has advantages over the direct and step-down methods, it is more difficult to use. For 20 service departments, the solution requires solving 20 equations with 20 unknown variables, which requires a computer. Before computers, organizations had to use the direct or step-down method; the continued popularity of these methods is evident today.

Table 9A.4

Reciprocal Method

To Division A	
From telecommunications ($255,172)(400/1,000)	$102,069
From data processing ($296,552)(600/2,000)	88,966
Total allocated costs to Division A	$191,035

To Division B	
From telecommunications ($255,172)(100/1,000)	$ 25,517
From data processing ($296,552)(900/2,000)	133,448
Total allocated costs to Division B	$158,965

SELF-STUDY PROBLEM

Reed Park, Inc., is a bottler/supplier of spring water to both commercial and residential customers; its corporate headquarters is located in Clearwater Springs, Colorado. The company began by selling to residential areas and small businesses in the region. In recent years, its sales have moved toward larger businesses. Customers pay a one-time subscription fee of $100 and $11 per bottle. Reed Park operates distribution centers (DCs) in three territories throughout the metro Clearwater Springs area. Metro center was the first DC established; the newest center, Metro West, was established four years ago and continues to show great growth potential.

Bottling and distribution operations are treated as separate entities. The costs associated with each are easily tracked and charged to the appropriate division. There have been no problems related to the accounting systems between the two divisions. However, the managers in the distribution division recently have started to raise questions regarding the accounting systems in place within their division.

Distribution center operations are relatively straightforward. Bottled water shipments are taken from the main bottling plant and stored at the DCs for delivery to customers at later dates. Most subscribing customers take delivery once every two weeks. Expenses associated with DC operations can be seen in the quarterly income statement (see Exhibit S-S 9.1). DC overhead includes lease, building maintenance, security, and other costs related to running the warehouse facility. Staff and administrative expenses include salaries of sales and support staff as well as the cost of materials used in running the office (i.e., office supplies, forms).

Each distribution center has its own sales staff. The corporate office handles the subscription process and informs the drivers and delivery employees regarding delivery type and schedule. The majority of corporate overhead allocated to DCs results from the processing and maintenance of subscriptions and schedules. Reed Park allocates these overhead costs based on the proportion of the book value of trucks at each DC facility to the total book value of the entire Reed Park delivery fleet. This allocation scheme was implemented when the company was founded to relate costs to the most significant cost item. Each DC is treated as a profit center, and DC management is evaluated based on its territory's net income performance.

Trucks are requested by distribution centers and purchased by the corporate offices under a corporate fleet contract with a major truck manufacturer. Like interest expense, the truck lease expense is shown as a separate corporate level expense and is not allocated to the DCs. (See Exhibit S-S 9.2 for relevant data.)

The bottled water industry is experiencing strong growth, as is Reed Park. Reed Park's business seems to be profitable, but all is not well within the ranks of the organization. Corporate has been pressuring DCs to expand their territories and increase delivery volume, but they have been reluctant to meet this request. Some DC managers are beginning to question the amount of overhead being charged to them; they complain that increased deliveries will only cause overhead costs to rise. DC drivers are also unhappy; they complain about being overburdened by their ever-expanding routes and the pressure to meet difficult delivery schedules.

Incentives Created by Overhead Allocations

Exhibit S-S 9.1

QUARTERLY INCOME STATEMENT
REED PARK THREE DISTRIBUTION CENTERS
(dollars in thousands)

	Metro		Metro East		Metro West	
Revenues		$865.0		$928.0		$766.4
Expenses						
Delivery wages	$ 34.2		$ 40.0		$ 33.6	
Overtime wages	4.2		3.2		4.4	
Staff & administrative	150.0		120.0		125.0	
DC overhead	75.0		80.0		125.0	
Fuel	24.0		28.1		26.0	
Truck maintenance	105.0		65.0		75.0	
Corporate overhead	235.7	(628.1)	283.0	(619.3)	391.3	(745.3)
Net income		$236.9		$308.7		$ 21.1

Cost Allocations

Exhibit S-S 9.2

Data for Reed Park Analysis

	Metro	Metro East	Metro West
Delivery employees	80	70	50
Delivery employee wages (per hour)	$8	$8	$8
Total subscriptions	8,533	7,200	5,040
Deliveries per quarter	51,198	43,200	30,240
Bottles delivered per quarter	75,000	78,000	62,400
Average miles driven per delivery	4	4.5	5.2
New subscriptions this quarter	400	700	900
Trucks based at distribution center	70	65	60
Truck dollar value	$700,000	$690,000	$670,000
Accumulated depreciation	350,000	270,000	90,000
Allocation base	350,000	420,000	580,000
Overhead allocation percentage	26%	31%	43%
Additional notes	• Trucks average	15 mpg	
	• Fuel cost	$1.20 per gallon	
	• Delivery charge	$11 per bottle delivered	
	• Subscription fee	$100 per subscription	

Judy Tsai, assistant to the controller, has been assigned the task of examining the situation and developing alternatives if, indeed, a solution is needed.

a. Describe the problems, if any, at Reed Park. Specifically, discuss items related to decision making, cost allocation, and incentives.

b. Describe some alternative ways to allocate corporate overhead.

c. Which allocation system would you choose? What effects do you believe that it would have on Reed Park's distribution operations?

d. Calculate net income for each DC under the system you have chosen and compare these results with those under the present system.

e. How does total profit of the three DCs compare across the original allocation and your proposed allocation scheme?

Solution

a. Reed Park's current overhead allocation system is creating tremendous incentive problems with distribution center managers. Corporate overhead is allocated based on the book value of delivery trucks; therefore, an internal tax is created when the distribution centers acquire new trucks. This system provides incentives for DC managers to attempt to make more and more deliveries with their current number of trucks. In addition, these managers have incentives to keep older, less reliable trucks in their delivery fleet. The increasing number of driver complaints and the high percentage of overtime pay found in the respective income statements are additional indications of these problems.

Other problems in the accounting system include the fact that the cost of bottled water and the cost of trucks are not being charged to the distribution centers. Since both of these are "free" (except for corporate overhead being allocated based on the depreciated cost of trucks), DC managers are likely making the wrong decisions.

b. **Equal overhead allocation**   Since corporate overhead results from functions that are necessary for the survival of each distribution center, this expense could be equally allocated among the three centers.

Allocation based on profits   To take into account the profitability levels of each of the centers, corporate overhead could be allocated based on the net profits of each DC. This allocation scheme leads to some degree of monitoring and cooperation among the centers because other divisions' profits affect allocated overhead.

Allocation based on total subscriptions   Since most of the corporate overhead expense results from the maintenance of subscriptions, corporate overhead can be tied to the total number of subscriptions held by each distribution center.

c. Reed Park should allocate corporate overhead based on total subscriptions. Since much of corporate expense results from processing and maintaining subscriptions, this

Exhibit S-S 9.3

QUARTERLY INCOME STATEMENTS
REED PARK THREE DISTRIBUTION CENTERS
Under Proposed Allocation Scheme
(dollars in thousands)

	Metro		Metro East		Metro West	
Revenues		$865.0		$928.0		$766.4
Expenses:						
Delivery wages	$ 34.2		$ 40.0		$ 33.6	
Overtime wages	4.2		3.2		4.4	
Staff & administrative	150.0		120.0		125.0	
DC overhead	75.0		80.0		125.0	
Fuel	24.0		28.1		26.0	
Truck maintenance	105.0		65.0		75.0	
Corporate overhead*	373.1	(765.5)	315.8	(652.1)	221.1	(575.1)
Net income		$ 99.5		$275.9		$191.3

Supporting notes

	Metro	Metro East	Metro West
Total subscriptions	8,533	7,200	5,040
Percentage of total	41.0%	34.7%	24.3%

*Corporate overhead allocated based on subscriptions.

allocation scheme ties the distribution of these costs to a more accurate cost driver. This method removes the disincentive for DC managers to request additional trucks, use older trucks for deliveries, and force drivers to work overtime. While the new allocation imposes an "internal tax" on the sale of subscriptions, it encourages distribution centers to sell subscriptions to customers who buy larger quantities.

d. Exhibit S-S 9.3 shows income statements for the three distribution centers under the proposed allocation scheme. Under the current allocation, Metro West is being unfairly penalized because of the high book value of its newer trucks. Alternatively, Metro center, with lower truck book values, appears more profitable due to the fact that it is not receiving a large enough portion of the corporate overhead expense. The proposed allocation method provides each distribution center with improved incentives for growth and profitability.

    However, such a change substantially alters the relative profitability of the three divisions. Metro is the big "loser" and Metro West the big "winner." Corporate headquarters should adjust the compensation formulas of the DC managers to ensure that bonuses are insulated from the new cost allocation scheme.

e. Total profit of the three DCs is the same ($566.7) for both allocation methods. The reason is that the total corporate overhead cost of $910 does not vary with the allocation method used. The same number of dollars is being allocated, and thus the total profit of the three DCs is invariant to the allocation method. The allocation method affects how the total pie is distributed to the DCs, not the size of the pie.

(Contributed by D. Lonczak, R. Bingham, M. Eisenstadt, and B. Sayers.)

NUMERICAL EXERCISES

NE 9.1
Cost Allocation and Income
(LO 2)

A company makes 200 units of A and 500 units of B. It sells all units of B and one-half of the units of A. There was no beginning inventory, but 100 units of A are in ending inventory. Product A sells for $5/unit and Product B sells for $10/unit. The variable cost of making Product A is $2/unit, and the variable cost of making Product B is $6/unit. There are no fixed costs other than $900 allocated to the two products.

    Calculate the income with $600 allocated to Product A and $300 allocated to Product B. Calculate the income with $300 allocated to Product A and $600 allocated to Product B.

NE 9.2
Effect of Allocation on Income
(LO 2)

A company has an agreement to sell Product A for 20% above cost. It also sells Product B for $10/unit. The variable cost of Product A is $4/unit and the variable cost of Product B is $6/unit. The company makes and sells 1,000 units of Product A and 2,000 units of Product B. The company has $5,000 of common costs to allocate to the two products.

What is the profit if all common costs are allocated to Product A? What is the profit if all common costs are allocated to Product B?

NE 9.3
Basic Steps of Cost Allocation
(LO 6)

A firm's maintenance department has fixed costs of $40,000 and variable costs of $15 per maintenance hour supplied to other divisions. The department expects to supply 1,000 hours of maintenance during the coming year.

What is the application rate per maintenance hour supplied? What is the marginal cost of another maintenance hour?

NE 9.4
Basic Steps of Cost Allocation
(LO 6)

What is the application rate in NE 9.3 if 2,000 maintenance hours are supplied and there is no effect on fixed costs?

NE 9.5
Basic Steps of Cost Allocation
(LO 6)

Use the data in NE 9.3. How are maintenance costs allocated to production departments A, B, and C, which use 200 hours of maintenance, 300 hours of maintenance, and 500 hours of maintenance, respectively?

NE 9.6
Segment Reporting
(LO 7)

Company C is composed of Division A and B. Division A has sales of $200,000 to outside buyers and $50,000 to Division B. Division B has sales of $300,000 to outside buyers. The costs for Division A are $120,000 and those for Division B are $200,000 excluding the purchases from Division A. Company C headquarters allocates costs of $30,000 to Division A and $10,000 to Division B.

What is the profit of Divisions A and B?

NE 9.7
Allocation of Service Department Costs
(LO 8)

Alpha Company has two service departments, A and B, whose costs are allocated to two production departments, C and D. The following table describes the usage of the allocation base of the service departments by the service and production departments:

	Service Dept. A	Service Dept. B	Production Dept. C	Production Dept. D	Total
Service Dept. A	500	100	800	600	2,000
Service Dept. B	1,000	2,000	3,000	4,000	10,000

Costs are $100,000 for Service Department A and $200,000 for Service Department B.

Allocate these costs to Production Departments C and D using the direct, step-down (Service Department A first), and reciprocal methods.

NE 9.8
Cost Reimbursement and Cost Allocation
(LO 2, 6)

A consultant has an agreement with Worldwide Foods to be reimbursed for all her costs while working on its project in addition to paying her $100 per hour. Other clients pay her a fee of $150 per hour with no cost reimbursement. During the year, she expects to have overhead costs of $150,000 and to work 2,000 hours for clients. Of those 2,000 hours, 400 hours are expected to be on the Worldwide Foods project. The overhead costs are the only expected costs and are allocated based on hours working for clients.

What does the consultant expect to earn during the year?

NE 9.9
Cost Allocations and Performance Measures
(LO 4)

Harrison Corporation allocates indirect costs to different products using the following allocation bases and application rates:

Allocation Base	Application Rate
Direct labor hours (DLH)	$10/DLH
Machine hours (MH)	$20/MH

Jim Ellers is responsible for manufacturing toy trucks at the lowest possible cost. The direct material costs of making toy trucks are $4 per unit. Jim has no control over the cost of the direct materials, but he can influence how the toy trucks are made. They could be made using 10 minutes of direct labor and 20 minutes of machine time. Another option is to use 30 minutes of direct labor and 5 minutes of machine time. The direct cost of labor is $12 per hour.

Which method of manufacturing the toy trucks will minimize their total cost?

NUMERICAL PROBLEMS

Beach Chair Corporation makes two types of beach chairs, reclining and straight-back. The direct costs per unit of the two chairs follow:

	Reclining	Straight-Back
Direct materials	$3	$5
Direct labor	5	2

NP 9.1
Effect of Allocation Base Choice on Profit
(LO 6)

The company has no beginning inventory. During the year, it plans and makes 10,000 reclining chairs and 20,000 straight-back chairs. The company sells all of the reclining chairs for $20 each but only half of the straight-back chairs for $18 each. Budgeted and actual manufacturing overhead costs during the year are $150,000.

a. Calculate the operating profit using direct material dollars as the allocation base for the manufacturing overhead.

b. Calculate the operating profit using direct labor dollars as the allocation base for the manufacturing overhead.

Pure Water Company operates as the municipal water supplier for Prairie Town. The town allows Pure Water to charge consumers of the water the costs to provide it plus 10%. Pure Water also sells bottled water to grocery stores. These sales are not regulated, and the company can charge what the market will bear. The costs of the two types of water per gallon are as follows:

NP 9.2
Choice of Allocation Bases with Cost Reimbursement
(LO 2, 6)

	Municipal Water	Bottled Water
Direct labor	$0.001	$0.10
Direct materials	0.001	0.01

The overhead costs to provide water are $2 million per month. Each month, Pure Water sells 10 million gallons to its municipal customers and 10,000 gallons of bottled water for $1 per gallon.

a. What is the company's profit if overhead costs are allocated by direct labor dollars?

b. What is the company's profit if overhead costs are allocated by direct material dollars?

A building contractor started and finished a 20-unit condominium complex during the year. Its direct costs per unit were $100,000, and its indirect costs per unit were $50,000. The indirect costs are for manufacturing overhead and are considered product costs. By the end of the year, the contractor had sold 12 units for $200,000 each. The contractor had additional indirect expenses of $500,000 that were considered period expenses.

Allocation and External Reporting
(LO 2, 6)

a. What is the building contractor's income for the year?

b. What is the contractor's ending inventory?

c. What is the contractor's income if all indirect costs are considered period expenses?

A lawyer allocates overhead costs based on her hours working with different clients. She expects to have $200,000 in overhead during the year and to work on clients' cases 2,000 hours during the year. In addition, she wants to pay herself $50 per hour for working with clients. She does not bill all clients based on covering overhead costs and her own salary however. Some clients pay her contingency fees; if she works with a client on a contingency-fee basis, she receives half of any settlement for her client. During the year, she works 1,200 hours that are

NP 9.4
Cost Allocation and Contingency Fees
(LO 2, 6)

billable to clients. The remaining hours are worked on a contingency basis. The lawyer wins $300,000 in settlements for clients, of which she receives half. Actual overhead was $210,000.

What does the lawyer earn during the year after expenses?

NP 9.5

Fixed Costs and Allocated Costs

(LO 1, 6)

The maintenance department's costs are allocated to other departments based on the number of hours of maintenance used by each department. The maintenance department has fixed costs of $500,000 and variable costs of $30 per hour of maintenance provided. The variable costs include the salaries of the maintenance workers. If other departments demand more maintenance, more maintenance workers can be added without affecting the fixed costs of the maintenance department. The maintenance department expects to provide 10,000 hours of maintenance.

a. What is the maintenance department's application rate?

b. What is the additional cost to the maintenance department of providing another hour of maintenance?

c. What problem exists if the managers of other departments can choose the amount of maintenance to be performed?

d. What problem exists if the other departments are allowed to outsource their maintenance services?

NP 9.6

Fixed Costs and Cost Allocation

(LO 4, 6)

The personnel department's costs are allocated to the other departments based on the number of direct labor hours. Personnel's expected fixed costs are $400,000 and its variable costs are $0.25 per direct labor hour. The department has sufficient capacity such that fixed costs will not change with increased direct labor. The expected annual usage of direct labor by other departments follows:

Departments	A	B	C	D
Direct labor hours	100,000	500,000	250,000	150,000

a. What is the application rate for the personnel department's costs?

b. What would the application rate be if Department B were closed?

c. Why would the managers of Departments A, C, and D be upset with the closure of Department B?

NP 9.7

Cost Allocation and Decision to Drop a Unit

(LO 3)

Cosmo Inc. operates two retail novelty stores, Mall Store and Town Store. Condensed monthly operating income data for Cosmo for November are as shown. Additional information regarding Cosmo's operations follows the statement.

	Total	Mall Store	Town Store
Sales	$200,000	$80,000	$120,000
Less variable costs	116,000	32,000	84,000
Contribution margin	$ 84,000	$48,000	$ 36,000
Less direct fixed expenses	60,000	20,000	40,000
Store segment margin	$ 24,000	$28,000	($ 4,000)
Less indirect fixed expenses	10,000	4,000	6,000
Operating income	$ 14,000	$24,000	($ 10,000)

* One-fourth of each store's direct fixed expenses would continue through December of next year if either store were closed.

* Cosmo allocates indirect fixed expenses to each store on the basis of sales dollars.

* Management estimates that closing Town Store would result in a 10% decrease in Mall Store sales, while closing Mall Store would not affect Town Store sales.

* The operating results for November are representative of all months.

a. A decision by Cosmo Inc. to close Town Store would result in a monthly increase (decrease) in Cosmo's operating income during next year of how much?

b. Cosmo is considering a promotional campaign at Town Store that would not affect Mall Store. Increasing monthly promotional expenses at Town Store by $5,000 in order to increase Town Store sales by 10% would result in a monthly increase (decrease) in Cosmo's operating income next year of how much?

c. One-half of Town Store's dollar sales are from items sold at variable cost to attract customers to the store. Cosmo is considering dropping these items, a move that would reduce Town Store's direct fixed expenses by 15% and result in the loss of 20% of its remaining sales volume. This change would not affect Mall Store. A decision by Cosmo to eliminate the items sold at cost would result in a monthly increase (decrease) in Cosmo's operating income next year of how much?

(CMA adapted)

Nixon & Ross, a law firm, is about to install a new accounting system that will improve the tracking of overhead costs to individual cases. Currently, overhead is allocated to individual client cases based on billable professional staff salaries. Attorneys who work on client cases charge their time to Billable Professional Staff Salaries. Attorney time spent in training, law firm administrative meetings, and the like is charged to an overhead account titled Unbilled Staff Salaries. Overhead is allocated to clients based on billable professional hours.

A summary of the costs for 2001 follows:

NP 9.8
Direct and Indirect Costs
(LO 3, 6)

Billable professional staff salaries	$ 4,000,000
Overhead	8,000,000
Total costs	$12,000,000

The overhead costs were as follows:

Secretarial costs	$1,500,000
Staff benefits	2,750,000
Office rent	1,250,000
Telephone and mailing costs	1,500,000
Unbilled staff salaries	1,000,000
Total costs	$8,000,000

Under the new accounting system, the firm will be able to trace secretarial costs, staff benefits, and telephone and mailing costs to its clients.

The following costs are incurred on the Lawson Company case:

Billable professional staff salaries	$150,000
Secretarial costs	25,000
Staff benefits	13,500
Telephone and mailing costs	8,000
Total costs	$196,500

a. Calculate the 2001 overhead application rate under the current cost accounting system.

b. How would this application rate change if the secretarial costs, staff benefits, and telephone and mailing costs were reclassified as direct costs instead of overhead, and overhead were assigned based on direct costs (instead of staff salaries)? *Direct costs* are defined as billable staff salaries plus secretarial costs, staff benefits, and telephone and mailing costs.

c. Use the overhead application rates from parts (a) and (b) to compute the cost of the Lawson case.

d. Nixon & Ross bills clients 150% of the total costs of the job. What would be the total billings to Lawson Company if the current overhead application scheme were replaced with the new overhead scheme?

e. Steve Nixon, managing partner, has commented that replacing the current allocation system with the direct charge method of the new accounting system will result in more accurate costing and pricing of cases. Critically evaluate the new system.

NP 9.9
Allocation of Central
Corporate Overhead
(LO 6, 7)

American Wood Products is the world's largest integrated timber grower and wood proces-sor. Its forest group manages and harvests timber from company-owned and public forests. Its lumber group buys cut trees from either the forest group or other timber companies and processes them into a full line of wood products, including plywood, lumber, and veneers. The building products group buys wood products (from the lumber group and other com-panies) as well as other building supplies, such as dry wall and roofing products, and dis-tributes these products worldwide to retailers. The senior managers in each group receive a bonus based on their group's profit before taxes.

Central corporate overhead is allocated to each group on the basis of actual sales revenues in each division. The current year's corporate overhead allocated to the three groups follows:

Corporate salaries and other	$ 50,000,000
Research and development	600,000,000
Interest	850,000,000
Corporate overhead	$1,500,000,000

Operating data for the last fiscal year are (in millions of dollars) are as follows:

	Forest Group	Lumber Group	Building Products Group	Total
Revenues	$5,000	$8,000	$12,000	$25,000
Operating expenses	3,500	7,000	11,500	22,000
Gross margin	$1,500	$1,000	$ 500	$ 3,000
Corporate overhead	300	480	720	1,500
Profit (loss) before taxes	$1,200	$ 520	($ 220)	$ 1,500
Group assets	$5,000	$2,000	$ 1,000	$ 8,000

Instead of allocating $1.5 billion of overhead to the groups on the basis of revenues, the controller is proposing that each of the overhead categories be allocated using a different al-location base, in particular the following:

Overhead Category	Allocation Base
Corporate salaries and other	Sales revenue
Research and Development	Gross margin
Interest	Group assets

a. Calculate each group's profits before taxes using the controller's proposed allocation scheme.
b. What are the pros and cons of allocating corporate overhead to operating divisions?
c. What are the advantages and disadvantages of the controller's proposed change rela-tive to the existing method?

NP 9.10
Allocation of Service
Department Costs
(LO 8)

A manufacturer has two service departments, power and maintenance, and two production departments, parts and assembly. The following table indicates costs, the allocation bases, and the usage of the allocation bases (budgeted = actual) of the two service departments by each other and the production departments.

Service Department	Cost	Allocation Base	Usage of the Allocation Base			
			Power	Maintenance	Parts	Assembly
Power	$30,000	KWH	5,000	8,000	15,000	20,000
Maintenance	40,000	Square meters	5,000	10,000	80,000	40,000

a. Use the direct method to allocate service department costs to the parts and assembly production departments.

b. Use the step-down method, beginning with the power department, to allocate service department costs to the parts and assembly production departments.

c. Use the reciprocal method to allocate service department costs to the parts and assembly production departments.

Mutual Fund Company (MFC) is considering centralizing its overnight mail function. Five departments within MFC use overnight mail service: trades processing, trades verifications, securities processing, accounts control, and customer service. Although these departments send different types of packages (weight and content), different departments often send packages to the same destinations. Currently, each department independently contracts for overnight mail service. The five departments' present rates are as listed:

NP 9.11
Estimation of Application Rates
(LO 3, 4, 5, 6)

Present Rates per Package

Department	Number of Pounds in Package				
	1	2	3	4	5
Trades processing	$ 7.25	$ 8.50	$ 9.75	$11.00	$12.25
Trades verifications	7.75	8.75	9.75	10.75	11.75
Securities processing	8.00	9.50	11.00	12.50	14.00
Accounts control	10.00	12.00	14.00	15.50	16.50
Customer service	16.00	18.00	20.00	22.00	24.00

MFC has requested each department to submit an estimate of its overnight mail for the coming year. The departments' estimates are as follows:

Estimated Usage

	Packages per Day	Annual Number of Packages*	Avg. Weight per Package (pounds)	Pounds per Year
Trades processing	100	25,000	5	125,000
Trades verifications	100	25,000	3	75,000
Securities processing	100	25,000	2	50,000
Accounts control	50	12,500	5	62,500
Customer service	10	2,500	1	2,500
Total	360	90,000		315,000

*Based on 250 days per year.

Using these volume estimates, MFC was able to negotiate the following corporate rates with EXP Overnight Express:

Corporate Rates per Package

Weight (pounds)	Rate
1	$ 7.75
2	8.70
3	9.65
4	10.65
5	11.60
6	12.55
7	13.55
8	14.50
9	15.45
10	16.45

The centralized overnight mail unit would be run as a cost center that would charge back all expenses to the five departments. The charge-backs would comprise two components:

1. The corporate rate per package charged by EXP (based on weight).
2. An overhead allocation per package.

MFC plans to use a "prospective" overhead rate. Pounds per package would be used as the allocation base. As each package comes in, overhead is charged. The rate is set at the beginning of the year and allows the overnight mail service to be costed as it is used. The common costs that compose overhead (labor, supervision, and other expenses) are as follows:

Overhead Expenses	
3 employees @ $11,000 per person per year	$33,000
1 supervisor @ $18,000 per year	18,000
Other costs (rent, utilities, etc.)	24,000
Total overhead	$75,000

At this time, there is much controversy and skepticism about the centralization of the overnight mail function. The managers of trades processing and trades verifications are most opposed to the proposed system. They claim that not only is this proposed system unfair but also that the annual cost savings created by this centralized system do not justify a change.

a. Calculate the overhead allocation rate that would be used with the centralized system.
b. Calculate the estimated cost overall and per department of MFC's overnight mail service under both the present system and the proposed centralized system.
c. Discuss why the managers of trades processing and trades verifications are opposed to the proposed centralized system. Do you agree with their criticisms?
d. Evaluate the proposed method of allocating overhead under the centralized system. Is there a better method to allocate cost? If so, what?
e. Do you think the proposed centralized system can be improved? If so, how?

(Contributed by A. DiGabriele, M. Perez, N. Rivera, C. Tolomeo, and J. Twombly.)

NP 9.12
Allocation of Service
Department Costs
(LO 8)

Donovan Steel has two profit centers, ingots and stainless steel. These profit centers rely on services supplied by two service departments, electricity and water. Ingots's and stainless's consumption of the service departments' outputs (in millions) is given in the following table:

	Service Departments		Profit Centers		
Service Departments	Electricity	Water	Ingots	Stainless Steel	Total
Electricity	2,500 kwh	2,500 kwh	2,500 kwh	2,500 kwh	10,000 kwh
Water	1,000 liters	800 liters	1,600 liters	1,400 liters	4,800 liters

The total operating costs of the two service departments are as follows:

Electricity	$ 80 million
Water	60 million
Total cost	$140 million

a. Service department costs are allocated to profit centers using the step-down method. Water is the first service department allocated. Compute the cost of electricity per kilowatt-hour using the step-down allocation method.
b. Critically evaluate this allocation method.

World Imports buys products from around the world for import into the United States. The firm is organized into a number of separate regional sales districts that sell the imported goods to retail stores. Eastern Sales District is responsible for sales in the northeastern region. Sales districts are evaluated as profit centers and have authority over what products to sell and the price they charge to retailers. Each sales district employs a full-time direct sales force. Salespersons are paid a fixed salary plus a commission of 20% of revenues on what they sell to the retailers.

Eastern District's sales manager, Joseé Krupsak, is considering selling an Australian T-shirt that the firm can import. She has prepared the following table of the estimated unit sales at various prices and costs. Corporate offices at World Imports provided the cost data of the imported T-shirts.

NP 9.13
Allocation of Corporate Overhead to Sales Districts
(LO 3, 7)

WORLD IMPORTS Eastern Sales District Proposed Australian T-Shirt Estimated Demand and Cost Schedules		
Quantity (thousands)	Wholesale Price	T-Shirt Imported Cost
10	$6.50	$2.00
20	5.50	2.20
30	5.00	2.50
40	4.75	3.00

The unit cost of the imported shirts rises because the Australian manufacturer has limited capacity and will have to add overtime shifts to produce higher volumes.

Corporate headquarters of World Imports is considering allocating corporate expenses (advertising, legal, interest, taxes, and administrative salaries) back to the regional sales districts based on the sales commissions paid in the districts. It estimates that the corporate overhead allocation rate will be 30% of the commissions (or for every $1 of commissions paid in the districts, $0.30 of corporate overhead will be allocated). District sales managers receive a bonus based on net profits in their districts. Net profits are revenues less costs of imports sold, sales commissions, other costs of operating the districts, and corporate overhead allocations.

The corporate controller, who is proposing that headquarters costs be allocated to the sales regions and included in bonus calculations, argues that all of these costs must ultimately be covered by the profits of the sales districts. Therefore, the districts should be aware of these costs and must price their products to cover the corporate overhead.

a.   Before the corporate expenses are allocated to the sales districts, what wholesale price will Joseé pick for the Australian T-shirts and how many will she sell? Show how you derived these numbers.

b.   Does the imposition of a corporate overhead allocation affect Joseé's pricing decision on the Australian T-shirts? If so, how? Show calculations.

c.   What are the arguments for and against the controller's specific proposal for allocating corporate overhead to the sales districts?

BFR is a ship-building firm that has just won a government contract to build 10 high-speed patrol boats for the Coast Guard for drug interdiction and surveillance. Besides building ships for the government, BFR operates a commercial vessel division that designs and manufactures commercial fishing and commuting ships. The commercial division and government division are BFR's only two divisions. The Coast Guard contract is BFR's only work in the government division.

NP 9.14
Incentives of Make-Buy Decisions in Cost-Plus Contracts
(LO 2)

The Coast Guard contract is a cost-plus contract. BFR will be paid its costs plus 5% of total costs to cover profits. Total costs include all direct materials, direct labor, purchased subassemblies (engines, radar, radios, etc.), and overhead. Overhead is allocated to the Coast Guard contract based on the ratio of direct labor expense on the contract to firm-wide direct labor.

BFR can either purchase the engines from an outside source or build them internally. The following table presents the costs of the commercial division and the Coast Guard contract for building the engines and purchasing them outside.

		Coast Guard Contract—Engines	
BFR Cost Structure (millions)			
	Commercial Division	**Manufactured Internally**	**Purchased Externally**
Direct labor	$14.600	$22.800	$18.200
Direct material		32.900	25.900
Purchased engines		0.000	17.000

Overhead for BFR is $83.5 million and does not vary whether the engines are purchased outside or manufactured inside. Overhead consists of corporate-level salaries, building depreciation, property taxes, insurance, and factory administration costs.

a. How much overhead is allocated to the Coast Guard contract if

   1. The engines are manufactured internally?

   2. The engines are purchased outside?

b. Based on the total contract payment to BFR, will the Coast Guard prefer BFR to manufacture or purchase the engines?

c. What is the difference to BFR in net cash flows of manufacturing versus purchasing the engines?

d. Explain how cost-plus reimbursement contracts affect the make-or-buy decision for subassemblies.

NP 9.15
Allocation of the Cost of Shared Resource and Incentives
(LO 1, 4)

Grove City Broadcasting owns and operates a radio and a television station in Grove City. Both stations are located in the same building and are operated as separate profit centers with separate managers who are evaluated based on station profits. Revenues of both the radio and television station are from advertising spots. The price of a standard 30-second ad is based on audience size, which is measured by an independent outside agency. The radio station sells a 30-second ad for $100. (Assume that all 30-second ads sell for $100 regardless of the time of day they are aired.) The $100 price is based on an expected audience size of 20,000 listeners. If the listener audience were doubled, the 30-second ad would sell for $200, or each radio listener is worth $0.005 ($100 ÷ 20,000) of advertising revenue per 30-second ad. Television viewers are worth $0.008 per 30-second ad.

The number of 30-second ads sold per month is 3,550 for the radio station and 3,200 for the TV station.

Sports Wire has approached both the radio and television managers about subscribing to its service (which brings all sports scores, news, and analyses to the station via an online computer system over standard telephone lines). The radio or TV station's sports announcers could download scores and news directly into their scripts. Sports Wire is more comprehensive and contains more sports stories than the current general news wires that Grove City is receiving. If one of the two stations bought Sports Wire, the price would be $30,000 per month. For an extra $5,000 per month, both the radio and TV stations could utilize it. If both stations used it, the $5,000 additional fee would include an extra computer terminal that would allow two users to be on the system at the same time without interfering with each other.

Sports Wire would increase the revenue per ad, not the number of ads each month. Grove City's radio manager believes that purchasing Sports Wire would allow him to increase his audience by 1,500 listeners per ad. The television manager believes her audience size would increase by 500 viewers per ad.

a. If the two managers did not cooperate, but each made the decision, assuming he or she were the sole user of the system, would either buy Sports Wire? Support your answer with detailed calculations.

b. If Grove City Broadcasting's owner had all the facts available to the two managers, would the owner buy Sports Wire?

c. The cost of the current wire services that Grove City purchases is allocated to the two stations based on the number of stories aired each month from the wire service. Grove

City Broadcasting's owner decides to purchase Sports Wire for both stations and to allocate its $35,000 cost based on the number of Sports Wire stories aired each month. At the end of the first month, the radio station used 826 Sports Wire stories and TV used 574. Allocate Sports Wire's cost to the radio and TV stations.

d. What is the allocated cost per Sports Wire story in the first month?

e. Given the allocation of Sports Wire cost, what behaviors can you predict for the radio and TV station managers?

f. Design an alternative allocation scheme that avoids the problems identified in part (e). Discuss the advantages and disadvantages of your allocation scheme.

Morris Corporation has two divisions, engineering and consulting. Both divisions charge customers by the hour of work performed. Engineering charges $100 per hour and consulting charges $200 per hour. Engineering bills 10,000 hours during the year to outside customers and 2,000 hours to the consulting division. Consulting bills 5,000 hours. Engineering's variable costs are $40 per billable hour, and annual fixed costs are $500,000. Consulting has variable costs of $60 per billable hour, not including the services purchased from engineering and annual fixed costs of $400,000. Engineering services are transferred to consulting based on the market rate. Central administration allocates $200,000 to each division.

Calculate the profit of each division using transfer prices and allocated costs.

NP 9.16
Segment Reporting
(LO 7)

Rose Hospital has two service departments, building services and food service, and three patient-care units, intensive care, surgery, and general medicine. Building services provides janitorial, maintenance, and engineering services as well as space (utilities, depreciation, insurance, and taxes) to all departments and patient-care units. Food service, which provides meals to both patients and staff members, operates a cafeteria and serves meals to patients in their rooms. Building services's costs of $6 million are allocated based on square meters and food service's costs of $3 million are allocated based on number of meals served. The following tables summarize the annual costs of the two service departments and the utilization of each service department by the other departments.

NP 9.17
Allocation of Service Department Costs
(LO 8)

ANNUAL COST* (millions)	
Building services	$6.0
Food service	3.0
Total overhead	$9.0

*Before allocated service department costs

Utilization Patterns							
	Allocation Base	Building Services	Food Service	Intensive Care	Surgery	General Medicine	Total
Building services	Square meters	2,500	15,500	10,000	20,000	40,000	88,000
Food service	Meals	12,000	10,000	3,000	4,000	98,000	127,000

The following table summarizes the allocation of service department costs using the step-down method with food service as the first service department to be allocated:

STEP-DOWN METHOD (Food Service First) (millions)			
	Intensive Care	Surgery	General Medicine
Food service	$0.09	$0.09	$2.52
Building services	0.88	1.83	3.59
Total	$0.97	$1.92	$6.11

Cost Allocations

(Round all allocation rates and all dollar amounts to two decimal places.)

a. Allocate the two service department costs to the three patient-care units using the direct method.

b. Allocate the two service department costs to the three patient-care units using the step-down allocation method with building services as the first service department allocated.

c. Write a short, non-technical memo to management explaining why the sum of the two service department costs allocated to each patient-care unit in part (b) differs from those computed using the step-down method starting with food service.

NP 9.18
Allocation of Service Department Costs
(LO 8)

Fidelity Bank has five service departments (telecom, information management, building occupancy, training & development, and human resources). The bank uses a step-down method of allocating service department costs to its three lines of business (retail banking, commercial banking, and credit cards). The following table presents the utilization rates of the five service departments and three lines of business. Also included in this table are the direct operating expenses of the service departments (in millions of dollars). Direct operating expenses of each service department do not contain any allocated service costs from the other service departments. For example, telecom spent $3.5 million dollars and provided services to other units within Fidelity Bank. Information management consumed 15% of telecom's services. The order in which the service departments are allocated is also indicated in the table. Telecom is the first department whose costs are allocated, followed by information management, and human resources is the last department's costs allocated.

FIDELITY BANK
Utilization Rates and Direct Operating Expenses of the Service Departments
(dollars in millions)

		Service Departments					Lines of Business		
	Direct Op. Exp.	Telecom	Info. Mgmt.	Building Occ.	Training & Dev.	Human Res.	Retail Banking	Comm. Banking	Credit Cards
1. Telecom	$3.5	—	0.15	0.05	0.05	0.05	0.20	0.15	0.35
2. Information mgmt.	9.8	0.20	—	0.05	0.10	0.10	0.20	0.20	0.15
3. Building occupancy	6.4	0.05	0.10	—	0.05	0.10	0.50	0.10	0.10
4. Training & dev.	1.3	0.15	0.15	0.05	—	0.05	0.10	0.30	0.20
5. Human resources	2.2	0.10	0.10	0.20	0.05	—	0.20	0.20	0.15

a. Using the step-down method and the order of departments specified in the table, what is the total allocated cost from information management to credit cards, including all the costs allocated to information management?

b. Information management costs are allocated based on gigabytes of hard disk storage used by the other service departments and lines of business. If, instead of being second in the step-down sequence, information management became fifth in the sequence, does the allocated cost per gigabyte increase or decrease? Explain precisely why it changes as it does.

c. If instead of using the step-down method of allocating service department costs, Fidelity uses the direct allocation method, what is the total allocated cost from information management to credit cards, including all the costs allocated to information management? (Note: Information management remains second in the list.)

ANALYSIS AND INTERPRETATION PROBLEMS

AIP 9.1
Choice of Allocation Bases for Levying Taxes
(LO 2)

The town of Seaside has decided to construct a sea aquarium to attract tourists. The cost of the measure is to be paid by a special tax. Although most of the townspeople believe that the sea aquarium is a good idea, there is disagreement about how the tax should be levied.

Suggest three different methods of levying the tax and the advantages and disadvantages of each.

AIP 9.2
Methods of Applying Overhead
(LO 3)

Rose Bach has recently been hired as controller of Empco Inc., a sheet-metal manufacturer. Empco has been in the sheet-metal business for many years and is currently investigating ways to modernize its manufacturing process. At the first staff meeting that Bach attended,

Bob Kelley, chief engineer, presented a proposal to automate the drilling department. He recommended that Empco purchase two robots that would have the capability of replacing the eight direct labor workers in the department. The cost savings outlined in Kelley's proposal included the elimination of direct labor cost in the drilling department plus a reduction of manufacturing overhead cost in the department to zero because Empco charges manufacturing overhead on the basis of direct labor dollars using a plant-wide rate.

Empco's president was puzzled by Kelley's explanation of the cost savings, believing it made no sense. Bach agreed, explaining that as firms become more automated, they should rethink their manufacturing overhead systems. The president then asked Bach to look into the matter and prepare a report for the next staff meeting.

To refresh her knowledge, Bach reviewed articles on manufacturing overhead allocation for an automated factory and discussed the matter with some of her peers. She also gathered the following historical data on the manufacturing overhead rates experienced by Empco over the years. Bach also wanted to have some departmental data to present at the meeting and, using Empco's accounting records, was able to estimate the annual averages presented for each manufacturing department in the 1990s.

Historical Data			
Date	Average Annual Direct Labor Cost	Average Annual Manufacturing Overhead Cost	Average Manufacturing Overhead Application Rate
1950s	$1,000,000	$ 1,000,000	100%
1960s	1,200,000	3,000,000	250
1970s	2,000,000	7,000,000	350
1980s	3,000,000	12,000,000	400
1990s	4,000,000	20,000,000	500

Annual Averages			
	Cutting Department	Grinding Department	Drilling Department
Direct labor	$ 2,000,000	$1,750,000	$ 250,000
Manufacturing overhead	11,000,000	7,000,000	2,000,000

a. Disregarding the proposed use of robots in the drilling department, describe the shortcomings of Empco's current system to apply overhead.

b. Do you agree with Bob Kelley's statement that the manufacturing overhead cost in the drilling department would be reduced to zero if the automation proposal were implemented? Explain.

c. Recommend ways to improve Empco's method to apply overhead by describing how it should revise its overhead accounting system:

1. In the cutting and grinding departments.

2. To accommodate the automation of the drilling department.

(CMA adapted)

Increased global competition has spurred most firms to take a hard look at their costs and to become "lean and mean." Rochco, a large industrial complex, has seen off-shore competition erode its market share. Over the past few years, this industrial site of more than 100 functional departments, some cost centers, and other profit centers has undergone several restructuring and labor reduction programs to become more cost competitive.

Five years ago, the many service groups supporting Rochco's manufacturing operations were broken up into well-defined business centers. Top management encouraged all centers to take over more decentralized decision making and mandated that the service groups create value to the firm beyond that provided by outside contractors or be shut down. Dennis Flynn, manager of building services department (BSD), was asked by Jim Corrado, general manager of Rochco operations, to describe how he would take his unit from its then-dismal position vis-à-vis outside cleaning contractors to being the cleaning service of choice for its customers. An aggressive five-year plan was developed with

AIP 9.3
Cost Reduction in Service Departments
(LO 4)

breakeven to be achieved in the third year. This task was not easy, considering that when benchmarked against outside cleaners, BSD's costs exceeded its competitors' prices by 53%.

The majority of Rochco properties are cleaned daily by BSD, which operates as a cost center. BSD allocates its expenses at full cost based on the number of labor hours of service consumed by site customers. More than 80% of BSD's cost is labor, not uncommon for a cleaning service. However, BSD's wage rates historically have been higher than those of its competitors due to Rochco's policy of paying in the upper bracket of local industry to attract good people. Flynn's operating budget two years ago was $17 million.

Labor turnover is higher in BSD than the Rochco average (20% versus 5% annually). The primary reason is that BSD is one of the few departments to hire labor from outside the company. The manufacturing departments tend to recruit personnel from BSD before looking externally for two reasons: BSD provides basic safety training and Rochco culture orientation to its people, and its people represent "screened" employees to the hiring departments, inspiring greater confidence that the employee is a good, reliable worker.

The manufacturing departments also use BSD workers to fill in when normal production workers are on vacation.

Last year, BSD reduced its full costs to less than 29% over market prices, ahead of the forecast of 37%. BSD's costs are now $15 million annually. There is more pressure than ever on all Rochco managers to reduce costs. In June, J. William Laurri, a manufacturing manager and one of BSD's largest customers, told Flynn that he was seriously considering going outside for cleaning services based on price. Laurri manages another cost center with challenging cost reduction goals and represents 50% of BSD's customer base. Flynn is concerned that the loss will irreparably damage BSD's progress toward its five-year break-even goal and raise costs to other departments to such an extent that most of his customers will switch to contract cleaners. Although BSD is still not competitive at full cost, it is almost competitive (within 2%) on a direct cost basis.

a.   Describe the cost accounting and control issues in this situation, which are driving Flynn, Corrado, and Laurri.

b.   Dennis Flynn is confident that his cost-cutting program will succeed by the target date if BSD keeps its current accounts. Should he discount BSD's services in order to keep Laurri?

c.   Should Jim Corrado insist that managers of the operating units continue to use BSD's services? What are the pros and cons of such an order?

(Contributed by S. Usiatynski, H. Merkel, and M. J. Joyce.)

AIP 9.4

Cost Allocation of Tuition Benefits in Universities

(LO 3, 4, 5)

Eastern University prides itself on providing faculty and staff a competitive compensation package. One aspect of this package is a faculty and staff child tuition benefit of $4,000 per child per year, for up to four years, to offset the cost of college education. The faculty or staff member's child can attend any college or university, including Eastern University, and receive the tuition benefit. If a staff member has three children in college one year, the staff member receives a $12,000 tuition benefit. This money is not taxed to the individual staff or faculty member.

Eastern University pays the benefit directly to the other university where the faculty/staff member's child is enrolled (or reduces the amount of tuition owed by the faculty/staff if the student is attending Eastern University) and then charges this payment to a benefits account. This benefits account then is allocated back to the various colleges and departments based on total salaries in the college or department.

Critically evaluate the pros and cons of Eastern University's present method to account for tuition benefits. What changes would you recommend?

AIP 9.5

Effect of Allocation Bases on Behavior

(LO 4)

Portable Phones, Inc., manufactures and sells portable, wireless telephones for residential and commercial use. Its plant is organized by product line, five telephone-assembly departments in total. Each of these five telephone-assembly departments is responsible for the complete production of a particular telephone line, including manufacturing some parts, purchasing other parts, and assembling the unit.

Each of the five assembly department managers reports to a product-line manager, who has profit responsibility for his or her product. These five product-line managers have authority over pricing, marketing, distribution, and production of the product. Each of the five assembly departments is a cost center within its respective product-line profit centers.

A key component of each telephone is the circuit board(s) containing the integrated circuit chips. Each assembly department purchases the basic boards and chips to be attached to its board(s) from outside vendors. The plant's board department receives the boards and chips in kits from each assembly department and assembles them into completed boards ready for assembly into the telephones. The board department (with a cost structure that is 80% fixed and 20% variable) uses a single, highly automated line of robotic-insertion machines to precisely position each chip on the board and soldering machines to solder the chips onto it. The board department is a common resource for the plant; all five of the assembly departments use it to assemble some or all of their boards. Since the board department has a single assembly line, it can assemble boards for only one type of telephone at a time. The assembly departments have authority to seek the most competitive supplier for all their parts and services, including circuit-board assembly.

The board department's assembly schedule is determined at the beginning of each month. The five assembly departments request a time during the month when they plan to deliver particular kits to the board department and the number of boards to be assembled. The board department manager then takes these requests and tries to satisfy them. However, the board department manager finds that she has a peak load problem; the assembly departments tend to want their boards assembled at the same time. The only way to satisfy these requests is to work overtime shifts during these peak periods, even though the board department has excess capacity at other times of the month.

The board department's total monthly costs (equipment depreciation, maintenance, direct labor, supervision, and engineering support) are assigned to the telephone-assembly departments based on an hourly rate. The board department's total monthly costs are divided by the number of hours of capacity in the month (e.g., if a particular month has 22 working days, this is equivalent to 352 hours, or 22 days × 2 shifts × 8 hours per shift) to arrive at a charge per hour. To provide each assembly department with incentives to have its kits (boards and chips) delivered to the board department in a timely manner, each assembly department is charged for the time from when the board department finished the last job (a batch of boards assembled for an assembly department) until it finishes the next job. For example, suppose that telephone assembly department A's telephones were finished at 9 A.M., Department B delivered its kits at 1 P.M., and the latter were completed at 7 P.M. the same day. Department B would be charged for 10 hours of the board department's costs, even though the board department was idle for 4 of the 10 hours.

When first installed, the board department was expected to be operating at full capacity, two shifts per day, six days per weak. Due to overseas outsourcing of some models and increased competition, it is now operating at about 70% of the initial planned capacity.

a. If you manage a telephone-assembly department, everything else being held constant, when during the month would you tend to request your circuit boards be assembled by the board department? Explain why.

b. Identify various dysfunctional behaviors likely to be occurring among the telephone-assembly departments and the board department.

c. What management changes would you suggest? In particular (but not limited to), what changes would you make to the accounting system? Explain why each change should be made. What would you hope to accomplish by the change?

EXTENDED ANALYSIS AND INTERPRETATION PROBLEMS

AIP 9.6
Development of Application Rates

Marfrank Corporation is a manufacturing company with six functional departments, finance, marketing, personnel, production, research and development (R&D), and information systems (ISD), each administered by a vice president. ISD was established two years ago, in 1999, when Marfrank decided to acquire a new mainframe computer and develop a new information system.

While systems development and implementation are ongoing processes at Marfrank, many of the basic systems needed by each of the functional departments were operational at the end of 2000. Thus, calendar year 2001 is the first year that ISD's costs can be estimated with a high degree of accuracy. Marfrank's president wants the other five functional departments to be aware of the magnitude of ISD's costs in the reports and statements prepared at the end of the first quarter of 2001. The allocation of ISD's costs to each department was based on its actual use of ISD services.

Jon Werner, vice president of ISD, suggested that ISD's actual costs be allocated on the basis of the pages of actual computer output. This basis was suggested since reports are what all of the departments use to evaluate their operations and to make decisions. The use of this basis resulted in the following allocation:

Department	Percentage	Allocated Cost
Finance	50%	$112,500
Marketing	30	67,500
Personnel	9	20,250
Production	6	13,500
R&D	5	11,250
Total	100%	$225,000

After the quarterly reports detailing the allocated costs were distributed, the finance and marketing departments objected to this allocation method. Both departments recognized that they were responsible for most of the output in terms of reports. However, they believed that these output costs might be the smallest of ISD costs and requested that a more equitable allocation basis be developed.

After meeting with Jon, Elaine Jergens, Marfrank's controller, concluded that ISD provided three distinct services: systems development, computer processing represented by central processing unit (CPU) time, and report generation. She recommended that a predetermined rate be developed for each of these services from budgeted annual activity and costs. The ISD costs then would be assigned to the other functional departments using the predetermined rate times the actual service provided. Any difference between actual costs incurred by ISD and costs allocated to the other departments would be absorbed by ISD.

Elaine and Jon concluded that systems development could be charged based on hours devoted to systems development and programming, computer processing based on CPU time used for operations (exclusive of database development and maintenance), and report generation based on pages of output. The only cost that should not be included in any of the predetermined rates would be purchased software; these packages were usually acquired for a specific department's use. Thus, Elaine concluded that purchased software would be charged at cost to the department for which it was purchased. In order to revise the first quarter allocation, she gathered the following information on ISD costs and services:

Information Systems Department Costs					
	Estimated Annual Costs	Actual First Quarter Costs	Percentage Devoted to		
			Systems Development	Computer Processing	Report Generation
Wages and benefits					
Administration	$100,000	$ 25,000	60%	20%	20%
Computer operators	55,000	13,000		20	80
Analysts/programmers	165,000	43,500	100		
Maintenance					
Hardware	24,000	6,000		75	25
Software	20,000	5,000		100	
Output supplies	50,000	11,500			100
Purchased software	45,000	16,000*	—	—	—
Utilities	28,000	6,250		100	
Depreciation					
Mainframe computer	325,000	81,250		100	
Printing equipment	60,000	15,000			100
Building improvements	10,000	2,500		100	
Total department costs	$882,000	$225,000			

*All software purchased during the first quarter of 2001 was for the benefit of the production department.

Information Systems Department Services

Annual capacity	Systems Development 4,500 hours	Computer Operations (CPU) 360 CPU hours	Report Generalization 5,000,000 pages
Actual usage during first quarter 2001			
Finance	100 hours	8 CPU hours	600,000 pages
Marketing	250	12	360,000
Personnel	200	12	108,000
Production	400	32	72,000
R&D	50	16	60,000
Total usage	1,000 hours	80 CPU hours	1,200,000 pages

a.
1. Develop predetermined rates for each of ISD's service categories (i.e., systems development, computer processing, and report generation).
2. Using the predetermined rates developed in part (a1), determine the amount that each of the other five functional departments would be charged for services provided by ISD during the first quarter of 2001.

b. With the method proposed by Elaine Jergens for charging the ISD costs to the other five functional departments, there might be a difference between ISD's actual costs incurred and the costs assigned to the five user departments.
1. Explain the nature of this difference.
2. Discuss whether Elaine's proposal will improve cost control in ISD.
3. Explain whether Elaine's proposed method of charging user departments for ISD costs will improve planning and control in the user departments.

(CMA adapted)

Independent Underwriters Insurance Co. (IUI) established a systems department two years ago to implement and operate its own data processing systems. IUI believed that its own system would be more cost effective than the service bureau that it had been using.

    IUI's three departments—claims, records, and finance—have different requirements with respect to hardware and other capacity-related resources and operating resources. The system was designed to recognize these differing demands. In addition, the system was designed to meet IUI's long-term capacity. The excess capacity designed into the system would be sold to outside users until IUI needed it. The estimated resource requirements used to design and implement the system are shown in the following schedule:

AIP 9.7
Allocation of Computer Costs

	Hardware and Other Capacity-Related Resources	Operating Resources
Records	30%	60%
Claims	50	20
Finance	15	15
Expansion (outside use)	5	5
Total	100%	100%

IUI currently sells the equivalent of its expansion capacity to a few outside clients.

    When the system became operational, management decided to redistribute the system department's total expenses to the user departments based on actual computer time used. The actual costs for the first quarter of the current fiscal year were distributed to the user departments as follows:

Department	Percentage Utilization	Amount
Records	60%	$330,000
Claims	20	110,000
Finance	15	82,500
Outside	5	27,500
Total	100%	$550,000

The three user departments have complained about the cost distribution since the systems department was established. The records department's monthly costs have been as much as three times the costs experienced with the service bureau. The finance department is concerned about the costs distributed to the outside user category, as these allocated costs form the basis for the fees billed to the outside clients.

James Dale, IUI's controller, decided to review the distribution method by which the systems department's costs have been allocated for the past two years. The additional information he gathered for his review is reported in Tables AIP 9.7A, AIP 9.7B, and AIP 9.7C.

James has concluded that the method of cost distribution should be changed to reflect more directly the actual benefits received by the departments. He believes that the hardware and capacity-related costs should be allocated to the user departments in proportion to the planned, long-term needs. Any difference between actual and budgeted hardware costs would not be allocated to the departments but remain with the systems department.

The remaining costs for software development and operations would be charged to the user departments based on actual hours used. A predetermined hourly rate based on the annual budget data would be used. The hourly rates that would be used for the current fiscal year are as follows:

Function	Hourly Rate
Software development	$ 30
Operations	
Computer related	200
Input/output related	10

James plans to use first-quarter activity and cost data to illustrate his recommendations, which will be presented to the systems department and the user departments for their comments and reactions. He then expects to present his recommendations to management for approval.

a. Prepare a schedule to show how the systems department's actual first-quarter costs would be charged to the users if James Dale's recommended method were adopted.

b. Explain whether James Dale's recommended system for charging costs to the user departments would accomplish the following:
   1. Improve cost control in the systems department.
   2. Improve planning and cost control in the user departments.
   3. Provide a more equitable basis for charging costs to user departments.

(CMA adapted)

Table AIP 9.7A

Systems Department Costs and Activity Levels

| | Annual Budget | | First Quarter | | | |
| | | | Budget | | Actual | |
	Hours	Dollars	Hours	Dollars	Hours	Dollars
Hardware and other capacity-related costs	—	$ 600,000	—	$150,000	—	$155,000
Software development	18,750	562,500	4,725	141,750	4,250	130,000
Operations						
Computer related	3,750	750,000	945	189,000	920	187,000
Input/output related	30,000	300,000	7,560	75,600	7,900	78,000
		$2,212,500		$556,350		$550,000

	Hardware and Other Capacity Needs	Software Development		Operations			
				Computer		Input/Output	
		Range	Average	Range	Average	Range	Average
Records	30%	0–30%	12%	55–65%	60%	10–30%	20%
Claims	50	15–60	35	10–25	20	60–80	70
Finance	15	25–75	45	10–25	15	3–10	6
Outside	5	0–25	8	3–8	5	3–10	4
	$100%		100%		100%		100%

Table AIP 9.7B

Historical Utilization by Users

	Software Development	Operations	
		Computer Related	Input/Output
Records	425	552	1,580
Claims	1,700	184	5,530
Finance	1,700	138	395
Outside	425	46	395
Total	4,250	920	7,900

Table AIP 9.7C

Utilization of Systems Department's Services (in hours)—First Quarter

Chapter **Ten**

Absorption Costing Systems

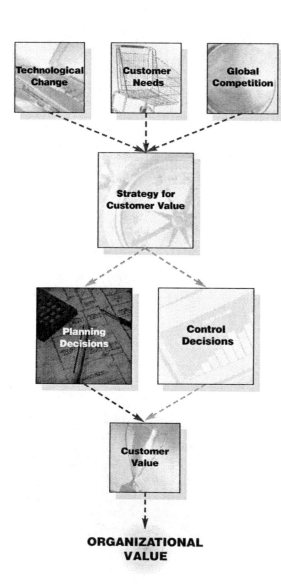

SANTA FE BELTS

Santa Fe Belts manufactures leather belts. Although belts can be made from pigskin, lambskin, or exotic animals such as crocodiles and sharks, the primary material used by Santa Fe Belts and most belt manufacturers is cowhide. The cowhide is composed of two layers, the top grain, which is the outer layer, and the split leather, which is the inner layer. The top grain is the preferred material for belts because it is the most durable and beautiful. The split leather does not have a natural grain, although a grain may be embossed on it to more closely resemble top grain.

The construction of a belt begins with the purchase of dyed cowhides. Santa Fe Belts buys both top grain for the production of

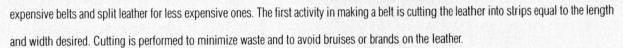

expensive belts and split leather for less expensive ones. The first activity in making a belt is cutting the leather into strips equal to the length and width desired. Cutting is performed to minimize waste and to avoid bruises or brands on the leather.

Most belts have two layers, an outside layer of leather and an inside liner to help them maintain shape. Naturally, the nicest leather is used for the outside layer. Some belts use top grain on the outside and split leather as a liner. The second activity of making the belt includes laminating and combining the two layers with glue. In addition, the edges of the leather strips are beveled and dyed. This activity is referred to as *combining*.

The third activity in belt production is punching holes and making the loop. Belts typically have five to seven holes with an additional hole for the buckle.

The fourth and final activity includes adding the buckle and stitching the belt and stamping it with the company logo and size. Buckles are typically made of silver-plated zinc, but brass, steel, copper, nickel, and aluminum are also used. The fourth activity is referred to as *finishing*.

Santa Fe Belts has two factories. Factory A makes belts to order. These belts tend to use top-grain leather and are more expensive. Factory A receives the design specifications from the customer and makes the belts accordingly, resulting in modifying machines and procedures for each order. The factory manager is responsible for negotiating a price for these special orders.

Factory B makes a standard split-leather belt that is sold to department stores. All machines in Factory B are dedicated to making the standard belt. Purchases by the stores tend to be large and unpredictable, so the factory maintains a relatively large inventory to meet customer demand.

Each factory is divided into the four activities: cutting, combining, punching, and finishing. Each factory also identifies direct material, direct labor, and overhead costs. Direct labor and overhead also can be identified with each activity. Costs are used for planning (pricing and product-mix decisions) and control (motivating, evaluating, and rewarding managers).

PRODUCT COSTING PROCEDURES IN ORGANIZATIONS

LO 1 Identify different types of production systems and corresponding absorption costing systems.

Chapter Three introduced activity-based costing (ABC) as a method to estimate the cost of products and services. Costs estimated through ABC are useful for making planning decisions related to product mix and pricing. Costs related to products must be not only estimated for planning purposes but also recorded when incurred. As we will see later in this chapter, ABC also can be used to record product costs as incurred. The initial examples of this chapter, however, use a single allocation base to record indirect product cost, to facilitate the learning of product costing procedures.

Chapter Nine described the procedures for allocating indirect costs to cost objects. In this chapter, the cost object of interest is the product or service of the organization. This chapter describes a particular, widely used, cost allocation system called *absorption costing*. **Absorption costing** is the process of allocating variable and fixed overhead costs to products. In manufacturing facilities, all manufacturing (variable and fixed) overhead is commonly allocated to the goods produced by the facility. If it costs $32 million to operate a factory that manufactures 28,000 units (including units still in inventory), the absorption cost system allocates the $32 million among the 28,000 units. Absorption cost systems lead to the same trade-offs between making planning decisions and control as other accounting method choices do, but most of the discussion of this trade-off is deferred to Chapter Eleven. The current chapter focuses on the mechanics of these cost systems.

Absorption cost systems are widely used in financial reporting to determine inventory valuation and the cost of goods manufactured. These systems initially were developed in manufacturing firms, and we will use this setting to describe these systems. However, the same concepts can be applied to the service sector, including financial institutions, and professional services organizations (such as advertising agencies, law firms, and public accounting firms). The chapter does not describe absorption cost systems in service industries, although several problems at the end of this chapter and other chapters illustrate absorption costing in non-manufacturing settings. Non-manufacturing settings tend to have simpler absorption costing systems as they do not have tangible work-in-process and finished goods inventories.

The two basic types of absorption cost systems are job-order systems and process cost systems. **Job-order systems** are used in departments that produce output in distinct jobs (job-order production) or batches (batch manufacturing). A "job" might consist of a single unit, such as the construction of an office building, or a batch of units, such as 200 windshield wiper motors for automobiles. (In a service organization, a job might be handling a client's lawsuit or processing a loan application at a bank.) The cost of each job is tracked separately, and job-order cost systems accumulate costs by jobs. Alternatively, in some assembly processes and continuous flow production processes, process cost systems are used. Production in these settings is continuous (e.g., an oil refinery), and distinct batches usually do not exist. Under **process costing,** manufacturing overhead is allocated equally to all the units produced.

In practice, there is great diversity in the way firms' accounting systems allocate costs to products, jobs, or activities. Even within batch manufacturing, no two systems are exactly alike. Many plants use hybrids of job-order and process costing. Each accounting system is tailored to the peculiarities of the department or plant. Accounting systems also adapt and change as firms modify their production processes. However, this chapter focuses on the similarities across all these systems. The central issue in cost systems is how to allocate indirect costs to products, jobs, or services.

Concept**Review**

1. What are the two different types of production processes?
2. What types of absorption cost systems are appropriate for different production processes?

Although both Santa Fe Belt factories make belts and have the same processes and machines, their operating methods are much different. Factory A makes belts as ordered from customers. Each order specifies the design and number of belts required. The factory treats each order as a batch. Each batch goes through the same four processes but may require different types of material, amounts of direct labor, and machine time. Given the way this factory operates, management has decided to use job-order costing to identify the direct costs of each batch and to allocate overhead costs to those batches.

Factory B processes belts as a continuous flow. It makes only the standard belt; batches are not distinguishable as they move through the factory. This factory uses process costing to determine the cost of the belts.

SANTA FE BELTS
(Continued)

JOB-ORDER COSTING

Job-order costing is the process of recording and accumulating the cost of making an identifiable product or batch of the same or similar products. A plant that manufactures different types of metal boxes in batches is used to illustrate job-order costing. Each box is produced in a batch requiring several different raw material inputs and several different classes of direct labor. Moreover, the boxes utilize various combinations of common resources such as machines, supervisors, shipping docks, and factory space. Each batch is referred to as a *job*; every job passes through a common machining process. The time spent in this machining center is recorded for each job and is used to allocate overhead costs to the job. In other words, the allocation base is machine hours, and jobs are the cost objects. Each job in the factory has a job-order cost sheet that records the costs associated with the products manufactured in the batch, and the number of machine hours spent to process the job. A typical job-order cost sheet is shown in Table 10.1

Job #5167 in Table 10.1 was started on March 13 and completed on May 23. The job sheet records all direct materials issued for the job, including the date, the type

LO 2 Understand a job-order cost system.

Table 10.1

Job-Order Cost Sheet

Job Number 5167								Date Started	3/13
								Date Completed	5/23
		Raw Materials					**Direct Labor**		
Date	Type	Cost	Qty.	Amount	Machine Hours	Type	Rate	Hrs.	Amount
3/13	103a	$30	205	$ 6,150	13	a65	$18	15	$ 270
3/14	214	50	106	5,300	111	a68	30	20	600
4/1	217	15	52	780	45	b73	10	81	810
4/23	878	5	229	1,145	28	c89	20	368	7,360
5/23					16	c89	20	419	8,380
Totals				$13,375	213				$17,420

Total direct materials	$13,375
Total direct labor	17,420
Overhead (213 machine hours @ $25/hour)	5,325
Total job cost	**$36,120**
Divided by: Number of units in batch	1,560
Average cost per unit produced	$ 23.15

of materials (represented by codes), the cost of the materials, and the quantity of materials. Direct labor related to Job #5167 is also recorded on the job-order sheet. This information is either obtained from workers' time cards or directly recorded on the job sheet by the worker. Notice that different types of labor (represented by codes), with different labor rates, worked on the job. Job #5167 accumulated $13,375 of direct materials costs and $17,420 of direct labor costs. Also recorded on the job sheet is the number of machine hours used by the job. In this plant, machine hours are used to allocate overhead costs at the rate of $25 per machine hour. The $25 per machine hour is a predetermined application rate. Chapter Nine discussed the calculation of application rates. Job #5167 used 213 hours of machinery. Multiplying 213 machine hours by $25 per machine hour yields $5,325 of overhead costs charged to this job. The total costs for this job are $36,120. With 1,560 units produced in this batch, the average cost is $23.15 per unit.

The allocation base for indirect manufacturing costs accumulated in the overhead account is machine hours. As discussed in Chapter Nine, the use of machine hours as the allocation base is similar to a tax on machine hours. This "tax" creates incentives to economize on machine hours. The example of Job #5167 illustrates several important features of job-order costing:

- All direct costs of manufacturing the job are traced directly to the job.
- Each job is charged for some indirect manufacturing overhead.
- At least one allocation base (such as machine hours) is used to distribute overhead costs to jobs.
- The application rate for overhead (here, the rate per machine hour) is set at the beginning of the year, before the first jobs are started. This overhead rate is based on an estimate of what factory overhead costs and machine hours will be for the coming year.
- Reported product costs are average, not variable or marginal, costs. Each job is assigned a portion of the overhead. Since overhead contains some fixed costs, overhead distributed to jobs includes some of the fixed costs.

Numerical Example 10.1

A customer orders a special tool (Job #676) that requires 5 units of part 103 at a cost of $40 per unit, 4 units of part 244 at a cost of $20 per unit, and 1 unit of part 566 at a cost of $100 per unit. The tool also requires five hours of direct labor at $18 per hour. Overhead is allocated to the job at a rate of $15 per direct labor hour. The job is started and finished on May 6. Prepare a job-order sheet for the tool.

Solution

Job Number 676					Date Started	5/6	
					Date Completed	5/6	
		Raw Materials				Direct Labor	
Date	Type	Cost	Qty.	Amount	Rate	Hours	Amount
5/6	103	$ 40	5	$200	$18	5	$ 90
	244	20	4	80			
	566	100	1	100			
				$380			

Total direct materials	$380
Total direct labor	90
Overhead (5 direct labor hours @ $15/hour)	75
Total job cost	**$545**

ConceptReview

1. What costs are recorded on a job-order cost sheet?

2. How are overhead costs added to the job-order cost sheet?

In developing its job-order cost system, Factory A of Santa Fe Belts must design a job cost sheet, train employees to make appropriate entries on it, and decide how to allocate overhead to the different batches. To keep its accounting system simple, Santa Fe Belts decides to accumulate overhead in a single cost pool and to allocate costs by direct labor hours. The application rate for the year is determined by dividing the estimated overhead costs ($800,000) for the year by the estimated direct labor hours (80,000 hours). Therefore, an application rate of $800,000/80,000 hours, or $10 per direct labor hour, is used. The overhead costs include supplies such as dye, thread, hangers, and labels.

SANTA FE BELTS
(Continued)

An example of a completed job-order cost sheet for Santa Fe Belts follows:

Job-Order Cost Sheet

Job Number 543   **Date Started** 6/30
Job Description   **Date Completed** 7/5
     1,000 belts using design #456G

Direct Material Costs

Date	Process	Part	Quantity	Unit Cost	Total
6/30	Cutting	Top grain leather	750 sq. ft.	$3.30/sq. ft.	$2,475
7/5	Finishing	Buckle (#356)	1,000	$0.80/buckle	800
Total Direct Materials Cost					$3,275

Direct Labor Costs

Date	Process	Hours	Cost/Hour	Total
6/30	Cutting	10	$10/hour	$100
7/2	Combining	15	8/hour	120
7/3	Punching	5	12/hour	60
7/5	Finishing	15	12/hour	180
Totals		45		$460

Total Cost of Job

Direct materials	$3,275
Direct labor	460
Overhead (45 hours)($10/hour)	450
Total costs	$4,185
Number of units	1,000
Manufacturing cost per belt	$4.185

COST FLOWS THROUGH THE ACCOUNTS

The job sheet illustrated in Table 10.1 is the underlying source document in the job-order cost system. For many years, manufacturing firms maintained job-order cost sheets manually with paper and ink. Today, they are electronic records in computer

LO 3   Identify how costs flow through different accounts.

Job-Order Cost Sheets and U.S. Steel

In the 1870s, Andrew Carnegie built the Edgar Thompson Steel Works in Pittsburgh, which was later to become part of U.S. Steel. One of Carnegie's many management innovations (and his obsession) was a detailed cost accounting system. Each department in the steel works listed the amount and cost of labor and materials used by each order as it passed through the department. Carnegie received daily reports showing the direct costs of the products produced and would repeat, "Watch the costs and the profits will take care of themselves."

Carnegie's cost sheets were called the marvel of ingenuity and careful accounting. He required his people to explain the most minute change in unit costs. Carnegie and his managers used these data to evaluate the performance of his people, maintain the quality and mix of raw materials, evaluate improvements in process and product, and price products. New orders would not be accepted until there had been a careful checking of the costs.

Source: A. Chandler, *The Visible Hand* (Cambridge, Mass.: Harvard University Press, 1977), pp. 267–68.

systems. Costs are commonly recorded through the use of bar codes and handheld computers.

Table 10.1 illustrates the job-order cost sheet for one job. Modern manufacturing plants can have hundreds, even thousands, of jobs in various stages of completion on the plant floor at any one time. The accounting system tracks the costs charged to each job. As costs are charged to individual jobs, the costs are entered simultaneously in a Work-in-Process Inventory account, which contains all costs for all unfinished jobs in the organization. Each job cost sheet can be thought of as a subsidiary account for the Work-in-Process account. The sum of the costs on the job cost sheets equals the balance of the Work-in-Process account.

The job-order cost sheet is not the original source document for product-related costs. Figure 10.1 diagrams the flow of costs from the original documents to the job-order cost sheet (as represented by Work-in-Process), to Finished Goods, and finally to Cost of Goods Sold. Labor costs are recorded based on the amount of time the employee works times a labor rate, which includes unemployment taxes, social security, and pension expenses. Employees who work on a job record the time spent on it and their labor rate on the job cost sheet. At the same time, labor costs are recorded by the same amount. Not all labor costs eventually appear on job cost sheets. For example, employees have down time when they are not working on any job but are still being paid. Also, some employees do not work directly on jobs. Any labor costs that do not end up on job cost sheets become part of the overhead account.

At the time of purchase, material costs initially are recorded as raw materials. The manager of the inventory warehouse controls the inventory; requisition slips

Figure 10.1   Schematic of a Job-Order Cost System

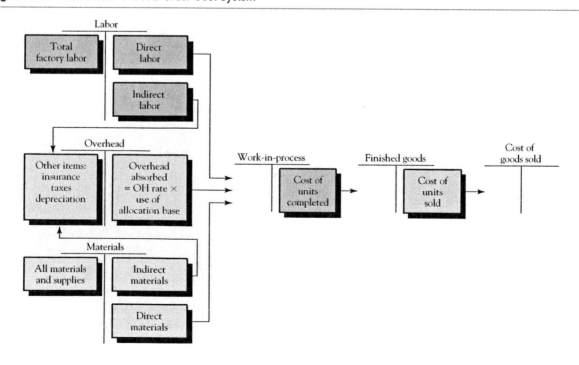

are necessary to move raw materials from the warehouse to the factory floor. At the time of requisition, the raw materials are recorded on the job-order cost sheet and are eliminated from the Raw Materials Inventory account. Some raw materials are not used directly on jobs but are used indirectly by multiple jobs. For example, raw materials used to check the setting of a machine are not directly related to a specific job and their cost is treated as overhead.

Overhead indirect manufacturing costs are also recorded in various overhead accounts (such as Insurance, Property Taxes, Depreciation, Accounting, Purchasing, Security, General Factory Management, and Utilities) before being allocated to job-order cost sheets through the use of allocation bases. In Figure 10.1, the Overhead accounts are aggregated into a single cost pool and allocated by a single allocation base. When overhead is allocated to a job-order cost sheet, the Overhead account is reduced by an equivalent amount. The application rates of the allocation bases are estimated at the beginning of the time period. Estimates of the application rate do not always accurately reflect the actual usage of the allocation base and the actual overhead costs; therefore, the overhead allocated to jobs usually does not equal the total costs in the Overhead account. The next section explains procedures to account for any differences between allocated overhead and actual overhead.

When a job is finished and transferred to finished goods inventory, the total job cost from the job-order cost sheet is transferred out of the Work-in-Process account and into the Finished Goods account. Similarly, when the goods are sold, the costs flow out of the Finished Goods account and into the Cost of Goods Sold account.

In a typical manufacturing plant, direct labor is about 30% of total plant costs, direct material is another 30%, and overhead is 40% of total plant costs.[1] These percentages can vary widely. In some cases, direct labor can be as low as 1 to 5 percent of total manufacturing costs and overhead as high as 80 percent. A study of manufacturing overhead costs in the electronics, machinery, and automobile components industries reports that manufacturing overhead is approximately three times the direct labor cost. Manufacturing overhead represents 26% of total manufacturing costs, direct labor is 8%, and direct material is 65% in the electronics plants studied.[2]

Numerical Example 10.2

The job cost sheet for a special product is as follows:

Job Number	711				Date Started	5/26	
					Date Completed	6/15	
		Raw Materials			**Direct Labor**		
Date	Type	Cost	Qty.	Amount	Rate	Hours	Amount
5/26	130	$30	6	$180	$18	5	$ 90
6/15	248	10	20	200	15	10	150
				$380		15	$240

Total direct materials	$380
Total direct labor	240
Overhead (15 direct labor hours @ $10/hour)	150
Total job cost	**$770**

---

[1] R. Howell, J. Brown, S. Soucy, and A. Seed, *Management Accounting in the New Manufacturing Environment* (Montvale, N.J.: National Association of Accountants, 1987).

[2] R. Banker, G. Porter, and R. Schroeder, "An Empirical Analysis of Manufacturing Overhead Cost Drivers," *Journal of Accounting and Economics* 19 (February 1995), pp. 115–37.

Overhead is allocated based on direct labor hours (DLH). The parts were in the Raw Materials Inventory before being used on Job #711. The product is sold on July 10. Identify the cost flows on May 26, June 15, and July 10.

Solution

Cost flows:

On 5/26:	$180 from Raw Materials Inventory to Work-in-Process
	$90 from Labor to Work-in-Process
	$50 from Overhead to Work-in-Process for overhead related to direct labor hours (5 DLH × $10/DLH)
On 6/15:	$200 from Raw Materials Inventory to Work-in-Process
	$150 from Labor to Work-in-Process
	$100 from Overhead to Work-in-Process for overhead related to direct labor hours (10 DLH × $10/DLH)
When finished:	$770 from Work-in-Process to Finished Goods
On 7/10:	$770 from Finished Goods to Cost of Goods Sold

Concept**Review**

1. When production begins, which account receives costs?
2. When production ends, which account receives costs?
3. Which account reflects the production costs of a product that is sold?

SANTA FE BELTS
(continued)

Santa Fe Belts has an inventory of leather and buckles. When an order arrives, the manager of the cutting process requisitions the leather necessary to make the belts. Similarly, the manager of the finishing process requisitions the buckles when the partially completed belts arrive in the finishing department. The manager of the raw materials inventory uses the requisition slips to verify the reduction in raw materials and their cost. The recipients record the cost and amount of raw materials used in their division on the job cost sheet. When the raw materials are recorded on the job cost sheet, they become part of the cost of Work-in-Process. In a similar fashion, direct labor and overhead become part of Work-in-Process when recorded on the job cost sheet. Upon completing the batch of belts, the total cost of the batch is recorded as part of Finished Goods Inventory. When delivered to the customer, the cost of the batch is recorded as Cost of Goods Sold.

Santa Fe Belts has a fiscal year ending June 30. Job #543 (described on page 335) is the only partially completed batch in Factory A. The Work-in-Process as of June 30 follows:

Direct materials	$2,475
Direct labor	100
Overhead (10 hours)($10/hour)	100
Total work-in-process	$2,675

ALLOCATION OF OVERHEAD TO JOBS

Chapter Nine outlined the following steps to allocate overhead (indirect product) costs: (1) defining the cost objects, (2) accumulating indirect costs in cost pools, (3) choosing an allocation base, (4) estimating an application rate, and (5) allocating indirect costs based on use of the allocation base. In this section, the cost objects are jobs, which are composed of individual or batches of products. The accumulation of indirect costs includes costs that are both fixed and variable with respect to the allocation base. The allocation base is some input into the production process, such as direct labor hours, machine hours, or material costs.

As described in Chapter Nine, the allocation base is chosen for making planning decisions and for control reasons. The application rate is predetermined based on budgeted overhead costs and the predicted use of the allocation base. The predetermined application rate allows for the allocation of overhead costs to jobs throughout the period, based on the usage of the allocation base. For instance, a firm's CD-ROM manufacturing department estimates its overhead costs for the upcoming year to be $1,000,000. The allocation base is machine hours used by the manufacturing jobs. It is predicted that 50,000 machine hours will be used in the next year. The predetermined application rate is established as $1,000,000/ 50,000, or $20 per hour. For each hour of machine time used by a job, overhead costs of $20 will be allocated.

These steps create an absorption cost system. All manufacturing costs are absorbed by the jobs if budgeted overhead costs and usage of the allocation base in the application rate are accurate predictions of the actual overhead costs and the actual allocation base usage. The predictions usually are not perfectly accurate, however, so allocated overhead costs do not equal actual overhead costs. In the following sections, we examine reasons why the application rate does not allocate all of the overhead costs, why we should be concerned about having applied (allocated) overhead different from actual overhead allocated to jobs, and how to account for these differences.

Over- and Underabsorbed Overhead

The application rate is a ratio of budgeted overhead costs to budgeted usage of the allocation bases. As long as the actual overhead costs divided by the actual usage of the allocation base (the actual application rate) equals the budgeted application rate, the allocated overhead costs equal the actual overhead costs. In reality, however, the estimated application rate rarely if ever equals the actual application rate. Therefore, the applied overhead does not equal the actual overhead. If allocated overhead costs are greater than actual overhead costs, the difference is called **overabsorbed overhead**. If allocated overhead costs are less than actual overhead costs, the difference is called **underabsorbed overhead**.

LO 4 Calculate over- and underabsorbed overhead.

Numerical Example	**10.3**

A tool manufacturer uses machine hours (MH) to allocate overhead costs. The company expects to use 1,000 machine hours during the month, and overhead costs are expected to be $100,000. Therefore, the application rate of $100,000/1,000 MH, or $100 per MH is used.

a. If the actual overhead costs during the month total $90,000 and actual machine hours total 900, what is the difference between applied and actual overhead?

b. If the actual overhead costs during the month total $98,000 and actual machine hours total 950, what is the difference between applied and actual overhead?

Solution

a.

Actual overhead costs	$90,000
Applied overhead costs ($100/MH)(900 MH)	90,000
Difference	$ 0

There is no difference between applied and actual costs because the actual application rate ($90,000/900 MH = $100/MH) equals the estimated application rate.

b.

Actual overhead costs	$98,000
Applied overhead costs ($100/MH)(950 MH)	95,000
Difference (underabsorbed)	$ 3,000

The actual application rate ($98,000/950 MH = $103.16/MH) is higher than the estimated application rate ($100 per MH). As a result, the overhead is underabsorbed.

There are many reasons why the actual application rate differs from the predicted one. This difference results in a discrepancy between actual and allocated overhead costs. One example is illustrated in Figure 10.2. The predicted and actual overhead cost functions are assumed to have a fixed cost component. The allocated overhead costs, however, are applied through the usage of an allocation base. If the allocation base is not used, no overhead costs are allocated, so the allocated cost function goes through the origin. The application rate is estimated by dividing the predicted overhead costs by the predicted usage of the allocation base. Therefore, the allocated cost line in Figure 10.2 goes through the point where the predicted overhead costs and the predicted usage of the allocation base meet. The allocated cost line has a slope equal to the application rate. If the actual usage of the allocation base turns out to be less than predicted, the amount of overhead costs allocated is less than the predicted amount. This relation can be seen on the vertical axis of Figure 10.2. Although actual costs are as predicted, the incorrect estimate of the usage of the allocation base causes underabsorbed overhead. Overabsorbed overhead occurs if the actual usage of the allocation base is greater than the predicted usage of the allocation base.

Numerical Example 10.4

A bicycle manufacturer estimates that the company will use 3,000 direct labor hours (DLH). Direct labor hours are used to allocate overhead. The company estimates that fixed overhead costs will be $30,000, and variable costs will be $20 per direct labor hour. At the end of the year, the company finds that it estimated fixed overhead and variable overhead per direct labor hour correctly but used 4,000 direct labor hours. What is the relation between actual overhead costs and allocated overhead costs?

Solution

Fixed costs	$30,000
Variable costs ($20/DLH)(3,000 DLH)	60,000
Total estimated overhead costs	$90,000

Figure 10.2

Cost Allocation with Fixed Costs

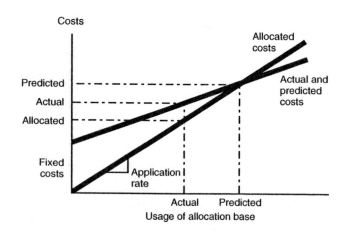

The application rate is $90,000/3,000 DLH, or $30 per DLH. The company actually uses 4,000 DLH, so (4,000 DLH)($30/DLH), or $120,000, of overhead is allocated to the products. The actual overhead, however, is as follows:

Fixed costs	$ 30,000
Variable costs ($20/DLH)(4,000 DLH)	80,000
Total actual overhead costs	$110,000

Therefore, the allocated overhead costs are $120,000 − $110,000, or $10,000 greater than the actual overhead costs. The overhead costs are overabsorbed.

Another reason for under- or overabsorbed overhead is simply an imprecise estimate of the overhead cost. Even if the expected usage of the allocation base is accurate, a misestimate of expected overhead leads to allocated overhead not being equal to actual overhead.

Numerical Example 10.5

An Internet bookseller allocates equal overhead to each book sold. At the beginning of the year, the bookseller estimates that 1 million books will be sold and that overhead will be $2 million. What is the over- or underabsorbed overhead if 1 million books are sold and overhead is $2.1 million?

Solution

The application rate is $2,000,000/1,000,000 books, or $2 per book. If 1 million books are sold, the bookseller allocates (1,000,000 books)($2/book), or $2,000,000. The underabsorbed overhead is $2,100,000 − $2,000,000, or $100,000.

Why Worry about Over- and Underabsorbed Overhead?

Differences between allocated and actual overhead exist due to inaccurate expectations about costs and cost driver usage. One option is to ignore the differences, but there are planning, control, and external reporting reasons for adjusting product costs for over- and underabsorbed overhead.

Many of the products have been sold by the time over- and underabsorbed overhead has been identified at the end of the period. Therefore, little opportunity exists to adjust prices of the products already manufactured. The organization can, however, use product costs adjusted for over- and underabsorbed overhead to make future pricing and product-mix decisions. If the over- and underabsorbed overhead occurred because of mistakes in estimates, these mistakes should be corrected before making subsequent planning decisions. If the over- and underabsorbed overhead results from a one-period aberration, no adjustments to product costs are necessary for planning purposes.

Planning Decisions

For instance, suppose a firm has a significant amount of underabsorbed overhead at the end of the year. If the underabsorbed overhead indicates a change in market demand for its products, the firm should investigate its products and those of its competitors to determine how best to adapt to its environment and create customer value. Alternatively, if the underabsorbed amount reflects excess capacity, management should evaluate whether this situation is short- or long-term in nature. If it is the latter, management must decide whether to eliminate the excess capacity or to find alternative uses for it. Therefore, organizations should use the warning signs provided by over- and underabsorbed overhead to improve their future planning decisions. In this way, they can better ensure that their activities continue to create organizational value.

Strategy for Customer Value

Over- and underabsorbed overhead costs also have control implications. Allocated costs are used as performance measures, creating incentives to influence the

**Control
Decisions**

overhead cost allocations. One way to affect allocated overhead costs is to influence the calculation of the application rate. If the application rate is calculated with biased estimates of overhead costs and allocation base usage, managers can avoid the allocation of some overhead costs. Unless the allocated overhead is adjusted for underabsorbed overhead, managers will be tempted to influence application rates with biased estimates. These biased estimates not only affect control but also harm planning efforts. For example, managers frequently are evaluated based on the income of their responsibility centers. If they can influence the overhead rate, they would prefer to estimate their usage of an allocation base in terms of the final impact on their center's income. Inaccuracies could lead to poor planning if the firm used these figures for pricing and product-mix decisions. Control also would be affected if the managers could influence reported income to their advantage. One way to mitigate these biased estimates is to reward managers for the accuracy of their predictions.

External reports to shareholders or tax authorities are based on actual costs, not on estimated costs. Allocated overhead costs reflect estimates of actual overhead costs. Ultimately, however, these estimates most be replaced by actual overhead costs for external reporting purposes. Therefore, some adjustment for over- and underabsorbed overhead must be made to the external reports. Also, cost reimbursement contracts frequently are based on actual costs, not estimated costs. Therefore, adjustments for over- and underabsorbed overhead are commonly made to determine the final bill for a cost reimbursement contract.

When allocated overhead costs are different from actual overhead costs, some decision must be made on accounting for the difference. The next section describes alternate procedures for dealing with over- and underabsorbed overhead.

Accounting for Over- and Underabsorbed Overhead

LO 5 Account for over- and underabsorbed overhead.

At the end of the accounting period, an accounting adjustment must be made to eliminate any over- or underabsorbed overhead for the reasons just described. The three methods to account for over- and underabsorbed overhead are: (1) adjust Cost of Goods Sold, (2) prorate among Work-in-Process, Finished Goods, and Cost of Goods Sold, or (3) recalculate the application rate and apply to all the jobs during the year. Each method has a different impact on current earnings. If net income is used as a performance measure for some managers, they will be concerned about the method of accounting for over- and underabsorbed overhead. Managers usually are not free to select any of the three methods. In general, if the over- or underabsorbed overhead is a material amount, managers cannot use the first method of simply adjusting the cost of goods sold.

The choice of method also depends on how the allocated over- and underabsorbed costs are being used. If the purpose of the allocation is to communicate costs for planning purposes, the method that most closely approximates the cost of using indirect resources should be used. If the purpose of the allocation is to control managers, the over- and underabsorbed overhead allocation should reflect controllability by the managers. The superiority of any of the following methods depends on the circumstances surrounding the allocation.

Adjusting Cost of Goods Sold

The simplest method of accounting for over- or underabsorbed overhead is to adjust Cost of Goods Sold. If overhead is overabsorbed, the Cost of Goods Sold account is reduced by the amount of overabsorption. If overhead is underabsorbed, the Cost of Goods Sold account is increased. No adjustments are made to the Work-in-Process or Finished Goods Inventory accounts at the end of the period. This method, however, cannot be used for external reporting if the over- and underabsorbed overhead has a material impact (more than 3 to 5%) of Cost of Goods sold.

Prorating

Through **proration,** the over- or underabsorbed overhead is allocated to the Work-in-Process, Finished Goods, and Cost of Goods Sold accounts proportionally to the size of those accounts at the end of the period. For example, if the ending balances of Work-in-Process, Finished Goods, and Cost of Goods Sold accounts are $10,000, $15,000, and $25,000, respectively, 20% of the over- or underabsorbed overhead would be allocated to Work-in-Process, 30% allocated to Finished Goods, and 50% to Cost of Goods Sold.

Recalculating the Application Rate

Recalculating the application rate and reallocating overhead to all products manufactured during the year is the most costly in terms of accounting efforts. The actual application rate is calculated and used to reallocate the entire overhead to the products. Recalculating the application rate and reallocating overhead may be required in some cost reimbursement contracts.

Numerical Example 10.6

At the end of the accounting period, a window manufacturer has the following account balances:

	Direct Costs	Allocated Overhead	Balance
Work-in-Process	$ 10,000	$ 2,000	$ 12,000
Finished Goods	25,000	5,000	30,000
Cost of Goods Sold	85,000	13,000	98,000
Total	$120,000	$20,000	$140,000

The amount of overhead allocated to these accounts during the period was $20,000 based on an application rate of $5 per direct labor hour (DLH), but actual overhead costs were $25,000.

a. What adjustments are made to the account balances if the underabsorbed overhead is completely allocated to cost of goods sold?

b. What adjustments are made to the account balances if the underabsorbed overhead is prorated?

c. What are the new balances if the overhead application rate is recalculated?

Solution

a. The underabsorbed overhead is $25,000 − $20,000, or $5,000. If the entire underabsorbed overhead were allocated to the Cost of Goods Sold account, the adjusted account balances would be as follows:

	Original	Allocation	Adjusted
Work-in-Process	$ 12,000	0	$ 12,000
Finished Goods	30,000	0	30,000
Cost of Goods Sold	98,000	$5,000	103,000
Total	$140,000	$5,000	$145,000

b. If the entire underabsorbed overhead were prorated, these would be the adjusted account balances:

	Original	Percentage	Allocation	Adjusted
Work-in-Process	$ 12,000	8.57%	$ 429	$ 12,429
Finished Goods	30,000	21.43	1,071	31,071
Cost of Goods Sold	98,000	70.00	3,500	101,500
Total	$140,000	100.00%	$5,000	$145,000

c. The actual number of direct labor hours to produce the items in each account can be calculated by dividing the allocated overhead by the application rate of $5 per DLH:

Work-in-Process $2,000/($5/DLH)	400 DLH
Finished Goods $5,000/($5/DLH)	1,000 DLH
Cost of Goods Sold $13,000/($5/DLH)	2,600 DLH
Total	4,000 DLH

The actual application rate is $25,000/4,000 DLH, or $6.25 per DLH. The overhead allocated in the following table is calculated by multiplying the actual application rate by the actual number of direct labor hours:

	Direct Costs	Allocated Overhead	Balance
Work-in-Process	$ 10,000	$ 2,500	$ 12,500
Finished Goods	25,000	6,250	31,250
Cost of Goods Sold	85,000	16,250	101,250
Total	$120,000	$25,000	$145,000

Concept**Review**

1. Why do actual overhead costs generally not equal overhead allocated based on a predetermined application rate?
2. Why should an organization be concerned about over- and underabsorbed overhead?
3. What three methods can be used to deal with over- and underabsorbed overhead?

SANTA FE BELTS
(Continued)

Factory A of Santa Fe Belts predicted that its overhead costs would be $800,000 and that the number of direct labor hours would be 80,000. The actual overhead costs, however, are $765,000, and actual direct labor hours are 75,000 hours. The underabsorbed overhead is as follows:

Actual overhead	$765,000
Allocated overhead ($10/hour)(75,000 hours)	750,000
Underabsorbed overhead	$ 15,000

The actual overhead application rate is $765,000/75,000 hours, or $10.20 per hour. Santa Fe Belts could use this actual application rate to recalculate the overhead allocated to each batch of belts but decides that this step would be a costly procedure without obvious benefits, given that it cannot recapture any costs from its customers. Instead, the Cost of Goods Sold account is increased by $15,000 to account for the underabsorbed overhead.

ABC AND MULTIPLE ALLOCATION BASES

LO 6   Use ABC to allocate overhead in a job-order system.

Until this point in the chapter, all overhead costs have been accumulated first in a single overhead account and then allocated to products using a single overhead rate. Figure 10.3 illustrates this overhead allocation procedure. When a single overhead rate is used, all of the overhead is accumulated in a single cost pool. As defined in Chapter Nine, a *cost pool* is a collection of accounts accumulated for the purpose of allocating the costs in the pool to other cost objects. These cost objects include departments, processes, products, and services.

From Chapter Three and the discussion of ABC, we know that indirect costs have varying relations with products. For example, some indirect product costs vary with the number of units produced; other costs vary with the number of batches. To adapt to an organizational environment with different types of indirect costs, costs can be accumulated in multiple cost pools related to different activities. A cost driver then is selected for each activity cost pool to allocate the indirect costs to the different products.

ABC can be used in a job-order costing system. Direct material and direct labor costs are recorded in a similar fashion. Overhead, however, would be added to the job cost sheet based on the use of multiple cost drivers.

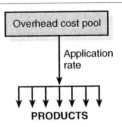

Figure 10.3 Single Overhead Cost Pool and Application Rate

Numerical Example 10.7

A printing company has received an order (Job #234) to print 20 books written by Sara Wilson on her family's history. The company will charge her based on cost plus 30%. It uses 10 reams of paper at $15 per ream and 20 covers at $5 each. To complete the job, 15 hours of labor at $20 per hour were used. The job was started on June 4 and finished on June 8. Overhead is allocated to the job based on ABC. The job used the following activities and cost drivers:

Activity	Cost Driver	Usage	Application Rate
Printing	Number of pages	4,000 pages	$0.05/page
Cropping	Number of pictures	80 pictures	$6/picture
Binding	Number of bindings	20 bindings	$10/binding
General	Direct labor hours	15 hours	$12/direct labor hour

a. Construct a job-order cost sheet for Job #234.

b. What price should Sara Wilson be charged?

Solution

Job Number	234			Date Started	6/4	
				Date Completed	6/8	
	Raw Materials			**Direct Labor**		
Type	**Cost**	**Qty.**	**Amount**	**Rate**	**Hours**	**Amount**
Paper	$15	10	$150	$20	15	$ 300
Cover	5	20	100			

Total direct materials	$250
Total direct labor	300
Overhead	
Printing (4,000 pages)($0.05/page)	200
Cropping (80 pictures)($6/picture)	480
Binding (20 bindings)($10/binding)	200
General (15 hours)($12/hour)	180
Total job cost	$1,610
Price ($1,610)(1.3)	$2,093

The advantages of using ABC in a job-order system include improved planning and control. Improved planning occurs as the cost drivers are more likely to capture the different ways that cost objects use overhead resources. If each cost driver is proportional to the activity costs in the cost pool, the job-order cost sheet reports a relatively accurate product cost.

Business**Analysis**

Activity-Based Costing in a Business School

How much does it "cost" to teach an undergraduate student for one year? Is it more expensive to teach Ph.D. students, MBAs, or undergraduates? Most universities do not have good answers to these questions despite complex and detailed accounting systems. Also, unlike manufacturing organizations, universities do not have products in the typical sense. Many interrelated costs and benefits result from the activities that a university undertakes. Activity-Based-Costing is one way that can provide insights into the cost and benefits of the outputs of a university system.

A case study at a large business school developed an ABC model of its accounting department. As in the manufacturing sector, the objective was to allocate overhead costs in a manner that captured how different cost objects consumed resources. The study determined that the business school, like most universities, had a number of features that made cost management more difficult:

* Decentralized decision making with critical decisions taken at lower levels.
* Complex accounting and budget systems geared to compliance reporting.
* A lack of clearly defined outcomes and products.
* Many interconnected activities (e.g., teaching, research, administration).
* The consumer and the producer of activities frequently the same.
* Interrelated costs and revenues in that certain activities only undertaken due to the receipt of specific funds tied to the activity.
* The impact of capacity constraints on cost and quality of activities.

The ABC model focused on the accounting department of the business school. The first stage developed a set of cost objects and cost pools. The cost objects were the various programs, research outputs, service outputs, and unused capacity. The cost pools were the faculty resource costs and non-faculty resource costs. Faculty costs (compensation, travel and research allowances, etc.) were subdivided into four

pools: teaching, research, service, and advising of doctoral students. Non-faculty costs were placed into three pools: teaching support, research support, and general administration. In the second stage, costs of the business school were identified and allocated in the same manner. These costs included the career center, computer technology, media services, and administrative offices. Once the costs of the various cost pools were assigned to the cost objects, the study examined specific cost objects to determine whether the ABC model provided insights not available from the existing approach to costing.

The following points summarize the results of the study:

* Significant differences exist in the per-student cost of the various academic programs. For instance, the cost of a Ph.D. student per year is approximately 3.5 times that of a masters program student in a combined undergraduate/masters program.
* Unused capacity represents a major cost. This unused capacity results from a number of factors ranging from undersubscribed classes and inefficient course scheduling.
* Space is a costly commodity at the business school, often comparable to the sum of all other costs.
* Programs and activities do not make uniform use of support services, but the cost of the latter tends to be spread uniformly across all areas based on head count.
* ABC offers one way to focus on the cost-benefit of activity spending and a better way to determine the efficiency in delivering teaching, research, and service outputs.

What factors might contribute to the higher annual total cost per student in the Ph.D. program compared to the five-year combined undergraduate/masters program? Why would the cost of capacity tend to be overlooked in a university environment? Why would university faculty and staff be hesitant perhaps about efforts to cost their activities?

Source: M. H. Granof, D. E. Platt, and I. Vaysman, "Using Activity-Based Costing to Manage More Effectively," Grant Report to The PricewaterhouseCoopers Endowment for The Business of Government, January 2000.

Control Decisions

Using multiple cost drivers through ABC also has some control benefits. When using only one allocation base, managers will overuse all the overhead resources not associated with the allocation base. By using more than one allocation base or cost driver, the organization can tax the use of more than one overhead resource. With multiple cost drivers, managers would have to make trade-offs in using overhead resources in the different activity cost pools. For example, if all costs of the department supporting Web pages are allocated based on the number of Web pages, managers will attempt to reduce the allocated costs by increasing the amount of information on each Web page. At the same time, the managers may use extra pictures and other expensive Web-page services if no allocated costs are associated with them.

Improved control also can occur if an organization has multiple goals. An organization can use multiple allocation bases or cost drivers to achieve these multiple goals more effectively. For example, if an organization is trying to decrease both de-

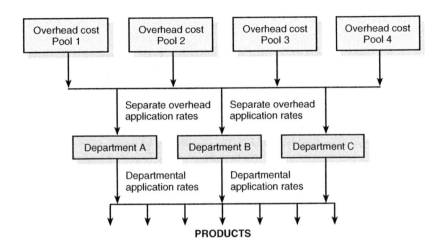

Figure 10.4

Two-Stage Cost Allocation
with Departmental
Application Rates

fects and the use of direct labor, both the number of defects and the number of direct labor hours can be used as allocation bases for different cost pools. Allocation bases are taxed through the allocation of overhead; therefore, managers will be motivated to reduce defects and reduce direct labor.

MULTI-STAGE ALLOCATION PROCESSES

Overhead costs might be allocated to products through multiple stages. A common approach is to allocate general overhead costs first to departments that directly provide products and services and then to allocate the departmental costs to the various products and services. Figure 10.4 illustrates this two-stage allocation process.

The allocation bases and application rates used to allocate costs from the departments to the products are specific to that department. One department might use machine hours, and another department might use the number of engineering hours to allocate the departmental overhead costs. Alternatively, the allocation base for each department could be the number of direct labor hours specific to that department.

Multi-stage allocation schemes also can be used in conjunction with ABC. The general overhead cost pools would represent general activities. Cost drivers that reflect usage of the general activities would be selected to allocate costs to departmental or more specific activity cost pools. An additional set of cost drivers to allocate costs to products then would be identified for the departments or specific activities.

There are control reasons for allocating general overhead initially to departments. Managerial responsibility often is oriented around departments. Departmental managers who are responsible for controlling the cost of their departments want to control costs allocated to them. Therefore, managers carefully use the allocation base upon which costs from the general overhead accounts are allocated to their departments.

LO 7 Use multi-stage allocation methods and departmental cost pools to allocate overhead.

Control Decisions

Numerical Example   10.8

A factory has three general overhead cost pools representing personnel, inventory, and general administration. Their costs, allocation bases, and application rates follow:

Cost Pool	Allocation Base	Application Rate
Personnel	Number of employees	$5,000/employee
Inventory	Cost of raw materials used	$0.05/$ of raw materials
General administration	Direct labor hours	$8/direct labor hour

The factory contains three departments, machining, painting, and assembly, which have the following costs (before allocated costs from general overhead cost pools) and usage of allocation bases:

Department	Internal Department Costs	Raw Materials	Employees	Direct Labor Hours
Machining	$900,000	$200,000	20	20,000
Painting	750,000	100,000	10	15,000
Assembly	850,000	100,000	30	25,000

Each department allocates overhead to products based on direct labor hours. How much overhead is allocated to a product that uses 1,000 direct labor hours of machining, 800 direct labor hours of painting, and 500 direct labor hours of assembly?

Solution

The first step is to allocate general overhead costs to the departments to determine total departmental costs. The allocated amounts in the following panel are calculated by multiplying the application rate by the usage of the allocation base:

Overhead Cost Pool	Application Rate	Allocated to:		
		Machining	Painting	Assembly
Personnel	$5,000/employee	$ 100,000	$ 50,000	$ 150,000
Inventory	$0.05/$ raw material	10,000	5,000	5,000
Gen. Ad.	$8/direct labor hour	160,000	120,000	200,000
Total allocated to departments		$ 270,000	$175,000	$ 355,000
Separate departmental costs		900,000	750,000	850,000
Total departmental costs		$1,170,000	$925,000	$1,205,000

The next step is to determine the application rates for the different departments:

Department	Costs	Direct Labor Hours	Application Rate
Machining	$1,170,000	20,000	$58.50/DLH
Painting	925,000	15,000	61.67/DLH
Assembly	1,205,000	25,000	48.20/DLH

The last step is to allocate the overhead from the different departments to the products based on the use of direct labor hours by the products. For the product in question, the allocated overhead follows:

Department	Application Rate	Direct Labor Hours	Overhead Costs
Machining	$58.50/DLH	1,000	$ 58,500
Painting	61.67/DLH	800	49,336
Assembly	48.20/DLH	500	24,100
Total allocated overhead costs			$131,936

Concept**Review**

1. Under what conditions will multiple allocation bases yield more accurate product costs than a single allocation base?

2. What is a control reason for first allocating costs to departments and then to products?

Santa Fe Belts is under pressure to change its cost allocation system. Pricing of specially ordered belts is based, in part, on the expected cost of making the belts. Some customers, who order special belts requiring a great deal of finishing labor, believe that the product that they order is burdened too heavily with overhead from other departments. Santa Fe's controller decides to reallocate overhead using departmental application rates. This allocation procedure requires her to estimate overhead costs and direct labor in each department. She makes the following estimates:

Department	Overhead Costs	Direct Labor Hours	Application Rate
Cutting	$250,000	10,000	$25.00/hour
Combining	320,000	40,000	8.00/hour
Punching	50,000	5,000	10.00/hour
Finishing	180,000	25,000	7.20/hour
Totals	$800,000	80,000	

She tests the departmental allocation method on Job #543 (on page 335). The following cost allocation occurs:

Department	Direct Labor Hours	Application Rate	Allocated Overhead
Cutting	10	$25.00/hour	$250
Combining	15	$8.00/hour	120
Punching	5	$10.00/hour	50
Finishing	15	$7.20/hour	108
Total allocated overhead			$528

When only one cost pool is used, the overhead allocation to Job #543 is $450. The difference of $78 appears to be large enough to warrant further testing. If sufficiently large differences do exist across different orders, the company will have to consider allocating costs by department.

PROCESS COSTING

Job-order cost systems are built around distinct jobs or batches in the manufacturing plant. In contrast, some manufacturing processes have continuous flow production. For example, a car manufacturer dedicated to making a single model operates a continuous production line. A vegetable canning company operates a continuous process of cleaning, chopping, cooking, and canning vegetables. A cement manufacturer continuously mixes the ingredients of cement and packages the mix. Each of these companies is devoted to making a single product (at least for a period of time) in a continuous process. Service organizations also have continuous flow processes. For instance, fast-food restaurants often maintain a continuous production of ready-to-go items.

LO 8 Calculate product costs using process costing.

Many restaurants prepare menu items continuously to have them ready on demand. The process ensures that all items are similarly made, to maintain quality and quantity standards. This continuous process saves time and cost, while meeting customer demands for quick and consistent menu choices.

**Planning
Decisions**

Since the production process is a continuous flow operation, discrete batches do not exist. In process costing, costs are assigned to identical products that are produced in a continuous flow through a series of manufacturing steps or *processes*. These processes are usually organized as separate cost centers for control purposes.

For product costing purposes, all the costs are associated with the same product. The cost allocation is not among different products but among units still in Work-in-Process Inventory and units transferred out of the process or out of the plant to Finished Goods Inventory or Cost of Goods Sold. Work-in-Process and Finished Goods are assets, Cost of Goods Sold is an expense. Therefore, the allocation affects the organization's profit.

On the one hand, process costing is inherently simpler and less costly to maintain than job-order costing. It requires no tracking and accounting for separate units or batches. On the other hand, the information provided is far more aggregated and less useful for decision making. In particular, costs for individual units or batches are not available and hence cannot be used to evaluate cost trends across different jobs of similar products.

The simplest example of process costing can be illustrated by dividing total manufacturing costs (including indirect and direct costs) of the period by the number of units produced. For example, if a car manufacturer makes 5,000 cars during a month and incurs $50,000,000 of manufacturing costs, the average cost per car is $50,000,000/5,000 cars, or $10,000 per car. The $10,000 is an average cost containing both variable and fixed costs. Therefore, the average cost provides no information about the incremental cost of making additional cars. The $10,000 average cost can be used, however, in external financial reports to indicate the cost of inventory and the cost of goods sold.

Process costing becomes more difficult when work-in-process exists at the end of the accounting period. If there is work-in-process at the end of the accounting period, some units have been partially processed but are not yet finished. Partially completed units have consumed some of the period's manufacturing costs. Dividing total manufacturing costs during the period by the number of units finished during the period ignores the resources consumed by partially completed units.

To recognize the partial completion of some units at the end of the period, the concept of equivalent units is used. An **equivalent unit** is a measure of production during a period of time; it is based on the *percentage of completion*. This percentage of completion is used to determine the equivalence in terms of finished units completed during the period. For example, completing 40% of the work to make 50 cars is equivalent to completing (0.40)(50), or 20 cars. By recognizing the percentage of completion of ending work-in-process, the work performed during the period can be described in terms of equivalent units.

Numerical Example 10.9

A computer workstation manufacturer began and completed 500 workstations during the period. In addition, another 50 workstations were worked on during the period. On average, these units were 60% completed. There was no beginning work-in-process. Manufacturing costs during the period were $5,000,000. How many equivalent units of work were performed during the period? What was the average cost of a completed workstation?

Solution

The total equivalent units completed during the period were as follows:

Units 100% completed	500
Partially completed units (0.60)(50)	30
Total equivalent units	530

The average cost per computer workstation is $5,000,000/530, or $9,434.

Business**Analysis**

CAE Inc.

CAE Inc., a group of advanced technology companies, is a global leader in the specialized markets of electronics, fiber processing technologies, and cleaning technologies. CAE's global headquarters is located in Toronto, Canada. Its Electronics Group designs and produces flight and land-based simulation systems as well as marine and energy control systems. Its Cleaning Technologies Division supplies cleaning and waste minimization equipment and services to the automobile and other industries. Its Fiber Processing Division works with the forestry industry to develop technologies to optimize the usage of fiber. The company has built its strength in each division by focusing on its customers, technological innovation, and the creation of organizational value.

To achieve these goals, CAE must provide solutions that match customer needs. This customer focus is one way that CAE can maintain a competitive edge in the global marketplace. CAE also must be mindful of costs. Therefore, CAE designs, develops, and produces its products in terms of "mass customization." While products might share common features to permit some economies of scale, CAE customizes its products to meet the requirements of individual clients. Working with its customers to meet current and anticipated demands allows CAE to remain both competitive and innovative. In the long run, this ability to meet customer needs translates into sustained shareholder value.

For example, CAE's Electronics Group maintains its niche by customizing simulation systems to meet the specifications of global customers as diverse as the British Royal Navy, Swissair, Ford Motor Company, and Federal Express. In terms of its costing system, CAE employs a detailed job-order system to accumulate and record costs to each specific contract. The system also must track contracts that span an extended time frame from initiation to completion.

Why does CAE use a job-order costing system instead of a much simpler process costing system? How does the costing system at CAE operate to support CAE's strategy and its goals to create customer and organizational value?

Source: www.cae.ca.

Once the average cost per unit is determined, it can be used to partition the period's production costs into costs associated with goods that are finished and goods that are still in work-in-process. In the case of the workstations in Numerical Example 10.9, the cost of those that are finished is (500 workstations)($9,434/

Televisions are mass produced even when firms try to meet customer requirements through mass customization. With continuous production, units are at various stages of completion throughout the period. To estimate the value of work-in-process, the firm converts the physical quantity of televisions into equivalent units based on percentage of completion.

workstation), or $4,717,000. The cost of the workstations in work-in-process at the end of the period is (30 workstations)($9,434/workstation), or approximately $283,000. The original $5,000,000 in manufacturing costs are allocated to the Finished Goods and Work-in-Process accounts. Costs allocated to Finished Goods are transferred to Cost of Goods Sold when the product is sold.

Additional complications in process costing arise when there is beginning work-in-process. In this case, the equivalent units of work performed during the period also must include the work necessary to complete the beginning work-in-process. The number of equivalent units of work performed during the period includes three components: (1) work to complete beginning work-in-process, (2) work on units that are both started and completed during the period, and (3) work on units that are started during the period but not completed (ending work-in-process).

Numerical Example 10.10

A manufacturer of televisions had 1,000 units in beginning work-in-process that were 30% completed at the end of last year. This year, the remaining 70% of the work on the 1,000 units was completed, and 10,000 more units were started and completed. In addition, 500 more units were started this period but were only 60% completed. Manufacturing costs during the period were $2,000,000. What was the cost per equivalent unit during the period?

Solution

The number of equivalent units of work performed during the period was as follows:

Work to complete beginning work-in-process (0.70)(1,000)	700
Work on unit started and completed	10,000
Work on ending work-in-process (0.60)(500)	300
Total equivalent units	11,000

The cost per equivalent unit is $2,000,000/11,000, or $181.82.

The allocation of costs between units that are finished and units still in work-in-process is complicated when beginning work-in-process exists. In addition to the production costs in the current period, the cost of the beginning work-in-process due to work performed in the previous period also must be allocated. The cost allocation procedure depends on the accounting cost flow assumption. The FIFO, weighted-average cost, and LIFO procedures lead to different cost allocations. Those procedures are explained briefly in the Appendix and in detail in financial accounting and cost accounting textbooks.

Process costing yields cost numbers for Work-in-Process, Finished Goods, and Cost of Goods Sold for external financial reporting. The use of process costs for planning purposes is limited if process costs include fixed and variable costs. Dividing total process costs by the number of equivalent units produced yields an average cost. In general, an average cost does not represent the variable cost of making the product.

Process costing is used for control because externally reported accounting numbers are frequently used to evaluate managers. If managers are evaluated based on the cost per equivalent unit, then minimizing the average cost per unit and maximizing profit are not necessarily consistent. Minimizing the average cost can lead to production levels beyond amounts that can be sold. This excess production creates non–value-added costs, such as inventory holding costs. Problems related to absorption costing systems, such as job-order or process costing systems, are described in Chapter Eleven.

Concept**Review**

1. What is the primary purpose of process costing?
2. How does the concept of equivalent units enable the calculation of the average cost per unit?

SANTA FE BELTS
(Continued)

Factory B of Santa Fe Belts uses a process costing system because its only product, the standard belt, has no distinguishable batches. Instead of tracking the cost of each belt as it is processed, this factory tracks only total manufacturing costs as they occur. At the end of each month, the total manufacturing costs are divided by the number of belts produced to determine the average cost per belt. For example, in January, total manufacturing costs were $40,000, and the number of standard belts manufactured during January was 10,000. The average cost per belt in January is $40,000/10,000 belts, or $4 per belt.

The president of Santa Fe Belts uses the $4 per belt cost to make pricing decisions for standard belts and to evaluate and reward managers at Factory B. However, problems are arising in both areas.

The $4 per belt is an average cost and includes fixed costs. The president would like to know the variable cost of making standard belts, but the process costing system does not reveal any information about variable costs. The president also is noticing an increase in inventory at Factory B and wonders whether rewarding the managers based on reducing the average cost of making the belt is affecting inventory decisions. The president decides to read the next chapter on problems with absorption costing systems.

You decide

SUMMARY

1 **Identify different types of production systems and corresponding absorption costing systems.** Job shops and batch manufacturers tend to use job-order cost systems, and assembly processes and continuous flow processes tend to use process costing.

2 **Understand a job-order cost system.** A job-order cost system is used to record the direct labor, direct material, and overhead costs related to a particular product or batch of products. Costs are separately accumulated on the job cost sheet while work is being performed on the product or batch.

3 **Identify how costs flow through different accounts.** Costs flow from raw materials, labor, and overhead accounts to work-in-process accounts during production, to finished goods accounts upon completion of production, and to cost of goods sold when sold.

4 **Calculate over- and underabsorbed overhead.** Over- and underabsorbed overhead occurs when the actual overhead costs are not equal to the applied overhead costs.

5 **Account for over- and underabsorbed overhead.** Over- and underabsorbed overhead can be (1) charged directly to cost of goods sold, (2) prorated among work-in-process, finished goods, and cost of goods sold, or (3) eliminated by recalculating the application rate using the actual overhead costs and allocation base usage.

6 **Use ABC to allocate overhead in a job-order system.** Overhead is divided into different activity cost pools and allocated to different products using different cost drivers and application rates for each cost pool.

7 **Use multi-stage allocation methods and departmental cost pools to allocate overhead.** Overhead initially is allocated to departmental cost pools and then to products based on the department's usage of the allocation base.

8 **Calculate product costs using process costing.** With process costing, the production costs are divided by the number of units to determine an average cost per unit. If there is partial completion of units during the period, equivalent units are used to divide into production costs.

9 **Prepare cost of goods manufactured and cost of goods sold schedules. (Appendix)** The cost of goods manufactured schedule includes raw material used (beginning raw materials + purchases − ending raw materials), direct labor, and manufacturing overhead to determine total manufacturing costs. The cost of goods manufactured equals the total manufacturing costs plus beginning work-in-process less ending work-in-process. The cost of goods sold equals the cost of goods manufactured plus the beginning finished goods inventory less the ending finished goods inventory.

KEY TERMS

absorption costing The inclusion of variable and fixed overhead in the product cost. *(p. 332)*

equivalent unit A measure of production, recognizing partial completion, that is used in process costing to identify work performed during a period of time. *(p. 350)*

first-in, first-out (FIFO) An inventory flow that assumes that the oldest units in inventory are sold first. *(p. 355)*

job-order systems A system of recording costs for a particular job, which could be a single unit or a batch. *(p. 332)*

last-in, first-out (LIFO) An inventory flow that assumes that the newest units in inventory are sold first. *(p. 355)*

overabsorbed overhead The amount by which overhead applied is greater than actual overhead cost incurred. *(p. 339)*

process costing   A system of determining product costs by dividing total costs by the number of equivalent units produced. *(p. 332)*

proration   The process of dividing over- or underabsorbed overhead into finished inventory, cost of goods sold, and work-in-process. *(p. 343)*

specific identification inventory valuation   An inventory flow that uses the historical costs of the actual

units transferred out of an inventory account. *(p. 354)*

underabsorbed overhead   The amount by which overhead applied is less than actual overhead cost incurred. *(p. 339)*

weighted-average cost   A per unit product cost determined by taking the weighted-average cost of all units in inventory. *(p. 355)*

APPENDIX

Cost of Goods Manufactured, Cost of Goods Sold, and Alternative Cost Flow Methods for Inventory

LO 9   Prepare cost of goods manufactured and cost of goods sold schedules.

This chapter examines the flow of costs for a particular job from Raw Materials, Work-in-Process, Finished Goods Inventory, and Cost of Goods Sold. The jobs are specifically identified. The manufacturing costs of a particular job move from account to account as the job is manufactured, finished, and sold. This flow of costs determines the cost of the goods manufactured and the cost of goods sold. This cost flow, in turn, affects net income. These relations are captured in two schedules: cost of goods manufactured and cost of goods sold.

The cost of goods manufactured is a schedule that identifies the manufacturing resources used to determine the total cost of goods manufactured during the period. Table 10A.1 is an example of a cost of goods manufactured schedule. In this schedule, the amount of raw materials used is calculated indirectly by using beginning and ending raw material balances and the purchases during the period:

Raw materials used = Beginning raw materials + Purchases −
Ending raw materials

In a similar manner, the cost of goods manufactured is calculated indirectly, using beginning and ending work-in-process and total manufacturing costs of the period:

Cost of goods manufactured = Beginning work-in-process +
Total manufacturing costs −
Ending work-in-process

The cost of goods manufactured in Table 10A.1 represents the cost of finished units transferred to the finished goods inventory. The cost of goods sold schedule in Table 10A.2 uses the $245,000 cost of goods manufactured to calculate the cost of goods sold. The cost of goods sold is calculated indirectly by using the beginning and ending finished goods inventory and the cost of goods manufactured during the month:

Cost of goods sold = Beginning finished goods inventory +
Cost of goods manufactured −
Ending finished goods inventory

The cost of goods sold in Table 10A.2 is then used to calculate the net income for the period.

In the cost of goods manufactured and cost of goods sold schedules, the cost of the ending inventories of the raw materials, work-in-process, and finished goods is used in determining the cost of goods sold. Several external reporting methods are acceptable in calculating the cost of ending inventories. Under the **specific identification inventory valuation** method, the ending inventory is determined by identifying the specific units of the raw materials, work-in-process, and finished goods and their respective historical costs. This procedure has been used implicitly in this

WESTERN COMPANY
Schedule of Cost of Goods Manufactured
Month of May 2002

Direct material		
Raw Material Inventory, May 1	$ 40,000	
May purchases of raw materials	100,000	
Available raw materials	$140,000	
Raw Material Inventory, May 31	50,000	
Raw materials used in May		$ 90,000
Direct labor		100,000
Manufacturing overhead		
Indirect labor	$ 30,000	
Utilities	10,000	
Depreciation	5,000	
General administration	15,000	
Total		60,000
Total manufacturing costs		$250,000
Work-in-Process, May 1		10,000
Work-in-Process, May 31		(15,000)
Cost of goods manufactured		$245,000

WESTERN COMPANY
Schedule of Cost of Goods Sold
Month of May 2002

Finished Goods Inventory, May 1	$180,000
Cost of goods manufactured (from Table 10A.1)	245,000
Cost of goods available for sale	$425,000
Finished Goods Inventory, May 31	150,000
Cost of goods sold	$275,000

textbook. However, this method might be expensive to implement as management must keep track of the batches from which each item came.

Alternative ways to measure the cost of ending inventory and the cost of goods sold exist. Under **first-in, first-out (FIFO,** the ending inventory is assumed to be the items produced most recently and is valued based on the cost of producing the most recent batches. The cost of goods sold, therefore, is based on the costs of the beginning inventory and items produced earlier in the period. Under **last-in, first-out (LIFO),** the ending inventory is assumed to be composed of items produced initially. The valuation of ending inventory under LIFO is based on the costs of items produced at the beginning of the accounting period and the costs of the beginning inventory. Therefore, the cost of goods sold is based on the cost of items most recently produced. The **weighted-average cost** method uses a weighted average of the cost of beginning inventory items and the cost of items produced during the accounting period to determine the cost of ending inventory and cost of goods sold. These methods are described in more detail in financial accounting texts.

Different inventory costing methods only provide different accounting numbers when there is an ending inventory and inventory costs (either manufacturing or wholesale) are changing over time. During periods of stable costs, the inventory costing method has no effect on accounting reports. If prices are changing rapidly, however, the inventory costing method can have a large effect on the valuation of inventory and the earnings reported by the organization. The choice of an inventory cost method is important as it affects external financial statements, taxes, and contracts based on the external financial statements.

During periods of rising costs, the FIFO method generally results in higher ending inventory costs. If an inventory costing method makes the cost of the ending inventory higher, the cost of goods sold is lower, and the net income is higher. During periods of rising costs, the LIFO method generally reports a lower cost of ending inventory, a higher cost of goods sold, and a lower net income figure. A lower net income is advantageous to reduce taxes, so LIFO is popular for tax reporting but is not allowed in many jurisdictions.

If external financial statements are used for performance evaluation, the inventory costing method also will affect internal decision making and control. For the remainder of this text, we assume that organizations use the specific identification inventory valuation method, but the use of other inventory costing methods should be recognized.

Numerical Example 10A.1

Portland Company, which makes cement, had the following bimonthly manufacturing output during 2002:

Month	Output in Tons	Manufacturing Costs	Cost per Ton
January/February	3,000	$ 60,000	$20.00
March/April	3,500	71,750	20.50
May/June	2,500	52,500	21.00
July/August	3,000	63,000	21.00
September/October	3,200	67,200	21.00
November/December	3,300	72,600	22.00
Totals	18,500	$387,050	$20.92

Beginning inventory = 5,000 tons at $20.00 pound, or a total of $100,000
Ending inventory = 6,000 tons

a. What is the cost of the ending inventory under the FIFO, LIFO, and weighted-average cost methods?

b. What is the cost of goods sold under each of the methods?

Solution

a. FIFO: The last 6,000 tons manufactured include 3,300 from November/December and 2,700 from September/October. These tons of cement cost (3,300 tons)($22/ton) + (2,700 tons)($21/ton), or $129,300.

LIFO: The last 6,000 tons include 5,000 units from beginning inventory and 1,000 units from January/February. These tons of cement cost (5,000 tons)($20/ton) + (1,000 tons)($20/ton), or $120,000.

Weighted-average cost: The average cost per ton including beginning inventory and manufacturing this year is ($100,000 + $387,050)/(5,000 + 18,500), or $20.72553/ton. The cost of the 6,000 tons of cement in ending inventory is ($20.72553/ton)(6,000 tons), or $124,353.

b. FIFO:

Beginning inventory, 1/1/02	$100,000
Manufacturing costs	387,050
Ending inventory, 12/31/02	(129,300)
Cost of goods sold	$357,750

LIFO:

Beginning inventory, 1/1/02	$100,000
Manufacturing costs	387,050
Ending inventory, 12/31/02	(120,000)
Cost of goods sold	$367,050

Weighted-average cost:

Beginning inventory, 1/1/02	$100,000
Manufacturing costs	387,050
Ending inventory, 12/31/02	(124,353)
Cost of goods sold	$362,697

Concept**Review**

1. How does the schedule for cost of goods manufactured relate to the cost of goods sold?

2. How do FIFO, LIFO, and the weighted-average cost methods affect the cost of ending inventory and cost of goods sold?

SELF-STUDY PROBLEM

IPX is a specialized packaging company that packages other manufacturers' products. Manufacturers ship their products to IPX in bulk. IPX then packages the products using high-speed, state-of-the-art packaging machines and ships the packages to wholesalers. A typical order involves packaging small toys in see-through, plastic, and cardboard packaging.

Over- and Underabsorbed Overhead

IPX uses a flexible budget to forecast annual plant-wide overhead, which is then allocated to jobs based on machine hours. The annual overhead budget is forecasted to be $6 million of fixed costs plus $120 per machine hour. The expected number of machine hours for the year is 20,000. The estimated application rate includes both fixed and variable overhead costs.

At the end of the year, 21,000 machine hours were used, and actual overhead incurred was $9.14 million.

a. Calculate the application rate set at the beginning of the year.

b. Calculate the amount of over- or underabsorbed overhead for the year.

c. Company policy is to write off any over- or underabsorbed overhead to the Cost of Goods Sold account. Will net income rise or fall this year when the over- or underabsorbed overhead is written off to Cost of Goods Sold?

Solution

a. The application rate equals the forecasted overhead divided by the forecasted usage of the allocation base (machine hours (MH)):

($6,000,000 + ($120/MH)(20,000 MH))/20,000 MH = $420/MH

b.

Actual overhead	$9,140,000
Absorbed overhead ($420/MH)(21,000 MH)	(8,820,000)
Underabsorbed overhead	$ 320,000

c. The underabsorbed overhead will increase the cost of goods sold and decrease net income.

NUMERICAL EXERCISES

BPA Accounting is performing an audit of the Chadwick Company. BPA uses a cost sheet to record the cost of each audit. Only professional services (by associates, managers, and partners) and overhead are recorded on the cost sheet. The cost sheets are then compared with the bid price of the audit to determine whether the audit was profitable and to improve future bid prices. BPA had bid $10,000 to do the Chadwick Company audit. During January,

NE 10.1
Job-Order Cost Sheet
(LO 2)

the following work was performed on the Chadwick audit: 10 hours of associate work at $30 per hour, 4 hours of manager work at $50 per hour, and 1 hour of partner time at $100 per hour. During February, the following work was performed at the same rates as in January to finish the audit: 100 hours of associate time, 50 hours of manager time, and 8 hours of partner time. Overhead is allocated at $20 per professional service hour provided.

a. Make a cost sheet for the Chadwick Company audit.

b. Was the Chadwick Company audit profitable for BPA Accounting?

NE 10.2

Estimated, Actual, and Allocated Overhead

(LO 4)

Philbrick Company makes recreational equipment. Overhead is allocated to the different products based on machine hours. At the beginning of the year, the company estimates that overhead will be $4 million and machine hours will be 200,000. During the year, the company actually has $4.3 million of overhead and 190,000 machine hours.

a. How much overhead is allocated?

b. What is the over- or underabsorbed overhead?

NE 10.3

Estimated, Actual, and Allocated Overhead

(LO 4)

The Dinkleberry law firm allocates overhead to different clients based on hours of work performed by Mr. Dinkleberry. At the start of the year, he estimates that the total overhead of the coming year will be $100,000. He also estimates that he will perform 2,000 hours of work for clients. During the year, he works 2,100 hours for clients and incurs $110,000 of overhead.

a. How much overhead is allocated?

b. What is the over- or underabsorbed overhead?

NE 10.4

Over- and Underabsorbed Overhead

(LO 4)

Alphonse Company allocates fixed overhead costs by machine hours and variable overhead costs by direct labor hours. At the beginning of the year, the company expects fixed overhead costs to be $600,000 and variable costs to be $800,000. The expected machine hours total 6,000, and the expected direct labor hours total 80,000. The actual fixed overhead costs totaled $700,000, and the actual variable overhead costs totaled $750,000. During the year actual machine hours totaled 5,500, and the actual direct labor hours totaled 90,000.

a. How much overhead is allocated?

b. What is the over- or underabsorbed overhead?

NE 10.5

Equivalent Units

(LO 8)

White Flour Company mills wheat into flour. Equivalent units are measured in terms of tons of flour produced. At the beginning of the year, the mill had 20 tons of flour that was 30% milled. During the year, another 500 tons of flour were completely milled. At the end of the year, the company has 40 tons of flour 80% milled.

How many equivalent tons of flour has White Flour Company milled during the year?

NE 10.6

Cost per Equivalent Unit

(LO 8)

A computer manufacturer has an assembly line for making computers. At the beginning of the year, the company had 300 computers on the assembly line that were 40% complete on average. The computer company started and completed another 5,000 computers. At the end of the year, another 500 computers were still on the assembly line and 30% complete on average. During the year, the computer manufacturer had costs of $2 million.

a. How many equivalent units were produced during the year?

b. What is the cost per equivalent unit of computers worked on during the year?

NE 10.7

Over- and Underabsorbed Overhead

(LO 4)

A company allocates overhead using direct labor hours. The expected number of direct labor hours is 4,000 for the coming year, and the expected overhead is $80,000. During the year, the company uses 3,600 direct labor hours and the actual overhead was $82,000.

What is the over- or underabsorbed overhead?

NE 10.8

Over- and Underabsorbed Overhead

(LO 4)

Anacom Company has expected overhead fixed costs of $100,000. The estimated variable overhead costs are $400,000, assuming the allocation base is 50,000 machine hours. Anacom has one overhead application rate that includes both variable and fixed costs. The actual machine hours total 60,000, and the actual overhead is $550,000.

What is the over- or underabsorbed overhead?

Multifirm has three different production departments, A, B, and C. Each department allocates overhead costs to products based on direct labor dollars. The production departments had the following expected overhead costs and direct labor dollars:

NE 10.9
Use of Multiple Application Rates
(LO 6)

Department	Expected Overhead Costs	Direct Labor Dollars
A	$400,000	$40,000
B	200,000	10,000
C	800,000	50,000

Product P requires $2,000 of direct labor in Department A, $1,000 in Department B, and $3,000 in Department C.

How much overhead is allocated to the product from the three production departments?

A company has no beginning work-in-process. During the year, it starts and completes 1,000 units and has 100 units in ending inventory that are 60% complete. The costs related to this product during the period are $10,000.

How many equivalent units were produced during the period? What was the average cost per equivalent unit?

NE 10.10
Equivalent Units and Process Costing
(LO 8)

A manufacturer has 500 units in beginning inventory that are 30% complete. During the year, the firm starts 5,000 units. It completes the 500 units in the beginning inventory and 4,200 of the 5,000 units started. The ending inventory is 80% complete.

How many uncompleted units are in ending work-in-process? How many equivalent units are produced during the year?

NE 10.11
Equivalent Units and Process Costing
(LO 8)

Prepare a cost of goods manufactured schedule for July from the following data:

NE 10.12
Cost of Goods Manufactured and Cost of Goods Sold Schedules
(LO 9)

Work-in-Process 7/1/2001	$ 10,000
Work-in-Process 7/31/2001	20,000
Raw Materials 7/1/2001	40,000
Raw Materials 7/31/2001	30,000
Raw materials purchased in July	100,000
Direct labor used in July	200,000
Manufacturing overhead in July	150,000

NUMERICAL PROBLEMS

Talbott Company has received an order (#324) for 100 widgets. On January 20, the shop supervisor requisitioned 100 units of part 503 at a cost of $5 per unit and 500 units of part 456 at a per-unit cost of $3 to begin work on the 100 widgets. On the same day, 20 hours of direct labor at $20 per hour were used to work on the widgets. On January 21, 200 units of part 543 at $6 per unit were requisitioned, and 10 hours of direct labor at $15 per hour were performed on the 100 widgets to complete the job. Overhead is allocated to the job based on $5 per direct labor hour.

Make a job-order cost sheet for the 100 widgets.

NP 10.1
Job-Order Sheet
(LO 2)

The following activities have been performed for Job #515:

NP 10.2
Job-Order Cost Systems
(LO 2)

- Requisition of 3 units of part #34 at $40 per unit and 2 hours of direct labor at $10 per hour on 5/16/2001.
- Requisition of 5 kg. of raw material #45 at $10 per kg. and direct labor of 3 hours at $12 per hour on 6/3/2001.
- Direct labor of 4 hours at $15 per hour on 6/10/2001 (the job is finished).

* Applied overhead at $12 per direct labor hour.
* The job is sold on 7/7/2001.

a. Make a job-order cost sheet for the activities.

b. Describe the changes in the account balances during May, June, and July for Raw Materials, Work-in-Process, Finished Goods, and Cost of Goods Sold.

NP 10.3
Job-Order Cost Flows
(LO 2, 3)

The job-order cost sheet for 1,000 units of toy trucks is as follows:

Job Number	555				Date Started	4/13	
					Date Completed	6/18	
		Raw Materials				**Direct Labor**	
Date	Type	Cost	Qty.	Amount	Cost	Hours	Amount
4/13	565	$3	1,000	$3,000	$18	20	$ 360
5/24	889	1	4,000	4,000	12	10	120
6/18	248	2	1,000	2,000	15	100	1,500
				$9,000		130	$ 1,980

Total direct materials	$9,000
Total direct labor	1,980
Overhead (130 direct labor hours @ $10/hour)	1,300
Total job cost	**$12,280**

All of the materials for the job were purchased on April 10. The batch of 1,000 toy trucks is sold on July 10.

    What are the costs of this job order in the Raw Materials, Work-in-Process, Finished Goods, and Cost of Goods Sold accounts on April 30, May 31, June 30, and July 31?

NP 10.4
Job Cost Flows
(LO 2, 3)

Tip Tap Company receives an order for 10,000 units of taps (a tool used to make threads in a block of steel). The taps require considerable machining on a blank (part #14). Blanks are sometimes ruined in the machining process, but the cost of the ruined blanks is treated as a part of the cost of the job. Direct labor hours are used to allocate overhead. Each blank, spoiled or good, requires the same amount of direct labor hours. The job-order cost sheet for the order follows:

Job Number	43				Date Started	4/20	
					Date Completed	6/20	
		Raw Materials				**Direct Labor**	
Date	Type	Cost	Qty.	Amount	Cost	Hours	Amount
4/20	14	$1	3,500	$ 3,500	$18	200	$ 3,600
5/14	14	1	4,000	4,000	18	220	3,960
6/20	14	1	3,300	3,300	18	200	3,600
			10,800	$10,800		620	$11,160

Total units worked on	10,800
Good units	10,000
Spoiled units	800
Total direct materials	$10,800
Total direct labor	11,160
Overhead (620 direct labor hours @$10/hour)	6,200
Total job cost	**$28,160**

All of the blanks for the job were purchased on March 10. The batch of 10,000 taps was sold on July 15.

What are the costs of this job order in the Raw Materials, Work-in-Process, Finished Goods, and Cost of Goods Sold accounts on March 31, April 30, May 31, June 30, and July 31?

A computer manufacturer has the following account balances at the end of the year:

Work-in-Process	$ 100,000
Finished Goods	800,000
Cost of Goods Sold	2,000,000
Total	$2,900,000

NP 10.5
Proration of Over- and Underabsorbed Overhead
(LO 5)

These accounts contain $900,000 of allocated overhead. Actual overhead, however, is $1,000,000.

a. What are the account balances after prorating the underabsorbed overhead?
b. If the manufacturing manager's performance bonus is based on income, what is the effect of proration on the manager's bonus?
c. If the manager had the discretion to prorate the underabsorbed overhead or to write it off to cost of goods sold, which choice would the manager prefer?

A chair manufacturer uses direct labor to allocate overhead. At the end of the year, the company had the following account balances with and without allocated overhead:

NP 10.6
Allocation of Over- and Underabsorbed Overhead
(LO 5)

Account	Direct Costs	Direct Labor Hours	Allocated Overhead	Ending Balance
Work-in-Process	$ 10,000	100	$ 5,000	$ 15,000
Finished Goods	40,000	300	15,000	55,000
Cost of Goods Sold	200,000	1,600	80,000	280,000
Totals	$250,000	2,000	$100,000	$350,000

Actual overhead during the year was $90,000. Estimated and actual direct labor hours are equal.

a. What are the ending account balances if the Cost of Goods Sold is adjusted for the over- and/or underabsorbed overhead?
b. What are the ending account balances if the over- and/or underabsorbed overhead is prorated?
c. What are the ending account balances if the application rate is recalculated to reflect actual overhead costs?
d. If the manager's performance is evaluated, in part, in terms of net income, which method to adjust for the over- and/or underabsorbed overhead would the manager prefer? Explain your answer.

A house-building contractor has the following three overhead cost pools:

NP 10.7
Multiple Overhead Rates
(LO 6)

General administration	$ 500,000
Utilities	100,000
Equipment	1,000,000
Total overhead	$1,600,000

Costs from each of these cost pools are then allocated to housing contracts using the following allocation bases:

Overhead Item	Allocation Base	Expected Usage
General administration	Direct labor dollars	$2,000,000 in direct labor
Utilities	Number of houses	40 houses
Equipment	Cost of house	$16,000,000 in total costs

How much overhead is allocated to a house that uses $20,000 of direct labor and has a total cost of $300,000?

NP 10.8
Allocation of Overhead by Department
(LO 7)

Puzzle Company makes jigsaw puzzles. Its manufacturing process includes using the departments related to gluing, cutting, and boxing. Each type of jigsaw puzzle must go through these departments. The overhead costs in each department are allocated by direct labor hours. Expected overhead costs and direct labor hours used to determine an allocation rate are as follows:

Department	Expected Department Costs	Expected Department Direct Labor Hours
Gluing	$ 90,000	10,000
Cutting	200,000	40,000
Boxing	110,000	50,000
Total overhead	$400,000	100,000

A job of 5,000 jigsaw puzzles requires 10 hours of gluing, 15 hours of cutting, and 12 hours of boxing.

a. How much overhead is allocated to the job if overhead is allocated by department?
b. How much overhead is allocated to the job if overhead is allocated by a single company-wide application rate?

NP 10.9
Job-Order Costing and Incremental Costs of Outsourcing
(LO 2)

Kitchen Rite is considering outsourcing the production of a steel chassis used in a kitchen appliance. It produces 2,000 chassis per month. An outside vendor can supply an identical chassis for $9.90. The chassis is manufactured in two steps. A stamping press punches out the part from sheet metal, bends the sides, and cuts holes in it—all in one operation. Then a welding machine welds the corners. Both the welding and stamping machines are used only to produce this one chassis. The following job-order cost sheet summarizes the costs of producing a single chassis:

	Cost per Unit
Steel plate	$ 4.75
Direct labor	
Stamping ($20/hour)	1.60
Welding ($30/hour)	2.50
Overhead	
Stamping (depreciation)	3.60
Welding (lease payment)	2.15
General plant	5.90
	$20.50

The stamping machine is old and has little economic value. A used equipment dealer is willing to remove the machine and haul it away at no cost. The stamping machine was purchased 13 years ago for $1,728,000. For both tax and reporting purposes, it is being depreciated using a 20-year life, straight-line method, and zero salvage value. The welding machine is leased for $4,300 per month, and the lease can be canceled at any time and the machine returned. However, an early termination penalty of $1,800 per month for the next 42 months must be paid.

General plant overhead consists primarily of the allocated cost of depreciation on the plant, property taxes, and fire insurance on the plant. Kitchen Rite currently has excess plant space. The manufacturing space freed up if the chassis is outsourced has no other use.

Employees are unionized and have a clause in their contract that prevents the firm from firing workers if their jobs are eliminated due to outsourcing. The employees working on the stamping machine will be placed on indefinite leave at 75% of their current pay. The employees operating the welding machine can be reassigned to other positions in the firm as job openings occur. Given the high demand for welders, these reassignments will occur within a few weeks of outsourcing the chairs.

Kitchen Rite has a tax loss for the current and previous two years.

Should Kitchen Rite outsource the chassis? Support your recommendation with a clear financial analysis of the facts.

Hurst manufactures custom replacement floor mats for automobiles. The mats are made of spun nylon on highly automated, expensive machinery. Hurst manufactures two mat styles, Plush and Deluxe. Hurst's unionized work force makes it difficult for the company to compete on price. So far, it has been able to compete successfully on quality, innovative design, and delivery schedule. However, the leaders of Hurst's union are aggressive and are seeking additional work-related job guarantees. Hurst management would like to reduce its dependence on unionized labor.

Hurst's manufacturing process is overhead driven. Most of the overhead arises from the common machinery that produces the Plush and Deluxe floor mats. Non-unionized engineers and technicians maintain the equipment, and the machinery requires expensive lubricants and filters, and large amounts of electricity and natural gas to operate. Each mat style is produced in batches of 10 mats each. Plush and Deluxe do not put differential demands on the equipment other than the amount of machine time required to produce each batch. The following table summarizes the operating data for each mat style.

NP 10.10
Choice of Allocation Base for Job-Order Costing
(LO 2)

	Plush	Deluxe
Machine minutes per batch of 10 mats	12	9
Direct labor per batch of 10 mats	$4	$6
Direct material per batch of 10 mats	$7	$5
Number of batches per year	14,000	9,000

Overhead is allocated to the two mat styles using a predetermined overhead rate estimated from a flexible budget at the beginning of the year. Fixed overhead is estimated to be $680,000, and variable overhead is estimated to be $1.50 per machine minute. Management is debating whether to use machine minutes or direct labor cost as the overhead allocation base to allocate overhead to the two mat styles.

a. Calculate two overhead rates. The first overhead rate uses machine minutes as the allocation base and the second uses direct labor cost as the allocation base. Round both overhead rates to two decimal places.

b. Calculate the *total* product cost per batch of Plush and Deluxe mats using the two overhead rates calculated in part (a).

c. Discuss the advantages and disadvantages of using machine minutes or direct labor cost as the allocation base for assigning overhead to the two mat styles.

Jacklin Stampings allocates overhead to products based on machine hours. It uses a flexible overhead budget to calculate a predetermined overhead rate at the beginning of the year. This rate is used during the year to allocate overhead to the various stampings produced. The following table summarizes operations for the last year:

NP 10.11
Overabsorbed Overhead and Overhead Rate
(LO 4)

Budgeted fixed overhead	$3,800,000
Overabsorbed overhead	$220,000
Actual machine hours	46,000
Variable overhead per machine hour	$100
Actual overhead incurred	$8,750,000

In setting the overhead rate at the beginning of the year, what budgeted volume of machine hours was used?

NP 10.12
Equivalent Units
(LO 8)

Department 100 is the first step in the firm's manufacturing process. Data for the current quarter's operations follow:

	Units
Beginning work-in-process (70% complete)	30,000
Units started this quarter	580,000
Units completed this quarter and transferred out	550,000
Ending work-in-process (60% complete)	60,000

How many equivalent units were completed during the current quarter in Department 100?

NP 10.13
Overhead Allocation Recalculated with the Actual Application Rate
(LO 5)

Jackson Industries makes an assortment of aircraft parts. It allocates overhead based on direct labor costs (DL$). At the beginning of the year, the company estimated that overhead costs would be $400,000 and direct labor costs would be $250,000. The application rate was estimated to be $400,000/$250,000, or $1.60 per DL$. The actual overhead costs were $420,000 and the actual direct labor costs $210,000. A batch of parts that used $10,000 of direct labor was completed during the year. It was sold based on a contract of actual costs plus 20%. The original bill was sent using the estimated application rate.

How much greater would the bill have been using actual overhead and direct labor costs?

NP 10.14
Over- and Underabsorbed Overhead
(LO 2, 4)

Rosen Company has two manufacturing departments, production and assembly, each of which has separate application rates. Rosen made the following estimates for its production and assembly department for calendar year 2002:

	Production	Assembly
Factory overhead	$ 300,000	$100,000
Direct labor cost	$1,000,000	$500,000
Machine hours	1,500	6,250
Direct labor hours	5,000	10,000

The company uses a budgeted application rate to apply overhead to orders. Machine hours are used to allocate overhead in the production department, and direct labor hours are used to allocate overhead in the assembly department.

a. What is the application rate for each department?

b. What are overhead costs for Job #77? A summary of this job follows:

	Production	Assembly
Direct materials used	$3,000	$2,000
Direct labor costs	$7,000	$2,500
Machine hours	100	250
Direct labor hours	500	750

c. Actual operating results for January 2002 are as follows:

	Production	Assembly
Factory overhead	$325,000	$65,000
Direct labor cost	$900,000	$600,000
Machine hours	1,550	6,250
Direct labor hours	5,000	7,500

Calculate the over- and/or underabsorbed overhead for each department.

Ware Paper Box manufactures corrugated paper boxes for use in the produce industry. It uses a job-order costing system. Operating data for February and March follow:

Job	Date Started	Date Finished	Date Sold	Total Mfg. Cost as of 2/28	Total Mfg. Cost in March*
613	1/28	2/5	2/15	$12,500	
614	2/5	2/17	2/20	17,200	
615	2/20	2/27	3/5	18,500	
616	2/25	3/10	3/20	10,100	$13,400
734	2/21	3/15	4/1	4,300	8,200
735	2/27	4/1	4/9	9,100	2,400
736	3/2	3/22	4/19		16,300
617	3/15	3/20	3/26		19,200
618	3/22	4/5	4/15		14,400

*Manufacturing costs incurred only in March; does not include any manufacturing costs incurred in prior months.

Calculate the following amounts:

a. Work-in-Process inventory as of 2/28.
b. Work-in-Process inventory as of 3/31.
c. Finished Goods inventory as of 2/28.
d. Finished Goods inventory as of 3/31.
e. Cost of goods sold for February.
f. Cost of goods sold for March.

NP 10.15
Work-in-Process, Finished Goods, and Cost of Goods Sold
(LO 3)

DeJure Scents manufactures an aftershave. In May, it had no beginning inventory and started 15,000 liters. May's ending work-in-process inventory of 2,000 liters was 50% complete. In May, manufacturing costs were $75,000.

a. Calculate the equivalent units.
b. Calculate the cost per equivalent unit.
c. Calculate the cost of the ending inventory and the cost transferred to finished goods inventory.

NP 10.16
Cost per Equivalent Unit
(LO 8)

Chemtrex is an agricultural chemical producer that uses process costing in its mixing department. At the beginning of July, it had 700,000 liters 70% complete in work-in-process. During July, it started another 4,000,000 liters and finished 3,700,000 liters. One million liters of ending work-in-process were 60% complete at the end of July.

Calculate the number of equivalent units of conversion work performed during July.

NP 10.17
Equivalent Units
(LO 8)

The following figures were taken from the records of Wellington Co. for the year 2002. At the end of the year, two jobs were still in process. Details about the two jobs follow:

NP 10.18
Work-in-Process and Proration of Over- and Underabsorbed Overhead
(LO 2, 4, 5)

	Job A	Job B
Direct labor	$10,000	$28,000
Direct materials	$32,000	$22,000
Machine hours	2,000	3,500
Direct labor hours	1,000	2,000

Wellington Co. applies overheads at a budgeted rate calculated at the beginning of the year. The budgeted rate is the ratio of budgeted overhead to budgeted direct labor costs. Budgeted figures for 2002 were as follows:

Budgeted direct labor costs	$250,000
Budgeted overhead	187,500

Actual figures for 2002 follow:

Direct labor	$350,000
Overhead	192,500
Finished goods inventory	75,000
Cost of goods sold	550,000

There were no opening inventories. It is the practice of the company to prorate any over- or underabsorption of overhead to Finished Goods Inventory, Work-in-Process, and Cost of Goods Sold based on the total dollars in these accounts.

a. Compute the cost of work-in-process before prorating over- and/or underabsorbed overheads.

b. Prepare a schedule of Finished Goods Inventory, Work-in-Process, and Cost of Goods Sold after prorating over- and/or underabsorbed overhead.

c. What is the difference in the operating income if the over- and/or underabsorbed overhead is charged to Cost of Goods Sold instead of being prorated to Finished Goods Inventory, Work-in-Process, and Cost of Goods Sold?

d. The manager's compensation is partially based on net income. What is the effect on the manager's compensation if the over- and/or underabsorbed overhead is charged to Cost of Goods Sold instead of being prorated? What managerial incentives could this system create if the manager were allowed to influence the application rate and/or the year-end adjustment of any over- and/or underabsorbed overhead?

NP 10.19

Work-in-Process and Proration of Over- and Underabsorbed Overhead

(LO 2, 4, 5)

Beaver Company has the following account balances after allocating overhead based on the predetermined application rate of $10 per machine hour:

Work-in-Process	$ 40,000
Finished Goods	60,000
Cost of Goods Sold	300,000
Total	$400,000

Work-in-process used 1,000 machine hours. The balance in Finished Goods was calculated using 1,500 machine hours. Cost of Goods Sold was calculated using 10,000 machine hours. The actual overhead was $115,000.

a. What is the over- and/or underabsorbed overhead?

b. What are the final account balances for Work-in-Process, Finished Goods, and Cost of Goods Sold if the overabsorbed overhead is (1) allocated completely to Cost of Goods Sold, (2) prorated among the three accounts, and (3) allocated based on a recalculation of the application rate using actual data?

NP 10.20

Activity-Based Costing in a Job-Order System

(LO 6)

An ice cream company has identified the following activities and calculated the following application rates:

Activity	Application Rate
Cleaning equipment	$100/batch
Purchasing ingredients	$50/purchase
Advertising	$500/advertisement
Renting factory space	$1,000/flavor

a. What level of overhead (unit, batch, product, facility) is each of these overhead activities?

b. How much overhead would a new flavor receive if it were made in five batches, required 20 purchases, and were advertised twice?

c. If there is plenty of factory space available for the production of more ice cream flavors, will the company likely choose too many or too few flavors?

GAMMA produces more than 100 different types of residential water faucets at its Delta, Florida, plant. This plant uses activity-based costing to calculate product costs. The following table summarizes the plant's overhead for the year and the cost drivers used for each activity center:

NP 10.21
Use of Activity-Based Costing to Allocate Overhead
(LO 6)

Summary of Plant Overhead and Activity Centers				
Activity Center	Cost (millions of dollars)	Cost Driver	Total Amount of Cost Driver	Activity Cost per Unit of Cost Driver
Material handling	$20.8	Direct materials	$130 million	$0.16
Purchasing	13.8	Part numbers	800	$17,250
Set-up labor	6.8	Batches	500	$13,600
Engineering	10.9	Number of products	125	$87,200
Occupancy	16.2	Direct labor	$ 90 million	$0.18
Total plant overhead	$68.5			

GAMMA manufactures an Explorer model. Its total product cost follows:

Direct labor			$121,700
Direct material			90,500
Material handling	$ 90,500	$ 0.16	14,480
Purchasing	9	17,250	155,250
Set-up	8	13,600	108,800
Engineering	1	87,200	87,200
Occupancy	121,700	$ 0.18	21,906
Total cost			$599,836
Number of units manufactured			12,500
Product cost per unit			$ 47.99

Calculate the product cost per unit of the Explorer faucet using absorption costing where plant overhead is assigned to products using direct labor dollars.

Frames, Inc., manufactures two types of metal frames, large and small. Steel angle iron is first cut to the appropriate sizes, and the pieces are then welded together to form the frames. The process involves a high degree of automation. There is considerable indirect labor by skilled technicians and engineers who maintain the automated equipment. There are two manufacturing departments, cutting and welding. The following reports detail the actual costs of production for the year:

NP 10.22
Use of Multiple Application Rates
(LO 6)

FRAMES, INC. Year Ending December 31			
Direct Costs			
Frame Type	Units Produced	Direct Labor	Direct Materials
Large	10,000	$ 480,000	$950,000
Small	30,000	1,140,000	800,000
Overhead Costs by Department			
Overhead Costs	Cutting	Welding	Total
Utilities	$ 58,000	$174,000	$ 232,000
Indirect labor	430,000	480,000	910,000
General factory costs			150,000
Total overhead costs			$1,292,000

(continued)

	Kilowatt Hours (000s)		
Frame Type	**Cutting**	**Welding**	**Total**
Large	530	1,040	1,570
Small	910	1,200	2,110
Total kilowatt hours	1,440	2,240	3,680

a. Compute the unit costs of large frames and small frames for the year using a single factory-wide overhead rate. The factory-wide overhead allocation base is direct labor cost.

b. Compute the unit costs of large frames and small frames for the year using different overhead rates for utilities, indirect labor, and general factory costs. Utility costs and indirect labor costs are allocated to frames using kilowatt hours. General factory costs are allocated to frames using direct costs (the sum of direct labor and direct materials).

c. Compute the unit costs of large frames and small frames for the year using departmental overhead rates for the cutting and welding departments. General factory overhead costs are evenly divided between the two departments before departmental overhead is allocated to the frames. Cutting department overhead costs are allocated based on the amount of direct materials cost. Welding department overhead costs are allocated based on kilowatt hours in the welding department.

b. Analyze why different unit costs result from the different methods of allocating overhead costs to the products. Which method is best?

NP 10.23
Departmental Rates to Allocate Overhead
(LO 7)

MumsDay Corporation manufactures a complete line of fiberglass attaché cases and suitcases. It has three manufacturing departments (molding, component, and assembly) and two service departments (power and maintenance).

    The sides of the cases are manufactured in the molding department. The frames, hinges, locks, and so on are manufactured in the component department. The cases are completed in the assembly department. Varying amounts of materials, time, and effort are required for each of the various cases. The power department and maintenance department provide services to the three manufacturing departments.

    MumsDay has always used a plant-wide overhead rate. Direct labor hours are used to assign the overhead to its product. The predetermined rate is calculated by dividing the company's total estimated overhead by the total estimated direct labor hours to be worked in the three manufacturing departments.

    Whit Portlock, manager of the cost accounting department, has recommended that MumsDay use departmental overhead rates. Portlock has developed the planned operating costs and expected levels of activity for the coming year. These figures by department are presented in the following schedules (thousands omitted):

	Manufacturing Departments		
	Molding	**Component**	**Assembly**
Departmental activity measures			
Direct labor hours	500	2,000	1,500
Machine hours	875	125	0
Departmental costs			
Raw materials	$12,400	$30,000	$ 1,250
Direct labor	3,500	20,000	12,000
Variable overhead	3,500	10,000	16,500
Fixed overhead	17,500	6,200	6,100
Total departmental costs	$36,900	$66,200	$35,850
Use of service departments			
Maintenance—estimated usage			
in labor hours for coming year	90	25	10
Power (in kilowatt hours)—			
estimated usage for coming year	360	320	120
Maximum allocated long-term			
capacity (in kilowatt hours)	500	350	150

	Service Departments	
	Power	**Maintenance**
Departmental activity measures		
Maximum capacity	1,000 KWH	Adjustable
Estimated usage in coming year	800 KWH	125 hours
Departmental costs		
Materials and supplies	$ 5,000	$1,500
Variable labor	1,400	2,250
Fixed overhead	12,000	250
Total service department costs	$18,400	$4,000

a. Calculate MumsDay's plant-wide overhead rate for the coming year using the same method as used in the past.

b. Whit Portlock has been asked to develop departmental overhead rates for comparison with the plant-wide rate. The following steps are to be followed in developing the departmental rates.

   1. The maintenance department costs should be allocated to the three manufacturing departments using labor hours.

   2. The power department's fixed costs should be allocated to the three manufacturing departments according to long-term capacity and the variable costs according to planned usage.

   3. Calculate departmental overhead rates for the three manufacturing departments using a machine-hour base for the molding department and a direct-labor-hour base for the component and assembly departments.

c. Should MumsDay use a plant-wide rate or departmental rates to assign overhead to its products? Explain your answer.

(CMA adapted)

Astin Car Stereos manufactures and distributes four different car stereos. The following table summarizes the unit sales, selling prices, and manufacturing costs of each stereo:

NP 10.24
Multiple Cost Drivers
(LO 6)

ASTIN CAR STEREOS				
Summary of Operations				
Fiscal Year 2001				
	A90	**B200**	**B300**	**Z7**
Sales price	$100	$120	$140	$180
Manufacturing cost (all variable)	$80	$90	$100	$120
Units sold	15,000	13,000	12,000	9,000

Selling and distribution (S&D) expenses of $1,270,000 are treated as a period cost and are written off to the income statement. To assess relative profitability of each product, S&D expenses are allocated to each product based on sales revenue.

Upon further investigation of the S&D expenses, one-half is for marketing and advertising. Each product has its own advertising and marketing budget, which is administered by one of four marketing managers. Z7, the premier product, is advertised heavily. Of the marketing budget, 40% goes to Z7, 30% to B300, 20% to B200, and 10% to A90.

The other half of the S&D expenses are composed of distribution and administration costs (25%) and selling costs (25%). The distribution and administration department is responsible for arranging shipping and billing customers. (Customers pay transportation charges directly to the common carrier.) It also handles federal licensing of the car radios. Upon analysis of the work in the distribution and administration department, each of the four products places even demands on the department and each consumes about the same amount of resources as the others. Selling costs consist primarily of commissions paid to independent sales people. The commissions are based on gross margin on the product (sales revenue less manufacturing cost).

a. Allocate all S&D expenses based only on sales revenue. Identify the most and least profitable products.

b. Allocate all S&D expenses based only on the advertising and marketing budget. Identify the most and least profitable products.

c. Allocate all S&D expenses using the advertising and marketing budget for advertising and marketing costs, the distribution and administration costs using the demand for these resources by the products, and the selling costs based on commissions. Identify the most and least profitable products.

d. Discuss the managerial implications of the various schemes. Which products are the most or least profitable under each of the three allocation schemes? Why do the different schemes result in different product line profits? Which product is really the most or least profitable?

NP 10.25

Job-Order Costing, Over- and/or Underabsorbed Overhead, and Departmental Rates

(LO 2, 4, 7)

Media Designs is a marketing firm that designs and prints customized marketing brochures. The design department designs the brochure and the printing department prints and binds it. Each department has a separate overhead rate. The following estimates for the two departments were made for calendar year 2001.

	Design	Printing
Overhead	$800,000	$500,000
Direct labor cost	$3,250,000	$410,000
Direct material cost	$8,500	$250,000
Direct labor hours	50,000	10,000

Media Designs uses a budgeted overhead rate to apply overhead to jobs. Direct labor hours are used to allocate overhead in the design department, and direct material cost is used to allocate overhead in the printing department.

a. What are the overhead rates for the design and printing departments?

b. A summary of the Matsui job follows:

	Design	Printing
Direct materials used	$3,000	$12,000
Direct labor costs	$46,200	$28,500
Direct labor hours	700	750

What are overhead costs for the Matsui job?

c. Actual operating results for 2001 follow:

	Design	Printing
Overhead	$802,000	$490,000
Direct labor cost	$3,193,000	$451,500
Direct material cost	$11,550	$230,000
Direct labor hours	51,500	10,500

Calculate the over- and/or underabsorbed overhead for each department.

NP 10.26

Cost of Goods Manufactured and Cost of Goods Sold Schedules

(LO 9)

Marion Company had the following bimonthly output:

Month	Output in Units	Manufacturing Costs	Cost per Unit
Jan/Feb	200	$ 4,000	$20
Mar/Apr	250	5,000	20
May/Jun	300	6,300	21
Jul/Aug	240	5,280	22
Sep/Oct	300	6,900	23
Nov/Dec	200	4,800	24
Total	1,490	$32,280	

The beginning inventory had 100 units at a cost of $18 per unit, or a total cost of $1,800. The ending inventory had 300 units.

a. What is the cost of the ending inventory under FIFO, LIFO, and weighted-average cost methods?

b. What is the cost of goods sold under each method?

Williams Company manufactures garage door openers. At the beginning of November, it had the following inventory accounts:

Raw Materials	$20,000
Work-in-Process	15,000
Finished Goods	30,000

NP 10.27

Cost of Goods Manufactured and Cost of Goods Sold

(LO 9)

At the end of November, the company had the following inventory accounts:

Raw Materials	$10,000
Work-in-Process	25,000
Finished Goods	50,000

During the month of November, the company purchased raw materials costing $100,000. The company also incurred direct labor costs of $200,000 and overhead of $50,000.

a. Make a schedule calculating the cost of goods manufactured during November.

b. Make a schedule calculating the cost of goods sold during November.

Smith Company has the following inventory balances at the beginning of 2001:

Raw Materials	$ 50,000
Work-in-Process	75,000
Finished Goods	100,000

NP 10.28

Cost of Goods Manufactured and Cost of Goods Sold

(LO 9)

At the end of 2001, the controller calculates the cost of goods sold to be $700,000 and the cost of goods manufactured as $750,000. Ending work-in-process for 2001 was estimated to be $95,000. During 2001, the company purchased $200,000 of raw materials and used $190,000 of them. Manufacturing overhead during 2001 was $300,000.

a. What was the ending Raw Materials balance in 2001?

b. What amount of direct labor was paid during 2001?

c. What was the ending balance of Finished Goods in 2001?

City Gravel Company has the following outputs, costs, and ending inventory for its five years of operations:

NP 10.29

Cost of Goods Sold and Different Cost Flow Methods for Inventory

(LO 9)

Year	Output in Tons	Manufacturing Costs	Cost per Ton	Ending Inventory (tons)
1998	300,000	$ 800,000	$1.00	20,000
1999	400,000	500,000	1.25	30,000
2000	500,000	750,000	1.50	50,000
2001	400,000	600,000	1.50	70,000
2002	800,000	1,400,000	1.75	80,000

a. What is the cost of goods sold in each year using FIFO?

b. What is the cost of goods sold in each year using LIFO?

c. What is the cost of goods sold in each year using weighted-average cost?

ANALYSIS AND INTERPRETATION PROBLEMS

The shop supervisor is complaining to the controller about all the time his workers are wasting in filling out job-order cost sheets. He estimates that 10% of his employees' time is spent recording labor hours spent on different jobs. Given that the direct labor costs of the

AIP 10.1

Job-Order Cost Sheets

(LO 2)

factory are $2 million per year, the supervisor estimates that the company is losing $200,000 a year completing the job-order cost sheets.

What alternatives exist to using worker time to complete job-order cost sheets?

AIP 10.2

Job-Order and Process Costing

(LO 1)

A management accounting professor was trying to explain the difference between job-order costing and process costing to her class. She pointed out that a job-order costing system is generally used when distinct batches or "jobs" can be identified. Alternatively, process costing is used for the continual processing of homogenous products. A student pointed out another difference between job-order and process costing. He noted that on the one hand, job-order costs are determined when the job is being performed by using predetermined overhead rates. On the other hand, process costs are normally determined at the end of the period based on the number of equivalent units produced and actual overhead costs.

What does the timing difference between job-order costing and process costing say about how job-order costs and process costs are used for planning purposes?

AIP 10.3

Modified Job-Order and Process Costing

(LO 1, 2)

Trophy Company makes medallions for the Olympic Festival. All of the medallions are exactly the same except for the type of metal that is stamped into them: gold, silver, and bronze. Each medallion goes through the same steps of cutting, stamping, polishing, and packaging. The controller is uncertain about whether to use a job-order system or a process costing system to determine the costs of the different types of medallions.

Provide arguments for the use of both types of costing systems. Suggest a hybrid costing system that would be suitable for Trophy Company.

AIP 10.4

Application Rates for Departments

(LO 7)

Glass Key Company manufactures hand-blown glass pieces. It has three glass-blowing departments (A, B, and C) that revolve around three different furnaces. The work performed in each department can be replicated by any of the other departments, but department C has newer and more expensive equipment that has a higher depreciation expense. Overhead costs are allocated to the different batches of glassware based on the direct labor hours. Each of the glass-blowing departments has its own application rate, with the rate in department C being the highest. Glass Key prices its product based on absorbed costs, so customers have been asking that their special orders be performed in departments A or B. As a result, department C, with the best equipment, is being used least.

What is wrong? What are some remedies for this problem?

AIP 10.5

Underabsorbed Overhead

(LO 5)

The end of the year has arrived and it is bonus time for the successful managers of Crescent Company. Divisional managers are evaluated by the profit of their respective divisions after the allocation of costs from headquarters. One of these allocations is the cost of data processing, which is performed centrally for all divisions. The data processing costs are allocated to the divisions based on the number of transactions processed. The application rate was calculated at the beginning of the year based on estimated data processing costs and the estimated transactions to be processed by all of the divisions. Near the start of the year, however, one of the divisions was unexpectedly sold to another company and did not use very much data processing before being sold. At the end of the year, all of the data processing costs have not been allocated. The company president has decided to allocate the underabsorbed data processing costs to the remaining divisions based on each division's actual usage of data processing during the year. In allocating the underabsorbed overhead to the divisions, some division managers cannot achieve their profit targets and will not receive their bonuses.

Is this type of cost allocation appropriate?

AIP 10.6

Process Costing and Underabsorbed Manufacturing Costs

(LO 5, 8)

Process costing can be performed with estimated cost and production data and actual cost and production data. A company estimated total manufacturing costs to be $4,000,000 and estimated equivalent units to be 20,000. Therefore, the estimated cost per equivalent unit was $200. Inventory costs were adjusted for completed units based on this $200 estimated cost per equivalent unit. At the end of the year, the actual manufacturing costs were $5,000,000, and the actual equivalent units produced were 22,000.

How would you determine and account for the underabsorbed manufaturing costs?

AIP 10.7

Application Rates and Depreciation Methods

(LO 2)

The frame-welding department of a large automotive company welds car frames as they pass down the assembly line. Four computer-controlled robots make the welds on each frame simultaneously. When installed last year, each robot was expected to have a five-year useful life before becoming obsolete and being replaced by newer, faster models with more advanced electronics. Over its life, each robot is expected to make 100 million welds. Each robot costs $8 million and has no salvage value at the end of its useful life, after taking into consideration the cost of dismantling and removing it.

The firm has an absorption costing system that costs each frame as it is produced. The accounting system supports both decision making and control. Straight-line depreciation is used for both internal and external reporting. Accelerated depreciation is used for tax purposes. As frames move through the welding stations, they are charged based on the number of welds made on each frame. Different car frames require different numbers of welds, with some frame models requiring up to 1,000. Each weld costs $0.11. This charge is set at the beginning of the year by estimating the fixed and variable costs in the welding department. The expected number of welds projected for the year is determined by multiplying the forecasted number of frames by the number of welds per frame. The expected number of welds is used to estimate total costs in the welding department. The cost per weld is then the ratio of the projected welding costs and the expected number of welds. Seventy-two million welds were projected for the current year.

The following statement illustrates the computation of the charge per weld:

FRAME WELDING DEPARTMENT			
Charge per Weld			
Current Year			
	Variable Costs (at 72 million welds)	**Fixed Costs**	**Total Costs**
Depreciation*		$ 6,400,000	$ 6,400,000
Welding rods	$ 700,000		700,000
Engineering services	300,000	200,000	500,000
Electricity	180,000		180,000
Factory overhead	85,000	55,000	140,000
Total	$ 1,265,000	$ 6,655,000	$ 7,920,000
÷ Expected number of welds	72,000,000	72,000,000	72,000,000
Cost per weld	$0.0176	$0.0924	$0.1100

* Depreciation per year = (4 robots × $8 million per robot) ÷ 5-year useful life

After reviewing this statement, Amy Miller, manager of the body fabricating division, which includes the welding department, made the following remarks:

> I know we use straight-line depreciation to calculate the depreciation component of the cost per weld now. But it would seem to make a lot of sense to compute robot depreciation using units-of-production depreciation. Each robot cost $8 million and was expected to perform 100 million welds over its useful life. That comes to $0.08 per weld. Thus, we should charge each weld at $0.08 plus the remaining fixed and variable costs as calculated on this statement. If I back out the $6.4 million depreciation from these figures and recompute the fixed costs per weld at 72 million welds, I get $255,000 divided by 72 million, or $0.00354. Add this to the variable cost per weld of $0.0176 plus the $0.08 depreciation, and our cost per weld is $0.1011, not the current $0.11. This reduces our costs on our complicated frames by as much as $10.
>
> The real advantage of using units-of-production depreciation, in my opinion, is that depreciation is no longer a fixed cost but becomes a variable cost. This has real advantages because when you lower your fixed costs, your break-even point is lower. Operating leverage is lower and, thus, the overall risk of the company is reduced.
>
> I think we should go to the plant controller and see if we can convince him to use a more realistic basis for calculating depreciation costs of the robots.

Evaluate Amy Miller's proposal.

EXTENDED ANALYSIS AND INTERPRETATION PROBLEMS

Targon Inc. manufactures lawn equipment. Targon manufactures its products in a batch rather than a continuous-flow process. Therefore, it uses a job-order cost system. The firm employs a full absorption accounting method for cost accumulation. The balances in selected accounts for the 11-month period ended August 31, 2002, follow:

AIP 10.8

Flow of Costs and Over- and/or Underabsorbed Overhead

Stores inventory	$ 32,000
Work-in-Process Inventory	1,200,000
Finished Goods Inventory	2,785,000
Factory Overhead	2,260,000
Cost of Goods Sold	14,200,000

The work-in-process inventory consists of two jobs:

Job No.	Units	Items	Accumulated Cost
3005-5	50,000	Estate sprinklers	$ 700,000
3006-4	40,000	Economy sprinklers	500,000
			$1,200,000

The finished goods inventory consists of five items:

Items	Quantity and Unit Cost			Accumulated Cost
Estate sprinklers	5,000 units	@	$22 each	$ 110,000
Deluxe sprinklers	115,000 units	@	$17 each	1,955,000
Brass nozzles	10,000 gross	@	$14 per gross	140,000
Rainmaker nozzles	5,000 gross	@	$16 per gross	80,000
Connectors	100,000 gross	@	$5 per gross	500,000
				$2,785,000

The factory cost budget prepared for the 2001–02 fiscal year follows. Targon applied factory overhead on the basis of direct labor hours.

The activities during the first 11 months of the year were quite close to budget. A total of 367,000 direct labor hours have been worked through August 31, 2002.

TARGON INC.
Factory Cost Annual Budget
For the Year Ending September 30, 2002

Direct materials	$ 3,800,000
Purchased parts	6,000,000
Direct labor (400,000 hours)	4,000,000
Overhead	
Supplies	190,000
Indirect labor	700,000
Supervision	250,000
Depreciation	950,000
Utilities	200,000
Insurance	10,000
Property taxes	40,000
Miscellaneous	60,000
Total factory costs	$16,200,000

The following summarizes the September 2002 transactions:

1. All direct materials, purchased parts, and supplies are charged to stores inventory. The September purchases follow:

Materials	$410,000
Purchased parts	285,000
Supplies	13,000

2. The direct materials, purchased parts, and supplies were requisitioned from stores inventory as follows:

	Purchased Parts	Materials	Supplies	Total Requisitions
3005-5	$110,000	$100,000	$ —	$210,000
3006-4	—	6,000	—	6,000
4001-3 (30,000 gross rainmaker nozzles)	—	181,000	—	181,000
4002-1 (10,000 deluxe sprinklers)	—	92,000	—	92,000
4003-5 (50,000 ring sprinklers)	163,000	—	—	163,000
Supplies	—	—	20,000	20,000
	$273,000	$379,000	$20,000	$672,000

3. The payroll summary for September is as follows:

	Hours	Cost
3005-5	6,000	$ 62,000
3006-4	2,500	26,000
4001-3	18,000	182,000
4002-1	500	5,000
4003-5	5,000	52,000
Indirect	8,000	60,000
Supervision	—	24,000
Sales and administration	—	120,000
		$531,000

4. Other factory costs incurred during September follow:

Depreciation	$62,500
Utilities	15,000
Insurance	1,000
Property taxes	3,500
Miscellaneous	5,000
	$87,000

5. Jobs completed during September and the actual output were as follows:

Job No.	Quantity	Items
3005-5	48,000 units	Estate sprinklers
3006-4	39,000 units	Economy sprinklers
4001-3	29,500 gross	Rainmaker nozzles
4003-5	49,000 units	Ring sprinklers

6. The following finished products were shipped to customers during September:

Items	Quantity
Estate sprinklers	16,000 units
Deluxe sprinklers	32,000 units
Economy sprinklers	20,000 units
Ring sprinklers	22,000 units
Brass nozzles	5,000 gross
Rainmaker nozzles	10,000 gross
Connectors	26,000 gross

a. Calculate the over- or underabsorbed overhead for the year ended September 30, 2002. Be sure to indicate whether the overhead is over- or underabsorbed.

b. Calculate the dollar balance in the Work-in-Process Inventory account as of September 30, 2002.

c. Calculate the dollar balance in the Finished Goods Inventory account as of September 30, 2002, for the estate sprinklers using a FIFO basis.

(CMA adapted)

AIP 10.9
Departmental Rates, ABC, and Product Costs in a Job-Order System

Joe Bell, president and chief executive officer of Dyna Golf, called a meeting of the executive committee of his board of directors. He is concerned about the price competition and declining sales of his golf wedge line of business. Mr. Bell summarizes the current situation by saying:

> As you know, we set target prices to maintain a gross margin on sales of 35%. On some products, such as our drivers, we have been able to achieve the target price. We have been able to achieve higher prices than a target 35% gross margin would dictate on our putters. But the wedge is a totally different story.
>
> Our factory is among the most efficient in the world. I think that some foreign companies are dumping wedges in the U.S. market, driving down prices and unit sales. We've been reluctant to cut our prices further for fear of what this will do to our gross margins. Fortunately, we have been able to offset the decline in sales of wedges by significantly raising the price of our putters. We were pleasantly surprised when our customers readily accepted the price increases of our putters and we have not experienced much reaction from our competitors on the putter price increases.

Steve Barber, an outside director on the board, asks:

> Joe, I don't pretend to know a lot about the golf club business, but how confident are you in your cost data? If your costs are off, won't your prices be off as well?

Joe Bell responds:

> That's a good point, Steve, and one I have been worried about. We have been modernizing our production facilities, and I have asked our controller, Phil Meyers, to look into it and report back after he has undertaken a thorough analysis. My purpose for calling this meeting was to update you on our current situation and let you know what we are doing.

Background   Dyna Golf has been in business for 15 years. Its one plant manufactures three different types of golf clubs: drivers, wedges, and putters. Dyna does not produce a complete club with a shaft and grip. It makes the metal head, which it sells to other companies that assemble and market the complete club. Dyna holds four patents on a unique golf club head design that forges together into one club head three different metals: steel, titanium, and brass. It also has a very distinctive appearance. These three metals weigh different amounts, and by designing a club head with the three metals, Dyna produces a club with unique swing and feel properties. The Dyna club is unique and covered by patents, but other manufacturers have recently introduced similar technology using comparable manufacturing methods.

The Dyna driver is sold to a single distributor that adds the shaft and grip and sells the driver to retail golf shops. Dyna first made its reputation with its driver. It became an instant hit with amateurs after a professional golfer won a major tournament using it. Based on its name recognition from its driver, Dyna introduced a line of putters and then wedges. The wedges are sold to three different distributors and the putters to six different distributors. Specialty, high-end putters, like Dyna's, have a retail price of \$120–\$180, and drivers have a retail price of \$350–\$500. Golfers like to experiment with new equipment, especially when they are playing badly. Therefore, it is not uncommon for golfers to own several putters and switch among them during the year. Putter manufacturers seek to capitalize on this psychology with aggressive advertising campaigns. It is less common for players to switch among wedges as they do with putters. Since it takes several rounds of golf to get the feel-and-distance control with a new wedge, most players do not experiment as much with wedges as they do with putters or even drivers.

Production Process   All three clubs (drivers, wedges, and putters) use the same manufacturing process. Each club consists of between 5 and 10 components. A component is a precisely machined piece of steel, brass, or titanium that Dyna buys from outside suppliers. The components are positioned in a jig, which is placed in a specially designed, computer-

Exhibit AIP 10.9A

DYNA GOLF
Basic Product Information

	Drivers	Wedges	Putters
Production	10,000 units in 1 run	15,000 units in 3 runs	5,000 units in 10 runs
Shipments	10,000 units in 1 shipment	15,000 units in 5 shipments	5,000 units in 20 shipments
Selling prices			
Target	$162.61	$134.09	$ 81.31
Actual	162.61	125.96	105.70

Exhibit AIP 10.9B

DYNA GOLF
Production Information

	Drivers	Wedges	Putters
Raw material	5 components @ $4 each = $20	6 components @ $5 each = $30	10 components @ $1 each = $10
Labor ($20/hr.)			
Set-up labor	10 hrs. per production run	10 hrs. per production run	11 hrs. per production run
Run labor	1/2 hr. per driver	1/3 hr. per wedge	1/4 hr. per putter

Exhibit AIP 10.9C

controlled machine. This machine first heats the components to a very high temperature that fuses them together, cools them, and then polishes the finished club.

The factory is organized into five departments: receiving, engineering, set-up, machining, and packing. Before a production run begins, receiving issues a separate order for each component comprising the club head and inspects each order when it arrives. Engineering ensures that the completed club heads meet the product's specifications and maintains the

DYNA GOLF
Other Overhead

Receiving department	$ 300,000
Engineering department	500,000
Machining department	700,000
Packing department	200,000
Set-up department	3,000
	$1,703,000

operating efficiency of the machines. Due to the preciseness of the production process, engineering is constantly having to issue engineering change orders in response to small differences in purchased components. Set-up first cleans out the machine and jigs, adjusts it to the correct settings to produce the desired club head, and then makes a few pieces to ensure that the settings are correct. Machining has several machines, any of which can be used to manufacture drivers, wedges, or putters once it is equipped with the proper jigs and tools. Packing is responsible for packaging and shipping completed units.

Exhibit AIP 10.9A summarizes the basic product information for the three products: production, shipments, target prices, and actual prices. For example, Dyna manufactured all 10,000 drivers in a single production run and shipped them all out in a single shipment. The 5,000 putters were manufactured in 10 separate runs and shipped in 20 shipments. Dyna set the target price for drivers to be $162.61 (wholesale price) and achieved it. However, it was not able to achieve its target price for wedges ($134.09 versus $125.96), but it exceeded its target price for putters ($105.70 versus $81.31).

Accounting System Exhibit AIP 10.9B summarizes material, set-up labor, and run labor for each of the three products. Each product is produced in the machining department by assembling the metal components. Drivers require 5 components, whereas wedges and putters require 6 and 10 components, respectively. Before the production begins, the machine must be set up, requiring set-up labor. Then to produce clubs, operating the machines requires both machine time and run labor time. Both set-up and run labor costs $20 per hour. Machining has a total budget of $700,000 consisting of the depreciation on the machine, electricity, and maintenance.

Exhibit AIP 10.9C summarizes the overhead accounts.

Phil Meyers, Dyna's controller, and Joe Bell meet a week after the meeting of the executive committee of the board of directors. Joe asks Phil to report on what he has found. Phil begins:

Joe, as you know, our current accounting system assigns the direct material costs of the components and the direct labor for run time to the three products. Then it allocates all overhead costs, including set-up time and machine costs, to the three products based on direct run labor dollars. Set-up labor is considered an indirect cost and is included in overhead. Based on these procedures, we calculate our product costs for drivers, wedges, and putters to be $105.70, $87.16, and $52.85, respectively.

I have been looking at our system and have become worried that our overhead rate is getting out of line. It is now more than 750% of direct labor cost. Since we have introduced more automated machines, we are substituting capital or overhead dollars for labor dollars. (Each driver now takes one-half hour per club, wedges take one-third hour per club, and putters take one-quarter hour per club of machine time.) The engineering department schedules its people based on change orders they receive. Drivers are pretty standard and generate only 25% of the change orders; wedges generate about 35%. Putters are our most complex production process and require the remainder of the change orders.

I'm thinking we should refine our accounting system along the following lines. First, we should break out set-up labor from the general overhead account and assign that directly to each product. We know how much time we are spending setting up each machine for each club-head run. Second, we should stop allocating receiving costs based on direct labor dollars but rather on raw material dollars. And third, the remaining overhead (excluding set-up and receiving) should be allocated based on machine hours. If we make these three changes, I think we'll get a more accurate estimate of our products' costs.

Joe Bell responded:

These seem to be some pretty major changes in our accounting system. I'll need some time to mull these over. Let me think about it, and I'll let you know in a few days how to proceed.

What advice would you offer Mr. Bell in examining changes to the accounting system? How does the accounting system affect pricing and product decisions at Dyna Golf?

Chapter**Eleven**

Variable Costing and Capacity Costs

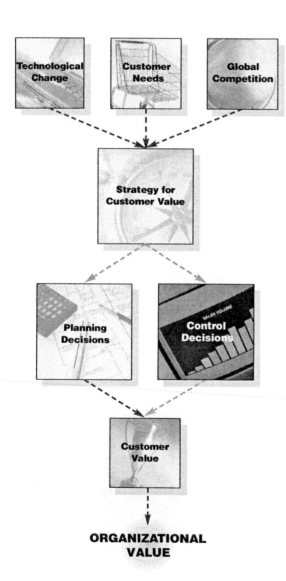

PIERPONT ELECTRONICS

Pierpont Electronics owns a group or warehouses with a total 2,500,000 square meters in an industrial park. The company purchases parts and assembles different electronic consumer products. Currently, Pierpont Electronics is operating assembly lines for computer modems, clock radios, and other small electronic items. It

has a small engineering department and views its primary competitive edge to be low-cost assembly. The organizational structure is closely tied to the products with a product manager for each major line. The product manager is responsible for purchasing, assembly, and sales and is evaluated based on the product line's profit. Most overhead allocated to the product manager comes from warehouse space, which is allocated based on the square meters used by the product.

Roberta Garcia, the product manager for the modem assembly lines, spends time locating more dependable and less expensive suppliers of parts, improving efficiency on the assembly line, and making sure that her customers (mostly retail electronics stores) are satisfied. Making and selling modems is a very competitive business with competition coming primarily from Asia. Roberta is working hard to create a profit for the product line. Year-end bonuses for her and her managers depend on generating a profit of $1,000,000. The profit goal for this year looks elusive after losing an important customer. In addition, she must bear the burden of the cost of warehouse space, which is allocated to her at $10 per square meter per year. Roberta is considering dropping a few modem models to conserve on space and reduce the allocation of overhead. Based on estimated sales of 200,000 units at $20 per unit, she expects this year's income to be the following:

Sales ($20 per unit × 200,000 units)	$4,000,000
Cost of goods sold ($14 per unit × 200,000 units)	(2,800,000)
Selling and other expenses	(500,000)
Expected profit	$ 700,000

The cost of goods sold is estimated by calculating an average cost per unit (assuming that 200,000 units are assembled and sold):

Parts	$ 4 per unit
Direct labor	3 per unit
Variable overhead	2 per unit
Fixed overhead ($10 per sq. m.)(100,000 sq. m.)/200,000 units	5 per unit
Cost per unit	$14 per unit

CRITICISMS OF ABSORPTION COST SYSTEMS

LO 1   Identify the problems with absorption costing systems.

Chapter Ten described two absorption cost systems, job-order costing and process costing. These systems have been widely used for most of the twentieth century. Indeed, some of their elements have been traced back to the Industrial Revolution. For as long as these systems have been used, they have been criticized for producing misleading information and creating incentives that are inconsistent with maximizing the firm's value. Despite these criticisms, absorption cost systems are the predominant systems used by manufacturing firms today. Service firms are not prone to many of these problems since they do not manufacture a product or hold inventories. This section analyzes absorption cost systems by examining some common complaints.

As described in Chapter One, cost systems serve numerous functions, including making planning and control decisions and external reporting. No single system can satisfy all the requirements of each function, so trade-offs among the requirements must be made. Costing systems are constantly being revised and updated as technology and firms' organizational structures change. The examination of the well-known problems in absorption cost systems and alternative cost systems provides a greater appreciation of the successful implementation of such systems. Also, one must be careful not to reject a particular type of cost system (e.g., absorption costing versus variable costing) simply because a particular firm or industry does not implement it well.

Incentive to Overproduce

Absorption cost systems include both variable and fixed costs in the product cost. The average cost of the product is determined by dividing the variable and fixed costs of making a product by the number of units produced. This procedure occurs in both job-order and process costing.

The average product cost, however, exhibits certain qualities that are not necessarily consistent with the opportunity cost of making the product. For example, as long as the variable cost per unit is constant, the average cost per unit decreases as more units are produced. This decrease is due to "spreading" fixed costs over more units. For example, if the fixed costs of operating a hotel are $100,000 per month, the fixed cost per room rented declines as more rooms are rented. If 5,000 rooms are rented during the month, the fixed cost per room is $100,000/5,000, or $20 per room. If 8,000 rooms are rented during the month, the fixed cost is $100,000/8,000, or $12.50 per room. As the number of units increases, the decline in the fixed cost per unit has nothing to do with a change in fixed costs; it simply reflects the increase in the number of units. Notice that the total costs of operating the hotel do not decrease as more rooms are rented. Rather, total costs increase to the extent that additional variable costs for maid services and other expenditures exist. Thus, declining average costs do not mean that total costs are falling.

Therefore, managers, who are evaluated based on the average cost per unit produced, have an easy way to reduce the average cost per unit: They simply increase the number of units produced as long as there are no capacity constraints and the variable costs per unit do not increase. Increasing the number of units produced is not necessarily bad for the organization. As long as all the units are sold and the contribution margin of each unit is positive, the organization should encourage increased production.

A problem arises, however, if all units produced cannot be sold. Excess units in inventory can lead to increased storage and handling costs. In Numerical Example 11.1, inventory handling costs are recognized.

Numerical Example   11.1

A plant with $1 million of fixed overhead costs makes CD-ROMs that have a variable cost per unit of $1. The plant makes only CD-ROMs and allocates all fixed costs to the product by the number produced. The firm can sell 200,000 a year for $10 each. There is no beginning inventory. The plant manager has the opportunity to make 200,000 units, 220,000 units, or 240,000 units. Handling excess inventory costs $0.10 per unit. Handling costs are expensed in the year that they are incurred. Which production level causes the highest reported income for the year?

Solution

	Production Levels		
	200,000	**220,000**	**240,000**
Fixed costs	$1,000,000	$1,000,000	$1,000,000
Variable costs ($1 per unit)	200,000	220,000	240,000
Total costs	$1,200,000	$1,220,000	$1,240,000
Average cost per CD-ROM	$6	$5.55	$5.17
Revenues (200,000 CD-ROMs)($10 per unit)	$2,000,000	$2,000,000	$2,000,000
Cost of goods sold			
(200,000 CD-ROMs)($6.00 per unit)	(1,200,000)		
(200,000 CD-ROMs)($5.55 per unit)		(1,110,000)	
(200,000 CD-ROMs)($5.17 per unit)			(1,034,000)
Excess inventory handling costs			
(220,000 − 200,000)($0.10 per unit)		(2,000)	
(240,000 − 200,000)($0.10 per unit)			(4,000)
Net income	$ 800,000	$ 888,000	$ 962,000

The production of 240,000 CD-ROMs results in the highest net income. The cost of goods sold is lower with excess production because some fixed costs are left in the ending inventory account. The fixed costs are not treated as an expense in the current period. As a result of producing 240,000 CD-ROMs, the average cost is $5.17, of which $4.17 is a fixed cost. Therefore, the ending inventory would have ($4.17 per CD-ROM)(240,000 − 200,000 CD-ROMs), or $166,800, of fixed costs in inventory. The cost of the ending inventory, including the fixed cost portion, remains an asset and will not become an expense until the units are sold in the future. When the inventory is sold, the fixed costs in inventory will be part of the cost of goods sold and will reduce future income. Increased production, however, also harms the organization because additional handling costs are incurred ($4,000 for the 40,000 CD-ROMs if 240,000 are made). In addition to the extra handling costs, the firm also incurs additional variable costs ($1 per CD-ROM) to produce the extra inventory.

Numerical Example 11.1 demonstrates that managers can increase short-term reported income and harm the organization at the same time. In the long term, reported income will be lower as the higher inventory costs are passed on to subsequent years. However, not all managers remain with the organization long enough to bear the costs of earlier overproduction. As long as managers are evaluated based on short-term income and have the potential to leave the organization, absorption costing creates an incentive to overproduce. Managers who are evaluated based on long-term performance and are committed to the organization for the long term have less incentive to overproduce.

In addition to the increased storage and handling costs of excess inventory, the opportunity cost of investing cash in the excess inventory also exists. The cash used to make excess inventory could be invested more profitably elsewhere, or it could be paid to the owners. The opportunity cost of capital, however, is not commonly reflected in managerial performance measures unless residual income is used to evaluate performance.

Overproduction is another example of the trade-off between planning and control. The organization would like the manager to use resources efficiently and not overproduce. However, short-term net income is commonly used to evaluate the manager; thus, the manager has an incentive to overproduce.

Several methods exist to mitigate the incentive to overproduce. The first is to charge managers for holding inventory. The net income reported in financial statements does not consider explicitly the opportunity cost of using cash to hold

Control Decisions

inventory. The residual income performance measure is one example of a charge for holding inventory because the manager is responsible for the opportunity cost of capital.

A second method is a strict senior management policy against adding to or building inventories. Compensation plans can contain a clause that bonuses tied to net income will not be paid if inventories exceed a certain amount. However, such strict constraints are cumbersome and costly to monitor. In some circumstances, such as new product introduction and unexpected orders, the organization prefers higher inventory levels.

A third approach is to choose performance measures other than short-term reported income to evaluate managers. Long-term profit, the change in share price, total sales, or percentage of defects also could be used as measures of managerial performance.

A fourth possibility is to use just-in-time (JIT) production systems to reduce inventory levels. In a JIT system, manufacturing typically does not begin until a customer orders the part or the final product. Intermediate products flow immediately from one stage of production to another without waiting in work-in-process inventories. If the production schedule is determined by demand, the plant manager or product line manager does not have the discretion to set production levels in excess of demand. In essence, a JIT system removes the responsibility from managers to set production levels. These responsibilities are replaced by demand-driven market orders. Typically, JIT systems reduce inventories and thus the incentive to overproduce to increase reported profits. JIT systems and their accounting implications are discussed in Chapter Twelve.

A final option is to change the costing system. Variable costing systems, discussed in the next section, reduce the incentives to overproduce.

Underutilization of Allocation Base Used to Allocate Fixed Costs

In absorption costing systems, fixed and variable overhead costs are allocated to products through an allocation base. The allocation of overhead costs simulates a tax on the allocation base. Managers who are evaluated based on product costs will use the allocation base sparingly since allocated costs increase product costs and act as a tax on the manager.

**Planning
Decisions**

The organization may not benefit, however, from the reduced usage of the allocation base. Cost allocations lead to good planning decision if the allocated costs approximate the opportunity cost of using the allocation base. The allocation of fixed costs to products through the usage of allocation bases is unlikely to approximate the incremental cost of using the indirect resources. By definition, fixed costs of the indirect resource do not change with the usage of the allocation base. For example, suppose the computing center uses the number of networked computers as an allocation base to allocate computer center costs to other departments. The computing center costs contain fixed costs that do not change with the number of networked computers. Therefore, the allocated costs of adding another networked computer is higher than the incremental cost of having the computing center purchase and support this computer. If the allocated cost is too high, departments will restrict their usage, compromising their operations by having too few networked computers. Numerical Example 11.2 demonstrates this problem.

Numerical Example 11.2

The expected fixed costs of operating the computing center total $1,000,000 per year. The expected variable costs, which reflect the incremental cost of additional PCs, are $5,000 per PC. The number of PCs in each department is used to allocate the computing center costs. The application rate, based on expected usage of 200 PCs, is ($1,000,000 + (200)($5,000))/200, or $10,000 per PC. The engineering department estimates the following benefits of having its own PCs:

Number of PCs	Expected Benefits	Marginal Benefits
1	$15,000	$15,000
2	27,000	12,000
3	35,000	8,000
4	41,000	6,000
5	44,000	3,000

What number of PCs would the engineering department choose if the allocation rate of $10,000 per PC were used? What is the net loss to the organization of using $10,000 per PC as the application rate instead of the variable cost per PC?

Solution

The engineering department will use only two PCs. The marginal benefit of using the third PC is $8,000, which is less than the allocated cost. To maximize the organization's profit, the engineering department should be using four PCs because the marginal benefit of using the fourth PC ($6,000) is still greater than the variable cost ($5,000). The additional benefit of having the third and fourth PCs in the engineering department is $41,000 − $27,000, or $14,000. The incremental cost of having two additional PCs is ($5,000)(2), or $10,000. The net loss of not having the two additional PCs is $14,000 − $10,000, or $4,000.

Misleading Product Costs

The allocation of fixed costs does not represent the incremental cost of using the allocation base if the allocation base has excess capacity. Product costs generated through an absorption costing system will not approximate the marginal cost of making the products. Therefore, managers who rely on product costs from an absorption costing system are likely to misprice products and choose inappropriate product mixes.

Planning Decisions

A common result of the misuse of product costs from full absorption cost system is the **death spiral,** which occurs when an organization drops a product because its full cost exceeds its price. Once the product is eliminated, the fixed overhead that had been allocated to it is redistributed to the remaining products. This redistribution might make other products appear to be unprofitable because of the increased overhead that these products now must bear. When these products are dropped, more overhead is again allocated to the remaining products. So the cycle continues until the organization has no profitable products left.

The death spiral is a threat to many traditional businesses, such as retail banks. Bricks-and-motar banks face significant costs to set up and maintain retail branches. Internet-based banks have low start-up costs and can choose the most lucrative parts of the banking business. With the loss of customers to the Internet, traditional banks must cover their infrastructure costs with fewer fee-paying customers. If the banks increase

The Internet has banks rethinking their strategy to deliver customer value. Online banks provide convenience and flexibility at low cost. They also have low infrastructure costs, while traditional banks must cover the costs of bricks-and-mortar operations. For traditional banks, a death spiral can ensue if service fees for regular operations continually increase and customers shift to cheaper, online services.

fees, more customers leave, and service costs rise again. This continuing cycle creates the danger of a death spiral for traditional banks. Numerical Example 11.3 describes the death spiral.

Numerical Example 11.3

A company makes two types of refrigerators, compact and full size. Excess capacity exists for which it has no alternative use. Fixed overhead costs are allocated based on direct labor dollars. The product profitability of each product is as follows:

	Compact	Full Size
Revenues	$500,000	$1,000,000
Direct costs	(300,000)	(450,000)
Fixed costs	(240,000)	(360,000)
Profit	($ 40,000)	$ 190,000

Management decides to drop the compact model because it appears to be unprofitable. What is the impact on the profitability of the full-size model?

Solution

By dropping the compact model, all of the fixed overhead is shifted to the full-size refrigerator. Its profitability is now as follows:

	Full Size
Revenues	$1,000,000
Direct costs	(450,000)
Fixed costs	(600,000)
Profit	($ 50,000)

Absorption costing systems do not lead necessarily to erroneous product costs. If a fixed cost resource is operating at capacity, profitable alternatives to use the facility might exist but have not been utilized because of limited capacity. In this case, the allocation of the fixed costs could represent the opportunity cost of not being able to use the facility for an alternative purpose. This allocation could lead to more accurate product costs. If an organization is not operating at capacity, variable costing can overcome the problems in control and planning described in this section. We examine this alternative costing system next.

Concept**Review**

1. Why is there an incentive to overproduce with an absorption costing system?
2. What alternatives are available to discourage overproduction?
3. Why does the allocation of fixed costs lead to underuse of its allocation base?
4. What causes the death spiral?

PIERPONT ELECTRONICS
(Continued)

Roberta would like to meet the profit goal of $1,000,000 for her product line of modems so that she and many of her employees can receive a bonus. After further analysis, her sales estimate for the year appears to be accurate and additional sales do not seem possible. A closer look at operations indicates no opportunities for easy cost savings. She could, however, squeeze operations into a smaller space and be charged less overhead. A 30% reduction in space used to 70,000 square meters would lower fixed overhead allocation and increase expected profit to $1,000,000. Roberta is afraid, however, that the reduced use of space would cause other costs to increase. Also, it makes little sense to reduce the use of space when the company already has excess warehouse capacity.

Another possibility is to increase production to transfer some fixed overhead to ending inventory. If Roberta were able to make 285,715 modems, the per unit cost would be reduced as follows:

Parts, direct labor, and variable overhead per unit	$ 9.00
Fixed overhead per unit	
($10 per sq. m.)(100,000 sq. m.)/285,715 units	3.50
Cost per unit	$12.50

This increases the expected profit to $1,000,000:

Sales ($20 per unit × 200,000 units)	$4,000,000
Cost of goods sold ($12.50 per unit × 200,000 units)	(2,500,000)
Selling and other expenses	(500,000)
Expected profit	$1,000,000

Roberta is not happy about this option because she might have to bear the storage costs of the extra inventory. Also, she does not believe that making excess inventory is ethically appropriate, so she is still in a quandary as to how to achieve the $1,000,000 profit goal.

VARIABLE COSTING

The cost of a product under **variable costing** includes only the variable costs of making the product. The variable costs include direct material, direct labor, and variable overhead. The fixed overhead costs are treated as period costs and are expensed in the period incurred. Therefore, the difference between absorption costing and variable costing is the treatment of fixed manufacturing costs: Fixed costs are included as part of product costs under absorption costing and are written off as period expenses under variable costing.

Variable costing has several advantages. The variable cost per unit approximates the marginal cost of making another unit if the organization is operating below capacity. This information is useful in pricing and product mix decisions. Prices above the variable cost per unit provide a positive contribution margin. The contribution margin per unit (price less variable cost per unit) is also used to direct scarce resources among products. Organizations prefer to make and sell products with higher per unit contribution margins, given constraints in the production process.

Variable costing also reduces the dysfunctional incentive to overproduce. With all fixed costs treated as period expenses, increased production does not spread the fixed costs across more units and allows fixed costs to reside in the inventory account at the end of the period. The incremental cost of making additional units approximately equals the recorded inventory cost. Overproduction of inventory has a negative effect on reported profit because of additional handling and storage costs.

LO 2 Recognize the advantages and disadvantages of variable costing and use it to generate income statements.

Planning Decisions

Numerical Example 11.4

A factory making electric fans has estimated and actual fixed costs of $50,000. Variable costs per unit total $6. The allocation base is the number of units produced. The sales price of the electric fan is $10 per unit. There is no beginning inventory. During the year, the factory makes and sells 20,000 electric fans. In December, the factory manager has the opportunity to make another 5,000 units, but they cannot be sold this year. What is the factory's profit with and without the additional 5,000 units under the absorption and variable costing systems? (Assume no handling and storage costs.)

Solution

Under the absorption costing system without the additional 5,000 units, the application rate is ($50,000 + ($6 per unit)(20,000 units))/20,000 units, or $8.50 per unit. The profit is as follows:

Sales ($10.00 per unit)(20,000 units)	$200,000
Cost of goods sold ($8.50 per unit)(20,000 units)	(170,000)
Profit	$ 30,000

Under the absorption costing system with the additional 5,000 units, the application rate is ($50,000 + ($6 per unit)(25,000 units))/25,000 units, or $8 per unit. The profit is as follows:

Sales ($10 per unit)(20,000 units)	$200,000
Cost of goods sold ($8 per unit)(20,000 units)	(160,000)
Profit	$ 40,000

The cost of the ending inventory of 5,000 units is ($8.00 per unit)(5,000 units), or $40,000.

Under the variable costing system without the additional 5,000 units, the application rate is the variable cost of $6 per unit and fixed costs are expensed. The profit is as follows:

Sales ($10 per unit)(20,000 units)	$200,000
Cost of goods sold ($6 per unit)(20,000 units)	(120,000)
Fixed costs	(50,000)
Profit	$ 30,000

Under the variable costing system with the additional 5,000 units, the application rate is still the variable cost of $6 per unit and fixed costs are expensed. The profit is still

Sales ($10 per unit)(20,000 units)	$200,000
Cost of goods sold ($6 per unit)(20,000 units)	(120,000)
Fixed costs	(50,000)
Profit	$ 30,000

The cost of making the additional 5,000 units is ($6 per unit)(5,000 units), or $30,000, which is recorded as the ending inventory cost.

Numerical Example 11.4 indicates that the reported profit under both absorption and variable costing is the same when there is no beginning or ending inventory. When ending inventory is added, the variable costing method still reports the same income, but the absorption costing system reports a higher income because it allocates some fixed costs to the ending inventory. The fixed costs allocated to the ending inventory become the cost of goods sold in the next period. The absorption costing just postpones the expense. Therefore, absorption costing may cause a lower reported profit in the next period, depending on the amount of ending inventory that remains.

A variable costing system also does not have product costs that fluctuate as the output volume changes. The per unit product cost is the variable cost per unit, which should not vary with normal fluctuations in output. Alternatively, the absorption costing system reports an average product cost. The average cost declines with higher levels of output as fixed costs are spread over more units.

The disadvantages of variable costing include misleading product costs if there is an opportunity cost of using fixed overhead resources. An opportunity cost exists if the fixed overhead resources are operating at capacity and alternative, profitable uses of the overhead resources exist. The allocation of these fixed costs provides a means to represent the opportunity cost of using the fixed overhead resources. If the cost of fixed overhead resources are sunk and without alternative use, however, the variable cost more closely approximates the cost of making the product.

If managers are evaluated based on product costs and are not responsible for fixed overhead costs, they tend to overuse the overhead resources generating the fixed costs. Managers avoid using variable overhead resources, which affect product costs, and attempt to use fixed overhead resources instead. This substitution leads to dysfunctional behavior for the entire organization if there is an opportunity cost in using those fixed overhead resources. For example, facility costs are often considered fixed. If these fixed costs are not allocated to managers, they want to use more space because the space is free to them, yet space probably is not free to the entire organization. Extra space could be rented or sold.

An implementation problem with variable costing is the choice of allocation base to use to allocate variable overhead costs. In Numerical Example 11.4, the allocation base is the output measure of the number of units produced. If the manufacturing facility makes multiple products that share common variable overhead resources, some input measure such as direct labor hours frequently is used as an allocation base. As long as an allocation base uses only one input metric, overhead can be classified as variable or fixed with respect to that allocation base. If multiple allocation bases are used, however, the definition of variable and fixed becomes less clear. For example, batch-level costs are fixed with respect to the number of units or other unit-level costs but vary with the number of batches and allocation bases such as the number of set-ups. Should batch-level costs be treated as variable and included in product costs, or should they be treated as fixed and excluded from product costs? These definitional problems become more acute when different levels of costs are recognized in activity-based costing.

Variable costing attracted much attention in the 1950s and 1960s. Some companies experimented with it, and some are still using it, but only for internal reports. Absorption costing remains the predominant method of costing in manufacturing organizations, although all firms treat some overhead as a

Business Analysis

Strategic Cost Management at National Bank

National Bank of Canada is the sixth largest of Canada's chartered banks. To compete with other major players, National Bank uses its cost management system to support its strategy of product differentiation and personalized customer service. In its credit card sector, the bank's cost management system reports costs on a product basis. This method contrasts with the more general approach within the banking industry of reporting costs on a functional or departmental basis.

Cost assignment at National Bank is complicated, especially because many costs are fixed, semifixed, or shared across products. For example, the cost of head-office operations and customer service representatives are not assigned easily to an individual credit card. With new products and card features constantly being added, it is more difficult to identify how a particular item affects the overall cost behavior of credit cards.

National Bank uses a full-cost system to allocate costs to credit card products. First, costs are assigned to more than 30 different activity centers. Next, costs are allocated to products based on a variety of cost drivers that include the number of cards outstanding, the number of cards in use, and bad debt levels. These allocated costs are used to determine product profitability, whether or not to launch a new product, relative profitability, marketing programs, and so on.

The cost system also provides a mechanism for the marketing and accounting groups to work together to ensure that new initiatives meet National Bank's strategic objectives and financial goals. To compensate for the potential loss of information from the fully allocated cost system, National Bank supplements these data with a direct cost model. The direct cost model is used to evaluate the short-term impact of new products on resource consumption. Both models motivate managers to challenge cost figures from the perspective of their own experience and conventional wisdom. While managers might have different ideas and expectations, the accounting system ensures that decisions are based on reasonable and realistic figures.

How does the management accounting system at National Bank support organization strategy and its implementation? What are the advantages and disadvantages of National Bank's full-cost system? What are the potential effects of the system on management behavior?

Source: A. Mersereau, "Controlling the Cost of Plastic," *CMA Management* 73, no. 6 (July–August 1999), pp. 26–30.

period expense rather than a product cost. For example, Allegheny Ludlum writes off depreciation, plant insurance, property taxes, and plant management salaries to income. These fixed costs are not part of Allegheny Ludlum's product costs and are treated as period costs. Also in Canada and the United States, research and development costs must be treated as a period cost for external reporting purposes.

For income tax calculations, absorption costing tends to be the allowed method. Thus, firms seeking to use variable costing for internal purposes must maintain two costing systems. This duplication increases their costs of doing business.

The preference for absorption costing implies that the benefits of switching to variable costing for some organizations are not as great as the costs. Most organizations have retained their absorption costing system even when potential problems with planning decisions and control exist.

Concept**Review**

1.   How are fixed costs treated with variable costing?
2.   What are the advantages of using variable costing?
3.   Why is variable costing not more widely used?

PIERPONT ELECTRONICS
(Continued)

Roberta is glad that she did not produce extra inventory to improve the reported profit. For internal reporting and performance compensation, corporate headquarters has announced a change in the calculation of profit for the different product lines. By requiring reports based on variable costing, there is no longer an advantage to overproduction. All fixed costs are to be reported in the period in which they are incurred. No opportunity would exist to spread fixed costs over both products sold and products held in inventory to improve income.

CAPACITY COSTS

LO 3   Identify problems in selecting the capacity of a fixed cost resource.

Planning Decisions

Absorption costing and variable costing provide alternative ways to account for fixed costs. Fixed costs primarily derive from prior decisions on capacity. Capacity decisions include decisions on the size of plants and the amount of equipment purchased. These fixed costs include depreciation of buildings and equipment, property taxes, security, and utilities. Other capacity decisions include the size of service units within the organization, such as computing, accounting, and marketing. Each of these capacity decisions generates fixed costs that are usually allocated to other units within the organization.

How much capacity should the firm acquire? Even with all the information available, this decision is difficult. The future demand for an organization's products is uncertain and tends to vary over time. The cost of too much capacity (acquiring more plants and equipment and hiring more employees) must be weighed against the cost of too little capacity (overtime pay, wear on facilities, and lost sales). The capacity decision for a common overhead resource becomes even more difficult when knowledge about future demand for the overhead resource is decentralized. Product managers likely have better information about the future demand for their products than do centralized decision makers. However, the latter usually are responsible for capacity decisions. Therefore, the organization should gather information from all potential users of the resource before making a capacity decision.

Gathering information for making a capacity decision leads to trade-offs between planning and control decisions. In particular, the organization prefers to receive accurate information from decentralized managers to make the appropriate resource capacity decision. It also prefers that decentralized managers use the resource in an efficient manner. The capacity decision, however, generates fixed costs that are allocated to the decentralized managers. For example, the decision to expand the warehouse generates additional depreciation expense and utilities that are fixed costs; therefore, the capacity decision influences their performance measures. This influence on managerial performance evaluation and rewards might lead managers to provide inaccurate estimates and to use the capacity in a less than optimal manner.

**Control
Decisions**

As described in the previous sections of this chapter, the allocation of fixed costs can lead to underutilization of the allocation base used to allocate the fixed costs. This problem occurs when an organization is operating below capacity. If resource capacity is set and is not flexible, no opportunity cost exists in using the excess capacity, yet managers choose to control their use of the resource because of the allocation of fixed costs. In the extreme, underutilization of the allocation base can lead to the death spiral. Not allocating fixed costs can resolve the underutilization problem when operating below capacity.

Not allocating the fixed costs of a resource when operating below capacity, however, leads to problems with the capacity decision. Managers overstate their future resource requirements and request additional capacity that satisfies all potential future resource needs. Therefore, the allocation of fixed costs related to capacity prevents managers from overstating their capacity needs. The allocation of fixed costs to managers also commits them to recovering a share of the capacity costs.

Once the capacity decision has been made, however, the efficient use of the resource becomes the important issue. If excess capacity exists, the organization wants to encourage use of the resource by allocating little or no costs. When excess capacity exists, the opportunity cost of using the resource is zero; therefore, its use should be encouraged.

In deciding whether to allocate the fixed costs of a capacity resource to its users, the firm makes a trade-off between the efficient investment in the common resource and its efficient utilization after acquisition. Allocating fixed costs helps control the problem of overinvestment in capacity, but at the expense of the possible underutilization of the asset after acquisition.

The following two sections provide methods to allocate fixed costs related to capacity.

Allocation of Overhead Based on Practical Capacity

In Chapter Ten, the predetermined application rate for overhead is calculated by dividing the expected overhead costs by the expected usage of the allocation base. By using the expected usage of the allocation base, the total overhead allocated should approximate the total actual overhead.

LO 4   Recognize the advantages and disadvantages of the practical capacity of the organization and use it to allocate overhead.

An alternative to a full absorption costing system is a partial absorption costing system. Under this system, all variable overhead is allocated, but only the fixed cost of overhead resources used is allocated. The fixed costs of unused overhead resources (excess capacity) are treated as expenses of the period and are not allocated to products. To allocate overhead based on capacity used, a fixed cost application rate is calculated by dividing the expected fixed overhead costs by the practical capacity of the shared resource. The **practical capacity** is the maximum level of operations that can be achieved without increasing costs due to congestion. For example, the practical capacity of a paper mill operating 24 hours a day is estimated to be 2,000 tons per week. The paper mill could produce 2,300 tons per week by increasing the speed of the machines, but that would lead to higher maintenance and replacement costs.

**Control
Decisions**

When the application rate to allocate fixed costs is based on practical capacity, the underabsorption of fixed overhead costs generally occurs. The capacity level of

Online shops must compete with other Internet sites and clicks-and-mortar retailers – those with both Internet and retail locations. Ever-changing customer needs, global links, and price competition make value creation more challenging. As well, online stores must ensure that product prices cover all costs, including their overhead costs.

the allocation base is usually higher than the expected level, so the application rate will be lower. A lower application rate leads to the allocation of less overhead. For example, suppose the practical capacity of the paper mill described earlier is 2,000 tons per week, but only 1,600 tons are used. Suppose the fixed costs of the mill are $300,000 per week. Using practical capacity, the application rate is $150 per ton ($300,000/2,000 tons). An amount of $240,000 is allocated to the paper produced because only 1,600 tons are manufactured. Any fixed cost that is not allocated is the cost of having excess capacity. The unallocated overhead is not absorbed in inventory but is treated as a separate period expense. In the paper mill example, the remaining $60,000 is the cost of excess capacity and is a period cost.

Numerical Example 11.5

The fixed costs of operating an online retail operation primarily are due to the cost of the facility. The expected and actual annual cost of the facility is $200,000. Its fixed cost of 20,000 square meters is allocated to the marketing and inventory divisions, which share the facility. The inventory division uses 10,000 square meters, and the marketing division uses 4,000 square meters. Currently, 6,000 square meters are unoccupied. What is the application rate using square meters as the capacity measure? How much of the fixed costs are allocated to the marketing and inventory divisions? How much is treated as the cost of excess capacity?

Solution

The application rate is as follows:

$200,000/20,000 square meters = $10 per square meter

Cost Object	Usage of Square Meters	Application Rate/ Square Meters	Allocation
Inventory	10,000 sq. m.	$10 sq. m.	$100,000
Marketing	4,000	10	40,000
Excess capacity	6,000	10	60,000
Totals	20,000 sq. m.		$200,000

The $60,000 allocated to unused capacity is a period expense.

Using practical capacity of the allocation base to determine the application rate has several advantages. The allocation of the fixed costs of a resource to a particular product or organizational unit is not affected by the use of the resource by other products or units. With full absorption costing systems, less use of the shared resource by some products or units means more fixed costs allocated to the other units and products that share the resource. A death spiral is less likely to occur because the cost of unused capacity is not imposed on the remaining units and their products.

Another advantage of using practical capacity of the allocation base is having a measure of the cost of unused capacity. Under a full absorption costing system, the cost of unused capacity is not easily identified. Knowledge about the cost of unused capacity is valuable in making decisions to change capacity.

Use of practical capacity to allocate fixed costs has some disadvantages. This procedure does not alleviate the incentive to overproduce. By producing more units than can be sold, some fixed costs remain in ending inventory at the end of the year instead of being expensed. Overproduction has a short-term, positive impact on income.

Another disadvantage of using practical capacity occurs if economies of scale exist. In this case, managers still have incentives to overinvest by building too large a facility. Knowing that the cost of the excess capacity is not allocated to them, they can lower their future allocated fixed costs. For example, suppose that a paper mill with practical capacity of 2,000 tons a week can be built. The mill incurs weekly fixed costs of $300,000. Due to economies of scale, a mill can be built with a capacity of 3,000 tons per week that generates $400,000 of fixed costs per week. The product managers know that they need only 2,000 tons of capacity per week, but by building the larger mill, they can lower their allocated fixed cost from $150 per ton to $133.33 per ton ($400,000/3,000 tons).

Managers also tend to underutilize the allocation base even if only some fixed costs are being allocated. If the organization is not operating at full capacity, the usage of the allocation base is taxed at a higher rate than the opportunity cost of using the overhead resource. In effect, the opportunity cost is zero. When allocation rates are higher than the opportunity cost of using the indirect resource, managers are motivated to use less of the indirect resource than they would if the opportunity cost of the indirect resource were allocated. This problem is described in Numerical Example 11.2.

Allocation Based on the Capacity Decision

To gather information on the capacity decision, the organization must provide appropriate incentives to encourage managers to reveal truthfully their future expected demand for a resource. If the managers are not charged for the resource, they prefer a larger resource capacity. However, if capacity costs are allocated to the manager, underutilization of the capacity occurs when excess capacity exists.

An alternative fixed cost allocation system allocates fixed costs based on requests for the resource when the capacity was acquired. Decentralized managers would be charged a fixed amount for the resource based on capacity requested rather than on the resource used, as long as resource consumption is less than requested. Any use of the resource more than requested is charged to the manager at a much higher rate. This rate discourages managers from requesting too little of the resource when the capacity decision is made.

This cost allocation procedure has several benefits. It encourages managers to reveal their expected use of the resource. If they request too much of the resource when they make the capacity decision, they will be burdened with a large allocated cost for that resource. If they request too little of the resource, they will face stiff penalties for its overuse.

This cost allocation procedure also tends to provide decentralized managers the right incentives in using the resource. Once the capacity decision has been made and the fixed cost allocation is predetermined, managers treat the resource as free until its usage reaches the requested amount. After reaching the requested amount, managers are charged considerably more for additional use. This cost allocation scheme approximately mirrors the opportunity cost of using the fixed resource. However, it too is not without problems. What charge do new users receive years after the capacity has been built? Or suppose that a new technology makes it more efficient for current users of the capacity to switch to the new technology. If they continue to be charged for their previous share of the old capacity, they will not make the shift. Should they be excused from their previous commitment?

LO 5 Describe trade-offs for decentralized managers to provide accurate information in making a decision on the capacity of a common resource and in using it efficiently.

Control Decisions

ConceptReview

1. How are application rates calculated using practical capacity?

2. What portion of the fixed overhead is allocated to products when application rates are calculated using practical capacity?

3. What are the advantages and disadvantages of using practical capacity to allocate fixed costs?

4. What other methods might be used to manage both the capacity decision and the efficient use of fixed resources?

PIERPONT ELECTRONICS
(Continued)

To get a clearer understanding of how overhead is allocated to her product line, Roberta has asked corporate headquarters to explain fixed overhead allocation. The following calculations were made:

Total annual fixed costs related to all of the facilities	$20,000,000
Total square meters of all facilities	2,500,000
Total square meters expected to be used during the year	2,000,000
Application rate ($20,000,000/2,000,000 square meters)	$10 per square meter
Applied to modem assembly ($10 per square meter)(100,000 square meters)	$1,000,000

Roberta recognizes that she is being charged for the cost of the unused capacity. She was not part of the capacity decision; therefore, she responds to corporate headquarters that the following allocation based on practical capacity is more appropriate:

Application rate ($20,000,000/2,500,000 square meters	$8 per square meter
Applied to modem assembly ($8 per square meter)(100,000 square meters)	$800,000

You decide

If corporate headquarters agrees with her argument, she will be $200,000 closer to reaching the goal of $1,000,000 profit for modem assembly and sales.

SUMMARY

1 **Identify the problems with absorption costing systems.** Absorption costing systems can cause overproduction, underutilization of allocation bases, and misleading product costs.

2 **Recognize the advantages and disadvantages of variable costing and use it to generate income statements.** With variable costing, only variable costs are treated as part of the product cost. Fixed costs are expensed in the period incurred. Variable costing reduces the incentive to overproduce and provides product costs closer to the opportunity cost when excess capacity exists. The disadvantages include the excessive use of fixed overhead resources and the exclusion of fixed opportunity costs in the product cost.

3 **Identify problems in selecting the capacity of a fixed cost resource.** In selecting the capacity of a fixed cost resource, the organization is committing resources for a period of time. If it sets capacity

too high, it will incur excessive fixed costs. If it sets capacity too low, it will incur additional overtime costs and excess wear on the facilities. The organization also may lose sales. Information about future demand for its products is critical in making the capacity decision.

4 **Recognize the advantages and disadvantages of the practical capacity of the organization and use it to allocate overhead.** The application rate is calculated by dividing fixed costs by the practical capacity of the allocation base. Allocated costs include only the cost of capacity used. Advantages include an allocated cost that is not affected by other users of the resource and the identification of the cost of unused capacity. Disadvantages include the incentive to overproduce and the underutilization of the allocation base.

5 **Describe trade-offs for decentralized managers to provide accurate information in making a decision on the**

capacity of a common resource and in using it efficiently. When the capacity decision for a common resource is being made, decentralized managers would like extra capacity if they were not charged for it through the allocation of costs. However, the allocation of the fixed costs of a common resource likely leads to underutilization of the resource, especially if significant excess capacity exists.

6 **Make decisions regarding the production and further processing of joint products. (Appendix)**   A process that produces joint products is profitable if the joint costs are less than the sales value of all the joint products. A joint product should be processed further if the incremental revenues exceed the incremental costs.

KEY TERMS

by-products   Joint products of relatively low value compared to other joint products. *(p. 397)*

death spiral   The process of dropping products without lowering overhead costs. *(p. 385)*

joint costs   The costs of the input and of the processing of the input to generate joint products. *(p. 395)*

joint products   Products generated from splitting a single material input. *(p. 395)*

net realizable value method   A procedure of dividing joint costs based on the sales value less the finishing costs of the joint products. *(p. 398)*

physical measure method   A procedure of dividing joint costs based on a physical characteristic of the joint products. *(p. 398)*

practical capacity   The highest rate at which an organization can operate without increasing congestion. *(p. 391)*

relative sales value method   A procedure of dividing joint costs based on the gross sales value of the joint products. *(p. 398)*

variable costing   Determining product costs based only on the variable cost of making the product. The fixed costs are treated as period costs and are written off directly to the income statement. *(p. 387)*

APPENDIX

Joint Costs

Joint products are produced from a single input, which is generally some raw material that is split into joint products. For example, hamburger and liver are joint products of a butchered cow. In a mining operation, gold and silver are joint products of the processed ore. Usually, but not always, joint products are produced in fixed proportions, meaning that more gold cannot be produced by making less silver. The production of joint products is demonstrated in Figure 11A.1.

Joint costs refer to the cost of the input and the cost of processing the input to generate the joint products. The cost of the petroleum and the refining costs are joint costs of making kerosene, gasoline, tar, and the other joint products that are separated through the distillation process. Joint costs are obviously part of the production cost of joint products, but there are no obvious ways to trace joint costs to specific joint products. In other words, what part of the cost of a barrel of petroleum can be traced to the gasoline distilled from it? All of the joint costs are necessary to make each of the joint products.

The inability to trace joint costs to joint products does not mean that joint costs cannot be allocated to them. To the extent that joint costs are manufacturing costs, GAAP suggests that these joint costs should be allocated to the joint products for

LO 6   Make decisions regarding the production and further processing of joint products.

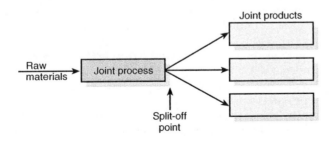

Figure 11A.1

Production of Joint Products

⁕ In department 3, the material is processed at a total additional cost of $40,000. Thirty percent of the processed pineapple turns into juice and is sold at $0.50 per kilogram after incurring $3,500 as selling costs. The remaining 70% is transferred to department 4.

⁕ Department 4 is used to pack the sliced pineapples into tins. Costs incurred here total $25,500. The cans are then ready for sale at $4 per kilogram.

Prepare a schedule showing the allocation of the processing cost of $120,000 between crushed and sliced pineapple using the net realizable value method. The net realizable value of the juice is added to the sales value of the sliced pineapples.

Zipp Cards buys baseball cards in bulk from companies producing them. Zipp buys the cards in sheets of 48 cards, cuts the sheets into individual cards, and sorts and packages them. Zipp then sells the packages to large discount stores. The following table provides information regarding the results from operations for 2000 and 2001.

NP 11.11
Absorption Costing and Overproduction
(LO 1)

ZIPP CARDS Summary of Operations 2000 & 2001 (one unit = 48 cards)		
	2000	**2001**
Unit sales	50,000	48,000
Price	$5.00	$4.90
Production in units (budgeted = actual)	50,000	75,000
Variable cost	$1.00	$1.00
Fixed manufacturing overhead	$160,000	$160,000

Volume is measured in terms of 48 card sheets processed. Budgeted and actual production in 2000 was 50,000 units. There were no beginning inventories on January 1, 2000. In 2001, budgeted and actual production rose to 75,000 units.

At the end of 2001, Zipp's owner was pleasantly surprised with the income statement the accountant had prepared for 2001. The president remarked, "I'm surprised we made more money in 2001 than 2000. We had to cut prices and we didn't sell as many units, but yet we still made more money. Well, you're the accountant and these numbers don't lie."

a. Prepare income statements for 2000 and 2001 using absorption costing.

b. Prepare a statement reconciling the change in net income from 2000 to 2001. Explain to the president why the firm made more money in 2001 than in 2000.

Medford Mug Company is an old-line maker of ceramic coffee mugs. It imprints company logos and other sayings on mugs for both commercial and wholesale markets. The firm has the capacity to produce 50 million mugs per year but as the result of a downturn has cut production and sales in the current year to 15 million mugs. The operating statement for 2000 follows:

NP 11.12
Absorption Costing and Overproduction
(LO 1)

MEDFORD MUG COMPANY Income Statement For the Year Ending 2000 (millions)		
Sales (15 million @ $2)		$30.0
Less: Cost of goods sold		
Variable cost (15 million @ $0.50)	(7.5)	
Fixed cost	(20.0)	(27.5)
Gross margin		$ 2.5
Less: Selling and administration		(4.0)
Operating profit		($ 1.5)

At the end of 2000, there was no ending inventory of finished goods.

The board of directors is very concerned about the $1.5 million operating loss and hires an outside consultant who reports that the firm suffers from two problems. First, Medford Mug's president receives a fixed salary and since she owns no stock, she has little incentive to worry about firm profits. The second problem is that Medford Mug has not aggressively marketed its product and has not kept up with changing markets. The board of directors makes her an offer to retire so that it can hire a new chief operating manager to turn the firm around. The current president accepts the offer to retire and the board immediately hires a new president with a proven track record as a "turnaround" specialist.

The new president's employment contract pays him a fixed wage of $50,000 a year plus 15% of the firm's operating profits (if any). Operating profits are calculated using absorption costing. In 2001, the new president doubles the selling and administration budget to $8 million (which includes his salary of $50,000). He designs a new line of "politically correct" sayings to imprint on the mugs and expands inventory and the number of distributors handling the mugs. Production is increased to 45 million mugs and sales of mugs climb to 18 million at $2 each. Variable costs per mug in 2001 remain at $0.50 and fixed costs at $20 million.

At the end of 2001, the president meets with the board of directors and announces that he has accepted another job. He believes that he has successfully put Medford Mug back on track and thanks the board for giving him the opportunity. His new job is helping to turn around another struggling company.

a. Calculate the president's bonus for 2001.

b. Evaluate the new president's performance for 2001. Did he do as good a job as the "numbers" in part (a) suggest?

NP 11.13

Absorption and Variable Costing Using FIFO

(LO 1, 2)

Smidt & Sons produces a single product and has the following operating data:

	1999	2000	2001
Units produced	22,000	16,000	15,000
Units sold	20,000	15,000	18,000
Fixed manufacturing overhead	$800,000	$880,000	$950,000
Variable manufacturing cost	$3.00	$3.10	$3.20
Variable selling costs	$0.25	$0.30	$0.35
Selling price	$45.00	$50.00	$53.00

The firm uses FIFO inventory costing and had no beginning inventory in 1999.

a. Calculate net income in each year using absorption costing.

b. Calculate net income in each year using variable costing.

c. Reconcile the annual differences between the two costing methods.

NP 11.14

Absorption and Variable Costing

(LO 1, 2)

BBG Corporation is a manufacturer of a synthetic chemical. Gary Voss, president of the company, has been eager to get the operating results for the just-completed fiscal year. He was surprised when the income statement revealed that income before taxes had dropped to $885,500 from $900,000 despite an increase in sales volume of 100,000 kg. The drop in net income occurred even though Voss had implemented two changes during the past 12 months to improve the company's profitability.

* In response to a 10% increase in production costs, the sales price of BBG's product was increased by 12%. This action took place on December 1, 1999, the first day of the 2000 fiscal year.

* The managers of the selling and administrative departments were given strict instructions to spend no more in fiscal 2000 than in fiscal 1999.

BBG's accounting department prepared and distributed to top management the following comparative income statements:

BBG CORPORATION
Statements of Operating Income
For the Years Ended November 30, 1999 and 2000
(000 omitted)

	1999	2000
Sales revenue	$9,000	$11,200
Cost of goods sold	$7,200	$ 8,320
Under- or overabsorbed overhead	(600)	495
Adjusted cost of goods sold	$6,600	$ 8,815
Gross margin	$2,400	$ 2,385
Selling and administrative expenses	1,500	1,500
Income before taxes	$ 900	$ 885

The accounting staff also prepared related financial information presented in the following schedule to assist management in evaluating the company's performance. BBG uses FIFO inventory method for finished goods.

BBG CORPORATION
Selected Operating and Financial Data
For 1999 and 2000

	1999	2000
Sales price	$10.00 per kg.	$11.20 per kg.
Material cost	$1.50 per kg.	$1.65 per kg.
Direct labor cost	$2.50 per kg.	$2.75 per kg.
Variable overhead cost	$1.00 per kg.	$1.10 per kg.
Fixed overhead cost	$3.00 per kg.	$3.30 per kg.
Total fixed overhead costs	$3,000,000	$3,300,000
Normal production volume	1,000,000 kg.	1,000,000 kg.
Selling and administrative (all fixed)	$1,500,000	$1,500,000
Sales volume	900,000 kg.	1,000,000 kg.
Beginning inventory	300,000 kg.	600,000 kg.
Production	1,200,000 kg.	850,000 kg.

a.   Explain to Gary Voss why BBG Corporation's net income decreased in the current fiscal year despite the sales price and sales volume increases.

b.   A member of BBG's accounting department has suggested that the company adopt variable costing for internal reporting purposes.
   1.   Prepare an operating income statement through income before taxes for the year ended November 30, 2000, for BBG Corporation using the variable costing method.
   2.   Present a numerical reconciliation of the difference in income before taxes using the absorption costing method as currently employed by BBG and the proposed variable costing method.

c.   Identify and discuss the advantages and disadvantages of using the variable costing method for internal reporting purposes.

(CMA adapted)

Matson manufactures a single metal dog cage that has a variable cost of $50 per cage. Budgeted and actual fixed overhead costs are $900,000. Cages sell for $60 each.
Calculate net income under both variable costing and absorption costing for each of the following independent cases:

NP 11.15
Absorption and Variable Costing
(LO 1, 2)

a.   Sales and production are 100,000 cages.

b.   Sales are 90,000 cages and production is 100,000 cages.

c.   Sales are 100,000 cages and production is 90,000 cages. The beginning inventory consists of 20,000 units manufactured last year. Last year 100,000 units were manufactured, 80,000 were sold, variable costs were $50 per cage, and fixed manufacturing overhead costs were $900,000. For inventory valuation purposes, all of this year's production is sold and 10,000 units in the beginning inventory are sold. LIFO is used.

NP 11.16
Absorption Costing and
Variable Costing
(LO 1, 2)

Alliance Tooling produces a single product in its plant. At the beginning of the year, there were no units in inventory. During the year, Alliance produced 120,000 units and sold 100,000 units at $26.75 per unit. Variable manufacturing costs are $13.50 per unit. Alliance pays $2.70 per unit for sales commissions and shipping. It has fixed costs of $720,000 for selling and administration. The tax rate is 40 percent.

a.   Prepare an income statement for Alliance Tooling using absorption costing.

b.   Prepare an income statement for Alliance Tooling using variable costing.

c.   Explain why the net income figures computed in parts (a) and (b) differ.

NP 11.17
JOINT PRODUCTS
(LO 6)

New View, a chemical processor, produces two chemicals, V7 and AC, from a decomposition of M68JJ. Each batch of M68JJ costs $22,000 and yields 300 kilograms of V7 and 400 kilograms of AC. Each unit of V7 can be sold for $35 and each unit of AC can be sold for $25. Either intermediate product can be processed further. It costs $2,000 to convert 300 kilograms of V7 into 240 kilograms of V7HX. Likewise, it costs $1,500 to convert 400 kilograms of AC into 320 kilograms of AC92. Each kilogram of V7HX can be sold for $50 and each kilogram of AC92 can be sold for $45. The $22,000 batch cost is allocated to the two intermediate products using kilograms.

a.   Prepare a financial statement assuming V7 and AC are sold and not processed further. Calculate the profit per batch of each intermediate product that includes the allocated batch cost.

b.   If neither V7 nor AC is processed further, should New View produce V7 and AC?

c.   Should New View further process V7 into V7HX and/or AC into AC92? Justify your answer with supporting calculations.

ANALYSIS AND INTERPRETATION PROBLEMS

AIP 11.1
Average Costs and Variable
Costs as Performance
Measures
(LO 1, 2)

The manager of a company's manufacturing unit is responsible for the costs of the manufacturing unit. The company president is in the process of deciding whether to evaluate the manufacturing manager based on the average cost per unit or the variable cost per unit. Quality and timely delivery would be used in conjunction with the cost measure to reward the manager.

What problems are associated with using the average cost per unit as a performance measure?

What problems are associated with using the variable cost per unit as a performance measure?

AIP 11.2
Allocation of Overhead Using
Practical Capacity
(LO 4)

Celestial Printing's president has decided to use the practical capacity of the firm's printers to determine the application rates per machine hour for overhead. She believes that the cost of unused capacity would be valuable information. As the controller begins to calculate application rates for the coming year, he is suprised to find that several more printers were purchased during the previous year despite there being considerable excess capacity.

How does the cost allocation system affect the behavior of managers?

AIP 11.3
Using Allocated Joint Costs
(LO 6)

Green Packing Company has recognized an increasing demand for frozen boneless chicken breasts. The frozen chicken breasts can be thawed and cooked quickly. This product is becoming very popular with people who do not want to deal with the bones and other parts of the chicken that have less meat. The company recently received an offer to buy frozen boneless chicken breasts for $1 per kilogram. Green Packing Company is not sure that the company should accept the offer, however, because the cost of chicken breasts is greater than $1 per kilogram (see next page).

Joint costs purchasing and butchering a chicken	
Cost of a chicken	$0.30
Butchering costs per chicken	0.10
Cost of de-boning, freezing, and packaging breasts per chicken	
(0.50 kg./chicken)	0.15
Cost of chicken breasts per chicken (0.50 kg.)	$0.55
Cost of chicken breasts per kilogram (2 × $0.55)	$1.10

All of the joint costs of purchasing and butchering the chicken are allocated to the chicken breasts in this analysis because the chicken breasts are specially ordered.

How should the company analyze this special order for chicken breasts?

ITI Technology designs and manufactures solid state computer chips. In one of its production departments, a six-inch circular wafer is fabricated by laying down successive layers of silicon and then etching the circuits into the layers. Each wafer contains 100 seperate solid state computer chips. After a wafer is manufactured, the 100 chips are cut out of the wafer, initially tested, and mounted into protective covers, and electrical leads are attached. A final quality control test is then performed.

AIP 11.4
Allocation of Cost of Scrap
(LO 6)

The intial testing process consists of successive stages of heating and cooling the chips and testing how they work. If 99% of each chip's circuits work properly after the testing, it is classified as a high-density (HD) chip. If between 75% and 99% of a chip's circuits work properly, it is classified as a low-density (LD) chip. If fewer than 75% of the circuits work, it is discarded. Twenty wafers are manufactured per batch. In each batch, 50% of the chips are HD, 20% LD, and 30% are discarded. HD chips are sold to defense contractors and LD chips to consumer electronic firms. Chips sold to defense contractors and chips sold to consumer electronic firms require different types of mountings, packaging, and distribution channels. HD chips sell for $30 each and LD chips sell for $16 each.

Each batch of 20 wafers costs $29,100: $8,000 to produce, test, and sort; and $21,100 for mounting, attaching leads, final inspection, and distribution costs ($14,500 for HD chips and $6,600 for LD chips). The $29,100 total cost per batch consists of direct labor, direct materials, and variable overhead.

The following report summarizes the operating data per batch.

ITI TECHNOLOGY
Operating Cost Summary for HD and LD Chips

	Total	HD Chips	LD Chips	Scrap
Percent of chips	100%	50%	20%	30%
Total costs	$29,100	$14,550	$5,820	$8,730
Revenue	$36,400	$30,000*	$6,400†	$ 0
Total costs	$29,100	$14,550	$5,820	$8,730
Profit per batch	$ 7,300	$15,450	$ 580	($8,730)

*$30,000 = 50% × 20 wafers × 100 chips per wafer × $30 per chip.
†$6,400 = 20% × 20 wafers × 100 chips per wafer × $16 per chip.

The cost of scrap is charged to a plant-wide overhead account, which is then allocated directly to the lines of business based on profits in the line of business.

a. Critically evaluate ITI Technology's method of accounting for HD and LD chips.

b. What suggestions would you offer ITI's management?

You are working as a loan officer at TransPacific Bank. While analyzing a loan request for a client, you come across the following footnote in the client's annual report:

AIP 11.5
Variable Costing
(LO 2)

Inventories are priced at the lower of cost or market of materials plus other direct (variable) costs. Fixed overheads of $4.2 million this year and $3.0 million last year are excluded from inventories. Omitting such overhead resulted in a reduction in net income (after taxes) of $720,000 for this year. Our tax rate is 40%.

You are preparing your presentation of the loan application to TransPacific's loan committee. Write a brief paragraph in nontechnical terms describing what the footnote means and how it affects the bank's decision regarding the evaluation of the would-be borrower's financial condition.

AIP 11.6
Variable and Absorption
Costing
(LO 1, 2)

Federal Mixing is a division of Federal Chemicals, a large diversified chemical company. Federal Mixing (FM) provides mixing services for both outside customers and other Federal Chemicals divisions. FM buys or receives liquid chemicals and combines and packages them according to the customer's specifications. FM computes its divisional net income on both a fully absorbed and variable costing basis. For the year just ending, it reported:

FM DIVISION Net Income	
Absorption costing	$13,800,000
Variable costing	12,600,000
Difference	$1,200,000

Overhead is assigned to products using machine hours.

There is no finished goods inventory at FM, only work-in-process (WIP) inventory. As soon as a product is completed, it is shipped to the customer. The beginning inventory was valued at $6.3 million and represented 70,000 machine hours. The ending WIP inventory was valued at $9.9 million and represented 90,000 machine hours.

Write a short, nontechnical note to senior management explaining why variable costing and absorption costing net income amounts differ.

EXTENDED ANALYSIS AND INTERPRETATION PROBLEMS

AIP 11.7
Overhead Costs from a
New Factory

Karsten is one of the premier carpet manufacturers in the world for both residential and commercial applications. Home sales and commercial sales each account for about 50% of total revenues. Karsten is organized into three departments: Manufacturing, Residential Sales, and Commercial Sales. Manufacturing is a cost center and the two sales departments are profit centers. The full cost of each roll of carpeting produced (including fully absorbed overhead) is transferred to the sales department ordering the carpet. The evaluation of the sales departments includes the fully absorbed cost of each roll as the transfer price.

The current manufacturing plant is operating at capacity. A new plant is being built that will more than double capacity. Within two years, management believes that its businesses will grow such that most of the excess capacity will be eliminated. When the new plant comes online, the plan is for one plant to produce exclusively commercial carpeting and the other to produce exclusively residential carpeting. This change will simplify scheduling, ordering, and inventory control in each plant. It also will create some economies of scale by producing longer mill runs. Nevertheless, it will take a couple of years before these economies of scale can be realized.

Each mill will produce carpeting in 12-foot-wide rolls of up to 100 yards in length. The output of each mill is measured in terms of yards of 12-foot rolls produced. Overhead is assigned to carpet rolls using carpet yards produced in the mill. The cost structure of each plant is as follows:

	Old Plant	New Plant
Normal machine hours per year	6,000	5,000
Normal carpet yards per hour	1,000	1,400
Normal capacity	6 million yards	7 million yards
Annual manufacturing overhead costs excluding accounting depreciation	$15,000,000	$21,000,000
Accounting depreciation per year	$6,000,000	$21,000,000

Karsten's new mill will run at higher speed and produce more carpet yardage per hour. Moreover, the new mill will use 15% less direct materials and direct labor because the new machines, being more automated, produce less scrap and require less direct labor per yard. A job sheet run at the old mill is:

Carpet no. A6106: (100-yard roll)	
Direct materials	$ 800
Direct labor	600
Direct costs	$1,400

Although the new mill has lower direct costs of carpet production than the old mill does, the new facility's higher overhead costs per yard have the sales department managers worried. They are already lobbying senior management to have the old mill assigned to produce their products. The Commercial Sales department manager argues: "More of my customers are located closer to the old plant than are Residential Sales' customers. Therefore, to economize on transportation costs, my products should be produced in the old plant." The Residential Sales department manager counters with the argument, "Transportation costs are less than 1% of total revenues. The new plant should produce commercial products because we expect new commercial products to use more synthetic materials and the latest technology at the new mill is better able to adapt to the new synthetics." Senior management is worried about how to deal with the two sales department managers' reluctance to have their products produced at the new plant. One suggestion put forth is for each plant to produce about half of Commercial Sales products and about half of Residential Sales products. However, this proposal would eliminate most of the economies of scale that would result from specializing production in each plant to one market segment.

a. Calculate the overhead rates for the new plant and the old plant, with overhead assigned to carpet based on normal yards per year.

b. Calculate the expected total cost of carpet no. A6106, if it is run at the old mill and if it is run at the new mill.

c. Put forth two new potential solutions that overcome the desire of the Residential and Commercial Sales department managers to have their products produced in the old plant. Discuss the pros and cons of your two solutions.

Carlos Sanguine, Inc., makes premium wines and table wines. Grapes are crushed and the free-flowing juice and the first-pressing juice are made into the premium wines (bottles with corks). The second- and third-pressing juices are made into table wines (bottles with screw tops). The data in Exhibit AIP 11.8A summarize operations for the year.

AIP 11.8
Overhead Costs and Dropping a Product with Joint Costs

Exhibit AIP 11.8B provides a breakdown of the manufacturing overhead expenses into General Winery costs and Production Facilities costs.

Based on the data in Exhibits AIP 11.8A and AIP 11.8B, the Accounting prepared the report shown as Exhibit AIP 11.8C.

Upper management was concerned that the table wines had such a low margin and some managers urged that these lines be dropped. Competition kept the price down at the $7.00 per case level. This information caused some managers to question how the competition could afford to sell the wine at this price.

Before making a final decision, upper management asked for an analysis of the fixed and variable costs by product line and their break-even points. When management saw Exhibit AIP 11.8D (p. 415), the president remarked, "Well, this is the final nail in the coffin. We'd have to almost triple our sales of table wines just to break even. But we don't have that kind of capacity. We'd have to buy new tanks, thereby driving up our fixed costs and break-even points. This looks like a vicious circle. By next month, I want a detailed set of plans on what it will cost us to shut down our table wines."

Exhibit AIP 11.8E (p. 415) summarizes the shutdown effects.

Based on the data, what should management do?

Exhibit AIP 11.8A

CARLOS SANGUINE, INC.
Summary of Operations for the Year

Tons of grapes	10,000
Average cost per ton	$190

	Premium Wines	Table Wines
Number of cases produced and sold	400,000	70,000
Selling price per case	$11.00	$7.00
Revenues	$4,400,000	$490,000
Grape costs	1,650,000	250,000
Packaging costs	1,000,000	140,000
Labor	200,000	35,000
Selling & distribution	400,000	35,000
Manufacturing overhead	400,000	87,500
Operating profit (loss)	$ 750,000	($ 57,500)

Note: Grape costs represent the cost of the juice placed into the two product categories and are calculated below. (A greater quantity of juice is required per case of premium wine than per case of table wine because there is more shrinkage in the premium wines than in table wines.)

	Gallons of Juice Used in Each Product	×	Total % of Juice	=	Grape cost	Grape Costs Per Product
Premium wines	13,200,000		86.84%		$1,900,000	$1,650,000
Table wines	2,000,000		13.16%		$1,900,000	250,000
Total	15,200,000		100%			$1,900,000

Note: Each product has its own Selling and Distribution (S&D) organization. Two-thirds of Selling & Distribution expenditures vary with cases produced. The remainder of the expenditures do not vary with output.

Exhibit AIP 11.8B

CARLOS SANGUINE, INC.
Manufacturing Overhead by Products

	Premium Wines	Table Wines	Total
General Winery costs*	$212,800	$37,200	$250,000
Production Facilities costs† (depreciation and maintenance)	187,200	50,300	237,500
Manufacturing overhead	$400,000	$87,500	$487,500

*General Winery costs do not vary with the number of cases or number of product lines. These costs are allocated based on cases produced.

†One-fourth of total production facilities costs varies with cases produced. The remainder is fixed costs previously incurred to provide the production capacity.

Exhibit AIP 11.8C

CARLOS SANGUINE, INC.
Product Line Cost Structure

	Cost Structure per Case			
	Premium Wines		Table Wines	
Net sales		$11.00		$7.00
Variable costs				
Grapes	$4.13		$3.57	
Packaging	2.50		2.00	
Labor	0.50		0.50	
Selling & distribution	1.00	8.13	0.50	6.57
Margin		$ 2.87		$0.43
Less manufacturing overhead		1.00		1.25
Operating profit (loss)		$ 1.87		($0.82)

Exhibit AIP 11.8D

CARLOS SANGUINE, INC.
Fixed and Variable Costs Per Product
and Product Break-Even Points

	Premium Wines		Table Wines	
Sales		$11.00		$7.00
Less variable costs				
Grapes	$4.13		$3.57	
Packaging	2.50		2.00	
Labor	0.50		0.50	
Selling & distribution	0.67		0.33	
Manufacturing overhead	0.13	7.93	0.13	6.53
Contribution margin		3.07		0.47
Less unitized fixed costs per unit				
Selling & distribution	0.33		0.17	
Manufacturing overhead	0.87	1.20	1.12	1.29
Profit (loss)		$ 1.87		($0.82)
Breakeven				
Fixed costs	(400,000 × $1.20)	$480,000	(70,000 × 1.29)	$ 90,300
Divided by contribution margin		$3.08		$0.47
Number of cases to break even		156,000		192,000

Exhibit AIP 11.8E

CARLOS SANGUINE, INC.
Effects of Discontinuing
Table Wines

1. No effect on the sale of premium wines is expected.
2. The juice being used in the table wines can be sold to bulk purchasers to use in fruit juices for $150,000 per year.
3. The table wine production facilities (tanks, refrigeration units, etc.) have no use in premium wine production. These facilities can be sold for $350,000 net of disposal costs.

AIP 11.9
Chooosing Cost Drivers to Reflect Variable Cost of Overhead

Industry Background   Ryetown Steel, Inc., is the nation's largest distributor of steel and fabricated steel products. Over the past two decades, the company's sales have grown substantially as most major metal users no longer purchase directly from the producing mills, but purchase instead through service centers such as Ryetown Steel. Also, distributors process the steel products to customer specifications, mainly cutting the steel to nonstandard dimensions. Consequently, service centers have gained tremendous market share at the expense of the integrated mills. Searching for ways to improve cash flow, increase productivity, properly manage inventories, and reduce storage space, metal users increased their reliance on service centers. With pressure to become more internally efficient, end users could no longer rely on the producer's erratic lead times and large minimum production quantities. As JIT deliveries became vogue, the steel service centers were positioned to expand their role in the market. From 1970–89, the steel service center market grew from 15% of total metal purchased to over 40%.

Ryetown Background   Ryetown is a full-line service center that carries nearly all grades produced. It is considered the "supermarket" of the steel service center industry. Ryetown has 26 full-line service centers throughout the United States. Its largest warehouse and headquarters is in Chicago, Illinois, the largest metal-consuming market in the United States. The 26 plants operate as investment centers, with the local plant manager having responsibility for market growth and return on investment. Each plant manager's ROI standard is different. For instance, if one plant shipped heavily to another plant, its ROI goal would be lower since the shipping plant incurred the investment and the variable cost, but was not credited for the profit revenue generated from the sale to the customer. For example, Chicago, a large

Variable Costing and Capacity Costs

Exhibit AIP 11.9A

Service Charges on
Interplant Sales, Emergency
Transfers, and Planned
Transfers of Plant Materials

Department	Product	Service Charge	CWT Charge*
10	H.R. Carbon Bars and Strip	$32.00	$0.90
10	C.F. Carbon Bars	32.00	1.10
10	Alloy Bars	32.00	0.90
10	Stainless Bars and Tubes	32.00	1.20
10	Aluminum Bars, Shapes & Tubes	32.00	1.40
10	Carbon & Alloy Tubing & Pipe	43.00	2.50
10	Structural Shapes and Tubes	43.00	0.80
10	Carbon Plate	43.00	1.30
	Cold Saw & Abrasive		
	Other Cut		
10	Alloy Plates & Sheets	43.00	1.60
	Cold Saw & Abrasive		
	Other Cut		
10	Stainless Plate	43.00	4.90
	Cost Saw & Abrasive		
	Burn		
	Shear & Other Cut		
10	Aluminum Plates	43.00	3.90
	Saw Cut		
	Other Cut		
10	Pattern Sheets	43.00	0.90
10	Production Sheets	43.00	1.20
10	Stainless Sheet & Coils	43.00	5.40
10	Aluminum Sheets	43.00	6.00
10	Steel Coils	43.00	0.40
	Edge		
	Slit		
	Slit & Cut-to-Length		
	Slit & Blank		
	Slit, Cut-to-Length & Shear		
	Slit & Edge		
	Cut-to-Length		
	Cut-to-Length, Box & Crate		
	Blanking		
	Cut-to-Length, & Shear		
	Cut-to-Length, Shear & Roll Flatten		
	Pickle		
	Pickle & Slit		
	Pickle, Slit & Cut-to-Length		
	Pickle, Slit Cut-to-Length & Shear		
	Pickle & Cut-to-Length		
	Pickle, Cut-to-Length & Shear		
10	Aluminum Coils	43.00	1.60
10	Magnesium & Titanium	43.00	16.80
10, 70	Miscellaneous Products	43.00	2.80

*CWT denotes "hundred weight."

export plant, has an ROI goal of just 9%. Buffalo, a large importer of material, has an ROI goal of 24%.

Ryetown considers one of its true strategic advantages to be the ability of the various plant locations to service large original equipment manufacturers throughout the United States by positioning its inventory to cater to the specific grades of steel used in the local markets. Until the early 1980s, Ryetown stocked almost every grade of steel used in the local markets. Until the early 1980s, Ryetown stocked almost every grade at each location, minimizing the need for interplant transfers. In 1975, 10% of the metal sold by Ryetown was transferred between plants. The shipping plant was compensated for its service with a predetermined service charge to help cover the variable cost of the shipping plant. These service charges consisted of a standard item charge and a per-hundred-weight charge. The per-hundred-weight charge was the same across the company regardless of

---

TO: Ms. J. Koster
PLANT: General Office
FROM: Mr. Russ Vack
DATE: October 16, 1991
SUBJECT: Transaction Variable Operating Expense

It is recommended that the transaction operating expense be based on two factors:

1. Item Expense
2. Process Expense

Item Expense
The expense of direct labor (DL) for the functions of receiving, assembly, crane, and loading, indirect labor (IDL), and other variable operating expense are more item-oriented than weight-oriented. Therefore, the dollar expense divided by operating items would generate an item charge to be applied to every item ordered, independent of the number of pieces in the order.

Exhibit AIP 11.9C on page 418 outlines the fixed item charges by various commodity groupings. The fixed item charge varies depending on whether the item is cut or uncut.

Process Expense
Processing expense is affected by many factors such as total weight, piece weight, commodity, complexity of cut, and so on. The current service charge plus hundred-weight charge is only valid for the average order, whatever that may be. A more accurate reflection of process cost would be to use processing time multiplied by the average hourly rate. This cost then would be charged to the transaction.

Example

$$\text{Cost of Transaction} = I_{exp} + T(R)$$

where:

I_{exp} = Item expense (per item ordered)
T = Standard time in hours
R = Average hourly rate

---

the processing time involved. In other words, whether an item was shipped unfabricated or was cut to a specific length, an identical charge was applied. Exhibit AIP 11.9A, on p. 416, shows a listing of charges.

By 1990, however, as Ryetown consolidated inventories to help preserve capital, it relied very heavily on interplant transfers, with almost 60% of the metal sold to customers transferred in from other plants. Furthermore, with an increasing number of customers demanding JIT deliveries, Ryetown fabricated more and more of its shipments in order to send the product directly to the customer's production assembly line.

In 1991, Ryetown's president, Jacqueline Koster, became concerned as to whether the service charges adequately reflected the marginal cost of the shipping plant. In September, Ms. Koster asked Mr. Russ Vack, senior industrial engineer, to evaluate the current service charge system and, if required, recommend a new system that would more accurately reflect the variable expense associated with interplant transfers. Mr. Vack's recommendations in October 1991 are outlined in Exhibit AIP 11.9B above with a summary in Exhibit AIP 11.9C (on p. 418). Exhibit AIP 11.9D (p. 418) lists hourly machine wage rates for a few selected commodity groups. Exhibit AIP 11.9E (p. 419) depicts a selected number of item transfers in the month of May 1991.

a. Compute the current and proposed charges using the sample data from May 1991 for the four commodity groups listed in Exhibit AIP 11.9E. Compute the total variance between these two alternatives.

b. Discuss the current system from the perspective of the Buffalo plant, the Chicago plant, and the company as a whole.

c. Will the new costing system affect the way in which local management operates?

d. What recommendations would you make to Ryetown's president? Why?

(Contributed by J. Engel, G. Niederpruem, and J. Stein.)

Exhibit AIP 11.9C

Summary of Proposed
Fixed Item Charges*

Charge per item by commodity groupings:

	Fixed Item Charge	
	Uncut	**Cut**
HR Carbon Bars and Strip	$25	$35
CF Carbon Bars	25	35
Alloy Bars	25	35
Nickel & Stainless Bars and Tubes	25	35
Aluminum Bars, Shapes and Tubes	25	35
Carbon and Alloy Tubing and Pipe	35	45
Structural Shapes and Tubes	35	45
Misc. Products	35	45
Carbon Plate	35	60
Alloy Plate and Sheet	35	60
Nickel and Stainless Plate	35	60
Aluminum Plate	35	60
Pattern Sheets	35	50
Production Sheets	35	50
Stainless Sheets and Coil	35	50
Aluminum Sheets and Coil	35	50
Steel Coils	35	50
Nickel Sheets	35	50

* Processing charges are computed using processing time multiplied by the average hourly rate for each commodity.

Exhibit AIP 11.9D

Machines Rates Per Hour

Commodity	Hourly Rate
Structurals	$25.00
Plates	28.00
Alloy bar	27.00
Stainless bar	30.00

Commodity	Gross Weight in Pounds	Assembly and Processing Time (hours)
Structural Shapes and Tubes		
200 pcs. 2″ × 20 × 1/4″–20′ (uncut)	12,760	.42
100 pcs. 6″ @ 8.2#–Channel 2′0″ Long (Cut)	1,640	1.17
10 pcs. 24″ @ 150#–Wide Flange Beams 14′0″ Long (Cut)	21,000	1.97
Carbon Plates		
10 pcs. 1/4″ × 48″ × 120″ (Uncut)	4,080	0.25
28 pcs. 2″ × 24″ Dia. (Cut)	9,533	3.43
100 pcs. 3/4″ × 24″ × 36″ (Cut)	18,378	2.63
Alloy Bars		
100 pcs. HR 4140–2″ Rd.–12′ Long (Uncut)	12,816	0.38
50 pcs. HR 4140–1″ Rd.–1′0″ Long (Cut)	134	0.40
1200 pcs. HR 4140–7″ Rd.–0′2″ Long (Cut)	26,180	129.40
Stainless Bar		
10 pcs. 1″ × 2″ × 12′ (Uncut)	816	0.15
25 pcs. 3½″ Rd. × 2′0″ Long (Cut)	1,636	1.47
100 pcs. 4″ Rd. × 10′0″ Long (Cut)	42,730	9.35

Exhibit AIP 11.9E

Sample of Items Transferred in the Month of May 1991

Chapter **Twelve**

Management Accounting in a Dynamic Environment

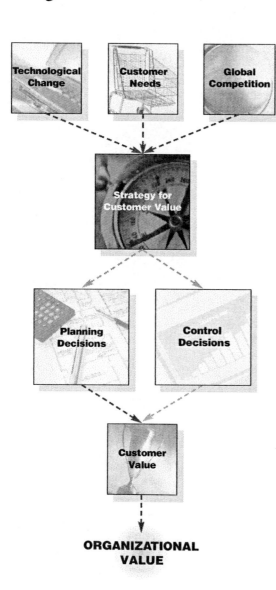

Technological Change

Customer Needs

Global Competition

Strategy for Customer Value

Planning Decisions

Control Decisions

Customer Value

ORGANIZATIONAL VALUE

LEARNING OBJECTIVES

1 Describe the factors in a dynamic environment that influence an organization.

2 Describe the way an organization's strategy is related to its structure.

3 Explain the role of management accounting in the organizational structure and in making planning decisions.

4 Identify major characteristics of total quality management.

5 Use quality costs for making planning and control decisions.

6 Explain the philosophy of just-in-time processes and accounting adjustments for JIT.

7 Create a balanced scorecard to articulate the strategy of the organization.

8 Identify when management accounting within an organization should change.

DEPARTMENT OF MOTOR VEHICLES

The Department of Motor Vehicles (DMV) is a division of the State Department of Transportation. The governor delegates the responsibility of operating the Department of Transportation to the secretary of transportation, who delegates responsibility for operating the DMV to a commissioner. Melody Kim is the current commissioner of DMV.

The DMV has three major responsibilities: (1) issuing drivers licenses, (2) registering and licensing motor vehicles that operate on public roads, and (3) maintaining and accessing records on those licenses. In addition to the central offices in the state capital, the DMV has offices in all the state's major communities.

When the secretary of transportation hired Melody to manage the DMV, he told her that things at the DMV must change. The citizens of the state have complained incessantly about long lines and unfriendly service. The state police also are unhappy about slow response times when they make inquiries about licenses. The DMV is one of the most visible of state agencies, and the citizens are unhappy with what they see. To show their displeasure with the state's operation of it, the voters recently passed a property tax limitation that makes the state government responsible for covering any shortages necessary to operate public schools. That requirement has left a diminishing amount of revenues available for other state services. Melody and the DMV will have to do a better job of serving the people and state police with less money.

INTEGRATIVE FRAMEWORK FOR CHANGE AND MANAGEMENT ACCOUNTING

L0 1   Describe the factors in a dynamic environment that influence an organization.

The major theme of this book is that management accounting is an integral part of an organization's strategy and implementation efforts to create customer value. An organization's strategy and management accounting system are dynamic. Organizations must continually adapt to changes in consumer demand, global competition, and a rapidly evolving technological revolution. Figure 12.1 summarizes the relationship between the external environment and an organization's efforts to create customer value. If the organization is successful, its value will increase.

External Forces Affecting the Organization

Customer Demand

Adapting to changes in customer demand is critical for an organization. Retail clothing stores exemplify the need to continually modify products to meet customers' changing demand. Consumers want the latest fashions, and failure to update inventory is usually disastrous for a clothing store.

Figure 12.1

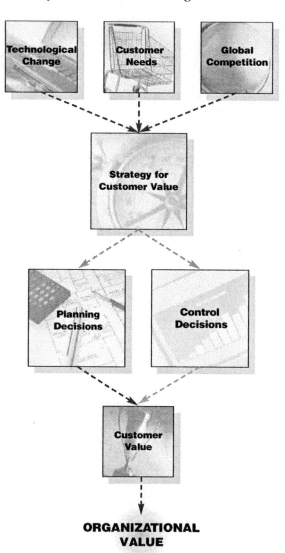

Meeting or even exceeding customer expectations is the key to success for an organization. Total quality management (TQM) is based on meeting customer expectations. Quality is defined by the customer and designed into the product. When an organization adopts TQM, it seeks to improve continually its operations and customer services. Later in this chapter, TQM and its implications for management accounting are described more fully.

Customer Needs

Technological Innovation

Keeping up with technological innovation is critical to an organization's competitiveness. Technological innovations, such as the Internet, have redefined many consumer product markets. Technological innovation is most apparent in the electronics and communication fields, but all industries have been revolutionized by technological change in the last 25 years. Farmers have genetically altered crops; construction firms use recently developed materials. Services, such as banking and stock trading, have been completely revised as the result of new technology.

Technological innovation also has altered the way products are designed, produced, and delivered. Technology has made cost-saving procedures such as just in time (JIT) feasible. JIT is one of the changes in organizational philosophy described in this chapter.

Technological Change

Global Competition

Increased global competition has forced many organizations that once faced protected domestic markets to become more cost competitive. Instead of making products domestically, many organizations now outsource parts and subcomponents globally. Market conditions change for a variety of reasons, including changes in government regulations and taxation policies. The North American Free Trade Agreement (NAFTA) reduced tariffs between Canada, Mexico, and the United States; as a result, companies have relocated production sites in search of lower costs. Not only has the flow of trade increased among the three countries but also the geographic dispersion of company operations has changed. Firms, such as DaimlerChrysler, Du Pont, and Samsung, have expanded operations in Mexico to take advantage of lower labor costs and duty-free access to the North American market. Some firms have shifted operations from Asia to North America to reap the benefits of freer trade. Emerging markets in the People's Republic of China have also set off chain reactions within organizations seeking to expand into these markets.

Global Competition

Organizational Strategy and Structure

Successful organizations will be those that adapt quickly to changing customer demand, technological innovation, and global competition. New profitable investments will appear, and some previously lucrative investments will become unprofitable. To identify profitable investment opportunities, an organization must develop an evolving strategy that recognizes the external forces affecting it and its own strengths and weaknesses.

LO 2   Describe the way an organization's strategy is related to its structure.

An organization's strengths and weaknesses can be described in terms of its current assets, relationships with suppliers and customers, and ability to innovate and change. An organization's assets include the current and long-term assets typically found on the balance sheet. In addition, brand-name recognition, patents, and employees are an organization's important "off-balance-sheet" assets. Brand-name recognition provides the organization consumer name recognition that lowers the information costs of introducing new products. Pepsi is recognized worldwide. When PepsiCo introduced Diet Pepsi, consumers already had an expectation of taste and quality before sampling the new product. Its existing brand-name capital

Strategy for Customer Value

Wal-Mart creates organizational value with a combined strategy to deliver both low-cost and high-quality products. Supplier relations are critical to providing customers with what they want when they want it. As Wal-Mart expands globally, it must adapt its strategy to different customer demands and supplier networks.

gives PepsiCo a cost advantage in introducing a brand that new entrants do not enjoy.

Relationships with suppliers and customers also affect an organization's ability to adapt in a dynamic environment. Partnering with suppliers can allow the organization to move quickly into new fields if suppliers have skills and resources that otherwise would be difficult for it to acquire. Mergers, especially in the communications and the computer industries (such as the recent merger of AOL and Time Warner), are formal methods of partnering to compensate for weaknesses. Time Warner and AOL each recognized that it lacked the strengths that the other possessed. Time Warner had program content, brands, and distribution channels, but it lacked agility in adapting to the Internet. AOL had established itself on the Internet but had inadequate distribution networks and was vulnerable because of its reliance on subscription fees.[1]

The ability to innovate and change also differs across organizations. Studies indicate that more educated managers are more willing to implement change. Knowledge of consumers and their preferences facilitates innovation. Flexibility in production and the delivery of products and services is also critical to being able to innovate and change.

An organizational strategy based on a dynamic environment and internal strengths and weaknesses is a general plan for achieving customer and organizational value. An organization achieves customer value through innovative product/service design, high-quality products and services, and/or low-cost production and delivery. For example, much of Wal-Mart's success results from its low cost in getting products from its suppliers to its stores. Successful organizations match their strengths with opportunities in the market to generate customer value. An organization with highly educated and creative employees is more likely to be successful in creating customer value through innovative products and service designs.

Control Decisions

The best strategies, however, are doomed to failure if they are not matched with the appropriate organizational structure. The organizational structure is composed of the control mechanisms that motivate individuals within the organization to act in accordance with the selected strategy. The three major elements of the organizational structure are assignment of responsibilities, measurement of performance, and compensation.

The assignment of responsibilities should be linked directly or indirectly to those with the specialized knowledge to make the decision. However, individuals with specialized knowledge cannot be relied on always to make decisions consistent with the organization's goals. Personal goals influence their decisions.

One solution to this problem is to transfer the knowledge to the individual who is more likely to make decisions consistent with organizational goals, yet information, like technical knowledge, is sometimes costly to transfer. In addition, individuals are reluctant to transfer knowledge on which their performance might be evaluated.

As described in Chapter Six, responsibilities are commonly assigned to separate planning decisions from control decisions. This separation of making planning decisions from control leads to mutual monitoring. For example, the manager responsible for writing payroll checks is generally different from the person who makes the payroll list. Each individual monitors the other to ensure the organization achieves its goals.

---

[1] "The Big Leap," *The Economist*, January 15, 2000, pp. 17, 22–24.

The second component of the organizational structure is the performance measurement system, which includes the accounting system. In addition to using accounting-based measures of performance, organizations also develop nonaccounting-based measures such as their share price, customer complaints, quality, and on-time delivery percentages. Performance measures should be consistent with the assignment of responsibilities. Managers' responsibilities and performance measures should reflect controllability. Managers of a profit center, for example, have some control over revenues and costs and are evaluated, in part, by the profit center's profit.

The third component of the organizational structure is the compensation system. Rewards are based on performance measures, which should be consistent with responsibilities and include compensation, promotions, titles, and perquisites such as assigned parking spaces, country club memberships, and company cars.

The three components of the organizational structure should be balanced as a three-legged stool. The balanced scorecard (described later in this chapter) is a comprehensive plan showing how the organizational structure is directly linked to the organization's goals and strategy.

Planning decisions are the means to achieve an organization's goals. Planning decisions include choosing organizational goals, hiring members for the organization, creating products and service designs, selecting activities for making and delivering products and services, and providing customer services. Each of these planning decisions is made based on appropriate information. Accounting is one source of information that assists managers in making planning decisions.

Planning Decisions

The development of innovative products and services and their sale at prices in excess of their costs are key ingredients to increasing organizational value. Good planning decisions based on sound information allow the organization to accomplish these goals.

Customer Value and Organizational Value

As described throughout this book, providing customer value is critical to an organization's success. Each organization must find ways to create innovative products or services, manufacture high-quality products, and/or provide the product at a low cost. Customers purchase a product only if they perceive its value and its attached services to outweigh the cost. Although the creation of customer value is necessary for organizational success, it is not sufficient.

Customer Value

ORGANIZATIONAL VALUE

To survive, an organization must have adequate funds. An organization receives funds from sales to consumers or from donations by benefactors (in the case of many not-for-profit organizations). The inflow of funds depends on the organization's ability to create customer value. To create organizational value and survive, it must be able to supply customer value at a cost less than or equal to the inflow of funds. In the case of profit organizations, value is captured in the profit concept of revenues less expenses.

Role of Management Accounting and Change

The role of management accounting in Figure 12.1 is to assist in control through the organizational structure and in making planning decisions. Management accounting plays an integral role in the organizational structure by assigning responsibilities through the budgeting process and by providing managerial performance measures. Management accounting also identifies the costs and benefits of different planning decisions, allowing managers to make choices that increase the organization's value.

Management accounting is closely related to the organization's structure; thus, management accounting must evolve with the organizational structure. Changes in the accounting system rarely occur in a vacuum. Alterations to the organizational

LO 3 Explain the role of management accounting in the organizational structure and in making planning decisions.

Business**Analysis**

Changes at US West

US West, a regional Bell telephone company based in Denver, Colorado, operates in more than 14 U.S. states and serves more than 25 million customers nationally. In September 1993, management announced the lay-off of 9,000 employees (15% of its work force), the consolidation of 560 service centers into 26, and the streamlining of the customer-order system. Also announced were plans to convert its network covering 14 states into a broadband system for high-speed data transfer and video on demand. US West invested $2.5 billion in Time Warner Entertainment. These moves were seen as evidence of US West's competition with cable companies and other carriers in the new telecommunications era.

In addition to announcing the strategy and organizational changes, US West also reported that it was changing from straight-line depreciation to accelerated depreciation. The one-time accounting change reduced assets by $3.2 billion. The reason for the change was that new technology has caused telephone assets to be replaced more often. " . . . [telephone companies'] assets aren't lasting as long as they were thought to, and need to be replaced."*

How do these announcements by US West illustrate the intertwined relationship of accounting choices (depreciation methods), organizational structure (consolidating service centers), strategy (providing broadband system), technology, and competition? What market forces require US West to adapt continually to remain competitive? What role does the management accounting system play in helping US West deal with its dynamic environment? Note, in June 2000 US West and Qwest merged creating a single company valued at $85 billion in stock.

* *The Wall Street Journal*, September 20, 1993, pp. A3–4.

Source: www.uswest.com.

structure, including changes in the accounting system, are likely in response to external shocks from technology and shifting market conditions.

The remainder of the chapter describes three concepts for implementing strategy that have become increasingly popular: TQM, JIT, and the balanced scorecard. These innovations have emerged in response to customer demand, new technology, and global competition. They are closely tied to organizational strategy and have important implications for the management accounting system.

Concept**Review**

1. What environmental forces affect organizations?
2. What should an organization consider in designing a strategy?
3. How does the organizational structure relate to strategy?
4. What is the role of management accounting in a dynamic environment?

DEPARTMENT OF MOTOR VEHICLES
(Continued)

Melody Kim began her term as commissioner of the DMV by analyzing its environment. Her customers are easily identified as the citizens of the state and the state police. Although the customers have not changed, their expectations have. They are no longer complacent about long waits and unfriendly service. Other organizations in the state have demonstrated that friendly and on-time service should be expected. Although global competition is not Melody's major worry, she has heard rumors that failure to correct problems might lead to outsourcing the DMV's operations. Melody must take advantage of recent technological changes and management philosophies to be a success.

Once she had developed an understanding of the DMV's environment, Melody was keen to develop a strategy that will enable the DMV to meet customer expectations and remain a viable part of the state's operations. She examined a number of alternatives, such as staff retraining, new technologies, and even outsourcing noncritical operations. She decided that the new strategy for the DMV must be customer focused. Customers require prompt and courteous service. Efficiency could be improved by adapting JIT techniques to the DMV's services. She wondered whether employees really understand that courteous service influences customer perceptions of quality. Perhaps the introduction of TQM would help employees to understand better exactly what quality means.

Melody recognized that change at the DMV is necessary but might be resisted. She decided that the new strategy should take advantage of new computer technology and management approaches. She also decided to begin with small initiatives that could be successful in the short term. She expected these initial projects to generate enthusiasm across the DMV for further improvements and help employees accept change. In particular, Melody decided to create an online registration process and introduce TQM and JIT techniques for service requests in DMV offices. To accomplish these tasks, she needed to reorganize the division. Some services could be centralized to better control them, but local offices have more knowledge about customer needs. Decentralization might be more appropriate in these areas. Consistency of service is important, so a trade-off between centralization and decentralization was necessary. In the end, she opted to give local offices more control over methods to improve face-to-face service with customers but to evaluate the offices based on cost and quality. Customers will be surveyed to determine satisfaction. Online registration and state police searches will be centralized to ensure consistency and efficiency of service. Survey feedback also will be tallied to evaluate these services and the achievement of the customer-focused strategy.

Total Quality Management and Quality Measures

To compete in a global market, organizations must be concerned about quality. Quality has become a major issue in both the profit and not-for-profit sectors of the economy. In attempting to improve quality, managers have had to grapple with what quality means and how to improve it. They also must design measurement systems to report improvements in quality. In this section, various definitions of quality are provided followed by a discussion of some quality measurement systems.

LO 4 Identify major characteristics of total quality management.

Quality means different things to different people. It could mean a luxurious product. On the one hand, a Rolls-Royce is perceived to be of higher quality than a Toyota Corolla because the Rolls-Royce has a smoother ride, leather interior, and wood on the dashboard. On the other hand, the Toyota Corolla could be considered of higher quality because it has fewer component failures than does a Rolls-Royce. Reliability is often used as a synonym for quality.

Conformity is another definition of quality. Using it, McDonald's hamburgers are of higher quality than are those at the local diner. McDonald's hamburgers taste the same no matter which outlet prepares them because of the standardization in purchasing materials and preparing hamburgers.

Quality also can be defined as having more options. A CD player that can be programmed to play multiple CDs is said to be of higher quality than one that can play only one.

Meeting customer expectations is another way to define quality. Xerox, for example, defines quality as 100 percent customer satisfaction. Customers have expectations with respect to all of a product's attributes: delivery schedules, operating characteristics, service, and so on. For example, a customer might expect a service technician to arrive on average within two hours of the service call. If the

Organizations and their customers define quality in a variety of ways. Some people consider a Rolls Royce to be high quality. Even if they cannot afford such luxury, a Rolls Royce is their quality benchmark. Others interpret quality differently, opting for a Toyota because of its reliable service record. Organizations compete effectively by developing the appropriate strategy to meet varied customer expectations.

service representative arrives in less than two hours, the organization has met the customer's expectations.

Joseph Juran, a noted quality expert, emphasizes that quality has multiple meanings, including product performance and satisfaction. Most quality experts define quality as meeting customer expectations, which include those concerning opulence, conformity, reliability, and the number of options.

The traditional approach to ensure product quality was to "inspect-it-in." Inspection stations and quality assurance inspectors were added along the production line to weed out defects. Notice that the organization defined quality as meeting a certain set of specifications, which may or may not have been of interest to the consumer. Statistical sampling methods were used to draw random samples from a batch and to reject the entire batch if a statistically large number of defective units were detected in the sample. Sections of the manufacturing plant stored defective items waiting to be reworked or scrapped. Organizations built a normal allowance for scrap and rework into their operating budgets. In some cases, if market demand exceeded production in a period, organizations might release marginally defective products. Those products that reached the market were corrected by the field service organization under warranty arrangements.

By the 1970s, two key factors had combined to make the traditional approach to quality obsolete in many industries. First, the cost of detecting problems and monitoring production via computer instrumentation fell relative to the cost of maintaining quality via direct labor inspectors. The cost of labor (including health-care benefits) made the cost of manually detecting and correcting errors expensive relative to performing these tasks electronically. Second, worldwide competition expanded to include nonprice forms of competition such as quality. Once the Japanese automobile companies had gained price competitiveness against North American companies, they turned their attention to achieving quality advantages. Both the lower cost of detecting defects and increased global competition have fostered the concept of *zero defects*. The goal of zero defects, while never achievable, has become the target. Each year, the standard becomes fewer defects than the year before.

To prevent customers from receiving defective goods, some organizations test their products with a sampling of potential customers. Intel distributes its computer chips to sophisticated users to "stress" the chips and to identify any potential defects before releasing the chip to the market at large. One such user discovered a flaw in the original Pentium chip and Intel made corrections prior to its widespread use.

The movement toward improved quality and customer satisfaction is called *total quality management (TQM)*. TQM is a management philosophy that includes involved leadership, employee participation, empowerment, teamwork, customer satisfaction, and continual improvement.

Through TQM, companies redesign their products to require fewer different parts, making it easier to maintain tighter controls on the quality of their suppliers. Production processes are reengineered to reduce defects. Robots and additional instrumentation are built into manufacturing to ensure more uniform production. In addition to these changes, major changes in the organizational structure occur, including modifying the performance evaluation and reward systems and the partitioning of responsibilities. Responsibilities are pushed down lower in the firm, closer to where the knowledge of customer preferences resides.

In summary, most TQM programs contain the following elements:

* *Quality is a firmwide process.* Every employee from the senior manager to the janitor must understand the quality work processes. Quality links customers to suppliers. The pursuit of excellence is a prime motivator in the company.
* *Quality is defined by the customer.* Customer satisfaction is a central goal of the organization. Customers expect reliability, conformity, timely delivery, and customer service.
* *Quality requires organizational changes.* The organizational structure (assignment of responsibilities, performance measurement, and reward systems) must encourage mutual cooperation and create incentives to improve quality. Senior managers should develop hands-on, specialized knowledge of how to improve quality. Workers should be empowered (i.e., given responsibilities) to make changes that increase quality.
* *Quality is designed into the product.* Quality must be designed into the product and processes from the initial product development through manufacturing to the final delivery of a quality product to the consumer. Designers and engineers should work with manufacturers, marketers, and accountants to design products that meet customer needs, are simple to manufacture, and are not too costly. Once products have been designed and engineered, many of the quality attributes have been predetermined.

If the organization's goal is to achieve customer satisfaction, some measures of quality are necessary to determine whether the organization is achieving its goal and to motivate and reward managers. Many measures of quality are not part of the management accounting system. Typical TQM quality measures include product design (number of new parts, number of total parts), vendor rating systems (number of defects, on-time delivery), manufacturing (defect rates, scrap, rework, on-time delivery), and customer satisfaction (surveys, warranty expense).

Moreover, quality is often measured in terms of defects. For example, a component part must be within 0.001 millimeters of a standard or it is termed *defective*. If

IBM's Quality Management Program

IBM redefined its business strategy as *market-driven quality*. The goal is "total customer satisfaction," guided by the following four market principles:

* Understand our markets.
* Commit to leadership in the markets we choose to serve.
* Execute with excellence across our enterprise.
* Make customer satisfaction the final arbiter.

To implement these principles, the following initiatives are followed:

* Research, understand, and segment total potential market needs. Commit to market leadership and deliver the right solutions at the right time.
* Remove defects in everything we do to achieve market-driven quality.
* Reduce the total time between customer wants/needs and fulfill those needs to the customer's total satisfaction.
* Give employees the authority and information they need to make timely decisions and carry out the activities necessary to ensure total customer satisfaction.
* Establish achievable business targets with a particular focus on quality and customer satisfaction.

Business Analysis

L0 5 Use quality costs for making planning and control decisions.

changing the machine that produces the part decreases the defect rate from five per thousand to three per thousand, quality is said to have increased. This concept of quality is based on achieving certain specifications. One drawback to defining quality in terms of defect rates is worker opportunism. Workers can appear to improve quality if they have the responsibility to redefine the standard or benchmark against which defect rates are evaluated. For example, suppose that defects are defined as being in excess of 0.0010 millimeters of a tolerance. If defects were redefined as being in excess of 0.0015 millimeters, fewer would result. If a part is produced with a tolerance of 0.0012 millimeters, under the old definition of 0.0010 millimeters it would be classified as a defect. Under the new definition of 0.0015 millimeters, it is not classified as a defect. Therefore, when installing quality improvement programs, an organization must ensure that the definition of defects is held constant.

Numerical Example 12.1

A farmer of gourmet tomatoes estimates that 10% of the 20,000 kilograms of tomatoes picked do not meet customers' specifications. After being picked, the tomatoes are placed on a conveyer belt for inspection and packaging. The inspection team identifies and removes 80% of the defective tomatoes. How many kilograms of defective tomatoes reach the farmer's tomato customers?

Solution

If 80% of the defective tomatoes are detected, 20% are not detected. Therefore, (0.20)(0.10), or 2%, reach the customers. Of the 20,000 kilograms of tomatoes picked, the farmer sends (0.02)(20,000 kilograms), or 400 kilograms, of defective tomatoes to customers.

**Planning
Decisions**

The benefits and problems of measuring quality must include the associated costs. Defect rates, on-time delivery, and customer complaints are easy for managers to understand and measure. Without a corresponding cost system, however, these diverse measures are difficult to aggregate. Managers do not know how to make trade-offs among quality decisions. For example, is it more costly to design and manufacture a product without defects or to focus on inspecting products and correcting defects from initial production? Is it cheaper to buy a scanning machine to obtain more accurate inspections or to stay with manual inspections? Managers need cost data to make these comparisons for planning decisions.

Part of the TQM philosophy is that improved quality actually can be less costly to the organization. The cost of selling defective products and not satisfying customers can be substantial: Errors must be corrected, disgruntled customers must be mollified, and some customers will seek other suppliers of the service or product. A reputation for shoddy work is often the death knell for organizations. Even if they discover a defect before it is sent to a customer, the cost of handling and fixing the problem can be quite high. In many cases, the defective product cannot be fixed and must be junked. The opportunity cost of not being able to sell a product because it is defective equals the costs of making the defect plus the forgone profit.

If defects can be reduced through better cost prevention efforts, organizations would no longer incur the large costs of fixing or throwing away defects. The TQM philosophy is consistent with the adage "an ounce of prevention is worth a pound of cure." For example, a little extra effort to make sure the Hubble space telescope's mirror was correctly ground would have saved the huge cost of sending a space shuttle mission to correct the problem.

Quality costs are typically categorized into four groups:

1. **Prevention costs** are incurred to eliminate defective units before they are produced. These costs include reengineering and design, use of high-quality parts, improved processes, and employee training.

2. **Appraisal costs** are incurred to eliminate defective units before they are shipped. These costs include inspecting and testing both raw materials and work-in-process.

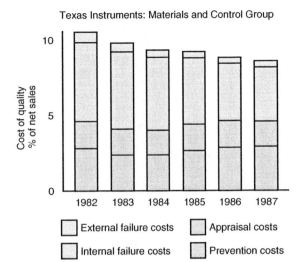

Texas Instruments: Materials and Control Group

Figure 12.2

Change in Quality Cost
Categories with TQM

☐ External failure costs   ▨ Appraisal costs

☐ Internal failure costs   ▨ Prevention costs

3. **Internal failure costs** are incurred when a defect is discovered before sending the product to the customer. These costs include handling and fixing the product or disposing of it. The opportunity cost of not being able to sell the disposed unit also should be included.

4. **External failure costs** are incurred when a customer receives a defective product. These costs include the cost of returns, warranty work, product liability claims, and the opportunity cost of lost sales from reputation effects.

The advantage of categorizing costs is to recognize trade-offs among different activities. The shift to TQM generally is accompanied by an increase in prevention costs that is more than offset by lower internal and external failure costs. In Figure 12.2, the quality costs for a division of Texas Instruments over a six-year period after the implementation of TQM is described.[2] Notice that the failure costs have declined over this time period. Although the prevention and appraisal costs remained about the same, the decline in failure costs indicates that resources were used more effectively. The net effect is higher quality at a reduced cost.

Most management accounting systems do not specifically identify quality costs. Many quality expenditures are imbedded in overhead accounts. Opportunity costs are commonly not reported at all. Therefore, a quality cost system frequently must be constructed outside the cost accounting system, which makes the cost of quality more difficult to identify and measure.

One of the benefits of measuring and identifying quality costs is to bring these expenditures to the attention of senior managers. Many companies have found that their quality costs exceed 10% of sales. Given that total quality costs often can be reduced through increased prevention efforts and a corresponding decline in failure costs, cost savings of 5 to 10% are extremely important to an organization in a globally competitive market.

Another benefit of measuring quality costs is to measure improvement in quality performance. Total quality costs should decline as an organization engages in TQM. If they do not, the organization should reexamine its TQM processes.

Numerical Example 12.2

Yee Corporation decides to perform an inventory of its quality costs for 2001. It identifies the following quality costs: employee training, $100,000; storing defective products, $70,000; responding to customer complaints, $50,000; lost sales due to dissatisfied customers, $110,000; inspections, $40,000; and quality engineering, $40,000. Categorize

---

[2]Harvard Business School Case 9-189-029.

the quality costs and estimate them for 2002 if a 20% increase in prevention costs would result in a 30% decrease in external failure costs. Appraisal and internal failure costs would remain the same.

Solution

Quality Cost Category	Quality Costs, 2001		Estimated Quality Costs, 2002
Prevention			
Employee training	$100,000		
Quality engineering	40,000	$140,000	(1.2)($140,000) = $168,000
Appraisal			
Inspections	40,000	40,000	40,000
Internal failure			
Storing defects	70,000	70,000	70,000
External failure			
Customer complaints	50,000		
Lost sales	110,000	160,000	(0.7)($160,000) = 112,000
Total quality costs		$410,000	$390,000

The investment in prevention should be made because it results in a total reduction in quality costs.

Explicit use of quality costs is not common for planning purposes. In principle, quality costs offer an opportunity to compare and trade off different quality efforts. Quality costs should be used to identify the optimal prevention and appraisal procedures. However, organizations seem to lack confidence in identifying and measuring quality costs. Also, organizations must understand the linkages between the cost categories. For example, how will an improved product design affect appraisal activities and reduce internal and external failure? Until senior managers can determine more confidently the advantages in tracking and using quality costs, they will be reluctant to invest in systems to measure and identify them.

Numerical Example 12.3

Compty Computer Company is having problems with the hard drive for its computer. A particular part fails about 2% of the time. It costs $2,000 to replace the part and to deal with customer dissatisfaction. The company could redesign the computer and leave out the part for $500,000 or perform extensive inspections on the part that would cost $20 per computer. What should the company do if it plans to make 30,000 computers during the coming year before this model becomes obsolete?

Solution

The cost of not redesigning the computer or increasing inspections is (0.02)(30,000 computers)($2,000 per defect), or $1,200,000. The cost of increasing inspections is ($20 per computer)(30,000 computers), or $600,000. The cost of changing the design ($500,000) is lower than the cost of either dealing with customer dissatisfaction ($1,200,000) or increasing inspection ($600,000) and is the preferred choice.

Companies are now explicitly incorporating quality-based criteria into their performance measurement schemes even if they do not adopt the total TQM philosophy. Such changes in performance evaluation, however, have their own problems. Quality is important and should be improved. As discussed earlier, it is an elusive concept with many different dimensions. It is both difficult to define precisely and to measure objectively.

Although much attention has been paid to quality improvement programs in firms, many of them have failed to achieve their objectives. A 1992 *Newsweek* article reported that a number of companies, including McDonnell Douglas aircraft and Florida Power & Light, had abandoned their TQM programs.[3] Wallace Co.

---

[3]J. Mathews and P. Patel, "The Cost of Quality," *Newsweek*, September 7, 1992, pp. 48–49.

won a national quality award in 1990 and filed for bankruptcy in 1992. Although quality should be a primary goal of an organization, it cannot ignore other goals. The balanced scorecard approach described later in this chapter encompasses the customer perspective and recognizes that other performance dimensions are important to increase organizational value.

To summarize, if followed to the letter, TQM is very much an attempt to restructure the organization. Responsibilities must be linked with knowledge. As global competition increases, customers are able to find products more to their liking and often at lower cost. Organizations must know what product attributes consumers most desire. Employees who have day-to-day contact with customers usually possess the detailed knowledge of customer preferences. Somehow this detailed knowledge must be transferred within the organization to the product planners and manufacturing managers. Alternatively, some of the responsibility for product design and distribution must be transferred to the lower-level workers who have the detailed knowledge of customer preferences. TQM programs attempt to do both. Multidisciplinary task forces are formed to conduct special studies and to improve quality. These task forces, composed of people from all levels of an organization, attempt to assemble specialized knowledge concerning customer preferences. Sometimes these task forces have the responsibility to change the product or processes. Worker empowerment transfers responsibilities to employees with specialized knowledge within the organization.

To successfully restructure the organization and assign responsibilities to the people with the knowledge about customer preferences, the performance evaluation and compensation systems also must be changed. Empowering workers with responsibilities requires systems to evaluate and reward their performance. Firms that implement TQM often do not garner the hoped-for benefits because they overlook the need to modify their performance measurement and reward systems to support the changes in responsibilities.

Although TQM has not been universally accepted, some aspects of it have become a part of almost every organization. Organizations might not completely follow TQM with all of its ramifications; however, almost every manager has heard of it and has become more aware of the competitive necessity to meet customer needs.

Concept**Review**

1. Explain the philosophy of total quality management (TQM).
2. What are the four categories of quality costs?
3. How are prevention and appraisal costs related to failure costs?

Before implementing any changes, Melody attended a seminar on TQM to determine how it could be used effectively at the DMV. The seminar leader focused on TQM in a manufacturing organization, but Melody was convinced that it could work for a service organization such as the DMV.

Melody puzzled over what quality means at the DMV. She thought of a number of ways to interpret quality and began to see that it is not easy to develop a clear definition. Perhaps this helps explain why her employees might not understand its importance. Customers do not have other sources for DMV services, so it is difficult to define quality in product terms. The DMV provides a service that customers do not take with them. She decided that what customers do take away are their perceptions of the level of service, which they currently view as unfriendly and discourteous. Thus, Melody defined quality as friendly, courteous service. To meet this quality goal, employees must take training programs

DEPARTMENT OF MOTOR VEHICLES
(Continued)

on interacting and reducing confrontation with customers. Supervisors must be instructed to monitor the behavior of clerks dealing with customers. The TQM program Melody implemented appeared to be a success. Both the DMV's employees and its customers were noticeably happier. As confrontations were reduced, the clerks were able to service customers at a faster rate.

To determine whether the TQM program was saving the DMV money, Melody had its controller estimate quality costs before and after its implementation. The controller defines quality costs as follows:

Prevention costs: Employee training costs

Appraisal costs: Supervisor salaries

Internal failure costs: Clerk downtime while mistakes in service are corrected

External failure costs: Time spent dealing with dissatisfied and irate customers

After implementing the TQM program, prevention and appraisal costs increased, but internal and external failure costs dropped by a larger amount. Therefore, TQM appears to be cost effective.

To verify that customers are satisfied with service at the DMV, Melody had them fill out a survey; it indicates that customers appreciate the smiling faces behind the counter but still are unhappy with the long lines and time necessary to get their licenses and registrations. Melody realized that she might have defined quality incorrectly. Customers are more concerned with speed of service. She decided to attend a conference on JIT.

Just-in-Time Processes

LO 6 Explain the philosophy of just-in-time processes and accounting adjustments for JIT.

With just-in-time (JIT) processes, production and demand are synchronized by not starting production until an order is received. In this way, products are *pulled* through the plant rather than *pushed* through by a master production schedule designed to keep the plant operating at full capacity. The goal of a JIT plant manager is to reduce the time the product spends in the plant. If total production time decreases, costs decrease as well because fewer inventories must be financed, stored, managed, and secured. To accomplish these goals, the plant is reorganized so that raw material and purchased parts are delivered to the factory right before they enter the production process; no intermediate work-in-process inventories exist. Units flow from one production cell to another with no interruptions, and all work is processed continually. Units spend time in the manufacturing plant only when actual work is being expended on them. Of course, the preceding description is for an ideal JIT installation. Figure 12.3 compares a traditional system with a JIT system.

JIT systems seek to minimize a product's **throughput time,** which is the total time from receiving the order to its delivery to the customer. Throughput time is the sum of the following:

* Processing time.
* Time waiting to be moved or worked on.
* Time spent in transit.
* Inspection time.

In a JIT manufacturing environment, the goal is to drive the last three items (waiting, transit, and inspection time) to zero. The sum of these last three items is

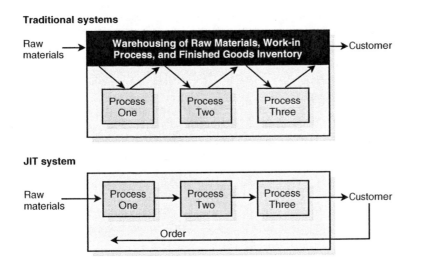

Figure 12.3

Traditional Systems versus
JIT Systems

referred to as *wasted* or *non–value-added time.* The benefits of reducing throughput time include smaller in-process inventories, leading to the following:

* Lower capital costs of holding inventories.
* Factory and warehouse space and cost savings.
* Reduced overhead costs for material movers and expediters.
* Reduced risk of obsolescence.
* Faster response time to customers and reduced delivery times.

To accomplish the goal of reducing throughput time and to achieve these benefits, the following changes must take place:

1. *Increase quality.* To prevent production down time, the quality of raw materials and the manufacturing process must be maintained at a high level. Their increased quality decreases the need to stop production due to defects. JIT and TQM share the common goal of continuous improvement. The success of JIT depends on good-quality management and production maintenance.

2. *Change factory layout.* The factory is redesigned to focus the production strategy on the corporate strategy. Standardization and more efficient workflow reduce time and duplication. Machines that perform the same function are not grouped in one department but are organized in terms of manufacturing cells to sequence similar parts through the machines. Dedicated JIT production lines manufacture a single type of product, sometimes called *dedicated flow lines.*

3. *Reduce set-up times.* If machines can be set up for a new production run very quickly (or instantaneously), parts do not have to wait for processing to begin. Moreover, inventories do not accumulate in front of the machine while it is being set up.

4. *Balance flow rates.* The rate of production in the various manufacturing cells must be the same. Otherwise, work-in-process inventories will build up below the cells with the faster flow rates.

5. *Change performance measurement and reward systems.* Employees are not measured and rewarded solely on efficiency measures, such as the number of units produced or keeping machines busy. Individual manufacturing cells are no longer rewarded for maximizing output. Such efficiency measures encourage workers to build inventories and to have them in front of their station as buffer stocks. A key performance measure in a JIT system is throughput time divided by process time. The closer this ratio comes to 1, the

less non–value-added time is involved. Employees are encouraged to work as multifunctional teams to achieve this goal and to participate in decision making and problem solving.

Numerical Example 12.4

Macve Motors is adopting a JIT system to reduce its throughput time, which is currently 10 days. With a JIT system, the firm believes that throughput time will fall to 6 days. This reduction will lower its costs of holding work-in-process inventory, the average value of which is $500,000. The capital cost of holding inventory is 10% per year. What is the impact on holding costs if the JIT system reduces throughput time as anticipated?

Solution

The annual cost of holding inventory is ($500,000)(0.10), or $50,000. With JIT, the throughput time is 60% of the current time. Inventory will be processed more quickly, and less capital will be devoted to holding inventory. The holding cost under a JIT system is ($500,000)(0.10)(0.60), or $30,000. Therefore, the annual cost decreases by 40%, or $20,000.

One important aspect of JIT involves redesigning the firm's relationships with its suppliers. In the past, managers believed that having multiple suppliers for each input increased competition and kept prices down. Firms had policies to divide total purchases among several sources, which required each input order received to be inspected to ensure quality and made coordinating timely delivery of supplies more difficult. In a JIT environment, firms have drastically reduced the number of suppliers, often going to long-term, sole-sourcing contracts by which a single supplier provides all of the firm's demand for a given input. The purchasing firm benefits from lower prices due to volume discounts, lower ordering costs (only a single-relationship contract is required), and higher quality assurance (audits of the supplier's process rather than the inspection of each shipment). Transportation costs are reduced because suppliers can establish long-term contracts with shippers. Risks of long-term, sole-sourcing contracts include price increases and delivery problems given the organization's dependence on a single supplier. JIT systems also impose negative externalities on society due to increased traffic congestion and pollution. Japan and parts of North America experience these problems as a result of the burden placed on the environment caused by frequent transport deliveries to manufacturing firms.

Buyers and sellers are integrating their computer systems so that buyers receive orders on a JIT basis. For example, "Motorola's Paging Product Group has won 60 percent global market share due partly to cooperation with suppliers that has brought significant advances in cost, quality, cycle time, and technology."[4] At Motorola, supply costs have fallen 8 to 10% annually for many years. Moreover, Ford and General Motors, among others, are shifting their purchasing operations to the Internet, which makes interactions between suppliers and purchasers easier and more flexible. Suppliers are encouraged to use the business-to-business network to remain competitive. The automakers' procurement costs are expected to decrease by as much as 20% while product cycles are shortened and consumers receive more customized vehicles.[5]

Initial interest in JIT arose as a result of automation, information technology, and global competition. Factory automation allows organizations to produce small batches of different products because setting up computer-programmed robots is much simpler than setting up traditional machinery. Robots are ready to manufacture a different product with the insertion of different software. With short set-up times, organizations can produce a variety of products to meet customized demand quickly.

---

[4]*Wall Street Journal,* December 12, 1995, p. A21:3.

[5]"Riding the Storm," *The Economist,* November 6, 1999, pp. 63–64.

Information technology provides much better coordination among different departments and between suppliers and customers. Bar-coding and scanning at the local supermarket are monitored by suppliers to allow for timely deliveries of products. Information technology in the form of programs such as materials requirement planning allows organizations to quickly ascertain resource requirements to make a product. A **materials requirement planning (MRP)** system is a computerized program that makes the necessary orders for raw materials and schedules the production to facilitate a short throughput time when an order arrives. MRP systems also can be tied to the organization's accounting system. Online marketplaces have developed in many industries and are being integrated into the MRP system. This integration standardizes the purchasing and production system, thereby reducing costs.

Planning Decisions

For planning purposes, the role of the accounting system also changes. Orders come before production begins; therefore, pricing decisions must be based on estimated rather than actual costs. Once the order has been accepted, no pricing reason for tracking the cost of filling the order exists. Product costs, however, still must be estimated for pricing purposes, so periodic cost checks should be made to ensure that pricing decisions reflect cost information.

Global competition is another reason for the growing popularity of JIT, which can result in lower costs and increased customer satisfaction. Ideally, manufacturing costs decrease as the result of reduced inventory holding and handling costs. However, lower costs do not always result from a switch to JIT, especially in the short term. Small batch runs and reconfiguring the factory layout may cause costs to increase. JIT is a long-term strategy that takes time to have an impact on an organization's performance.

Global Competition

Customer satisfaction should increase as a result of more timely delivery of products as well as the improved quality and reliability of products. By reducing throughput time, the organization often can deliver goods more quickly. Lower inventory levels can have the opposite effect, however; if a problem develops during the production process, the organization does not have inventory on hand to satisfy immediate customer demand. As long as the organization faces shocks to either production or demand, such as labor strikes, weather-related interruptions in the flow of raw materials, or changing prices for its products, satisfying customers with timely delivery can be a problem.

Customer Value

When organizational strategy changes to incorporate the JIT philosophy, the management accounting system also must adapt to altered responsibilities, performance evaluation, and reward systems. For control purposes, performance measures should coincide with the goals of JIT. Reducing throughput time is a primary performance measure for JIT organizations. Traditional performance measures to minimize input costs are inappropriate in a JIT system because they encourage building inventory. Instead, JIT organizations need to encourage production sufficient to cover only demand. The savings from reduced throughput time increase organizational value in the long term if they offset the costs imposed on other organizational activities.

Strategy for Customer Value

Team effort is important in JIT environments, so performance measures should reflect cooperative goals. Employees should be rewarded for achieving higher team performance measures rather than higher individual performance measures. A JIT approach also lends itself to mutual monitoring to ensure that managers are aware of the costs imposed on other organizational activities when they work to decrease throughput time.

Control Decisions

In a JIT environment, accounting is simpler. The detailed tracking of transactions in a job-order costing system is replaced with a streamlined accounting system similar to process costing. Chapter Ten discussed these two costing systems. The elimination of job cost sheets for every batch shortens throughput time because employees do not need to spend time recording costs. Having line workers fill out job order sheets as they work on a product is a non–value-added activity.

Figure 12.4

Schematic of a Just-in-Time System

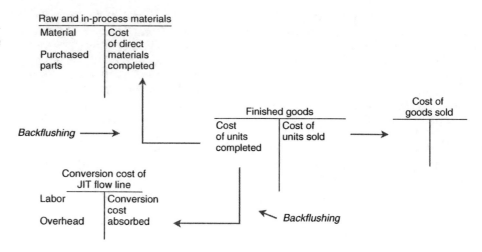

Firms that have adopted these JIT accounting systems have significantly reduced the number of accounting transactions; some have reduced their journal entry volume 20% because detailed payroll posting to jobs is eliminated. Also, jobs are no longer tracked through the work-in-process accounts as they move from department to department.

Inventory is in the form of work-in-process for a short time; therefore, less attention is paid to the valuation of partially completed products. The only time an organization may want to value work-in-process is at the end of the accounting period for external reporting purposes. Balance sheets identify the organization's assets at a particular point in time. Generally, some work-in-process exists at that point, and its full cost must be determined.

Accounting in a JIT system is tailored to the organization's needs and circumstances. A general approach to JIT accounting is called *backflushing,* which has the following features:

* One raw materials and in-process materials inventory account (RIP) is used.
* No separate work-in-process account exists, and work-in-process tracking is eliminated.
* Raw materials and purchased parts issued to production are charged to RIP.
* One account for labor and overhead costs (conversion costs) exists for each JIT flow line.
* Material costs are charged directly to products.
* Conversion costs are assigned based on machine or throughput time directly to the finished goods inventory account (FG).
* When units are completed, RIP is reduced for material costs, and FG is charged for the materials.

Figure 12.4 presents a schematic diagram of the cost flows in a JIT accounting system.

Numerical Example   12.5

Ryan Inc. manufactures a control assembly for Ford Motor Company's auto steering columns. Ryan uses a JIT production system. All conversion costs for the JIT line, such as direct and indirect labor, depreciation, and other overhead items, are budgeted at $8.8 million. This year Ryan expects to produce 2.2 million control assemblies, each of which has overhead of $4 per unit. Last week, factory labor was $38,000, and $59,000 of materials were purchased and used to produce 10,000 control assemblies. These units were shipped and billed to Ford Motor. Summarize the accounting entries for these activities.

Solution

The activities are summarized as follows:

Change in materials inventory	$ 0
Total conversion costs incurred	78,000 [$38,000 + $4(10,000 units)]
Change in finished goods inventory	0
Cost of goods sold incurred	137,000 [$78,000 + $59,000]

JIT processes and accounting systems also have problems. Firms hold inventories to smooth out fluctuations in supply or demand in the event that a labor strike occurs, bad weather prevents delivery of raw materials, or demand unexpectedly increases. These inventories allow the firm to avoid the opportunity costs of stockouts and lost sales. Factory reorganization, improved product and process quality, and strengthened purchasing relationships with suppliers can smooth out some of the fluctuations but cannot eliminate all shocks to the system. Random fluctuations beyond the control of management, such as weather-related and demand-related shocks, require firms to carry some inventories to buffer against lost sales. Few organizations have been able to completely eliminate raw materials inventory. For example, after installing JIT at one Hewlett-Packard plant, raw material inventory ranged from a two-day to a five-day supply on hand, and finished inventory on hand fell from a 2.8 months' supply to a 1.3 month's supply. However, production tripled, and the actual dollar value of inventory on hand increased.

A JIT accounting system that does not track work-in-process requires other systems to track inventory. At the Hewlett-Packard plant, the number of accounting entries was drastically reduced. However, the accounting system was no longer able to track inventory levels, which meant that inventory had to be physically counted (some every six weeks) to supply managers information on specific inventory levels. Inconsistent with the basic JIT philosophy, these inventory counts are non–value-added activities that disrupted the production process by forcing workers to stop production and count the inventory.[6] Although simplification and lower costs are advocated as advantages of a JIT accounting system, many firms have not adapted their management accounting systems to JIT. This reluctance to simplify reinforces the fact that firms use their accounting systems for many decision-making and control purposes. Simplification and the lack of tracking might affect the firms' ability to make good decisions and might create weaknesses in the control system.

Concept**Review**

1. What are the advantages of a just-in-time (JIT) system?
2. Why is a short throughput time so important for JIT?
3. How should performance measures change with the adaptation of JIT?

DEPARTMENT OF MOTOR VEHICLES (Continued)

The JIT conference that Melody attended was very exciting. Once again, the emphasis was on manufacturing firms, but she gained many insights that would work for the DMV. She decided that throughput is one concept applicable to the DMV's operations. She defined throughput as the time a customer spends in the DMV office. She asked her staff for their input on the flow of customers. She believed that she could encourage managers to reduce throughput time by linking their evaluation to this measure,

---

[6]R. Calvasina, E. Calvasina, and G. Calvasina, "Beware of Accounting Myths," *Management Accounting*, December 1989, pp. 41–45.

so she decided to evaluate the managers of the local offices according to the average throughput time for a customer obtaining a license or registration. To gain the enthusiasm of local managers for this new evaluation measure, she gave them the responsibility to change procedures to achieve a quicker throughput time. The local managers came up with the following ideas:

Using prefilled-out forms so customers have only to sign the forms if the information is correct.

Training to develop flexible, multiskilled employees, who can supplement other overburdened employees.

Using part-time labor during busy times.

Allowing registration via mail and the Internet.

Throughput time declined sharply and customers have been happier. The main question is whether there are also cost savings. Melody was eager to learn whether the more efficient use of employees through JIT actually will lead to lower costs.

BALANCED SCORECARD

L0 7 Create a balanced scorecard to articulate the strategy of the organization.

Strategy for Customer Value

An organization's strategy provides its direction, such as goals for introducing new products, customer satisfaction, market share in specific areas, and efficiencies in production. A strategy, however, is seldom specific enough to describe the steps necessary to achieve the goals. A more detailed plan identifying the inputs necessary to achieve the goals is required. A **balanced scorecard** translates the strategy into a plan of action that identifies specific objectives and performance measures to help determine whether the organization is moving in the right direction.

As outlined in Chapter Six, the balanced scorecard combines planning and control efforts in its design. It is a planning mechanism because it identifies the sequence of objectives that, if met, allow the organization to achieve its goals. The balanced scorecard also provides control by establishing performance measures and targets for each objective. It articulates the organization's strategy and communicates it in a language that everyone in the organization can understand.

The balanced scorecard derives its name from the balance that it attempts to achieve among objectives and performance measures. In particular, the balanced scorecard attempts to achieve balance between (1) short- and long-term objectives, (2) outcome and driver performance measures for cause-and-effect objectives, (3) financial and nonfinancial performance measures, and (4) all of the organization's stakeholders.

Many observers of corporate culture have loudly criticized the emphasis on short-term performance measures in corporations. Quarterly earnings announcements appear to have undue influence on the actions of corporate managers. The focus on short-term performance measures can reduce the organization's value because it results in a reluctance to invest in activities that benefit the organization in the long run. Plant maintenance and employee training are examples of expenditures that harm short-term financial results but benefit the organization in the long term. A balanced scorecard should have a mix of both short-term and long-term performance measures.

The ultimate objective of a profit organization is to generate value for the owners, yet value for them is the outcome of satisfying customers, operating efficiently, and having the infrastructure necessary to accomplish all of these activities. Secondary objectives must be accomplished before organizational value can be created. Each organizational objective has driver performance measures and outcome performance measures. **Driver performance measures** are measures of input activities to achieve the objective. For example, the number of employee training sessions is a driver performance measure for the objective of increasing employee skills to serve customers. **Outcome performance measures** are measures to determine whether the objective has been realized. For the objective of increasing employee skills to serve customers, an outcome performance measure could be the number of different services that an employee can offer a customer. Outcome performance measures of one objective can be driver performance measures of another objective. For example, the number of different services an employee can offer a customer is a driver performance measure for the objective of customer satisfaction. Driver and outcome performance measures reflect the cause-and-effect nature of the balanced scorecard.

As described in previous chapters, an organization should not rely solely on financial performance measures, which are reported periodically and are lag indicators of performance. They also tend to be outcome performance measures. Nonfinancial performance measures are important as driver performance measures to help achieve a financial outcome; they provide a broader picture of the organization's activities.

The balanced scorecard is linked closely to the organization's strategy. It also recognizes the organization's multiple stakeholders who contribute to strategic success. These stakeholders include the shareholders or owners, customers, suppliers, employees, and society. The organization's objectives should reflect the interests of these stakeholders. Indeed, most corporate mission statements mention these stakeholders. Objectives related to the stakeholders are captured in the balanced scorecard through four perspectives: financial, customer, internal business process, and learning and growth. Each of these perspectives has objectives, performance measures, targets, and initiatives. A typical balanced scorecard is described in Figure 12.5.

Financial Perspective

The financial perspective of the balanced scorecard represents the organization's shareholders/owners. The financial perspective objectives in a profit organization are oriented toward providing shareholders a return on their investment. Typical performance measures include profit, sales growth, and measures of risk. Not-for-profit organizations monitor financial objective measures such as gifts and tax revenues.

ORGANIZATIONAL VALUE

In the balanced scorecard, the objectives of the financial perspective coincide with the creation of organizational value. Value creation is the ultimate goal within the framework of this book. Driver performance measures for achieving organizational value come from the other perspectives: customer, internal business processes, and learning and growth.

Customer Perspective

The customer perspective of the balanced scorecard is concerned with adding customer value. This can be achieved by providing innovative and high-quality products and services at low prices. The balanced scorecard should highlight the organization's strategy to add customer value. Typical outcome performance drivers for the customer perspective include customer satisfaction surveys and market share. Driver performance measures include on-time delivery and reduced defects, which are outcome performance measures of the internal business process perspective.

Customer Value

Figure 12.5

Balanced Scorecard
Example

Strategy: To be the leading organization in our industry through constant innovation and adaptation to our environment. We will measure success in terms of value creation for our shareholders and customers, by the learning and growth of our employees, and by our good corporate citizenship.

Objectives	Initiatives	Performance Measure	Target
Financial Perspective			
Increase shareholder wealth	Develop new products	Return on assets	25%
Provide growth	Increase online sales	Percentage growth in sales	30%
Customer Perspective			
Increase market share	Increase advertising	Percentage market share	10%
Increase customer satisfaction	Increase postsales service	Percentage satisfied through survey	99%
Internal Business Process Perspective			
Reduce throughput time	Reduce non–value-added activities	Average throughput time	4 hours
Provide on-time delivery	Streamline delivery process	Percentage on-time delivery	90%
Reduce defects	Develop employee quality teams	Percentage defects	0.01%
Learning and Growth Perspective			
Develop a multiskilled workforce	Provide employee training	Percentage of employees with multiple skills	80%
Improve information systems	Hire new employees in computing	Number of employees in computing	20
Reduce employee turnover	Pay higher salaries	Percentage annual turnover	10%

Internal Business Process Perspective

The internal business process perspective focuses on the organization's value chain. The objectives of the internal business process perspective deal with issues of efficiency and quality. TQM, JIT, and activity-based management are processes that support this perspective. Activities should be analyzed to determine whether they add value and how to perform them most efficiently. Typical outcome performance measures for the internal business process perspective include number of defects, throughput time, and on-time delivery. Driver performance measures include the outcome measures of the learning and growth perspective.

Learning and Growth Perspective

An organization's infrastructure is the focus of the learning and growth perspective. An organization needs the right people, systems, and facilities to support them to achieve its goals. Without learning and growth in the organization, the organization is not able to adapt to a dynamic environment. To adapt successfully, an organization must have ongoing employee training, requisite technology and information systems, and facilities to meet new customer demands. Driver performance measures include employee training efforts, information system implementations, and equipment and facility purchases.

Relations among Perspectives

Each of the different perspectives of the balance scorecard should be directly or indirectly related to all others and to the overall organizational strategy. Typically, the development of a balanced scorecard starts with the financial perspective and cascades down to the learning and growth perspective, but the cause-and-effect relation flows in the opposite direction.

The organization's strategy is the starting point and dictates the financial perspective objectives. To achieve these objectives, the organization must look at its relationships with its customers and determine how it can add value to them. Adding value to customers comes from the efficient and quality operations of its internal processes, yet processes cannot operate efficiently without the appropriate learning and growth within the organization. Identifying these links is critical to the successful implementation of a balanced scorecard.

DEPARTMENT OF MOTOR VEHICLES (Continued)

Although TQM and JIT are contributing to improvements at the DMV and to its customer-focused strategy, Melody wonders whether a more comprehensive approach might be necessary. It is difficult to determine how these techniques link together and how they contribute to the DMV's long-term goals. She also is concerned that gaps still exist and that objectives possibly conflict. She decides next to capture her strategy and objectives in a balanced scorecard. One reason for this exercise is to determine whether she has the proper resources and procedures in place to achieve customer satisfaction at low cost. In addition, she believes that DMV employees are more likely to buy into her strategy if they can understand how her plans are linked to the DMV's goals. The performance measures and targets of the balanced scorecard can help her to determine whether the organization and its managers are moving in the right direction.

Melody creates the following balanced scorecard for the DMV:

Objectives	Initiatives	Performance Measure	Target
Financial Perspective			
Reduce costs	Increase online registration	Percentage online registration	20%
Customer Perspective			
Increase customer satisfaction	Implement TQM and JIT	Percentage satisfied through survey	95%
Internal Business Process Perspective			
Reduce throughput time	Use prefilled forms, flexible employees	Average throughput time	20 min.
Increase on-time police response	Create accessible computer database	Average time to respond	3 min.
Reduce complaints	Create employee quality teams	Percentage of customers dissatisfied	1%
Learning and Growth Perspective			
Develop a multiskilled workforce	Provide employee training	Percentage of employees with multiple skills	90%
Develop online registration	Hire new employees in computing	Number of employees in computing	10
Respond to employees	Provide a suggestion box	Number of suggestions per month	50

You decide

WHEN SHOULD MANAGEMENT ACCOUNTING BE CHANGED?

LO 8 Identify when management accounting within an organization should change.

An ideal management accounting system does not exist. Each organization has different circumstances that lead to different management accounting systems. Also, management accounting must continually deal with trade-offs among internal users, who prefer information for making planning and control decisions, and external users, who want information describing the firm's performance. Finally, each organization is continually adapting to meet the demands of a dynamic environment. Organizations are in a continual state of flux; thus, management accounting must continually adapt.

Certain warning signals indicate that the management accounting process is not working well and that the system must be changed. One sign is dysfunctional behavior on the part of managers due to inappropriate performance measures. Managers make decisions to influence performance measures in a positive way. If these performance measures are not consistent with the organization's goals, management might make decisions that do not coincide with organizational goals. When organizational managers are acting at cross-purposes with each other, the management accounting system is not working and should be changed.

Another signal of problems with the management accounting process is poor planning decisions. If product mix and pricing decisions based on management accounting information are not adding to organizational value, the management accounting system might not be estimating costs well. One indication of a poor management accounting system is the inability to win bids to sell products that are the company's specialty but the ability to win bids to sell products for which the company has no comparative advantage. John Deere Component Works had this problem and realized that the management accounting system was not allocating overhead properly.[7]

Management accounting systems must change as organizations do. Warning signs, such as lost sales, can indicate that the system is not working properly and is reducing organizational value. John Deere faced such a situation when it changed its manufacturing processes, but not its accounting system. A dysfunctional management accounting system is often the symptom of underlying problems that the organization should investigate and resolve.

Organizations should not look necessarily to the latest management accounting fads to give them direction in changing their management accounting systems. TQM, JIT, and activity-based management, for example, are appropriate for certain types of organizations and in particular environments. Some features of each approach might be beneficial, while others might not contribute to the creation of organizational value in every case. Each organization must continually evaluate and improve its management accounting system to meet the challenges of a dynamic environment and a changing organization.

[7]Harvard Business School Case 9-187-107.

SUMMARY

1 Describe the factors in a dynamic environment that influence an organization. Consumer demand, technology, and global competition are factors in a dynamic environment that lead to changes in organizations.

2 Describe the way an organization's strategy is related to its structure. An organization's strategy determines its structure. For example, an innovative product strategy is usually best accomplished in a decentralized organization.

3 Explain the role of management accounting in the organizational structure and in making planning decisions. Management accounting through budgets is used to assign responsibilities. It is also used to measure performance and to assist in making planning decisions.

4 Identify major characteristics of total quality management. Total quality management (TQM) is a philosophy that places customer satisfaction first. Continual improvement, involved leadership, and employee participation and empowerment are all part of TQM.

5 Use quality costs for making planning and control decisions. The comparison of quality costs over time provides a benchmark to determine whether TQM efforts are successful. Quality costs should also be used to make planning decisions comparing different quality efforts.

6 Explain the philosophy of JIT processes and accounting adjustments for JIT. The JIT philosophy is to produce to order rather than produce for inventory. To be successful, the organization must have a short throughput time to meet demand. JIT has no job order costs. Accounting performance measures should be selected to encourage faster throughput time and to discourage increased inventory.

7 Create a balanced scorecard to articulate the strategy of the organization. A balanced scorecard describes objectives in a cause-and-effect sequence to achieve the organization's strategy. Performance measures and targets are identified for each objective.

8 Identify when management accounting within an organization should change. Management accounting must continually adapt to dynamic environments and organizations. Warning signals within the management accounting system are dysfunctional behavior by managers and poor planning decisions.

KEY TERMS

appraisal costs Costs related to the identification of defective units before they are shipped to customers. (*p. 430*)

balanced scorecard The articulation of an organization's strategy through a sequence of objectives with corresponding performance measures. (*p. 440*)

driver performance measures Input or lead measures of objectives within a balanced scorecard. (*p. 441*)

external failure costs Costs incurred when a customer receives a defective product. (*p. 431*)

internal failure costs Costs incurred when a defect is discovered before a customer receives it. (*p. 431*)

materials requirement planning (MRP) Computer programs that allow organizations to quickly ascertain resource requirements to make a product. (*p. 437*)

outcome performance measures Output measures of objectives in a balanced scorecard. (*p. 441*)

prevention costs Costs incurred in the production process to reduce defects. (*p. 430*)

throughput time The total time from receipt of an order to delivery. (*p. 434*)

SELF-STUDY PROBLEM

Jose Morales operates a small sewing shop that makes dresses and pants. He receives orders for the dresses and pants from large clothing companies that contract with firms like his to manufacture the clothing that the companies sell to retailers. The clothing companies provide the patterns and specifications for a clothing item for Jose. Any dresses and pants that do not meet specifications are returned to him. The business is extremely competitive. Jose is forced to operate on small margins because the clothing companies are threatening to send the manufacturing to other countries. He has managed to keep his business operating by promising a low number of defects and timely delivery. Jose has achieved a low number of defects by careful inspection of all clothing leaving the shop. He has been less successful in achieving timely delivery.

Jose hired 20 seamstresses to do the sewing. Prior to sewing, however, the cloth must be cut. Once the sewing has been completed, buttons and snaps are added. The dresses and pants are then inspected, pressed, and packaged.

Describe how Jose might use TQM and JIT. Outline the advantages and disadvantages of each management philosophy.

Solution

Jose Morales must maintain the quality of his product to survive, so TQM appears to be relevant for him. TQM suggests a different approach, however, to achieving fewer defects. Instead of discovering defects at final inspection, Jose should attempt to reduce defects before they happen. Providing training for employees and better sewing machines could help reduce initial defects. With fewer initial defects, Jose can save on the cost of spoiled units discovered after completion. In the long term, TQM can save on costs, but in the short term, the training and new machines will be costly.

Jose has a problem delivering his clothes on time. JIT suggests that production should start after the receipt of an order rather than producing for inventory. Jose already has been following this rule, but he needs to shorten his throughput time. One method of shortening throughput time is to have small groups of seamstresses work in teams with individuals doing the cutting, adding the snaps and buttons, pressing, and packaging. Work-in-process could be reduced, allowing defects to be identified and processes corrected more quickly. The team members could become multiskilled to assist each other when needed. All of these actions would increase throughput. Jose would have to change the organizational structure, however, to achieve JIT, and many employees might temporarily resent moving to a new evaluation system.

NUMERICAL EXERCISES

NE 12.1
Quality Costs and Defect Rates
(LO 5)

A manufacturer of recordable CDs is concerned about the quality of a recent production run. The company ships a complete batch of CDs to the same retailer to monitor quality. In a recent batch, a retailer reported one defective disc. The firm's management believes that 1% of its discs do not meet its quality specifications. Of these, it is convinced that 90% are identified and removed prior to shipping.

If inspection is on a per batch basis, what is the size of the questionable batch?

NE 12.2
Estimation of Quality Costs
(LO 5)

Spectra Company is examining its quality spending for the current year. It has summarized its spending as follows: prevention, $150,000; appraisal, $50,000; internal failure, $100,000; and external failure, $180,000. Next year, Spectra plans to increase its spending on prevention activities by 25%. This increased spending will reduce external failure costs by 40%. The costs for appraisal and internal failure will both increase by 5% as a result of cost increases in Spectra's operations.

What is the projected cost of quality for the upcoming year? Is the increased spending on prevention activities beneficial in terms of overall costs of quality?

NE 12.3
Quality Costs
(LO 5)

For the last five years, a firm has measured (in dollars) the following quality costs by categories:

Category	1997	1998	1999	2000	2001
Prevention	$5000	$6000	$7000	$8000	$9000
Appraisal	5000	5000	6000	7000	8000
Internal failure	9000	9000	7000	5000	3000
External failure	9000	8000	7000	6000	5000

a. Given these costs, is it likely that the company's defect rate has gone up or down? Explain.

b. If these costs reflect all the relevant quality costs, have the increased costs of prevention and appraisal yielded a net benefit to the company?

NE 12.4
Inspection Decision with Quality Costs
(LO 5)

A company is considering additional final inspection costs of $1 per unit before delivery to customers. The additional inspection should reduce the defect rate from 3% to 1%. If a defective unit is found, it is scrapped at no additional cost. The manufacturing costs before the final inspection total $200 per unit. Management believes that the external failure costs are $40 per defective unit.

Should management incur the additional inspection costs?

NE 12.5
Throughput Time and Inventory Costs
(LO 6)

A company that has a throughput time of 32 days wants to reduce this time to 8 days. To do so, it will need to change its layout at a cost of $150,000. It believes that its inventory level will drop by 25% once these changes take effect. The capital cost of holding inventories is 10% per year based on the average inventory level of $1,500,000.

Should the company adopt the new layout?

Solarcom uses a JIT production system to manufacture its solar-powered CD players and has adopted backflushing to streamline its accounting system. It accumulates all conversion costs for the JIT line in one account; these costs are estimated to be $2 million for the current year. Solarcom estimates that it will produce 500,000 CD players this year. Last week, plant labor was $15,000, and $25,000 of materials were purchased and used to produce 10,000 CD players. All units were shipped and billed to a major retail chain.

> Provide a summary of the accounting entries for last week's production activities.

NE 12.6
JIT Systems
(LO 6)

NUMERICAL PROBLEMS

A large retailer purchases furniture directly from the manufacturer in North Carolina. The retailer insists that 99% of the furniture arriving at the retail shops pass inspection. The manufacturer knows that 0.6% of the furniture is damaged during shipping and 2% is defective before shipping.

> To satisfy the retailer, approximately what percentage of defects must be discovered after manufacturing but before shipping takes place?

NP 12.1
Defect Rates and Inspection
(LO 5)

A building contractor estimates the following quality costs: prevention, $100,000; appraisal, $50,000; internal failure, $40,000; and external failure, $200,000. The contractor is considering one of the following two courses of action: (1) increasing prevention costs by 50%, which should lead to a 10% decline in internal failure costs and a 40% decline in external failure costs; and (2) increasing appraisal costs by 100%, which should increase internal failure costs by 20% and decrease external failure costs by 50%.

> Which action causes the lower quality costs?

NP 12.2
Quality Costs and Benefits
(LO 5)

Holder Company is experiencing problems with the handle on the carafe of its Euro-design coffeemaker. The handle breaks and must be replaced 5% of the time. It costs $50 to replace each carafe; Holder replaces the carafe and ships it by express courier to appease customers who cannot use their coffeemakers while awaiting a replacement. Holder is considering the use of a specialty plastic for the handle that would not break even under extreme use. The new plastic would increase its production costs by $10,000 per year. An alternative to the new plastic is to examine each carafe to see whether the handle is defective. It would cost $3 per carafe to add this inspection. This year, Holder plans to manufacture and sell 5,000 coffeemakers. Next year it plans to replace the model with a new design.

> What should Holder do?

NP 12.3
Defect Rates and Inspection Costs
(LO 5)

O'Reilly Manufacturing produces three models of a product, super, supreme, and ultra. These models are basically the same design but have different quality standards applied in the production process. Frequent production line stops, adjustments, and start-ups cause a certain amount of scrap costs. Scrap also occurs when inspectors reject a product for not meeting its specifications. Once rejected, the product has no commercial value and is hauled away. All costs incurred to produce a scrapped product are charged to a scrap account, which is part of overhead. The firm's budgeted operating statement by product is as follows:

NP 12.4
Scrap Costs
(LO 5)

O'REILLY MANUFACTURING Budgeted Operating Statement for 2001				
	Super	**Supreme**	**Ultra**	**Total**
Unit volume	85,000	42,000	13,000	
Selling price	$205	$225	$235	
Revenue	$17,425,000	$9,450,000	$3,055,000	$29,930,000
Less				
Raw materials	$ 8,500,000	$4,200,000	$1,300,000	14,000,000
Direct labor	5,312,500	3,150,000	975,000	9,437,500
Overhead	3,478,245	2,062,395	638,360	6,179,000
Total cost	$17,290,745	$9,412,395	$2,913,360	$29,616,500
Profits	$ 134,255	$ 37,605	$ 141,640	$ 313,500

448

Management Accounting in a Dynamic Environment

Other information:

• Overhead costs are allocated to products based on direct labor dollars.
• Direct labor cost is $25 per hour.

Overheads consist of

Depreciation	$3,500,000
Indirect labor	450,000
Scrap	1,679,000
Other	550,000
Total	$6,179,000

Additional data:

	Super	Supreme	Ultra
Direct labor hours per unit	2.5 hours	3 hours	3 hours
Total scrap	$850,000	$504,000	$325,000
Profit per unit	$1.58	$0.90	$10.90

Management is concerned about the relatively low profit per unit on the supreme line as compared to the ultra line. It is considering a variety of marketing strategies to increase the sales of ultras since the profit margins are substantially higher.

Critically analyze management's conclusion that profits are substantially higher on ultra. Present supporting figures to back up your analysis and conclusions.

NP 12.5
ISO 9000 Certification
(LO 4)

Stowbridge Division is analyzing the expansion of its total quality management program, which is already in place. One of its customers, Amlan Equipment, is asking all of its suppliers to become ISO 9000 qualified; this is a process that certifies that the firm meets various quality standards. Once its suppliers are ISO 9000 qualified, Amlan can reduce its inspection costs because it can depend on quality parts from its suppliers. Only its suppliers that obtain certification will receive more business from Amlan.

Amlan purchases a stainless steel rotor from Stowbridge. To meet the ISO 9000 certification requirements, Stowbridge estimates that it will have to incur additional costs. The following annual incremental costs will be necessary as long as it wants to obtain ISO 9000 certification:

Annual Incremental Costs for ISO 9000 Certification	
Training	$74,000
Inspection	$96,000
Prevention	$62,000
Direct materials	10%
Direct labor	15%

The budgeted selling price and standard cost data per rotor related to the manufacture of the current quality of rotor is provided:

Selling price	$14.00
Less standard costs	
Direct materials	4.30
Direct labor	2.40
Manufacturing overhead (all fixed)	2.05
Selling and administrative (all variable)	1.60
Unit cost	$10.35
Unit profit	$ 3.65

Unless Stowbridge receives ISO 9000 certification, it will lose Amlan's business of 120,000 units per year. Management estimates that the higher quality of the rotor achieved as a result of ISO certification will allow Stowbridge to add 14,000 rotors to its current sales from new and existing customers. Stowbridge is currently selling 480,000 rotors per year, including the Amlan sales. The current sales of 480,000 units amount to 63% of plant capacity. The additional 14,000 units sold can be manufactured without exceeding plant capacity. After receiving ISO 9000 certification, the higher-quality process would apply to all rotors produced.

Should Stowbridge seek ISO 9000 certification? Support your recommendation with an analysis of the costs and benefits of ISO 9000 certification.

Toby Manufacturing produces three different products in the same plant and uses a job-order costing system to estimate product costs. It uses a flexible budget to forecast overhead costs. Total budgeted fixed factory overhead is $450,000 and variable overhead is 120% of direct labor dollars. There is no beginning or ending inventory.

NP 12.6
Allocation of Costs Based on Throughput Time
(LO 6)

Projected volumes, selling prices, and direct costs for the three products for the next calendar year follow:

	Product AAA	Product BBB	Product CCC
Projected number of units	6,000	3,000	1,000
Direct materials per unit	$22	$25	$30
Direct labor per unit	$11	$12	$16
Selling price	$98	$115	$140

The manufacturing process requires six operations. Between operations, intermediate products are moved and warehoused until the next production stage. Each of the three products requires 10 days of processing time to complete all six operations, but each has a different throughput time because of different waiting times between operations. *Throughput time* is defined as the total time from ordering the raw materials for the product until the product is completed and shipped. Product AAA has the shortest throughput time (20 days) because the large volume allows more accurate forecasts and more continuous scheduling of production. Total throughput time for product BBB is 40 days and for product CCC is 50 days. Products BBB and CCC have longer warehousing times of work-in-process because of more frequent scheduling changes and more frequent supplier delays.

Half of what is currently treated as fixed overhead cost involves the warehousing function.

a. Prepare a pro forma income statement by product line for the year based on full absorption costing. Product costs should include overhead assigned on direct labor cost.

b. Prepare a revised pro forma income statement by product line using throughput time to allocate fixed overhead related to warehousing.

c. Comment on the differences.

Tagway 4000 is a computer manufacturer based in Montana. One component of the computer is an internal battery used to keep track of time and date while the computer is turned off. Tagway produces the batteries in house; the division, which produces 1,000,000 of them each year, is treated as a cost center. The division manager is compensated based on her ability to keep total costs low and to meet quality control measures of number of defects and delivery time. She has a base salary of $144,000 and is eligible for a $34,000 bonus if total costs are less than or equal to $2,000,000 without including her compensation. She is eligible for a $40,000 bonus if there are 32 or fewer defects per 1,000,000 units produced. Finally, she is eligible for a $22,000 bonus if batteries are delivered on time. On-time delivery is defined as averaging two days between the order from the assembly department and delivery to the assembly department.

NP 12.7
Compensation and Quality
(LO 5)

The basic cost of producing a battery is $1.55. However, current methods have an inherent defect rate of 1,032 per 1,000,000. The cost of improving the defect rate involves using higher-quality materials and more experienced labor. Based on currently available inputs, improving the defect rate below 32 per 1,000,000 is impossible. The cost of removing each defect from 1,032 defects to 32 defects per 1,000,000 is $450. In other words, the cost to

450   *Management Accounting in a Dynamic Environment*

reduce defects to the desired level of 32 per 1,000,000 is $450,000. This production method also delivers the batteries in an average of four days. The cost of overtime necessary to lower the average to three days is $90,000. The cost of speeding delivery another day is $95,000, making the cumulative cost of lowering the average to two days $185,000. The marginal cost of reducing the average delivery a third day is $115,000, making the total cost of reducing the average delivery time to one day $300,000.

a. Create a table showing the production costs related to defect rates of 1,032, 500, 100, 50, and 32 per 1,000,000 and average delivery times of four, three, two, and one days. Do not include the manager's salary. Note the minimum cost.

b. Create a table showing the manager's compensation related to defect rates of 1,032, 500, 100, 50, and 32 and average delivery times of four, three, two, and one days. Note the maximum compensation level.

c. Comment on the ideal number of defects and delivery times necessary to achieve the minimum costs and the maximum compensation level.

NP 12.8
Choice of Quality Spending Levels
(LO 5)

Aqua Company has extremely high external failure costs for all level of defects. The company must achieve zero defects in products sent to customers through either prevention efforts or appraisal and correction efforts. The company makes 1,000 units; the following data relate to prevention efforts and costs:

Defects	Prevention Costs
100	$ 1,000
50	3,000
20	10,000
10	50,000
5	100,000
0	300,000

Inspection of all units after production costs $50,000. The cost of correcting defective units (internal failure costs) depends on the number of defective units.

Defects	Internal Failure Costs
100	$130,000
50	60,000
20	20,000
10	10,000
5	5,000
1	0

a. What is the optimal level of prevention, appraisal, and correction?

b. If the cost of inspecting all units is $500,000, what is the lowest cost strategy?

NP 12.9
JIT and Backflush Costing
(LO 6)

Abco manufactures car radio antennas. It produces the retractable wand that other firms assemble with a motor, wiring, housing, and switch for sale to automakers. Abco receives deliveries of steel rod and tubing each day. These materials are cut, threaded, crimped, and assembled into final wands on continuous flow production lines. Twice a day, it ships finished wands to customers who assemble the complete antenna unit.

On March 16, rod and tubing valued at $2,040 were delivered for the 11-cm. antenna model. These materials were converted into wands and the following shipments made:

Completed units shipped in the morning	160
Completed units shipped in the afternoon	180

Labor and overhead on March 16 totaled $980. Each completed 11-cm. wand has a conversion cost of $4.80. Abco uses JIT accounting and backflushes RIP and conversion costs directly to cost of goods sold when the units are shipped because wands are not started until Abco receives an order.

What accounting entries are made on March 16 for the 11-cm. wands?

The Lunatic Fringe operates a chain of hair salons. Each salon manager has four measures in their balanced scorecard. If managers meet all four targets they get a $10,000 bonus. They receive $7,500 for meeting three targets, $5,000 for meeting two targets, and $2,500 for meeting one target. The following table defines the four targets:

NP 12.10
Balanced Scorecard
(LO 7)

Lunatic Fringe Balanced Scorecard		
Objectives	**Performance Measure**	**Target**
Financial Perspective		
Increase shareholder wealth	Return on assets	20%
Customer Perspective		
Provide customer satisfaction	Percentage satisfied through survey	95%
Internal Business Process Perspective		
Provide on-time delivery	Percentage customers not waiting for appointment	90%
Learning and Growth Perspective		
Reduce employee turnover	Percentage annual turnover	20%

The Lunatic Fringe's West End salon had the following operating statistics for the fiscal year:

Net income	$139,500
Total assets	$634,000
Number of customer surveys	672
Number of customer surveys "satisfied"	646
Number of customers	915
Number of customers served on time	833
Employee turnover	5
Number of employees	15

How much bonus will Lucy Chan, the West End manager, receive?

ANALYSIS AND INTERPRETATION PROBLEMS

Avon (http://avon.avon.com/) manufactures and sells cosmetics primarily to women using a sales force consisting of part-time women (sales representatives) selling the products through in-home sales parties and the Internet. Sales representatives host parties in their homes where they demonstrate the products and then take orders. The sales representatives are paid on a commission basis.

Discuss the factors currently affecting Avon's business.

AIP 12.1
Factors Influencing an Organization
(LO 1)

In the 1960s, there were many banks, each with multiple branches. In the 1990s and 2000s, numerous bank mergers have occurred, and branch banks have been consolidated. Discuss the factors driving banks to change their strategy and thus their organizational structure.

AIP 12.2
Relation between Organization Strategy and Organization Structure
(LO 2)

Describe various ways that the management accounting system assists in planning decisions.

AIP 12.3
Management Accounting and Planning Decisions
(LO 3)

AIP 12.4

Choice of TQM

(LO 4)

Wonderful Toy Company is celebrating its 100th anniversary this year. The company has been successful in designing and making educational toys for department stores and small hobby stores. The sales manager recently returned from a national convention where he heard that many other toy manufacturers are implementing TQM. The president of the company, the great grandson of the company's founder, does not think that the company needs TQM. He states, "We have been in business for 100 years, and this company has been very profitable. Our customers must be happy with us because they are still buying our products. Why should we change the way we do business?"

Evaluate the president's statement.

AIP 12.5

JIT and the Role of Accounting

(LO 6)

The president of Kelly Windows believes avidly in JIT. Kelly Windows manufactures bay windows. The president wants no inventory or work-in-process on the floor at the end of each day. Windows are manufactured only after being ordered, and throughput time is quick enough to complete most orders during the day of the order. The president is also trying to eliminate all non–value-added activities. She considers accounting to be non–value-added and wants to reduce accounting activities sharply if not completely.

As the controller, how can you defend the accounting activities that your department performs?

AIP 12.6

Measurement of Quality Costs

(LO 5)

Precision Machines' president wants to convert to TQM. The industrial machinery produced by Precision Machines is critical to its customers. Customers who receive defective machinery incur very high costs, which Precision Machines usually has to pay because of warranties or lawsuits. The president believes that TQM will help the organization satisfy its customers. As part of the change to TQM, the president has asked you, the controller, to devise a system for measuring the different categories of quality cost: prevention, appraisal, internal failure, or external failure.

Describe the costs in each of these categories. For which categories will it be the most difficult to make cost estimates?

AIP 12.7

JIT and Stock-Out Costs

(LO 6)

James Industries is considering a shift to JIT. The president believes that reducing inventory can save considerable costs, but the marketing manager is worried. She recognizes that the inventory holding costs, such as storage and the opportunity cost of cash consumed to hold inventory, are high and will be reduced if the company changes to JIT. She believes that the president has forgotten about stockout costs, which occur when customers want to purchase an item that is not immediately available and go elsewhere to make the purchase.

How should the company measure stockout costs? What can be done to minimize them?

AIP 12.8

Design of a Balanced Scorecard

(LO 7)

Old Town Roasters (OTR) owns and operates a chain of 12 coffee shops around town. OTR's strategy is to provide the highest quality coffee and baked goods in a warm, friendly environment. The OTR provides its customers Internet access and current newspapers. Some shops are open 24 hours a day, especially those located around college campuses. Each shop manager is responsible for deciding the hours that the store is open, the selection of baked goods to stock, and the number of Internet terminals to provide in the store.

Design a balanced scorecard to evaluate and reward the manager of each shop.

AIP 12.9

Design of a Balanced Scorecard

(LO 7)

The Pottery Store is a chain of retail stores in upscale malls that sells pottery, woodcarvings, and other craft items. The typical customer is shopping for a gift and spends between $50 and $200. Buyers located in the corporate office contact artists around the country and buy inventory for the stores. Corporate headquarters sets the final selling price for each item and determines when to mark them down for sales. Each store manager is responsible for store staffing and layout. Store managers do not have responsibility for choosing the merchandise, store hours (set by the mall), or pricing decisions.

a.   Design a balanced scorecard for the store managers.
b.   How would your answer to (a) change if the store managers also had decision-making responsibilities for both selecting the merchandise to carry in the store and pricing?

AIP 12.10

Factors Suggesting Management Accounting Change

(LO 8)

What telltale signs suggest that the management accounting process requires change?

EXTENDED ANALYSIS AND INTERPRETATION PROBLEMS

Software Development, Inc. (SDI), produces and markets software for personal computers including spreadsheet, word processing, desktop publishing, and database management programs. It has annual sales of $800 million.

AIP 12.11
Quality Costs

Producing software is a time-consuming, labor-intensive process. Quality is an extremely important aspect of success in computer software markets. One aspect of quality is program reliability. Does the software perform as expected? Does it work with other software in terms of data transfers and interfaces? Does it terminate abnormally? In spite of testing the software extensively, programs always contain some bugs. After the software has been released, SDI stands behind the product with phone-in customer service consultants who answer questions and help the customer work around existing problems in the software. SDI also has a software maintenance group that fixes bugs and sends revised versions of the programs to customers.

SDI has been tracking the relationship between quality costs and quality. The quality measure that it uses is the number of documented bugs in a software package. A bug is identified when a customer calls in with a complaint and the SDI customer service representative determines that it is a new problem. The software maintenance programmers then set about to fix the program and eliminate the bug. To manage quality, SDI tracks quality costs. It has released 38 new or major revisions in existing packages in the last three years. Exhibit AIP 12.11A on page 454 reports the number of defects (bugs) documented in the first six months following release. It also lists total product cost and quality cost per software package release.

Product costs include all costs incurred to produce and market the software, excluding the quality costs in Exhibit AIP 12.11A. Quality costs consist of training, prevention, and software maintenance and customer service costs. Training costs are expenditures for educating the programmers and updating their training. Better educated programmers produce fewer bugs. Prevention costs include the expenditures for testing the software before it is released. Maintenance and customer service costs are for the programmers charged with fixing the bugs and reissuing the revised software and the customer service representatives answering phone questions. The training and prevention costs are measured for the period during which the software was being developed. The number of defects and maintenance and service costs are measured in the first six months following release.

All numbers in Exhibit AIP 12.11A have been deflated by lines of computer code in the particular program release. Programs with more lines of code cost more and have more bugs. Studies have found that lines of code provide an acceptable way to control for program complexity. Thus, the numbers in Exhibit AIP 12.11A are stated in terms of defects and cost per 100,000 lines of code.

Exhibit AIP 12.11B (see page 454) plots the relationship between total quality cost and number of defects. SDI's vice president of quality likes to use Exhibit AIP 12.11B to emphasize that costs and quality are inversely related. She is fond of saying, "Quality pays! Our total costs are a declining function of the number of defects. The more we spend on quality, the lower are our costs."

Critically evaluate the vice president's analysis.

In 1995, Global Oil Corporation's Marketing and Refining (M&R) Division was the fifth largest U.S. refiner with 7,700 Global-branded service stations selling about 23 million gallons per day, or 7% of U.S. gasoline. All stations were company owned. In 1990, M&R ranked last among divisions in profitability and was annually draining $500 million of cash from the corporation.

AIP 12.12
Balanced Scorecard

In 1993, M&R reorganized from a centralized functional organization (refineries, transportation, warehousing, retail, and marketing) into 17 geographic business units (sales and distribution) and 14 service companies. The functional organization had been slow to react to changing market conditions and the special customer needs that differed across the country. The new decentralized organization was designed to better focus on the customer. New marketing strategies could be better tailored to local markets by giving local managers more decision-making authority.

The company implemented a new corporate strategy to focus on the less price-sensitive customer who would not only buy Global gas but also shop in its convenience gas store outlets simultaneously with the reorganization. Global's new strategy was to redesign its convenience stores so that they would become a "destination shop," offering one-stop shopping for gas and snacks.

Exhibit AIP 12.11A

SDI Defects and Quality Costs by Program Release*

Program Release	Number of Defects	Product Cost	Training Cost	Prevention Cost	Software Maintenance & Customer Service Cost	Total Costs
1	66	$3,455	$442	$ 770	$2,160	$6,827
2	86	3,959	428	447	2,658	7,492
3	14	3,609	417	1,167	687	5,880
4	73	3,948	211	655	2,334	7,148
5	17	3,104	290	1,013	544	4,951
6	48	3,179	253	547	1,556	5,535
7	80	3,112	392	508	2,633	6,645
8	41	3,529	276	577	1,563	5,945
9	50	3,796	557	634	1,666	6,653
10	67	3,444	365	947	2,140	6,896
11	42	3,922	453	869	1,444	6,688
12	64	3,846	378	1,108	1,942	7,274
13	71	3,014	555	762	2,384	6,715
14	1	3,884	301	773	423	5,381
15	18	3,183	378	1,080	857	5,498
16	85	3,475	528	1,010	2,572	7,585
17	17	3,445	357	666	631	5,099
18	50	3,203	285	427	1,546	5,461
19	22	3,839	239	1,080	891	6,049
20	73	3,060	540	1,054	2,309	6,963
21	52	3,182	329	1,079	1,867	6,457
22	75	3,075	395	832	2,697	6,999
23	35	3,456	447	969	1,518	6,390
24	53	3,987	355	651	2,042	7,035
25	25	3,836	309	1,160	1,036	6,341
26	6	3,886	234	794	252	5,166
27	78	3,846	418	833	2,800	7,897
28	82	3,106	409	1,092	2,871	7,478
29	39	3,506	448	899	1,342	6,195
30	47	3,545	450	442	1,450	5,887
31	30	3,376	456	784	1,260	5,876
32	17	3,740	542	420	607	5,309
33	67	3,479	411	821	2,018	6,729
34	51	3,773	351	1,145	1,873	7,142
35	74	3,034	497	671	2,389	6,591
36	25	3,768	268	887	1,094	6,017
37	14	3,168	356	645	837	5,006
38	77	3,561	492	1,167	2,597	7,817
Average	48	$3,509	$390	$ 826	$1,671	$6,395

*Per 100,000 lines of computer code

Exhibit 12.11B

SDI Total Costs by Defects

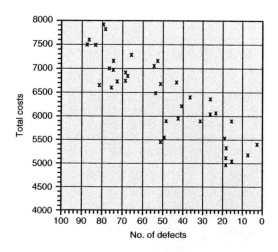

The old organization used a variety of functional measures: manufacturing cost, sales margins and volumes, and health and safety metrics. After changing its corporate strategy and organizational structure, M&R decided to change its performance metrics and began investigating the balanced scorecard.

Balanced Scorecard The balanced scorecard (BSC) is a series of performance measures that track the key elements of a company's strategy.[8] Based on the adage of "what you measure is what you get," a company's BSC seeks to complement traditional financial performance measures with operational measures of customer satisfaction, internal processes, and internal innovation. After setting the company's vision and strategy, four general sets of measures are identified:

1. **Financial Perspective**
   Return on capital
   Cash flow
   Earnings per share growth

2. **Customer Perspective**
   Customer satisfaction
   Innovation
   Competitive price

3. **Internal Processes**
   Safety
   Rework
   Time to market for new products

4. **Learning and Growth**
   Rate of improvement
   Employee satisfaction
   Percentage of revenue from new products

A BSC has been compared to the instrument panel in an airplane. Each gauge provides specific information on the plane's location (altitude, speed, direction), and its operating condition (fuel, cabin pressure, temperature). Like an airplane's control panel, a BSC helps managers steer their business toward achieving its mission.

BSC at M&R M&R formed project teams of managers to design performance metrics for their operations. Thirty-two different metrics were identified. These included financial (return on assets [ROA], cash flow, volume, growth), customer (share of segment, mystery shopper), internal (safety incidents, refinery ROA, inventory level), and learning (strategic skills acquisition, quality of information system). The "mystery shopper" is a third-party vendor who purchases gas and snacks at each station monthly. During each visit, the mystery shopper rates the station on 23 items related to external appearance, rest rooms, and so forth. A brochure describing the BSC was prepared and distributed to M&R's 11,000 employees in August 1994. Extensive meetings with employees explained the new metrics and the BSC concept.

Compensation Plans All salaried employees of M&R are to receive a bonus up to 10% if Global ranked first among its seven competitors on ROA and earnings per share (EPS) growth. In addition to this existing plan, a new program was added to award bonuses up to 20% of their salary to managers. The size of the bonus depended on the average performance of three factors:

* Global's competitive ranking on ROA and EPS growth.
* M&R's balanced scorecard metrics.
* The business unit's balanced scorecard.

In 1995, M&R generated more income per barrel of oil than the industry average, and its ROA exceeded the industry's average.

a.   Critically evaluate M&R's implementation of the balanced scorecard. Identify any of its strengths and weaknesses.

b.   Was the adoption of the balanced scorecard at M&R responsible for its turnaround financial performance?

Source: R. Kaplan, "Mobil USM&R (A): Linking the Balanced Scorecard," Harvard Business School Case 9-197-025 (May 7, 1997).

---

[8]R. Kaplan and N. Norton, "Putting the Balanced Scorecard to Work," *Harvard Business Review,* September–October 1993, pp. 136–47.

Chapter **Thirteen**

Investment Decisions

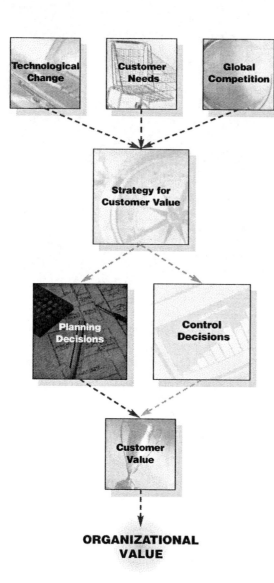

SLIM'S ICE CREAM PARLOR

Slim Tarver owns the only ice cream parlor in town. He eats a lot of his own ice cream and is not so slim, but he recognizes that many people are concerned about their health and the fat content of ice cream. Therefore, he wonders whether a frozen yogurt machine might encourage more customers to come to his ice cream parlor. There is plenty of space to put the frozen yogurt machine, and the additional business could be very profitable. He visits a supplier and learns that a new frozen yogurt machine costs $10,000 and is expected to last five years. Slim could pay cash for the machine but decides to borrow the amount from his bank at 8% interest.

To determine whether the frozen yogurt machine would be profitable, Slim estimates the impact of the machine on his reported income for each of the next five years:

Revenues from selling frozen yogurt	$5,000
Cost of ingredients	(1,500)
Additional utility costs	(500)
Interest expense (0.08) ($10,000)	(800)
Straight-line depreciation on machine ($10,000/5)	(2,000)
Profit per year	$ 200

Although these estimates indicate that the frozen yogurt machine will generate a profit, Slim is not sure that he has included everything in his calculations.

LONG-TERM INVESTMENT DECISIONS

Chapters Two to Five described different planning decisions and how management accounting facilitates those planning decisions. Those decisions tend to have short-term implications. In other words, the cash flow is received or paid within a year of the decision. Long-term investment decisions tend to differ from short-term ones in two ways: (1) the long-term investment decision usually involves a larger cash outlay and has more implications on the organization's strategy and (2) the long-term investment decision has cash-flow implications for many years.

The size and strategic implications of a long-term investment decision make those decisions much more critical to the organization. Therefore, the decision process for these investments is carefully controlled within organizations. The control aspects of the long-term investment decision are described in the next section.

The multiyear, cashflow implications of the long-term investment decision introduce additional complications in comparing the costs and benefits of the decision. Cash flows received or paid in different years are not directly comparable. The remainder of this chapter and the Appendix describe procedures used to adjust the costs and benefits form different time periods to make them comparable.

Capital Budgeting Process

L0 1   Describe the steps of the capital budgeting process.

Control Decisions

Strategy for Customer Value

Capital budgeting is a process of evaluating and choosing long-term investments. Given the size of long-term investments, the organization should take special care in making these decisions. Typically, the capital budgeting process includes (1) initiation or identification of the investment proposal, (2) ratification, (3) implementation, and (4) monitoring. These are the same decision-making steps described in Chapter Six.

The initiation process begins with the identification of possible investment opportunities. Different members of the organization can make proposals, but usually individuals with the most information initiate investment proposals. These proposals include a description of the investment opportunity and the predicted effect of the investment on cash flows. Large investment proposals often include the predicted effect on the balance sheet and income statement. Initiation is a planning process.

Once the proposal has been developed, a ratification process begins. For control purposes, different individuals in the organization are likely responsible for determining which investment proposals to accept. The parties responsible for ratifying a long-term investment proposal verify the cash-flow estimates. They also analyze the risk of the proposal. The long-term investment proposal often involves a substantial amount of cash; therefore, the organization's economic viability may be at risk.

The parties responsible for ratification also should examine competitor reaction to the proposal. Initiators of long-term investment proposals often do not identify competitors and assume that competitors will not change their behavior. In competitive markets, profitable projects are not easily found. Any investment project that appears profitable will soon have many competitors, which will drive down the original organization's future cash inflows. Therefore, the effect of competition should be recognized in estimating future cash flows. Firms must have some competitive edge, such as low-cost manufacturing, excellent researchers, or quality customer service, to be able to consistently find profitable investment projects. When analyzing investment projects, it is important to understand the source of the expected profits.

The final aspect of ratification is to ensure that the investment is consistent with the organization's strategic goals. An investment proposal may appear to be profitable but could shift the organization's emphasis away from its primary purpose. Ratification is a control process.

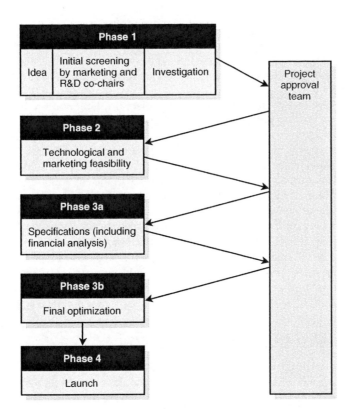

Figure 13.1

Capital Budgeting Steps at
Cyto Technologies

If the investment proposal is ratified, implementation follows. Cash and other resources are invested, and operations related to the investment begin. Implementation is a planning process.

During and subsequent to the implementation stage, the investment project is monitored. The monitoring process determines whether the investment proposal is fulfilling expectations; if it is not, the project may be closed down before the planned termination. Once the investment project is completed, an audit of the project is performed to evaluate the performance of its managers and to determine appropriate adjustments to the capital budgeting process in the future. Monitoring is a control process.

These steps in the capital budgeting process are generally followed by all organizations with some minor variations. Cyto Technologies, a biotech company, uses the process described in Figure 13.1 up to implementation.[1] Notice that there are several stages of ratification by the project approval team before the launch (implementation). The company also would have a monitoring process following the launch.

A presidential commission recently examined capital budgeting by the federal government and how it could be improved to better meet the needs of citizens and taxpayers. The study noted that the long-term benefits of such spending tended to be overlooked due to the political nature of these expenditures and the short-term focus of government decisions makers. Also, the report stated, the federal government did not have a clear policy to distinguish capital spending from operating budgets. The commission recognized two features of government spending that make the capital budget process more difficult. First, capital expenditures frequently have objectives not readily measured in financial terms, such as public welfare, defense, and foreign affairs. Second, the federal government is not subject to the same market discipline as are firms in the private sector. The commissioner's

[1]S. Kalagnanam and S. Schmidt, "Analyzing Capital Investments in New Products," *Management Accounting,* January 1996, pp. 31–36.

overall recommendations comprise four stages: Strategy and planning includes five-year plans, cost/benefit analyses of proposed spending, and integration of these strategic plans into performance plans and reviews. Decision making incorporates life cycle planning, an emphasis on improved asset management, and full funding of projects. Reporting introduces audited financial reports and asset inventories to monitor capital spending and project implementation. Evaluation includes a report card to evaluate past decisions and to determine whether projects meet preestablished benchmarks. Proposed benchmarks include returns in excess of the cost of capital, such as the interest rate on long-term government debt, the market rate expected by investors, and appropriate qualitative criteria.[2]

Management accountants perform many roles in the capital budgeting process. A management accountant usually helps put the investment proposal together. At Cyto Technologies shown in Figure 13.1, the feasibility study in Phase 2 includes a measure of the return on investment. In Phase 3, product costs are estimated and final return measures are estimated. The project approval team at Cyto Technologies includes the head of finance and accounting. Once a project is ratified, an accountant identifies, measures, and communicates information to assist the implementation process. Accounting reports also are used in the monitoring process. Management accountants should be active participants in all phases of the capital budgeting process.

Opportunity Cost of Capital

LO 2 Identify the opportunity cost of capital.

Planning Decisions

Chapter Two defined *opportunity cost* as the forgone opportunity of using a resource. The opportunity cost of using a resource depends on its alternative uses. The opportunity cost is the basis for making planning decisions. If a firm is made better off by an action, in the sense that it is not forgoing a better alternative, the proposed action is preferred.

The Chapter Two discussion of opportunity cost focused on decisions with short-term implications. The options to use labor or materials are assumed to occur during the same time period. There is no reason, however, to presume that all alternatives will occure in the same time period. One can defer accepting a current job offer and return to school for additional years of study prior to taking a job. The current stock of raw materials can be used in current production or stored and used next year. In general, all decisions have a time element. At any point in time up to accepting the pending alternative, the option of delaying or forgoing the alternative and continuing to search for better ones is always available.

Many decisions explicitly involve trading off cash inflows and cash outflows over time. For example, the decision to invest in research and development (R&D) involves postponing current cash payments to investors to fund R&D. It is hoped that the investment in R&D will lead to higher cash payments to investors in the future (when the R&D projects produce profitable new products). The decision to buy a government savings bond involves trading current consumption for future consumption. In fact, most decisions span several time periods and therefore involve cash flows over different time periods.

The decision to earn a university degree involves comparing costs and benefits over time. Instead of working and earning a salary, students pay tuition in anticipation of obtaining a higher-paying job in the future than they could now obtain. Students sacrifice current income and make payments on books and tuition to invest in their human capital to earn higher wages in the future. The sacrifices occur during the four years of study while the benefits of higher wages accrue over the remainder of their working career. The opportunity cost of going to a university includes making a full-time salary immediately. The cash flows from the various alternatives occur in different time periods.

[2]*Report of the President's Commission to Study Capital Budgeting* (Washington, D.C.: Government Printing Office, February 1999), pp. 1–61.

Calculating the opportunity cost of alternatives that involve cash flows occurring at different points of time is complicated because a dollar today is not equivalent to a dollar tomorrow. Time is money! A dollar received today can be invested and earn interest and therefore is worth more than a dollar tomorrow.

No matter the currency—yen, euros, or pounds, organizations around the globe consider the opportunity cost of cash invested in capital projects. This process requires the comparison of cash flows over time and the estimation of risk. Multinational firms also consider the political, economic, and social factors that differ across countries.

The **opportunity cost of capital** is a term used to describe the forgone opportunity of using cash. Like other resources, the opportunity cost of capital depends on whether the cash has another use and whether it is replaceable. Cash always has another use. If no other investments are available, it can be used to retire debt or pay dividends to the owners. Cash is also replaceable. Financial markets exist for issuing debt and equity. Therefore, the opportunity cost of capital is the replacement cost of cash or the cost of borrowing or issuing shares. The cost of borrowing money is the interest payment. The cost of issuing share capital is the expected return to shareholders. The opportunity cost of capital is described in terms of a percentage return or interest rate.

Not all organizations can borrow cash at the same interest rate. Those that are riskier and less likely to repay the loan must pay a higher interest rate to borrow cash. The same is true with issuing stock. Shareholders of risky stock expect a higher return than do shareholders of less risky stock. The relation between risk and the cost of capital is discussed later in the chapter. In the next few sections, the opportunity cost of capital is provided as an interest rate.

The purpose of recognizing the cost of capital is to make comparisons of cash flows over different periods of time. The ability to compare cash flows over different time spans is extremely important in evaluating investment decisions. The analysis of investment alternatives involving cash flows received or paid over time is called *capital budgeting*.

The Appendix to this chapter describes how to compare and aggregate cash flows that occur in different time periods. In general, cash now is worth more than cash in the future. The later the cash flows, the lower their present value. To compare cash flows in the future with cash flows in the present, the future cash flows must be discounted. The discount factor for a future cash flow is $(1/(1 - r)^n)$, where r is the opportunity cost of capital and n is the number of periods until the cash flow occurs. Note that the discount factor decreases with the opportunity cost of capital and the number of time periods. For example, if r equals 10% and n equals two years, the discount rate is $(1/(1 + 0.10)^2)$, or 0.826. One dollar received in two years is worth 82.6 cents today if the interest rate is 10%. If the opportunity cost of capital is higher, say 12%, and more periods are involved, say four years, the discount rate is $(1/(1 + 0.12)^4)$, or 0.636. One dollar received in four years at 12% is worth only 63.6 cents today. The capital budgeting process should consider the opportunity cost of capital and discount future cash flows for comparison with present cash flows. The next section describes methods that treat future and present cash flows in the same manner and that do not discount future cash flows.

Concept**Review**

1. What are the steps in the capital budgeting process?

2. How does the opportunity cost of capital affect long-term investment decisions?

INVESTMENT CRITERIA IGNORING THE OPPORTUNITY COST OF CAPITAL

Some managers find the discounting of future cash flows confusing or difficult. To make investment decisions, they might choose instead to use the payback method or the accounting rate of return (ROI) on an investment. These methods are described in the next section.

Payback

LO 3 Estimate the payback period of an investment and identify its weaknesses in making investment choices.

Planning Decisions

A simple method of evaluating projects is the **payback** method. Payback is the number of years or months that it takes for cash inflows from an investment to equal the initial investment cost. Suppose that a project's initial investment cost is $200,000 and subsequent yearly cash inflows are $50,000, $100,000, and $100,000, and $200,000 after taxes. This project has a payback of two and one-half years. At the end of the second year, the project has returned $150,000 ($50,000 + $100,000). The third year's cash flow is $100,000, or $50,000 per six months. Therefore, in two and one-half years, the cash inflows just equal the initial investment of $200,000. Home improvement firms implicitly use this logic to entice homeowners to update their heating systems, insulation, and windows. For example, salespeople often suggest that an investment of $2,000 in a new furnace will translate into yearly savings of $500 for heating costs. Thus, they claim that the project "pays for itself" in four years. The great advantage of payback is its simplicity. It is easy to compute and to understand. One needs no assumptions about the appropriate opportunity cost of capital for the particular project. Simplicity, however, is also payback's handicap.

Payback ignores the opportunity cost of capital. Two projects with the same payback are viewed as equally attractive, even though all the payback might occur in the last year for one project while it might be spread evenly over time for the other. For example, suppose that two projects each require $300,000 investments. One pays $100,000 for each of three years; the other pays nothing for two years and $300,000 in the third year. Each has a three-year payback, but the first is more valuable because the $100,000 payments in years 1 and 2 can be earning interest.

Payback also ignores all cash flows beyond the payback period. Thus, payback ignores the project's "profitability." Two projects with the same investments and same cash flows per year up to the payback year have the same payback. However, if one investment has no cash flows beyond the payback year and the other investment does, clearly the latter investment is better.

Finally, payback lacks a benchmark for deciding which projects to accept and which to reject. What payback cutoff should the firm use as a criterion for project selection? Is a three-year payback good or bad?

Some managers believe that it is difficult to accurately forecast cash flows beyond three or four years and that little weight should thus be placed on these cash flows. Payback simply ignores them. One criticism of U.S. managers is that they are too short-term oriented. They are not willing to take risks and look at long-term payoffs. The exclusive use of payback to evaluate investment projects motivates managers to focus on short-term cash flows and to ignore long-term rewards.

Numerical Example 13.1

A $4 million investment in a motel has expected net cash flows (cash inflows less cash outflows) of $1 million in each of the next five years. What is the investment's payback? What does the payback method ignore?

Solution

The investment has a payback of four years, but the payback ignores the cash flows in the fifth year and the time value of money.

Accounting Rate of Return

Another method for project evaluation is the accounting rate of return, which is also called the **return on investment (ROI)**. The ROI of an investment project is the accounting income from the investment divided by the cost of the investment:

ROI = Income / Investment

The ROI formula looks quite simple, but some questions arise about how to measure the numerator and denominator. For example, the choice of different accounting methods influences the income measure. There is a question of whether to include interest and taxes in estimating income. In general, interest is not included in income, but less agreement exists on the treatment of taxes. The investment also can be measured in multiple ways. For example, some companies estimate ROI using only fixed assets as a measure of investment. Other companies include all assets, such as inventories and accounts receivable, as part of the investment. The investment also can be measured at the beginning or the end of the income period or as an average over the investment's life.

The choice of how to measure income and investment for calculating the ROI should depend on how the ROI is being used. If it is used as a performance measure, the measures of income and investment should reflect controllability. If interest, taxes, current assets, or fixed assets are controllable, they should be included in the ROI calculation. If the ROI is being used for making a capital budgeting decision, comparisons should be made with the opportunity cost of capital. Interest is part of the opportunity cost of capital; thus, it should be excluded from the income figure. The investment should include all assets because of the forgone opportunity of using the cash invested in the assets for other purposes.

How to estimate ROI for an investment with income over many years is also unclear. An ROI could be measured for each year. For example, suppose a $10,000,000 investment is expected to yield income of $900,000 for each of the next five years. The straight-line depreciation method is used on the original investment, so the average investment declines each year. Table 13.1 shows the ROI for each year of this investment using the average investment each period. The ROI increases from 10% the first year to 90% the last year. The investment is not described by a single ROI; therefore, it is difficult to compare to other investments.

A multiperiod alternative of estimating the ROI of a project is to divide the average annual income over all the years by the average annual investment in the project, as shown at the top of the next page.

L0 4 Calculate the accounting rate of return (ROI) and identify its weaknesses in making investment choices.

Year	Net Income	Average Book Value of Investment	ROI
1	$900,000	$9,000,000	10%
2	900,000	7,000,000	13
3	900,000	5,000,000	18
4	900,000	3,000,000	30
5	900,000	1,000,000	90

Table 13.1

Average Net Income, Average Book Value of Investment, and Annual ROI

$$ROI = \frac{\text{Average annual income from project}}{\text{Average annual investment in the project}}$$

$$= \frac{\$900,000}{\$5,000,000}$$

$$= 18\%$$

The ROI has the advantage of being easy to calculate once income and investment have been defined. The ROI also relates to the firm's accounting statements, which are familiar to managers. The problem with ROI is that its use often can lead to incorrect investment decisions.

Decisions based on ROI are incorrect because they ignore the time value of money. In calculating the ROI, the average annual income from the project is computed. A dollar of income received today is treated the same as a dollar of income received in the future. The fact that these dollars are worth different amounts is ignored in computing accounting ROI.

ROI also relies on accounting numbers rather than cash flows. For example, depreciation is often a major component of income, but it has no cash flow implications other than its impact on income taxes. The following numerical example indicates how depreciation can influence the measurement of ROI.

Numerical Example 13.2

An investment of $300,000 generates cash inflows of $150,000 during each of the next three years. The investment is fully depreciated using the straight-line method over the three years. There are no other accrual effects, so the annual net income of the investment is $150,000 − $100,000, or $50,000. The average investment is used as the denominator to calculate the ROI. What is the ROI for each year and what is the multiyear ROI? How would the sum-of-the-years' digits method affect the calculation of ROI?

Solution

Using the straight-line method:

Year	Income	Average Investment	ROI
1	$50,000	$250,000	10%
2	50,000	150,000	33
3	50,000	50,000	100

The multiyear ROI is $50,000/$150,000, or 33%.

The sum-of-the-year's-digits method causes depreciation to be $150,000 in the first year, $100,000 in the second year, and $50,000 in the third year. Therefore, the ROI for each year is as follows:

Year	Income	Average Investment	ROI
1	$ 0	$225,000	0%
2	50,000	100,000	50
3	100,000	25,000	400

The average annual income is $50,000, but the average investment over the three years is $100,000, so the multiyear ROI is $50,000/$100,000, or 50%. Note that accounting methods affect the ROI, making it less desirable.

Concept**Review**

1. What are the limitations of using the payback method to evaluate investments?
2. How can a multiyear ROI be calculated?
3. What are the limitations of using ROI to evaluate investments?

Slim decides that he should try all methods of evaluating the investment in the frozen yogurt machine. To estimate the payback period, he first must estimate cash flows per year from his proposed investment. His original estimate of $200 of income per year includes $2,000 of depreciation expense, which does not involve any cash flow (ignoring taxes). Therefore, the cash flow per year of the $10,000 investment is estimated to be $2,200. The payback period is as follows:

$10,000/$2,200 per year = 4.55 years

The ROI of the investment is calculated by taking the average investment over the five-year investment period and dividing by the annual income. The average investment equals $10,000/2, or $5,000. The estimated annual income of $200 includes an $800 interest expense that should be eliminated. The income before deducting the interest expense is $1,000. Therefore, the ROI for the frozen yogurt machine is as follows:

ROI = $1,000/$5,000 = 20%

Slim is not sure how to interpret either of these measures and recognizes that neither method includes the opportunity cost of capital. Therefore, he decides to continue reading.

NET PRESENT VALUE OF CASH FLOWS

Capital budgeting decisions should consider the opportunity cost of capital. Future cash flows should be discounted when they are compared with present cash flows. The discounting of future cash flows is accomplished through the following equation:

LO 5   Calculate the net present value (NPV) of cash flows.

Present value = $[1/(1 + r)^n]$ × Future cash flow

Where r is the opportunity cost of capital and n is the number of time periods that separate the present and the future cash flow. The opportunity cost of capital reflects the interest rate of borrowing money for the organization.

Numerical Example 13.3

Carbon Corporation, which has an opportunity cost of capital of 10%, is considering an investment project that should yield the following cash flows:

Year from Now	Cash Inflow
1	$44,000
2	50,000
3	20,000

What is the present value of these cash inflows?

Solution

The present value of the cash inflow is based on this equation: Present value = $[1/(1 + r)^n]$ × Future cash flow.

Cash Inflow	Discount Factor	Present Value
$44,000	$1/(1 + 0.1)^1 = 0.90909$	$40,000
50,000	$1/(1 + 0.1)^2 = 0.82645$	41,322
20,000	$1/(1 + 0.1)^3 = 0.75131$	15,026
Total present value of cash inflows		$96,348

The purpose of discounting future cash flows is to compare them with present cash flows. The **net present value** of an investment proposal compares all cash inflows and outflows by discounting them to the present. An investment that has a positive net present value increases the organization's value and should be made.

An investment generally involves a cash outflow in the present with subsequent cash inflows. The initial investment outflow is already in present dollars; therefore, no need exists to discount the outflow. The present outflow can be compared to the discounted future cash inflows. In Numerical Example 13.3, the total present value of all the future cash inflows is $96,348. If the initial investment costs $100,000, the net present value is −$100,000 + $96,348, or −$3,652. The investment proposal has a negative net present value, and accepting it will reduce the organization's value. The costs (initial cash investment outflow) are higher than the benefits (discounted future cash inflows).

If the initial investment for Numerical Example 13.3 is $80,000, the net present value is −$80,000 + $96,348, or +$16,348. The investment proposal has a positive net present value and would increase the organization's value. The benefits exceed the costs of the investment.

The general rule for making long-term investment decisions is to accept proposals that have a positive net present value and reject proposals that have a negative net present value. Other nonquantifiable factors also should be considered such as the welfare of employees, the reaction of competitors, government actions, and the organization's strategic goals.

**Planning
Decisions**

Numerical Example 13.4

A new drill press costs $20,000. The annual cost savings of having it are expected to be $8,000 over the next three years. At the end of the three years, the drill press is expected to be sold for $2,000. The company's borrowing rate is 12%. What is the net present value of this investment?

Solution

Year	Cash Flows	Discount Factor	Present Value
0	($20,000)	$1/(1 + 0.12)^0 = 1.00000$	($20,000)
1	8,000	$1/(1 + 0.12)^1 = 0.89286$	7,143
2	8,000	$1/(1 + 0.12)^2 = 0.79719$	6,378
3	10,000	$1/(1 + 0.12)^3 = 0.71178$	7,118
Net present value			$ 639

The net present value of the investment in the drill press is positive. Therefore, it should be purchased.

Estimating Cash Flows for Calculating Present Values

Future cash flows are discounted and compared to present cash flows to determine the net present value of an investment. If the net present value of the proposed investment is more than zero, the investment should be undertaken. Although this concept appears straightforward, estimating future cash flows involves potential problems. Considerable information often must be gathered to make reasonable estimates of future cash flows. Cash flows beyond five years are usually difficult to predict accurately in a changing world. In addition to the uncertainty in estimating future cash flows, the factors described in the next section also affect future cash flow estimates.

LO 6 Identify noncash income accounts that should be excluded in calculating the net present value.

Discount Cash Flows, Not Accounting Earnings

Present value analysis discounts cash flows, not accounting earnings. The focus is on cash flows, not accounting earnings, because earnings contain accounting accruals and deferrals. The accounting process keeps certain cash flows out of earnings. The purchase cost of fixed assets is not treated as an expense until depreciated; that is, earnings do not contain amounts spent until the economic benefits of the investments are received. Likewise, sales are recorded when the legal liability arises, not when the cash is collected. Therefore, dollars *earned*, as computed by accounting earnings, do not reflect the dollars actually received. We discount cash flows, not accounting earnings, because cash flows can be invested in the bank and thereby generate interest. Accounting earnings, however, cannot be used to open a bank account. You cannot go to the store and buy soft drinks and pretzels with accounting earnings; only cash or an equivalent is accepted.

When United Airlines announced its bid to acquire the assets of US Airways, its stock shares fell by approximately 15%. Market investors negatively perceived the offer to pay a premium of more than 100% on the shares of US airways. While United analyzed improved future cash flows resulting from increased capital utilization and economies of scale, investors apparently were wary of the potential reduction in reported accounting earnings due to roadblocks such as labor union difficulties and differences in corporate cultures and information systems.[3]

Adjust Cash Flows to Reflect the Need for Additional Accounts Receivable and Inventory

Many businesses carry significant amounts of accounts receivable and inventories, which represent tied-up cash that could be earning interest if it were invested in the bank. Therefore, cash invested in accounts receivable and inventory should be included in the business's investment. For example, many businesses allow customers to make purchases on credit. In these cases, the business must invest additional cash to finance these outstanding accounts. Alternatively, to the extent that the firm acquires goods and services on credit, the accounts payable offsets the cash needed to finance current assets. If cash flows are estimated by adjusting earnings for depreciation and other noncash expenses, the additional amounts invested in working capital (current assets − current liabilities) must be included to derive the cash flows in the period.

LO 7 Adjust cash flows to reflect the additional accounts receivable and inventory required.

Investments in working capital can also decline as a result of new investments. Firms that implement advanced manufacturing technologies, including just-in-time (JIT) systems, frequently experience lower inventory levels and improvements in cash flows given the reduced need to finance these assets. For example, a study of more than 90 firms that had formally implemented JIT reported that more than 80% had decreased levels of raw materials and work-in-process inventories. Almost 66% of the firms indicated a decline in finished goods inventories. Overall, approximately 50% of the firms indicated that the decrease in work-in-process inventory had been significant since implementing JIT.[4]

Include Opportunity Costs but Not Sunk Costs

As in other planning decisions, opportunity costs should be used in capital budgeting. The opportunity cost of an investment might not be limited to its purchase price. A new investment project also might impose costs on other parts of the organization. For example, an investment in a new product could affect sales of other products. An investment in a new machine should consider the disposal cost of the machine being replaced. If a new investment project uses existing resources, the benefit forgone of using those resources for some other project is part of the cost of the new investment. The opportunity cost concept is still valid with capital budgeting.

---

[3]"Flying into Thin Air," *The Economist*, May 27, 2000, p. 67.

[4]R. R. Fullerton and C. S. McWatters, "The Production Performance Benefits from JIT Implementation," *Journal of Operations Management* (2001).

Sunk costs, in contrast, should be ignored in capital budgeting. If a new investment project uses resources that already have been purchased and have no other uses, the purchase price of those resources should not be included in the investment decision.

Exclude Financing Costs

LO 8   Exclude financing charges when calculating the net present value of an investment.

The interest and principal payments on debt should not be included in the discounted future cash flows. The costs of financing the project are implicitly included in discounting the future cash flows. If the project has a positive net present value, the cash flows from the project yield a return in excess of the firm's cost of capital, which more than compensates the firm for the financing costs. Dividend payments also should be excluded in calculating cash outflows.

Taxes and Depreciation Tax Shields

LO 9   Estimate tax cash flows for capital budgeting.

Taxes are usually a significant cash flow item in most discounted cash flow analyses. A corporate income tax rate of 34% implies that about one-third of any project's profitability is taxed away. Therefore, taxes and ways to minimize them become an important element in capital budgets.

Most U.S. firms use different depreciation methods for external reports for shareholders and for the Internal Revenue Service (IRS). The IRS allows firms to elect straight-line depreciation for shareholder reports and accelerated depreciation for tax returns. In Canada, the federal government's capital cost allowance (CCA) system dictates the depreciation that can be taken for tax purposes. The CCA system is also a tool of public policy that the government uses to encourage capital investment by providing accelerated depreciation for selected assets and industries. Other accounting methods also cause the income reported to shareholders to differ from the firm's taxable income. For example, the expected cost of product warranties is included in financial reports to shareholders when the product is sold. However, the cost of the warranty work is deductible for tax purposes only when the actual warranty cost is incurred. When calculating a project's net present value, it is important to use the tax accounting rules rather than the external financial reporting rules to estimate income taxes. Taxes are a cash flow. The accounting rules used to compute taxes affect tax payments. The accounting methods used only for shareholder reports, however, do not affect tax cash flows.

The primary difference between cash flows and income for tax purposes is **depreciation,** which is the allocation of the historical cost of a fixed asset over time. The depreciation of the fixed asset is treated as an expense in calculating taxable income but is not a cash outflow. The cash outflow took place when the fixed asset was acquired.

The amount of depreciation that can be recognized each year is determined by the tax code. Generally, organizations prefer to recognize as much depreciation for tax purposes as possible to reduce income and, therefore, reduce their present tax liability. Depreciation is not a cash flow but affects cash flow through the calculation of taxable income. The reduction in cash payments due to depreciation is called the **depreciation tax shield.**

Some simple algebra illustrates the indirect cash-flow effect of depreciation and the calculation of the tax shield.

Let

t = Tax rate

R = Revenue

E = All cash expenses (except depreciation)

D = Depreciation (allowed for tax purposes)

Using this notation, we can write the following familiar formulas:

$$\text{Net income} = \text{NI} = (R - E - D)(1 - t)$$
$$\text{Taxes} = \text{TAX} = (R - E - D)\,t$$
$$\begin{aligned}\text{Cash flow} = \text{CF} &= R - E - \text{TAX}\\ &= R - E - (R - E - D)\,t\\ &= (R - E)(1 - t) + D\,t\end{aligned}$$

Notice that the last term in the cash flow equation, Dt, is the depreciation tax shield. This amount is the annual depreciation charge, D, times the tax rate t. The product of the two is *added* to the annual after-tax operating net cash flow, $(R - E)$ $(1 - t)$, to arrive at the after-tax net cash flow. From the last formula, we can see that the higher the depreciation expense, the higher is the firm's cash flow because the tax liability is lower. In this sense, depreciation is said to be a tax shield since it results in lower taxes and thus, a higher after-tax cash flow. The total amount of depreciation that can be deducted from taxes is limited to the asset's original cost. Therefore, the sooner the depreciation is taken (assuming the firm has positive taxable income), the higher is the present value of the depreciation tax shield. Accelerated tax depreciation methods, which allow earlier recognition of depreciation, increase a project's net present value.

Numerical Example 13.5

An asset with a five-year life and no salvage value is purchased for $500,000. The tax rate is 34%, and the interest rate is 5%. What is the present value of the tax shields under the straight-line and double-declining-balance depreciation methods?

Solution

Table 13.2 displays the calculation of the present value of the tax shields under the straight-line and double-declining-balance depreciation methods. Double-declining-balance depreciation writes off the $500,000 original cost faster than does straight-line depreciation. Therefore, its tax shield has a higher present value by $5,061. In other words, by using double-declining-balance depreciation instead of straight-line depreciation for tax purposes, the net present value of the project is increased by $5,061. This amount represents about 1% of the asset's cost.

Adjusting the Discount Rate for Risk

In the previous sections, the opportunity cost of capital is provided as an interest rate. The opportunity cost of capital is the cost of replacing cash through borrowing or issuing stock. Some organizations are less likely to repay loans; therefore, the opportunity cost of capital is higher for some organizations than for others.

LO 10   Recognize the effect of risk on the discount rate.

Table 13.2 Comparing the Net Present Value of Depreciation Tax Shields of Straight-Line to Double-Declining-Balance Depreciation ($500,000 asset, no salvage, five-year life, 34% tax rate, 5% interest)

	Straight-Line Depreciation				Double-Declining-Balance Depreciation			
Year	Depreciation Expense	Tax Shield (Dt)	PV of Tax Shield	DDB Rate*	Book Value at Beg. of Yr.	Depreciation Expense	Tax Shield (Dt)	PV of Tax Shield
1	$100,000	$34,000	$ 32,381	0.4	$500,000	$200,000	$68,000	$ 64,762
2	100,000	34,000	30,839	0.4	300,000	120,000	40,800	37,007
3	100,000	34,000	29,370	0.4	180,000	72,000	24,480	21,147
4	100,000	34,000	27,972	0.4	108,000	43,200	14,688	12,084
5	100,000	34,000	26,640		64,800	64,800	22,032	17,263
	$500,000		$147,202			$500,000		$152,263

*DDB rate (double-declining-balance rate) is twice the straight-line rate, or 40% = 2 × ⅕.

Organizations that are riskier have a higher cost of capital than do less risky ones. Investment projects that are riskier and, therefore, make the organization riskier should be treated as having a higher cost of capital. In other words, risky projects should be discounted at higher interest rates than safe projects.

Investment projects in developing countries often are considered to be riskier yet profitable. Many of the risks involved are difficult to quantify. For example, firms are exposed to political and government instability, potential asset expropriation, loss of firm reputation, and lax standards of business conduct. These types of projects should be discounted at a higher interest rate than similar investments in advanced economies. Some firms attempt to mitigate the risks in other ways. For example, firms purchase risk insurance or outsource activities to organizations that specialize in the assumption of these operating risks.[5]

The definition of risk, its measurement, and the choice of risk-adjusted discount factors are the subject of corporate finance. We will not concern ourselves with how to derive a risk-adjusted discount rate. For any given risky cash flow stream, we assume that an equivalent risk-adjusted interest rate exists.

The risk of an investment occurs because of the uncertainty of its future cash flows. The cash inflows of an investment depend on many factors that are not perfectly predictable. Future cash flows may depend on the weather, the economy, the entry of competitors, or the fickle nature of customer demand. Since the cash flows are uncertain, one of many possible cash flows can result. Instead of discounting the highest or lowest cash flow that can occur, we discount the **expected** (or average) **cash flow**. For example, if the cash flows next year can be either $100 or $200 with equal probability, we would discount the expected cash flow of $150. The expected cash flows should be discounted using a risk-adjusted discount rate appropriate for the risk inherent in the project.

In its first quarter report for 2000, Nortel Networks describes the discount rate used for capital budgeting as follows: "The discount rates used to discount projected net returns were based on a weighted average cost of capital relative to Nortel Networks and the high technology industry, as well as the product-specific risk. . . . Product-specific risk includes the stage of completion of each project, the complexity of the development work completed to date, the likelihood of achieving technical feasibility, and market acceptance." Along with this information, Nortel emphasizes that its forecasts are based on assumptions that are "inherently uncertain and unpredictable." In its *2000 First Quarter Report*, Nortel reports discount rates of 21 and 22 for various projects. These rates reflect the fact that Nortel operates in a "highly volatile and rapidly growing industry which is characterized by vigorous competition for market share and rapid technological development carried out amidst uncertainty over adoption of industry standards and protection of intellectual property rights." As a result of aggressive competition and short product life cycles, it is also Nortel's practice to integrate all projects and acquisitions into its businesses. It does not track these projects independently, making the determination of their long-term impact more difficult.[6]

Concept**Review**

1. Why should cash flows rather than future earnings be discounted?
2. Why should accounts receivable and inventory levels be considered when making a capital budgeting decision?
3. Why should finance charges not be included when making a capital budgeting decision?
4. Why does depreciation act as a tax shield?

---

[5]"Doing Business in Difficult Places," *The Economist*, May 20, 2000, pp. 85–88.
[6]Nortel Networks Limited, *2000 First Quarter Report*, March 31, 2000, pp. 10, 32, and 39.

5. How does the risk of the investment project affect the discount rate used for capital budgeting?

Slim now knows how to calculate the net present value of the investment in the frozen yogurt machine, but he must reconsider his estimate of cash flows before discounting them. He realizes that the machine is not the only investment that he must make to provide his customers with frozen yogurt. He also must have some ingredients on hand to make the frozen yogurt, but he estimates that the amount of extra ingredients that he will need to hold is relatively small. He decides not to worry about that cost.

SLIM'S ICE CREAM PARLOR
(Continued)

Slim also realizes that the opportunity cost of capital is implicitly included in the discounting process. The annual interest payments of $800 should not be included in the discounted cash flow estimates. The 8% interest rate does appear to be the correct risk-adjusted interest rate.

The space to be taken by the frozen yogurt machine had no alternative use, so no facility costs are applied to the investment project. Slim needs, however, to consider the potential effect of the frozen yogurt on the sales of his other products. After careful consideration, he decides that the net effect of selling frozen yogurt on his other products will be approximately zero. Some ice cream buyers will switch to frozen yogurt, but having frozen yogurt will bring in more customers, some who will buy ice cream.

Slim has forgotten to adjust his cash flow estimates for tax effects. The taxable income is $200 and the tax rate for Slim is 30%. Therefore, he must pay annual taxes of ($200) (0.30), or $60. Slim's annual cash flow analysis after eliminating the depreciation and interest and adding the income taxes is as follows:

Revenues from selling frozen yogurt	$ 5,000
Cost of ingredients	(1,500)
Additional utility costs	(500)
Income taxes at 30% (0.30) ($200)	(60)
Cash flows per year for five years	$ 2,940
Initial investment	$10,000

Slim then estimates the present value of these cash flows over the next five years using a discount rate of 8%.

Year	Cash Flows	Discount Factor	Present Value
0	($10,000)	$1/(1 + 0.08)^0 = 1.00000$	($10,000)
1	2,940	$1/(1 + 0.08)^1 = 0.92593$	2,722
2	2,940	$1/(1 + 0.08)^2 = 0.85734$	2,520
3	2,940	$1/(1 + 0.08)^3 = 0.79383$	2,334
4	2,940	$1/(1 + 0.08)^4 = 0.73503$	2,161
5	2,940	$1/(1 + 0.08)^5 = 0.68058$	2,001
Net present value			$ 1,738

Based on the calculation of a positive net present value of $1,738, Slim is pleased to invest in the frozen yogurt machine.

Korean *Chaebols* and the "Next Generation" of DRAM Chips

Korean *chaebols* (large conglomerates) have invested heavily in the production of computer chips. Samsun, Hyundai, and LG have all been players in the market for 64-megabit DRAM chips. The business is extremely competitive with severe swings in prices as demand increases and decreases. After a downturn in 1996, market sales reached record high levels in 1999, increasing by almost 50% from the previous year. Most of the companies in the business still are trying to recover their investments in their old fabrication plants, which cost up to $1.5 billion (U.S.).

The industry, however, is dynamic, with emerging customer needs. While demand for PC chips is strong, demand for chips suitable in wireless communications has triggered a surge in the market. Computer makers now want 256-megabit DRAM chips. Industry watchers are uncertain about which producers can afford the move to the next generation of DRAM chips. The cost of a new fabrication plant and equipment to make the next generation of chips is estimated to be more than $3 billion. In 1999, Intel reported capital expenditures of more than $3 billion for chip-making plants and $3.1 billion in related research and development (R&D). NEC of Japan is likely to follow Intel's investment. Many firms are forging global alliances with these market leaders to share the R&D costs, reduce production costs, and create a global standard. The question is which Korean *chaebol*, if any, will make the investment. With recent investments in process improvements, the Koreans have been able to offset price fluctuations with higher production yields. Some estimates give these firms about a 20% cost advantage over their Japanese competitors, but exchange rates can change rapidly. The Koreans have a difficult capital budgeting decision.

If the opportunity of cost of capital is 15%, how much in annual cash flows above operating expenses must the new fabrication plants generate just to break even? What are the strategic implications of not investing in fabrication plants to make the next-generation chips?

Sources:

INTERNAL RATE OF RETURN

LO 11 Estimate the internal rate of return (IRR) of an investment project.

Planning Decisions

The internal rate of return method finds the interest rate that equates the initial investment cost to the future discounted cash flows. In other words, the internal rate of return makes the net present value equal to zero. If the project's internal rate of return exceeds a certain cut-off rate (e.g., the project's cost of capital), the project should be undertaken. On the surface, the **internal rate of return (IRR)** method for comparing different projects appears to be similar to the net present value (NPV) method.

The IRR is quite easy to calculate if an initial cash outflow (the cost of the investment) is followed by a cash inflow in one year. For example, suppose a firm can invest $1,000 today and receive $1,070 in a year. The internal rate of return (IRR) sets the investment cost equal to the discounted future cash flow:

$$\text{Investment cost} = (\text{Cash inflows in one year})/(1 + \text{IRR})$$

$$\$1,000 = \frac{\$1,070}{1 + \text{IRR}}$$

$$(1 + \text{IRR}) = \frac{\$1,070}{\$1,000}$$

$$\text{IRR} = 0.07 = 7\%$$

In this simple example, the internal rate of return on an investment of $1,000 today that generates a $1,070 payment in one year is 7%. If the cost of capital is 5%, clearly this investment offers a return in excess of its opportunity cost. The NPV of this investment is as follows:

$$\text{NPV} = -\$1,000 + \frac{\$1,070}{1.05}$$

$$= -\$1,000 + \$1,019.05$$

$$= \$19.05$$

If the IRR exceeds the opportunity cost of capital, the NPV of the investment is positive, and the investment should be undertaken. If the IRR is less than the opportunity cost of capital, the NPV of the investment is negative, and the investment should be rejected.

The advantage of the IRR method is that an investment project's return is stated as an interest rate. For some people, saying that a project's return is 14% is clearer than saying a project has a net present value of some monetary amount such as $628,623.

However, the IRR and NPV methods do not always give consistent answers. The IRR and the NPV potentially will lead to different investment decisions if investments are mutually exclusive. Mutually exclusive investments involve a group of investments of which only one can be chosen. For example, a manufacturing firm usually chooses only one of many possible methods to make a part. With mutually exclusive investments, a manager would like to rank the alternative investments. Consider the following two *mutually exclusive* investments:

LO 12   Identify problems with using the internal rate of return to evaluate investment projects.

1. Invest $1,000 today and receive $1,070 in a year.
2. Invest $5,000 today and receive $5,300 in one year.

We know that investment 1 has an IRR of 7% and an NPV of $19.05. The IRR of investment 2 is as follows:

$$\$5,000 = \$5,300/(1 + IRR)$$
$$(1 + IRR) = \frac{\$5,300}{\$5,000}$$
$$IRR = 0.06 = 6\%$$

Investment 2's NPV follows:

$$NPV = -\$5,000 + \frac{\$5,300}{1.05}$$
$$= -\$5,000 + \$5,047.62$$
$$= \$47.62$$

Which investment is better? The IRR criterion says investment 1 is better because it has the higher IRR. The NPV criterion says investment 2 is better because it has the higher NPV. How should a person decide? Which is more valuable, a rate of return or cash? Net present value indicates how much cash in today's dollars an investment is worth, or the *magnitude* of the investment's return. The IRR indicates only the *relative* return on the investment. A 20% return on $1,000 ($20) is preferable to a 200% return on $1 ($2).

The NPV and IRR methods also may rank investment projects differently due to a difference in the length of time or duration of cash flows. Consider the following two *mutually exclusive* investments:

1. Invest $1,000 today and receive $1,200 in one year.
2. Invest $1,000 today and receive $1,500 in three years.

The NPV of these two projects for different discount rates is presented in Figure 13.2. The IRR of each of the two investments is the discount rate where each line crosses the *x* axis. For the first investment, the IRR equals 20%. For the second investment, the IRR is between 14% and 15%. Even though the IRR of the first investment is higher, the NPV of the second investment is higher if the discount rate is below 12%. Above 12%, the NPV of the first investment is higher.

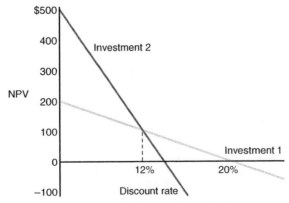

Investment 1: Invest $1,000 today and receive $1,200 in one year.
Investment 2: Invest $1,000 today and receive $1,500 in three years.

Figure 13.2

Comparing the NPV of Two Investments

The net present values in Figure 13.2 decline as the discount rate rises because only the cash inflows are affected by the change in the discount rate. The cash outflows occur in the present; hence, they are not affected by the discount rate. The cash inflows, however, occur in the future, and their present values will decline with an increase in the discount rate. The NPV of investment 2 declines more rapidly because the present value of cash flows in the more distant future is more sensitive to changes in the discount rate.

Perhaps the most serious problem with the IRR method is its implicit assumption regarding the *reinvestment rate*. The reinvestment rate is the interest rate used to compound cash flows received or paid over the life of the project. In the discounted cash flow method, each cash flow is discounted at the opportunity cost of capital. The implicit assumption is that intermediate cash flows are being reinvested at the opportunity cost of capital. If the opportunity cost of capital is expected to be higher or lower in future years, nonconstant discount rates can be used. The IRR method assumes that all intermediate cash flows are being automatically reinvested at the project's constant IRR. Thus, the IRR method implicitly assumes that all the intermediate cash flows can be invested in a stock of projects identical to the one being considered and that the same IRR can be achieved. If the current project is a one-time opportunity, then there are no future projects like it in which to reinvest the current project's cash flows. Therefore, the IRR method overstates a project's rate of return if other investments with the same reinvestment rate do not exist. This serious problem with the IRR makes its use dangerous to evaluate alternative investments.

Another problem that may arise with the IRR occurs when an organization sets a hurdle rate higher than the cost of capital. A **hurdle rate** is a benchmark that an organization establishes as an investment criterion. To be acceptable, the planned IRR must be higher than the hurdle rate. For example, an organization may establish a hurdle rate of 20% but its cost of capital is 10%. The organization accepts only those investment proposals with a hurdle rate higher than 20%, but the organization is forgoing the opportunity to invest in projects with an IRR between 10% and 20%, which have positive NPVs.

In summary, the IRR provides the correct decision rule for investments if the cost of capital is used as the benchmark. If the IRR is higher than the cost of capital, the investment should be made. The IRR fails, however, to duplicate the NPV ranking of mutually exclusive investment projects. In addition, requiring investment projects to exceed a hurdle rate that is higher than the cost of capital forgoes the opportunity to invest in positive NPV projects. Therefore, the IRR should be used with caution.

The IRR is not always easy to calculate if unequal cash inflows occur over multiple years. Computers can solve for the IRR, but a trial-and-error method also can be used to approximate it. The trial-and-error method calculates the NPV for a particular discount rate. If the NPV is positive, a higher discount rate is tried. If the NPV is negative, a lower discount is tried. This process continues until a discount rate is found that results in an NPV value of approximately zero.

Numerical Example   13.6

A company is considering an investment that requires an initial cash outlay of $100,000. The investment is expected to return $70,000 in the first year and $55,000 in the second year. What is the investment's IRR?

Solution

An initial estimate of 10% gives the following NPV:

$$-\$100{,}000 + (\$70{,}000/(1 + 0.1)) + (\$55{,}000/(1 + 0.1)^2) = \$9{,}090$$

The NPV (at 10%) is positive; thus, a higher estimate for the IRR, say 20%, is used:

$$-\$100{,}000 + (\$70{,}000/(1 + 0.2)) + (\$55{,}000/(1 + 0.2)^2) = -\$3{,}473$$

The NPV (at 20%) is negative; thus, a lower estimate for the IRR, say, 17%, is used:

$$-\$100,000 + (\$70,000/(1 + 0.17)) + (\$55,000/(1 + 0.17)^2) = \$7$$

This NPV (at 17%) is very close to zero, so the IRR is approximately 17%.

Concept**Review**

1. How is the internal rate of return (IRR) determined?

2. What are some problems in using the IRR to evaluate investments?

Slim is thrilled with his new skills in using the time value of money, so he decides to calculate the IRR of the frozen yogurt machine. He uses the trial-and-error method and begins with his interest rate of 8% to calculate the NPV.

SLIM'S ICE CREAM PARLOR
(Continued)

Discount Rate	Net Present Value
8%	$1,738
10	1,146
12	599
14	93
16	(374)

You decide

Slim finds that the IRR is a little higher than 14%, which exceeds his opportunity cost of capital.

CAPITAL BUDGETING METHODS USED IN PRACTICE

The discounting of cash flows to make capital budgeting decisions has become common practice.[7] By the mid-1960s, about one-third of large companies used discounted cash flow methods. Today, almost every large company uses them. Discounted cash flow methods include both net present value and internal rate of return. In the survey referred to, the IRR was more commonly used than was the NPV. As described earlier, the IRR rate of return does not always rank projects in the same order as NPV. Given the survey findings, however, this disadvantage of the IRR seems to be less important than its intuitive appeal.

The following reasons likely account for this trend toward using discounting methods: (1) they are theoretically superior, (2) they are a mainstay in business school curricula, and (3) inexpensive calculators and PCs are available with programs that compute NPV and IRR. Finally, when interest rates are high, as they were in the 1980s, discounting methods are more critical in comparing dollars from different time periods.

Technology has had a major impact on organizations. For example, computers have made discounted cash-flow techniques common practice, enabling firms to quickly estimate the financial return of capital projects. Specialized software also permits firms to evaluate the costs and benefits of investment opportunities and their contribution to organizational value.

---

[7]T. Klammer, B. Koch, and N. Wilner, "Capital Budgeting Practices—A Survey of Corporate Use," *Journal of Management Accounting Research*, Fall 1991, pp. 113–30.

SUMMARY

1 **Describe the steps of the capital budgeting process.** The steps of the capital budgeting process include initiation, ratification, implementation, and monitoring.

2 **Identify the opportunity cost of capital.** The opportunity cost of capital is the forgone opportunity of using cash, which is the interest rate on borrowing money to replace the cash.

3 **Estimate the payback period of an investment and identify its weaknesses in making investment choices.** The payback period is the time required for the investment to generate cash flows equal to the initial investment. The payback method does not consider the time value of money or cash flows beyond the payback period.

4 **Calculate the accounting rate of return (ROI) and identify its weaknesses in making investment choices.** The accounting rate of return, or ROI, is the average income from a project divided by the average investment cost. The ROI is an accounting measure and does not consider the time value of money.

5 **Calculate the net present value (NPV) of cash flows.** The NPV of cash flows is calculated by discounting all future cash flows to the present and comparing the present value of the cash inflows with the present value of the cash outflows.

6 **Identify noncash income accounts that should be excluded in calculating the net present value.** Cash, not accounting income, should be discounted to estimate the NPV of an investment. Income items such as depreciation do not affect cash flows.

7 **Adjust cash flows to reflect the additional accounts receivable and inventory required.** New investments often require increased amounts of accounts receivable and inventory. Increases in accounts receivable and inventory resulting from a new investment should be treated as part of the investment cost.

8 **Exclude financing charges when calculating the net present value of an investment.** Interest and principal payments on debt should not be included in discounting future cash flows because the discounting implicitly includes financing charges.

9 **Estimate tax cash flows for capital budgeting.** Taxes are an important part of cash flow estimates. Noncash expenses, such as depreciation, do affect cash flows indirectly through their effect on taxable income.

10 **Recognize the effect of risk on the discount rate.** The cash flows of higher risk investment projects should be discounted at a higher interest rate.

11 **Estimate the internal rate of return (IRR) of an investment project.** The IRR is the discount rate that sets the NPV of the cash flows equal to zero.

12 **Identify problems with using the internal rate of return to evaluate investment projects.** The IRR and NPV do not always rank investment projects in the same manner. The difference in rankings could be due to the relative size of the investment and the duration of the cash flows. In addition, the IRR method assumes that intermediate cash flows can be reinvested at the internal rate of return.

13 **Use annuity tables to relate present and future values. (Appendix)** The annuity tables allow for the calculation of the present value and future value of constant streams of cash over finite periods.

KEY TERMS

capital budgeting   A process of evaluating and choosing long-term investments. (*p. 458*)

depreciation   The allocation of the historical cost of a fixed asset over time. (*p. 468*)

depreciation tax shield   The reduction in taxes due to the decrease in taxable income from depreciation. (*p. 468*)

expected cash flow   The sum of each cash flow that can occur weighted by its probability of occurrence. (*p. 470*)

hurdle rate   The benchmark rate of return that is established by the organization as an investment criterion. (*p. 474*)

internal rate of return (IRR)   The discount rate that makes the net present value of an investment equal to zero. (*p. 472*)

net present value (NPV)   The net present value of cash flows is calculated by discounting all future cash flows to the present and comparing the present value of the cash inflows with the present value of the cash outflows. (*p. 466*)

opportunity cost of capital   The forgone opportunity of using cash for another purpose. (*p. 461*)

payback   The time required to generate cash inflows equal to the initial investment. (*p. 462*)

return on investment (ROI)   The income divided by the assets generating the income. (*p. 463*)

APPENDIX

Interest Rate Mathematics

This Appendix develops the mathematical relations for converting cash flows received or paid at different times. By deriving the various formulas, the logic of the calculations is made clearer. In the following examples, the interest rate is given. Determining the appropriate interest rate to relate dollars from different time periods is discussed in the chapter.

LO 13 Use annuity tables to relate present and future values.

Future Values

The *future value* of cash today is the initial amount plus interest that is earned during the interim period. If we assume an interest rate of 5% and an initial investment of $1,000, the future value of the $1,000 in one year is the initial investment of $1,000 plus interest of $50 (5% of $1,000), or $1,050. What is the future value of $1,000 in two years with an interest rate of 5%? At the end of the first year, one has $1,050 ($1,000 principal plus $50 of interest). This amount is then reinvested to yield $1,102.50 ($1,050 principal plus interest of $52.50). Of the $52.50 of interest in the second year, $50 is interest on the original $1,000 and $2.50 is interest on the first year's interest ($50 × 5%). Or at the end of the second year the value of the investment is

$$\$1,000 + 2(0.05 \times \$1,000) + [0.05 \times (0.05 \times \$1,000)] =$$
$$\$1,000 + \$100 + \$2.50 = \$1,102.50$$

The fact that interest is earned on the interest in the second year is called *compounding*. The formulas that we will derive are often called *compound interest formulas*. The future value of $1 at different interest rates for different periods of time is provided in Table 13A.5 on page 487.

We now will generalize the preceding illustration. Let PV represent the amount of money invested today at r% per year and let FV represent the amount that will be available at the end of the two years. The general formula relating present dollars to dollars in two years at r% per year is as follows:

$$PV (1 + r)^2 = PV (1 + 2r + r^2) = FV$$

The $2r$ term represents interest for two years on the original investment of PV, and r^2 is the interest on the interest (compound interest). The general formula for leaving money in the bank for n years and allowing the interest to accumulate and earn interest is as follows:

$$PV (1 + r)^n = FV \qquad \text{(Future value formula)}$$

All of the formulas of interest rate mathematics are simple algebraic manipulations of this basic formula.

Numerical Example 13A.1

A mother, who recently gave birth to a daughter, has decided to put $1,000 in the bank for her daughter's university fund. The fund earns 6% a year for 18 years before being withdrawn from the bank. How much will the $1,000 be worth in 18 years?

Solution

$$PV (1 + r)^n = FV$$
$$\$1,000(1 + 0.06)^{18} = \$2,854 = FV$$

The $1,000 will be worth $2,854 in 18 years.

Present Values

Suppose that instead of asking how much money a person will have at the end of n years, the person asks how much money must be invested today at r% per year to have a defined future value at a specific future point in time? For example, how much money must be invested today, at a 5% interest rate, to be able to buy a $25,000 boat in six years? The amount of money that must be invested today to equal a certain amount in the future at a given interest rate is called the *present value* (PV). In present value calculations, the future value (FV) and interest rate (r) are known, but present value (PV) is unknown. Rearranging the future value formula yields the present value formula:

$$PV = \frac{FV}{(1 + r)^n} \qquad \text{(Present value formula)}$$

To solve for the boat example,

$$PV = \frac{\$25,000}{(1 + 0.05)^6}$$
$$= \frac{\$25,000}{1.3401}$$
$$= \$18,655$$

Therefore, if an individual invests $18,655 in the bank at 5% and allows the principal and interest to compound, at the end of six years that person will have $25,000. The present value of $1 received at different time periods in the future at different rates is provided in Table 13A.3 on page 485.

Numerical Example 13A.2

A recent university graduate would like to go back to school in 10 years and earn an MBA. He estimates that a two-year MBA degree will cost $70,000 in 10 years. He can put money in a bank that will earn 5% annually for the next 10 years. How much money will he have to put in the bank to have $70,000 in 10 years?

Solution

$$PV = \frac{FV}{(1 + r)^n}$$
$$= \$70,000/(1 + 0.05)^{10}$$
$$= \$42,974$$

The university graduate must deposit $42,974 in the bank today to have $70,000 in 10 years.

Present Value of a Cash Flow Stream

The future value and present value formulas (which are the same formula) allow for the comparison of cash flows from different time periods. So far, we have been dealing with just a single cash flow invested today or received in the future. Now suppose a person has a series of cash flows occurring *at the end of each year* for the next n years. That is, FV_1 is the cash received at the end of the first year, FV_2 is the cash received at the end of the second year, and FV_n is the cash received at the end of the nth year. What is the present value of this cash flow stream? Apply the preceding present value formula to each cash flow and sum them:

$$PV = \frac{FV_1}{(1 + r)^1} + \frac{FV_2}{(1 + r)^2} + \frac{FV_3}{(1 + r)^3} + \cdots + \frac{FV_n}{(1 + r)^n}$$

Suppose the individual is offered $500 at the end of the first year, $1,000 at the end of the second year, and $1,500 at the end of the third year. How much is this stream of cash flows worth today? Using the preceding formula:

$$PV = \frac{\$500}{(1 + 0.05)^1} + \frac{\$1,000}{(1 + 0.05)^2} + \frac{\$1,500}{(1 + 0.05)^3}$$

$$= \frac{\$500}{1.05} + \frac{\$1,000}{1.1025} + \frac{\$1,500}{1.157625}$$

$$= \$476 + \$907 + \$1,296$$

$$= \$2,679$$

Therefore, the person would be indifferent between receiving the cash flow stream of $500, $1,000, and $1,500 in the next three years and $2,678.98 today if the interest rate is 5%.

Each of the cash flows, FV_t, is said to be *discounted* (or divided) by $(1 + r)^t$ where t is the year in which the cash flow is received. Notice that $1 \div (1 + r)^t$ is always less than 1 for all positive interest rates. Therefore, a dollar received in the future is worth less than a dollar today. We will see that discounting is central to the concept of comparing alternatives involving cash flows received at different points of time. By discounting the future cash flows from each alternative to present values (or dollars today), we then can determine which alternative is best.

Numerical Example 13A.3

An insurance company is offering a new retirement policy. It is willing to pay $100,000 in 30 years, another $200,000 in 40 years, and a final payment of $300,000 in 50 years. What is the value of this retirement policy now to someone with an annual interest rate of 8%, assuming the person knows with certainty that he or she will live another 50 years?

Solution

$$PV = \$100,000/(1 + 0.08)^{30} + \$200,000/(1 + 0.08)^{40} + \$300,000/(1 + 0.08)^{50}$$

$$PV = \$9,938 + \$9,206 + \$6,396 = \$25,540$$

The present value of the retirement policy is $25,540.

Perpetuities

A *perpetuity* is an infinite stream of equal payments received each year. Some government bonds issued by the British government promise to pay a fixed amount of cash each year forever. How much would investors be willing to pay for such bonds? All of the future payments, FV_1, FV_2, . . . , FV_n are the same and equal to FV. Substituting FV into the general formula yields the following:

$$PV = \frac{FV}{(1 + r)^1} + \frac{FV}{(1 + r)^2} + \frac{FV}{(1 + r)^3} + \cdots$$

$$= \left(\frac{FV}{1 + r}\right)\left(1 + \frac{1}{(1 + r)^1} + \frac{1}{(1 + r)^2} + \frac{1}{(1 + r)^3} + \cdots\right)$$

From algebra, we know that the sum of an infinite series has the following expression:

$$\left(1 + \frac{1}{(1 + r)^1} + \frac{1}{(1 + r)^2} + \frac{1}{(1 + r)^3} + \cdots\right) = \frac{1 + r}{r}$$

Substituting this term into the preceding formula gives

$$PV = \left(\frac{FV}{1 + r}\right)\left(\frac{1 + r}{r}\right)$$

$$PV = \frac{FV}{r} \qquad\qquad \text{(Perpetuity formula)}$$

This formula is the basic one for a perpetuity, or an infinite cash flow stream, when the interest rate is $r\%$. If the British government bonds pay 100 pounds (£) per year in perpetuity and the interest rate is 5%, then investors would be willing to pay:

$$PV = \frac{£100}{0.05}$$
$$= £2.000$$

Numerical Example 13A.4

Antonio's eccentric aunt just died. He learned that he was included in her will. Instead of a lump-sum payment, however, she left Antonio an unusual contract through an insurance company, which must pay him $1,000 per year beginning at the end of this year for an infinite number of years. Before Antonio dies, he can designate an heir to continue to receive these $1,000 payments. What is the present value of the contract if the interest rate is 8%?

Solution

$$PV = \frac{FV}{r}$$

$$PV = \$1,000/0.08 = \$12,500$$

The present value of the contract equals $12,500.

Annuities

An *annuity* is a stream of *equal* cash flows for a *fixed* number of years. Many financial instruments are annuities. For example, car loans and mortgage payments involve a fixed number of equal monthly payments. Corporate bonds pay a fixed amount twice a year over the term of the bond (usually 20 years). To derive the formula for an annuity, let FV again denote the annual cash flow received at the end of each of the next n years. The present value of an annuity of n cash flows of FV each is as follows:

$$PV = \frac{FV}{(1 + r)^1} + \frac{FV}{(1 + r)^2} + \frac{FV}{(1 + r)^3} + \cdots \frac{FV}{(1 + r)^n}$$

This formula can be rearranged into the following formula:[8]

$$PV = FV\left(\frac{(1 + r)^n - 1}{r(1 + r)^n}\right) \qquad \text{(Present value of annuity formula)}$$

---

[8] To derive the formula for this annuity stream, notice that mathematically, an annuity is equivalent to the difference between the following two streams:

Year	0	1	2	3	$\cdots$	n	$n + 1$	$n + 2$	$\cdots$
Cash flow 1	0	FV	FV	FV	$\cdots$	FV	FV	FV	$\cdots$
Cash flow 2	0	0	0	0	$\cdots$	0	FV	FV	$\cdots$

That is, an annuity cash flow stream = cash flow stream 1 − cash flow stream 2. We know how to value cash flow stream 1 using the perpetuity formula:

$$\text{Present value of cash flow 1} = \frac{FV}{r}$$

The present value of cash flow stream 2 is as follows:

$$\text{Present value of cash flow 2} = \left(\frac{1}{(1 + r)^n}\right)\left(\frac{FV}{r}\right)$$

That is, the present value of cash flow stream 2 is the present value of a perpetuity discounted back from n years because the first perpetuity payment is not received for n years. The first term in the preceding formula discounts the value of the perpetuity to recognize that the first payment is not received immediately. Now take the difference between the two formulas:

$$PV \text{ of an annuity} = PV \text{ of cash-flow stream 1} - PV \text{ of cash-flow stream 2}$$

$$= \frac{FV}{r} - \left(\frac{1}{(1 + r)^n}\right)\left(\frac{FV}{r}\right)$$

$$= FV\left(\frac{(1 + r)^n - 1}{r(1 + r)^n}\right) \qquad \text{(Present value of annuity formula)}$$

To illustrate the application of the formula, suppose you can afford to pay $1,000 per year for 10 years. How large a loan can you take today? The interest rate is 5%. Using our annuity formula, we get the following:

$$PV = \$1,000 \left(\frac{(1.05)^{10} - 1}{0.05(1.05)^{10}}\right)$$

$$= \$1,000 \left(\frac{0.628895}{0.081445}\right)$$

$$= \$7,722$$

Therefore, the bank will lend $7,722 today, with payments of $1,000 per year for 10 years.

Another useful formula is the future value of an annuity. For example, if a person invests $1,000 a year for 18 years, how much money will this person have for a child's university education? We start with the present value of an annuity and then convert this amount to a future value by taking the present value formula for an annuity and multiplying it by $(1 + r)^n$, or

$$\text{Future value of annuity} = FV\left(\frac{(1 + r)^n - 1}{r(1 + r)^n}\right)(1 + r)^n$$

$$= FV\left(\frac{(1 + r)^n - 1}{r}\right) \quad \text{(Future value of annuity formula)}$$

To solve for how much money this will supply for the child's education, we substitute into the preceding formula:

$$\$1,000 \left(\frac{(1.05)^{18} - 1}{0.05}\right)$$

$$= \$1,000 (28.132)$$

$$= \$28,132$$

Therefore, with interest left to accumulate in the bank, the person will have more than $28,000 by investing $1,000 a year for 18 years at an interest rate of 5%. The future and present values of a $1 annuity for different interest rates and different periods of time are presented in Tables 13A.6 (p. 488) and 13A.4 (p. 486), respectively.

Numerical Example   **13A.5**

Karen Wu is considering the purchase of a home. She wants to borrow $100,000 from the bank. Instead of the normal monthly mortgage payments, the bank is willing to let Karen repay the loan in equal annual payments at 12% interest over the next 20 years. How much will Karen have to pay each year?

Solution

$$PV = FV\left(\frac{(1 + r)^n - 1}{r(1 + r)^n}\right) \quad \text{or} \quad FV = PV/\left(\frac{(1 + r)^n - 1}{r(1 + r)^n}\right)$$

$$FV = \$100,000/(((1 + 0.12)^{20} - 1)/(0.12(1 + 0.12)^{20}))$$

$$FV = \$13,388$$

Karen will have to pay $13,388 at the end of each of the next 20 years.

Multiple Cash Flows Per Year

So far we have considered cash flows that occur only once per year. How do we handle cash flows that occur more frequently, say monthly? We could add up the monthly flows and treat them as a single annual cash flow on the last day of the year, yet this ignores the interest that we could earn on the monthly receipts. To illustrate, consider the difference between the following two options: (1) receiving 12 monthly payments or (2) receiving a single $12,000 payment at the end of the year. Before we can calculate which option is worth more, we first must understand the relation between monthly and annual interest rates. If the annual interest rate is 5%, what is the interest rate per month? You might be tempted to say $0.05 \div 12 = 0.004166$, but this is wrong. A dollar invested at the monthly interest rate, r_m, must accumulate to the same amount at the end of the year as a dollar invested at the annual interest rate, r. Therefore, the following formula must hold:

$$(1 + r_m)^{12} = (1 + r)$$
$$(1 + r_m) = (1 + r)^{1/12}$$
$$r_m = (1 + r)^{1/12} - 1$$
$$= (1.05)^{1/12} - 1$$
$$= 0.004074$$

Now we can return to the original question and value the two options. The monthly interest rate just derived is 0.004074, and the annual interest rate is 0.05. Using the present value of the annuity formula to calculate the stream of 12 monthly $1,000 payments,

$$FV = \left(\frac{(1 + r)^n - 1}{r(1 + r)^n} \right) = \$1,000 \left(\frac{(1.004074)^{12} - 1}{0.004074(1.004074)^{12}} \right)$$
$$= \$1,000 \left(\frac{1.05 - 1}{0.004074(1.05)} \right)$$
$$= \$1,000 \, (11.68817)$$
$$= \$11,688.17$$

The present value of the single $12,000 payment is

$$\frac{FV}{(1 + r)^n} = \frac{\$12,000}{(1.05)^1} = \$11,428.57$$

Therefore, the 12 payments of $1,000 are worth $259.60 more today than a single $12,000 payment at an annual interest rate of 5%.

The preceding example illustrates that the earlier a payment is received, the more valuable it is. The example also introduces the notion of the *compounding interval*, which is the period of time when interest is calculated and then compounded in the next period. The compounding interval could be a year, a month, or a day. The key point is that the annual interest rate cannot be used to discount cash flows received more frequently than yearly. Some banks quote interest rates in annual terms, say 5%, but then compound the interest monthly. In this case, the *effective* annual interest rate is as follows:

$$\left(1 + \frac{r}{12} \right)^{12} - 1 = \left(1 + \frac{0.05}{12} \right)^{12} - 1$$
$$= (1.0041666667)^{12} - 1$$
$$= 0.05116$$

Therefore, if the bank has a stated annual interest rate of 5% but compounds monthly, the *effective* interest rate is 5.116%. If the bank states that its interest rate is 5% but compounds interest *daily*, the *effective* annual rate is 5.127%.[9] The preceding discussion illustrates that depositors who want the highest *effective* interest rate always choose the shortest compounding interval among banks offering the same stated annual interest rate.

It is not necessary to memorize the major formulas for converting cash flow streams into either present or future values. Appendix tables on pp. 485-488 contain the present and future values that correspond to the formulas. These tables greatly simplify the computation of present values. Also, most computer spreadsheet

---

[9] $0.05127 = \left(1 + \dfrac{0.05}{365} \right)^{365} - 1$

	Cash flow In	Discount Factor	Source of Factor	Present Value
Years 1–20	$1,000	12.462	Table 13A.4	$12,462
Years 1–10	1,000	7.722	Table 13A.4	7,722
Year 21	3,000	0.359	Table 13A.3	1,077
Total present value				$21,261

Table 13A.1

Example of Using Compound Interest Tables (Interest rate = 5%)

		Net Cash Flow	Discount Factor	Present Value
Years 1–2	Forgone wages + cost of school	($45,000)	1.859	($ 83,655)
Years 1–30	Additional wages with MBA	55,000	15.372	845,460
Years 1–2	Higher MBA wages not earned in first two years*	(55,000)	1.859	(102,245)
Net present value				$659,560

Table 13A.2

Decision to Obtain an MBA Degree

*The present value of $55,000 for two years is being deducted in this line because the line above includes the first two years.

programs and pocket calculators compute present values and future values. For example, suppose you want to compute the present value of the following cash flows (at $r = 5\%$): $2,000 for the first 10 years, $1,000 for the next 10 years, and $3,000 at the end of year 21. Table 13A.1 above outlines the calculations.

The first thing to note is that to simplify the calculations, the $2,000 stream for years 1–10 and the $1,000 stream for years 11–20 are equivalent to a $1,000 stream for the first 20 years and a $1,000 stream for the first 10 years. The discount factors for these two streams are taken from the annuity table (Table 13A.4 on p. 486). The single $3,000 payment in year 21 is discounted using the present value factor from the present value table (Table 13A.3 on p. 485). Adding the three discounted cash flows yields a present value of $21,261. Recall that $21,261 is the *opportunity cost* or value of the three cash flow streams ($2,000 for the first 10 years, $1,000 for the next 10 years, and $3,000 at the end of year 21) when the market rate of interest is 5%.

Numerical Example 13A.6

Juan Perez has $5,000 to invest for two years. One bank offers 5% annual rate compounded monthly and another bank offers 6% compounded annually. Which is the better investment?

Solution

A 5% annual rate is equivalent to a monthly rate of $(1 + 0.05)^{1/12} - 1$, or 0.0040741. The value of $5,000 over 24 months at 0.40741% is $5,000(1 + 0.0040741)^{24}$, or $5,512. The value of $5,000 over two years at an annual rate of 6% is $5,000(1 + 0.06)^2$, or $5,618. Investing the $5,000 at 6% annually has the higher future value.

Numerical Example 13A.7

Judy Radski is considering returning to school to get an MBA degree. Her current wages total $25,000 per year. Tuition, books, and fees will cost $20,000 per year for two years. Upon completing the MBA, her starting salary will be $80,000. The MBA degree is expected to add $55,000 per year to her salary until retirement. However, she must give up two years of current salary while in graduate school in addition to paying tuition, books, and fees. At a current age of 30 and with an expected retirement age of 60, does it makes sense to go back and get the MBA? The market rate of interest is 5%.

Solution

In Table 13A.2 above, the net present value of her MBA, the difference between the present value of the cash inflows and outflows, is calculated.

In Table 13A.2, the additional wages of $55,000 are treated as an annuity beginning in year 1 and then a two-year annuity beginning in year 1 of $55,000 is subtracted. This method is the simplest approach to perform the calculation. The computations in Table 13A.2 assume that all cash flows occur at the end of the year. To keep the example simple, the additional wages from having the MBA degree are assumed to be constant at $55,000 per year over the career. Given these assumptions, the decision to get an MBA is worth $659,560 in today's dollars. That is, the present value of the additional wages from receiving the MBA is higher than the amount forgone (wages plus schooling costs) to acquire the degree.

SELF-STUDY PROBLEM

Avroland is an amusement park in California. It currently uses a computer system to perform general accounting functions, including tracking ticket sales and payroll as well as employee and maintenance scheduling functions. The original system, when purchased two years ago, cost $300,000 and has been depreciated for tax purposes using straight-line depreciation with an expected useful life of four more years and a zero salvage value. However, due to recent expansion, the computer system is no longer large enough. Upgrading it to increase the storage capacity and processing speed to accommodate the extra data processing demands would cost $65,000 and would become obsolete in four years. These system additions also would be depreciated using straight-line depreciation and would have a zero salvage value. The company's accountant estimates that the firm will increase operating spending by $28,000 a year after taxes for data processing, payroll (including Avroland personnel), and annual updates of software for the upgraded system. Alternatively, the firm could outsource payroll to a local payroll processing firm at the cost of $40,000 a year after taxes. This outsourcing would free enough capacity in the computer to prevent having to upgrade it. Assume a real cost of capital of 4% and a tax rate of 40%.

What should Avroland do?

Solution

The relevant costs to Avroland for processing payroll internally include the cost of upgrading the computer plus the variable cost of processing the information minus the tax savings from depreciating the upgraded machine. The relevant cost for outsourcing payroll is the cost of the outside service firm. Over the next four years, Avroland's cash flows would be as follows under the two possibilities:

Keep Payroll Inside						
	Year 0	Year 1	Year 2	Year 3	Year 4	NPV
Cost of upgrade	$65,000					
Labor plus software		$28,000	$28,000	$28,000	$28,000	
Tax savings from deprec.*		(6,500)	(6,500)	(6,500)	(6,500)	
Total cash outflows	$65,000	$21,500	$21,500	$21,500	$21,500	
Discount rate	1.000	0.962	0.925	0.889	0.855	
Present value at 4%	$65,000	$20,683	$19,878	$19,113	$18,383	$143,067

Outsource Payroll						
Annual cost of service		$40,000	$40,000	$40,000	$40,000	
Discount rate	1.000	0.962	0.925	0.889	0.855	
Present value at 4%		$38,480	$37,000	$35,560	$34,200	$145,240

* $\dfrac{\$65,000}{4 \text{ years}} \times 40\%$ tax rate $= \$6,500$

Note: The depreciation of the original system will remain whether the system is upgraded or payroll is outsourced. Therefore, it is not relevant to the decisions under consideration.

Since the net present value of the cash outflows is lower by keeping the payroll inside rather than outside the firm, the computer should be upgraded.

Table 13A.3 Present Value of $1

Present value of $1 received at the end of n periods at an interest rate of $r\%$

Periods	3%	4%	5%	6%	7%	8%	9%	10%	12%	14%	16%	18%	20%	25%	30%	35%	40%
1	0.971	0.962	0.952	0.943	0.935	0.926	0.917	0.909	0.893	0.877	0.862	0.847	0.833	0.800	0.769	0.741	0.714
2	0.943	0.925	0.907	0.890	0.873	0.857	0.842	0.826	0.797	0.769	0.743	0.718	0.694	0.640	0.592	0.549	0.510
3	0.915	0.889	0.864	0.840	0.816	0.794	0.772	0.751	0.712	0.675	0.641	0.609	0.579	0.512	0.455	0.406	0.364
4	0.888	0.855	0.823	0.792	0.763	0.735	0.708	0.683	0.636	0.592	0.552	0.516	0.482	0.410	0.350	0.301	0.260
5	0.863	0.822	0.784	0.747	0.713	0.681	0.650	0.621	0.567	0.519	0.476	0.437	0.402	0.328	0.269	0.223	0.186
6	0.837	0.790	0.746	0.705	0.666	0.630	0.596	0.564	0.507	0.456	0.410	0.370	0.335	0.262	0.207	0.165	0.133
7	0.813	0.760	0.711	0.665	0.623	0.583	0.547	0.513	0.452	0.400	0.354	0.314	0.279	0.210	0.159	0.122	0.095
8	0.789	0.731	0.677	0.627	0.582	0.540	0.502	0.467	0.404	0.351	0.305	0.266	0.233	0.168	0.123	0.091	0.068
9	0.766	0.703	0.645	0.592	0.544	0.500	0.460	0.424	0.361	0.308	0.263	0.225	0.194	0.134	0.094	0.067	0.048
10	0.744	0.676	0.614	0.558	0.508	0.463	0.422	0.386	0.322	0.270	0.227	0.191	0.162	0.107	0.073	0.050	0.035
11	0.722	0.650	0.585	0.527	0.475	0.429	0.388	0.350	0.287	0.237	0.195	0.162	0.135	0.086	0.056	0.037	0.025
12	0.701	0.625	0.557	0.497	0.444	0.397	0.356	0.319	0.257	0.208	0.168	0.137	0.112	0.069	0.043	0.027	0.018
13	0.681	0.601	0.530	0.469	0.415	0.368	0.326	0.290	0.229	0.182	0.145	0.116	0.093	0.055	0.033	0.020	0.013
14	0.661	0.577	0.505	0.442	0.388	0.340	0.299	0.263	0.205	0.160	0.125	0.099	0.078	0.044	0.025	0.015	0.009
15	0.642	0.555	0.481	0.417	0.362	0.315	0.275	0.239	0.183	0.140	0.108	0.084	0.065	0.035	0.020	0.011	0.006
16	0.623	0.534	0.458	0.394	0.339	0.292	0.252	0.218	0.163	0.123	0.093	0.071	0.054	0.028	0.015	0.008	0.005
17	0.605	0.513	0.436	0.371	0.317	0.270	0.231	0.198	0.146	0.108	0.080	0.060	0.045	0.023	0.012	0.006	0.003
18	0.587	0.494	0.416	0.350	0.296	0.250	0.212	0.180	0.130	0.095	0.069	0.051	0.038	0.018	0.009	0.005	0.002
19	0.570	0.475	0.396	0.331	0.277	0.232	0.194	0.164	0.116	0.083	0.060	0.043	0.031	0.014	0.007	0.003	0.002
20	0.554	0.456	0.377	0.312	0.258	0.215	0.178	0.149	0.104	0.073	0.051	0.037	0.026	0.012	0.005	0.002	0.001
21	0.538	0.439	0.359	0.294	0.242	0.199	0.164	0.135	0.093	0.064	0.044	0.031	0.022	0.009	0.004	0.002	0.001
22	0.522	0.422	0.342	0.278	0.226	0.184	0.150	0.123	0.083	0.056	0.038	0.026	0.018	0.007	0.003	0.001	0.001
23	0.507	0.406	0.326	0.262	0.211	0.170	0.138	0.112	0.074	0.049	0.033	0.022	0.015	0.006	0.002	0.001	0.000
24	0.492	0.390	0.310	0.247	0.197	0.158	0.126	0.102	0.066	0.043	0.028	0.019	0.013	0.005	0.002	0.001	0.000
25	0.478	0.375	0.295	0.233	0.184	0.146	0.116	0.092	0.059	0.038	0.024	0.016	0.010	0.004	0.001	0.001	0.000
26	0.464	0.361	0.281	0.220	0.172	0.135	0.106	0.084	0.053	0.033	0.021	0.014	0.009	0.003	0.001	0.001	0.000
27	0.450	0.347	0.268	0.207	0.161	0.125	0.098	0.076	0.047	0.029	0.018	0.011	0.007	0.002	0.001	0.000	0.000
28	0.437	0.333	0.255	0.196	0.150	0.116	0.090	0.069	0.042	0.026	0.016	0.010	0.006	0.002	0.001	0.000	0.000
29	0.424	0.321	0.243	0.185	0.141	0.107	0.082	0.063	0.037	0.022	0.014	0.008	0.005	0.002	0.000	0.000	0.000
30	0.412	0.308	0.231	0.174	0.131	0.099	0.075	0.057	0.033	0.020	0.012	0.007	0.004	0.001	0.000	0.000	0.000
35	0.355	0.253	0.181	0.130	0.094	0.068	0.049	0.036	0.019	0.010	0.006	0.003	0.002	0.000	0.000	0.000	0.000
40	0.307	0.208	0.142	0.097	0.067	0.046	0.032	0.022	0.011	0.005	0.003	0.001	0.001	0.000	0.000	0.000	0.000
60	0.170	0.095	0.054	0.030	0.017	0.010	0.006	0.003	0.001	0.000	0.000	0.000	0.000	0.000	0.000	0.000	0.000

Table 13A.4 Present Value of an Annuity

Present value of a stream of $1s received at the end of each of the next n periods at an interest rate of r%

Periods	3%	4%	5%	6%	7%	8%	9%	10%	12%	14%	16%	18%	20%	25%	30%	35%	40%
1	0.971	0.962	0.952	0.943	0.935	0.926	0.917	0.909	0.893	0.877	0.862	0.847	0.833	0.800	0.769	0.741	0.714
2	1.913	1.886	1.859	1.833	1.808	1.783	1.759	1.736	1.690	1.647	1.605	1.566	1.528	1.440	1.361	1.289	1.224
3	2.829	2.775	2.723	2.673	2.624	2.577	2.531	2.487	2.402	2.322	2.246	2.174	2.106	1.952	1.816	1.696	1.589
4	3.717	3.630	3.546	3.465	3.387	3.312	3.240	3.170	3.037	2.914	2.798	2.690	2.589	2.362	2.166	1.997	1.849
5	4.580	4.452	4.329	4.212	4.100	3.993	3.890	3.791	3.605	3.433	3.274	3.127	2.991	2.689	2.436	2.220	2.035
6	5.417	5.242	5.076	4.917	4.767	4.623	4.486	4.355	4.111	3.889	3.685	3.498	3.326	2.951	2.643	2.385	2.168
7	6.230	6.002	5.786	5.582	5.389	5.206	5.033	4.868	4.564	4.288	4.039	3.812	3.605	3.161	2.802	2.508	2.263
8	7.020	6.733	6.463	6.210	5.971	5.747	5.535	5.335	4.968	4.639	4.344	4.078	3.837	3.329	2.925	2.598	2.331
9	7.786	7.435	7.108	6.802	6.515	6.247	5.995	5.759	5.328	4.946	4.607	4.303	4.031	3.463	3.019	2.665	2.379
10	8.530	8.111	7.722	7.360	7.024	6.710	6.418	6.145	5.650	5.216	4.833	4.494	4.192	3.571	3.092	2.715	2.414
11	9.253	8.760	8.306	7.887	7.499	7.139	6.805	6.495	5.938	5.453	5.029	4.656	4.327	3.656	3.147	2.752	2.438
12	9.954	9.385	8.863	8.384	7.943	7.536	7.161	6.814	6.194	5.660	5.197	4.793	4.439	3.725	3.190	2.779	2.456
13	10.635	9.986	9.394	8.853	8.358	7.904	7.487	7.103	6.424	5.842	5.342	4.910	4.533	3.780	3.223	2.799	2.469
14	11.296	10.563	9.899	9.295	8.745	8.244	7.786	7.367	6.628	6.002	5.468	5.008	4.611	3.824	3.249	2.814	2.478
15	11.938	11.118	10.380	9.712	9.108	8.559	8.061	7.606	6.811	6.142	5.575	5.092	4.675	3.859	3.268	2.825	2.484
16	12.561	11.652	10.838	10.106	9.447	8.851	8.313	7.824	6.974	6.265	5.668	5.162	4.730	3.887	3.283	2.834	2.489
17	13.166	12.166	11.274	10.477	9.763	9.122	8.544	8.022	7.120	6.373	5.749	5.222	4.775	3.910	3.295	2.840	2.492
18	13.754	12.659	11.690	10.828	10.059	9.372	8.756	8.201	7.250	6.467	5.818	5.273	4.812	3.928	3.304	2.844	2.494
19	14.324	13.134	12.085	11.158	10.336	9.604	8.950	8.365	7.366	6.550	5.877	5.316	4.843	3.942	3.311	2.848	2.496
20	14.877	13.590	12.462	11.470	10.594	9.818	9.129	8.514	7.469	6.623	5.929	5.353	4.870	3.954	3.316	2.850	2.497
21	15.415	14.029	12.821	11.764	10.836	10.017	9.292	8.649	7.562	6.687	5.973	5.384	4.891	3.963	3.320	2.852	2.498
22	15.937	14.451	13.163	12.042	11.061	10.201	9.442	8.772	7.645	6.743	6.011	5.410	4.909	3.970	3.323	2.853	2.498
23	16.444	14.857	13.489	12.303	11.272	10.371	9.580	8.883	7.718	6.792	6.044	5.432	4.925	3.976	3.325	2.854	2.499
24	16.936	15.247	13.799	12.550	11.469	10.529	9.707	8.985	7.784	6.835	6.073	5.451	4.937	3.981	3.327	2.855	2.499
25	17.413	15.622	14.094	12.783	11.654	10.675	9.823	9.077	7.843	6.873	6.097	5.467	4.948	3.985	3.329	2.856	2.499
26	17.877	15.983	14.375	13.003	11.826	10.810	9.929	9.161	7.896	6.906	6.118	5.480	4.956	3.988	3.330	2.856	2.500
27	18.327	16.330	14.643	13.211	11.987	10.935	10.027	9.237	7.943	6.935	6.136	5.492	4.964	3.990	3.331	2.856	2.500
28	18.764	16.663	14.898	13.406	12.137	11.051	10.116	9.307	7.984	6.961	6.152	5.502	4.970	3.992	3.331	2.857	2.500
29	19.188	16.984	15.141	13.591	12.278	11.158	10.198	9.370	8.022	6.983	6.166	5.510	4.975	3.994	3.332	2.857	2.500
30	19.600	17.292	15.372	13.765	12.409	11.258	10.274	9.427	8.055	7.003	6.177	5.517	4.979	3.995	3.332	2.857	2.500
35	21.487	18.665	16.374	14.498	12.948	11.655	10.567	9.644	8.176	7.070	6.215	5.539	4.992	3.998	3.333	2.857	2.500
40	23.115	19.793	17.159	15.046	13.332	11.925	10.757	9.779	8.244	7.105	6.233	5.548	4.997	3.999	3.333	2.857	2.500
60	27.676	22.623	18.929	16.161	14.039	12.377	11.048	9.967	8.324	7.140	6.249	5.555	5.000	4.000	3.333	2.857	2.500
120	32.373	24.774	19.943	16.651	14.281	12.499	11.111	10.000	8.333	7.143	6.250	5.556	5.000	4.000	3.333	2.857	2.500
360	33.333	25.000	20.000	16.667	14.286	12.500	11.111	10.000	8.333	7.143	6.250	5.556	5.000	4.000	3.333	2.857	2.500

Table 13A.5 Future Value of $1

Future value of $1 invested today at r % interest and allowed to compound for n periods

Periods	3%	4%	5%	6%	7%	8%	9%	10%	12%	14%	16%	18%	20%	25%	30%	35%	40%
1	1.030	1.040	1.050	1.060	1.070	1.080	1.090	1.100	1.120	1.140	1.160	1.180	1.200	1.250	1.300	1.350	1.400
2	1.061	1.082	1.103	1.124	1.145	1.166	1.188	1.210	1.254	1.300	1.346	1.392	1.440	1.563	1.690	1.823	1.960
3	1.093	1.125	1.158	1.191	1.225	1.260	1.295	1.331	1.405	1.482	1.561	1.643	1.728	1.953	2.197	2.460	2.744
4	1.126	1.170	1.216	1.262	1.311	1.360	1.412	1.464	1.574	1.689	1.811	1.939	2.074	2.441	2.856	3.322	3.842
5	1.159	1.217	1.276	1.338	1.403	1.469	1.539	1.611	1.762	1.925	2.100	2.288	2.488	3.052	3.713	4.484	5.378
6	1.194	1.265	1.340	1.419	1.501	1.587	1.677	1.772	1.974	2.195	2.436	2.700	2.986	3.815	4.827	6.053	7.530
7	1.230	1.316	1.407	1.504	1.606	1.714	1.828	1.949	2.211	2.502	2.826	3.185	3.583	4.768	6.275	8.172	10.541
8	1.267	1.369	1.477	1.594	1.718	1.851	1.993	2.144	2.476	2.853	3.278	3.759	4.300	5.960	8.157	11.032	14.785
9	1.305	1.423	1.551	1.689	1.838	1.999	2.172	2.358	2.773	3.252	3.803	4.435	5.160	7.451	10.604	14.894	20.661
10	1.344	1.480	1.629	1.791	1.967	2.159	2.367	2.594	3.106	3.707	4.411	5.234	6.192	9.313	13.786	20.107	28.925
11	1.384	1.539	1.710	1.898	2.105	2.332	2.580	2.853	3.479	4.226	5.117	6.176	7.430	11.642	17.922	27.144	40.496
12	1.426	1.601	1.796	2.012	2.252	2.518	2.813	3.138	3.896	4.818	5.936	7.288	8.916	14.552	23.298	36.644	56.694
13	1.469	1.665	1.886	2.133	2.410	2.720	3.066	3.452	4.363	5.492	6.886	8.599	10.699	18.190	30.288	49.470	79.371
14	1.513	1.732	1.980	2.261	2.579	2.937	3.342	3.797	4.887	6.261	7.988	10.147	12.839	22.737	39.374	66.784	111.120
15	1.558	1.801	2.079	2.397	2.759	3.172	3.642	4.177	5.474	7.138	9.266	11.974	15.407	28.422	51.186	90.158	155.568
16	1.605	1.873	2.183	2.540	2.952	3.426	3.970	4.595	6.130	8.137	10.748	14.129	18.488	35.527	66.542	121.714	217.795
17	1.653	1.948	2.292	2.693	3.159	3.700	4.328	5.054	6.866	9.276	12.468	16.672	22.186	44.409	86.504	164.314	304.913
18	1.702	2.026	2.407	2.854	3.380	3.996	4.717	5.560	7.690	10.575	14.463	19.673	26.623	55.511	112.455	221.824	426.879
19	1.754	2.107	2.527	3.026	3.617	4.316	5.142	6.116	8.613	12.056	16.777	23.214	31.948	69.389	146.192	299.462	597.630
20	1.806	2.191	2.653	3.207	3.870	4.661	5.604	6.727	9.646	13.743	19.461	27.393	38.338	86.736	190.050	404.274	836.683
21	1.860	2.279	2.786	3.400	4.141	5.034	6.109	7.400	10.804	15.668	22.574	32.324	46.005	108.420	247.065	545.769	1,171.356
22	1.916	2.370	2.925	3.604	4.430	5.437	6.659	8.140	12.100	17.861	26.186	38.142	55.206	135.525	321.184	736.789	1,639.898
23	1.974	2.465	3.072	3.820	4.741	5.871	7.258	8.954	13.552	20.362	30.376	45.008	66.247	169.407	417.539	994.665	2,295.857
24	2.033	2.563	3.225	4.049	5.072	6.341	7.911	9.850	15.179	23.212	35.236	53.109	79.497	211.758	542.801	1,342.797	3,214.200
25	2.094	2.666	3.386	4.292	5.427	6.848	8.623	10.835	17.000	26.462	40.874	62.669	95.396	264.698	705.641	1,812.776	4,499.880
26	2.157	2.772	3.556	4.549	5.807	7.396	9.399	11.918	19.040	30.167	47.414	73.949	114.475	330.872	917.333	2,447.248	6,229.831
27	2.221	2.883	3.733	4.822	6.214	7.988	10.245	13.110	21.325	34.390	55.000	87.260	137.371	413.590	1,192.533	3,303.785	8,819.764
28	2.288	2.999	3.920	5.112	6.649	8.627	11.167	14.421	23.884	39.204	63.800	102.967	164.845	516.988	1,550.293	4,460.109	12,347.670
29	2.357	3.119	4.116	5.418	7.114	9.317	12.172	15.863	26.750	44.693	74.009	121.501	197.814	646.235	2,015.381	6,021.148	17,286.737
30	2.427	3.243	4.322	5.743	7.612	10.063	13.268	17.449	29.960	50.950	85.850	143.371	237.376	807.794	2,619.996	8,128.550	24,201.432
35	2.814	3.946	5.516	7.686	10.677	14.785	20.414	28.102	52.800	98.100	180.314	327.997	590.668	2,465.190	9,727.860	36,448.688	130,161.112
40	3.262	4.801	7.040	10.286	14.974	21.725	31.409	45.259	93.051	188.884	378.721	750.378	1,469.772	7,523.164	36,118.865	163,437.135	700,037.697

Table 13A.6 Future Value of an Annuity of $1

Future value of a stream of *n* $1s invested today at *r* % interest and allowed to compound for *n* periods

Periods	3%	4%	5%	6%	7%	8%	9%	10%	12%	14%	16%	18%	20%	25%	30%	35%	40%
1	1.000	1.000	1.000	1.000	1.000	1.000	1.000	1.000	1.000	1.000	1.000	1.000	1.000	1.000	1.000	1.000	1
2	2.030	2.040	2.050	2.060	2.070	2.080	2.090	2.100	2.120	2.140	2.160	2.180	2.200	2.250	2.300	2.350	2
3	3.091	3.122	3.153	3.184	3.215	3.246	3.278	3.310	3.374	3.440	3.506	3.572	3.640	3.813	3.990	4.173	4
4	4.184	4.246	4.310	4.375	4.440	4.506	4.573	4.641	4.779	4.921	5.066	5.215	5.368	5.766	6.187	6.633	7
5	5.309	5.416	5.526	5.637	5.751	5.867	5.985	6.105	6.353	6.610	6.877	7.154	7.442	8.207	9.043	9.954	10
6	6.468	6.633	6.802	6.975	7.153	7.336	7.523	7.716	8.115	8.536	8.977	9.442	9.930	11.259	12.756	14.438	16
7	7.662	7.898	8.142	8.394	8.654	8.923	9.200	9.487	10.089	10.730	11.414	12.142	12.916	15.073	17.583	20.492	23
8	8.892	9.214	9.549	9.897	10.260	10.637	11.028	11.436	12.300	13.233	14.240	15.327	16.499	19.842	23.858	28.664	34
9	10.159	10.583	11.027	11.491	11.978	12.488	13.021	13.579	14.776	16.085	17.519	19.086	20.799	25.802	32.015	39.696	49
10	11.464	12.006	12.578	13.181	13.816	14.487	15.193	15.937	17.549	19.337	21.321	23.521	25.959	33.253	42.619	54.590	69
11	12.808	13.486	14.207	14.972	15.784	16.645	17.560	18.531	20.655	23.045	25.733	28.755	32.150	42.566	56.405	76.697	98
12	14.192	15.026	15.917	16.870	17.888	18.977	20.141	21.384	24.133	27.271	30.850	34.931	39.581	54.208	74.327	101.841	139
13	15.618	16.627	17.713	18.882	20.141	21.495	22.953	24.523	28.029	32.089	36.786	42.219	48.497	68.760	97.625	138.485	195
14	17.086	18.292	19.599	21.015	22.550	24.215	26.019	27.975	32.393	37.581	43.672	50.818	59.196	86.949	127.913	187.954	275
15	18.599	20.024	21.579	23.276	25.129	27.152	29.361	31.772	37.280	43.842	51.660	60.965	72.035	109.687	167.286	254.738	386
16	20.157	21.825	23.657	25.673	27.888	30.324	33.003	35.950	42.753	50.980	60.925	72.939	87.442	138.109	218.472	334.897	541
17	21.762	23.698	25.840	28.213	30.840	33.750	36.974	40.545	48.884	59.118	71.673	87.068	105.931	173.636	285.014	466.611	759
18	23.414	25.645	28.132	30.906	33.999	37.450	41.301	45.599	55.750	68.394	84.141	103.740	128.117	218.045	371.518	630.925	1,064
19	25.117	27.671	30.539	33.760	37.379	41.446	46.018	51.159	63.440	78.969	98.603	123.414	154.740	273.556	483.973	852.748	1,491
20	26.870	29.778	33.066	36.786	40.995	45.762	51.160	57.275	72.052	91.025	115.380	146.628	186.688	342.945	630.165	1,152.210	2,089
21	28.676	31.969	35.719	39.993	44.865	50.423	56.765	64.002	81.699	104.768	134.841	174.021	225.026	429.681	820.215	1,556.484	2,925
22	30.537	34.248	38.505	43.392	49.006	55.457	62.873	71.403	92.503	120.436	157.415	206.345	271.031	538.101	1,067.280	2,102.253	4,097
23	32.453	36.618	41.430	46.996	53.436	60.893	69.532	79.543	104.603	138.297	183.601	244.487	326.237	673.626	1,388.464	2,839.042	5,737
24	34.426	39.083	44.502	50.816	58.177	66.765	76.790	88.497	118.155	158.659	213.978	289.494	392.484	843.033	1,806.003	3,833.706	8,032
25	36.459	41.646	47.727	54.865	63.249	73.106	84.701	98.347	133.334	181.871	249.214	342.603	471.981	1,054.791	2,348.803	5,176.504	11,247
26	38.553	44.312	51.113	59.156	68.676	79.954	93.324	109.182	150.334	208.333	290.088	405.272	567.377	1,319.489	3,054.444	6,989.280	15,747
27	40.710	47.084	54.669	63.706	74.484	87.351	102.723	121.100	169.374	238.499	337.502	479.221	681.853	1,650.361	3,971.778	9,436.528	22,046
28	42.931	49.968	58.403	68.528	80.698	95.339	112.968	134.210	190.699	272.889	392.503	566.481	819.223	2,063.952	5,164.311	12,740.313	30,866
29	45.219	52.966	62.323	73.640	87.347	103.966	124.135	148.631	214.583	312.094	456.303	669.447	984.068	2,580.939	6,714.604	17,200.422	43,214
30	47.575	56.085	66.439	79.058	94.461	113.283	136.308	164.494	241.333	356.787	530.312	790.948	1,181.882	3,227.174	8,729.985	23,221.570	60,501
35	60.462	73.652	90.320	111.534	138.237	172.317	215.711	271.024	431.663	693.573	1,120.713	1,816.652	2,948.341	9,856.761	32,422.868	104,136.251	325,400
40	75.401	95.026	120.800	154.762	199.635	259.057	337.882	442.593	767.091	1,342.025	2,360.757	4,163.213	7,343.858	30,088.655	120,392.883	466,960.385	1,750,091

NUMERICAL EXERCISES

An investment opportunity that costs $40,000 generates $20,000 in cash inflows each of the next four years.

 What is the payback period for the investment?

An investment that costs $100,000 generates $20,000 in income over the next five years. The original cost of the investment is depreciated using straight-line depreciation over the five years with no salvage value.

 What is the multiyear ROI for the investment?

What is the net present value of cash inflows of $30,000 in one year, $40,000 in two years, and $80,000 in three years if the opportunity cost of capital is 8%?

What is the net present value of an investment that costs $50,000 and generates $20,000 in cash inflows in the first year and $40,000 in the second year given a 10% cost of capital?

A company buys a machine for $60,000 that is fully depreciated over three years using the straight-line method.

 What is the value of the depreciation tax shield if the tax rate is 40%?

What is the IRR for an investment of $1,000 that yields $1,300 in one year?

What is the IRR of an investment of $1,000 that yields cash flows of $600 in each of the first two years?

What is the value of a 10-year annuity in 10 years if the interest rate is 6% and each annuity payment is $100?

What is the present value of a 12-year annuity if the interest rate is 8% and the annuity payment is $1,000?

A mother wants to put sufficient money in the bank to cover university expenses for her son in 15 years. She estimates that in 15 years, $100,000 will be necessary to pay for the university costs. The bank pays 8% compounded annually.

 How much does she need to deposit today to have sufficient money in 15 years?

Your grandfather put $1,000 in the bank for you 48 years ago. The bank paid 6% interest compounded annually during this time period.

 How much is your grandfather's deposit worth today?

NE 13.1
Estimation of the Payback Period
(LO 3)

NE 13.2
Calculation of the Accounting Rate of Return
(LO 4)

NE 13.3
Net Present Value of Cash Flows
(LO 5)

NE 13.4
Net Present Value of Cash Flows
(LO 5)

NE 13.5
Depreciation Tax Shields
(LO 9)

NE 13.6
Internal Rate of Return
(LO 11)

NE 13.7
Internal Rate of Return
(LO 11)

NE 13.8
Use of Annuity Tables
(LO 13)

NE 13.9
Use of Annuity Tables
(LO 13)

NE 13.10
Future Value of an Annuity
(LO 5, 13)

NE 13.11
Compounded Interest
(LO 5, 13)

NUMERICAL PROBLEMS

A law firm is considering dismissing one of its junior lawyers. The firm presently has enough space for more lawyers, but this junior lawyer is perceived as a net loss to the firm. To dismiss him, however, the firm would have to pay $100,000 now for severing his employment contract early. The lawyer has a salary of $80,000 and currently brings in $200,000 per year in revenues. The firm, however, estimates that indirect costs related to him are $180,000 per year. The alternative is to wait two more years to dismiss him at the end of his contract and not have to make any severance pay. The discount rate is 10%.

 What should the law firm do?

NP 13.1
Decision with Discounting Cash Flows
(LO 5)

NP 13.2
Annuity
(LO 5, 13)

Suppose that the opportunity cost of capital is 10% and you have just won a $1 million lottery that entitles you to $100,000 at the end of each of the next 10 years.

a. What is the minimum lump-sum cash payment you would be willing to take now in lieu of the 10-year annuity?

b. What is the minimum lump sum you would be willing to accept at the end of the 10 years in lieu of the annuity?

c. Suppose that three years have passed and you have just received the third payment. You have seven years left when the lottery promoters approach you with an offer to settle up for cash. What is the minimum you would accept (at the end of year 3)?

d. How would your answer to part (a) change if the first payment came immediately (at $t = 0$) and the remaining payments were at the beginning instead of at the end of each year?

NP 13.3
Retirement Decision and Annuities
(LO 5, 13)

Mr. Jones intends to retire in 20 years at the age of 65. As yet, he has not provided for retirement income and wants to set up a periodic savings plan to do this.

If he makes equal annual payments into a savings account that pays 4% interest per year, how large must his payments be to ensure that after retirement he can draw $30,000 per year from this account until he is 80?

NP 13.4
Present Value of Interest and Principal
(LO 5, 13)

You are thinking about borrowing $100,000 for 10 years at 12%. Annual interest payments are required at the end of each year, and the principal ($100,000) is to be repaid at the end of the 10 years.

What is the present value of the principal payment, and what is the present value of the interest payments?

NP 13.5
Net Present Value and Internal Rate of Return
(LO 5, 9, 11)

A company is considering buying a corporate jet for $5,000,000. The jet will save employee time and eliminate the need to buy plane tickets. These benefits are worth approximately $800,000 per year. The cost of operating the plane is $100,000 per year. The plane will last for 10 years and can be sold for $1,000,000 at the end of the tenth year. Assume an interest rate of 10% and no taxes.

a. What is the NPV of this project?

b. What is the IRR of this project if the jet will have zero value at the end of the tenth year?

c. Assume that the jet is depreciated $500,000 per year for the 10 years and is sold for $1,000,000 at the end of the tenth year. Also assume that the tax rate on income is 40%. What is the NPV of the jet?

NP 13.6
Decision to Sell Division
(LO 5, 13)

Several years ago, your firm paid $25,000,000 for Clean Tooth, a small, high-technology company that manufactures laser-based tooth-cleaning equipment. Unfortunately, due to extensive production line and sales resistance problems, the company is considering selling the division as part of a modernization program. Based on current information, the following are the estimated accounting numbers if the company continues to operate the division:

Estimated sales revenues—next 10 years	$500,000 per year
Estimated cash expenses—next 10 years	450,000 per year
Current offer for the division from another firm	250,000

Assume the following:

* The firm is in the 0% tax bracket (no income taxes).
* No additional expenses are associated with the sale.
* After year 10, the division will have sales (and expenses) of 0.
* Estimates are completely certain.

Should the firm sell the division for $250,000?

NP 13.7
Present Value of Payments
(LO 5, 13)

Farmers in a valley are subject to occasional flooding when heavy rains cause the river to overflow. They have asked the federal government to build a dam upstream to prevent the flooding. The construction cost of this project is to be repaid without interest over a period of years. The cost of the dam is $30,000. No payments at all are to be made for the first five years. Then $1,000 is to be paid at the end of each year for 30 years to pay off the $30,000.

Are the farmers receiving a subsidy? Why? If the interest rate is 10%, what is the approximate present value of the subsidy (if any)? Show all calculations.

You have just purchased a house and have obtained a 30-year, $200,000 mortgage with an interest rate of 10%.

a. What is your annual mortgage payment, assuming that you pay equal amounts each year?

b. Assuming that you bought the house on January 1, what is the principal balance after one year? After 10 years?

NP 13.8
Mortgage Payments and Refinancing
(LO 5, 13)

PQR Coal Company has several conventional and strip mining operations. Recently, new legislation has made strip mining, which produces coal of high sulfur content, unprofitable, so those operations will be discontinued. Unfortunately, two years ago PQR purchased $1 million of earth-moving equipment for the strip mines, which is not particularly well suited to conventional mining.

Mr. Big, the president, suggests that since the equipment can be sold for $500,000, it should be scrapped. In his words, "I learned a long time ago that when you make mistakes, it's best to admit them and take your lumps. By ignoring sunk costs, you aren't tempted to throw good money after bad. The original value of the equipment is gone."

A new employee, Ms. Embay, has suggested that the equipment should be adapted to the conventional operations. She argues, "We are about to spend $800,000 on some new conventional equipment. However, for a smaller expenditure of $250,000, we can adapt the old equipment to perform the same task. Of course, it will cost about $20,000 per year more to operate over the assumed 10-year life of each alternative. But at an interest rate of 10%, the inclusion of the present value of $20,000 per year for 10 years and the initial $250,000 are still less than $800,000 for new equipment. While it's true that we should ignore sunk costs, at least this way we can cut our losses somewhat."

Who is correct? Why?

NP 13.9
Replace or Modify Equipment
(LO 5, 6, 13)

The National Direct Student Loan (NDSL) program allows university students to borrow funds from the federal government. The contract stipulates that the annual percentage rate of interest is 0% until 12 months after the student ceases his or her formal education (defined as at least half-time enrollment), at which time interest is 4% per year. The maximum repayment period is 10 years. For the purposes of the following questions, assume that the student borrows $10,000 in the beginning of the first year and completes his or her education in four years. Loan repayments begin one year after graduation.

a. Assuming that the student elects the maximum payment period, what are the uniform annual loan repayments? (Assume that all repayments occur at the end of the year.)

b. If the rate of interest on savings deposits is 6%, what is the minimum amount that the student must have in a bank account one year after graduation to make the loan payments calculated in part (a)?

c. Are recipients of NDSL receiving a subsidy? If so, what is the present value of the subsidy when the loan is taken out?

NP 13.10
Student Loan Payments and Subsidies
(LO 5, 13)

A home in your neighborhood identical to your home sold last week for $150,000. Your home has a $120,000 assumable, 8% mortgage (compounded annually) with 30 years remaining. An assumable mortgage is one that the new buyer can assume at the old terms and continue to make payments at the original interest rate. The house that recently sold did not have an assumable mortgage; that is, the buyers had to finance the house at the current market rate of interest, which is 15%.

What price should you ask for your home?

NP 13.11
Value of a Home with an Assumable Mortgage
(LO 5, 13)

Suppose that you are the manager of a mortgage department at a savings bank. Under the state usury law, the maximum interest rate allowed for mortgages is 10% compounded annually.

a. If you granted a $50,000 mortgage at the maximum rate for 30 years, what would be the equal annual payments?

NP 13.12
Mortgage Department Decisions
(LO 5, 13)

b. If the bank's cost of capital is 12%, how much money does the bank lose by issuing the mortgage described in (a)?

    c. The usury law does not prohibit banks from charging "points." One "point" means that the borrower pays 1% of the $50,000 loan back to the lending institution at the inception of the loan. That is, if one point is charged, the repayments are computed as in part (a), but the borrower receives only $49,500. How many points must the bank charge to earn 12% on the 10% loan?

NP 13.13
Decision to Make or Buy Electricity
(LO 5, 13)

A company that purchases electric power from the local utility is considering the alternative of generating its own electricity. The current cost of obtaining the company's electricity from the local utility firm is $42,000 per year. The cost of a steam generator (installed) is $140,000, and the annual maintenance and fuel expenses are estimated at $22,000 per year. The generator is expected to last for 10 years, at which time it will be worthless. The cost of capital is 10%, and the company pays no taxes.

    a. Should the company install the electric generator? Why or why not?

    b. The engineers have calculated that with an additional investment of $40,000, the excess steam from the generator can be used to heat the company's buildings. The current cost of heating the buildings with purchased steam is $21,000 per year. If the generator is to be used for heat as well as electricity, additional fuel and maintenance costs of $10,000 per year will be incurred. Should the company invest in the generator and the heating system? Show all calculations.

NP 13.14
Internal Rate of Return
(LO 5, 11, 12)

Jasper, Inc., is considering two mutually exclusive investments (A and B). Alternative A has a current outlay of $300,000 and returns $360,000 next year. Alternative B has a current outlay of $165,000 and returns $200,000 next year.

    a. Calculate the internal rate of return for each alternative.

    b. Which alternative should Jasper take if the required rate of return for those projects in the capital market is 15%?

    c. Why are the projects ranked differently in terms of internal rate of return and net present value?

NP 13.15
Decision to Sell or Keep an Asset
(LO 5, 13)

Abby Landlord owns a dilapidated 30-year-old apartment building in Los Angeles. The net cash flow from renting the apartments last year was $200,000. She expects those net cash flows from renting the apartments to continue for the remaining useful life of the apartment building, which is 10 years. In 10 years, the value of the property is expected to be $100,000. A developer wants to buy the apartment building from Abby, demolish it, and construct luxury condominiums. He offers Abby $1,500,000 for the apartments. Her opportunity cost of capital is 16%. Assume there are no taxes.

    Evaluate the developer's offer and make a recommendation to Abby.

NP 13.16
Decision to Replace a Machine
(LO 5, 9 13)

Baltic Company is considering the purchase of a new machine tool to replace an older one. The machine being used for the operation has a tax book value of $80,000 with an annual depreciation expense of $8,000. The older machine tool is in good working order and will last, physically, for at least an additional 10 years. It can be sold today for $40,000 but will have no value if it is kept for another 10 years. The proposed new machine will perform the operation so much more efficiently that Baltic Company engineers estimate that labor, material, and other direct costs of the operation will be reduced $60,000 a year if it is installed. The proposed machine costs $240,000 delivered and installed, and its economic life is estimated to be 10 years with zero salvage value. The company expects to earn 14% on its investment after taxes (14% is the firm's cost of capital). The tax rate is 40%, and the firm uses straight-line depreciation.

    Should Baltic buy the new machine?

NP 13.17
Investment in Pollution Control Devices
(LO 5, 6, 13)

Overland Steel operates a coal-burning steel mill in New York state. Changes in the state's air quality control laws will result in this mill incurring a $1,000 per day fine, which is paid at the end of the year, if it continues to operate. The mill currently operates every day of the year.

    The mill was built 20 years ago at a cost of $15 million and has a remaining undepreciated book value of $3 million. The mill's expected remaining useful life is 30 years.

The firm can sell the mill to a developer who wants to build a shopping center on the site. The buyer would pay $1 million for the site if the company demolishes the mill and prepares the site for the developer. Demolition and site preparation costs are estimated at $650,000.

Alternatively, the firm could install pollution control devices and other modernization devices at an initial outlay of $2.75 million. These improvements do not extend the useful life or salvage value of the plant, but they do reduce net operating costs by $25,000 per year in addition to eliminating the $1,000 per day fine. Currently, the net cash flows of sales less the cost of operating the plant are $450,000 per year before any fines.

Assume the following:

* The opportunity cost of capital is 14%.
* There are no taxes.
* The annual cash flow estimates given are constant over the next 30 years.
* At the end of the 30 years, the mill will have an estimated salvage value of $2 million whether or not the pollution equipment is installed.

Evaluate the alternatives available to management and make a recommendation as to which one is preferable. Support your conclusions with neatly labeled calculations when possible.

Scottie Corporation has been offered a five-year contract to produce 100 castings a year at a price of $200 per casting. Producing the castings will require an investment in the plant of $35,000 and operating costs of $50 per casting produced. For tax purposes, depreciation will be on a straight-line basis over five years with a full year's depreciation being taken in both the beginning and ending years. The tax rate is 40% and the opportunity cost of capital is 10%.

Should Scottie accept the contract?

NP 13.18
Depreciation and Taxes
(LO 5, 9)

A punch press currently in use has a book value of $1,800. It needs design modifications totaling $16,200, which would be capitalized at the present time and depreciated. The press could be sold for $2,600 now, but it could be used for three more years if the necessary modifications were made. At the end of the three years, it would have no salvage value.

A new punch press can be purchased at an invoice price of $26,900 to replace the present equipment. Freight-in will amount to $800, and installation will cost $500. These expenses will be depreciated, along with the invoice price, over the life of the machine. Due to the nature of the product manufactured, the new machine also will have an expected life of three years and will have no salvage value at the end of that time.

Using the old machine, the operating profits before taxes and depreciation (revenues less costs) are $10,000 in the first year and $8,000 in each of the next two years. Using the new machine, the operating profits before taxes and depreciation (revenues less costs) are $18,000 in the first year and $14,000 in each of the next two years.

The corporate income tax rate is 40%, which is the same rate applicable to gains or losses on sales of equipment. Both the present and proposed equipment would be depreciated on a straight-line basis over three years. The opportunity cost of capital is 10%.

Should the company modify the old machine or purchase the new one?

NP 13.19
Decision to Replace a Machine
(LO 5, 9)

The City of Toledo has received a proposal to build a new multipurpose outdoor sports stadium. The expected life of the stadium is 20 years and will be financed by a 20-year bond paying 8% interest annually. The stadium's primary tenant will be the city's Triple-A baseball team, the Red Hots. The plan's backers anticipate that the site will also be used for rock concerts and university and high school sports. The city does not pay any taxes and its cost of capital is 8%. The costs and estimated revenues follow.

NP 13.20
Capital Budgeting Decision
(LO 5, 13)

Cash Outflows	
Construction costs	$12,000,000
General maintenance (including labor)	250,000 per year
Cash Inflows	
Red Hots' minimum lease payments	650,000 per year
Concerts	600,000 per year
University and high school sports	50,000 per year

a. Should the city build the stadium? (Assume that payments are made at the end of the year.)

    b. The Red Hots have threatened to move out of Toledo if they do not get a new stadium. The city comptroller estimates that the move will cost the city $350,000 per year for 10 years in lost taxes and parking and other fees. Should the city build the stadium now? State your reasoning.

NP 13.21
Payback Period
(LO 3)

Kline Corporation is evaluating two investment projects, a tennis club and a squash club. The tennis club would require $10,000,000 to build. Kline management projects annual cash inflows from the tennis club to be $2,000,000. The squash club would be smaller and would require $2,000,000 to build. Management projects annual cash inflows from the squash club to be $500,000.

    a. What is the payback period for each of the investments?

    b. Based on the payback period, which investment should be chosen?

    c. What are the problems with making the investment decision based on the payback period?

NP 13.22
Accounting Rate of Return (ROI)
(LO 4)

Kline Corporation in NP 13.21 is thinking about investing in either a tennis club or a squash club. The tennis club would cost $10,000,000 and generate annual cash flows of $2,000,000 per year. The initial cost of the tennis club would be depreciated over 10 years using straight-line depreciation. The squash club would cost $2,000,000 and generate annual cash flows of $500,000 per year. The initial cost of the squash club would be depreciated over 20 years using straight-line depreciation. Depreciation is the only adjustment to cash flow for the calculation of income for both investments. Each investment would have zero salvage value after being fully depreciated.

    a. What is the ROI of each investment during the first year, using the investment at the beginning of the year as the denominator?

    b. What is the multiyear ROI for each investment?

    c. What are the problems with using ROI to evaluate investments?

NP 13.23
Adjustments to Cash Flows for Accounts Receivables and Inventory
(LO 7)

Hammer Company is considering opening a car dealership. The business would be completely funded by borrowing. At the end of the first two years, the car dealership is expected to have accounts receivable balances of $50,000 and $75,000, and inventory balances of $300,000 and $400,000, respectively. Income for the first two years is expected to be $200,000 and $500,000, respectively.

    How would the income numbers be adjusted for the accounts receivable and inventory balances if income is converted into cash flows?

ANALYSIS AND INTERPRETATION PROBLEMS

AIP 13.1
Capital Budgeting and Opportunity Costs
(LO 6)

Geico is considering expanding an existing plant on a piece of land that it already owns. The land was purchased 15 years ago for $325,000; its current market appraisal is $820,000. A capital budgeting analysis shows that the plant expansion has a net present value of $130,000. The expansion will cost $1.73 million; the discounted cash inflows are $1.86 million. The expansion cost of $1.73 million does not include any provision for the cost of the land. The manager preparing the analysis argues that the historical cost of the land is a sunk cost, and since the firm intends to keep the land whether or not the expansion project is accepted, the current appraisal value is irrelevant.

    Should the land be included in the analysis? If so, how?

AIP 13.2
Decision to Drop a Product
(LO 6)

Declining Market, Inc., is considering the problem of when to stop production of a particular product in its product line. Sales of the product have been declining and all estimates are that they will continue to decline. Capital equipment used to manufacture the product is specialized but can be readily sold as used equipment.

    Discuss what is wrong, if anything, with the decision rule for this case that says this:

    "Keep producing the product as long as its contribution to net earnings is positive." ["Contribution to net earnings" is $(1 - t)$ (sales − variable cost − depreciation on equipment used to manufacture product), where t is the tax rate.]

Sharp Razor Company invested in the production of a new type of razor blade three years ago. The production has been implemented, and the new blade has been sold for two years. The president of the company has asked the controller to perform an ex post audit of the investment in the new type of razor blade. An ex post audit is an examination of an investment after it has been made. The controller is complaining that the president just wants her to work overtime and there is no reason for this after-the-fact analysis. She points out that the investment already has been made and is now a sunk cost.

How can an ex post audit of a capital budgeting decision help an organization?

AIP 13.3
Ex Post Audit of a Capital Budgeting Decision
(LO 1)

Don Phelps recently started a dry cleaning business. He would like to expand it and add a coin-operated laundry. The expansion of the building and the washing machines and dryers will cost $100,000. The bank will lend the business $100,000 at a 12% interest rate. Don could get a 10% interest rate loan if he uses his personal house as collateral. The lower interest rate reflects the increased security of the loan to the bank because the bank could take Don's home if he does not pay the loan back. Don currently can put money in the bank and receive 6% interest.

Provide arguments for using 12%, 10%, and 6% as the opportunity cost of capital for evaluating the investment.

AIP 13.4
Identification of the Opportunity Cost of Capital
(LO 2)

The controller and the president are arguing about how to adjust for risk when evaluating investments. The president thinks that the best way to evaluate risk is to measure the payback period of an investment. The shorter the payback period, the lower is the risk. The controller believes that the net present value still should be used to evaluate investments. To adjust for risk, the discount rate is simply increased.

Provide arguments for and against each of these alternative methods.

AIP 13.5
Payback Period and Risk
(LO 3, 10)

The president of the company is not convinced that the interest expense should be excluded from the calculation of the net present value. She points out that "interest is a cash flow. You are supposed to discount cash flows. We borrowed money to completely finance this project. Why not discount interest expenditures?" The president is so convinced that she asks you, the controller, to calculate the net present value including the interest expense.

How can you adjust the net present value analysis to compensate for the inclusion of the interest expense?

AIP 13.6
Finance Charges and Net Present Value
(LO 8)

EXTENDED ANALYSIS AND INTERPRETATION PROBLEMS

Davenport Farms is a family-owned, fruit-growing operation. The farm currently includes 300 acres of orchards of apples, pears, and cherries and a warehouse for packing and storing fruit. Tom Davenport is the manager and owner of the farm, which has been in the family for several generations.

The farm operation requires a variety of heavy machinery including 10 tractors, eight trucks of varying sizes, a sprayer for insecticides, and a bulldozer for removing tree stumps. The warehouse also has considerable equipment for grading, sorting, and packing the fruit. Part of the warehouse is dedicated to storage and is refrigerated in an atmosphere with low oxygen content to reduce spoilage.

Davenport Farms has 20 permanent employees to maintain the equipment, prune trees, apply insecticides, and irrigate the trees. During picking seasons, however, the farm hires large numbers of migrant workers to pick and work in the warehouse.

Davenport Farms has had several successful years, and Tom is considering an expansion. Recently a 20-acre parcel adjacent to Davenport Farms became available for sale for $100,000. The land is currently bare and would have to be developed for irrigation and planted with apple trees. Development of the land for irrigation would take several months and cost $20,000 in materials. Apple trees can be planted immediately after the land is developed. Tom assumes that his existing labor force could provide the labor for developing and planting the trees.

Tom has not decided whether he would plant dwarf or full-sized apple trees. Dwarf apple trees produce fruit earlier (in the sixth year after planting) and require less space (100 per acre can be planted). The disadvantage is that dwarf apple trees do not last as long as full-sized trees and will have to be replaced after 20 years. Full-sized apple trees begin producing in the eleventh year after planting and are replaced after 40 years, but only 50

AIP 13.7
Davenport Farms

496   *Investment Decisions*

trees per acre can be planted. Annual cash expenses per acre are the same for each type of tree and each type of tree generates the same number of apples. The cost of both types of seedling apple trees is $5 per tree. Tom plans to hold the land for 40 years and sell it for $200,000. Tom has made the following estimates of costs and benefits of buying the land and planting either dwarf or full-sized trees for the next 40 years:

	Planting Dwarfs	Planting Full-Sized
Land costs (now)	($100,000)	($100,000)
Development costs (now)	(20,000)	(20,000)
Planting costs		
Dwarf ($5 per tree) (100 per acre)		
(20 acres) = $10,000 now	(10,000)	
In 20 years	(10,000)	
Full-sized ($5 per tree) (50 per acre)		
(20 acres) = $5,000 now		($5,000)
Stump removal and disposal		
(in 20 years)	($100,000)	
Other cash expenses ($20,000 per year)		
(40 years) = $800,000	($800,000)	($800,000)
Cash revenues		
Dwarf ($70,000 per year (Years		
6–20 and 26–40)	2,100,000	
Full-sized ($70,000 per year)		
(Years 11–40)		2,100,000
Sale of land	200,000	200,000
Total	$1,240,000	$1,275,000

Based on these estimates, the initial cash requirements to purchase and develop the land and plant dwarf trees is $130,000. If full-size trees are planted instead, the initial cost is $125,000. Tom has $40,000 of cash available to make this investment. The rest of the costs can be covered by a mortgage from the local bank, which charges 10% interest for mortgages of this type. Tom will need to borrow $90,000 if he plants dwarf trees and $85,000 if he plants full-size trees. He figures that his cost of capital is the interest rate that the bank charges.

a.   Using the net present value analysis, should Tom buy the land? If so, which type of trees should he plant?

b.   What other factors should be considered in making this land acquisition that are not captured in the present value analysis?

AIP 13.8
Performance Measures and Investment Opportunities

Sarah Adams manages Executive Inns of Toronto, a 200-room facility that rents furnished suites to executives on a monthly basis. The market is people relocating to Toronto who are waiting for permanent housing. Sarah's compensation contains a fixed component and a bonus based on the net cash flows from operations. Sarah seeks to maximize her compensation. While Sarah likes her job, and has learned a lot, she expects to be working for a financial institution within five years.

Sarah's occupancy rate is running at 98%. She is considering a $10 million addition to her present building to add more rental units. She has very good private knowledge of the future cash flows. In year 1, cash flows will be $2 million and then will decline by $100,000 per year. The following table summarizes the expansion's cash flows:

Year	Net Cash Flow (millions)
0	($10)
1	$2.0
2	1.9
3	1.8
4	1.7
5	1.6
6	1.5
7	1.4
8	1.3
9	1.2
10	1.1

Based on the preceding data, Sarah prepares the following analysis of the discounted cash flow of the addition:

Year	Net Cash Flow (millions)	Discount Factor	Present Value of Cash Flow
0	($10)	1.000	($10)
1	$2.0	.893	1.79
2	1.9	.787	1.51
3	1.8	.712	1.28
4	1.7	.636	1.08
5	1.6	.567	.91
6	1.5	.507	.76
7	1.4	.452	.63
8	1.3	.404	.53
9	1.2	.361	.43
10	1.1	.322	.35
Total			($.72)

The discount factors are based on a weighted-average cost of capital of 12%, which accurately reflects the inn's non-diversifiable risk.

Sarah Adams' boss, Kathy Judson, manages the Inn Division of Comfort Inc. which has 15 properties located across North America. Kathy does not have the detailed knowledge of the Toronto hotel/rental market, as does Sarah. She has some general knowledge, but neither as detailed nor as accurate as Sarah does. (For the questions below, ignore taxes.)

a. The Inns Division has a very crude accounting system that does not assign the depreciation of particular inns to individual managers. Therefore, Sarah's annual net cash-flow statement is based on the operating revenues less operating expenses. Neither the cost of expansion nor the depreciation of the inn expansion is charged to her operating statement. Given the facts provided so far, what decision do you expect Sarah to make regarding building the $10 million addition? Explain why?

b. Sarah prepares the following report for Kathy Judson to justify the expansion project:

Year	Net Cash Flow (millions)	Discount Factor	Present Value of Cash Flow
0	($10)	1.000	($10)
1	2	0.893	1.79
2	1.9	0.797	1.51
3	1.9	0.712	1.35
4	1.8	0.636	1.14
5	1.8	0.567	1.02
6	1.8	0.507	0.91
7	1.8	0.452	0.81
8	1.8	0.404	0.73
9	1.7	0.361	0.61
10	1.7	0.322	0.55
Net Present Value			$0.43

Kathy realizes that Sarah's projected cash flows are most likely optimistic. However, she does not know how optimistic, or whether or not the project even has a positive net present value. She decides, therefore, to change the performance measure used to compute Sarah's bonus. Sarah's compensation now will be based on residual income. Kathy also changes the accounting system to track asset expansion and depreciation on the expansion. Sarah's profits from operations now will be charged for straight-line depreciation of the expansion using a 10-year life (assume a zero salvage value). Calculate Sarah's expected residual income from the expansion for each of the next 10 years.

c. Based on your calculations in part (b), will Sarah propose the expansion project? Explain why.

d. Instead of using residual income as Sarah's performance measure in part (b), Kathy uses net cash flows from operations less straight-line depreciation. Will Sarah seek to undertake the expansion? Explain why.

e. Reconcile any differences in your answers for parts (c) and (d) above.

Chapter**Fourteen**

Standard Costs and Variance Analysis

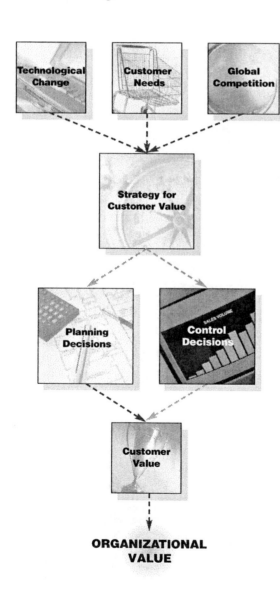

EDWARD ODELL, CONTRACTOR

Edward Odell started as a carpenter working on new homes. He soon tired of broken thumbnails and chilled bones and decided to become a contractor. He subcontracted with others to do most of the work on the new houses but maintained a crew to do the wood framing. Ed was successful while the local economy was doing well, but new

housing starts are very sensitive to interest rates and the economy. At times he had to lay off his crew. He believed that there must be something to do with the crew during down time in the local economy, so he approached a Japanese company about exporting wall sections to Japan.

Traditional home construction in Japan has always conserved wood, which is a relatively scarce resource there. But recently demand has increased for more substantial houses with walls built using 2″ × 4″s (1 ½ inches × 3 ½ inches) instead of smaller boards. Ed believed that he could successfully make and ship wall sections using 2″ × 4″s to Japan.

Ed received an initial order for 1,000 wall sections; they were 8 feet by 12 feet with drywall on one side. He leased some warehouse space and began construction. The first order was a real learning experience. The wall sections were relatively easy to make, but moving and shipping them led to many problems given their size and weight. Also, the Japanese company would accept wall sections made only of clear fir (no knots) even though the 2″ × 4″s would eventually be hidden behind the drywall and the exterior covering. Ed lost money on this first order, but the Japanese company was interested in more and larger orders, which were for a variety of different sizes of wall sections.

Ed believed that he could do better the next time with a little more control of the manufacturing system. In particular, he was certain that he could save costs by reducing excess scrap and slack time for his workers. He had heard that standard costing systems might help him achieve those goals and make the new orders more profitable.

Ed reorganized his business by putting Jeff Pringle in charge of buying lumber, drywall, and other supplies. Barbara Kaplan was put in charge of the framing, and Chet Slocum was assigned to manage the drywall process. Ed remained in charge of administration and marketing.

STANDARD COSTS

Historical costs are useful for satisfying financial reporting requirements, such as deriving unit product costs for valuing inventories (balance sheet) and cost of goods sold (income statement). Historical costs also can be a useful starting point for estimating opportunity costs, yet historical costs do not provide any built-in controls or benchmarks as to what costs should be. They state only what the costs actually were. An over- or underabsorbed overhead number conveys some information about whether the plant has met expectations with respect to overhead. However, no benchmarks exist as to whether direct labor or direct materials are too high or too low, except by comparing the actual results to the same numbers from prior periods.

Control Decisions

Standard costs provide these benchmarks. They represent the expected future cost of a product, service, process, or subcomponent. Once standards are set, managers can gauge performance by comparing actual operating results against the standards. The difference between an actual and standard cost is called a **variance.** Variances provide useful information for senior management in determining whether the production system is operating efficiently. Variances are an important part of the control process. Like budget variances discussed in Chapter Eight, standard cost variances are attention getters. They alert senior managers that something is not going according to plan. Variances also provide information for performance evaluation. In addition to their role in control, standard costs are useful in making planning decisions such as product pricing, make-versus-buy, and plant resource allocation. This chapter primarily examines standard costs in production settings, but standard costing is used in service organizations and other nonmanufacturing activities, such as marketing and sales. Standard costing techniques assist organizational members in creating customer and organizational value by meeting cost and quality objectives.

This chapter describes the use of standard costs for planning and control. The conflict between planning and control, which you have seen in previous chapters, also exists in standard cost systems. The focus of this chapter is on the costs and benefits of standard cost systems.

Reasons for Standard Costing

LO 1 Provide reasons for using standard costs.

Historical costs often can prove misleading for planning purposes. They can be out of date if operating conditions, material prices, or wages have changed or are expected to change. Operating conditions in the past might not provide a valid basis for forecasting the future, especially when new products are introduced or a new manufacturing process is implemented.

Planning Decisions

Organizations frequently use standard costs instead of historical costs in a wide variety of planning decision contexts: product pricing, contract bidding, outsourcing, and assessing alternative production technologies. Standard costs are part of the budgeting system, which organizations utilize to coordinate their operating plans for the coming year. The estimated product cost at the beginning of the year is a standard cost. Standard costs convey information about product costs among the different parts of the organization. For example, marketing managers usually rely on standard costs to make selling decisions.

Standard costs also provide information for control. As part of the budgeting process, standard costs might be the basis for contracts among the organization's managers. Manufacturing managers agree to supply a certain number of units of the product at a standard cost. Service department managers agree to supply their services at a standard cost. Managerial performance is evaluated based on managers' success in achieving these standard costs. Achieving standard costs can lead to bonuses and rewards and, in some cases, promotions.

Large variances between actual and standard costs indicate that a particular activity differs significantly from what was expected when the standard was set.

Variances are treated as signals that activities might be out of control and corrective action might be necessary. Not all variances necessarily indicate a problem, however; they also might indicate that the environment has changed and the standards are no longer appropriate. The variance itself does not tell the manager exactly what is wrong. Further investigation is usually necessary to determine its cause. **Management by exception** is a management strategy that focuses management effort on significant variances. When actual costs are close to the standard costs, managers assume that the activity is operating as planned and no further investigation is necessary.

Surveys indicate that most large manufacturing firms use standard costs. Standard cost systems are common in large organizations, but some managers question their costs and benefits. Some firms are scaling back on their reliance on standard costs, changing how they estimate standard costs, or even abandoning their standard cost systems. Many organizations supplement their standard cost reports with nonfinancial information. The problems generally reflect the trade-off between using standard costs for planning decisions and control. This trade-off is outlined in the next section.

Setting and Revising of Standards

No commonly accepted method for deriving standard costs exists. Some experts argue that standard costs should be attainable, meaning the cost that is achievable if normal effort and environmental effects prevail. Others argue that the standards should be those that will occur with extra effort. How difficult the standards should be to attain and how much weight to place on their achievement for performance evaluation purposes are important issues in the design of the firm's organizational structure. These issues involve trading off the costs and benefits of tight versus loose standards. One survey reported that 50% of the firms said that they set standards to be the expected actual costs yet difficult to attain, 42% say that standards were set based on average past performance, and 8% said that they set the standard as the maximum theoretical efficiency level.[1]

If the standard cost is to reflect the cost of using a resource, standard setting and revision require communication with individuals who have specific knowledge. The standard cost should contain all specific knowledge pertaining to the resource. Standards that are the most accurate estimates of costs are the most useful in conveying information within the firm about alternative resource utilization.

The accuracy of the standard as a measure of cost, however, is often compromised for control reasons. Usually managers with the specific knowledge for updating the standard are evaluated, at least in part, based on the difference between their actual performance and the standard. Managers are reluctant to reveal information that might be used later to penalize them. This issue was described in Chapter Eight in terms of motivating managers to reveal private knowledge in setting next year's budget when their performance will be judged relative to the budget.

Planning decisions require assembling the specialized knowledge that often resides only with the person or unit of the firm that later will be judged by the standard. For example, the purchasing department has the specialized knowledge to set the purchase price standard. If that department also has the responsibility to set the purchase price standard, the standard becomes less useful in evaluating the purchasing department manager's performance. One solution is to separate the setting of the standard from approving, ratifying, and monitoring it.

LO 2 Describe planning and control issues in setting standards.

Planning Decisions

---

[1]W. Cress and J. Pettijohn, "A Survey of Budget-Related Planning and Control Policies and Procedures," *Journal of Accounting Education* 3 (Fall 1985), p. 66. A related study finds "a large majority of profit center budget targets are set so they can and will be achieved"; see K. Merchant, *Rewarding Results: Motivating Profit Center Managers* (Boston: Harvard Business School Press, 1989), p. 30.

Usually, the accounting or industrial engineering department has the responsibility to set or change standards. Individuals responsible for the standard cost variance have some ability to influence the standards, which are reviewed and revised each year as part of the annual budgeting cycle. In the study referred to earlier, 79% of the respondents said that three or more of the following groups participated in setting the standards: industrial engineering, purchasing, personnel, accounting, top management, and line managers with specific cost responsibility. Standard costs were reviewed for possible revision annually by 62% of the firms and quarterly by 15% of them.[2]

A common approach to derive standard costs is a bottom-up technique. Usually, the manager who will be held responsible for meeting the standards submits an initial estimate of it. Industrial engineers, controllers, and higher-level managers then review and ratify the standard. Sometimes industrial engineers submit the initial estimate of the standard. In all cases, setting and revising standards involve assembling specific knowledge from various individuals in the firm. The standard cost of each type of labor, material, and overhead is estimated, and the standard cost of the complete product is built up from the sum of these individual costs.

Target costing is a top-down approach. It starts with the long-term price, estimated by marketing, required to achieve a desired market share. The required return on investment (profits) is subtracted from this price to derive a total target product cost. This total target cost then is divided into subcomponent costs, including selling and distribution costs. These subcomponent costs become the targets or standards to be achieved if the firm is to meet its goals for market penetration, cost reduction, and return on capital. Target costs then become part of the performance evaluation system.[3] Chapter Four discussed target costing in more detail.

Once standards are set, they are used to judge performance by calculating the variance between the actual cost and the standard cost. In general, most firms produce three sets of standard cost variances: direct labor variances, direct materials variances, and overhead variances. Since direct labor and materials are quite similar, their calculations and incentive effects are discussed together in the next two sections. Overhead variances are more complicated and are described generally in the section "Overhead Standard Costs and Variances." Specific overhead variance calculations are described in the Appendix to this chapter.

The variances described in this chapter are generic to a wide cross-section of applications. Not every department, plant, and company will use all the variances in this chapter. Some organizations develop other variances; for example, many firms also calculate sales and marketing variances. Variances and their analysis are tailored to the organization's specific requirements. The following discussion illustrates the types of variances possible and their advantages and disadvantages.

Concept**Review**

1. Why do organizations use standard costing?

2. How are standards set?

---

[2]Cress and Pettijohn, "A Survey," p. 74.

[3]See Y. Kato, "Target Costing Support Systems: Lessons from Leading Japanese Companies," *Management Accounting Research* 4 (March 1993) pp. 33–47; T. Hiromoto, "Another Hidden Edge: Japanese Management Accounting," *Harvard Business Review*, July–August 1988, pp. 22–26; and M. Sakurai, "Target Costing and How to Use It," *Journal of Cost Management for Manufacturing Industry*, Summer 1989, pp. 39–50.

Ed thinks that standard costing fits his business quite well. Making wall sections requires a series of repetitive actions by workers, and the material requirements are fairly easy to measure. He hopes the standard costs will do two things for him: (1) determine product costs for the different sizes of wall sections so he can do a better job of pricing and (2) encourage managers and workers to use the materials and their time more efficiently.

To implement the standard costing system, Ed calls in his managers and explains the problems. To encourage them to pay attention to the standards, he tells them that he will give them bonuses if their department performs better than the standards. Jeff Pringle will be responsible for the material price variances, and Barbara and Chet will be responsible for the direct labor variances and the material quantity variances, respectively. Then he asks them for input on establishing the standards. Jeff believes that lumber prices are going up in the future, so the standard price of the lumber should be higher than today's price. Barbara and Chet think the standards should recognize some scrap and slack labor time.

Ed realizes that his managers are not going to be completely forthcoming in establishing standards. Therefore, he decides to set them based on his knowledge of prices and the process of making wall sections. The following standards for direct labor and direct materials are used for making the 8 feet by 12 feet wall section:

EDWARD
ODELL,
CONTRACTOR
(Continued)

Direct labor cost	$8 per hour
Direct labor time per unit	3 hours
Material costs	
Lumber	$0.10 per board foot
Drywall	$2 per sheet
Material per unit	
Lumber	72 board feet
Drywall	3 sheets

The estimated direct costs per unit are as follows:

Direct labor ($8 per hour) (3 hours)	$24.00
Direct materials	
Lumber ($0.10 per board foot) (72 board feet)	7.20
Drywall ($2 per sheet) (3 sheets)	6.00
Total direct costs per unit	$37.20

DIRECT LABOR AND DIRECT MATERIALS VARIANCES

Within an organization, variances are used primarily to identify problems in following a prescribed plan. Variances are calculated to help managers determine the cause and responsibility for the problem. By partitioning variances into component variances, cause and responsibility become easier to identify. This section describes how standard cost variances for direct labor and materials are decomposed and calculated.

LO 3   Calculate direct labor and direct materials variances.

Direct labor and materials costs are composed of a price per unit and a quantity. In other words, the cost of direct labor is the wage rate per hour (price per unit) times the number of hours worked (quantity). The cost of direct materials used is the purchase price per unit of the materials times the quantity of units used. Any variance between the actual and standard costs is due to the difference in the actual price per unit and/or actual quantity from the standard price or quantity. Recognizing the dual effect of price and quantity on costs allows the direct labor and materials variances to be decomposed into two parts: (1) variance due to the actual price per unit differing from the standard price per unit and (2) variance due to the actual quantity differing from the standard quantity.

Direct Labor Variances

The **direct labor variance** is the difference between the actual direct labor costs and the standard direct labor costs for a period of time. The direct labor variance can be decomposed into a **wage rate variance** and a **labor efficiency variance.** The following equations define the wage rate and labor efficiency variances so that the sum of the two variances equals the direct labor variance:

$$\text{Direct labor variance} = \text{Actual cost of labor} - \text{Standard cost of labor}$$
$$= (\text{Actual wage rate} \times \text{Actual hours}) - (\text{Standard wage rate} \times \text{Standard hours})$$
$$\text{Wage rate variance} = (\text{Actual wage rate} - \text{Standard wage rate}) \times \text{Actual hours}$$
$$\text{Labor efficiency variance} = (\text{Actual hours} - \text{Standard hours}) \times \text{Standard wage rate}$$
$$\text{Direct labor variance} = \text{Wage rate variance} + \text{Labor efficiency variance}$$

The wage rate variance focuses on the difference between the actual wage rate and the standard wage rate. The labor efficiency variance highlights the difference between the actual direct labor hours and the standard direct labor hours.

To demonstrate the calculation of direct variances, an example of the printing costs of the Smith *art book* is used. The standard costs to make a batch of 1,000 books are reported in Table 14.1.

The standard costs to make the 1,000 copies of the Smith *art book* are used as benchmarks for comparison with actual costs. Table 14.2 describes the actual costs.

Table 14.1

Standard Cost Sheet

Smith *art book:* 1,000 copies

Direct Materials				Direct Labor			
Type	Quantity	Price	Amount	Type	Hours	Wage	Amount
Paper	800 kg.	$2	$ 1,600	Typesetters	80	$15	$ 1,200
Covers	2,000	3	6,000	Printers	55	40	2,200
Binding	500 kg.	4	2,000	Binders	70	20	1,400
Totals			$9,600				$ 4,800

Total direct materials	$ 9,600
Total direct labor	4,800
Total overhead ($100 per printer hour)	5,500
Total cost	$19,900
Number of copies	÷ 1000
Cost per book	$19.90

Table 14.2

Actual Cost Sheet

Smith *art book:* 1,000 copies

Direct Materials				Direct Labor			
Type	**Quantity**	**Price**	**Amount**	**Type**	**Hours**	**Wage**	**Amount**
Paper	810 kg.	$2.10	$1,701	Typesetters	85	$15.40	$ 1,309
Covers	2,010	2.90	5,829	Printers	53	41.00	2,173
Binding	490 kg.	4.20	2,058	Binders	72	19.50	1,404
Totals			$9,588				$ 4,886

Total direct materials	$ 9,588
Total direct labor	4,886
Total overhead ($100 per printer hour)	5,300
Total cost	$19,774
Number of copies	÷ 1000
Cost per book	$ 19.77

The actual costs are $19,774, which is $126 less than the standard cost of $19,900. The $126 is called a **favorable variance**. A favorable variance occurs when the actual costs are less than the standard costs. An **unfavorable variance** occurs if actual costs are more than standard costs.

The existence of a $126 favorable variance for printing the 1,000 copies of the Smith *art book* does not tell the manager much about the cause of the variance. To understand the total cost variance better, the cost variance can be broken into parts representing the prices and quantities of each of the inputs of the manufacturing process. For example, the direct labor variance for the typesetters can be decomposed into a wage rate variance and a labor efficiency variance:

Wage rate variance = (Actual wage rate − Standard wage rate) ×
Actual hours

Typesetters ($15.40 − $15.00) × 85	$34 U
Printers ($41.00 − $40.00) × 53	53 U
Binders ($19.50 − $20.00) × 72	36 F
Total	$51 U

Note: U denotes unfavorable variance and F denotes favorable variance.

Labor efficiency variance = (Actual hours − Standard hours) ×
Standard wage rate

Typesetters (85 − 80) × $15.00	$75 U
Printers (53 − 55) × $40.00	80 F
Binders (72 − 70) × $20.00	40 U
Total	$35 U

Notice that the sum of the wage variance and the efficiency variance ($51 + $35 = $86) is the difference between the total standard labor costs ($4,800) and the actual labor costs ($4,886). The relation among the direct labor variances is described in Table 14.3.

The variance analysis indicates that the unfavorable labor variances are primarily due to typesetter labor costs. The sum of the wage rate variance and the labor efficiency variance for printers is favorable and for binders only slightly

LO 4   Identify potential causes of different favorable and unfavorable variances.

Table 14.3

Relations among Direct
Labor Variances

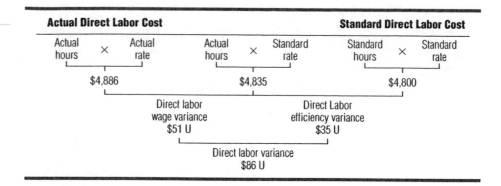

Figure 14.1

Direct Labor Variances

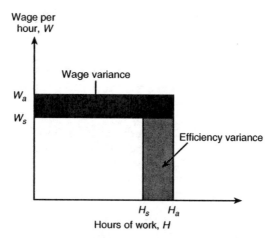

W_a is the actual wage H_a is the actual hours
W_s is the standard wage H_s is the standard hours

$$\text{Total labor variance} = W_aH_a - W_sH_s$$
$$\text{Wage variance} = (W_a - W_s) \times H_a$$
$$\text{Efficiency variance} = (H_a - H_s) \times W_s$$

unfavorable. The typesetter labor costs exceeded standard because (1) $0.40 more per hour was paid than expected and (2) 5 hours more typesetter hours were used than expected. If management believes that the standards are correct, the typesetter labor variances indicate that the person responsible for assigning typesetters to the Smith *art book* assigned these with a higher actual wage rate per hour than expected. Also, the typesetters' supervisor allowed more typesetting hours than expected. The costs of these two "errors" are $34 for paying too much per hour and $75 for using too many hours. Clearly, management's ability to draw these inferences depends on its belief that the standards are indeed unbiased forecasts of what the typesetting wage rates should have been and how many hours of typesetting should have been used.

The foregoing analysis is illustrated graphically in Figure 14.1. In the figure, the rectangle $W_s \times H_s$ represents what the labor should have cost and the rectangle $W_a \times H_a$ represents what the labor actually cost. The total typesetting labor variance is the difference between the actual typesetting cost and what it should have cost, $W_aH_a - W_sH_s$. This difference is the shaded areas in Figure 14.1, which are decomposed into a wage variance (the top shaded rectangle) and an efficiency variance (the shaded rectangle on the right).

Numerical Example 14.1

A CPA firm estimates that an audit will require the following work:

Type of Auditor	Expected Hours	Cost per Hour	Standard Costs
Manager	10	$50	$ 500
Senior	20	40	800
Staff	40	30	1,200
Totals	70		$2,500

The following were the actual hours and costs:

Type of Auditor	Actual Hours	Actual Cost per Hour	Actual Costs
Manager	9	$52	$ 468
Senior	22	38	836
Staff	44	30	1,320
Totals	75		$2,624

Calculate the direct labor, wage rate, and labor efficiency variances for each type of auditor and interpret them.

Solution

The direct labor variance for each type of auditor follows:

Type of Auditor	Actual Costs	Standard Costs	Direct Labor Variance
Manager	$ 468	$ 500	($ 32) F
Senior	836	800	36 U
Staff	1,320	1,200	120 U
Totals	$2,624	$2,500	$124 U

The wage rate rate variance for each type of auditor follows:

Manager ($52 per hour − $50 per hour) (9 hours)	$18 U
Senior ($38 per hour − $40 per hour) (22 hours)	(44) F
Staff ($30 per hour − $30 per hour) (44 hours)	0
Total wage rate variance	($26) F

The labor efficiency variance for each type of auditor is as follows:

Manager (9 hours − 10 hours) ($50 per hour)	($ 50) F
Senior (22 hours − 20 hours) ($40 per hour)	80 U
Staff (44 hours − 40 hours) ($30 per hour)	120 U
Total labor efficiency variance	$150 U

Note that the direct labor variance equals the sum of the wage rate and labor efficiency variances. The favorable wage rate variance means that, on average, the auditors were paid less than expected, although managers were paid more than expected. The unfavorable labor efficiency variance means that, on average, the auditors took longer to complete the audit than expected. The manager, however, spent less time on the audit than expected.

Large variances, either favorable or unfavorable, can mean that the activity is out of control. An accounting variance can indicate that either the operating unit deviated from an appropriate standard or faulty assumptions were used to develop the standard. In the first case, direct labor supervisors did not operate at the levels assumed in the standards. Direct labor was used more or less efficiently than expected. In the second case, the standards were set at a level that could not be attained even if the supervisor used the direct labor as efficiently as possible. A large unfavorable variance does not mean necessarily that the person responsible is performing below expectations.

LO 4   Identify potential causes of different favorable and unfavorable variances.

Large favorable variances are not necessarily good news because they could signal that quality is being reduced. For example, one way to generate favorable labor efficiency variances is to use too few labor hours and produce lower-quality products. Likewise, favorable wage rate variances might mean that lower-skilled, lower-paid workers were employed, a decision that could compromise product quality. Managers and supervisors do not investigate all variances since the cost to investigate and gather further information may be greater than any additional benefits from doing so. Variance investigation is examined in more detail later in the chapter.

The personnel department is held responsible for the wage rate variance if that department is responsible for hiring workers with specific job skills at a given standard wage rate. In other cases, a shop floor supervisor who schedules different workers with varying skills and wage rates to produce the product is held responsible for wage rate variances. A supervisor who can change the mix of workers and, thus, the cost of the job by substituting more or fewer skilled workers at different wage rates is usually assigned the total direct labor variance. In this case, there is no reason to compute separately a wage variance and an efficiency variance except to provide information about what caused the labor variance.

The extent to which wage and efficiency variances are used to measure performance depends on the reliability of the underlying standards, the inherent variability of the wages and hours due to random fluctuations, and how much of the variance is potentially controllable by the manager. Some organizations place large weight on variances in performance evaluations; others place little or no weight on them.

Numerical Example 14.2

The CPA firm in Numerical Example 14.1 awards bonus compensation to managers based on their ability to meet budgeted costs. Each manager's bonus is adjusted for the direct labor variance by adding or deducting 50 percent of the direct labor variances, excluding those related to managerial labor, to the performance bonus.

What is the manager's bonus for the audit engagement?

Solution

The direct labor variance for senior and staff auditors is as follows:

Type of Auditor	Actual Costs	Standard Costs	Direct Labor Variance
Senior	$ 836	$ 800	$ 36 U
Staff	1,320	1,200	120 U
Totals	$2,624	$2,500	$156 U

The wage rate variance for senior and staff auditors follows:

Senior ($38 per hour − $40 per hour) (22 hours)	($44) F
Staff ($30 per hour − $30 per hour) (44 hours)	0
Total wage rate variance	($44) F

The labor efficiency variance for senior and staff auditors follows:

Senior (22 hours − 20 hours) ($40 per hour)	$ 80 U
Staff (44 hours − 40 hours) ($30 per hour)	120 U
Total labor efficiency variance	$200 U

The direct labor variance is $156 Unfavorable. Therefore, 50 percent of $156, or $78, is deducted from the audit manager's bonus. This bonus scheme motivates the manager to control costs. This manager used more senior and staff hours than anticipated. However, these additional hours were not offset by the lower total wage rate paid to senior auditors. The system is effective if the manager has the ability to change the mix of the audit team members to meet the budget. The audit manager still might consider that the bonus scheme is unfair if the firm's personnel department establishes wage rates.

Direct Materials Variances

Direct materials variances are similar to those computed for direct labor. As with direct labor, the total direct materials variance can be decomposed into a **material price variance** and a **material quantity variance**. The calculations are identical to those for direct labor:

Direct material variance = Actual cost of material − Standard cost of material = (Actual price × Actual quantity) − (Standard price × Standard quantity)

Price variance = (Actual price − Standard price) × Actual quantity

Quantity variance = (Actual quantity − Standard quantity) × Standard price

Direct material variance = Price variance + Quantity variance

Figure 14.2 illustrates how the total materials variance is decomposed into a material price variance and a material quantity variance under the assumption that *all materials purchased are used immediately in production.* As in Figure 14.1, this difference is the shaded areas in Figure 14.2.

The material price variance typically is reported to the purchasing manager and is one measure of the purchasing manager's performance. To be timely, the price variance should be calculated at the time of purchase. The time of purchase and the time the material is used may be different. Other performance measures for the purchasing department or its manager include the percentage of on-time delivery of materials and material quality.

The quantity variance is reported to the manager responsible for the efficient use of materials (usually the shop supervisor) and is one performance measure of this manager. Other performance measures for the shop supervisor include quality of output and timely manufacturing.

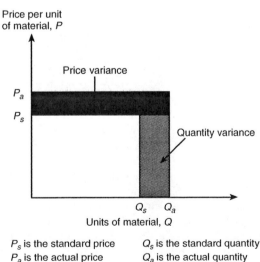

Figure 14.2

Direct Materials Variances (materials used as purchased)

P_s is the standard price Q_s is the standard quantity
P_a is the actual price Q_a is the actual quantity

Total materials variance = $P_a Q_a - P_s Q_s$
Price variance = $(P_a - P_s) \times Q_a$
Quantity variance = $(Q_a - Q_s) \times P_s$

Table 14.4

Relation among Direct
Material Variances

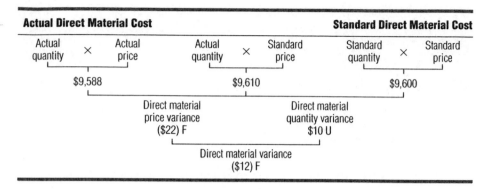

The calculation of material price variances is demonstrated using the standard cost data for the Smith *art book* in Table 14.1 and the actual cost data in Table 14.2. The total direct material variance is $9,588 − $9,600, or $12 favorable. This variance can be decomposed into the material price variance and the material quantity variance. The material price variances for each of the materials for the Smith *art book* are as follows:

$$\text{Material price variance} = (\text{Actual price} - \text{Standard price}) \times \text{Actual quantity}$$

Paper ($2.10 per kg. − $2.00 per kg.) (810 kg.)	$ 81 U
Covers ($2.90 − $3.00) (2,010)	(201) F
Binding ($4.20 − $4.00) (490 kg.)	98 U
Total material price variance	($ 22) F

The material quantity variance for each of the materials follows:

$$\text{Material quantity variance} = (\text{Actual quantity} - \text{Standard quantity}) \times \text{Standard price}$$

Paper (810 kg. − 800 kg.) ($2 per kg.)	$20 U
Covers (2,010 − 2,000) ($3)	30 U
Binding (490 kg. − 500 kg.) ($4 per kg.)	(40) F
Total quantity variance	$10 U

Table 14.4 demonstrates the relation among the direct material variances.

In a standard cost system, materials are recorded in the Raw Materials Inventory account at standard cost. That is, inventory is stated at standard price, not actual price. The material price variance is recorded in a separate ledger account. This variance usually is written off to the Cost of Goods Sold account at the end of the year instead of flowing through inventory and product costs. For example, suppose that 100 kilograms of copper are purchased for $12 per kilogram when the standard price is $10 per kg. The purchase is recorded in the Raw Materials Inventory account at $1,000, and the $200 difference is recorded separately in a materials price variance account (at the time of purchase). Future products using this copper are charged $10, not $12, per kilogram. By recording the $200 in a separate account and writing it off directly to cost of sales, the unit cost of the products using the copper is not distorted by the price variation of $2 per kilogram.

The advantage of recording raw materials at standard cost is that downstream users in the plant see only standard costs. Likewise, labor is charged to products and jobs at standard cost. If standard costs are unbiased forecasts of future costs, then using standard costs gives downstream managers more accurate information regarding the opportunity cost of the raw material. Of course, this discussion assumes that standard raw material prices are more accurate predictors of opportunity costs than are actual raw material prices. Using standard costs also reduces the risk borne by downstream "purchasers" of the product, such as the marketing department. At the beginning of the year, downstream users know what they will be charged for raw materials throughout the year. Price changes or inefficient use of materials do not affect the downstream users. The use of standard costs thus removes uncontrollable factors from the performance measures of downstream users.

Figure 14.3

Direct Materials Variances (materials purchased but not used yet)

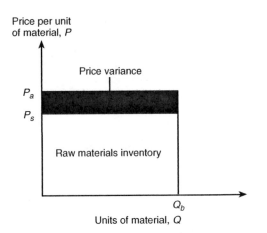

P_a is the actual price Q_b is the actual quantity bought
P_s is the standard price

Price variance $= (P_a - P_s) \times Q_b$

Figure 14.3 depicts the more usual case in which raw material is bought, placed in raw materials inventory, and then used at a later date. In Figure 14.3, the material price variance is isolated as soon as the raw material is purchased. The raw materials inventory is stated thereby at the standard cost per unit. The price variance is reported as soon as the material is bought, not when it is used at some later date. Once the material price variance is isolated at purchase, all the remaining withdrawals from the Raw Materials Inventory account are stated at the same standard cost per unit.

Given that the direct material is recorded at standard cost when it is used, there is no further material price variance. The only direct material variance that is calculated at the time of use is the material quantity variance, which is the difference between the actual and standard amount of materials used at the standard cost per unit.

Numerical Example   14.3

A tire manufacturer has a standard quantity of 3 kilograms (kg.) of fiberglass cord per automobile tire. The standard price is $1 per kg. During the month, the purchasing manager bought 98,000 kg. of fiberglass cord for $102,000. The plant used 95,000 kg. of it to manufacture 30,000 tires during the month. What are the material price and quantity variances for the fiberglass cord?

Solution

The material price variance is calculated at the time of purchase. The actual purchase price per kilogram is $102,000/98,000, or $1.04082 per kg. Therefore, the material price variance is ($1.04082 per kg. − $1.00 per kg.) (98,000 kg.), or $4,000 unfavorable.

The material quantity variance is calculated when the material is used. In this case, 95,000 kg. were used. But (3 kg. per tire) (30,000 tires), or 90,000 kg., should have been used according to the standard. The material quantity variance is (95,000 kg. − 90,000 kg.) ($1 per kg.), or $5,000 unfavorable.

The material price and quantity variances often are interrelated. For example, if substandard materials are purchased at a price below the standard price, an unfavorable material quantity variance usually results because more material than standard is used. If a less expensive exterior house paint is purchased, more of it probably will be required to provide the same coverage that a higher-quality, higher-priced paint would provide. A variance in one area is likely to be related to other variances. A favorable material price variance might cause an unfavorable material quantity variance, or a favorable labor efficiency variance from one type

L0 4   Identify potential causes of different favorable and unfavorable variances.

of labor might be the result of another unfavorable labor efficiency variance if another type of labor is substituted. A favorable materials price variance and a resulting unfavorable materials quantity variance can cause unfavorable labor efficiency variances if extra material and labor are used due to the substandard materials. Therefore, as a performance measurement system of the manufacturing process, the variances must be analyzed as an integrated whole.

Concept**Review**

1. What are the two components of direct labor and material costs?
2. What is the relation between standard and actual costs when the variance is favorable?
3. What type of manager is likely to be responsible for labor wage and efficiency variances?
4. What type of manager is likely to be responsible for material price and quantity variances?
5. Under what conditions would the material quantity variance be unfavorable?

EDWARD ODELL, CONTRACTOR (Continued)

The latest order to Ed for 8 feet by 12 feet wall sections is for 3,000 units. Given the standards that he has set for constructing the wall sections, Ed has estimated the total direct costs of making the 3,000 wall sections to be (3,000 units)($37.20 per unit), or $111,600. Ed is pleased to find that the actual direct costs of completing the order are only $107,990. The total direct cost variance for the order is $111,600 − $107,990, or $3,610 favorable. He figures that the standard costing system is working. The following information used to calculate direct cost variances, however, makes him wonder what is happening:

Purchases
    Lumber 300,000 board feet at $0.09 per board foot
    Drywall 15,000 sheets at $1.90 per sheet
Actual labor used: 10,000 hours at $7.00 per hour
Standard labor: (3,000 units)(3 hours per unit) = 9,000 hours
Actual direct material used
    Lumber 230,000 board feet
    Drywall 9,100 sheets
Standard material
    Lumber (3,000 units)(72 board feet per unit) = 216,000 board feet
    Drywall (3,000 units)(3 sheets per unit) = 9,000 sheets

The variances for direct costs for the order are as follows:

Wage rate variance: ($7.00 − $8.00)(10,000 hours)	($10,000) F
Labor efficiency variance: (10,000 − 9,000)($8.00/hour)	8,000 U
Material price variance for materials used for order	
Lumber ($0.09 − $0.10)(230,000 board feet)	(2,300) F
Drywall ($1.90 − $2.00)(9,100 sheets)	(910) F
Material quantity variance	
Lumber (230,000 − 216,000)($0.10 per board foot)	1,400 U
Drywall (9,100 − 9,000)($2 per sheet)	200 U
Total direct cost variance	($ 3,610) F

Jeff Pringle, the purchasing manager, is especially pleased with himself. The material price variances for both the lumber and drywall are favorable. He estimates that the material price variance would be even higher if the material price variance were calculated based on the amount purchased rather than the amount used. Both Barbara Kaplan and Chet Slocum report favorable wage rate variances to offset unfavorable labor efficiency and material quantity variances. They both claim that the unfavorable quantity variances are due to poor-quality materials.

The variance analysis worries Ed. The total cost of making the order is less than the total standard cost, but certain aspects of the analysis make him feel his problems are not over. The managers' concerns about the quality of materials are especially bothersome, given the Japanese customer's requirement for high quality. Also, Barbara and Chet apparently have hired lower-waged workers to complete the order. Are these workers capable of producing work to meet the quality requirements of the customer? Also, why did Jeff purchase far more materials than were needed for the order? Eventually, they will use the materials, but holding the inventory will be costly. Standard costing is proving to be more complex than expected.

INCENTIVE EFFECTS OF DIRECT LABOR AND MATERIALS VARIANCES

Standard costs and variances, when used as part of the performance evaluation system, create incentives for managers to control costs. Standards are part of the performance evaluation system, as described in Chapter Six. If the standard cost system is not designed properly and is not integrated consistently with the other parts of the organizational structure including assignment of responsibilities, performance measures, and compensation, however, dysfunctional behavior can ensue.

When used as performance measures, standard cost variances create subtle incentive effects. The following section describes five effects: (1) the incentive to build inventories and/or lower quality, (2) externalities, (3) uncooperative effort, (4) mutual monitoring incentives, and (5) satisficing behavior.

LO 5 Recognize incentive effects of standard costs.

**Control
Decisions**

Incentive to Build Inventories

The evaluation of purchasing managers based on direct materials price variances creates incentives for these managers to build inventories. Price discounts often are granted for large volume purchases. Therefore, one way to generate favorable price variances is to purchase raw materials in lot sizes larger than necessary for immediate production and to hold these inventories until they are needed. However, it is costly to hold inventory due to warehousing, material handling, obsolescence, and financing costs.

The incentive to hold large inventories can be reduced by charging the purchasing department for the cost of holding inventories. For example, suppose a firm's opportunity cost of capital is 13% per year and warehousing and handling costs are 15% of the cost of the inventory per year. Charging the purchasing department 28% per year of the average dollar balance in the Raw Materials Inventory account reduces the incentive to purchase in large lots. In other words, the inclusion of inventory holding costs in the purchasing department's performance

Organizational members frequently impose externalities on others due to the interdependence of organizational tasks. Teamwork motivates individuals to recognize this interdependence, but requires cooperation to be effective. Team meetings and team-based performance measures encourage cooperation, and mitigate shirking. Shirking also is reduced when the organization supports and rewards team accomplishments.

report reduces its incentive to buy in large lots just to get price concessions.

Most firms do not charge purchasing managers for inventory holding costs since many holding costs are not part of the external reporting system. An alternative mechanism for controlling inventory-building behavior is to adopt techniques such as just-in-time (JIT) purchasing methods described in Chapter Twelve. That is, the purchasing department can order materials only as they are needed for production.

Externalities

Externalities occur within an organization when the behavior of one individual affects other individuals within the organization. Purchasing managers can impose externalities on production by purchasing substandard materials. The lower-quality materials frequently cause more labor hours and more skilled workers (paid higher wages) to process the substandard materials. The substandard materials impose downstream costs on the production managers as a result of the consumption of additional production resources for rework or machine down time.

To offset the purchasing manager's incentive to acquire low-quality raw materials, purchases are inspected when received, engineering specifications are set for each product, and purchasing is not allowed to buy materials that deviate from these standards. Alternatively, part of the purchasing manager's performance evaluation can be tied to the amount of rework generated in production and/or the raw material quantity variance. The purchasing manager then has incentives to reduce rework and quality variances by purchasing higher-quality products. However, purchasing managers cannot control all reasons for rework and quality variances, so they might not consider including the variances in the performance evaluation scheme to be appealing or fair.

Production managers also can impose externalities on purchasing by requesting that materials be purchased on short lead times and in small lot sizes to reduce the amount of materials in storage. Also, engineering can increase the actual price of the purchases by making frequent design changes. These examples are just a few of the types of externalities that purchasing and production can impose on each other.

Uncooperative Effort

Evaluating individuals within an organization based on different variances can discourage cooperative effort. In some firms, every employee is evaluated based on a labor efficiency variance. In other words, the output of each individual is measured and compared with a standard to determine how the employee is rewarded. The employees in these factories frequently are reluctant to support others if their evaluation reflects only what they produce individually.

An alternative is to measure variances for a team or department within the organization. Team performance measures encourage cooperative effort but can lead to shirking on the part of some individuals. For example, a group project for a class is given a single grade that all the students in the group share. Some individuals take advantage of the group grading system by shirking their duties because they know that other responsible students in the group will complete the group task.

To encourage cooperative effort and avoid shirking, many organizations calculate variances and measure performance at multiple levels. For example, an individual worker would be evaluated based on an individual labor efficiency variance and a departmental labor efficiency variance. Bonuses would be paid for both individual and group accomplishments.

Mutual Monitoring Incentives

The usual method of monitoring behavior within firms is for superiors to monitor subordinates. Another important form of monitoring occurs between managers who are not in a direct reporting relationship with each other. As discussed in Chapter Nine, monitoring can occur between managers at the same level in the same subunit or between managers in different subunits. Mutual monitoring occurs when managers or workers at the same level monitor each other.

If the purchasing department manager is held responsible for materials variances (including the quantity variance), the purchasing manager has the incentive to monitor the production supervisor's usage of materials. Likewise, the production supervisor monitors the quality of the materials the purchasing manager buys. A purchasing manager rewarded on the basis of both the price and quantity variance will help to devise ways in which the production manager can economize on the use of materials. Also, the production manager will try to devise ways in which the purchasing manager can purchase materials to reduce purchase costs. Therefore, in designing the performance evaluation and reward systems, organizations can create mutual monitoring incentives that encourage managers to acquire and utilize their specialized knowledge to improve the performance of other managers.

Satisficing Behavior

If standards are used as a benchmark for evaluating managers, the reward system often is tied to achieving the standard. A manager who works sufficiently hard to achieve the standard is paid a bonus. In this type of reward system, managers have incentives to achieve the standard but go no further. This drawback is called **satisficing behavior.** There is an additional disincentive to perform beyond the standard. Next year's standards usually are based on past performance and would be harder to achieve if they are raised as a result of exceptional performance. The organization, of course, would like managers to continually improve and not stop when the standard is met.

Satisficing behavior also can affect quality if employees are motivated to meet production quotas but sacrifice quality to do so. For example, a manufacturer of trenching equipment realized that its standard cost system created incentives for employees to beat the production quota and standard time allowed by disregarding quality. Quality problems were noticed much later in the production process. To mitigate this dysfunctional behavior, management introduced detailed variance control tables that related quality problems to earlier production stages. This system changed incentives because employees were then held responsible for defects discovered later in the process.[4]

Managers also need to react to competitors. If the manager focuses only on the internal standard instead of the competition, the organization will not change to

---

[4]M. Thomas and J. Mackey, "Activity-Based Cost Variances for Just-in-Time," *Management Accounting,* April 1994, pp. 49–54.

meet new demands. Rewarding managers for simply achieving the standard encourages them to think that the status quo is appropriate. Rewards of this nature do not promote innovation. Therefore, management rewards based on achieving the standard are less appropriate in rapidly changing industries with new, innovative products. However, the problem is not the use of standards as performance measures but in the way the compensation schemes reward performance. Compensation schemes should motivate managers to continuously improve beyond the standard by providing higher payments for greater improvement.

ConceptReview

1. How do standard cost variances encourage the creation of excess inventory?
2. How does standard costing create externalities and discourage cooperative effort?
3. How can mutual monitoring be encouraged?
4. What is satisficing behavior and how is it related to standard costs?

EDWARD ODELL, CONTRACTOR
(Continued)

Ed realizes that his standard costing system has affected the behavior of his managers, but some behavior was perverse. Jeff Pringle was able to obtain favorable material price variances because he received discounts by purchasing more raw materials than required. To overcome this problem, Ed decides to charge Jeff for the average amount of raw materials in inventory. The quality of the raw materials and the workmanship present another issue that Ed has to reconsider. Henceforth, incoming raw materials will have to pass an inspection. This will reduce the externalities imposed by Jeff on the other two managers. Ed also will retain the responsibility for hiring and training workers to try to improve the quality of workmanship.

Ed also decides to encourage cooperative behavior by tying part of each manager's bonus to the profit of the entire company. Bonuses will be a percentage of total profit rather than a fixed amount if a certain level of profit is achieved. By making the bonuses a percentage of total profit, satisficing behavior on the part of managers should be less likely.

With these adjustments, Ed hopes that his standard costing system will lead to less perverse behavior. He still wants to control direct costs but not at the risk of reduced quality, excess inventory costs, and management dissension.

OVERHEAD STANDARD COSTS AND VARIANCES

The previous discussion in this chapter described standards for direct labor and direct materials. Standards also are established for overhead costs. Overhead standard costs are used for both planning and control purposes and provide information about the cost of using overhead resources. Standard product costs used for pricing decisions include standard overhead costs, which also provide benchmarks for evaluating managers who control overhead resources.

Overhead cost variances are more difficult to calculate and interpret than are the direct material and labor variances because "quantity" and "price" are not inherent characteristics of overhead. Instead, quantity and price are defined in terms of the allocation base used to allocate overhead costs. The *quantity* of overhead is defined as the level of usage of the allocation base. The *price* of overhead is the application rate of the allocation base. The next section describes different measures of quantity for the allocation base. The subsequent section describes variances in terms of budgeted, applied, and actual overhead. The calculation of specific overhead variances is left to the Appendix to this chapter.

Expected, Standard, and Actual Usage of the Allocation Base

Before describing overhead variances, it is useful to review some concepts and terminology involving the concept of volume. Most plants or departments within them do not produce a single homogeneous product but a diverse set of outputs. In this case, volume is not measured in terms of output but in terms of a common input such as direct labor dollars, machine time, or raw material dollars.

Once an input measure such as machine time is selected as the definition of plant or departmental volume, three different ways are used to quantify input volume: expected usage, standard usage, and actual usage of the input. The first volume measure, **expected usage,** is set at the beginning of the year based on the amount of production expected to occur during the year. More expected output volume implies more expected input usage. If a car repair shop measures volume through the usage of direct labor hours, the number of expected direct labor hours are estimated at the beginning of the year based on the number of cars estimated repaired during the year.

Expected usage of the allocation base is estimated for budgetary purposes. The overhead application rate generally is calculated by dividing the expected overhead costs by the expected usage of the allocation base.

Standard usage is the amount of the input used if each unit of product actually manufactured consumed precisely the standard units of input allowed. Given the output actually produced, standard usage measures the amount of input that should have been used. For example, suppose that the allocation base selected is direct labor hours. After each job is manufactured, the number of units actually produced times the standard number of direct labor hours per unit is the standard usage. Standard usage relates inputs to outputs.

The third input volume concept is **actual usage.** This volume measure is the actual amount of an allocation base used (e.g., actual machine hours, actual direct labor hours, actual direct labor dollars). Actual usage focuses simply on inputs.

The three input volume measures (expected, standard, and actual usage) differ in terms of when they are computed. Expected usage is estimated before the fiscal year begins and before production starts. Both standard and actual usage are computed after production is completed.

> L O 6 Measure expected, standard, and actual usage of an allocation base to apply overhead and determine overhead variances.

Pizza and students seem to go hand in hand. The local chain usually prepares the group's favorite pizza according to standards for ingredients and time. These standards ensure that customers receive the same pizza every time they order. Standards also provide the chain with targets for efficiency and effectiveness.

Numerical Example 14.4

Pizza Company makes two types of frozen pizzas, pepperoni and cheese. It allocates overhead to these two products based on the number of direct labor hours (DLH). The direct labor hours per unit for making a pepperoni pizza is 5 minutes, or 1/12 of an hour. The direct labor hours per unit for making a cheese pizza is 4 minutes, or 1/15 of an hour.

At the start of the year, Pizza Company expected to make 12,000 pepperoni pizzas and 6,000 cheese pizzas. During the year, it actually made 9,000 pepperoni pizzas and 7,500 cheese pizzas. The time cards indicate that direct laborers worked for 1,300 hours. What are the total expected standard and actual direct labor hours?

Solution

Expected number of DLH	
Pepperoni (12,000)(1/12)	1,000
Cheese (6,000)(1/15)	400
Total	1,400
Standard number of DLH	
Pepperoni (9,000)(1/12)	750
Cheese (7,500)(1/15)	500
Total	1,250
Actual number of DLH	1,300

Budgeted, Applied, and Actual Overhead

The previous section described three measures of usage of an allocation base. There are also three equivalent measures of overhead costs: budgeted, applied, and actual. **Budgeted overhead costs** (expected overhead costs) are the overhead costs expected at the beginning of the period; they are estimated using the organization's expected level of operations during the coming period. Budgeted overhead costs are divided by the expected usage of the allocation base to calculate the application rate for the allocation base.

Applied overhead costs are the overhead costs that are applied to cost objects through the standard usage of the allocation base. In Chapter Ten, the allocation of overhead occurs with the actual usage of the allocation base. With standard costing, however, the standard usage of the allocation base is used to allocate overhead costs. A standard costing system predetermines all components (direct labor, direct materials, and overhead) of the product cost. If 3 direct labor hours (DLH) are the standard for making a particular product and the allocation base is direct labor hours, the overhead allocated to the product is 3 DLH times the application rate per direct labor hour. Even though the product actually may have required 4 DLH, the standard number of direct labor hours is used to apply the overhead.

The **actual overhead costs** are the actual costs of overhead resources. These costs include cash outlays and depreciation of fixed assets.

Budget, applied, and actual overhead costs usually differ. Budgeted and applied overhead costs differ because the actual output (and, thus, the standard input usage) and the expected output are not equal. Only if the expected usage of the allocation base equals the standard usage of the allocation base will the budgeted and applied overhead costs be equal.

The difference between applied (allocated) overhead costs and actual overhead costs is described in Chapter Ten as under- or overabsorbed overhead. In a standard costing system, the difference between the applied and actual overhead costs is called the **total overhead variance.** Many factors can cause the total overhead variance; for example, the adoption of JIT often alters the firm's operations so that the existing overhead allocation base does not measure accurately how overhead resources are consumed. Unexpected price changes for overhead items also contribute to the overhead variance. Moreover, multiple managers frequently are responsible for overhead resources. Overhead is incurred in many parts of the organization, and different management levels make decisions that influence these overhead costs. For instance, the personnel department frequently negotiates the wage rates for workers in production areas. Top management generally determines plant capacity. In both cases, lower-level managers might be held responsible for the overhead costs related to these decisions. Therefore, partitioning the total overhead variance into components can allow for better identification of the cause and responsibility for the total overhead variance. One method of partitioning the total overhead variance is described in the Appendix to this chapter.

Numerical Example 14.5

A company makes two types of plastic pipe, 2.5-centimeter and 5-centimeter diameter. Overhead is allocated based on kilograms of plastic in the pipe. The standards for the two types of pipe are as follows:

Type	Standard Kilograms per Unit	Expected Units	Expected Kilograms of Plastic
2.5-cm.	2	500,000	1,000,000
5-cm.	3	600,000	1,800,000
Totals			2,800,000

The budgeted overhead for the period is $1,400,000. During the period, 450,000 units of 2.5-cm. pipe are made using 1,050,000 kilograms (kg.) of plastic. The company also makes 650,000 units of 5-cm. pipe using 1,900,000 kg. of plastic. Actual overhead costs are $1,300,000. The application rate is $1,400,000/2,800,000 kg., or $0.050 per kg. What is the total overhead variance?

Solution

The total overhead variance is the difference between the actual overhead costs ($1,300,000) and the applied overhead costs. To calculate the applied overhead costs, the standard kilograms of plastic first must be determined. The standard kilograms time the application rate ($0.50 per kg.) equals the overhead applied.

Type	Standard Kilograms per Unit	Actual Units	Standard Kilograms of Plastic	Overhead Applied
2.5-cm.	2	450,000	900,000	$ 450,000
5-cm.	3	650,000	1,950,000	975,000
Totals			2,850,000	$1,425,000

The total overhead variance is $1,300,000 − $1,425,000, or $125,000 overabsorbed (favorable).

Incentive Effects of Overhead Standards and Variances

Managers of overhead resources are responsible for providing quality services to the organization at the lowest possible cost. Standard costs for overhead are established, in part, to provide benchmarks for evaluating the managers of the overhead resources. If overhead standards are used to evaluate and reward managers, they will have an effect on managerial behavior.

Control Decisions

The preferred effect of standard overhead costs is the reduction in overhead costs. The manager of the overhead resources can create favorable overhead variances by reducing overhead costs below the standard levels. Of course, maintaining the quality of the overhead service is still important to the organization, so there is a danger that the manager might trade off cost savings and quality inappropriately.

Increasing output also can create favorable overhead variances. This increases the standard usage of the allocation base, which results in more applied overhead.

If actual overhead costs do not increase proportionally with the allocation base, a favorable overhead variance occurs with higher output levels. For example, applied costs increase more rapidly than actual costs if some costs are fixed with respect to the allocation base.

One organizational mechanism to overcome this overproduction incentive is the separation of responsibilities so that overhead resource managers do not control output levels. If they do not control output levels, they should be evaluated only on the portion of the overhead variance caused by cost savings or overruns. Partitioning the overhead variances to identify responsibility for different portions of the overhead variances is discussed in the Appendix.

Concept**Review**

1. How do expected, standard, and actual usage of the allocation base differ?
2. Why are standard overhead costs different from budgeted overhead costs?
3. What are some incentive effects of using overhead standards and variances for control?

EDWARD ODELL, CONTRACTOR
(Continued)

Once Ed has designed a standard costing system to control the direct costs, he turns to overhead costs. They were small when he was only a building contractor for new houses and he was able to work out of his house. The building of wall sections, however, has forced him to rent a warehouse. In addition, he has manager salaries and other indirect costs to pay. Overhead costs are rising more rapidly than his direct costs, and he needs some mechanism to control the overhead.

During the budgetary process for the year, Ed estimated the total overhead costs for the company to be $400,000. He decided to use standard direct labor hours (DLH) to allocate overhead to the various types of wall sections because direct labor hours were related to the number of managers, a major overhead expense. He estimated that the company would use 100,000 standard DLH based on expected production. The standard application rate, therefore, was $400,000/100,000 standard DLH, or $4 per standard DLH.

Given that the 8 feet by 12 feet wall section had a standard of 3 DLH per unit, the total number of standard hours for the order of 3,000 units was (3,000 units)(3 DLH per unit), or 9,000 hours. Other orders during the year have caused an additional use of 86,000 standard DLH for a total of 95,000. Therefore, during the year (95,000 standard DLH)($4 per DLH), or $380,000 of overhead has been applied to products. The actual overhead for the year, however, is $405,000. Therefore, the overhead variance is $405,000 − $380,000, or $25,000 underabsorbed (unfavorable).

Ed is unsure what to do about this variance. It is not clear who is responsible. Many of the overhead decisions were actually his. He is also not sure whether the overhead costs are variable or fixed. The overhead variance requires further investigation.

VARIANCE INVESTIGATION

L0 7 Identify factors that influence the decision to investigate variances.

The management accounting system routinely reports variance calculations in both monetary terms and as a percentage of the standard cost. These reports are only the first step in the decision-making process in a standard costing system. Variances provide information for planning and control purposes; in both cases, the variance figures alone rarely provide sufficient information for making good decisions.

Variances are intended to identify problems in existing processes that require attention, but variances often occur when processes are operating correctly. Random fluctuations in the costs of materials, labor, or overhead can cause a variance. A manager is seldom certain whether a problem or a random fluctuation caused the variance. Large variances are more likely to indicate a problem than are small variances.

**Planning
Decisions**

Small deviations between actual costs and standard costs are expected and unavoidable. Moreover, random variances tend to offset each other over time. Positive random variances approximately equal negative random variances, so aggregating random variances over time should lead to actual costs being close to standard costs. If variances do not offset each other over time, some factor other than randomness likely caused the variances. Aggregating variances over time provides supervisors with more confidence about the origins of the variance.

Even knowing that a problem other than random variation underlies a variance, the manager seldom can identify the nature of the problem by just looking at the variance figures. Looking at all the variances provides more information. Certain combinations of variances indicate certain problems. For example, favorable material price variances and unfavorable material quantity and labor efficiency variances are consistent with the purchase of cheap, low-quality materials. Even an analysis of all the variances does not reveal the complete story, however.

To understand the cause of a variance, a manager must investigate its source. Investigations include questioning responsible parties and looking at noncost data, such as the percentage of defects and quality measures of raw materials. For example, the IBM call center in Greenock, Scotland, provides support to IBM's European customers. The call center is evaluated on both financial and nonfinancial measures. It tracks the cost per call and compares it to the budgeted cost. The budgeted figure includes the telephone charges (callers make a local call in their own country and IBM pays any difference for long-distance charges), overhead, and adjustments to the account for the level of service. Nonfinancial measures include the call drop-out rate (the percentage of callers who do not wait in the queue), the average response time, and the average duration of each call. IBM supplements both sets of measures with customer surveys to establish a customer satisfaction index. The data are summarized and compared to budget estimates and to the results of other call centers. If a significant variance is noted in the reported data, IBM managers can investigate further by requesting additional information. For example, an increase in the cost per call might be related to calls of longer duration. Both items might signal that the call center was handling more complex questions requiring a higher level of service and more skilled telephone operators. The variances are one way that IBM determines whether the needs of its customers, an important strategic focus, are met.[5]

The decision to investigate is a decision in itself. Investigations are often costly, involving labor and sometimes the shutdown of processes during the investigation. Therefore, not every nonzero variance should be investigated. The manager often uses a decision rule based on the size of the variance to determine when to investigate. Large variances are less likely the result of random fluctuations and, therefore, often deserve further investigation. The decision problem is determining how large the variance must be to make an investigation worthwhile. Organizations frequently establish benchmarks or rules of thumb for variance investigation. These decision rules include, for example, investigating variances that are more than 10% of the standard cost or more than a specific dollar value, say $500. In addition, firms investigate variances that have continued over a period of time, using

[5]G. Brown, J. Innes, and N. Tagoe, "Performance Measurement in a Telephone Call Centre," *Management Accounting* 77, no. 1 (January 1999), pp. 41–42.

control charts to track them. Statistical models can be helpful in determining when a variance should be investigated. These models are discussed in advanced management accounting and operations management courses.

Factors that affect the decision rule to investigate variances include the size of the random fluctuations, the cost of investigation, the cost of not investigating, and the ease of correcting the problem if it exists. If random fluctuations tend to be high, only very large variances would distinguish a variance caused by randomness from a variance caused by a problem. If an investigation is costly, the manager is much less likely to investigate small variances. If the cost of not investigating is high, however, small variances are more likely to be investigated. For example, if the material quantity variance is caused by theft, the lack of investigation in all likelihood leads to more theft and a high cost to the organization. Therefore, small variances probably are investigated. The ease of correcting the problem, if it exists, also influences the investigation decision. High correction costs mean that even if the problem is discovered, the organization may not fix it because the benefits of doing so are less than the costs. Therefore, there is less reason to investigate the problem. Instead, the organization may choose to revise the standard. The new standard recognizes the existence of the problem, so the manager no longer is responsible for the variance that is considered too costly to fix.

Innovations in process technologies make production problems easier to detect and even correct. These innovations also affect variance investigation because it is increasingly possible to avoid future problems with timely intervention and preliminary variance information. The decision to investigate a variance relates to the opportunity cost concept outlined in Chapter Two. The organization must weigh the value of the increased information against the cost to produce it. In the current environment, technologically advanced expert systems can correct problems detected by the variance. These systems thus separate the variance investigation decision from the correction of the detected problem. Other models of variance investigation collapse these actions into one and might not lead to the correct cost/benefit decision in today's environment.[6]

Concept**Review**

1. Why are investigations of variances often appropriate?
2. What are some factors that influence the decision to investigate?

EDWARD ODELL, CONTRACTOR
(Continued)

You decide

To investigate the $25,000 overhead variance, Ed must use the assistant controller for 10 days. The assistant controller has some free time and is paid a fixed salary, so Ed figures the cost of using him will be only about $400. The potential cost savings from correcting a problem with overhead could be much larger, but Ed is not sure that a problem exists. The variance could have been caused by not estimating the overhead costs or the number of standard direct labor hours correctly. Ed decides to go ahead with the investigation. The assistant controller finds that much of the variance is caused by misestimates but does find a way to save $1,000 per year by more careful use of electricity. Therefore, Ed's decision to investigate saves $1,000 less the $400 investigation cost, or $600.

---

[6]These issues are examined in P. K. Sen, "Another Look at Cost Variance Investigation," *Issues in Accounting Education* 13, no. 1 (February 1998), pp. 127–37. Variance investigation models are provided for a variety of production settings.

COSTS AND BENEFITS OF USING STANDARD COSTING SYSTEMS

Standard cost systems are expensive to implement and operate. Detailed standards must be maintained for each labor and material input (standard prices and quantities), but these standards also must be revised in a timely fashion. Rapid technological change and continuous improvement initiatives (total quality management programs are described in Chapter Twelve) make standards quickly obsolete. In addition, investigating cost variances is expensive in terms of the cost of the manager's time.

Standard cost systems also create incentive problems. Workers tend to focus on existing standards rather than to seek continuous cost reductions. In addition, standard cost systems can cause overproduction and lower quality and can discourage cooperative effort.

Standard cost variances also are not particularly timely; they are usually reported monthly or quarterly. This information may be too late to correct problems.

For many companies, however, the benefits of standard costs through improved control and planning decisions exceed the costs of using standard costs. As mentioned earlier, most large U.S. companies use standard costs. A survey of 198 Japanese companies in four automated industries concludes that most Japanese firms are maintaining their standard costs.[7]

Although some companies might be abandoning their detailed standard cost systems, they often maintain some standard costs. These firms still see opportunities to use standard costs for planning and control purposes. A standard cost system must be designed carefully to maximize firm value. Carelessly designed standard cost systems, which serve as performance evaluation schemes, can lead to dysfunctional behavior.

> ## Business**Analysis**
>
> ### NEC Revises Its Standard Cost System
>
> NEC, a large diversified Japanese electronics firm, installed its standard cost system in the 1950s, when it was in a stable market supplying a small number of products, mainly telephones and switching equipment, to Nippon Telegraph & Telephone. But by the 1980s, NEC was supplying a vast number of different electronic products subject to rapid technological obsolescence to worldwide markets.
>
> It is very expensive to keep the standard costs up to date as products and the production technology changes. The life expectancy of any one cost standard is now much shorter. NEC still uses its standard cost system as a factory management tool but is not using standard costs on a product-by-product basis.
>
> What factors caused NEC to change its standard cost system?
>
> *Source:* T. Hiromoto, "Another Hidden Edge: Japanese Management Accounting," *Harvard Business Review*, July–August 1988, pp. 22–26.

LO 8   Summarize the costs and benefits of using standard costs.

Concept**Review**

1. Why are standard costs difficult to implement in a rapidly changing business environment?
2. What evidence indicates that for many organizations, the benefits of using standard costs outweigh the problems of using them?

---

[7]P. Scarbough, A. Nanni, Jr., and M. Sakurai, "Japanese Management Accounting Practices and the Effects of Assembly and Process Automation," *Management Accounting Research* 2 (March 1991), pp. 27–46.

SUMMARY

1 Provide reasons for using standard costs. Standard costs are used for planning purposes by communicating expected costs to member of the organization. Standard costs also are used for control by establishing benchmarks to evaluate processes and managers.

2 Describe planning and control issues in setting standards. For planning purposes, the person with the best knowledge of a process should establish standards. Conflict exists, however, if that individual also is evaluated based on those standards.

3 Calculate direct labor and direct materials variances. Direct labor and material variances are divided into variances related to differences between actual and standard prices and variances related to differences between actual and standard quantities.

4 **Identify potential causes of different favorable and unfavorable variances.** All variances are potentially due to incorrect standards. Favorable price variances (standard prices higher than actual prices) also are caused by purchasing large amounts of materials to get discounts or purchasing lower-quality items. Unfavorable price variances (actual prices more than standard prices) could result from rush orders or paying for higher-quality materials or labor. Efficient use of labor or materials or the use of higher-quality labor or materials could cause favorable quantity variances (actual quantity used less than the standard quantity). Unfavorable quantity variances (actual quantity used more than the standard quantity) could be the result of the inefficient use or theft of direct resources or the use of lower-quality labor or materials.

5 **Recognize incentive effects of standard costs.** Standard costs have the potential to cause overproduction and lower quality, externalities to other parts of the organization, uncooperative effort, mutual monitoring, and satisficing behavior.

6 **Measure expected, standard, and actual usage of an allocation base to apply overhead and determine overhead variances.** At the beginning of the period, the expected usage of the allocation base and the application rate are calculated based on budgeted numbers. Standard usage is the standard input per unit times actual units produced and is used to apply overhead. Actual usage is measured throughout the period based on the observed usage of the allocation base. The total overhead variance is the difference between the actual overhead and the overhead applied.

7 **Identify factors that influence the decision to investigate variances.** The decision to investigate a variance is based on the size of the random variation, the cost of investigation, the cost of not investigating, and the ease of correcting the problem if one exists.

8 **Summarize the costs and benefits of using standard costs.** Standard costs can improve planning and control, but standard costing systems are expensive to implement and adjust if the product mix is changing rapidly. In addition, standard costs potentially cause adverse incentive effects such as overproduction, uncooperative behavior, and satisficing behavior, depending on how the performance reward systems use the standard costs.

KEY TERMS

actual overhead costs Indirect costs actually incurred by the organization. *(p. 520)*

actual usage The number of times an allocation base actually is used. *(p. 519)*

applied overhead costs The dollar amount of overhead allocated to different products or other cost objects. *(p. 520)*

budgeted overhead costs The expected indirect costs used to establish application rates. *(p. 520)*

direct labor variance The difference between actual and standard labor costs. *(p. 506)*

direct materials variance The difference between actual and standard material costs. *(p. 511)*

expected usage The number of times an allocation base is expected to be used. *(p. 519)*

favorable variance The result when actual costs are less than standard costs. *(p. 507)*

fixed overhead budget variance The difference between budgeted and actual fixed overhead. *(p. 528)*

fixed overhead variance The difference between applied and actual fixed overhead. *(p. 528)*

fixed overhead volume variance The difference between applied and budgeted fixed overhead. *(p. 528)*

labor efficiency variance The difference between actual and standard direct labor hours times the standard wage rate. *(p. 506)*

management by exception A management style that focuses management effort on large cost variances. *(p. 503)*

material price variance The difference between the actual price and the standard price of raw materials times the actual amount used or purchased. *(p. 511)*

material quantity variance The difference between the actual and the standard quantity of materials used times the standard price. *(p. 511)*

satisficing behavior Behavior of employees seeking to achieve satisfactory levels of performance measures but not trying to excel. *(p. 517)*

standard costs Benchmarks based on expected future costs. *(p. 502)*

standard usage The number of times a cost driver should have been used given the actual number of units of output. *(p. 519)*

target costing A cost goal chosen given a competitive sales price and an expected profit margin. *(p. 504)*

total overhead variance The difference between total actual and applied overhead. *(p. 520)*

unfavorable variance The result when actual costs are higher than standard costs. *(p. 507)*

variable overhead efficiency variance The difference between actual and standard usage of the allocation base times the standard application rate for variable overhead. *(p. 527)*

variable overhead spending variance   The difference between actual and standard application rates for variable overhead times the actual usage of the allocation base. *(p. 527)*

variable overhead variance   The difference between the actual and applied variable overhead. *(p. 527)*

variance   The difference between actual and standard costs. *(p. 502)*

wage rate variance   The difference between the actual wage rate and the standard wage rate times the actual hours. *(p. 506)*

APPENDIX

Overhead Variances

The total overhead variance is the difference between the overhead allocated and the actual overhead. Many reasons exist for a nonzero overhead variance. Standards and application rates could be wrong, the production level could be higher or lower than expected, or overhead departments might not be operating efficiently. Decomposing the total overhead variance into its components provides information about the cause of the total overhead variance.

A common procedure is to partition the total overhead variance into variances related to variable and fixed overhead. The **variable overhead variance** is defined as the actual variable overhead less the applied variable overhead; it is calculated as follows:

Actual variable overhead − Applied variable overhead

$$U_a VR_a \qquad - \qquad U_s VR_s$$

where

U_a = Actual usage of the allocation base

VR_a = Actual variable overhead application rate (actual variable overhead cost/actual usage of the allocation base)

U_s = Standard usage of the allocation base

VR_s = Standard variable overhead application rate

The equation for the variable overhead variance is similar to the variance equations for the direct costs. The usage of the allocation base is a quantity measure, and the application rate is a price for using the allocation base. Therefore, the variable overhead variance also can be divided into a price and quantity variance.

The **variable overhead spending variance** is a price variance caused by the actual application rate being different from the standard application rate:

Variable overhead spending variance = $U_a(VR_a - VR_s)$

For managers responsible for the efficient provision of variable overhead resources, the standard application rate is a benchmark for evaluating performance. An unfavorable variable overhead spending variance indicates that the actual variable costs are higher per unit of the allocation base than expected. An unfavorable variance does not mean that the manager of the overhead resource is doing a poor job; overhead resources might have become more expensive than expected or the quality of the overhead services provided higher. An unusual variance, however, can be interpreted as a signal to investigate. For example, the prices of overhead items might change unexpectedly, such as sudden increases in the price of oil that affect the cost of gasoline and lubricants used in equipment. Wage rates of supervisory staff might rise as a result of revised labor contracts. Upon investigation, these changes might signal that existing standards are no longer appropriate.

The **variable overhead efficiency variance** is a quantity variance related to the usage of the allocation base:

Variable overhead efficiency variance = $VR_s(U_a - U_s)$

L0 6   Measure expected, standard, and actual usage of an allocation base to apply overhead and determine overhead variances.

The standard usage of the allocation base determines the amount of variable overhead that is applied. If actual usage of the allocation base is higher than the standard usage, variable overhead is underabsorbed and the variable overhead efficiency variance is unfavorable. In general, the responsibility for the variable overhead efficiency variance should rest with the users of the allocation base. For example, the variable overhead costs of the personnel department frequently are allocated to production departments based on standard direct labor hours. The manager of the production department is generally responsible for the difference between the actual and standard direct labor hours. The manager of the personnel department, however, could be responsible if the quality of the workers hired led to the inability to achieve direct labor standards. The variable overhead efficiency variance and the direct labor efficiency variance must be in the same direction (favorable or unfavorable) when the allocation base is direct labor hours. Once again, further investigation is necessary to determine whether a problem exists and who is responsible. In some cases, adoption of automated equipment makes direct labor hours inappropriate as the allocation base.

The **fixed overhead variance** is the actual fixed overhead less the applied fixed overhead. Fixed overhead, unlike variable overhead, should not change with the allocation base. The fixed overhead variance can be decomposed into two additional variances: the **fixed overhead budget variance** and the **fixed overhead volume variance.** Managers responsible for fixed overhead resources generally are evaluated based on the difference between actual fixed overhead expenditures and budgeted fixed overhead, which is the fixed overhead budget variance. An unfavorable fixed overhead budget variance indicates that more resources than expected were expended on fixed overhead. For instance, fixed expenses, such as property taxes and equipment leases, might be higher than expected.

The fixed overhead variance is decomposed using the following equations:

$$
\begin{aligned}
\text{Fixed overhead variance} &= \text{Actual fixed overhead} - \text{Applied fixed overhead} \\
&= (\text{Actual fixed overhead} - \text{Budgeted fixed} \\
&\quad\ \text{overhead}) + (\text{Budgeted fixed overhead} - \\
&\quad\ \text{Applied fixed overhead}) \\
&= \text{Fixed overhead budget variance} + \\
&\quad\ \text{Fixed overhead volume variance}
\end{aligned}
$$

The fixed overhead volume variance also can be written as follows:

$$
\begin{aligned}
\text{Budgeted fixed overhead} - \text{Applied fixed overhead} &= U_e FR_s - U_s FR_s \\
&= FR_s(U_e - U_s)
\end{aligned}
$$

where

U_e = Expected (or budgeted) usage of the allocation base

FR_s = Standard fixed overhead application rate

U_s = Standard usage of the allocation base

The difference between the expected usage (U_e) and the standard usage (U_s) of the allocation base is due to the volume of output being different than expected. Therefore, the fixed overhead volume variance is an estimate of unused or overused capacity. If the number of units produced is less than expected, the standard usage of the allocation base is less than expected. Less fixed overhead costs are applied than expected and the volume variance is unfavorable. Given that the volume variance depends on the output of the organization, the manager responsible for fixed overhead resources should not be held responsible for the volume variance. Instead, the manager in control of output levels should be responsible for the volume variance. This manager has an incentive to overproduce because increased output makes the volume variance more favorable as more fixed costs are applied to units produced. The volume variance, however, is not a measure of the opportunity cost of unused capacity. The opportunity cost is estimated by the contribution margin on products and services that could have been sold but were not. Therefore, performance based on the volume variance encourages managers to build inventories that might not be sold. Organizational value is decreased instead of increased.

Numerical Example 14A.1

A company that services office machines applies variable and fixed overhead to jobs based on standard labor hours. The company has the following budget numbers related to the allocation base:

Type of Service	Expected Service Units	Standard Labor per Service Unit	Total Expected Labor Hours
Copiers	5,000	1 hour	5,000
Fax machines	1,000	2 hours	2,000
Total			7,000

The standard numbers related to the allocation base given actual output follow:

Type of Service	Actual Service Units	Standard Labor per Service Unit	Total Standard Labor Hours
Copiers	4,500	1 hour	4,500
Fax machines	1,100	2 hours	2,200
Total			6,700

The actual number of labor hours used to service the copiers and fax machines was 6,800. Budgeted and actual variable and fixed overhead costs were as follows:

Overhead	Budgeted Costs	Actual Costs
Variable	$20,000	$22,000
Fixed	15,000	14,000

Calculate the application rates for variable and fixed overhead, the amount of variable and fixed overhead applied, the variable overhead spending and efficiency variances, and the fixed overhead budget and volume variances.

Solution

The application rates are calculated by dividing the budgeted (or expected) overhead by the expected use of labor hours:

Variable overhead application rate = $20,000/7,000 hr. = $2.857 per hr.

Fixed overhead application rate = $15,000/7,000 hr. = $2.143 per hr.

The applied fixed overhead and variable overhead are calculated by multiplying the application rates times the standard hours:

Variable overhead applied = (6,700 hr.)($2.857 per hr.) = $19,142

Fixed overhead applied = (6,700 hr.)($2.143 per hr.) = $14,358

The variable overhead variance is the difference between the actual variable overhead ($22,000) and the applied variable overhead ($19,142), or $2,858 unfavorable. The variable overhead variance can be further decomposed into the variable overhead spending variance and the variable overhead efficiency variance. The actual application rate for variable overhead is the actual variable overhead costs ($22,000) divided by the actual labor hours (6,800), or $3.235 per hr.

Variable overhead spending variance $= U_a(V_a - V_s) = 6{,}800$ hr. ($3.235 per hr. $- \$2.857$ per hr.) $=$ $\$2{,}570$ U

Variable overhead efficiency variance $= V_s(U_a - U_s) = \$2.857$ per hr. ($6{,}800$ hr. $- 6{,}700$ hr.) $= \$286$ U

The sum of these two variances equals $2,856, which differs slightly from the variable overhead variance $2,858 due to rounding error.

The fixed overhead variance is the difference between the actual fixed overhead ($14,000) and the applied fixed overhead ($14,358), or $358 favorable. The fixed overhead variance can be decomposed into the fixed overhead budget variance and the fixed overhead volume variance.

Fixed overhead budget variance $=$ Actual $-$ Budgeted fixed overhead $= \$14{,}000 - \$15{,}000 = \$1{,}000$ F

Fixed overhead volume variance $=$ Budgeted $-$ Applied fixed overhead $= \$15{,}000 - \$14{,}358 = \$642$ U

The sum of the fixed overhead budget and volume variances equals the total fixed overhead variance.

SELF-STUDY PROBLEM

Tippa Canoe Company makes fiberglass canoes. The fiberglass resin is molded initially to the shape of a canoe and is then sanded and painted. Metal or wooden seats and frames are added for stability. Jeff Littlehorse, the owner, started Tippa Canoe several years ago in his garage. He did much of the initial manual labor with the help of a few friends. The company has since expanded into a large warehouse and has hired new employees. As a result of the expansion, Jeff is no longer directly involved with production and is concerned about his ability to plan for and control the company. He is considering the implementation of a standard cost system.

a. Describe the procedures Jeff should use in setting standards for direct labor and direct materials.

b. Describe how Jeff could use standards for planning purposes.

c. Describe how Jeff could use standards for motivating employees as well as the problems in using standards as performance measures.

d. Why are some of Jeff's friends, who have worked with him from the beginning, not excited about a change to a standard cost system?

Solution

a. Direct material standards should be established for the fiberglass resin and the wood and metal for the seats and the frame. For planning purposes, the standards for quantity and price should reflect expectations, but Jeff is no longer familiar with production and must ask employees about expected quantities and prices. The purchasing manager has information on prices, and the manufacturing manager has information on quantities. The direct labor standards are based on expectations from the personnel manager and the manufacturing manager.

b. If accurate estimates of prices and quantities are provided, Jeff can use the information to plan for cash flows. The standards also can be used to plan for appropriate inventory levels given planned manufacturing efforts.

c. The standards can be used as benchmarks to evaluate the performance of employees. One problem with using standards as performance measures is the difficulty of obtaining accurate standards from the individuals being evaluated. Standards also can provide incentives to increase inventories, discourage cooperative behavior, and lead to satisficing behavior.

d. Some of Jeff's friends, who are still working in the expanded organization, probably will be unhappy with the standard costing system. They will no longer be judged directly by their friend Jeff but through the use of standards that appear to be impersonal and lacking in trust. Jeff's friends, however, must recognize that he cannot observe directly what is happening in the company given the expanded operations. Standard costing systems are not established because of a lack of trust; their use conveys information among the different members of the organization.

NUMERICAL EXERCISES

A Web page consultant estimates the following hours to create a page for a small retail store:

NE 14.1
Direct Labor Variances
(LO 3)

Staff Member	Expected Hours	Cost per Hour	Standard Cost
Senior designer	10	$25	$250
Junior designer	20	20	400
Secretarial staff	10	10	100
Totals	40		$750

The actual hours and costs were as follows:

Staff Member	Actual Hours	Actual Cost per Hour	Actual Costs
Senior designer	9	$30	$270
Junior designer	22	18	396
Secretarial Staff	12	11	132
Totals	75		$798

Calculate the direct labor, wage rate, and labor efficiency variances for each staff member.

The Web page consultant in Numerical Exercise 14.1 receives a bonus based on the direct labor variances. If the wage rate variance is unfavorable, 50 percent of this amount is deducted from the bonus. If it is favorable, 100 percent is added to the bonus received. The labor efficiency variance is added or deducted in total from the bonus.

What is the impact of the variances calculated in Numerical Exercise 14.1 on the consultant's bonus?

NE 14.2
Direct Labor Variances and Compensation
(LO 3)

Muffin Mania Bakery has a standard quantity of 1 kilogram (kg.) of flour for one batch of muffins. The standard price is $0.50 per kilogram. During the month, the bakery manager bought 3,000 kg. of flour for $1,600. The bakery used 2,500 kg. of flour to produce 2,400 batches of muffins during the month.

What are the material price and quantity variances for the flour?

NE 14.3
Direct Materials Variances
(LO 3)

Microchip makes two types of microchips for PCs, supra and magna. Microchip allocates overhead to these two products based on the number of direct labor hours. The direct labor hours per unit for making a supra chip is 5 minutes, or 1/12 of an hour. The direct labor per unit for making a magna chip is 4 minutes, or 1/15 of an hour. At the start of the year, Microchip expected to make 12,000 supra chips and 24,000 magna chips. During the year, it actually made 15,000 supra chips and 18,000 magna chips. The time cards indicate that direct labor was 2,500 hours.

What are the total expected, standard, and actual direct labor hours?

NE 14.4
Expected, Standard, and Actual Usage
(LO 3)

A company makes two types of tomato salsa, chunky and super chunky. Overhead is based on kilograms (kg.) of tomatoes in the salsa. The standards for the two types of salsa follow:

NE 14.5
Overhead Variance
(LO 6)

Type	Standard Kilograms per Unit	Expected Units	Expected Kilograms of Tomatoes
Chunky	1.0	500,000	500,000
Super chunky	1.5	600,000	900,000
Totals			1,400,000

The budgeted overhead for the period is $700,000. During the period, 450,000 units of chunky are made using 525,000 kg. of tomatoes. In addition, 650,000 units of super chunky are made using 1,000,000 kg. of tomatoes. Actual overhead costs are $800,000. The application rate is $700,000/1,400,000 kg., or $.50 per kg.

What is the total overhead variance?

NE 14.6
Raw Materials Variances
(LO 3)

Medical Instruments produces a variety of electronic medical devices. It uses a standard cost system and computes price variances at the time of purchase. One product, a thermometer, measures patient temperatures orally. It requires a silver lead with a standard length of 5 inches per thermometer. To make the leads, hollow silver tubing is purchased at $4 per inch, cut into the required length, and then assembled into the thermometer.

No silver tubing was in inventory when a batch of 200 thermometers was scheduled for production. The purchasing department bought 1,200 inches of silver tubing for $4,680 for this 200-unit batch of thermometers; 1,100 inches were used in production.

Compute the materials price and quantity variances for silver tubing and comment on the meaning of each.

NE 14.7
Direct Material Variances
(LO 3)

During November, Todco planned to produce 3,000 units of its single product, teragram. The standard specifications for one unit of teragram include six kilograms (kg.) of material at $0.30 per kilogram. Actual production in November was 3,100 units. The accountant computed a favorable materials purchase price variance of $380 and an unfavorable materials quantity variance of $120.

Based on these data, calculate how many kilograms of material were used in the production of teragram during November.

(CMA adapted)

NE 14.8
Direct Material and Labor Variances
(LO 3)

An ice cream maker produces 10,000 liters of strawberry ice cream in a month. The standard number of hours of direct labor per 1,000 liters is 40 at a standard wage rate of $10 per hour. The standard quantities and prices of ingredients per 1,000 liters of ice cream are 1,200 liters of cream at $1 per liter, 30 kilograms (kg.) of strawberries at $0.50 per kilogram, and 1,000 containers at $0.05 per container. During the month, the ice cream maker produced 11,000 liters of strawberry ice cream. The wage rate of direct labor was $12 per hour for 420 hours. The actual price of the cream was $0.90 per liter and 13,000 liters were used. The actual price of strawberries was $0.60 per kilogram; 300 kg. were used. The number of containers used was 11,200, and the actual price was $0.06 per container.

Calculate all of the direct material and labor variances.

NE 14.9
Direct Material and Labor Variances
(LO 3)

To manufacture a product requires a standard of 10 direct labor hours (DLH) per unit. The standard labor rate is $20 per hour. The product requires a standard of 25 kilograms (kg.) of material. The standard price of materials is $5 per kilogram. The actual production of 100 units uses 900 DLH at a total direct labor cost of $16,200 and 2,300 kg. of material at a total direct material cost of $9,200.

Calculate all direct labor and material variances.

NE 14.10
Application of Overhead
(LO 6)

At the beginning of the year, a firm sets standards for making 1,000 units with 10,000 direct labor hours. The application rate for overhead is $40 per standard direct labor hour. During the year, the firm actually makes 1,200 units.

How much overhead is applied?

NE 14.11
Overhead Variances
(LO 6) (Appendix only)

A company uses machine hours to apply both variable and fixed overhead. Budgeted variable overhead is $100,000. Budgeted fixed overhead is $200,000. The budgeted machine hours are 1,000. During the period, 1,200 machine hours are used, but only 1,100 standard hours occurred. The actual variable overhead is $105,000 and the actual fixed overhead is $205,000.

Calculate all of the overhead variances.

NUMERICAL PROBLEMS

NP 14.1
Direct Variances
(LO 3)

Arrow Industries employs a standard cost system in which direct materials inventory is carried at standard cost. Arrow has established the following standards for the direct costs of one unit of product:

	Standard Quantity	Standard Price	Standard Cost
Direct materials	8 kg.	$1.80 per kg.	$14.40
Direct labor	0.25 hour	$8.00 per hour	2.00
			$16.40

During May, Arrow purchased 160,000 kg. of direct material at a total cost of $304,000. The total factory wages for May were $42,000, 90% of which were for direct labor. Arrow manufactured 19,000 units of product during May using 142,500 kg. of direct material and 5,000 direct labor hours.

a. Calculate the direct materials price variance for May.

b. Calculate the direct materials quantity variance for May.

c. Calculate the direct labor wage rate variance for May.

d. Calculate the direct labor efficiency variance for May.

e. The production manager's bonus is based, in part, on the direct labor variance and the direct material quantity variance. The manager's bonus is adjusted (increased or decreased) by 10% of the direct labor variance and the direct material quantity variance. What is the impact of the variances on the manager's bonus?

(CMA adapted)

A company purchased 36,000 kilograms (kg.) of plastic pellets for $8,640. These pellets are used in injection molding machines to produce plastic parts. The pellets have a standard cost of $0.25 per kilogram. Of these pellets, 30,000 kg. were used in two jobs. The first job called for 14,000 kg. of pellets but actually used 15,000 kg. The second job also used 15,000 kg., but it called for 15,500 kg. The company uses a standard cost system, calculates price variances at purchase, and had no beginning inventory of this plastic pellet.

At the end of the two jobs and before any more of the plastic pellets are used, prepare a table that indicates the financial disposition of the historical cost of the pellets (i.e., account for the $8,640).

NP 14.2
Raw Material Variances
(LO 3)

Hospital Software sells and installs computer software used by hospitals for patient admissions and billing. For each client engagement, Hospital Software takes its proprietary software and modifies it for the client's specific demands. Prior to each installation, it estimates the number of hours of programming time that each job will require and the cost of the programmers. Programmers record the amount of time that they spend on each engagement and at the end of each installation, variance reports are prepared.

For the Denver General Hospital account, Hospital Software estimates the following labor standards:

NP 14.3
Direct Labor Variances
(LO 3)

	Standard Hours	Standard Rate per Hour
Junior programmer	85	$23
Senior programmer	33	31

After the job was completed, the following costs were reported:

Junior programmer (98 hours)	$2,352
Senior programmer (36 hours)	1,044

a. Calculate the labor efficiency and labor wage rate variances for the junior and senior programmers on the Denver General Hospital account.

b. The manager of the project receives a bonus based on labor cost and efficiency. The bonus is adjusted (increased or decreased) by 50 percent of the total direct labor variance. What is the impact of this project on the manager's bonus?

c. What incentives might this bonus system create?

NP 14.4
Standard Costs
(LO 1, 2, 3)

Ogwood Company is a small manufacturer of wooden household items. The corporate controller plans to implement a standard cost system for Ogwood and has information from several co-workers that will assist him in developing the standards.

One of Ogwood's products is a wooden cutting board. Each cutting board requires 1.25 board feet of lumber and 12 minutes of direct labor time to prepare and cut the lumber. The cutting boards are inspected after they are cut. They are made of a natural material that has imperfections; therefore, one board is normally rejected after cutting for every five that are accepted. Four rubber footpads are attached to each good cutting board. A total of 15 minutes of direct labor time is required to attach all four footpads and finish each cutting board. The lumber for the cutting boards costs $3.00 per board foot, and each footpad costs $0.05. Direct labor is paid at the rate of $8.00 per hour.

a. Develop the standard cost for the direct cost components of the cutting board. The standard cost should identify the following for each direct cost component of the cutting board:
   1. Standard quantity.
   2. Standard rate.
   3. Standard cost per unit.
b. What are the advantages of standard cost systems?
c. Explain the role of each of the following persons in developing standards:
   1. Purchasing manager.
   2. Industrial engineer.
   3. Cost accountant.

(CMA adapted)

NP 14.5
Direct Materials Variance
(LO 3, 4)

Howard Binding manufactures two types of notebooks, large and small. Both types of notebooks are made of the same cloth cover (direct material), but they require different quantities. The standard cost sheet for each is as follows:

	Large	Small
Cloth covering	3 meters @ $0.30 per meter	2 meters @ $0.30 per meter
Ring holder	1 @ $0.12 each	1 @ $0.12 each
Direct labor	0.15 hour @ $6.00 per hour	0.10 hour @ $6.00 per hour

At the beginning of the month, the purchasing department bought 35,000 meters of cloth for $10,850. There were no beginning inventories. During the month, 5,000 large and 8,000 small notebooks were produced. The production records for the month indicate the following actual production quantities:

	Large	Small
Cloth covering	16,000 meters	15,500 meters
Ring holders	5,000 @ $0.12 each	8,000 @ $0.12 each
Direct labor	800 hours @ $5.80 per hour	780 hours @ $6.10 per hour

a. Calculate the cloth covering price variance (1) at purchase and (2) when the materials are actually used.
b. Discuss why the two price variances calculated in part (a) differ and which is superior (and why).

NP 14.6
Overhead Variances
(LO 6) (Appendix only)

The technology support department of Acme Company services the firm's PCs and printers. It applies variable and fixed overhead to jobs based on standard labor hours. The department has the following budget numbers related to the allocation base:

Type of Service	Expected Service Units	Standard Labor per Service Unit	Total Expected Labor Hours
PCs	1,000	1 hour	1,000
Printers	3,000	2 hours	6,000
Total			7,000

The standard numbers related to the allocation base given actual output are as follows:

Type of Service	Actual Service Units	Standard Labor per Service Unit	Total Standard Labor
Copiers	850	1 hour	850
Fax machines	3,500	2 hours	7,000
Total			7,850

The actual number of labor hours used to service the copiers and fax machines was 7,800 hours. Budgeted and actual variable and fixed overhead costs follow:

Overhead	Budgeted Costs	Actual Costs
Variable	$14,000	$12,000
Fixed	28,000	26,000

Calculate the application rates for variable and fixed overhead, the amount of variable and fixed overhead applied, the variable overhead spending and efficiency variances, and the fixed overhead budget and volume variances.

The Toronto engine plant of Eastern Corporation manufactures engine blocks for automobiles. It produces three types, four-, six-, and eight-cylinder blocks. An engine block is the basic component of an automobile engine and contains the cylinders into which the pistons are fitted. After assembling the block with the head, pan, pistons, spark plugs, rods, camshaft, and valves, the motor is ready to be fitted with the fuel and exhaust systems and installed in the automobile. The engine block is cast from a single block of steel. The cylinders are bored by high-precision, computer-controlled machine tools. Then other machine tools tap and thread the block to attach the other engine components. The cylinder boring department is the key process after the engine block is cast.

NP 14.7
Budgeted, Standard, and Actual Machine Hours
(LO 6) (Appendix only)

Overhead is tracked to departments. The allocation base in the cylinder boring department is machine hours, or the number of hours each block spends in the computer-controlled machine tool having its cylinders bored. Each of the three motor blocks requires the following standard machine hours per block:

Four-cylinder blocks	0.50
Six-cylinder blocks	0.70
Eight-cylinder blocks	0.90

Each block requires some set-up time to mount and correctly position the block in the computer-controlled machine tool. Hence, an eight-cylinder block does not require twice the machining time of a four-cylinder block. Also, a cylinder in a four-cylinder block is larger and requires more boring time than does a cylinder in a six- or eight-cylinder block.

At the beginning of the year, management forecasts the number of blocks to be manufactured based on the projected unit sales of car models requiring four-, six-, and eight-cylinder engines. The plant plans to produce 95,000 engine blocks using 67,500 machine hours. The expected production by block type and the standard machine hours per block are given in the following table.

Calculation of Expected Usage of Machine Hours Toronto Engine Plant's Cylinder Boring Department		
Product	**Expected Production**	**Standard Machine Hours per Block**
Four-cylinder blocks	25,000	0.50
Six-cylinder blocks	40,000	0.70
Eight-cylinder blocks	30,000	0.90
Expected machine hours	95,000	

During the year, production plans change as customer preferences become known. An unexpected increase in gasoline taxes causes consumers to shift toward smaller, more fuel-efficient automobiles with smaller engines. Fewer eight-cylinder engines are made and more four- and six-cylinder engines are manufactured. The following table presents the actual operating results for the year.

Calculation of Actual and Standard Machine Hours Toronto Engine Plant's Cylinder Boring Department		
Product	**Actual Blocks Produced**	**Actual Machine Hours**
Four-cylinder blocks	27,000	14,200
Six-cylinder blocks	41,000	29,000
Eight-cylinder blocks	28,000	25,000
	96,000	68,200

What are the budgeted, standard, and actual machine hours?

NP 14.8
Expected, Standard, and Actual Volume and Volume Variance
(LO 6) (Appendix only)

Printers, Inc., manufactures and sells a mid-volume color printer (MC) and a high-volume color printer (HC). Each MC requires 100 direct labor hours to manufacture; each HC requires 150 direct labor hours. At the beginning of the year, the production schedule includes 700 MCs and 500 HCs. At the end of the year, 720 MCs and 510 HCs were produced. In producing MCs, 1,400 hours too many were used and 3,000 hours fewer than standard were used to manufacture HCs. Expected fixed overhead is $2.9 million and expected variable overhead is $10 per direct labor hour.
    Calculate the following:

a. Expected volume.
b. Standard volume.
c. Actual volume.
d. Overhead rate.
e. Fixed overhead volume variance and discuss its meaning.

NP 14.9
Direct Variances
(LO 3, 4)

ColdKing Company is a small producer of fruit-flavored frozen desserts. For many years, ColdKing's products have had strong regional sales on the basis of brand recognition. However, other companies have begun marketing similar products in the area, and price competition has become increasingly aggressive. John Wakefield, the company's controller, is planning to implement a standard cost system for ColdKing. He has gathered considerable information from his co-workers on production and materials requirements for Cold-King's products. John believes that the use of standard costing will allow ColdKing to improve cost control and make better pricing decisions.
    ColdKing's most popular product is raspberry sherbet. It is produced in 10-gallon batches, and each batch requires 6 quarts of good raspberries. The fresh raspberries are sorted by hand before entering the production process. Due to imperfections in the raspberries and normal spoilage, 1 quart of berries is discarded for every 4 quarts of acceptable berries. Three minutes is the standard direct labor time for sorting that is required to obtain 1 quart of acceptable raspberries. The acceptable raspberries then are blended with the other ingredients. Blending requires 12 minutes of direct labor time per batch. After blending, the sherbet is packaged in quart containers. John has gathered the following price information:

⁕   ColdKing purchases raspberries at a cost of $0.80 per quart. All other ingredients cost a total of $4.50 per 10-gallon batch.
⁕   Direct labor is paid at the rate of $9.00 per hour.
⁕   The total cost of material and labor required to package the sherbet is $0.38 per quart.

a. Develop the standard cost for the direct cost components of a 10-gallon batch of raspberry sherbet. The standard cost should identify the following for each direct cost component of a batch of raspberry sherbet:
    1. Standard quantity.
    2. Standard rate.
    3. Standard cost per batch.

b. As part of the implementation of a standard cost system at ColdKing, John plans to train those responsible for maintaining the standards in the use of variance analysis. He is particularly concerned with the causes of unfavorable variances.
   1. Discuss the possible causes of unfavorable materials price variances and identify the individual(s) who should be held responsible for these variances.
   2. Discuss the possible causes of unfavorable labor efficiency variances and identify the individual(s) who should be held responsible for these variances.

(CMA adapted)

Turow Trailers assembles horse trailers. Two models, G7 and V8, are manufactured. While labor intensive, the production process is not very complicated. The single plant produces all the trailers. Forty-eight work teams of two or three workers assemble entire trailers; 16 supervisors oversee the work teams. Material handlers deliver all the parts needed for each trailer to the work team. Personnel, accounting, inspection, purchasing, and tools are the other major overhead departments. Some operating statistics for 2000 and 2001 are provided:

NP 14.10
Overhead Variances
(LO 6) (Appendix only)

	2000	2001
Expected volume (DLH)*	1 million	1 million
Overhead budget		
Fixed overhead	$2.1 million	$2.2 million
Variable overhead per DLH	$7	$8
Units produced		
G7	11,000	8,000
V8	12,000	6,000
Standard DLH per unit of		
G7	40	40
V8	50	50
Actual overhead incurred	$9.0 million	$8.1 million
Actual direct labor hours	1.0 million	0.7 million

*DLH = direct labor hours.

a. Calculate all the overhead variances for both 2000 and 2001.
b. Discuss who in the plant should be held responsible for each of the overhead variances.

NP 14.11
Direct Materials Variances
(LO 3)

A pharmaceutical firm plans to make a new drug that requires 4.5 grams of compound AN7-X1 per batch of 250 tablets. AN7-X1 has a standard price of $2 per gram. An initial inventory of 8,000 grams of AN7-X1 is purchased for $17,200. The firm produces 1,000 batches of the new drug and uses 4,600 grams of AN7-X1. All variances are calculated as soon as possible.
   Calculate the price and quantity variances for AN7-X1.

NP 14.12
Direct Labor Variances
(LO 3)

Software Associates (SA) is a computer software consulting firm that specializes in designing and implementing integrated marketing database warehousing programs. Honora Catalog is a client. In preparing its bid for Honora, SA estimates its total labor cost for this project to be $222,500 broken down as follows:

	Budgeted Hours	Budgeted Wage	Budgeted Cost
Partner	100	$175	$ 17,500
Associate	300	120	36,000
Senior analyst	600	90	54,000
Analyst	1,000	40	40,000
Programmer	3,000	25	75,000
Total			$222,500

After the completion of Honora's contract, the following data are reported:

	Actual Hours	Actual Cost
Partner	90	$ 15,750
Associate	280	35,000
Senior analyst	750	63,750
Analyst	1,400	49,000
Programmer	3,600	82,800
Total		$246,300

a. Prepare a performance report (variance analysis) for Honora Catalog's project.

b. Analyze the variances and provide a plausible explanation for SA's performance on Honora's project.

NP 14.13
Direct Labor Variances
(LO 3)

Marian Health Care is a large hospital system outside Chicago that offers both hospitalization (inpatient) and clinic (outpatient) services. It has a centralized admissions office that admits and registers clients, some of whom are seeking inpatient hospital services and others outpatient clinic services. Marian uses a standard cost system to control its labor costs. The standard labor time to admit an inpatient is 15 minutes. Outpatient admissions have a standard labor time of 9 minutes. The standard wage rate for admissions agents is $14.50 per hour. During the last week, the admissions office admitted 820 inpatients and 2,210 outpatients. Actual hours worked by the admissions agents last week were 540 hours, and their total wages paid were $8,235.

a. Prepare a financial report that summarizes the operating performance (including the efficiency) of the admissions office for last week.

b. Based on the financial report you prepared in part (a), write a short memo summarizing your findings and conclusions from this report.

NP 14.14
Overhead Variances
(LO 6) (Appendix only)

The milling department uses standard machine hours to allocate overhead to products. Budgeted volume for the year was 36,000 machine hours. Fixed overhead is budgeted to be $720,000, and variable overhead is estimated to be $10 per machine hour.

During the year, two products are milled. The following table summarizes operations:

	Product 1	Product 2
Units milled	10,500	12,000
Standard machine hours per unit	2	1
Actual machine hours used	23,000	13,000

Actual overhead incurred during the year was $1.1 million, of which $750,000 was fixed and the remainder variable.

Calculate all relevant overhead variances for the department. Write a memo that describes what each one means.

NP 14.15
Overhead Variance and Capacity
(LO 6) (Appendix only)

You work in the strategy analysis department of On-Call, a worldwide paging firm offering satellite-based digital communications through sophisticated pagers. On-Call is analyzing the possibility of acquiring AtlantiCom, a paging firm in Maine.

AtlantiCom's latest quarterly report disclosed a total overhead variance (underabsorbed overhead) of $1.3 million. The engineering staff of On-Call, familiar with AtlantiCom's network, estimates that AtlantiCom has quarterly overhead costs of $6.5 million that can deliver 800,000 message packets per quarter. A message packet is the industry standard of delivering a fixed amount of digital information within a given time period.

In valuing AtlantiCom, senior management at On-Call wants to know whether it has excess capacity, and, if so, how much.

As a percentage of AtlantiCom's current capacity of 800,000 message packets, estimate its over- or undercapacity last quarter.

Betterton Corporation manufactures automobile headlight lenses and uses a standard cost system. At the beginning of the year, the following standards were established per 100 lenses (a single batch):

NP 14.16
Variance Calculations
(LO 3, 4, 6) (Appendix only)

	Input	Amount
Direct material	100 kg. @ $2.00 per kg.	$200
Direct labor	5 hours @ $18 per hour	90
Factory overhead		
Fixed overhead	$4 per direct labor hour	20
Variable overhead	$6 per direct labor hour	30
Total cost per batch of 100 headlight lenses		$340

Expected volume per month is 5,000 direct labor hours for January and 105,000 headlight lenses were produced. There were no beginning inventories. The following costs were incurred in January:

Fixed factory overhead		$39,000
Variable factory overhead		20,000
Direct labor	5,400 hours	99,900
Direct material used	102,000 kg.	
Direct material purchased	110,000 kg.	209,000

a. Calculate the following variances:
   1. Variable overhead spending variance.
   2. Fixed overhead volume variance.
   3. Fixed overhead budget variance.
   4. Variable overhead efficiency variance.
   5. Direct materials price variance at purchase.
   6. Direct labor efficiency variance.
   7. Direct materials quantity variance.
b. Discuss how the direct materials price variance computed at purchase differs from the direct materials price variance computed at use. Outline the advantages and disadvantages of each.

Shady Tree produces two products, M1s and M2s. It has no beginning inventories or ending work-in-process inventories of either M1s or M2s. A single plantwide overhead rate is used to allocate overhead to products using standard direct labor hours (DLH). This overhead rate is set at the beginning of the year based on the following: fixed factory overhead is forecast to be $3 million and variable overhead is projected to be $20 per direct labor hour. Management expects plant volume to be 200,000 standard DLH. The following are the standard direct labor hours for each product:

NP 14.17
Fixed Overhead Volume Variance
(LO 6) (Appendix only)

SHADY TREE MANUFACTURING
Direct Labor Standards per Product

	M1	M2
Standard DLH per unit	3	5

The variable overhead variances and fixed overhead budget variance for the year were zero. The following table summarizes operations for the year:

SHADY TREE MANUFACTURING
Summary of Operations for the Year

	M1	M2
Units produced	30,000	12,000
Units sold	20,000	10,000

540

Standard Costs and Variance Analysis

a. Calculate the plantwide overhead rate computed at the beginning of the year.

b. Calculate the fixed overhead volume variance for the year.

c. What is the dollar impact on accounting earnings if the fixed overhead volume variance is written off to the Cost of Goods Sold account?

d. What is the dollar impact on accounting earnings of prorating the fixed overhead volume variance to inventories and cost of goods sold compared to writing it off to cost of sales?

e. Suppose that *at the beginning of the year,* management at Shady Tree Manufacturing wants to increase accounting earnings in a particular year *without changing production or sales levels.* Describe how it might do this (assuming that its external auditors would allow such action). Use the facts presented to illustrate your answer.

NP 14.18
Variances and Absorption and Variable Costing
(LO 3, 4, 6) (Appendix only)

Mopart division produces a single product. Its standard cost system assigns indirect costs on the basis of standard direct labor hours (DLH). At the expected volume of 4,000 DLH, the standard cost per unit is as follows:

Selling price	$38.00
Direct materials, 3 kg. @ $5	$15.00
Direct labor, 0.4 hr. @ $20	8.00
Variable indirect costs, 0.4 hr. @ $6	2.40
Fixed indirect costs, 0.4 hr. @ $4	1.60
Total	$27.00

For the month of March, the following actual data were reported:

Units produced	9,000
Number of direct labor hours	3,800
Actual wage rate	$20.50
Direct materials used (kg.)	28,000
Average price of materials used	$5.50
Average selling price	$38.75
Number of units sold	8,800.00
Variable indirect costs	$21,500.00
Fixed indirect costs	$15,800.00
Variable selling and administrative costs	$34,500.00
Fixed selling and administrative costs	$28,000.00

There was no beginning inventory.

a. Analyze the results of operations for the month of March. Support your analysis with both reason and data. Exposition and easy-to-follow tables are important.

b. Present two income statements in good format using absorption costing and variable costing net income.

c. Reconcile any difference in net income between the two statements.

d. What is the opportunity cost of the unused normal capacity?

NP 14.19
Variance Calculations
(LO 3, 4, 6) (Appendix only)

Anpax, Inc., manufactures two products, L7 and Q2. Overhead is allocated to products based on machine hours. Management uses a flexible budget to forecast overhead. For the current year, fixed factory overhead is projected to be $2.75 million and variable factory overhead is budgeted at $20 per machine hour. At the beginning of the year, management developed the following standards for each product and made the following production forecasts for the year:

ANPAX, INC.
Current Year Standards and Production Forecasts

	Products			
	L7		**Q2**	
Budgeted number of units produced	25,000		35,000	
Production standards				
Direct labor per unit	10 hours	$15 per hour	12 hours	$15 per hour
Direct materials per unit	85 kg.	$1 per kg.	95 kg.	$1 per kg.
Machine hours per unit	4		5	

There were no beginning or ending inventories. Actual production for the year was 20,000 units of L7 and 40,000 units of Q2. Other data summarizing actual operations for the year follow:

Direct labor	700,000 hours	$9.8 million
Direct materials	5.0 million kg.	$5.5 million
Machine hours	270,000	
Fixed overhead	$3.4 million	
Variable overhead	$5 million	

a. Calculate the overhead rate for the current year.
b. Calculate materials and labor variances. Report only quantity (efficiency) variances and price variances.
c. Calculate the overhead variances.
d. Your boss (a nonaccountant) asks you to explain in nontechnical terms the meaning of each overhead variance.

ANALYSIS AND INTERPRETATION PROBLEMS

Critically evaluate the following quotation:

> More research is needed to explain the tenacity with which businesses cling to accounting performance information. More empirical research into the consequences of managing information is also in order, but there already is much evidence that businesses impair their competitiveness and profitability today by managing with the information found in standard cost variances, flexible budgets, product costs, return on investment, and more. Less well understood is why "world-class" manufacturing companies persist in using accounting-based financial performance measures.

(*Source:* H. T. Johnson, "Performance Measurement for Competitive Excellence," in *Measure for Manufacturing Excellence*, ed. R. Kaplan [Boston: Harvard Business School Press, 1990], p. 84.

AIP 14.1
Criticism of Standard Cost Variances
(LO 1, 2)

A number of companies use the following ratio to measure operating efficiency:

Earned direct labor dollars
─────────────────────────
Actual direct labor dollars

AIP 14.2
Labor Efficiency Ratio
(LO 2, 5)

Earned direct labor dollars are the number of units produced times the standard direct labor dollars per hour. For example, the machine department produced four jobs today:

Job Number	Number of Units Produced	Standard Labor Dollars per Unit	Earned Direct Labor Dollars
101	100	$3	$ 300
102	200	2	400
103	150	1	150
104	100	2	200
Total earned direct labor dollars			$1,050

Actual direct labor dollars for today is $1,350.

$$\frac{\text{Earned direct labor dollars}}{\text{Actual direct labor dollars}} = \frac{1,050}{1,350} = 0.777$$

The higher the ratio, the more output per actual direct labor dollar. Operating managers are rewarded for high values of this ratio. Discuss the advantages and disadvantages of using this ratio to measure and reward performance of factory management.

AIP 14.3
Setting of Standard Costs
(LO 2)

Associated Media Graphics (AMG) is a rapidly expanding company involved in the mass reproduction of instructional materials. It is organized into a number of production departments responsible for a particular stage of the production process, such as copyediting, typesetting, printing, and binding. Ralph Davis, owner and manager of AMG, has made a concentrated effort to provide a quality product at a competitive price with delivery on the promised due date. Expanding sales have been attributed to this philosophy. Ralph is finding it increasingly difficult to supervise personally the operations of AMG and is beginning to institute an organizational structure that would facilitate management control.

One change recently made was the designation of operating departments as cost centers, with control over departmental operations transferred from Ralph to each departmental manager. However, quality control still reports directly to him, as do the finance and accounting functions. A materials manager was hired to purchase all raw materials and to oversee the inventory handling (receiving, storage, etc.) and record-keeping functions. The materials manager is also responsible for maintaining an adequate inventory based on planned production levels.

The loss of personal control over AMG's operations caused Ralph to look for a method of efficiently evaluating performance. Donna Cress, a new management accountant, proposed the use of a standard cost system. Variances for material, labor, and manufacturing overhead then could be calculated and reported directly to Ralph.

a. Assume that AMG is going to implement a standard cost system and establish standards for materials, labor, and manufacturing overhead. Identify and discuss for each of these cost components
  1. Who should be involved in setting the standards.
  2. The factors that should be considered in establishing the standards.
b. Describe the basis for assignment of responsibility under a standard cost system.

AIP 14.4
Standard Overhead Rates
(LO 6) (Appendix only)

Spectra, Inc., produces personal computer color monitors. The firm makes 19-inch monitors with the following cost structure:

Direct materials	$220
Direct labor	150

Due to the rapidly changing market for computer monitors, standard costs, overhead rates, and prices are revised quarterly. While the direct labor component of standard cost has been relatively constant over time, direct material costs, especially the cost of the circuit boards, fluctuate widely. Therefore, for pricing purposes, management reviews costs each quarter and forecasts next quarter's costs using the current quarter's cost structure. Management also uses this method for revising overhead costs each quarter. Overhead is applied to product using direct labor cost. Fixed overhead is incurred fairly uniformly over the year. The overhead rate next quarter is the ratio of actual overhead costs incurred this quarter divided by this quarter's direct labor cost. Data for the last six quarters follow:

	2000				2001		
	Q1	Q2	Q3	Q4	Q1	Q2	Q3
Actual unit sales	200	200	190	180	190	250	
Total direct labor	$30,000	$30,000	$28,500	$27,000	$28,500	$37,500	
Actual overhead	$101,000	$102,000	$98,000	$95,000	$97,000	$118,000	
Overhead rate	$3.35	$3.37	$3.40	$3.43	$3.52	$3.40	$3.15

The president of the company, responding to the auditor's suggestion that it set its projected costs on an annual basis, replied: "Annual budgeting is fine for more static companies like automobiles. But the computer industry, especially peripherals, changes day by day. We have to be ahead of our competitors in terms of revising our product price in response to cost changes. If we waited eight months to react, we'd be out of business."

Do you agree with the president or the auditor? Critically evaluate Spectra's costing system. What changes would you suggest, and how would you justify them to the president?

Western Sugar processes sugar beets into granulated sugar that is sold to food companies. It uses a standard cost system to aid in the control of costs and for performance evaluation. To compute the standards for next year, the actual expense incurred by expense category is divided by the number of bushels of sugar beets processed to arrive at a standard cost per bushel. These per bushel standards then are increased by the expected amount of inflation forecast for that expense category. This year, Western Sugar processed 63 million bushels of beets. The calculation of next year's standard costs is as follows:

AIP 14.5
Overhead Variances
(LO 2, 6) (Appendix only)

WESTERN SUGAR
Standard Costs for Next Year
(thousands of dollars)

	This Year's Cost	Cost per Bushel	Inflation Adjustment	Standard Cost per Bushel
Direct labor	$ 33,000	$0.524	4%	$0.544
Sugar beets	58,000	0.921	3.5%	0.953
Variable overhead	24,000	0.381	5%	0.400
Fixed overhead	43,000	0.683	2%	0.696
Total	$158,000	$2.509		$2.593

Next year, actual production is 68 million bushels. At the end of next year, the following report is prepared:

WESTERN SUGAR
Actual Results Compared to Standard Next Year
(thousands of dollars)

	Actual Cost	Standard Cost per Bushel	Standard Cost	Variance
Direct labor	$ 38,100	$0.544	$ 36,992	$1,108 U
Sugar beets	64,829	0.953	64,804	25 U
Variable overhead	28,211	0.400	27,200	1,011 U
Fixed overhead	45,227	0.696	47,328	2,101 F
Total	$176,367	$2.593	$176,324	$ 43 U

Senior management was not surprised at the small variances for labor and sugar beets. The processing plant has good operating controls and there had been no surprises in the sugar beet market or in the labor market. Its initial forecasts proved to be good. Management was delighted to see the favorable total overhead variance ($1,090 F = $1,011 U + $2,101 F). Although variable overhead was over budget, fixed overhead was below budget and more than offset the overbudget variable overhead. There was no major change in the plant's production technology to explain this shift (such as increased automation), and, therefore, senior management was prepared to attribute the favorable total overhead variance to better internal control by the plant manager.

a. What do you think is the reason for the overhead variances?

b. Is it appropriate to base next year's standards on last year's costs?

EXTENDED ANALYSIS AND INTERPRETATION PROBLEMS

AIP 14.6
Volume Measures

The gear-cutting department of Universal Transmissions cuts the teeth into gears. These gears then are finished in other departments and assembled into farm and construction equipment transmissions (tractors, combines, bulldozers). The department contains three identical cutting machines that were purchased two years ago. Each machine's expected use is 2,400 hours a year. The production budget for the year is as follows:

	GEAR-CUTTING DEPARTMENT		
	Budgeted Production		
	For January 1, 2001–December 31, 2001		
Gear Type	**Budgeted Production (no. of gears)**	**Standard Minutes per Gear**	**Budgeted Minutes**
A7474	965	36	34,740
B7682	290	21	6,090
C4983	993	24	23,832
D7575	514	44	22,616
F8390	733	39	28,587
H6363	547	54	29,538
H8983	989	32	31,648
J3839	354	33	11,682
K9828	546	52	28,392
L2738	922	48	44,256
L7378	494	26	12,844
L9383	313	11	3,443
M7483	199	52	10,348
M8992	950	50	47,500
Q2839	423	52	21,996
R093	588	37	21,756
S2829	719	45	32,355
S2882	488	25	12,200
T8390	373	57	21,261
U1920	185	34	6,290
Y7382	647	37	23,939
Total			475,313

The operating budget for the gear-cutting department for 2001 follows:

	GEAR-CUTTING DEPARTMENT	
	Operating Budget	
	For January 1, 2001–December 31, 2001	
	Fixed Costs	**Variable Costs per Machine Hour**
Cutting oil		$ 3.21
Depreciation	$ 632,000	
Engineering	232,890	
Maintenance	69,840	4.56
Operators	25,400	36.34
Plant overhead	124,400	1.20
Utilities	26,800	2.21
Total	$1,111,330	$47.52

Costs in the gear-cutting department are assigned to gears based on standard gear-cutting machine minutes. At the beginning of the year, the cost per minute on these machines is set by dividing budgeted costs in the department (budgeted fixed costs plus budgeted variable costs per machine minute times projected minutes for the year) by projected minutes for the year. The following table summarizes actual operations by gear type:

GEAR-CUTTING DEPARTMENT
Summary of Operations
For January 1, 2001–December 31, 2001

Gear	Actual Production	Standard Minutes per Gear	Standard Minutes of Volume	Actual Minutes of Volume	Percentage Variance Actual from Standard
A7474	1,041	36	37,476	41,528	11%
B7682	304	21	6,384	6,160	(4)
C4983	937	24	22,488	24,671	10
D7575	543	44	23,892	26,359	10
F8390	724	39	28,236	29,546	5
H6363	544	54	29,376	26,970	(8)
H8983	958	32	30,656	29,631	(3)
J3839	331	33	10,923	10,142	(7)
K9828	596	52	30,992	28,823	(7)
L2738	1,007	48	48,336	49,494	2
L7378	536	26	13,936	14,484	4
L9383	335	11	3,685	3,936	7
M7483	208	52	10,816	10,657	(1)
M8992	1,020	50	51,000	55,543	9
Q2839	462	52	24,024	23,125	(4)
R093	603	37	22,311	22,761	2
S2829	675	45	30,375	28,110	(7)
S2882	447	25	11,175	12,371	11
T8390	351	57	20,007	19,989	0
U1920	191	34	6,494	6,332	(2)
Y7382	585	37	21,645	20,167	(7)
Total			484,227	490,799	

a. Identify the various measures of volume (e.g., actual volume) that can be used in the gear-cutting department for 2001. For each volume measure identified, provide the 2001 empirical magnitude.

b. Calculate the cost per minute in the gear-cutting department for 2001.

c. An outside company offers to provide gear cutting for gear A7474 for $63 each. This price includes pickup and delivery, and it guarantees the same quality and timeliness of delivery as the gear-cutting department does. Analyze the outside offer and make a recommendation as to whether or not the offer should be accepted. Be sure to identify any assumptions underlying your recommendation.

Maidwell Company manufactures washers and dryers on a single assembly line in its main manufacturing plant. The market has deteriorated over the last five years, and competition has made cost control very important. Management has been concerned about the materials cost of both washers and dryers. No model changes have been made in the past two years, and economic conditions have allowed the company to negotiate price reductions for many key parts.

Maidwell uses a standard cost system in accounting for materials. Purchases are charged to inventory at a standard price, and purchase discounts are considered an administrative cost reduction. Production is charged at the standard price of the materials used. Thus, the price variance is isolated at time of purchase as the difference between

AIP 14.7
Direct Material Variance Analysis

gross contract price and standard price multiplied by the number purchased. When a substitute part is used in production rather than the regular part, a price variance equal to the difference in the standard prices of the materials is recognized at the time of substitution in the production process. The quantity variance is the actual quantity used compared to the standard quantity allowed with the difference multiplied by the standard price.

The materials variances for several of the parts that Maidwell uses are unfavorable. Part No. 4121 is one of the items that has an unfavorable variance. Maidwell knows that some of these parts are defective and will fail (normal defective rate is 5% of normal input). The failure is discovered during production. The original contract price of this part was $0.285 per unit; thus, Maidwell set the standard unit price at $0.285. The unit contract purchase price of Part No. 4121 was increased $0.04 to $0.325 from the original $0.285 due to a parts specification change. Maidwell chose not to change the standard but treated the increase in price as a price variance. In addition, the contract terms were changed from payment due in 30 days to a 4% discount if paid in 10 days or full payment due in 30 days. These new contractual terms were the consequence of negotiations resulting from changes in the economy.

Data regarding the usage of Part No. 4121 during December is as follows:

Purchases of Part No. 4121	150,000 units
Unit price paid for purchases of Part No. 4121	$0.325
Requisitions of Part No. 4121 from stores for use in products	134,000 units
Substitution of Part No. 5125 for Part No. 4121 to use obsolete stock (standard unit price of Part No. 5125 is $0.35)	24,000 units
Units of Part No. 4121 and its substitute (Part No. 5125) identified as being defective	9,665 units
Standard allowed usage (including normal defective units) of Part No. 4121 and its substitute based upon output for the month	153,300 units

Maidwell's material variances related to Part No. 4121 for December were reported as follows:

Price variance	$7,560.00 U
Quantity variance	1,339.50 U
Total materials variances for Part No. 4121	$8,899.50 U

Bob Speck, the purchasing director, claims that the unfavorable price variance is misleading. He says that his department has worked hard to obtain price concessions and purchase discounts from suppliers. In addition, he has indicated that engineering changes have been made in several parts, increasing their price, even though the part identification has not changed. These price increases are not his department's responsibility. Bob declares that price variances no longer measure the purchasing department's performance.

Jana Buddle, the manufacturing manager, thinks the responsibility for the quantity variance should be shared. She states that manufacturing cannot control quality associated with less expensive parts, substitutions of material to use up otherwise obsolete stock, or engineering changes that increase the quantity of materials used.

The accounting manager, Mike Kohl, has suggested that the computation of variances be changed to identify variations from standard with the causes and functional areas responsible for the variances. Mike recommends the following system of materials variances and the method of computation for each:

Variance	Method of Calculation
Economic variance	Quantity purchased times the changes made after setting standards. Standards are the result of negotiations based on changes in the general economy.
Engineering change variance	Quantity purchased times change in price due to part specification changes.
Purchase price variance	Quantity purchased times change in contract price due to changes other than parts specifications or the general economy.
Substitutions variance	Quantity substituted times the difference in standard price between parts substituted.
Excess usage variance	Standard price times the difference between the standard quantity allowed for production minus actual parts used (reduced for abnormal scrap).
Abnormal failure rate variance	Abnormal scrap times standard price.

a. Discuss the appropriateness of Maidwell Company's current method of variance analysis for materials. Indicate whether the claims of Bob Speck and Jana Buddle are valid.

b. Compute the materials variances for Part No. 4121 for December using the system recommended by Mike Kohl.

c. Indicate who would be responsible for each of the variances in Mike's system of variance analysis.

(CMA adapted)

Thoughts on
Business**Analysis**

Chapter Two

Page 52 Firms with higher fixed costs, such as full-service brokerage houses, are likely to develop pricing strategies to cover the fixed and variable costs of their operations. Fixed costs relate to the higher infrastructure costs of these firms. Clients can be differentiated according to pricing schemes based on the level of service that they demand. Online trading firms have lower infrastructure costs and are more likely to pursue a low-price strategy to capture customers who will trade off higher levels of service for lower costs.

As firms try to compete in the long term, clients likely will become more demanding and expect firms to offer more at lower cost. In the long run, as commission fees drop, both existing and new firms will have more difficulty in competing successfully. Commission fees might be pushed lower to capture market share at the expense of long-run profits. In the end, successful firms will need to implement a strategy that delivers customer value in other ways, such as financial advice and banking privileges.

Chapter Three

Page 79 Given a cost structure that is predominantly at the product, facility, and batch levels, ATT should enter into pricing agreements that reflect the inexpensive unit-level costs. ATT could consider fixed monthly fees for unlimited long-distance telephone calls. Reducing the customer's marginal cost of a telephone call to zero, however, may have a large impact on the usage of long-distance calls. A large increase in long-distance calls could lead to capacity costs. Therefore, a fixed monthly fee for a limited number of calls during peak-use periods and an unlimited number of calls during nonpeak-use periods may be an alternative pricing strategy.

ATT must recognize that long-distance communication could evolve in many different directions in the next 10 years. The company must be prepared to keep pace with the technological changes. If wireless communication becomes the future standard, ATT must be prepared with satellite networks and control over sufficient wavelengths. If long-distance communication continues using wires, ATT must consider ways to reach local customers either through cables or the acquisition of local telephone companies (Baby Bells).

Chapter Four

Page 108 If an organization does not have the in-house personnel or expertise, it might prefer to outsource its advertising activity to an outside agency, such as Omnicom. Advertising agencies offer industry expertise, a broad range of services, and lower costs due to their economies of scale.

When making the decision to outsource, an organization must weigh the advantages and disadvantages of this choice. Advantages include the items previously mentioned, as well as potential time savings by outsourcing the activity to experts. Disadvantages include not developing and maintaining this expertise within the firm (contributing to organizational growth), the potential loss of confidentiality (the reason advertising agencies

generally cannot work for competing firms), and possible cost increases once the organization becomes dependent on the agency. In addition, there is no guarantee that the agency will develop a successful advertising campaign. Any decision to change agencies or revert to in-house production also could lead to lost sales if it is not carried out effectively.

Page 117 To some extent, the retail stores and Internet sites of Office Depot compete with each other. However, prices must be comparable; if they are much lower at one site, the other site will be driven out of business as customers discover the lower prices.

By using the synergies of having both retail shops and Internet sites, Office Depot can operate at lower costs than can some of its competitors. These lower costs can be passed on to customers in the form of lower prices, but an analysis of competitors and customer value should be made to determine whether lower prices are necessary. If Office Depot's prices are already the lowest and there is no danger of other companies competing at lower prices, Office Depot could maintain its existing prices, especially if customers believe they are getting a fair value for the service provided.

Page 119 Adjusting customer service based on customer profitability is a common practice. Big tippers get the best seats in restaurants. The practice should be performed with care, however. Less profitable customers are likely to resent inferior service when they can observe others receiving first-class service. Differential service levels should not be blatant. Airlines often use curtains between first class and coach to hide the different services offered.

An alternative to offering different levels of services is to educate and motivate less profitable customers to become more profitable. Bank customers may not realize the additional benefits that they receive when they deposit more money with the bank.

Chapter Five

Page 147 Ryanair, like other low-cost carriers, might establish its airfares by determining the marginal cost of carrying passengers, examining competitors' fares, and analyzing customers' price sensitivity. Customers might be willing to pay more than the firm's marginal cost if the alternative flight is a full-cost fare with a major carrier.

The low-cost carriers must be careful not to price their flights too low so that they do not cover their long-run fixed costs. In addition, customers might react negatively to future price increases, once low prices have been established. Low-cost carriers also face threats from larger firms that enter this market and try to lure customers by offering lower fares. The larger firms might consider that they can pursue this strategy in the short run, gain passengers, and place the smaller firms in a difficult position in terms of maintaining both market share and profits. Low-cost airlines, however, often can compete better with lower fares as they have lower fixed costs, operate more efficiently, and frequently have less unionized labor. They also tend to choose routes that are less popular for the major carriers.

Break-even analysis provides a tool to determine the required number of passengers (or passenger revenues) for a particular flight to be potentially profitable. By using various combinations of prices and passengers, the airline can determine when it is better to add an additional flight to a specific route or enter a new market, especially when this decision might reduce the number of passengers on existing flights. Break-even analysis also provides the airline initial insights into market potential before it undertakes a more in-depth study.

Chapter Six

Page 185 Ratification, such as United Health Group's authorization procedure, is not the only method of control. In most modern, decentralized organizations, only decisions with a very large impact on the organization require ratification. Control is achieved through monitoring. In the case of United Health Group, doctors can be monitored by using performance measures. Doctors could be evaluated, for example, based on the total costs of services their patients receive. These performance measures could be adjusted for doctors with different types of clientele. Those doctors who have predominantly older patients would be expected to have patients with higher service costs. The number of referrals per patient could be another performance measure.

Chapter Seven

Page 203 Given that all of the responsibility centers are oriented toward external customers, each center manager must make decisions related to sales. Therefore, the responsibility centers are either profit or investment centers, depending on the amount of discretion each manager has with respect to expansion.

Organizing around customers rather than functions or products focuses managers on customer needs. In a rapidly changing area such as technology, an organization must be ready to move quickly in generating new products and services for customers. Organizing around customers, however, means that managers must contract with centralized service departments to provide internal services such as accounting, purchasing, or maintenance. The alternative is for each center to have its own internal service departments, which could lead to some redundancies within the organization.

Chapter Eight

Page 245 Ericsson must react quickly to customer demands and technological change. Thus, it has adapted its organizational structure to create a firm that can more quickly react and adapt to these changes. For example, the firm has reduced management levels, created teams to share market information more efficiently and effectively, and decentralized decision making. The management accounting system must support the firm's decision-making and control mechanisms and reflect the firm's need for quick decisions and up-to-date information. Thus, the management accounting system has been altered to reflect the emphasis on activities, business segments, and key performance indicators. The system de-emphasizes the annual budget and uses a continuous one. In addition, Ericsson uses a series of nonfinancial performance indicators to measure the achievement of its strategic goals.

Ericsson's summary of Key Performance Indicators (KPI) measures five categories: customers, finance, employees, internal efficiency, and innovation.

The following measures are examples that Ericsson has selected to use:

EXAMPLES OF MEASUREMENTS

Customers: Customer satisfaction, market share, brand name awareness

Finance: Sales growth, profitability, cash flow

Employees: Skills development, employee turnover

Internal efficiency: Capital turnover, reliability of deliveries to customers, reliability of deliveries to the market

Innovation: Number of patent applications

These data are reported to the corporate executive team for regular follow-up.

Source: www.ericsson.com/infocenter

Chapter Nine

Page 296 Hitachi uses cost allocation for control purposes. The company attempts to reduce the use of direct labor by using it as a cost driver. If planning were the primary motivator for overhead allocation, the company would use a cost driver more closely associated with overhead costs.

Allocating overhead costs to estimate product costs is not as useful in the consumer electronics industry as in some industries. Consumer electronics products have a very short product life. By the time overhead costs were allocated, the company might already be moving to the next generation of products.

The strategy of automation permeates Hitachi. Products and processes are designed to minimize direct labor. By allocating overhead based on direct labor, the company discourages the use of direct labor.

Chapter Ten

Page 346 Factors that might contribute to the higher cost of Ph.D. students compared to those in a combined undergraduate/masters program are the small size of Ph.D. classes, the more senior rank of faculty who teach in the Ph.D. program, and special incentives and compensation for professors who teach in this program (extra salary, reduced teaching loads, etc.). Although not included in this study, extra costs also typically include the greater financial aid given to Ph.D. students.

The cost of capacity tends to be overlooked in a university environment for a number of reasons. First, universities have no market mechanisms to highlight inefficiencies and wasteful use of capacity. Second, in most universities, space is a free good to the extent that the internal cost of this space does not reflect its full cost or the comparable cost if this space were acquired in the rental market. Third, in some situations, the decision to allocate space to a specific activity is linked to other decisions, such as accommodating preferred class times and elective courses.

University faculty and staff might be reluctant about efforts to cost their activities since many of these activities might be difficult to measure and capture quantitatively. For example, courses or research programs that are reported to be high cost might be considered unnecessary or inappropriate when the university is dealing with cost constraints. Financial measures might not reflect the contribution of these items in other ways (reputation of the university, ability to attract high-quality professors and students) and might lead to decisions that are contrary to the university's long-run mission. Finally, as in all organizations, individuals react to what is measured and might not like the focus placed on their activities. However, cost measurement might also motivate university members to better manage the costs of the resources that they consume.

Page 351 CAE uses a job-order costing system to support its production process. It customizes its products to meet the requirements of individual clients. CAE also remains cost competitive by manufacturing products that share common features to permit economies of scale. A job-order costing system provides a mechanism to track these costs to individual customers, projects, and contracts. In addition, the system enables CAE to track costs over extended time periods. This system provides a mechanism for cost control and details to ensure that the project meets customer demands. Finally, job-order costing information is an important input for pricing. CAE must offer competitive pricing, technological innovation, and mass customization.

CAE's job-order costing system supports the company's goals of innovation and competitiveness in that it provides both the firm and its customers detailed information regarding production costs. These details include the ability to track the cost of special features that customers require. The cost information assists CAE in setting prices competitively that at the same time cover all costs. By highlighting activity costs, the detailed tracking supports CAE's goals to create organizational value. In this way, CAE can work to eliminate non-value-added activities and their costs, increasing both customers and organizational value.

Chapter Eleven

Page 389   The management accounting system supports National Bank's strategy and the implementation of that strategy by providing critical information on the cost of delivering value to customers. For example, the system enables the bank's management to analyze the cost of different products, services, and types of customers. The bank's management accounting system has evolved to center around the customer in conjunction with National Bank's strategic focus on personalized customer service.

National Bank's full-cost system has certain advantages. It ensures that pricing strategies and the introduction of new products consider the fixed costs of the bank's infrastructure. This system emphasizes that these costs must be covered in the long run. Another advantage is to curb the enthusiasm of marketing personnel to develop new products without adequate attention to their long-term as well as short-term impact. A disadvantage of the system is that it requires many decisions regarding which costs are fixed and which are variable. Also, it might not fully consider that certain costs are sunk and incurred regardless of the strategy pursued. Another disadvantage is that it might create situations in which short-term, profitable initiatives are overlooked due to the full-cost analysis. National Bank's direct cost model offsets this disadvantage.

Potential effects on management behavior are the reluctance to take risks that are beneficial in terms of the bank's strategic goals and the efforts of managers to use resources in such a way as to minimize allocated costs. A positive impact of the system is to make managers more careful in the use of resources whose costs are allocated to them.

Chapter Twelve

Page 426   When organizations make strategic changes to meet new consumer demand, incorporate technological change, and respond to global competition, they must generally change their structure. With a change in organizational structure comes a change in the accounting system. The accounting system must adapt to support planning decisions. In this case, the accelerated depreciation system reflects the shorter life of the fixed assets. The performance measurement system must also change to encourage managers to enact the new strategy.

The telecommunications market is changing so rapidly because of a host of international competitors. Companies have been purchasing other companies to obtain a competitive and technological advantage. On June 30, 2000, US West was acquired by Qwest Communications.

The management accounting system helps US West deal with its dynamic environment by providing performance measures that align the interests of organizational members with US West's strategic goals. In a dynamic environment, the management accounting system also changes to respond to technological innovations and shifting market conditions such as the recent merger with Qwest.

Chapter Thirteen

Page 472   If a company must invest $3 billion to construct these new fabrication plants, it must recover a minimum of (0.15) ($3 billion), or $450 million, annually just to cover the cost of the investment.

Failure to make the investment, however, could be disastrous for companies that want to continue to be competitors in the new chip market. By not participating in the fabrication of the next level of DRAM chips, a company will lose any technological advantage that it has and forfeit any opportunity to participate in subsequent generations of chips.

Chapter Fourteen

Page 525   NEC has had a standard cost system for approximately 50 years, but it has changed its system to adapt to market conditions and technological innovations. Short product life cycles and rapid technological obsolescence make standard cost systems expensive to maintain. In addition, the information provided by a standard cost system might not be adequate for decision making and control purposes due to the short life expectancies of products and the need for price changes to match those of its competitors.

Answers to
ConceptReviews

Chapter One

Page 10

1. Management accounting must adapt to changes in the organization, which is changing because of technological changes, customer needs, and globalization.
2. Technological innovations allow an organization to communicate information better and to operate more efficiently.
3. Globalization forces organizations to continually innovate to meet the demands of its customers.
4. If an organization cannot meet customer demand, it cannot generate revenues to remain in operation.

Page 12

1. Customer value is the well-being that occurs when a customer consumes a product or service.
2. An organization can create customer value by offering products and services at a cost that is less than the well-being generated by consuming the product or service.

Page 16

1. Organizations form to achieve goals that a person cannot attain individually.
2. The three basic processes are assigning responsibilities, measuring performance, and rewarding individuals.
3. Planning decisions are made to select activities to implement the strategy. Control decisions encourage members of the organization to follow the organization's strategy.

Page 20

1. Management accounting provides information for internal users; financial reporting provides information primarily for parties outside the organization.
2. Management accounting provides information for improved planning decisions.
3. Management accounting helps align the interests of the members of the organization with the goals of the organization by measuring performance.
4. The growth of large corporations and the separation of managers and owners made management accounting more important and more sensitive to a changing environment.

Page 23

1. The communication of information within the organization is affected when the same information is used to evaluate members of the organization.
2. Historical costs may differ from the market value of an asset.
3. Maximizing profit based on historical cost is not always consistent with maximizing shareholder wealth.

Page 26

1. The controllers are responsible for the organization's accounting system; the internal auditors monitor the organization to determine whether prescribed operational procedures are being followed.

2. A code of ethics provides direction for management accountants when they make a subjective decision that affects multiple stakeholders.

Chapter Two

Page 40

1. Only differential costs and benefits are relevant to a decision because all other costs and benefits are the same for each alternative.
2. Future costs and benefits are not known for certain and often involve factors that are not easily quantified in dollar terms.
3. The alternative use of resources should be considered in determining the opportunity cost.
4. Sunk costs are the effect of past decisions that cannot be changed.

Page 46

1. The cost of starting operations and making the first few units includes the purchase and setting up of machinery and training of labor.
2. When the capacity of resources is reached, the cost of the additional use of those resources becomes very high.
3. The marginal cost identifies the cost of making one more unit and should be used for making a decision of whether to make additional units.
4. The average cost does not provide the cost of making additional units and should not be used in deciding whether to increase output.

Page 48

1. The fixed cost does not change with the rate of output.
2. Variable costs approximate the marginal cost at a normal rate of operations.

Page 52

1. The account classification method separates accounts into variable and fixed. The summation of the costs of all of the fixed accounts is the fixed cost. The summation of the costs of all of the variable accounts divided by the expected output is the variable cost per unit of output.
2. The high/low method uses the costs of the highest and lowest output periods to estimate variable and fixed costs.

Chapter Three

Page 72

1. The cost object is the recipient of traced costs. A cost object is chosen based on the decision being made.
2. The product cost can be used to determine whether a particular product is profitable. A product that has a selling price less than its cost should be dropped from the product mix.

Page 75

1. Direct product costs are traced to a single product; while indirect product costs are related to multiple products.

2. Direct product costs are normally classified as either direct labor or direct materials.

3. Direct material costs can be estimated using pricing lists of suppliers. Engineers are often called on to estimate the number of direct labor hours necessary to complete a product. The direct labor hours times the wage rate provides an estimate of direct labor costs.

Page 78

1. Indirect product costs are not specific to a single product but are related to multiple products.

2. Unit-level costs increase with the number of units produced. Batch-level costs increase with the number of batches. Product-level costs increase with the number of different products. Facility-level costs are fixed unless another facility is purchased.

Page 81

1 The six steps are to (1) identify the activities that generate indirect product costs, (2) estimate the cost of the activities, (3) select a cost driver for each activity, (4) estimate the cost-driver use by all products, (5) calculate a cost-driver application rate, and (6) apply activity costs to each product.

2. Ideally the cost-driver use should be proportional to the activity costs.

Page 85

1. The first step of ABC is to identify activities and the cost drivers for each activity. The estimated cost of each activity is divided by the estimated usage of its respective cost driver to determine an application rate for each cost driver. Costs are then applied based on the usage of the cost drivers by the different products.

2. The advantage is that ABC recognizes different levels of indirect costs and generally provides a more accurate estimate of the cost of a product. A disadvantage is that ABC is more costly to estimate.

Page 89

1. Estimated indirect costs are divided by the estimated usage of the cost driver to determine an application rate. The application rate then becomes the cost of using the cost driver.

2. The problem with tracing indirect costs using a single cost driver is that all indirect costs do not necessarily vary with the use of that cost driver. Therefore, the estimated product costs are not necessarily a good estimate.

Chapter Four

Page 107

1. Strategic decisions have long-term implications and recognize external forces and the organization's strengths and weaknesses. Short-term decisions assume that the organization's existing resources are fixed and only marginal changes can be made.

2. The critical success factors that add customer value are innovative product/service design, high-quality products and services, and low-cost production.

Page 109

1. Activity-based management helps identify the critical activities that lead to customer value.

2. If external parties can provide certain activities at a lower cost, those activities can potentially be outsourced.

Page 114

1. Trade-offs exist among the different phases of the product life cycle. Increased costs in one phase can lead to decreased costs in other phases.

2. Most costs are committed during the design and engineering stage.

Page 118

1. Receiving, inspecting, warehousing, purchasing, and dealing with defective parts are activities that add to the cost of working with a supplier.

2. Suppliers can be linked through EDI for more prompt service and lower accounting costs. Timely delivery for JIT production with appropriate packaging can also reduce costs.

Page 119

1. Customers that buy small quantities and require much service are more expensive.

2. Organizations can educate their customers as to what is costly behavior and reward them for avoiding such behavior with additional services or lower prices.

Page 125

1. The rule for selecting a price to maximize value is to produce the quantity at which marginal cost equals marginal benefit.

2. In a competitive environment, an organization has little opportunity to influence the price because multiple producers of similar products exist.

3. Cost-based pricing is used in regulated industries and when the supplier does not want to bear the risk of making a product with an uncertain cost.

Chapter Five

Page 138

1. Short-term decisions are made frequently, assume that the organization's resources are relatively fixed, and are based on incremental analysis. Strategic decisions are made infrequently, and are often tied to the annual budgeting process.

2. In the short term, most fixed costs are sunk, so the focus is on variable costs.

Page 145

1. The basic equation for CVP analysis is Profit = (Price per unit)(Number of units) − (Variable cost per unit)(Number of units) − Fixed costs

2. The purpose of break-even analysis is to estimate the output quantity necessary to have a zero profit to determine whether a project is potentially profitable.

3. The major assumptions of CVP analysis include a separation of costs into fixed and variable, and constant prices and variable cost per unit over the total range of output.

4. To use CVP analysis with multiple products, constant proportions or a "basket" of the multiple goods must be assumed.

Page 146

1. Variable costs become the lower boundary for pricing in the short term when the organization is operating below capacity.

2. When an organization operates at capacity, the opportunity cost of making a product is greater than the variable cost. Therefore, the lower boundary for short-term pricing should be higher than the variable cost.

Page 151

1. Incremental costs should be considered when deciding to add a product.

2. Avoidable costs identify those costs that would be eliminated if the product were dropped.

3. If the purchase price of the product is less than the cost of making the product, the product should be purchased.

4. A product should be processed further if incremental revenues are greater than incremental costs.

5. Organizations prefer to sell products with higher contribution margins per unit.

Page 154

1. The product that yields the highest contribution margin per use of the constraint should have priority.

2. An organization should make sure that an activity that is a bottleneck is always in operation. Expanding the capacity of the bottleneck is another method to increase the rate of operation.

Chapter Six

Page 172

1. The two internal roles of management accounting are improving planning decisions and assisting in control.

2. Large organizations have greater control problems because they must motivate more individuals to act in the best interests of the organization.

Page 175

1. Top-level managers delegate some of their responsibilities to subordinates who delegate some of their responsibilities to their subordinates.

2. People with the best knowledge have the capabilities to make the best planning decisions.

3. By transferring knowledge to managers who will act in the best interests of the organization, the linking of knowledge with responsibilities and control are both achieved.

Page 181

1. The costs include time and effort. The benefits include monetary rewards, status, and relationships with people with similar interests.

2. Monitoring costs are incurred to assist in the control of the organization.

3. Performance measures are used to evaluate individuals and subunits of an organization.

4. A good performance measure is consistent with the goals of the organization and reveals the actions of the individual being evaluated.

5. Good performance measures should lead to extra rewards.

Page 184

1. The four steps of the decision process are initiation, ratification, implementation, and monitoring. Alternating steps are either a planning decision process (initiation, implementation) or a decision control process (ratification, monitoring).

2. Separation of planning and control activities allows for mutual monitoring.

Chapter Seven

Page 197

1. The controllability principle is used because it rewards and penalizes each member of an organization for those activities that they can control.

2. The advantage of a relative performance measure is that comparisons can be made across individuals facing a similar environment. The disadvantage is that there are always winners and losers no matter how all the managers did, so it may lead to competition rather than cooperation among managers.

Page 202

1. A cost center either has a fixed set of inputs from which to maximize outputs (type 1) or a fixed output to be achieved by minimizing the cost of inputs (type 2).

2. Minimizing cost may have adverse effects on quality, so quality measures should be used in conjunction with cost measures.

3. Profit center managers normally have control over both inputs and the sale of outputs.

4. The profit of investment centers does not normally include interest on long-term debt, so performance measures should capture the cost of capital.

5. Many responsibility centers have characteristics of more than one type of responsibility center. For example, managers of some responsibility centers have the right to make minor expansions of their responsibility center, but do not have the right to make large expansions.

Page 208

1. ROI allows for the comparison of performances across managers of different amounts of assets and is in the form of an easily understood percentage. The problems include measurement errors resulting from the use of historical costs, manipulation, incentives to underinvest, and not including the discounting of cash flows.

2. Residual income has all of the problems of ROI except underinvestment. Residual income has the advantage of explicitly recognizing the cost of capital.

Page 217

1. Transfer pricing allows decentralized managers to make transfer decisions among themselves. Transfer-pricing systems improve decision control by assigning costs to the responsibility center managers responsible for costs.

2. Transfer prices provide managers with information on the cost of internal services so they can plan accordingly. The transfer price should equal the opportunity cost of providing the product or service to ensure that the appropriate planning decision is made to benefit the entire organization.

Page 221

1. Set the transfer price to recognize more of the profits in the country with the lower tax rate. If the country of the supplying division has the lower tax rate, a higher transfer price transfers profit to the supplying division and lowers after-tax profit. If the country of the purchasing division has the lower tax rate, a lower transfer price transfers profit to the purchasing division and lowers after-tax profit.

2. If the local government is threatening to expropriate the assets of high-profit, foreign-owned companies, these companies may want to choose high transfer prices for their imports and low transfer prices for their exports. If multinationals choose transfer prices solely to minimize taxes or for political considerations, they must devise alternative measures of performance to motivate managers of foreign subsidiaries.

Chapter Eight

Page 244

1. Budgeting facilitates the transfer of information within the organization to improve planning decisions. Budgeting also forces managers to plan in a periodic manner.

2. The budget is used to distribute responsibilities by specifying how much can be spent on different items. Budgeting also establishes benchmarks for evaluating performance.

3. Conflict might occur because the gathering of information for planning purposes is influenced by how the information is to be used for evaluating performance.

Page 249

1. Short-term budgets are both planning and control tools. Long-term budgets reduce managers' focus on short-term performance and are primarily used for planning purposes.

2. A line-item budget restricts the responsibilities of a manager by forcing the manager to make purchases in prespecified amounts.

3. The cost of budget lapsing is the need to continually budget for multiperiod projects and not to allow managers to make trade-offs across different time periods. The benefit of budget lapsing is greater control on short-term spending.

4. Managers who can control the size of operations should be evaluated based on static budgets; managers who do not control the size of operations should be evaluated based on flexible budgets.

5. Zero-base budgeting is useful when there is new management resulting in a greater need of information flow.

Page 260

1. The first step of the budget process is normally the estimation of sales.

2. Production requirements are equal to sales plus expected ending inventory less beginning inventory.

3. A financial budget identifies the cash flows to and from investors and creditors of the organization.

4. Pro forma financial statements are the expected financial statements at the end of the budgeting period.

Chapter Nine

Page 285

1. Cost allocation is the process of assigning indirect costs to cost objects. Examples are the assignment of the cost of internal services such as maintenance and computer services to the users of those services such as production units, and the assignment of machinery costs to the multiple products that use the machine.

2. Common resources are used by multiple cost objects. Therefore, common resources are difficult to trace to cost objects.

Page 289

1. The allocation of all manufacturing overhead costs, but not indirect selling and administrative costs, to products is traditionally done for external financial and tax reporting. It is used to calculate the current period's financially reported profits.

2. Organizations prefer to allocate as much overhead as possible to products that are being produced under cost reimbursement contracts.

Page 291

1. Cost allocations should approximate the opportunity cost of using the overhead resource for planning purposes.

2. Cost allocations are used to communicate information to and penalize the party causing the externality (assuming it is negative).

Page 293

1. Cost allocations may coincide with the distribution of resources and limit the amount of resources that the manager controls.

2. Cost allocations affect the performance measures of managers and discourage managers from using the allocation base used to allocate the costs.

3. Mutual monitoring is monitoring that is performed by peers within the organization. Cost allocations are like prices that occur within the organization and reveal the efficiencies of other units within the organization.

Page 301

1. Cost objects are chosen depending on the type of decision being made.

2. A cost pool is an aggregation of costs related to a specific activity.

3. The allocation base is used to distribute costs of a cost pool among the different cost objects.

4. The application rate is calculated as follows: estimated size of the cost pool divided by the estimated usage of the allocation base.

5. As the cost objects use the allocation base, costs are allocated to the cost objects based on the application rate.

6. A cost driver reflects the cause of the costs in the cost pool, while the allocation base may be chosen for control reasons. Both are used to apply costs of common resources to multiple cost objects.

Page 303

1. The purpose of segment reporting is to measure the performance of the organization's different subunits and groups of products.

2. Transactions with other subunits of the organization affect the segment reports of the interacting subunits. For segment reports, these transactions should be treated as if they were with external parties.

Chapter Ten

Page 332

1. The two types of production processes are job-order production and continuous-flow production.

2. Job-order costing is used for job-order production, and process costing is used for continuous flow production.

Page 335

1. The job-order cost sheet records direct materials, direct labor, and overhead.

2. The overhead costs are added using an allocation base.

Page 338

1. Once production begins, the Work-in-Process account begins receiving costs.

2. At the end of production, the costs are transferred to the Finished Goods account.

3. At the time of sale, the costs are transferred to the Cost of Goods Sold account.

Page 344

1. Actual overhead costs or usage of the allocation base may be different than estimated.

2. Over- and underabsorbed overhead reflect how actual operations differed from expected operations and may be used to adjust future estimates. These future estimates are used to make product mix and pricing decisions. Over- and underabsorbed overhead may also reflect control problems.

3. Over- and underabsorbed overhead can be treated as (1) Cost of Goods Sold, (2) prorated among the Work-in-Process, Finished Goods, and Cost of Goods Sold, or (3) eliminated by recalculating the application rate using actual numbers and reallocating the overhead.

Page 348

1. The quality of the cost drivers in reflecting the costs of the cost pools determines the accuracy of product costs. Multiple allocation bases yield more accurate product costs if products use overhead resources in different ways.

2. By allocating costs first to departments, the manager becomes responsible for those costs and has incentives to reduce them.

Page 352

1. The primary purpose of process costing is to identify the average cost of the product.

2. Equivalent unit calculation is used when partially completed units exist at the beginning and end of the accounting period.

Page 357

1. The schedule for cost of goods manufactured generates the costs transferred to Finished Goods. The Cost of Goods Sold is calculated by adding the costs transferred to Finished Goods to the beginning inventory of Finished Goods less the ending inventory of Finished Goods.

2. FIFO assumes that cost of the early units of inventory should be transferred to Cost of Goods Sold first. LIFO assumes that the cost of the latest units of inventory should be transferred to Costs of Goods Sold first. The weighted-average cost method combines the costs of the beginning and recently added inventory.

Chapter Eleven

Page 386

1. The incentive to overproduce occurs because overproduction leads to more fixed costs being retained in inventory and a higher short-term profit.

2. To discourage overproduction, charge the cost of extra inventory to the person responsible for the inventory decision, or use JIT.

3. By definition, the marginal cost of a resource that is a fixed cost is zero. When a manager is charged through a cost allocation for using a fixed cost resource, the manager tends to use less of the resource.

4. The death spiral is caused by dropping products but not avoiding costs that must then be allocated to the remaining products.

Page 390

1. Fixed costs are treated as period expenses.

2. Variable costing removes the incentive to overproduce and identifies the contribution margin.

3. Variable costing may lead to problems in identifying fixed and variable costs. Variable costing still requires the choice of an allocation base

Page 393

1. The application rate is equal to the estimated overhead costs divided by the usage of the allocation base when operations are at capacity.

2. The portion of fixed costs allocated is equal to the portion of capacity used.

3. The advantages are identifying the cost of unused capacity and not burdening existing products or departments with costs due to capacity decisions. The disadvantage is that using practical capacity still does not alleviate the overproduction problem.

4. Fixed costs could be allocated based on requested capacity at the time of the capacity decision. Managers would be motivated to accurately report capacity requirements by penalizing them if they used more of the capacity than they requested.

Chapter Twelve

Page 426

1. Major forces that currently affect organizations include technological innovations, customer demand, and global competition.

2. An organization should design a strategy that will provide customer value given technological innovations and global competition.

3. The organizational structure is created to implement the strategy. The designation of responsibilities, performance measures, and rewards are all chosen to support the strategy.

4. The role of management accounting is to assist in control and planning decisions. The management accounting system must change as the organization changes.

Page 433

1. The philosophy of TQM is to improve continually in lowering costs and providing better products and service for customers.

2. The four categories of quality costs are prevention, appraisal, internal failure, and external failure.

3. Prevention efforts should reduce the total number of defects and, therefore, failure costs. Appraisal efforts identify defects before they reach the customer. Therefore, internal failure costs may rise, but external failure costs decline.

Page 439

1. The advantages of JIT include reduced inventory and storage costs and a quicker response to customer demand through faster throughput times.

2. A short throughput time allows the organization to provide products and services to customers with minimal delay.

3. Performance measures should be chosen to encourage fast throughput time and a team effort. The performance measures should discourage the building of inventory.

Chapter Thirteen

Page 461

1. The steps in the capital budgeting process are initiation or identification of investment opportunities, ratification, implementation, and monitoring.

2. The opportunity cost of capital represents the forgone opportunity of the cash invested in the project generating a return on another investment. The opportunity cost of capital affects long-term decisions because it is used to discount future cash flows.

Page 464

1. The limitations are that the payback period does not use the time value of money and does not recognize cash flows beyond the payback period.

2. A multiyear ROI is calculated by dividing the annual average income by the average investment during the life of the investment.

3. The limitations are that ROI does not recognize the time value of money and is influenced by accounting methods.

Page 470

1. Cash flows should be discounted because unlike accounting earnings, they can be invested and generate a return.

2. Most capital budgeting decisions have an effect on the level of other asset accounts. More cash invested in accounts

receivable and inventory generates an opportunity cost of capital.

3. Finance charges are not included because they are implicitly recognized by the discount rate.

4. Depreciation lowers income, which reduces cash that must be paid in taxes. Therefore, depreciation affects cash through taxes.

5. Higher-risk projects should be discounted by higher interest rates.

Page 475

1. The internal rate of return is determined by finding the discount rate on cash flows that sets the net present value to zero.

2. The internal rate of return may cause incorrect decisions when mutually exclusive investment choices must be made. The internal rate of return also may be difficult to calculate.

Chapter Fourteen

Page 504

1. Organizations use standard costing to communicate expected costs for planning purposes. The primary reason, however, is to control processes and individuals by using standard costs as benchmarks.

2. There is no generally accepted method for setting standards. Some organizations set standards very tightly and others set standards that are easily attainable. Information from those with knowledge about the processes should be obtained to establish standards.

Page 514

1. The two components are quantity and unit prices.

2. A favorable variance means that standard costs are greater than actual costs.

3. The personnel manager is likely to be responsible for the labor wage variance; the operations manager should be responsible for the efficiency variance.

4. The material price variance is the responsibility of the purchasing manager, and the quantity variance is the responsibility of the operations manager.

5. The material quantity variance is unfavorable when more than the standard material is used. It can be caused by carelessness in using the material or by the poor quality of the material.

Page 518

1. Purchasing managers can reduce the material price variance by purchasing large amounts to get discounts.

2. A manager responsible only for one variance will act to influence that variance to the detriment of the rest of the organization. An example is a purchasing manager purchasing low-quality material to obtain a favorable price variance, but the quantity variance will likely be unfavorable when employees try to work with the poor-quality material.

3. By making managers responsible for multiple variances over which they have some control, they will monitor other managers who influence those variances.

4. Satisficing behavior occurs when employees work hard enough only to satisfy standards. If a reward is paid when the standard is met, a disincentive exists to perform beyond the standard.

Page 522

1. The expected usage is based on estimates at the beginning of the period. The standard usage is based on the standard per unit times the actual units. The actual usage is what occurs.

2. Standard overhead costs differ from budgeted overhead costs because the expected usage of the allocation base is different than the actual usage.

3. Overhead standards are intended to motivate managers to use overhead resources efficiently. Favorable fixed overhead variances, however, can be obtained through overproduction.

Page 524

1. Variances represent deviations from plans, and managers should understand them.

2. The decision to investigate depends on the size of random fluctuations, the opportunity cost of investigation, the opportunity cost of not investigating, and the ease of correcting the problem if it exists.

Page 525

1. Standard costs are frequently based on past experiences and take time to institute. A rapidly changing business environment means that there is not a long history to examine and not enough time to institute a standard costing system.

2. Standard costs are still being used by a large number of companies.

Photo**Credits**

Index

Index